The Russia Reader

THE WORLD READERS
A series edited by Robin Kirk and Orin Starn

Also in this series:

THE ALASKA NATIVE READER
Edited by Maria Williams

THE INDONESIA READER
Edited by Tineke Hellwig and Eric Tagliacozzo

THE
RUSSIA
READER

HISTORY, CULTURE, POLITICS

Edited by Adele Barker and Bruce Grant

DUKE UNIVERSITY PRESS   *Durham and London*   2010

© 2010 Duke University Press
All rights reserved
Printed in the United States of America on acid-free paper ⊖
Typeset in Monotype Dante by Keystone Typesetting, Inc.
Library of Congress Cataloging-in-Publication Data appear on
the last printed page of this book.

Contents

VIII   *Building a New World from Old*

IX   *Rising Stalinism*

X   *The Great Terror*

Acknowledgments

For a project of this scope we want to acknowledge a familiar cohort of friends and colleagues who offered counsel on the hundreds of sources we sorted through, as well as a sizable number of editors, literary agents, permissions experts, families of writers, and families of translators who showed uncommon generosity in allowing us to use many of the essays found in this volume.

Foremost we thank Peter Maggs, professor of law at the University of Illinois, Urbana-Champaign, who kindly responded to queries on the rapidly shifting terrains of Russian, American, and European copyright laws. Though the standard disclaimer obtains as always—only we, as editors, bear the responsibility for the final product—Peter's counsel greatly advanced our education in copyrights. We can never adequately repay him. Janice Pilch, also at UIUC, shared a particularly useful guide we are grateful for. We thank the librarians Michael Brewer (Arizona), Diana Greene (NYU), and Patricia Polansky (Hawai'i) for their patience in repeat consultations and for the rich materials they provided.

Copyright permissions is a special field in which we acquired a long education for this project. We are particularly grateful to all who have worked to make these selections available to a wider range of readers: Lidia Isaakovna Babel, Christopher Barnes, Susan Bean, Justin Cavin, Charlotte Douglas, Ruslan Dzhopua, Peter Filardo, Mischa Gabowitsch, Moshe Gammer, Andrei Gul'tsev, Rick Hibberd, Jana Howlett, Fazil' Iskander, Galina Iudina, Veronique Jobert, Eve Levin, Anatoly Liberman, Masha Lipman, Leonid Livak, Marie-Christine MacAndrew, Stephanie Munson, Charlotte Pomerantz Marzani, Kevin O'Brien, Carolyn Pouncy, Antonina Nikolaevna Pirozhkova, Valerii Pisigin, Judith Roche, Mohsen Shah, G. S. Smith, Nikki Smith, Daniela Steila, Lev Timofeev, Doug Vogt, Angel Vu, Nikita Vysotskii, Anna Webber, Donald Weber, Alexander Yanov, and Leora Zeitlin. The Communal Group of the Kommunalka website, Ilya Utekhin, Alice Nakhimovsky, Slava Paperno, and Nancy Ries, graciously let us use some of their documents and interviews. Our special thanks to Elena Vadimovna Larina in Moscow whose help in gathering permissions was incalculable.

We extend similar thanks to the many who volunteered their time for translations, including Michael Brewer, Kenny Cargill, Jane Costlow, Sibelan Forrester, Rachel Glassberg, Rebecca Gould, Rebecca Holz, Natasha Kolchevska, Kelly Kozik, John Leafgren, Sara Lomasz Flesch, Del Phillips, Ezekiel Pfeifer, Lesa Randall, Alexander Rindisbacher, Hans-Juerg Rindisbacher, G. S. Smith, Stephanie Wesley, and Jane Zavisca. Larissa Rudova deserves special mention for her characteristic generosity in joining or overseeing a number of these translation projects. Deep thanks to Del Phillips for the long hours he spent helping review and edit translations and for his help in contacting Russian sources for copyright. Kenny Cargill came to our aid with a superb set of last-minute translations. His generosity was matched only by his superb library research skills.

The photographs that appear in this volume are the product of many hands. Ronald Bulatoff and Carol Leadenham at the Hoover Institution Archives took a particular interest in helping us, providing us with key background on the archival holdings and helping us gain permissions from copyright holders. Similarly our thanks to the staff at the Library of Congress Photo Archive Division, to Maria Vasil'evna Ivanova of the Tret'iakov Gallery in Moscow, to Evgenia Petrova of the Russian Museum, and Vera A. Prianishnikova of the National Library of Russia. Friends, students, colleagues, and sometimes complete strangers took time out to sift through their collection of photos for us. We thank Olga Cullinan, Nelson Hancock, Kate Kuhns, Garth Poole, Nancy Ries, and Donald Weber, who all made time to provide material. Rick Hibberd shared a wealth of photos from his years in the Soviet Union. Liza Malott Pohle let us use her photo of the caskets containing the remains of the Romanovs taken just minutes after the official service was over.

Among those friends and colleagues who gave their time and energy to recommend or review individual text selections, we thank Nicholas Breyfogle, Catherine Ciepiela, Jane Costlow, Alexei Elfimov, Sibelan Forrester, John Garrard, Alexander Genis, Nelson Hancock, Jane Harris, Adeeb Khalid, Catriona Kelly, Alexander Knysh, Nancy Kollman, Robert Lee, Scott Levi, Ralph Litzinger, Stephen Lovell, Douglas Northrop, Serguei Oushakine, Nancy Ries, Irina Sandomirskaia, Uli Schamiloglu, Robert Weinberg, and David Wolff.

We would like to take this opportunity to thank our anonymous reviewers at Duke University Press. Our volume benefited enormously from the care and intelligence with which they read, and improved upon, this work.

Finally, Ted Berklayd and Kristina Nazimova (NYU), and Kristy Schmidt and Mia Schnaible (University of Arizona) provided superb assistance at all stages of this project. With uncommon grace Sarah Monks gave up weekends and taught Adele the finer points of computer technology. The interns at Duke University Press, in particular Alex Greenberg, Julie Greenberg, and Vanessa Doriott, helped us tremendously in the final stages of this very large volume while simultaneously carrying a full course load themselves. Miriam Angress's technical and organizational skills kept the volume on track through the production process. Our thanks to our editor, Valerie Millholland, who encouraged us along the way, understanding that big countries deserve big books.

General Introduction

Adele Barker and Bruce Grant

Winston Churchill once said of Russia, "[It] is a riddle wrapped in a mystery inside an enigma." Indeed until the spectacular end to the former Soviet Union in 1991, there had perhaps been no other part of the world that was so consistently known for being so inconsistently known. Russians and observers alike may never have agreed on how best to define the historically changing space that stretches from Eastern Europe to the Pacific, but the chronicling of those disagreements has rarely flagged in its industry. Rich, telling, and voluminous, the effort to know Russia has recently become richer still, with ever greater access to the considerable erudition of the Russian legacy and with Russians themselves taking advantage of the greater freedom to publish and to represent their own worlds. Bringing together some of the best writing from and about Russia, *The Russia Reader* suggests that it may now be time to let go of Churchill's enigma without losing any of the force of the riddles.

The cold war that so many remember today as one of the guiding landmarks of twentieth-century geopolitics created borders, boundaries, and barriers around a vast political space, constraining global flows and giving rise to the language of enigma that encased Russia for so long. Those barriers to travel and political voice were not new; indeed they rivaled those of tsarist Russia chronicled so extensively by travelers, such as the archly intuitive Marquis de Custine, whose *Voyages en Russie*, published in France in 1839, was not released in the land he visited until Gorbachev's perestroika, or the philosopher Jeremy Bentham, who was inspired to build his famous high-surveillance prison panopticon only after experiencing the everyday effects of Russian imperial rule firsthand.

Yet for all the forms of isolation and closure seemingly axiomatic of Russian life, Russian space was never as hermetically sealed nor as clearly defined as popular imaginations have contended. The historic heart of Russia—to use one of the canons of nationalist politics that would have us understand all nations as ageless social bodies with a collective mind, limbs, and a personal

Map 1. The Russian Empire in 1914.

biography—was never technically in Russia at all. At least by the time empires started giving rise to nation-states, Kyivan Rus' was in contemporary Ukraine and had ongoing relations with Western Europe through trade and dynastic marriage. Until the eighteenth century, in fact, Russia, as it came to be known, was not really "Russia" at all but a configuration of competing feudal arrangements and princely appendages stretching across the great steppe, a vast land crossed constantly by the heirs of Slavic tribes, Mongol invasions, and Byzantine rulers, as well as countless religious leaders. In the twentieth century, when cold war ideologies suggested images of an iron curtain that sealed off Soviet Russia (by then only one of fifteen republics in the gigantic Soviet Union that stretched across eleven time zones), few appreciated the extent to which Soviet ideologists built their new world in the same spirit of imitation and contestation that figured in all modernizing state ambitions around the globe. Lenin came up with his idea for the electrification of the famously underdeveloped Russian countryside after seeing a postcard of Niagara Falls; Trotsky conceived of the dictatorship of the proletariat after reading Max Weber; Stalin commissioned musical comedy motion pictures after consuming reels of Busby Berkeley productions; and Khrushchev made the slogan "We will catch up to and surpass America" (*Dogonim i peregonim Ameriku*) into a much misunderstood comment, suggesting that the Soviet Union would "bury" (*pokhoronim*) America. His idea, ironically, was that the Soviet Union

Map 2. Map of the USSR after World War II.

would become *more* like its arch rival, not less. Nor was it solely ever a question of East borrowing from West. Imitation traveled in all directions across the unstable boundaries of time and space. British Quakers were the first to build Bentham's prisons, and it was the launching of the *Sputnik* space rocket in 1957 that jolted Europe and its allies into realizing just how well the Soviet Union had put modernism's ambitions into practice.

Looking back on Russian history with the kind of freedoms afforded by recent world events and the vigor with which Russian historians themselves have been generating new insight, one can see that borders were never as firmly closed in tsarist Russia or the later Soviet Union as most tend to think. Even at its height the vast Russian Empire stretched in directions that no central government might ever have controlled. From the earliest Chinese diplomatic chronicles until the start of the twentieth century, for example, the Russian Pacific coast was a complex, dynamic mix of cross-Bering indigenous exchange, East Asian traders, galleys arriving from the Indian Ocean, and American industrialists prospering in Vladivostok—a space where sovereign Russian overseers were only one party among many. Soviet citizens may have been vastly more limited than their Western European counterparts in freedom of movement and freedom of expression, but they were hardly isolated in the multilingual, multiconfessional communist state. Russians predominated demographically and culturally, but they were only one group among

Map 3. Map of the contemporary Russian Federation.

the many modern citizens of the industrial giant. It was when those borders seemed the most impenetrable that intellectual and creative life strove most dramatically to retain independence and to provide the ongoing alternative narrative to that produced by the Party for all its citizens.

Throughout Russian history borders and boundaries have raised difficult and often troubling questions of identification. Peter the Great looked his countrymen in the eye and exhorted them to catch up to and be more like Western Europe. Slavophiles, taking issue with Westernizers, sought the meaning of Russia's destiny elsewhere, in its religiosity, in its people, and turned away from those who wished to remold themselves as Westerners. Two hundred years later the Bolshevik leaders embarked on another mission, no less radical than that which Peter the Great had instituted: the creation of the new Soviet man and woman, the reengineering of the Russian to accompany the new revolutionary order that was being forged. At the beginning of the twentieth century Russia's émigré population in Western Europe and Harbin, China, confronted these questions in spades as they found themselves in new and alien homelands. Recently the question has reemerged as political realities have once again shifted. What does it mean to be Russian in the wake of the collapse of the Soviet Union? Exhorted by the Party to be Soviets first and citizens of their own republic second, Russians have had to confront yet again what being Russian means.

In keeping with the best new work in cultural geography, *The Russia Reader* takes as its subject not just a place, but an idea, or better, a set of ideas that have long traveled by aid of the imagination of Russians and their observers over many years. This leads us from medieval steppes and the lionized Russian peasants of communal lore, to the White Guards of Harbin, the borough of Queens of the émigré writer Sergei Dovlatov, and to the nuclear physicists who shuttle regularly today between Los Alamos, New Mexico, and Novosibirsk.

Not surprisingly we were faced with an excess of riches as we made the difficult decisions about what to include in this volume, and sadly, after much debate, what to set aside. Readers will find that many of their favorite Russian authors are not represented here. Trusting the bounty of Russian classics available in English translation, we chose instead to include writing not generally available in English translation.

Our aim was to show the complex layers of Russian and Soviet history and the social forces that presaged the changes that were to come. The texts that appear here speak from a variety of perspectives: that of the traveler, the ruler, the revolutionary, the gentry, the peasantry, American and European scholars, literary figures, émigrés, and veterans. As often as possible we strove to incorporate eyewitness accounts, from Yevtushenko caught in the throng at Stalin's funeral to the witness on the ground during the Revolution in Petrograd in 1917, and the villager who writes a desperate plea to Aleksandr Kerensky, the head of the provisional government a year later, asking what the revolution is and what is going on. We strove to present a slightly different portrait of Russia than that provided in traditional introductory readers by reintroducing voices that have not always been heard: men in the trenches during World War I writing letters home and to the tsar; a woman rising out of grinding poverty, for whom the Revolution was a godsend; and a librarian at the Lenin Library in Moscow in the 1960s who provides an insider's view of how Soviets were instructed to deal with foreigners. We wanted to look at Russia's often surprising history, at the seemingly abrupt changes of course it has taken, from as many perspectives as possible. Thus we present the letter written by Anna Zakharova defending her role as a prison camp official.

Our task in assembling these readings has been made much easier by the availability of archival sources and documents that prior to 1991 were closed to both Russians and foreigners alike. Several documents appear here from the Archives of the USSR Committee on State Security (KGB), the Archives of the Communist Party, and the Foreign Ministry that were opened during the Yeltsin era in the belief that the Russian people deserved to know their own history.

Alongside the events and people who have been part of Russia's history, we took care to contextualize the kinds of archetypes that foreign observers have so long located in Russia: bathing practices, mushroom gathering, drinking, the holy fool, the organic communism of the peasant *mir*, and the sovereign tyrant. It must be conceded that many first-person Russian accounts have often been no less enthusiastic to present such iconic figures to their readership, making twentieth-century Russian history in particular—with its spectacular murders, betrayals, and atrocities—into a kind of tabloid genre for specialists and nonspecialists alike. As the Bulgarian scholar Vladislav Todorov observed of post-Soviet life, it is in the most recent chroniclings of gangland, robber-baron society that this tradition reached its apogee. "The East aestheticizes its monstrosity to the West—its ruins, its fakes, its own end," Todorov writes. "The West pays for the danger because the West has been investing in the thrills of the ruins from the very beginning. Danger impregnated with money becomes a thriller." Indeed for much of the twentieth century Soviet citizens admonished Western scholars for seeking out only what was negative in Soviet society. By contrast, we have worked to find a balance between downplaying the sensational and still heeding the sometimes stunning heights and depths of historic events. This has led us to pay particular attention to the textures of daily life, what many Russians call *byt*, chronicles of the everyday that have taken up so many of the richest but often underattended pages of Russian literature, ethnography, and philosophy. As a result, over thirty selections for this volume appear in English for the first time.

In the same spirit of making Russia's differences more familiar, we take Soviet culture seriously. This simple appreciation of seventy years of social history should be self-evident, but it is remarkably difficult to come by in legions of recent studies from both sides of the Atlantic and from the former Soviet Union itself. Accustomed to denouncing the Soviet monolith for the sake of human freedoms, Western scholars and émigrés long ago made the dismissal of Soviet culture a commonplace. The moral ends were noble, but the scholarly means often did little to help us understand how the Soviet government so successfully won over millions of loyal followers from among its constituencies, generating what the anthropologist Katherine Verdery has called a "cognitive organization of the world" and what Sovietologist Vera Dunham termed those "glutinate forces" that held the Soviet Union together. With the breathless rush of perestroika, scholars of all stripes seemed to leave these seven decades behind them, turning to questions of new international orders, the development of civil society, rampant consumerism, and more recently the use of force in a newly robust post-Soviet Russia in ways unpopular with various world communities. And yet we would do well to remember that those forces—political, ideological, and economic—that held the Soviet

Union together for seventy-four years did not disappear in a moment of political transition. Complex notions of what constitutes sovereignty, empire, borders, and boundaries are as paramount now, perhaps even more so in the wake of the collapse of the state, as they were under Soviet rule. By taking up the question of Soviet culture as a cosmology unto itself, we look to advance our understandings of Russia's place in the complex system that was the Soviet Union, a system that endured for so many decades and is still reflected in much political decision making among the post-Soviet leadership.

The Russia Reader contains a predominance of essays written by and for Russians themselves. Most simply we have aimed for the best writing available to capture the history, culture, and politics of the continually changing set of persons, events, and ideas that make up Russia today. This is a volume that reaches out to the traveler who values considered insight and to the scholar and student who value pleasurably clear writing. It is a collection that took shape from the stacks of libraries we were able to cull on three continents; from the books that changed us and the ones we didn't realize we had been waiting to read; from Soviet-era political handbooks plucked from rubbish piles in Siberia and books in the best new independent Russian bookstores; from the pages of popular best-sellers and suggestions from academic colleagues who said they could not teach about Russia without including "just this article." We have aimed to juxtapose sometimes directly oppositional texts, configuring a diverse set of views from almost a millennium of written record. The result, we hope, is an ecumenical mix of writing on, from, and about a place where, like many others, historical event, cultural pluralism, and political experiment collide in the practices of daily life.

I

Icons and Archetypes

Who are Russians and where did they come from? As long ago as two millennia, Slavic peoples were said to occupy the northeastern realms of the Eurasian continent, competing with Finnic and Lithuanian northerners for preeminence in vast lands. More popularly, ancestors of modern Russians, often called "the eastern Slavic tribes," are thought to have come from what is now present-day Poland between the seventh century and the ninth. Rus' is the name most often given to the people who gained political ascendancy in Kyiv at this time, with the year 988 marking the founding of the Russian Orthodox branch of Christianity.

Whether Polish or Ukrainian in its origins, a collective of roaming tribes, or a seemingly absolutist state, Russian space has long been multicultural, multiconfessional, and regularly contested. At its height the Russian Empire covered one-sixth of the world's land mass. While Russians' well-known nineteenth-century efforts to stabilize control through intensive Russification of their non-Russian subjects gained them a reputation for harshness, the pluralism of the mammoth political enterprise was never far from view. In the census of 1897, the tsar officially recognized 104 "nationalities," 146 officially active languages, and dozens more of each waiting in the wings for their moment of recognition. Yet in an age of modernity, with the rise of empires and the forging of the nation-states that would succeed them, the notion of countries as persons unto themselves, with their own natural environments, landscapes, personalities, possessions and, not least, souls, came to Russia as it did to all corners of the globe. This is the Russia of imperial majesty and onion domes, Siberian snowscapes and fearsome forests, fearless leaders and iron rule.

The essays in this section furnish illustrations of these famous Russian icons and archetypes, as much as they aim to partially undo them. What exactly does it mean to be Russian, asks Aleksandr Blok in his poem "The Scythians," which opens our volume. Does Russia more properly belong to Europe or to Asia, and what does it mean, Blok asks, to be part of an Asiatic *mentalité*? If Blok located Russia's sense of self among the tribes that once spread across the southern steppe, the nineteenth-century philosopher Aleksei Khomiakov champions the cause of the inward-looking Slavophiles who saw a distinctive Russian character free of foreign influence in response to the more expansive Westernizers who, since at least the time of Peter the Great, have argued for particular brands of liberal reform. Regardless of what side one took in the debate, the question remains whether any political body, not least one as extensive as that of the eighteenth- or nineteenth-century Russian Empire, could meaningfully forge such a coherent collective at all.

In the twentieth-century world of nation-states, the notion of nation-as-person was everywhere read back into Russian history and society. The very idea of the nation (in Russian, *natsiia*) comes from the Latin root *natio*, "to be born," as does the Russian term for "people" (*narod*). One hears in the mysterious Russian soul, in the *zagadochnaia russkaia dusha*, one of many metaphysical shelters wherein Soviet citizens sought safety as a response to a state that had ambitiously promised a world of rationality for all.

Popular writers, both Russian and foreign, have spared little ink in suggesting Russia's strangenesses. The Marquis de Custine, journeying to Russia from France in the nineteenth century, is perhaps among the most famous in this line of gentlemen travelers. During the cold war even the more apolitical scholars managed to frame culture as an explanation for history. In the 1950s the psychologist Geoffrey Gorer and the anthropologist Margaret Mead advanced "the swaddling hypothesis," suggesting that places like Russia, where infants were tightly bound in blankets to prevent them from injuring themselves, created a host of primal frustrations, making their citizens prone to irrational outbursts later in life.

More favorably, essays such as Susan Buck-Morss's take us a long way from a cold war of primal outbursts and mysterious unknowns. What if, she asks, the Soviet Union was never as closed to the flows of shared European political ideals or global capital as most area specialists suggest? To what extent have the binary categories of East and West obscured more than they have revealed? The disarming proposition is that, far from engineering a world of two solitudes, the United States and the USSR spent much of the twentieth century actively imitating each other.

Aside from questions of character that encased Russia in a cloak of mystery or of cold war rhetoric, or a little of both, resides the more fundamental question of geography. Andreas Kappeler takes as his point of departure the fact that the first Russian state was located in what is today Ukraine. His is part of the much larger debate over whether Russia properly belongs to Europe or to "the slave soul" of a more absolutist Asia.

A couple painting nested dolls in their apartment, 1930s. Courtesy of Rick Hibberd. Source: The Artistic Pedagogical Museum of Toys, Sergiev Posad, Russia.

Whatever history may offer us by way of clarifications and corrections, Russian society has no doubt long invested in a series of icons and archetypes that have provided meaningful coherence to millions. Debates over what these archetypes mean arise in organized politics and in clouds of steam, with vodka, birch branches, and the company of fellow travelers.

The Scythians (1918)

Aleksandr Blok

On 29 January 1918, frustrated with the slow pace of the Brest peace negotiations intended to keep the new Soviet Russia out of World War I, Aleksandr Blok (1880–1921), one of Russia's most gifted lyrical poets, wrote "The Scythians" ("Skify"). The poem is a mix of history, destiny, promise, and threat, a challenge made to Europe to settle scores or face the consequences from a Russia rising from the ashes of revolution.

For all his creative gifts, Blok was never fully embraced by the worlds he lived in. He was born into an aristocratic family who felt betrayed by his revolutionary sympathies (the poem opens with an epigraph from his uncle, the famous Slavophile Vladimir Solov'ev), and the nascent Bolshevik literary establishment was suspicious of his religious and mystical leanings. The poem is a deft commentary on Russia's famously divided soul. If there is an Asiatic bent to the Russian character, Blok implies, this might be a character best not tangled with. Two centuries of Mongol domination (1237–1480), he suggests, taught Russians a thing or two. But the true song in Russia's "barbarian lyre" comes from what Blok held to be its pre-Slavic, "proto-Indo-European" Scythian legacy, referring to the nomadic pastoralist peoples whose reach embraced vast swaths of contemporary southern Russia and Ukraine during Classical Antiquity (600 BCE–300 CE), an influence attested to in elaborate archaeological finds. The Scythians, Blok reminds us, were a dynamic, multiethnic force, a world of the future, rather than peoples of a fallen past. Europe would do well to heed their call.

Panmongolism! The name, though savage, yet rings caressful in my ear.
—Vladimir Solov'ev

Mere millions—you. We—teem, and teem, and teem.
    You want to fight? Come on, then—try it!
We're—Scythians—yes! With Asiatic mien
    We watch you, gloating, through our slit-squint eyelids.

For you—long years. For us—alone one hour.
    We, like brute serfs, in blind obedience,
Have held our shield between two warring powers—
    The Mongols and the Europeans!

For years, long years, your ancient furnace forged
    And dulled the avalanches' rumble,
And what a wanton tale of woe was yours
    When Lisbon and Messina crumbled!

A thousand years you've watched this East of ours,
    Amassed and melted down our jewels,
Contemptuously, have counted but the hour
    When you could train your guns on to us!

That hour has struck. Misfortune beats her wings,
    You multiply your insults daily.
The day will come when nothing more remains,
    Not one trace, of your *Paestums*, maybe!

Old world! Before you fall in ruins—think,
    While yet you writhe in sweetest torture,
How Oedipus, before the ageless Sphinx's
    Enigma, once, was moved to caution!

So, Russia—Sphinx—triumphant, sorrowed, too—
    With black blood flows, in fearful wildness,
Her eyes glare deep, glare deep, glare deep at you,
    With hatred and—with loving-kindness!

Yes, so to love, as lies within our blood,
    Not one of you has loved in ages!
You have forgotten that there is such love
    That burns and, burning, lays in ashes!

We love them all—cold numbers' heartless heat,
    The gift of heavenly visions in us,
We understand them all—keen Gallic wit
    And gloomy-weighed Germanic genius.

Remember all—the streets of Paris' hell,
    The gentle coolnesses of Venice,
The lemon groves—their distant, perfumed smell—
    And, smoke-enswathed, Cologne's immenseness . . .

We love the flesh—its taste, its pinkish tone,
　　The scent of flesh, too—choking, deathsome . . .
Are we to blame, then, if we crunch your bones
　　When our unwieldy paws caress them?

It's nothing new for us to seize the rein,
　　To curb our prancing, fiery chargers,
To bend their stubborn will, to break them in,
　　And let them know that we're the masters . . .

Come on, then, come!—into the arms of peace.
　　Have done with war and all its horrors.
Before it's all too late—now, comrades, sheathe
　　Your age-old sword, and we'll be—brothers!

And if not—well, we've nothing left to lose,
　　We, too, can be perfidious traitors.
For years, long years, you'll stand—accursed, accused
　　Of crippled coming generations.

We'll blaze a trail—we'll beat a broad-flung track
　　Through the dense woods that fringe, behind you,
The gentle brow of Europe. We'll be back—
　　Our Asiatic mugs will find you.

Come on, then—on, unto the Urals. We'll
　　Prepare meanwhile the field of battle
Where cold machines of calculated steel
　　Shall meet the savage Mongol rabble.

But as for us—we'll no more be your shield;
　　Ourselves no longer sword unsheathing,
Through narrow eyes we'll scan the battlefield
　　And watch the mortal combat seething.

We shall not turn aside when raging Huns
　　Go delving into dead men's pockets,
Turn churches into stables, burn the towns,
　　And roast their white-flesh comrades' bodies . . .

For the last time—Old world, come to! The feast
　　Of peace-fraternal toil awaits you.
For the last time—the fair, fraternal feast.
　　And our barbarian lyre invites you.

On Russian Distinctiveness and Universality (1880)

Fyodor Dostoyevsky

Throughout the nineteenth century one of the most famous debates in Russian society was held between self-proclaimed Slavophiles and Westernizers. Though a wide variety of thinkers marched under the Slavophile banner, they shared a concern that Peter the Great's founding of St. Petersburg and the relocation of the imperial capital from Moscow to create "a window on Europe" had created a moral vacuum in Russian life typified by imitations of Western European custom. Philosophers from Petr Chaadaev onward thus called for a return to pre-Petrine values, stressing Russian communalism and religious orthodoxy. By the late nineteenth century more radical thinkers such as Nikolai Danilevskii used the premises of Slavophilia to call for the creation of pan-Slavist nationalist movements. In his famous "Pushkin Speech," extracted at the outset of the text here and first given at the unveiling of a Pushkin monument in Moscow on 8 June 1880, Fyodor Dostoyevsky (1821–81) offers an encomium to the Russian poet that is artful in its political navigation. Setting aside decades of debate, Dostoyevsky insists that the longstanding disagreements between Slavophiles and Westernizers over Russia's future was simply "a big misunderstanding." In Dostoyevsky's rendering, his countrymen had "admitted the genius of other nations" into their souls. At the same time, this melting pot of East and West created something entirely new, whereby Russia, by "becoming a brother to all human beings," was embodying a universal human standard. Russian distinctiveness, Dostoyevsky insisted, could be found in this very ecumenism.

That he used Pushkin as the platform for his speech points to the reverence in which Pushkin has been held from the nineteenth century up to the present. Heralded as Russia's first national poet, he was the first to incorporate the living, spoken Russian language into his art, thus creating an artistic legacy thoroughly Russian, independent of foreign influences. In the characters Pushkin created, Dostoyevsky sees both the kernel and the apotheosis of true Russian types. In Tatiana from Eugene Onegin *he finds the image of spiritual and moral nobility reflective of the Russian people as a whole. While Pushkin has often been used throughout Russian and Soviet history for political ends, the character of Tatiana has remained for Russians the image of what is good and morally sound about the Russian character, the personification of its highest ideals.*

(From a speech on Pushkin published in the August 1880 issue of *Writer's Diary*, a journal that Dostoyevsky single-handedly wrote and edited.)

I shall state it emphatically: there has never been a poet with such a universal responsiveness as Pushkin. The point is not just in his responsiveness, but in its amazing depth, and in the reincarnation of his spirit in the spirit of foreign nations, in an almost perfect, and therefore also miraculous, reincarnation, because no such phenomenon has taken place anywhere else in any other poet. This can be found only in Pushkin, and in this sense, I repeat, he is an unheard-of phenomenon and, in our opinion, even a prophetic one, for it was precisely here that his national Russian force expressed itself the most: precisely in the national quality of his poetry, the national quality in furthest development, that of our future, which exists at present in concealment, and it expressed itself prophetically. For what is the strength of the spirit of Russian nationality if not Russia's striving toward its ultimate goals of worldwide and international universality? When Pushkin became a national poet, as he came in close contact with the people's strength, he acquired a presentiment of the great future mission of that force. Here he is prescient, here he is a prophet.

(1880)

In fact what has Peter's reform meant to us, not only for the future, but also for what has already taken place, what has happened, what has appeared before our eyes? What did that reform signify to us? For us it was not merely the adoption of European costumes, customs, inventions, and European science. Let us penetrate into the essence of what took place, let us look closely. Yes, it is very possible that Peter originally began to carry it out only in the narrowest utilitarian sense, but subsequently, when he developed his idea to its furthest limit, he doubtlessly yielded to some secret intuition, which pulled him, in this matter, toward future goals that were indubitably far greater than narrow utilitarianism.

In exactly the same way the Russian people also did not accept the reform merely out of utilitarianism, but rather they already sensed with their foresight, almost immediately, some kind of very remote, incomparably higher goal than mere narrow utilitarianism.

The Russian people, I repeat, of course felt this goal unconsciously, but immediately and fully. We strove toward a vital, universal, humanistic union.

We admitted the genius of other nations into our soul, not in a hostile fashion (as it might appear it would have to be), but in a friendly manner. We took in all nations, not making discriminatory distinctions between nations, being able from the first to abolish contradictions and to excuse and reconcile differences. We thereby demonstrated our readiness and inclination (which appeared to us ourselves only then) to a universal international uniting with all the nations of the great Aryan family. Yes, the mission of the Russian people is certainly all-European and worldwide. To become truly Russian, to become fully Russian can in the last analysis only mean (I emphasize this) becoming a brother to all human beings, a universal human being, if you wish. Oh, all that Slavophilism and Westernism of ours is only a big misunderstanding, although historically it was inevitable. To a true Russian, Europe and the fate of the great Aryan clan are as precious as Russia herself, as the fate of our native land, because worldwide universality is our fate, not through conquest by the sword, but by the strength of brotherhood and our brotherly striving toward a uniting of people. If you try to understand our history after Peter's reform, you will find traces and signs of this idea, of my dream, if you wish, in the character of our relations with European nations, even in our governmental policy. What has Russia been doing these two entire centuries in its policy, if not serve Europe much more than herself? I do not think this happened only because of the incompetence of our politicians. The nations of Europe do not have any idea how precious they are to us! And in the future, I believe this, we, that is, of course not we, but the Russian people of the future, will come to understand down to the last one that to become real Russians will mean precisely this: to strive to reconcile European conflicts, finally and definitely, and to show to the Europeans how to put an end to their European anguish inside our Russian soul, which unites all humanity, to enclose in it with brotherly love all our brothers, and in the end maybe even to speak the final word of the great, general harmony, of the ultimate brotherly assent of all peoples to the law of Christ's gospels.

I know all too well that my words may seem enthusiastic, exaggerated, fanatical. Let it be so; I do not regret that I spoke them. They had to be spoken, and they are essential particularly now, especially now, when we are celebrating and honoring our great genius, who embodied this very idea in his artistic work. This idea had been expressed previously more than once; I am not saying anything at all new. This may seem smug: "That is the fate decreed for us, for our beggarly, rough land? We are fated to speak a new word to humanity?" Am I talking about economic power, about glory of the sword or science? I am speaking only about the brotherhood of human beings and about how the Russian heart may be predestined more than all other nations for universal, brotherly fellowship. I see signs of this in our history, in our talented people, in the artistic genius of Pushkin.

Let our land be impoverished. "Christ walked up and down in the serf's guise and blessed it" [from a poem by Tyutchev]. Why should we not accept his last word? Was He Himself not born in a manger? I repeat: at least we can point to Pushkin, to the universality of his genius. He was able to embrace foreign geniuses in his heart as if they were close relatives. At least in his artistic creation, he revealed irrefutably this universality of the Russian spirit, and there is an important lesson in this. If this idea is a fantasy, at least in Pushkin there is something on which to base it. If he had lived longer, maybe he would have shown immortal and great images of the Russian soul that would be understandable to our European brothers. He would have drawn them to us much more closely than they are now. Maybe he would have succeeded in explaining to them all the truth of our strivings, and they would have understood us better than they do now. They might have sensed what we are, they would have stopped looking at us distrustingly and condescendingly, as they look on us still. If Pushkin had lived longer, perhaps there would be less misunderstanding and quarreling even among ourselves. But God decided otherwise. Pushkin died in the full spread of his powers, and doubtless carried away with him some great secret into the grave. And now, we, without him, are trying to divine what that secret is.

To Russia (March 1854)

Aleksei Khomiakov

Aleksei Khomiakov (1804–60) was one of the leading figures of the mid-nineteenth-century Russian Slavophile movement. Though he is widely respected for his poetry, he was just as active in theology as he was in the arts. He carried on lively correspondences with Western religious scholars, particularly with the Anglican theologian William Palmer of England, debating the virtues of their respective Christian traditions. To be called to Russia, as Khomiakov spells out here, means more than just returning from "beyond the waves of the angry Danube." It means a profound cleansing of the soul, one that has been burdened by the indolence of Western social mores. To be called to Russia suggests a meeting of fellow travelers whose collective cooperation triumphs over individualism (leading to Khomiakov's oft-cited notion of sobornost', literally "cathedrality" or "shared struggle"). For historians and followers of the Slavophile movement, sobornost' could also be instantiated in the Russian peasant mir, *or commune, and the broader* obshchina, *from the root word* obshchii, *signaling that which is shared. Soviet writers would later suggest that it was precisely codes of* sobornost' *that made Russians receptive to notions of collectivity in the Communist era. Khomiakov wrote his poetry at a time when to be a poet was also part of a higher calling, that of prophet, thus suggesting the important spiritual and philosophical role of art as well as its mission in helping to define Russia's place in history.*

> To sacred struggle thee hath summoned
> The Lord who gave to thee His love,
> And granted thee a fateful strength,
> That thou might crush the base intention
> Of powers blind, mindless, untamed.
>
> Arise, O thou my native country,
> For thy brethren's sake! God summons thee
> Beyond the waves of angry Danube

To where, lapping about land's limit,
Aegean waters do resound.

Remember, though—to be God's weapon
For earthly men is heavy toil;
He sternly calls His slaves to judgment,
And upon thee, alas! So many
Horrendous sins are now imposed!

With dark injustice art thou blackened,
And branded art with slavery's yoke;
With godless flattery, noxious falsehood,
With indolence, moribund and shameful,
And every vileness art thou filled!

O thou, unworthy to be chosen,
Chosen thou art! Hasten to wash
Thyself with waters of repentance,
So that no punishment redoubled
Should break like thunder on thy head!

With soul humbled in genuflection,
And head prostrated in the dust,
Offer thy prayers of meek submission;
The injuries of festering conscience
Heal with the unction of thy tears!

And then arise, true to thy calling,
Speed to the heat of bloody arms!
Do doughty battle for thy brethren,
In doughty hand hold fast God's standard,
Smite with thy sword, for it is God's!

Translated by G. S. Smith

Moscow and Petersburg: 1842

Aleksandr Herzen

Aleksandr Herzen (1812–70) was one of the founding fathers of Russian socialism. He was a prolific writer and activist whose widely read works spawned equally wide debate—among liberal democrats who rejected his endorsement of violent overthrow and among anarchist revolutionaries who considered him too soft. His lobbying efforts greatly contributed to the emancipation of the serfs in 1861, significantly changing the legal status of millions of formerly hereditary, indentured laborers across the Russian countryside. In his writing he eschewed grand abstraction, preferring to focus on what he understood as the Realpolitik of the day and the concerns of average citizens outside of politics. He was the consummate dialectician in search of compromise.

Readers can decide for themselves how Herzen's dialectics play out in one of the greatest of Russia's parlor dramas of recent centuries, arguing a tale of two cities. By the time of its first recorded mention in 1147, Moscow (in Russian, Moskva) was, like so many medieval European towns to its west, becoming encircled in walls to protect it from invading forces. But unlike other European towns that grew into capitals over the succeeding centuries, Moscow held on to its walls, redesigning and rebuilding the surrounds of today's Kremlin in the seventeenth century. Moscow was a city of wood and onion domes, where the shape of the latter recalled the burning of the former in the hundreds of fires that had consumed the city over its long history. By contrast, in Peter the Great's design St. Petersburg (in Russian, Sankt-Peterburg) was to become everything that Moscow was not. This knowing contrast did not set the cities apart, but tied them inexorably from that moment onward. They embody the two most famous poles of Russian consciousness, and in their differences capture talk about its soul.

Petersburg is a marvel. I examined it closely, scrutinized its academies, its chancelleries, its barracks, its arcades . . . and I understood little. Not having any specific obligations, not involved in the bustle of civic affairs, nor in the field and guard assignments of peacetime military pursuits, I was at leisure, stepping back, so to speak, to examine the city. I saw the various strata of people: people who, with Olympian brush of the pen, can give out a Stanislav Award or remove someone from their post; people who are constantly writing (that is, bureaucrats); people who almost never write (that is, Russian men of letters); and people who not only never write, but also never read (the officers-for-life of the Imperial Guard). In Petersburg, I saw lions and lionesses, tigers and tigresses, I saw types of people who resemble neither beast nor human. But in Petersburg they are at home, like fish in water. Finally, I saw poets in Department III of the Sub-Chancellery . . . and I saw Department III of the Sub-Chancellery which studies poets. But Petersburg remained an enigma to me, as before. Now, when it has begun to fade in my mind into the mist which God has been drawing around it for an entire year, so that one cannot see from afar what is going on, I cannot find the means to explain the puzzling existence of a city which is founded on every sort of contrast and contradiction, physical and moral. . . . This, however, is evidence of its modernity. The entire period of Russian history since Peter the Great is an enigma, our present way of life is an enigma. . . . Ours is a chaos of forces with no uniform origin gnawing at each other, a chaos of opposing tendencies. Something European sometimes surfaces, something grand and humane finds its way through. It then either sinks into the swamp of the inertly suffering Slavic character that apathetically accepts everything (the rule of the whip, the abrogation of their rights, the invasion of the Tatars and then Peter himself) and which, for that reason, in essence, accepts nothing. Or else, it sinks into wild notions about our exceptional national character, notions that have recently crawled out of graves and have grown no wiser beneath the damp earth.

From the day Peter saw that there was only one salvation for Russia—to cease being Russia—from the day he resolved to move us into world history, Petersburg became necessary and Moscow superfluous. The first inevitable step for Peter was the transference of the capital out of Moscow. With the founding of Petersburg, Moscow became secondary; it lost its former meaning for Russia, heralding only nothingness and emptiness until 1812. In the future it could be . . . Who knows what it could be, and most likely there will be much good in the future. But we are talking about the past and the present. Moscow was of no significance for mankind, and for Russia it had the significance of a whirlpool, sucking its best energies and unable to make anything from them. After Peter, Moscow was forgotten, wrapped in the respect and favor in which one regards a little old grandmother, depriving her of any sort of participation in the running of the estate. Moscow served as a way-station between Petersburg and the next world for the gentry who had served their time, like the anticipation of the silence of the grave.

For its part, Moscow felt no indignation toward Petersburg. On the contrary, it has always tried to keep up with Petersburg, imitating and disfiguring its fashions and customs. The entire younger generation was serving in the

Red Square, Moscow, circa 1918. Courtesy of the Library of Congress, Prints and Photographs Division, LC-USZ62–95770.

Guards at that time; all the talented people who emerged in Moscow would set off for Petersburg to write, work, or to perform some function. And suddenly this Moscow, the existence of which had been forgotten, became entangled again in the history of Europe. Now it burned down, now it was built back up; its name found itself in the bulletins of the Grande Armée, Napoleon rode along its streets. Europe again remembered Moscow. Fantastic tales about how it had been built spread throughout the world. Who did not have this charming story about how the phoenix had risen up out of the ashes pounded into their ears? It must be confessed that Moscow had been poorly constructed; the architecture of its buildings is ugly, horribly pretentious; its buildings, or, better still, its farms, are small, plastered all over with columns, overloaded with pediments, enclosed by fences. . . . What was it like before, was it really much worse? There were good people who thought that such a powerful jolt would awaken the life of Moscow; they thought that an original and educated national character would develop in Moscow, little darling that she is, now stretched across forty versts [approximately twenty-six and a half miles] from Troitsa in Golenishchevo to Butyrok. The city must be resting on its laurels. But at this point no one is foreseeing another Napoleon.

In Petersburg, people in general, and persons individually, are extremely foul. It is impossible to love Petersburg, yet I feel that I would not live in any other Russian city. In Moscow, on the other hand, everyone is extremely kind, but it is just that they live with a deathly boredom. In Moscow there is a sort of half-wild, half-educated genteel way of life of the sort that gets worn down in the suffocating atmosphere of Petersburg. It is nice to look at it, as at any particular thing, but one immediately tires of it. The Russian gentry does not know comfort—it is wealthy, but dirty. The gentry is provincial and pompous in Moscow, which is why it is in a state of continual anxiety. It strives after, reaches for Petersburg's customs, but Petersburg does not even have its own customs. There is nothing original or unique in Petersburg, unlike in Moscow where everything is original, from the absurd architecture of St. Basil's Cathedral to the taste of *kalach* bread. Petersburg is the embodiment of the general, abstract concept of a capital city. It differs little from all other European cities insomuch as it looks like all of them; Moscow resembles not a single one. Moscow, instead, is a gigantic evolved kind of wealthy Russian village. Petersburg is a parvenu; it has no time-honored memories, nor does it have a sincere connection with the country that it was called forth from the swamp to represent. It has police, offices, merchants, a river, a royal court, seven-story buildings, Guards, paved walkways, and gaslights that really illuminate the streets. It is content with its comfortable way of life, which has no roots and which stands, like Petersburg itself, on pilings that hundreds of thousands of workers died hammering in.

There is a deathly silence in Moscow. The people systematically do nothing. They work, they live, and they rest again before more work. After ten o'clock you will not find a single cab, you will not run into another person on the street. At every turn one is reminded of the disconnected, eastern Slavic way of life. In Petersburg there is a perpetual flow of vanities, yet everyone is so busy that they do not even live. Petersburg's activity is senseless, but the habit of being seen as active is a great thing. Moscow's lethargic sleep gives Muscovites their Beijing / *Kuku Nor* static character, which would depress even Father Joacinth himself.[1] A resident of Petersburg has narrow or ignoble goals, but he achieves them, he is not content with the present, he works. A resident of Moscow, extremely noble at heart, does not have any sort of goal, is for the most part satisfied with himself, and when he is dissatisfied, he does not know how to get from general, indefinite, vague ideas to actually finding the sore spot. In Petersburg every man of letters is a peddler; there is not a single literary circle there that has as its unifying bond an idea rather than a personality or a profit motive. The men of letters in Petersburg are two times less educated than those in Moscow; when they come to Moscow they are astonished at the intellectual evening parties and conversations there. Meanwhile all publishing activity takes place in Petersburg. Journals are published there, the censors are smarter there, Pushkin and Karamzin wrote and lived there; even Gogol belonged more to Petersburg than to Moscow. There are people of strong conviction in Moscow, but they sit there idly with their arms folded. In Moscow there are literary circles that unselfishly spend their time demonstrating to each other the correctness of some useful idea, for example, that the West is decaying and Rus' is blossoming. Only one journal worth reading is published in Moscow, that being *The Muscovite.*

A resident of Moscow loves crosses and ceremonies, a resident of Petersburg—positions and money. A resident of Moscow loves aristocratic connections, a resident of Petersburg—connections with government functionaries. If they drape a Stanislav Award around the neck of a Muscovite, he will wear it on his paunch. In the case of a Petersburg resident, a Vladimir medal is put on like a dog collar with a clasp or like a noose on someone who has just come to an abrupt end at the gallows.[2] In Petersburg one can live about two years without guessing the religion to which it adheres—here even Russian churches have taken on a certain Catholic aspect. In Moscow you will know and hear Orthodoxy and its brazen voice the day after you arrive. In Moscow a great many people go to mass every Sunday and holiday; there are even those who go to matins too. In Petersburg no male goes to matins, only Germans attend mass at their own church. Newly arrived peasants go to mass. In Petersburg there is only one set of relics: Peter's Cabin. In Moscow lie the relics of all the Russian saints who did not get a place made for them in Kyiv, even those whose deaths are the subject of controversy to this day, Tsarevich Dmitrii, for example. All of these sacred objects are protected by the walls of the Kremlin while the walls of the Peter and Paul Fortress in Petersburg protect artillery fortifications and the mint.

Separated from the political action, living on old news, having no key to government activities, nor the instinct to divine them, Moscow moralizes. Dissatisfied with many things, it provides responses on many issues voluntarily. . . . Suddenly an oversized Aleksandr Ivanovich Khlestakov [a minor civil servant who is mistaken for a government inspector in Nikolai Gogol's comedy *The Inspector General*, 1836] shows up: Moscow bows from the waist, glad for the visit, gives balls and dinners and retells all the same bons mots. Petersburg, in whose center everything takes place, is pleased by no one and surprised by nothing. If all of Vasil'evskii Island were blown up with gunpowder, this would create less agitation than the arrival of Prince Khozrev-Mirza in Moscow. Ivan Aleksandrovich means nothing in Petersburg, you cannot fool anyone there, neither with power nor with authority—in Petersburg they know where and with whom power lies. Up to the present any foreigner in Moscow is taken for a great person; in Petersburg every great person is taken for a foreigner. During its entire life Petersburg has only rejoiced once: It very much feared the Frenchman, and when Wittgenstein saved it, Petersburg ran to meet him. In most decent Moscow an announcement appears in the paper that the city is to be moved to emotion on such-and-such a day, or rejoice on such-and-such a day: It is enough for the governor-general to give the order for the regimental band to be brought out or a religious procession to be arranged. Muscovites weep over the fact that there is a famine in Riazan', residents of Petersburg do not weep because they do not even suspect the existence of Riazan'. If they have even a vague notion of the interior provinces, they most likely do not know that people eat bread there.

A young resident of Moscow does not acquiesce to social proprieties. He acts the liberal, and it is precisely in these fits of liberalism that one sees the incorrigible Scythian. This liberalism takes its leave of Muscovites the moment they pay a visit to the secret police. A young resident of Petersburg is formal, like business paper; at the age of sixteen he is playing the role of a diplomat, and to some extent even that of a spy. He remains steadfast in this role for his whole life. In Petersburg everything happens terribly quickly. Five days after his arrival in Petersburg Polevoi [a controversial editor, writer, and historian] became a loyal subject; in Moscow he would have been ashamed, and he would have been a free-thinker for another five years or so. In general, Muscovite wishy-washy liberals are beginning to seek jobs in Petersburg, to curse enlightenment and to bless divorce. Petersburg, like an Egyptian incubator, once it opens up the shell, claims itself not to blame for the kind of chick it hatches. Belinskii, who in Moscow preached national roots and autocracy, outdid Anacharsis Cloots himself a month after arriving in Petersburg.[3] Petersburg, like all people with positive attitudes, does not listen to chatter, but demands action. That is why noble Muscovite talkers often become most ignoble doers. Overall there are no liberals in Petersburg, and if one appears, he does not end up in Moscow—he is sent directly off to hard labor or to the Caucasus.

There is something tragic, somber, and majestic in the destiny of Petersburg. This favorite child of the northern giant, a titan in whom the energy and cruelty of the 1793 National Convention and its revolutionary power were concentrated, is the favorite child of the tsar, who renounced his own country for its benefit and who oppressed it in the name of Europeanism and civilization. Petersburg's sky is always gray; the sun, which shines on good and evil alike, on Petersburg alone does not shine. The marshy soil gives off humid air, the damp coastal wind whistles along the streets. I repeat, every autumn

Nevskii Prospect, Petrograd (St. Petersburg), circa 1918. Courtesy of the Library of Congress Prints and Photographs Division, LC-USZ62–95769.

Petersburg can expect a squall to flood it. In the destiny of Moscow, there is something bourgeois and banal: The climate is not bad, but it is not good either; the buildings are not short, but then they are not tall. Take a look at Muscovites near Novinskii or in Sokol'niki on the first of May: They are neither hot nor cold, all is well with them, and they are content with their carnival booths, with their carriages, with themselves. Then look at Petersburg on a good day: The unhappy inhabitants run hurriedly from their burrows, throw themselves into carriages, and gallop off to dachas, to islands. They become intoxicated by the greenery and the sunshine like the prisoners in *Fidelio*. But the habit of worrying does not leave them: They know that it will start raining in an hour, and that they, chancellery toilers, bureaucratic laborers by day, have to be at their posts the next morning. A person who is shivering from the severe cold and the dampness, a person who lives in an endless fog and frost, looks at the world differently. The government, which is concentrated in this frost and which has taken from it its hostile and sullen character, is evidence of this. An artist who developed in Petersburg selected the image of the savage, irrational force destroying people in Pompeii as a target for his brush—this is Petersburg's inspiration![4] In Moscow there is a beautiful view once every verst. Yet you can walk all around flat Petersburg from one end to the other and not find even a single mediocre view. After walking around, you come back to the embankment of the Neva and say that all of Moscow's views are nothing compared to this. In Petersburg they like luxury, but they do not like anything superfluous; in Moscow it is precisely only the superfluous that is regarded as luxury. That is why every building in Moscow has columns, while there are none in Petersburg; every resident of Moscow has several footmen, badly dressed and doing nothing, while a resident of Petersburg has one, neat and adroit.

It must be confessed that it is impossible to be brought up in more opposite ways than were Petersburg and Moscow. During its entire life Petersburg has seen only revolutions in the seraglio, overthrows and celebrations, and has no knowledge at all of our ancient way of life. Moscow, which grew up under the Tatar Yoke and which took control of Rus' not by its own merit, but due to the lack of merit of other parts, came to a stop on the last page of the *Koshikhinskii Times* and knows about the subsequent overthrows only through rumor. In due course a courier arrives and brings a dispatch—and Moscow believes what is in print: who is tsar and who is not tsar. It believes that Biron is a good person, and then that he is an evil person; it believes that God himself came down to earth in order to put Anna Ivanovna on the throne, and then Anna Leopoldovna, and then Ivan Antonovich, and then Elizaveta Petrovna, and then Petr Fedorovich, and then Ekaterina Alekseevna in place of Petr Fedorovich. Petersburg knows very well that God would not come to meddle in these dark matters; it saw the orgies of the Summer Gardens, Duchess Biron rolling in the snow, and Anna Leopoldovna sleeping with her lover on the balcony of the Winter Palace, and then exiled; it saw the funeral of Peter the Third and the funeral of Pavel the First. It has seen much and knows much.

Nowhere have I given myself over to such sorrowful thoughts as often as I have in Petersburg. Crushed by serious doubts, I would sometimes wander across its granite and be close to despair. Such moments bind me to Petersburg, and because of them I came to love Petersburg just as I ceased to love Moscow. Moscow is unable to rip you apart or cause you to suffer. Petersburg can force any honest person a thousand times to curse this Babylon; in Moscow one can live for years and never hear cursing anywhere, except for the Uspenskii Cathedral. That is how Moscow is worse than Petersburg. Petersburg maintains a physically and morally feverish state. In Moscow health is magnified to such an extent that an organic plastic movement replaces all living activity. In Petersburg there is not a single fat person, except for Commandant Zakharzhevskii, even then he is fat from a contusion. From this it is clear that anyone who wants to live in body and spirit should choose neither Moscow nor Petersburg. In Petersburg he would die halfway through a natural life, and in Moscow he would go insane.

"So what, the devil with it," you will say. "You've been talking and talking, and I haven't even figured out who you give preference to." Rest assured that I have not figured it out either. In the first place, one cannot select either Petersburg or Moscow for residence right at this moment. Instead the matter is settled by fate that chooses a place of residence for us. In the second place, every living thing has such a multitude of features, so amazingly welded together into a single fabric, that any sharp opinion is one-sided nonsense. There are aspects of life in Moscow that are possible to like, as there are in Petersburg, but there are many more of the sort which make one not like Moscow or hate Petersburg. Likewise, good features can be found everywhere, even in Beijing and Vienna: There are those three good people on whose account God several times forgave the sins of Sodom and Gomorrah, but did no more than forgive. One should not get carried away by this. Everywhere where many people live, where people have been living for a long time, one can find something humane, something grand and poetic. Grand is the sound of Muscovite bells and processions at the Kremlin, grand are the long parades in Petersburg, grand are the gatherings of Buddhists in the East, reading their sacred books by the light of one hundred and twelve torches. There is little of this poetic aspect to us, we want . . . We want all sorts of things.

They are now predicting a railroad line between Moscow and Petersburg. May God grant it! Through this channel Petersburg and Moscow will rise to the same level, and, most likely, caviar will be cheaper in Petersburg, and in Moscow they will find out two days earlier which issues of foreign journals are forbidden. That will be something!

Translated by John Leafgren

Notes

1. Nikolai Iakovlevich Bichurin, 1777–1873, a Sinologist and translator who took monastic vows and became Father Joacinth. Author, among other works, of *The History of Tibet* and *Kuku Nor.*

2. The system of Russian orders dates back to the reign of Peter the Great. Empress Catherine II established the Order of St. Vladimir to reward military and civil achievements and longtime service. In 1831 the Polish Order of St. Stanislav was added.

3. Pseudonym of Jean Baptiste, 1755–94, political figure in the French Revolution.

4. A reference to the Russian artist Karl Briullov (1799–1852), who painted *The Last Day of Pompeii* (1830–33).

"Great Russians" and "Little Russians" (2003)

Andreas Kappeler

One of contemporary Russia's paradoxes is that it traces its origins to a place that is today the capital of another country, Ukraine. Historians and politicians alike commonly cite the founding of Kyivan Rus' in 880 as the shared origin of the contemporary Russian, Belorussian, and Ukrainian peoples. But this shared creation myth never entirely produced a doctrine of equality, not least when Kyiv itself and much of the broader surrounding territory was annexed into the Russian Empire in the late eighteenth century. Ukraine, a place whose name is most often translated as "at the border" but can also mean "cut off" or "removed," has long wrestled with this official peripheral status in light of its otherwise commanding size and natural resources. Despite the country's independence from the former Soviet Union (and correspondingly from Russia) in 1991, many Russian politicians have lobbied for a continued dominant voice in Ukrainian affairs given the enormous Russophone community there, comprising roughly half of the Ukrainian population. For some, to imagine the two countries as separate is simply an act of cognitive dissonance. In recent years Russia and Ukraine have conducted sometimes tense negotiations over the status of the sizable Russian Black Sea fleet anchored in Stavropol' on the Crimean Peninsula. While this was provisionally settled in 1997 with Russian recognition of Ukrainian sovereignty and the Ukrainian deeding of a twenty-year harbor lease to the Russian Navy, smaller skirmishes over usufruct rights continue. In the Crimea, among other Ukrainian sites, where Russia begins and where it ends (or historically speaking, where Russia began and where it rules today) depends on who you ask.

In 1762 the Ukrainian writer Semen Divovych wrote a dialogue in Russian verses titled "A Talk between Great Russia and Little Russia." At the time, "Little Russia" was the official name for Ukraine. In the beginning "Great Russia" asks "Little Russia":

> What kind of a people are you and whence have you come?
> Tell me, tell me your origins, from what have you derived?

"Little Russia" explains her heroic past, from the time of the Khazars, to rule under the kings of Poland, until her voluntary submission under the Russian ruler Aleksei Mikhailovich who guaranteed restoration of her old privileges. "Great Russia" replies:

> You know, with whom you speak, or do you forget it?
> I am Russia! Why do you disregard me? . . .
> As if you would belong to another Russia, not to me!

"Little Russia" answers:

> I know, that you are Russia,
> and this is my name, too.
> Why do you frighten me? I am brave myself.
> I have become subject not to you, but to your lord. . . .
> Do not think that you yourself are my ruler,
> But your lord and my lord are in command of both of us.
> And the difference between us is only in adjectives,
> You the Great and I the Little live in bordering countries.
> That I am called Little and you Great
> Is not a strange thing to you or to me.
> For your borders are wider than mine, . . .
> Yet we are equal and form one whole,
> We swear allegiance to one, not to two lords—
> Thus I consider you equal to myself.

"Little Russia then explains her merits and refutes "Great Russia's" accusation of having betrayed Russia with Hetman Mazepa [Ukrainian Cossack leader who abandoned his allegiance to the Russian Empire]. In the end "Great Russia" is convinced:

> Enough, I accept now your truth,
> I believe all you said, I respect and recognize your
> Braveness. . . .
> I won't give up my friendship with you forever.
> We will live in the future in inseparable concord
> And we will serve loyally one state.

In 1762, when this dialogue was written, the Tsarist state under Empress Catherine II began systematically to integrate "Little Russia," which consisted of the Hetmanate of the Dniepr Cossacks on the left bank of the Dnipro / Dniepr River (with Kyïv / Kiev on the right bank). The Cossacks had enjoyed considerable autonomy within Russia since "Little Russia's" voluntary union with Muscovy more than a century earlier. The "Conversation between Great Russia and Little Russia" reacts to "Little Russia's" danger of

A village twenty miles outside of Kyiv, ca. 1918. Courtesy of the Library of Congress, Prints and Photographs Division, LC-USZ62–97673.

being subordinated to "Great Russia" and emphasizes the dynastic, prenational character of the Tsarist Empire, which embraced "Great Russia" and "Little Russia" as equal partners. However, Semen Divovych's dialogue, written in the middle of the eighteenth century, does not reflect the reality of political interrelations between Russia and the Ukrainian hetmanate of this epoch, but, rather, the wishful thinking of the Cossack elite. It can be considered the swan song of the autonomous Hetmanate. In the following decades "Little Russia" lost practically all her traditional rights and privileges and became a normal part of the Tsarist Empire, as was also the case with the right bank Ukraine which was annexed by Russia in the second partition of Poland in 1793.

This equality between Ukraine and Russia lost its foundation in the nineteenth century when nationalism emerged in Russia. The "Little" or "Southern Russians" were considered integral parts of the Russian state, the Russian people and, consequently, the Russian nation. When Ukrainian intellectuals began to develop their own national movement, which brought into question an all-Russian nation, the Ukrainian language and culture were persecuted and subjected to repressive Russification (1863–1905). The February revolution of 1917 and the creation of an independent Ukrainian National Republic (1918–20) seemed to change the character of Ukrainian-Russian relations. This was also true, to a similar extent, for the Ukrainian Soviet Republic during the 1920s. This kind of relationship ended under Stalin, who bludgeoned Ukraine with terror and degraded her to an obedient little sister of the great Russian brother.

Only in 1991, when Ukraine emerged from the collapse of the Soviet Union as an independent republic, could the prospect of equality with Russia reappear on the political agenda. It was not until May 1997, after several delays, that Russian President Boris Yeltsin and Ukrainian President Leonid Kuchma signed a "Treaty on Friendship, Cooperation, and Partnership" between the two countries. It begins by stating:

> Ukraine and the Russian Federation . . . based on the close historic ties and the relationship of friendship and cooperation between the peoples of Ukraine and Russia . . . considering that the strengthening of friendly relations, good-neighborliness, and mutually beneficial cooperation corresponds to substantial interests of their peoples and serves the cause of peace and international security . . . filled with a determination to ensure the irrevocability and continuation of the democratic processes in both states . . . have agreed as follows:

> Article 1: As friendly, equal, and sovereign states, the High Contracting Parties shall base their relations upon mutual respect and trust, strategic partnership and cooperation.

Article 1 is followed by 40 other articles which regulate the principles of equality, of reciprocal recognition, and respect for the sovereignty and territorial integrity of the two states.

After 225 years Divovych's wish was finally fulfilled, that Russia recognized independent Ukraine as an equal partner. For Russia the recognition of Ukraine was a difficult step. The Duma and the Federative Council ratified the Treaty on Friendship only in December 1998 and February 1999. However, despite what the treaty may say, Russian-Ukrainian relations even today are not completely normal or equal. Nevertheless, initial political tensions have eased in recent years.

When Ukraine declared its independence in August 1991 and confirmed it in a referendum on 1 December, which passed with over 90 percent of the votes, it delivered a mortal blow to the Soviet Union. Russian government and society were shocked. Russian politicians (among them not only imperial nationalists like the Russian vice-president Alexander Rutskoi, but also prominent democrats like the mayors of Moscow and Leningrad, Gavriil Popov and Anatolii Sobchak, and Yeltsin's close adviser, Gennadii Burbulis) reacted with open threats. The media in Russia and abroad feared war, even nuclear war, between the two most important post-Soviet states. On the eve of the Ukrainian referendum, Soviet President Mikhail Gorbachev declared, "we cannot even contemplate that Ukraine would leave the Union, because that would be big trouble for the Union, but even bigger trouble, a catastrophe, for Ukraine." The chief editor of the liberal newspaper *Moskovskie novosti* (*The Moscow News*) said shortly before the final collapse of the Soviet Union that "millions of Russians are convinced that without Ukraine not only can there be no great Russia, but there cannot be any kind of Russia at all." Ukrainian politicians responded by insisting on independence. President Kuchma commented in 1995 that "Ukraine wanted to have an equal partnership with Russia. . . . There are forces in Russia which do not want to understand that Ukraine is a sovereign state and this is our main worry in relations with Russia."

However, the sensationalistic horror scenarios prominent in the Russian and Western press did not come to pass. On the contrary, Ukraine and Russia (with the notable exception of Chechnya) during the first decade after the collapse of the Soviet Union were spared from wars and violent interethnic conflicts—in contrast to the situation in the Caucasus or in former Yugoslavia. Nevertheless, Russo-Ukrainian tensions should not be underestimated. Many significant issues arose between Ukraine and Russia during the 1990s including:

1. Problems connected with the heritage of the Soviet army, especially their nuclear weapons, which evoked fears in Central and Western Europe, namely due to the memory of the Chernobyl catastrophe of 1986;

2. The conflict over who would inherit the Soviet Black Sea Fleet, provisionally settled in 1997;

3. The problem of the Crimean Peninsula in the Black Sea with the important marine harbor Sevastopol'. Crimea had been part of the Russian Republic for centuries, and only in 1954 was it transferred to the Ukrainian SSR. It is populated by a majority of ethnic Russians;

4. The existence of over 11 million ethnic Russians in the Ukrainian state, especially in its Eastern and Southern regions. They constitute over 20 percent of the population of Ukraine;

5. Cultural and linguistic rights of the Russian speaking population of Ukraine, which consists of approximately 50 percent of the general population;

6. The economic dependence of Ukraine on Russian petroleum and natural gas;

7. Diverging opinions about the character of the Commonwealth of Independent States (CIS): Ukraine succeeded in preventing Russian efforts toward tighter integration of CIS members.

Relations between Russia and Ukraine, the two largest nations in Europe (territorially), are extremely relevant for the future of Europe and the world. Despite the "Treaty on Friendship, Cooperation, and Partnership" in 1997, contemporary attitudes threaten their relationship. These attitudes are largely the product of history. To better understand their relationship, it is necessary to closely examine this history.

. . . .

In the conversation of 1762 Ukraine bears the name "Little Russia." The term "Little Russia" (*Malorossiia*) did not mean, as Semen Divovych thought, the difference in size between the two areas. Since the fourteenth century the Orthodox patriarch of Constantinople designated two church provinces of Rus', Halych / Kiev and Vladimir / Moscow, with the terms "he mikra Rosia" ("Little Russia" which is inner or southern Russia) and "he megale Rosia" ("Great Russia" which is outer or northern Russia). Names of church provinces occasionally were transferred to different regions of Rus', but disappeared in the beginning of the fifteenth century. The term "Great Russia" begins to reappear in sources during the sixteenth century, the term "Little Russia" by its very end.

Around 1600 Ukrainian-educated churchmen studying Greek sources took up the term *Malorossiia* and introduced it into the title of the orthodox metropolitan of Kiev, elected in 1620. As in the late middle ages, "Little Russia" meant the East Slavic lands of the Polish-Lithuanian commonwealth (Ruthenian or *rusyn*). Ukrainian churchmen began also to use more frequently the term "Great Russia." In the 1640s, when communication with Moscow became more intensive, the terminology was adopted in Russia. In 1654, "Great Russia" and "Little Russia" appeared for the first time in the official title of the Muscovite Tsar. Only from this time forward did the Russian government use "Little Russia" (*Malorossiia*) to express the idea that left-bank Ukraine, and later other Ukrainian regions, belonged to Russia.

In the dialogue from 1762, "Little Russia" represented the Hetmanate of left-bank Ukraine, or more precisely, its elites whose aim was to attain equal rights with "Great Russia" in the framework of the Tsarist Empire. "Great Russia" in this context meant the ethnically Russian part of Russia. Not until the nineteenth century did the term "Little Russia" gradually acquire the pejorative meaning of the inferior part of Russia. *Malorossy* ("Little Russians") then became a negative designation by nationally conscious Ukrainians for Ukrainian people who were loyal to the Tsarist state and integrated themselves into the Russian culture and language.

The partners of the treaty of 1997 were Ukraine and the Russian Federation as sovereign republics. Only during the second half of the nineteenth and the beginning of the twentieth century did the terms "Ukraine" and "Ukrainians," which had been used since the middle ages for particular regions, gradually become the common self-designation of the emerging nation. "Ukraine" has served as the official name for the region only since 1917, at first for the Ukrainian National Republic, and then for the Ukrainian Soviet Socialist Republic. Only after the Second World War did "Ukraine" include Ruthenians (*rusyny*) from Western Ukraine, when, for the first time, nearly all areas with a Ukrainian-speaking majority were united into one state.

In 1997, *Rossiia* (Russia) referred to the new state, *Rossiiskaia Federatsia* (the Russian Federation). In Russian, *Rossiia* is distinguished from the ethnonym *russkii* (Russian). *Rossiia* means a supranational identity which includes several ethnic groups, among them the Russians (*russkie*). So in principle, the new Russian state is a supranational federation of several peoples. The term *Rossiia* is taken from the Tsarist Empire where it was first used in the sixteenth century and became the official designation of the multinational state in the eighteenth century. In the later Soviet period the equivalent of the supranational imperial nation was the supranational Soviet nation or people (*sovetskii narod*).

The dichotomy between the ethnic nation based on language, culture, and common history (*russkie*) and the political or civic nation of subjects or citizens (*rossiane*) is crucial, although in practice the two conceptions continuously intermingle. The notion of *Rossiia,* the common designation for the multinational Tsarist Empire and for the present Russian state, is closely related to the older terms *Rus'* and *russkii*. In Ukrainian, English, or German *Rossiia* (Russian) and *russkii* (Russian) are designated by the same term. Ukrainians often identified the Russian state (*Rossiia*) with the Russian people (*rossiis'kyi narod*). In contrast to the Russian nation, the Ukrainian ethnicity and state nation are designated by only one name, "Ukraine" and "Ukrainian."

In the nineteenth and early twentieth centuries, the term *Rossiia* designated a multinational state, just as the ethnic term "Russian" (*russkii*) officially comprised not only ethnic Russians, but all Eastern Slavs, including "Great Russians," "Little Russians" (Ukrainians), and "White Russians" (Belorussians). In this sense the Ukrainians were part of an all-Russian cultural

Orthodox community which was an important pillar of Tsarist ideology. Modern Russian nationalism, which was constructed after the Crimean War, the Polish rebellion of 1863, and the apparition of a public sphere by political journalists like Mikhail Katkov and Ivan Aksakov, combined to form the concept of a Russian ethnic nation with the political concept of the Russian (*rossiiskii*) Empire aimed at the new project of an ethnically homogeneous Russian nation-state.

"Little Russians" or Ukrainians in the beginning of the twentieth century were regarded by many educated Russians as integral parts of the Russian nation. Assimilation to the Russian language and culture since the eighteenth century had been common among Ukrainian elites, but only after the Polish uprising of 1863 did Russification of Ukrainians become an explicit goal of Tsarist policy. The effects of this policy were strengthened by the impact of modernization. This option of merging into an ethnic Russian nation was also propagated, at least in theory, by the Russophiles of Austrian Galicia, who were for decades the most important branch of the Ruthenian national movement. If Russification in the Tsarist Empire or later in the Soviet Union had been successful, such assimilation processes could have interrupted or even ended Ukrainian nation building. An example for such an evolution were the Occitans or Provencals of France, with whom the Ukrainians of Russia sometimes compared themselves or were compared to by Russians.

In the Soviet Union, the supranational Russian Empire (*Rossiiskaia imperiia*) was replaced by a new supranational Soviet entity. Under this umbrella Ukrainians, Russians, and other nations had to live harmoniously as socialist nations, liberated from the antagonisms of capitalism. With the Stalinist return to national values, the old all-Russian (East Slavic) project and partially Russian nationalism were revived. Russians once again became "the leading people" of the state, the older brothers in the Soviet family of peoples. Their language, culture, and history got a superior status, and Russification again was furthered by the state. In 1954 Khrushchev tried to promote Ukrainians to the role of the second brother or junior partner, but after his fall Russification again was furthered by the state.

In the history of Ukrainian-Russian interrelations the ambiguity of the Tsarist and Soviet Empires has always been a crucial issue. Their original character was supranational, and it is quite problematic to identify them with Russia and the Russians. If we take seriously their supranationality, Russian-Ukrainian relations do not concern the interactions of Ukrainians with the Tsarist or Soviet state. The identification of the Empire with the Russians is contested by many Russians today who contend that the Russian people suffered more than most of the Tsarist and Soviet state under Imperial rule.

As Geoffrey Hosking states, the position of an imperial nation impeded the formation of a Russian ethnic and civic nation.

On the other hand, Russian nationalism from the start had a strong statist and imperial character. Most members of the elites in both Tsarist and Soviet times were Russians or Russified non-Russians. Many Russians in the late Tsarist and the late Soviet state considered themselves members of the ruling, imperial Russian nation. Believing their language and culture were superior to other peoples in the Empire, they therefore felt it their duty to civilize the non-Russian ethnicities of the territory. For many Russians today these notions of Russia and the Soviet Union are still interchangeable. From the perspective of many Ukrainians, Russians are perceived as representatives of the state, as agents of the Empire. The Russian nation is identified with the Tsarist and Soviet state. Thus, in the history of Russian-Ukrainian relations, conceptions of the state, peoples, and nations have intermingled, making it impossible to separate them analytically.

Bathing the Russian Way

from Folklore to the Songs of Vladimir Vysotskii

In The Russian Primary Chronicle *a story is told of St. Andrew's sojourn among the Slavs in the ninth century. So struck was he by the bathing practices he observed among the early Russians that he set down the following: "Wondrous to relate . . . I noticed their wooden bathhouses. They warm them to extreme heat, then undress, and after anointing themselves with an acid liquid, they take the young branches and lash their bodies. They actually lash themselves so violently that they barely escape alive. Then they drench themselves with cold water, and thus are revived. . . . Indeed, they make of the act not a mere washing, but a veritable torment."*

St. Andrew was not the least nor the last of those who traveled to Russia and observed Russian bathing practices. In the mid-eighteenth century the Abbé Chappe d'Auteroche arrived in Russia from France and wrote an account of his visit to a public bathhouse, not without certain salacious details. Catherine II, herself hardly the standard-bearer for prudishness, condemned the engravings of Russian bathing practices in d'Auteroche's volume as indecent and in the Statute of 1782 outlawed mixed public bathing.

Whatever the response it has elicited among foreigners, the Russian bathhouse or banya, *has been one of the most deeply engrained cultural practices of the Russian people since the earliest days of the Kyivan state. For Russians themselves its meaning has resided in much more than that small wooden building where people came to wash themselves. It has been the site of beliefs and practices, stories and superstitions, and rituals associated with birth, marriage, and death. It was, for all intents and purposes, a magical place, so much so that even the hours when one could take a steam bath were closely regulated. Failure to adhere to these rules meant that the unwary bather might intersect with the* bannik, *or bath spirit, who was said to haunt the premises after midnight. One was prohibited from bathing alone, and one took care to remove one's belt and cross and any other amulets one might be wearing. A word uttered inside the bathhouse automatically acquired magical properties, and thus the bathhouse became the place one went if one desired to acquire occult powers.*

The original bathhouses were similar to what Vladimir Vysotskii describes here as the "black" bathhouses, detached, low-lying wooden structures dependent on a fire lit inside to provide heat. A stove in a corner is made of large round stones that, when heated, are lifted with iron rods and placed in a wooden tub. Once the fire is built, the bather then removes the fire and flushes out the smoke before beginning the bath. Hence the soot and the term "black bathhouse" (chernaia bania). The key to the entire process is the steam (par) which forms after the water is poured over the hot stones. When the bathhouse fills up with steam, the bather begins to beat himself with a venik (a broom made of twigs, usually birch). From there one heads out either to roll in the snow, dive into the river or lake, or (the least extreme variant of the three) throw cold water from a well over oneself. The entire procedure can be repeated any number of times.

Over the centuries certain improvements were made in the bania, resulting in the appearance of "white" bathhouses with an internal heating element or chimney and tiered seating made of wood. To this day Russians are divided over whether the black bathhouse with its smoke and aromatic interior is superior to the more modern white version.

Initially a part of the culture of rural Russia, bathhouses became an important part of Russian urban life from the eighteenth century on. Most noble palaces in St. Petersburg by the second half of the eighteenth century could boast having a bania. In Moscow the Sandunovskaia Baths, still operational today, date from the early nineteenth century and during Soviet times functioned as one of the chief bathing places for people living in communal apartments who had to share toilet, bath, and kitchen space with sometimes seven or more families. The bania's popularity in Russia, however, is linked to more than hygiene. As in the past, it is part of Russian cultural practice. Men in particular spend hours there, talking, drinking beer, and eating dried fish in between periodic forays into the steam room (parilka). For Russian urban dwellers the bania is as much a part of the culture of bonding as of bathing.

We present here two excerpts on the bania, one a song that is part of the wedding rituals practiced for centuries among Russia's peasantry. The bride is invited by her girlfriends to partake of a steam bath on the eve of the day of her wedding. Sung by her friends, the song takes the form of a lament as the bride leaves behind her virginity, her maidenly happiness, her beauty and youth. Although a wedding is the last thing one might expect a young girl to mourn, the reality of life in Russian traditional culture meant that the girl often left her home and her village to live with in-laws she didn't know and where heavy labor often awaited her.

A very different bath song is that by Vladimir Vysotskii (1938–80), beloved poet, bard, actor, composer, and cultural icon who walked the thin line between acceptance and dissent during the Brezhnev era. Here Vysotskii describes the bath of a man, a former prisoner in the Gulag, for whom incarceration in the camps was only a part of his larger incarceration in the Soviet Union as a whole. Hoping that the bath and the birch switches will scrub away the past, he comes to realize that not even a Russian bania *can erase the scars of Soviet life. Vysotskii died of heart failure brought on by acute alcoholism at the age of forty-two. Part of his great appeal to Russian audiences was his gravelly voice and method of delivery. Recordings of Vysotskii performing his own music can be found online through several official Vysotskii websites.*

"S legkim parom" ("I hope you enjoyed your bath"), Russians say to each other after they emerge from the bania.

"The Bath," from Russian Wedding Rituals

I

> Come into our steamy little bath,
> Don't be angry please,
> We didn't stoke up the bath just for you,
> Not just for you was it prepared
> But for our wonderful little friend.
> From the bathhouse to the bedchamber
> Are small footbridges of guilder rose
> And cross beams of raspberry wood
> And finely molded columns
> Topped with gold.
> And on them sit small birds
> Singing plaintively
> Oi, such sad songs with bitter tears.

II

> We stand here, beautiful maidens
> On the oak floors.
> Our line of maidens shall go as far as the white swan
> Ai, it sickens me!
> We will call you by name
> We will call you forth by your patronymic.
> You Taisia, daughter of Antipishen,
> You are our little dove,
> Come to our hot steam bath.
> Our hot steam bath is stoked.
> And we have the steam bath twigs
> And we have laid them along the path
>
> The spring water has been carried in;
> The bathwaters have been prepared for you;

The first bathing is aspen scented,
And the second of rowan wood
And the third of cherry wood.
With the first bathing you will bathe yourself with aspen leaves
Beautiful maiden, you will wash away your bitter tears.
With the second bathing you will wash away your anguish,
From your white face.
And with the third bathing, beautiful maiden,
You will wash away your virginal beauty.

Translated by Delbert Phillips

"Bathhouses Black and White," by Vladimir Vysotskii

WHITE BATHHOUSE (1968)

Stoke me up a *bania*, woman.
I'll bake till I'm red-hot, burn up.
Perched at the shelf's very edge,
I'll wipe away any doubt in myself.

There I'll linger beyond sense or sanity.
A pail of cold water—and all's left behind.
And that tat from the "cult of personality"[1]
Will show blue on my left breast.

> Stoke me up a white *bania*.
> I'm not used to this wide world no more.[2]
> I'll give in to the heat, and in delirium,
> The hot steam will loosen my tongue.

I've felled so much faith, so much forest,
All the grief and the highways I've known!
On my left breast is Stalin in profile,
On my right—my Marinka, full face.

Oh, the years I vacationed in "paradise"[3]
For my unconditional faith!
In trade for my utter stupidity,
I was given this miserable life.

> Stoke me up a white *bania*.
> I'm not used to this wide world no more.

In the baths. Courtesy of Rick Hibberd.

> I'll give in to the heat, and in delirium,
> The hot steam will loosen my tongue.

I remember, how in the wee hours one morning,
I cried out to my brother—Help me!
And then a couple of handsome guards
Led me from this "Siberia" to that one.[4]

And then later, in the swamp or the quarry,
Having swallowed our share of coal dust and tears,
We inked the profiles closer to our hearts,[5]
So he'd hear just how they were bursting.

> No, don't stoke me a white *bania*.
> I'm not used to this wide world no more.
> I'll give in to the heat, and in delirium,
> The hot steam will loosen my tongue.

Oh, I shudder from the story so faithful!
The steam's chased all thoughts from my mind.
And from the fog of an icy past,
I plunge into a searing haze.

From my mind's depths thoughts began stirring.
I got branded for nothing, it seems.
And across my chest I thrash with birch switches,
That vestige of those dark times.

> Stoke me up a white *bania*.
> So I can get used to this wide world once more.
> I'll give in to the heat, and in delirium,
> A pail of cold water will loosen my tongue.
> Stoke it up! . . .
> No, don't stoke it! . . .
> Stoke it up! . . .

BLACK BATHHOUSE (1967)

Hoard!
Go on. Hoard your foolish thoughts. Hoard!
Stoke it up!
Go on. Stoke up a black *bania*. Stoke it up!
Start your wailing!
You'll be the death of me anyway, so go on and wail.
Stoke it up!
Any way you want it, just stoke it up.

> Today my suffering will be over. I'll feel my old self again.
> But I doubt that I can get myself clean.

Now, don't sleep!
Where'd you get that long shirt for me?
Stoke it up!
Today I'll get cleaned up, white as hell.
Splash it on.[6]
Splash it on those smoke-stained walls. Splash it on.
Stoke it up,
You hear?! Stoke me up a black *bania*. C'mon, stoke it up.

> Today my suffering will be over. I'll feel my old self again.
> But I doubt that I can get myself clean.

Cry out!
Driven to the edge by the bottle, like hounds on an elk.
Quiet now!
My hangover's long since gone.

Hang in there!
It was you, who was duped into selling me out!
Stoke it up,
So I'll be clean as a pup by the day's end.

> Today my suffering will be over. I'll feel my old self again.
> But I doubt that I can get myself clean.

Buy me out'a here!
Even if it's just one guard, pay him off!
Stoke it up!
You hear me now?! Stoke me a *bania* early in the morn. Stoke it up!
Start your wailing!
You'll be the death of me anyway, so go on and wail.

Stoke it up! Any way you like it, just stoke it up.

> Today my suffering will be over. I'll feel my old self again.
> But I doubt that I can get myself clean.

Translated by Michael Brewer

Notes

1. Cult of personality (*kul't lichnosti*) is the Thaw-era term for the phenomenon of leader worship practiced during the Stalin period. This is a reference to that time.
2. The Russian *belyi svet* literally means "white world," but is used in folkloric texts to mean "wide world." In this song, the "wide" world is contrasted with the world of the Gulag, to which the singer has become accustomed.
3. "Paradise" is a darkly ironic reference to the Gulag.
4. Literally "from Siberia to Siberia" (*iz Sibiri v Sibir'*), but meaning "to the camps." The prisoner is taken from one Siberia (the USSR—a symbolic one) to another (Siberia—the real one).
5. "Profiles" here refers to tattoos of Stalin.
6. This is a reference to the ritual of splashing water (or beer or other liquid) on the fire or the walls in the *bania* to create steam and increase the humidity.

A Cosmopolitan Project (2000)

Susan Buck-Morss

Since 1991 an ample literature has made commonplace the stereotype that the former Soviet Union "lost" the cold war to its capitalist rivals and today looks westward for economic and political examples. But what if, as Susan Buck-Morss asks, the Soviet Union was never as closed to the flows of shared European political ideals or global capital as most area specialists tend to think? To what extent have the binary categories of East and West obscured more than they have revealed? Resisting the classic view of twentieth-century history as a tale of how the United States and the USSR were locked in a cold war competition between polar opposites—pitting capitalist against communist, free market against command economy—we are set instead on a path where "the Cold War discursive binary of totalitarianism and democracy is challenged at its core." Rigorously asking after the commonalities of cold war enemies rather than their differences, she suggests that socialism in this century did not buckle under the weight of its inherent limitations but failed, paradoxically, "because it mimicked capitalism too faithfully." The provocative result offers a fundamental rethinking of Soviet cultural history.

At the start of the First Five Year Plan, Soviet engineers came to visit Albert Kahn Co., Inc., of Detroit, the famous industrial architects who had built Henry Ford's River Rouge plant as well as factories for General Motors, Packard, Oldsmobile, Chrysler, and De Soto.

> It was in 1928 . . . [that] the most extraordinary commission ever given an architect came in the door unannounced. In that year a group of engineers from the U.S.S.R. came to the Kahn office with an order for a $40,000,000 tractor plant [at Chelyabinsk], and an outline of a program for an additional two billion dollars' worth of buildings. About a dozen of these factories were done in Detroit; the rest were handled in a special office with 1,500 draftsmen in Moscow.

According to Anthony Sutton, the Cold War historian who documented this case, "The 'outline of a program' presented to the Kahn organization in 1928

was nothing less than the First and Second Five-Year Plans of 'socialist construction.'" In authorizing this act of extreme cosmopolitanism, Stalin envisioned a U.S. capitalist firm as designer of Soviet socialist industrialization.

A factory to produce Fordson tractors was prefabricated in Detroit by the
Albert Kahn Company and shipped to Stalingrad in 1929, where it was assembled under the direction of American engineers. A contract "under which
the Kahn Company became consulting architects to the Soviet Union" was
signed in early 1930. "The Kahn group undertook design, architectural, and
engineering work for all heavy and light industrial units projected by Gosplan. Kahn's chief engineer in the U.S.S.R., Scrymgoeur, was chairman of the
Vesenkha building committee. Scrymgoeur wrote:

> The Albert Kahn unit was engaged to control, teach and design all light
> and heavy industry. . . . By the end of the second year we controlled in
> Moscow, and from Moscow branches in Leningrad, Kharkov, Kiev, Dnie-
> propetrovsk, Odessa, Sverdlovsk and Novo-Sibirsk 3,000 designers and
> completed the design of buildings costing (these are Soviet figures) 417
> million rubles.

The Soviets seem to have taken advantage of competitive bidding, however,
and the Albert Kahn Company did not retain a monopoly. Henry Ford, already
a figure of heroic proportions in the Soviet Union, was included in the Soviet
plan, given six months to design an assembly line for the Gorky Auto Plant to
be built at Nizhni Novgorod. The agreement, signed on May 31, 1929, was for
Ford to furnish technical assistance (until 1938) for the plant, which was to be
completed by 1933 and which would produce the Model A (called by the
Soviets Gaz-a), the Ford light truck (Gaz-aa), and the heavy truck (amo-3).
Soviet engineers were to be provided facilities at the River Rouge factory for
the study of Ford production methods. In the economically depressed years of
the early 1930s, U.S. firms and personnel were grateful for the Soviet business.
"Ford was happy to see $30 million worth of parts and throw in invaluable
technical assistance for nothing. Technical assistance in production of axles,
tires, bearings, and other items required payment but, as the marginal cost to
American companies was slight, the Soviets reaped a gigantic harvest of
technological knowhow for almost no outlay." The Austin Company of Cleveland designed not only the plant at Nizhni Novgorod but the "Worker's City"
that surrounded it, complete with community housing, nursery, public bath,
Palace of Culture, and crematorium.

> In mid-1929 the A. J. Brandt Company of Detroit undertook an extensive
> two-year reorganization and expansion of Amo [the automobile plant in
> Moscow]. . . . The production equipment was entirely American and

German. In late 1929 Amtorg [the Soviet trade organization in New York] placed an order on behalf of Amo with the Toledo Machine and Tool Company for $600,000 of cold-stamping presses. In 1932 an order was placed with Greenless Company of Rockford, Illinois for multi-cylinder lathes. In 1936 a second technical-assistance agreement was concluded for Amo with the Budd Manufacturing Company of Philadelphia and the Hamilton Foundry and Machine Company of Ohio to produce 210,000 chassis and bodies per year for a new zis-model automobile.

The technology transfer included trained personnel high up in the Soviet economic administration: "Soyuzstroi [the All-Union Construction Trust] had responsibility for about one-quarter of new construction [in the Soviet Union] until 1933 when it was broken into smaller units attached to individual combinats. The Director of Soyuzstroi was Sergei Nemets, formerly an engineer with the Philadelphia construction company of Stone and Webster Inc. The Chief Engineer of Soyuzstroi was Zara Witkin, whose early projects included the Hollywood Bowl and several large Los Angeles hotels."

Even the Soviet "Dream City" of Magnitogorsk was built according to design specifications created in the United States and supervised by a team of American engineers. In March 1930, Arthur McKee and Co. of Cleveland won the foreign bid to turn the building site at Magnitogorsk, an iron lode in the middle of an empty steppe in southern Russia, into the largest mining-energy-chemical-metallurgical complex in the world. It was to be modeled after the U.S. Steel Company's plant in Gary, Indiana, an integrated design that provided a linear flow from raw materials to finished products.

> McKee undertook to design the entire steel plant, including all auxiliary shops and the iron-ore mine . . . [and to be] responsible for directing work on the site until the factory and mine were put into operation, for consulting on equipment orders, for building an electric power station and a dam, and for training Soviet engineers both at the site and in the United States. The Soviet government agreed to pay McKee 2.5 million gold rubles.

The fact that the United States had no diplomatic relations with the USSR was an obstacle to doing business. Germany, which had recognized the Soviet Union and established trade relations with the Rapallo Treaty in 1922, continued to provide serious competition until Hitler came to power in 1933—not coincidentally the year that the United States finally granted recognition to the Soviet regime.

> Although design and layout during this period [1929–32] was American, probably one-half of the equipment installed was German. Of this, a large

amount was manufactured in Germany to American design on Soviet account. In quantity, American-built equipment was probably second and British third. . . . Cement mills were largely from one firm in Denmark, ball bearings from one firm in Italy and another in Sweden, small ships from Italy, and aluminum technology from a French company.

Sutton concludes that "for the period from 1930 to 1945" Soviet technology *was* Western technology "converted to the metric system." The fact that Stalin's First and Second Five Year Plans amounted to the largest technological transfer in Western capitalist history was not something that either side advertised, nor did they care to remember this collaboration during the Cold War years. Although part of the public record, it remained an embarrassment for both the United States and the Soviet Union as superpower enemies.

And there is more to the story.

Payment for the technology transfer demanded hard currency. Soviet grain exports fell precipitously during the early 1930s, due to the intense famines caused by forced collectivization. The Soviet government found an alternative commodity in the European oil paintings and "household goods" of the aristocracy that had been confiscated after the October Revolution. In 1928 the Soviet government embarked on a major effort to sell Russian art abroad in order to gain hard currency to pay for the imports of the First Five Year Plan. The story of this extravagant international exchange was not documented until 1980. In the words of its historian, Robert Williams, "American buyers have been as reluctant to discuss their purchases as the Soviet government has been to discuss (or even admit) their sales." Yet the Soviet decision was clearly made at the top: "Tractors were needed more than Titians, Fords more than Fabergé." Millions of dollars' worth of masterpieces of art and thousands of tons of antiques—jewelry, icons, porcelain, rare book manuscripts, Easter eggs, silver, brocades—were sold abroad, and the largest buyers were U.S. citizens.

In the twelve months between April 1930 and April 1931 alone, Andrew W. Mellon, Secretary of the Treasury of the United States, bought close to seven million dollars' worth of Hermitage paintings from the Soviet government, a figure that equals half of what the Soviet Union paid in hard currency for imports during that year and "roughly one third of the official total of Soviet exports to the United States in 1930." Included were two Renaissance masterpieces of Jan van Eyck, five Rembrandts, four Van Dycks, two Halses, as well as paintings by Botticelli, Chardin, Perugino, Poussin, Rubens, Titian, Velásquez, and, the most expensive purchase, Raphael's *Alba Madonna,* for which

Mellon paid almost 1.7 million dollars, at the time the highest price ever paid for a single painting. These purchases were kept secret, laundered through a complex web of American entrepreneurs and Soviet officials, at the heart of which were M. Knoedler & Company (art gallery and dealer) and Amtorg (the Soviet trade representative), both based in New York City. Knoedler was owned by the entrepreneur Armand Hammer, whose pencil and asbestos factories in the Soviet Union were nationalized in 1930 but who, with his special Soviet connections, turned to selling Russian art objects through department stores in the United States, including, in January 1933, Lord and Taylor.

Because the Soviet Union lacked diplomatic recognition in the United States, Amtorg, the delegation for the Commissariat of Foreign Trade, had to maintain the legal fiction of being a private corporation of the state of New York, where it was based. As for the Secretary of the Treasury's part in the major deal, "for five long years there were only rumors of such a purchase and denials by Mellon." According to his lawyer, "Mr. Mellon wanted to keep the thing a surprise until the right moment. It probably would not have been good politics for the Secretary of the Treasury to spend millions for rare paintings at a time when the government was swamped with unemployment, bank failures, and general distress." The "right moment" was forced upon Mellon in 1935 when, for years suspected of a conflict of interest, he was charged by the Internal Revenue Service for failing to pay over three million dollars in taxes in 1931. "At issue was the taxable status of Andrew Mellon's paintings [donated to his own charitable trust] which he claimed as a deduction on his 1931 income return." Only after Mellon had written to President Roosevelt that he planned to bequeath his paintings to the government and offered to build a museum for them did the Board of Tax Appeals dismiss charges of tax fraud. "In March 1937, five months before Andrew Mellon's death, President Roosevelt accepted his donation of this entire art collection and a National Gallery of Art in which to house it in the name of the American people." With the opening of the National Gallery in Washington, the Hermitage paintings were once again on public display as "nationalized" property—this time on the other side, and in the capitalist manner.

The British art dealer Joseph Duveen, testifying at Mellon's trial, criticized the Soviet government for its policy, as a result of which "the Hermitage is no more the greatest collection in the world, it has gone to pieces. I do not see how a nation could sell their great pictures of that kind. . . . [Art objects] are not a commodity. You cannot buy a picture like you buy a load of copper or a tin mine." From the Soviet side the argument was not convincing. A Soviet museum curator was quoted as saying that such sales were a perfectly accept-

Raphael, *The Alba Madonna,* ca. 1510, Andrew W. Mellon
Collection. Image © 2006 Board of Trustees, National Gallery of
Art, Washington. Courtesy of the National Gallery of Art.

able socialist method to "turn diamonds into tractors." There was a strange
poetic justice in this economic circuit. Mellon, who made an early fortune
from steel mills in Pittsburgh, spent it on oil paintings the sale of which
enabled construction of the steel mills at Magnitogorsk. Thus the profits of
capitalism (surplus value withheld from the wages of American workers)
moved (via the Mellon family fortune) to finance (via the capitalist firm of
McKee Construction Company) the building of technologically advanced
socialist factories, an increase in what Marx called "constant capital" that in
turn increased the value of Soviet labor. Meanwhile, in the counterdirection,
cultural "treasures" that had been owned by the Russian aristocracy and
nationalized by the Bolsheviks became (via Mellon's "philanthropic" cover-up
of tax evasion) the property of the United States government—and the American public received socialized culture in the form of a national museum. How
should this strange merging of supposedly antithetical systems be reckoned?
What is the proper accounting, when the sale of one Raphael (at 1.7 million
gold dollars) buys more than half of the design of one Magnitogorsk (at 2.5
million gold rubles), which translates into jobs for tens of thousands of Soviet

workers, and the production (by 1938) of millions of tons of finished metal? How does one make political sense out of an economic exchange whereby the U.S. Secretary of the Treasury uses his private millions to "build social-ism" in Stalin's Russia—at the same time as the output of steel mills in the United States is falling precipitously due to a Great Depression that, to Stalin's delight, affects capitalism alone? How does one square with ideological rhet-oric the irony of the fact that pre-1929 production levels in the United States were not recovered until World War II when, to Stalin's surprise and against the intent of the Nazi-Soviet nonaggression pact, the steel mills of Magnito-gorsk and Pittsburgh, again at full throttle, found themselves producing weapon materials for the same warring side?

II

From Kyiv through Muscovy

Russia is sewn together by its rivers. In Siberia the Lena, the Yenisei, and the Ob' flow north into the Arctic Sea, whose waters are frozen for much of the year. Farther west the Volga, the longest river in Europe, flows south for 2,300 miles from the Valdai Hills in the north into the Caspian Sea at Astrakhan'. But it was down other rivers, the Dvina and the Dnepr', that the Norsemen known as Varangians came in the eighth century CE, looking for trade routes to the south and east to Constantinople and beyond. What little we know about these people from the north suggests that they were part traders, part soldiers of fortune, and that they quickly assimilated with the Slavic peoples living in the areas along important trade routes. From the Slavs they acquired valuable items—slaves, amber, salt, honey, furs, and wax—that they took with them to Constantinople and then east along the Volga. In return they brought back silk fabrics, fruits, spices, and wine. Legend has it that the first ruler of Novgorod, Riurik, was in fact a Varangian, invited by the local population in 862 to rule over the city torn apart by dissension. True or not, the legend points to the Scandinavian origin of many of the early princes of Rus'.

Despite their presence as traders and settlers among early Slavic peoples, Varangian culture and way of life were only minimally absorbed by the early Slavic communities. The origin of the name "Russia," however, is most likely Scandinavian. The early Russians and the land on which they lived were known as "Rus'," a word related to "Rotsi," the Finnish word used to describe the Swedes and etymologically close to the Germanic root *rod,* meaning "to row." Apart from this there is little direct evidence of Scandinavian influence on early Russian culture, perhaps because by the end of the eleventh century the Varangians had become so well assimilated through intermarriage that they were virtually indistinguishable from the Slavs over whom, according to the early Russian chronicles, they had been invited to rule.

The more discernible and permanent influence on early Russian culture came from the Byzantine Empire, the eastern branch of the Roman Empire. From here Russia received Christianity as well as the models for its earliest art, architecture, and literature. George Fedotov in "Slavic Byzantium" discusses the importance of this inheritance and specifically what it meant that early Russia received Christianity and its texts in the vernacular thanks to the Greek monks Cyril and Methodius, who in the ninth century designed for the early Slavs an alphabet originally known as Glagolitic that became the foundation for the later Cyrillic alphabet used by most Slavic peoples today. In addition, the two brothers began the work of translating the Scriptures, services, and saints' lives from Greek into the language then known as Slavic. Newly Christianized peoples did not always enjoy the luxury of receiving their religion in a language they could understand. In his *History of the English Church and People* the Venerable Bede (672–735) recounts stories of monks sitting in the scriptoria in the monasteries in winter, painfully attempting to copy down the Latin texts even as their knuckles froze. But even with the spring thaw Christianity remained frozen in a language that was inaccessible to the laymen in the outposts of the Roman Empire.

The early Russian Chronicles recount the arrival of Byzantine iconographers to Kyiv in the eleventh century to teach the newly Christianized people the art of icon painting. After Prince Vladimir sent his emissaries out to the surrounding lands to determine what religion he should accept, they reported that upon entering the Byzantine churches they "knew not whether [they] were in heaven or on earth, for surely there is no such splendor or beauty anywhere on earth." No doubt Vladimir's emissaries had seen not only the frescoes on the walls but the devotional pictures or icons that decorated the Byzantine churches as well.

Of all the arts it was icon painting that developed most fully in medieval Russia from the late tenth century onward. Originally imitative of Byzantine styles, Russia's icons and saints' lives over time acquired the original and distinctive features of the land to which they had traveled. The icons that decorated Russia's churches functioned in much the same way as did the stone carvings on the portals and walls of the Gothic cathedrals of Europe and became the means by which a predominantly illiterate population could read the stories from the Bible. Painted on wood, often depicting scenes from the saint's life, they were the Bible in visual, tactile form. The art that the early Russians inherited from the Byzantine Empire was the handmaiden of religion, and as such only religious figures—Christ, the Mother of God, saints, and apostles—could be depicted. Moreover these religious paintings were meant to function symbolically, with no attempt being made at realistic portrayal. The Christ child as bouncing baby familiar from the paintings of Botticelli was nowhere present in the Byzantine style, whose art reflected the theology of Christ's divinity.

On Russian soil, however, different styles and belief practices soon came to dominate. Increasingly Christ acquired a more humanized form, as did the Mother of God (*bogoroditsa*), whose maternal, human traits gradually overshadowed the original Byzantine depictions. Colors became brighter, and the icons themselves gradually acquired their own distinct local hues. Local saints were introduced into the panoply of the venerated. In this way Russia made the Byzantine inheritance its own.

Icons were meant to be worshipped. In the absence of the saint or holy figure, worshippers prayed to his or her symbolic representation. The icon was their entrance to the world beyond this earth, and as such Russians worshipped their icons with their eyes open. So much were these images a part of daily life that they were found not only in churches but increasingly in people's homes, regardless of class. Every Russian home, whether a peasant hut or a nobleman's estate, had an icon corner, or *krasnyi ugol*, lit by candles.

Indisputably, Russia's greatest contributions to iconography were the works of the early fifteenth-century monk Andrei Rublev, who humanized the figure of Christ and lifted his icons out of immobility by creating two-dimensional figures who look straight at the viewer. His greatest achievement, however, and that of Russian icon painting in general, is his *Trinity* (*Troitsa*), based on the Old Testament story of three angels disguised as young men who visit Abraham and Sarah near the oak of Mamre in the desert. The icon also symbolically re-creates the Trinity from the New Testament and simultaneously becomes a call to spiritual unity for Russia at a time when the country was under the domination of the Tatar-Mongol yoke.

Politically early Rus' consisted of principalities that vied with each other for power. The major towns from this era—Kyiv, Chernigov, Novgorod, Volynia, Polotsk, Smolensk, and Riazan', to name but a few—functioned as capitals of their principalities. It was in Kyiv, however, that the secular and political power of Rus' was concentrated. It was here that Prince Vladimir had his people baptized en masse in the Dnepr' River, here that the Crypt Monastery was founded by Saints Antonius and Theodosius, here where many of the first Russian Chronicles were recorded and where Iaroslav the Wise ruled (1036–54) under whose tutelage Kyiv became the political and ecclesiastical center of Rus'.

Sitting in the monasteries of Kyiv patiently writing down the annals, the monks created a tapestry of early Russian life that was necessarily incomplete, informed as it was by their ecclesiastical visions. We are left to wonder how the peasant who tilled the soil or worked in a small town lived and what daily life was like in early Rus'. As in medieval Europe, the average person's life was written out of the chronicles into which the lives and deeds of the princes and religious figures were inscribed. Similarly in France in the twelfth century one encounters beautifully illuminated art in the medieval breviaries and books of hours depicting peasants working in the fields and people going about their daily lives, and yet the doors were rarely opened to reveal the actual texture of the lives painted on the pages. In Rus' we encounter similar problems, as the scribes exercised their own decision making, if not outright censorship, over what material to include and what to leave out. Sometimes entire years are left blank in the Chronicles either because the annalists determined that nothing important happened that year or because they chose silence as one of the ways they responded to the nomadic incursions that they viewed as punishment for their sins. From time to time the doors part to reveal something of the everyday, of popular morality, of fears and superstitions. We learn that eclipses were seen as evil omens, that bad roads were then, as now, ubiquitous, and that princes worried over building bridges, paving roads, and constructing viable portages. We hear that plans were under way in the eleventh century to build a girls' school at a local convent. We know that people took public welfare seriously, particularly after Christianity was introduced, and were instructed to give to the poor on holidays and church feast days.

To get at the heart of beliefs and customs, however, we can turn to Russian folklore, much of which has its origins in pre-Christian Russia. Out of this tradition come the fairy tales, laments, chants, riddles, and songs that celebrate the agricultural feast days of the calendar year and that marked life passages, rituals connected with courtship, marriage, and death. Out of this folkloric tradition come Russia's *byliny*, the oral epics recounting the adventures of their larger-than-life heroes (*bogatyri*) who felled dragons and the enemy on the steppe. As was common for any people whose lives were centered on agriculture and depended on the seasons, Russian folklore is infused with nature. From early sources we read about the pre-Christian deities Dazhbog and Khors (both linked with the sun), Stribog (winds), Perun (thunder), and Mokosh (a female deity perhaps representing Damp Mother Earth). Although there is little written evidence as to how precisely these forces of nature functioned in early Russian society, it seems clear that they were not worshipped in the way we understand worship today, nor was there a hierarchical order to the panoply of gods. In the passage from the epic poem *The Igor Tale* (*Slovo o polku igoreve*) reprinted here, Igor's wife, Yaroslavna, invokes them to bring her husband home, reflecting these pre-Christian beliefs that predated the founding of the Kyivan state.

In 1240 the supremacy of the Kyivan state was dealt a precipitous blow as it came under attack by the Tatar-Mongol hordes who established rule over the Russian princes for the next 240 years. Unlike the Turkic peoples who had periodically launched forays into the periphery of Rus', the Mongols moved their entire world westward as they sought to expand their empire. The initial damage they left in their wake—cities razed, churches burned—was paradoxically proceeded by the Mongols' granting self-rule and religious toleration. From their capital in Sarai on the Volga River they installed overseers in various cities whose function was to manage the collecting of tribute. The Golden Horde, as the Tatar-Mongol rule was known, lasted as long as it did partly because it left the day-to-day running of governmental affairs basically as it had been prior to the Mongol conquest. One historian has even noted that many Russians went about their lives at the time as if the Mongol presence did not even exist. Yet its impact on the political and economic life of the time was far-reaching. Trade relations, particularly with the West, initially nearly ceased. The Russian princes also curried favor with the Tatars, knowing that they could not fight invaders simultaneously on both eastern and western fronts. Prince Aleksandr Nevskii of Novgorod, later of Vladimir, cooperated with the Tatars so as to better defeat the Swedes in 1240, thereby giving his native city Novgorod an outlet to the Baltic. Two years later he defeated the German Teutonic knights in the battle on the ice immortalized by Sergei Eisenstein in his film *Aleksandr Nevskii*.

It was only in 1480 that Russia finally managed to free itself from Tatar domination. By this time the political and religious canvas of Russia had changed dramatically. First and foremost the center of power had shifted north to Moscow. If, as the historian James Billington has suggested, this was a retreat into the security of the forest zone away from the vulnerability of the open steppes, it was also a response to a gradual and complicated shifting of allegiances. The Kyivan state had been much weakened by the infighting of its local princes, whose lack of unity was matched only by that of the steppe nomads themselves, who possessed the capacity to inflict much greater damage than they did. But there were other reasons that accounted for Moscow's growing supremacy. Politically and geographically from the thirteenth century through the fifteenth Moscow transformed itself from an unknown trading post first mentioned in the Chronicles only in 1147 to the center of political and spiritual power. Some of this was accomplished through its absorption of rival principalities and its expansion into new territories. In the early fourteenth century the metropolitan of the Russian Church transferred his see from the city of Vladimir to Moscow, thus making Moscow the center of Russian religious power.

There were other reasons for Moscow's rise as well. Its princes initially curried favor with the Tatars, becoming their principal agents in the collecting of tribute, and even used Tatar forces to solidify their power over their rivals. Gradually, however, the Moscow princes turned their strength against the Tatars, and in 1480 Ivan III, Prince of Moscow, took the money Moscow was supposed to give to the Horde and used it to rebuild the Kremlin, previously destroyed by the Tatars.

With the rise of Muscovy came the consolidation of power into the hands of one principality and one ruler. It was Ivan IV who, in an elaborate ceremony, had himself crowned first tsar of all Russia in 1547. He ruled over a state that has traditionally been seen as rigid, autocratic, and defined by ritual and law, perhaps more Byzantine than the Byzantines. "Rules for Russian Households," an excerpt from a book of household rules titled *The Domostroi* written in the 1550s, conveys the degree to which rules and codification had infiltrated every area of life in Muscovy, from the court to the home to the growing state bureaucracy and the service class. Further, by the mid-seventeenth century serfdom had become fully entrenched in Russia. From all evidence of this centralization of power it is tempting to conclude that the tendency toward autocracy has long been embedded in the Russian national consciousness. Aleksandr Solzhenitsyn argued that Russians have a natural proclivity toward authoritarian systems of government. Historians, however, remind us that there was shared power among the tsar and his boyars (advisors) and that arbitrary decision making on the part of the tsar was balanced by a political process not often seen from the outside. The historian George Vernadsky is of the opinion that absolutism and autocracy came into being in Russia not out of any natural inborn propensity but in response to the Mongol yoke and the need on the part of Russia's rulers to free themselves from its rule. Long before Peter the Great came to the throne Russia was expanding its territories and needed a firm organizational structure with which to secure its holdings. Looking at Muscovite absolutism through a slightly different lens affords us the opportunity to rethink the notion that certain systems of government are inherent in particular cultures and peoples.

Early Russian history and culture serve to remind us that Russian identity throughout the centuries has been a complex amalgam of geography, politics, and emotional resonance whose balance has shifted depending on factors as varied as the threat from foreign invaders, abuse of power by a tsar, and later the turning toward the West. When Stalin called upon his people during World War II to fight *za Stalina, za rodinu* (for Stalin, for the Motherland), and faced with a crisis of confidence in his own leadership, he reached deep into Russia's past for an image of collective identity that transcended politics. Much of the spirit of that identity was first formed in Kyivan and Muscovite Russia.

The Igor Tale (late twelfth-century)

Anonymous

In 1185 Prince Igor, from the town of Novgorod Seversk, set out with his retinue to wage battle against the Polovtsians, or Cumans, one of the several nomadic Turkic tribes that threatened the security of the southern steppe in Kyivan Rus'. Outnumbered and ill prepared, Igor and his men were defeated and Igor taken prisoner. Several months later he escaped and returned to his wife and townspeople.

The abortive expedition against the Polovtsians received only slight mention in the early Russian Chronicles. His raid, however, was recast and given artistic form in a poem that has since been heralded as the pearl of early Russia's written literary tradition, the Slovo o polku Igoreve, *known in English as* The Igor Tale. *Exactly when the poem was composed is unknown, as it was discovered only in the eighteenth century in a manuscript collection. Its authenticity has been disputed by some scholars; others have defended its authenticity based on philological evidence. It has been called an epic, yet on closer examination it seems an unlikely candidate for epic status. Unlike the heroes of other epic poems, such as Odysseus and Beowulf, Prince Igor possesses no superhuman abilities. Moreover in a stunning departure from his predecessors he fails to defeat the enemy, and thus bears a stronger resemblance to the hero of the French* Chanson de Roland, *whose forces succumb to the Saracens. What then accounts for the remarkable place this poem occupies in Russian literary tradition?*

As a political statement, the poem tells us much about the age. Early Rus' consisted of principalities, each with its own ruling prince. This political makeup was threatened not merely by the steppe nomads and their periodic incursions against the Russian land but by the disunity among the princes themselves. The Igor Tale is a *call to the princes to cease their internecine warfare and unite in their struggle against the steppe. Artistically it fuses folklore and written tradition, pagan and Christian. We learn more here about the pre-Christian pagan deities of the early Slavs than we do from virtually any other written record at this time. The Christian references in the poem seem decidedly less integrated than those in the animistic tradition, and thus it has been suggested that the work may have undergone some editing at the hands of a pious monk after it was composed. As to its original author, like most of early Russian literature* The Igor Tale *was composed anonymously, though it has been suggested that it may have been written by a member of Igor's court or one of his retinue (druzhina) in battle since many of the descriptions in the poem are those of an eyewitness.*

Reprinted here is a short excerpt from the poem in which Igor's wife, Yaroslavna, beseeches the forces of nature to bring her husband back from captivity. Nature heeds her call. The only example of secular literature to have emerged from an era in which all literature was religious, the poem remains a unique poetic testament of the folklore and belief patterns that infused the age.

One can hear the voice of Iaroslavna.
Like a cuckoo she sings early in the morning:
"Like a cuckoo," she says, "I will fly along the Danube
I will dip my beaver sleeve in the Kaiala River
And will cleanse the bleeding wounds of the prince
On his mighty body."
In the morning Iaroslavna cries again
Along the walls of Putivl, saying:
"Oh, wind, great wind!
Why, lord, do you blow so fiercely?
Why do you carry on your light wings
Khan's arrows against the forces of my beloved?
Are you not satisfied with blowing the clouds up high
Or with rocking ships upon the blue sea?
Why, lord, did you scatter my happiness
Over the feather grass [of the prairie]?"

In the morning Iaroslavna cries again
Along the walls of Putivl, saying:
"Oh, Dnieper, famed river!
You have pierced the stone mountains
Of the Polovtsian land!
You have carried Sviatoslav's boats against Kobiak's forces.
Bring, oh lord, my beloved to me
So that I might stop sending tears every morning to the sea."
In the morning Iaroslavna cries again
Along the city walls of Putivl, saying:
"You bright, you beautiful sun!
You warm everyone equally,
You are beautiful equally to all.
Why did you, oh lord, spread your burning rays

On the forces of my beloved?
Why did your rays increase their thirst in a waterless prairie
And thereby close their quivers with misfortune?"
The sea splashed [with fury] at midnight
Hurricanes advance through the mist.
God shows the road to Igor,
From the Polovtsian to the Russian land,
To the ancestral golden throne.
The evening glow now has faded.
Igor sleeps, Igor keeps vigil.
In his thought Igor surveys the land
From the Great Don to the Little Donets.
At midnight the horse was ready.
Across the river Ovlur whistled
A warning for the prince to get ready.
Prince Igor will not remain a prisoner!
As he called, the earth trembled,
The grass rustled,
And the Polovtsian tents began to stir.
Like an ermine Prince Igor sped to the reeds
And like a white duck he swam across the water.
Then he leaped on a swift horse,
Jumped off it like a roaming wolf,
Sped towards the valley of the Donets,
Flew like a falcon under the clouds
Killing geese and swans for breakfast, lunch, and dinner.
When Igor flew like a falcon
Ovlur followed him like a wolf,
Shaking off the cold dew.
They both exhausted their horses.
The Donets said: "Prince Igor!
Great glory awaits you.
[Great] disappointment awaits Konchak,
While happiness is in store for the Russian land."
And Igor replied: "Oh, Donets!
Great glory awaits you, too,
For rocking a prince on your waves,
For spreading for him green grass
Along your silver banks,
For covering him with warm haze

Under the shadow of a green tree,
For disguising him on water as a white duck,
As a seagull on the stream,
And as a black duck in the air."
"Entirely different," he said, "is the Stugna River.
Its stream is weak.
Because it has swallowed up other rivers
Its mouth is also wide.
The Dnieper imprisoned young prince Rostislav
On the bottom of its banks.
And Rostislav's mother mourns the young prince.
Flowers have withered from sorrow,
While trees have bent to the ground in grief."

This is not the chattering of the magpies,
It is Gzak and Konchak following Igor's trail.
Crows did not caw at that time,
The daws became silent
And even magpies stopped chattering.
Everything crawled on all fours,
And with their noise the woodpeckers showed the way to the river,
And nightingales with their gay song announced the dawn.
Said Gzak to Konchak:
"If the falcon should reach the nest
We will shoot the falconet with our gilded arrows."
And Konchak replied to Gzak:
"If the falcon should reach the nest
We will enmesh the falconet with [the charms of] a beautiful girl."
And said Gzak again to Konchak:
"If we enmesh him with [the charms of] a beautiful girl,
We will lose both the falconet and the beautiful girl,
And the birds will start fighting us in the Polovtsian land."
Boian, the song-maker of old times,
Said the following of the wars of Sviatoslav,
The grandson of Iaroslav, son of Oleg:
"It is difficult for a head to be without shoulders
It is equally difficult for a body to be without the head."
It is difficult for the Russian land to be without Igor.
The sun shines in the sky.
Prince Igor has returned to the Russian land.

Maidens sing on the Danube
Their voices reach Kiev across the sea.
Igor rides along the Borichev
[To the church of] the Holy Virgin of Pirogoshch.
The countryside is rejoicing,
Cities are jubilant,
Singing songs first to the old princes
And then to the young.
Let us sing glory to Igor, son of Sviatoslav,
To Wild Bull Vsevolod,
To Vladimir, son of Igor.
Hail to the princes and their troops
Who fight against pagan forces for Christendom.
Glory to the princes and to their troops—Amen.

The Russian Primary Chronicle (1040–1118)

Anonymous

The earliest history of the Kyivan state is contained in the chronicle known as The Tale of Bygone Years *(Povest' vremmenykh let). Originally set down by monks who were among the few who were literate at the time, the chronicle is a mélange of folklore, legend, and historical fact providing origins, lineages, and religious identification for the early Russian people dating from the year 852. It is a chronological compendium of legal documents, treaties, astronomical observations, accounts of the struggle with the tribes in the southern steppe, and instructions of princes to their people. Compiled originally in the Kyivan Crypt Monastery, it has generally been considered the work of six monks. Two names in particular are associated with it: Nikon, who worked on it from 1060 to 1073, and Nestor, who beginning in 1113 made final edits and added the introduction. Not surprisingly much that they recount is heavily filtered through their system of Christian belief. Establishing historical and Christian legitimacy for the early Slavs was paramount for the annalists as they embarked on writing the Russian land and the Slavs into the Old Testament story of Noah dividing the lands of the earth among his sons.*

It is in the Chronicles that we learn of the founding of the Russian state by a group of Scandinavian traders and plunderers known as Varangians. Looking for trade routes south and east, they traveled down the Russian waterways. Some settled along the rivers and moved inland, while others proceeded on to attack Byzantium.

The Chronicles also provide the account of how Russia came to accept Eastern Christianity, and it is here that their religious bias is most telling. According to legend, Prince Vladimir of Kyiv was visited by several delegations representing different faiths: the Bulgars, who resided along the Volga and had accepted Islam in 922; the Germans, who came as emissaries of the pope at Rome; the Khazars from southern Russia, who had been converted to Judaism in the mid-ninth century; and the Greeks from Byzantium, who offered Eastern Christianity to the Russian people. According to the Chronicle, Vladimir sent emissaries to each of these peoples to determine which religion he should accept. They returned overwhelmed by the beauty of the Eastern Church and its liturgy. Yet Vladimir's conversion in 988 and the subsequent baptism of his people was as much a political act as a religious choice. It cemented a political alliance between the early Russian state and the Byzantine Empire that served, at least temporarily, as a buffer from the Turkic tribes on the eastern steppe and offered stimulus to trade relations.

Vladimir was visited by Bulgars of Mohammedan faith, who said, "Though you are a wise and prudent prince, you have no religion. Adopt our faith, and revere Mahomet." Vladimir inquired what was the nature of their religion. They replied that they believed in God, and that Mahomet instructed them to practice circumcision, to eat no pork, to drink no wine, and, after death, promised them complete fulfillment of their carnal desires. "Mahomet," they asserted, "will give each man seventy fair women. He may choose one fair one, and upon that woman will Mahomet confer the charms of them all, and she shall be his wife. Mahomet promises that one may then satisfy every desire, but whoever is poor in this world will be no different in the next." They also spoke other false things which out of modesty may not be written down. Vladimir listened to them, for he was fond of women and indulgence, regarding which he heard with pleasure. But circumcision and abstinence from pork and wine were disagreeable to him. "Drinking," said he, "is the joy of the Russes. We cannot exist without that pleasure."

Then came the Germans, asserting that they were come as emissaries of the Pope. They added, "Thus says the Pope: 'Your country is like our country, but your faith is not as ours. For our faith is the light. We worship God, who has made heaven and earth, the stars, the moon, and every creature, while your gods are only wood.'" Vladimir inquired what their teaching was. They replied, "Fasting according to one's strength. But whatever one eats or drinks is all to the glory of God, as our teacher Paul has said." Then Vladimir answered, "Depart hence; our fathers accepted no such principle."

The Jewish Khazars heard of these missions, and came themselves saying, "We have learned that Bulgars and Christians came hither to instruct you in their faiths. The Christians believe in him whom we crucified, but we believe in the one God of Abraham, Isaac, and Jacob." Then Vladimir inquired what their religion was. They replied that its tenets included circumcision, not eating pork or hare, and observing the Sabbath. The Prince then asked where their native land was, and they replied that it was in Jerusalem. When Vladimir inquired where that was, they made answer, "God was angry at our forefathers, and scattered us among the gentiles on account of our sins. Our land was then given to the Christians." The Prince then demanded, "How can you hope to teach others while you yourselves are cast out and scattered abroad by the hand of God? If God loved you and your faith, you would not be thus dispersed in foreign lands. Do you expect us to accept that fate also?"

Then the Greeks sent to Vladimir a scholar, who spoke thus: "We have heard that the Bulgarians [a Turkic state on the Volga as distinct from the Bulgarians in the Balkans] came and urged you to adopt their faith, which pollutes heaven and earth. They are accursed above all men, like Sodom and Gomorrah, upon which the Lord let fall burning stones, and which he buried and submerged. The day of destruction likewise awaits these men, on which the Lord will come to judge the earth, and to destroy all those who do evil and abomination. For they moisten their excrement, and pour the water into their mouths, and anoint their beards with it, remembering Mahomet. The women also perform this same abomination, and even worse ones." Vladimir, upon hearing their statements, spat upon the earth, saying, "This is a vile thing."

. . . .

When the Prince arrived at his capital, he directed that the idols should be overthrown, and that some should be cut to pieces and others burned with fire. He thus ordered that Perun [the god of thunder and lightning in the Slavic pantheon] should be bound to a horse's tail and dragged down Borichev to the stream. He appointed twelve men to beat the idol with sticks, not because he thought the wood was sensitive, but to affront the demon who had deceived man in this guise, that he might receive chastisement at the hands of men. Great art thou, oh Lord, and marvelous are thy works! Yesterday he was honored of men, but today held in derision. While the idol was being dragged along the stream to the Dnieper, the unbelievers wept over it, for they had not yet received holy baptism. After they had thus dragged the idol along, they cast it into the Dnieper. But Vladimir had given this injunction: "If it halts anywhere, then push it out from the bank, until it goes over the falls. Then let it loose." His command was duly obeyed. When the men let the idol go, and it passed through the rapids, the wind cast it out on the bank, which since that time has been called Perun's sandbank, a name that it bears to this very day.

Thereafter Vladimir sent heralds throughout the whole city to proclaim that if any inhabitants, rich or poor, did not betake himself to the river, he would risk the Prince's displeasure. When the people heard these words, they wept for joy, and exclaimed in their enthusiasm, "If this were not good, the Prince and his boyars would not have accepted it." On the morrow, the Prince went forth to the Dnieper with the priests of the Princess and those from Kherson, and a countless multitude assembled. They all went into the water: some stood up to their necks, others to their breasts, and the younger near the bank, some of them holding children in their arms, while the adults waded farther out. The priests stood by and offered prayers. There was joy in heaven and upon earth to behold so many souls saved. But the devil groaned, lamenting, "Woe is me! how am I driven out hence! For I thought to have my dwelling-place here, since the apostolic teachings do not abide in this land. Nor did this people know God, but I rejoiced in the service they rendered unto me. But now I am vanquished by the ignorant, not by apostles and martyrs, and my reign in these regions is at an end."

When the people were baptized, they returned each to his own abode. Vladimir, rejoicing that he and his subjects now knew God himself, looked up to heaven and said, "Oh God, who has created heaven and earth, look down, I beseech thee, on this thy new people, and grant them, oh Lord, to know thee as the true God, even as the other Christian nations have known thee. Confirm in them the true and inalterable faith, and aid me, oh Lord, against the hostile adversary, so that, hoping in thee and in thy might, I may overcome his malice." Having spoken thus, he ordained that wooden churches should be built and established where pagan idols had previously stood. He thus founded the Church of St. Basil on the hill where the idol of Perun and the other images had been set, and where the Prince and the people had offered their sacrifices. He began to found churches and to assign priests throughout the cities, and to invite the people to accept baptism in all the cities and towns.

Slavic Byzantium (1946)

George P. Fedotov

In this excerpt the eminent Russian religious historian George Fedotov discusses some of the unique features of early Russian religious tradition. Key to an understanding of religious life from the time of Kyivan Rus' up through the fifteenth century was the persistence of a variety of local beliefs and traditions long after Christianity officially came to the land in 988. When Prince Vladimir ordered all non-Christian statues thrown over the hill into the Dnepr' River in Kyiv on the eve of his people's mass conversion to Christianity, the act spelled only the symbolic death of what the Russians called "paganism" in Kyivan Rus'. For centuries these local belief patterns continued to exist side by side with Christianity, a phenomenon that became known as dvoeverie, *or "twofold belief."*

Fedotov also weighs in on the question that has nipped at Russia's heels since the time of Peter the Great, namely, its identity in relation to the West. This volume began with the poet Aleksandr Blok's assertion in "The Scythians" that his country's sense of identity is rooted in the East, in cultures more ancient than those out of which Europe would be formed. Fedotov believes that there has long been a tendency among Russian nationalists to "overestimate the level of ancient Kyivan culture." He argues instead that Russia's Eastern inheritance stunted the development of a true "intellectual culture" and scientific thinking among the Russians. It is a conversation that still continues today.

About 1000 A.D. (tradition says 988) Russia was officially converted to Christianity by the baptism of the Kievan Prince Vladimir and his subjects. Of course, it was only the beginning of the Christian mission, supported by the state, among Slavic and Finnic tribes of the eastern European plain. Yet from the very outset Vladimir had to make a choice of tremendous historical significance: between the Eastern and Western forms of Christianity, between Byzantium and Rome. The Christian Church was still united at the time of the conversion. But the relations between its Greek and Latin halves were hopelessly spoiled and were moving toward the final break of 1054. Vladimir chose the Greek Church—not perhaps without hesitation—and thus determined the destiny of Russia. She became a province of Byzantine culture and the bearer of the Eastern Orthodoxy, the usual name for the Greek form of Catholicism. The whole Russian mind and heart were shaped by this Eastern Christian mould. After 1054 official ecclesiastical relations with Western Catholic Europe became practically impossible: after the Mongolian conquest of 1240, the political and cultural ties with the West were almost severed. These two facts are the source of both the originality and the limitations of Russian culture; of both its greatness and its flaws.

After 1037—the previous years are shrouded in mist—the Russian Church was headed by the Metropolitan appointed by the Patriarch of Constantinople. It was, indeed, an ecclesiastical province of Constantinople standing under the supreme jurisdiction of the ecumenical Patriarch. The decisions of the Greek councils, the Greek Canon Law, and the Greek ritual were obligatory on Russian territory. With two exceptions, the Metropolitans of Kiev of the pre-Mongolian time were Greek by nationality and subjects of the Byzantine Emperor. In Russia they found no political counterbalance to the Greek influence. The loose monarchy of Kiev, after reaching its climax under Vladimir, who died in 1015, and his son Iaroslav, who died in 1054, began to split into a multiplicity of local principalities, not dissimilar, at first glance, to the feudal Europe of the same time. Their ties were very weak, and of moral rather than legal character; the primacy of the prince of Kiev was merely honorary. In every local state the prince had to face many social forces: his retainers (*druzhina*), the landed and commercial aristocracy (*boyars*), and popular assembly (*veche*). The Church was the most powerful of these social elements and the princes could not even dream of dominating it. If they had an influence upon the election of the diocesan bishops, the appointment of the Metropolitan was still outside their sphere. Canonically, the Greek element was predominant. Modern Russian scholars have discovered some traces of Western institutions in the ancient Russian Church (the ecclesiastical tithes, for instance); they were due to continuous political and cultural relations with the West during the pre-Mongolian period. But they are not strong enough to change the predominance of the Greek institutions, as well as the Greek doctrines and forms of worship, in the Russian Church. The Church was born in the body of Byzantinism and to determine these Byzantine elements in ancient Russian Christianity will be our next task.

. . . .

Nobody can understand the destiny of Russian culture and religion without being aware of a primordial difference between Russia and the Christian West. Both had inherited their culture and their religion from the ancient

Hellenistic world: the one from the Latin source, the other from the Greek. The Greek tradition was undoubtedly richer and more original: the Romans were disciples and imitators of Greece. Besides, Rome had long lost its political existence and even had ceased to be a cultural center, whereas Byzantium was a powerful and flourishing state. It would seem that all conditions were turned in favor of the southern and eastern Slavs against the Latinised Germans and Celts, and we could expect the blossoming of medieval culture in Russia instead of in France, Germany, or England. Yet the contrary was the case. The poverty of intellectual culture in ancient Russia is amazing. For seven centuries—that is, until the seventeenth—we know of no scientific work in Russian literature, not even a dogmatic treatise. The whole of literary production had a practical, moral, or religious character, with the exception of the Chronicles, whose great artistic value vividly emphasizes, by contrast, the complete lack of scientific culture. Modern Russian historians, of a new nationalistic brand in the USSR, are unanimous in overestimating the level of ancient Kievan culture, which, according to them, was not inferior to and even surpassed the contemporary western civilization. Their complete failure to substantiate their claim constitutes by itself a new proof of the poverty, at least the intellectual poverty, of that culture.

What is the reason for this anomaly which has had such tragic consequences for Russian life? Was it a natural organic incapacity of the Russians—or Slavs in general—for rational thinking? Yet in the last century Russia developed a rich production in all branches of science second only to the few most civilized nations of the West. Was it the perennial struggle against the nomad tribes of the steppes which exhausted all the national energies? But a never-ceasing feudal war was the background of the medieval monastic schools and universities of the West. Was it the geographical remoteness from the areas of ancient classical culture? Yet Scandinavia and northern Europe in general were still more distant from Rome than Russia from Byzantium. However, the last consideration brings us nearer the truth. Russia, in fact, did not receive, together with Greek Christianity, the classical culture of Greece. Byzantium itself still possessed the ancient treasures; it did not transmit them to Russia, or rather, Russia did not care to receive them. What was the reason? Here again comparison with the West gives an illuminating answer.

The western barbarians, before they were able to think their own thoughts and to speak their own words—about 1100 A.D.—had been sitting for five or six centuries on the school bench, struggling with the foreign Latin language, learning by heart the Latin Bible and the Latin grammar with Vergil as the introduction to the Bible. Men of the dark ages had no independent interest in culture. They were interested only in the salvation of their souls. But Latin gave them the key to salvation. As the language of the Church, Latin was a sacred tongue and everything written in it became invested with a sacred halo. Hence the popularity of Ovid in medieval monasteries, and the Latin versifying of Irish saints, such as Columban, who in their severe asceticism and primitive rudeness of life did not yield to the anchorites of Egypt and Syria. For the Irish the Trivium and Quadrivium were the way to the Latin Bible.

The Slavs converted by the Greeks did not need a similar vehicle to Christianity: they received the Bible and divine service in Slavonic translations. In the second half of the ninth century, two Greek brother missionaries, Saint Cyril and Saint Methodius, performed with their disciples a great work of translating Greek sacred books into Old Slavonic, which at that time could be considered more or less as a common Slavic literary idiom. In the next century the cultivated circle around the Bulgarian Tsar Simeon completed the work of the Cyrillic generation by translating some works of theological and scientific content. A Slavonic library was thus created from which medieval Russia was spiritually fed. Russia received her ecclesiastical organization from Greece but the books and perhaps the first priests came from Bulgaria. The bulk of this literature was more than sufficient for the needs of a newly converted people. Some of these books even exceeded the level of their understanding. Upon this store of learning, obtained from abroad, Russia lived for centuries; most of the additions, new translations from the Greek, came from the same South Slavic source, the Serbs and Bulgarians. There was no religious motive to look in Greek libraries for a new supply. The available Slavonic literature had an overwhelmingly practical and didactic character. Theoretical interests had not been awakened. And the Russian intellect was dwarfed in its development for a long time, not because of the predominance of mystical tendencies, as has often been claimed, but because of the absence of external occasions for exercise. So the Slavonic Bible and the Slavonic liturgy proved to be an ambiguous gift to Russian culture. At the same time, it cannot be denied that these were a priceless endowment for Russia's spiritual life. The people could listen to the word of God and pray to Him in an idiom very near their own. The Gospel was accessible in some measure even to the illiterate. It is obvious then that the fruits of the Christian mission in Russia were, from the very beginning, richer than those yielded by the western Latin soil. It would be no exaggeration to suppose that the imprint of the Gospel was deeper there than in Teutonic and even Romance nations. And this *a priori* conclusion is, indeed, confirmed by the general impression one receives from the documents of ancient Russian literature.

The same must be said of other Slavic nations who inherited the Cyrillo-

Methodian tradition. The Bulgarians of the tenth century, the medieval Serbs, and in a lesser degree the Czecho-Moravians through the eleventh century conveyed to the Russians not only a selection of Greek literature, but also some original works of Bulgarian and perhaps even Czech authorship. To single these works out of the bulk of original Russian literature, with the exception of a few names, is very difficult. Future investigation has to determine accurately the extent and character of the Bulgarian and Czech contributions to Russian religious and cultural life. We can here venture only two remarks, based upon the authentic documents. First, the writings of the Bulgarian authors, such as Clement and Constantine the Junior, are marked by evangelical moralism, inspired by Chrysostom. Second, they preserve and develop the great Cyrillo-Methodian concept of the national calling and the particular gifts of every nation within the oecumenical Church. Both features, so essential to Russian Christianity, were thus originated in the Slavic West and found in Russia an extremely fertile soil.

Russia through Arabian Eyes (tenth century)

Ibn Fadlan

In the early tenth century Islam spanned a territory reaching from Spain in the west to India in the east. What had begun as a religion of Bedouin herders had been transformed into a culture and way of life increasingly shared by a large part of the known world. Emissaries from its religious and cultural centers were sent out to the north and east to proselytize, and thus it was that Ibn Fadlan's tenth-century account of his journey from Baghdad to the kingdom of the Bulgars along the Volga River came to be written. From all accounts, the king of the Bulgars wished to bring his people under one monotheistic religion, perhaps for both trade and political purposes. Dispatched as a religious emissary to the Bulgars by the caliphate of Baghdad, Ibn Fadlan followed a circuitous route north, first heading east and then doubling back west in order to avoid hostile tribes, eventually arriving in the land of the Bulgars.

In the course of his journeys Ibn Fadlan encountered a tribe of people known as Rus'. We know from the early Russian Chronicles that the Rus', or Varangians, had originally come south from Scandinavia in search of trade routes and plunder in the eighth century. By the time of Ibn Fadlan's journey in the tenth century they had made their way out to the lands of the Volga Bulgars, where they secured booty and destroyed homes. The hope that he might receive protection through a shared religion may have been one of the motivating factors behind the Bulgar king's invitation to Baghdad.

Ibn Fadlan's descriptions of the Rus' are those of a devout Muslim who saw himself as the bearer of culture, enlightenment, and faith among those he encountered on his travels. The importance the Muslim faith attaches to cleanliness and ablutions is contrasted here with the washing practices of the Rus', a subject that alternately fascinates and appalls the emissary. If he journeyed with religious intent, however, he was also an ethnographer of uncommon distinction. Although Arab travelers and merchants preceding him had left accounts, albeit sketchy, of their travels, Ibn Fadlan was the first to record in careful and precise detail all that he saw. If at times he exaggerated, he did so no more than was normal in other accounts of the day. What also emerges from reading about his travels is a description of a trade route whose trajectory from northwest to southeast had begun to rival the famous Silk Road to China.

I saw the Rūs (*ar-Rūsīyah*) who had come on their trading missions and taken up quarters on the river Ātil. I have never seen men more physically perfect than they, being tall as date palms, blond and ruddy and wearing neither tunics nor caftans. A man among them, however, wears a garment (*kisā'*) with which he wraps up one side of his body, and it is through this opening that he lets one of his hands out. Every one of them has an ax (*fa's*), a sword and a knife, and he is never without the items just mentioned.

. . . .

If one of them becomes ill, they pitch a tent for him at some distance from them. They place him in it, and leave him some bread and water. They do not come close to him, nor do they speak to him. Rather they do not visit him throughout the period of his illness, especially if he happens to be poor or a slave. If he recovers and is on his feet again, he returns to them. If he dies, they burn him, but if he happens to be a slave, they leave him as he is, so that dogs and birds of prey devour him.

When they catch a thief or a robber, they lead him to a large tree, fasten a rope around his neck and hang him on it. He remains hanging until he crumbles to pieces as a result of prolonged exposure to the winds and rains.

I used to be told that at the time of death they do certain things to their chiefs, the least of which is burning. I was eager to find out about such matters, when news reached me of the death of an illustrious man from among them. They put him in his grave and roofed it over for ten days until they were finished with the cutting and sewing of his clothes.

In the case of a poor man, they construct a small boat, place him in it and burn it. As for a rich man, they gather his wealth and divide it into three parts. One third is given to his family, one third is set aside for the cutting and sewing of his garments, and one third for the procurement of the *nabīdh* which they drink on the day his slave girl kills herself and is burned with her master.

They are inordinately fond of *nabīdh*, drinking it night and day. Sometimes one of them dies with the cup in his hand.

When a chief from among them dies, his family says to his young male and female slaves: "Which of you will die with him?" One of them then says: "I will!" Once he says that, it becomes binding on him, and he is unable to go back on his word, ever. Even should he desire to do so, it is not permitted. Most of those who do this are female slaves.

When the man, whom I mentioned before, was dead, they said to his slave girls: "Who will die with him?" And one of them said: "I!" They then put two girls in charge of her, to guard her and be with her wherever she went, even to the point that they sometimes washed her feet with their own hands. They then turn to matters pertaining to him, such as the cutting of his clothes [and] doing whatever is necessary. Meanwhile, the slave girl drinks and sings every day, and is joyous and cheerful.

When the day came on which he and the girl were to be burned, I went to the river where his boat was, and indeed it had already been taken out of the water, and was supported by four pillars made of *khadhank* and other types of wood. A structure similar to large wooden scaffoldings (*anābīr*) was placed around it. Then the boat was dragged up until it was placed on top of the wooden scaffolding. They then began to walk back and forth, uttering words which I did not understand while he was still in his grave from which they had not taken him out. They then came with a bed (*sarīr*), put it on the boat and covered it with quilted mattresses of Byzantine brocade, as well as with cushions of Byzantine brocade. Then came an old woman whom they call the angel of death and spread out on the bed the above mentioned furnishings. She took charge of sewing it and putting it in good shape. She is the one who kills the slave girls. I saw her as a young, old witch (*jawān bīrah*), massive and somber.

When they came to his grave, they brushed the dust from the wood and then set the wood aside. They pulled him out wearing the garment in which he had died. I saw that he had turned black already from the cold of that country. They had placed *nabīdh*, fruit and a three-stringed lute (*ṭanbūr*) in the grave with him. They now took all this out. Indeed, he had neither started to decompose, nor had he suffered any change other than that of his color.

They dressed him in trousers (*sarāwīl*), leggings (*rān*), a tunic (*qurtaq*) and a brocaded caftan (*khiftān*) with gold buttons. On his head they placed a cap made of brocade sable fur, and brought him along until they carried him into the tent (*qubbah*) which was located on the ship. They seated him on the quilted mattress and propped him up with the cushions. They then brought *nabīdh*, fruit and aromatic herbs and placed them with him.

They came with bread, meat and onions and threw them in front of him. They brought a dog, cut it in two and threw it into the boat. They then brought all his weapons and laid them at his side. Then they took two horses, ran them until they broke out in a sweat, then they cut them up with the sword and threw their meat into the ship.

They then came with two cows, cut them up likewise and threw them in it. They then fetched forth a cock and a chicken, killed them both and threw them into the ship.

The slave girl who wants to be killed wanders back and forth, entering one after another of their huts. The man in the hut has sexual union with her, saying to her: "Say to your master that I did this out of love for you."

When it was the time of the afternoon prayer on Friday, they brought the girl to something they had set up similar to the frame of a door (*malban al-bāb*). She then placed both her feet on the palms of the men's hands, and she was lifted up, peeped over the door frame and uttered certain words. They brought her down and raised her up a second time, and she did as she had done the first time. They then lowered her and raised her aloft a third time. She performed as she had done the two previous occasions. They handed her a chicken, and she cut off its head and flung it aside. They took the chicken and threw it into the ship.

I asked the interpreter about what she had done, and he said: "The first time they lifted her up she said: 'Behold! I see my father and my mother.' The second time they did so, she said: 'Behold! I see all of my dead relatives seated.' On the third occasion, she said: 'Lo! I see my lord sitting in paradise, and paradise is beautiful and green, and with him are men and slaves, and he is calling me. Take me to him.'" They took her in the direction of the ship. She took off two bracelets that she had been wearing and handed them over to the woman whom they call the angel of death, the one who is to kill her. She removed two anklets that she had on and gave them to the two girls who had been waiting on her and who were the daughters of the woman known as the angel of death.

They raised her up to the ship, but did not let her into the tent. Men came carrying shields and wooden staves. They then gave her a bowl of *nabīdh*. She sang over it and drank it. The translator said to me: "With that she is bidding farewell to her women companions." Then she was handed another cup. She took it, and made her song over it rather long and drawn out, while the old woman was inciting her to drink it and enter the tent in which was her master.

I saw her overcome with confusion. She wanted to enter the tent, but had inserted her head between it and the ship. The old woman took her head, directed her into the tent and entered with her.

The men began beating the shields with their staves lest the sound of her cry be heard, and the other slave girls become greatly distressed and no longer seek death with their masters. Six men then entered the tent, all of whom had sexual intercourse with the girl. They then laid her down at the side of her master, and two of them seized her feet, and two of them her hands while the old woman, who is called the angel of death, placed a rope around her neck, the two ends of which pointed in opposite directions, and handed it to two men to pull on. She stepped forward, holding a dagger with a wide blade, and began sticking it in and pulling it out in different places between the ribs of the girl. Meanwhile, the two men were simultaneously strangling her with the rope until she was dead.

The nearest relative of the dead man then appeared, took a piece of wood and lighted it at the fire. He then walked backward with the back of his head toward the ship and his face toward the people, holding the burning wood in one hand while he kept the other hand over his anus, for he was naked. [This was kept up until] he had set fire to the wood that was stacked under the ship, after they laid the slave girl they had killed at the side of her master.

The people than came forward with sticks and firewood. Each one of them had with him a piece of wood, the end of which he had set on fire, and which he now threw upon the wood packed beneath the ship. This spread to the firewood, then to the ship, then to the tent, [and finally to] the man and the slave girl and everything therein. There then began to blow a mighty and frightful wind, and the flames of the fire were intensified, and its blaze flared up. At my side was a man of the *Rūs,* and I heard him speak to the interpreter who was with me. I asked the interpreter what he had said, and he replied: "He says: 'You, O Arabs, are foolish.'" "How so?" I asked. "Indeed," he said, "you take the person that is the most beloved to you and the most respected among you and leave him in the ground, so that the earth, the insects and the worms consume him, while we burn him with fire in an instant, and he enters paradise forthwith, from that very moment."

Rules for Russian Households (sixteenth century)

Attributed to the monk Sylvestr

One of the most compelling works to come out of sixteenth-century Russia was a book of household management called The Domostroi, *purported to be written or edited by a priest named Sylvestr from the Cathedral of the Annunciation in Moscow. More than a book of etiquette, it is a compendium of rules and regulations to be followed on the domestic and moral planes in a large household belonging to the upper class in Muscovite Russia. It covers topics ranging from moral instruction ("How One Should Honor Tsars and Princes," "How One Should Visit Monasteries, Hospitals, Prisons," "How to Teach Children and Save Them with Fear") to the day-to-day duties involved in running a large, extended household ("How a Woman Should Care for Clothing," "How to Brew Beer, Make Mead, and Distill Vodka," "What to Do with Waste Produced in Kitchens, Bakeries, and Workrooms") and the economy of social and gender hierarchy ("How to Teach Your Servants to Run Errands," "How to Maintain Domestic Order," "How a Person Should Live by Gathering His Resources Together").* The Domostroi *holds to the belief that life runs more smoothly both economically, morally, and socially when highly ritualized and codified. Like most how-to books of the day, it sets forth goals and ideals rather than reflecting the reality of daily life.*

The political and social fabric of Muscovy may explain the appearance of this work at this particular time in Russian history. By the mid-sixteenth century Moscow had consolidated its power, the Tatar-Mongol hordes had been defeated, and Muscovy was expanding eastward into Siberia and had acquired areas formerly under Tatar control such as Astrakhan and Kazan.

As the state proceeded to reestablish its political prerogatives both at home and abroad, its values came to be reflected in the daily life and moral fabric of the well-to-do family. Hierarchy was strictly adhered to; social mobility increasingly became a function of dynastic alliances obtained primarily through marriage and one's ability to curry the tsar's favor. Women's lives were strictly circumscribed. For the most part women were confined to separate quarters of the house and were bound by strict rules as to whom they could visit and what they could say. What lay behind this virtual imprisonment was the belief that women ought not to be free to form emotional bonds with other men since marriage was in essence a political event, with personal compatibility taking second place to political, social, and economic alliances. Yet even as women lived in a world of diminished horizons their honor and legal rights were nevertheless protected by law.

If The Domostroi *reflected the ideology of the state, it may also have provided a refuge from it. Its appearance coincided with the rule of Ivan IV (1533–84), which, along with periods of reform, ushered in protracted political rivalries between the princes and the boyars as the tsar's behavior became increasingly characterized by paranoia and cruelty. Dusting off the icons and keeping the guests sober allowed, at least on paper, for sculpting a kind of order out of chaos.*

How One Should Decorate One's Home with
Holy Icons and Keep a Clean House

Every Christian should put holy and venerable pictures, icons painted according to the church's rules, on the walls of every room. These icons should be arranged and decorated beautifully. Place candles in candelabra before the holy images during every service.

When the service is done, extinguish the candles and cover all the icons with veils to ensure cleanliness, promote piety, and protect them from dust.

Always dust icons with a feather duster and wipe them with a soft sponge. Always keep the shrine clean.

When you go to touch the holy images make sure you are worthy—that is, pure in conscience.

While glorifying God, during the holy service and during prayers, light candles and burn sweet-smelling frankincense and incense. Set up the holy icons according to the Rule.

The saints will feel honored when you treat their icons in this manner. You must always so revere them—during prayer, vigils, worship, and any other divine service, confessing, pleading with tears and a contrite heart, for the remission of your sins.

. . . .

How One Should Invite Priests and Monks to One's House to Pray

On holy days, depending on who is present, let those in charge invite priests (as many as they can afford) into the home. The priests will complete the

Seventeenth-century Muscovite dress. From Adam Olearius, *Vermehrte Moscowitishce und Persianische Reisebeschreibung* (Schleszwig, 1656). Courtesy of Rare Books Division, Department of Rare Books and Special Collections, Princeton University Library.

ritual appropriate to the occasion. They will pray for the tsar and grand prince N., autocrat of all the Russias, for his tsaritsa and grand princess N., for their royal children, for the boyars, and the whole army of Christians, for its victory over enemies and for the freedom of those imprisoned, for bishops, priests, and monks, for all Christians, and for all that is profitable for the man of the house, his wife, children, and servants. If asked, they will sanctify water with the life-giving cross, with miracle-working icons, and with holy relics. For a sick person they will also consecrate oil to bring health and healing.

When a sick person is in the house, let the homeowner invite seven or more priests and as many deacons as he can find. They will pray over commemorative beer for health and over frumenty to bring peace of mind. After someone departs this life, the priest or deacon will cense every room, sprinkling it with holy water and making the sign of the cross. Then those in the house, praising God according to the divine liturgy, should at once set up a table so that the priests and monks, along with the rest of the guests and the neighborhood poor, may eat and drink. Then all, contented and replete, will go to their homes praising God.

It is up to the master of the house or his representatives to offer someone food or drink or to send something to another's table according to the recipient's worth or rank or the quality of his counsel. All such decisions belong to the master and not to others. If, out of affection or in response to some service that has been rendered, someone who is not in charge feels he should give food and drink to another, he may do so if he later pleads his master's forgiveness for it. But to take food or drink secretly from the table or sideboard or to send it without the master's permission or blessing is blasphemy and self-worship; those who do it dishonor everything.

> When you are asked by someone to a wedding-feast, do not sit down in the place of honour. It may be that some person more distinguished than yourself has been invited; and the host will come and say to you, "Give this man your seat." Then you will look foolish as you begin to take the lowest place. No, when you receive an invitation, go and sit down in the lowest place, so that when your host comes he will say, "Come up higher, my friend." Then all your fellow-guests will see the respect in which you are held. For everyone who exalts himself will be humbled, and whoever humbles himself will be exalted. [Luke 14:8–11]

When many dishes are placed before you, do not immediately begin to eat, lest someone more honored than you has been invited. If you know your status is highest, you may begin, but you should take note of how much food is offered. At the homes of some devout people, food and drink are plentiful, and their guests can partake fully; with others you should eat only if they insist. If someone—insensitive, graceless, unlearned, and ignorant—begins to stuff himself without considering how much food is available, he will be cursed, mocked, and dishonored by God and man.

How One Should Express Gratitude to God While Entertaining Guests

At the start of the meal, the priests should glorify the Father, the Son, and the Holy Ghost, then the Virgin Mother of God. If those present eat gratefully, in silence or while engaged in devout conversation, the angels will stand by invisibly and write down the diners' good deeds. Their food and drink will be sweet. But if those present utter blasphemy as they begin to eat, the food will turn to dung in their mouths. If they indulge in scurrilous conversation, dirty words, jesting, or any diversion—harps or dancing, clapping, galloping about, games, irreligious songs—then just as smoke drives away bees, so will the angels of God leave that table and that disgusting conversation. The demons will appear, rejoicing. Their desires will be loosed and all kinds of things that please Satan will happen.

Such people outrage God with dice and chess; they amuse themselves with the Devil's games. They throw God's gift of food and drink—the fruits of the earth—away in scorn, then tipple; they beat each other and pour a new round. They scorn God's gift; when the devils write down their deeds, the record is carried to Satan; the demons rejoice together at the destruction of Christians. All such deeds will stand on Judgment Day.

O, woe to the doers of such deeds! When the Jews sat in the desert to eat and drink, then, having stuffed themselves, got up to play and fornicate, the earth devoured twenty-three thousand of them.

Tremble, o people! Do God's will just as it is written in the Law. From such wicked dishonor, Lord, protect every Christian.

Eat, then, and drink in praise of God. Do not overeat or get drunk or act frivolously. If you set food or drink before anyone, or they set any food before you, do not denigrate anything, or say, "This is rotten (sour, tasteless, too salty, bitter, moldy, raw, overcooked)." If you do, the evil you say will be laid upon you. Rather, praise God's gift of food and eat gratefully. Then God will smell fragrance in you and will make bad food sweet.

If any item of food or drink is not needed, rebuke the servant who made it so that in the future such a thing will not happen.

My Early Life (1564–79)

Ivan IV

He has been more commonly known in Russian history as Ivan Groznyi, or Ivan the Dread, a title he conferred upon himself to laud his strength as a ruler and underscore the homage and respect he demanded from his subjects. Among Russia's rulers his name stands out for the terror he inflicted on his enemies and for extremes of behavior suggestive of a person beset by his own devils. In 1581 in a heated argument he bludgeoned to death his son and heir, an act recorded by the artist Ilya Repin in his painting Ivan the Terrible Killing His Son. *Profoundly pious, Ivan was prone to extremes of sadism and cruelty that invite comparisons with the Stalin era. It was not accidental that four centuries after Ivan's rule, part II of the film* Ivan the Terrible, *made in 1946 by Sergei Eisenstein, was banned under Stalin, ostensibly for historical inaccuracies but in fact for parallels that no one could fail to miss between the cruelty and misuse of power on the part of both rulers.*

Ivan IV's reign was marked by often puzzling contradictions between legal reform and increased political representation on the one hand and adherence to rigid dogma and terror on the other. The Russian lands, both under Ivan and under his predecessors, expanded significantly, north to the Baltic and east to the Volga and into Siberia, where lucrative furs and minerals were to be found. Principalities that had formerly been independent came under Moscow's rule, and by 1556 Kazan and Astrakhan and thus the Caspian Sea and the Volga trade routes had been brought under Moscow's control. Yet even as his realm expanded, Ivan sought to consolidate his own power in ways that suggest his psychological instability. Under his rule the oprichnina was formed, originally a geographical area north and northwest of Moscow designated by Ivan as his own private domain. Gradually, however, the word came to denote the elite army that Ivan established, whose task it was to eliminate any region or group of people perceived as hostile to his policies. Indicative of the formalism and traditionalism that marked Ivan's rule were two books widely read at the time: The Domostroi, *an excerpt from which appears in this section, and the* Chetia-Mineia, *an exhaustive collection of Church writings and saints' lives meant to serve as an encyclopedia of knowledge for the Russian Church.*

Ivan IV was the first prince to be crowned tsar of all Russia, a title that cemented

Moscow's already established place as chief among Russia's principalities. He viewed his own role as that of God's representative on earth and tolerated no interference in his decision making from either secular advisors or the Church. Circulating at the time was the theory of Moscow as the Third Rome, a theory that propagated the notion that the leadership of the Christian world had been passed down to Moscow from Rome and from Byzantium. Some scholars believe that this philosophy gave Russia's sixteenth-century rulers permission to exercise unlimited powers of rule. Others believe that this same philosophy exhorted Russia's rulers to aspire to rule with justice and mercy.

Much remains unknown about Ivan's life, including what level of education he attained. Even the authenticity of the correspondence between him and his close advisor, Prince Andrei Kurbskii, has been disputed. Kurbskii's flight to Lithuania in 1564, a country with which Moscow was at war, produced a series of seven letters between himself and Ivan IV over a period of fifteen years, from 1564 to 1579. While purporting to defend himself, Ivan in fact unintentionally incriminated himself by acknowledging his psychological difficulties and attributing them to the palace intrigue that surrounded him as a young child. Whether or not the letters themselves are apocryphal, they provide insight into the Muscovite ideology that informed Ivan's rule, an ideology best summed up by an apologist of the day who stated that "a realm without dread is like a horse without a bridle."

I will prove in the greatest detail what evil I have suffered from my youth even unto the present day. For this is clear (even if you were young in those years, yet none the less this you can know): when, by the decree(s) of God, our father, the great sovereign, Vasily, having exchanged the purple for the angel's form, had left all that was perishable and the fleeting earthly kingdom and come to the heavenly [realm], to that everlasting eternity, to stand before the Tsar of Tsars and the Lord of Lords, I remained with my only (-begotten) brother Georgiy, who has departed this life in sanctity. I was then three years old and my brother was one, and our mother, the pious Tsaritsa Elena, was left in such miserable widowhood—as though in the midst of flames, she suffered on all sides now unmitigated strife stirred up against her by all peoples—by the foreign peoples encircling [our realm], Lithuanians, Poles, Perikopians, Nadchitarkhan, and Nogais, and Kazan',—now manifold misfortune(s) and suffering(s) [inflicted by] you traitors; for, like unto you, you mad dog, Prince Semen Bel'sky and Ivan Lyatsky ran away to Lithuania; [from there] whither did they not run like men possessed? To Tsargrad and to Crimea and to the Nogai [Tatars] and on all sides they raised strife against the Orthodox. But they had no success. Thanks to the intervention of God and the most pure Mother of God and the great miracle-workers, and because of the prayers and the blessing of our parents, all these things, like the counsel of

Ahitophel, were scattered. In like manner later did the traitors raise up our uncle, Prince Andrey Ivanovich, against us, and with those traitors did he go to Novgorod (so, these are they whom you praise! You call them our "well-wishers" and "those that lay down their lives for us"!). And at that time did these [traitors] secede from us and adhere to our uncle, Prince Andrey, and at their head was your brother [i.e. cousin], Prince Ivan, the son of Prince Semen, the son of Prince Petr Romanovich Lvov, and many others. And likewise with the help of God did this plot miscarry [*lit.* this counsel was not achieved]. Well then, is that the "well-wishing" of those whom you praise? Thus do they "lay down their lives for us" by wishing to destroy us and raise our uncle to the throne? But later, in their treacherous manner, they began to hand over our patrimony to our Lithuanian enemy—the towns of Rado-goshch, Starodub, Gomel'—thus do they "wish us well"? When there is no one in the land with whom to wreak destruction at home [*lit.* from the land] and to turn glory to deceit, then do they cast in their lot with [*lit.* join in love with] foreigners, only so that they may wreak destruction of which no memory shall remain!

Thus by God's will did it come to pass that our mother, the pious Tsaritsa Elena, went from the earthly kingdom to the heavenly; and we and our brother Georgiy, who has departed this life in sanctity, remained as orphans, [having lost] our parents and receiving no human care from any quarter; and hoping only for the mercy of God, we put our trust in the mercy of the most pure Mother of God and the prayers of all the Saints and the blessing of our parents. But when I had entered upon my eighth year of life [*lit.* from birth] and when thus our subjects had achieved their desire, namely to have the kingdom without a ruler, then did they not deem us, their sovereigns, worthy of any loving care, but themselves ran after wealth and glory, and so leapt on one another [in conflict]. And what did they [not] do then! How many boyars and well-wishers of our father and *voevodas* [a tsar's appointed official in a city or district] did they massacre! And the courts and the villages and the posses-sions of our uncles did they seize and they set themselves up in them! And [the majority of] my mother's treasure did they transfer to the Great Trea-sury, furiously kicking out [at each other] and stabbing with sharp imple-ments; but the remainder they shared amongst themselves. Your grandfather, Mikhailo Tuchkov, did this. And so Prince Vasily and Prince Ivan Shuisky of their own accord did appoint themselves my guardians and thus did they raise themselves to the throne; and all those who had been our father's and our mother's main traitors did they release, one after the other, from imprison-ment and win over [*lit.* reconcile] to their side. And Prince Vasily Shuisky began to live in the court of our uncle, Prince Andrey Ivanovich, and in that court—as it were in a Jewish synagogue—they seized Fedor Mishurin, the private *d'yak* [secretary] of our father and of us, and having put him to shame they murdered him. And they banished Prince Ivan Fedorovich Bel'sky and many others to various places and rose up in arms against the Church and, deposing the Metropolitan Daniel from the metropolitanate, they sent him into banishment; thus did they achieve their desire in all things and themselves began to rule. But as for us, together with our only (-begotten) brother Georgiy, who has departed this life in sanctity—they began to feed us as though we were foreigners or the most wretched menials. What sufferings did I [not] endure through [lack of] clothing and through hunger! For in all things my will was not my own [*lit.* I had no will]; everything was contrary to my will and unbefitting my tender years. I (will) recall one thing: whilst we were playing childish games in our infancy Prince Ivan Vasil'evich Shuisky is sitting on a bench, leaning with his elbows on our father's bed and with his leg up on a chair; and he did not even incline his head towards us, either in parental manner, or even as a master—nor was there any element of servility to be found [in his attitude to us]. And who can endure such arrogance? How can I enumerate such countless sore sufferings as I put up with in my youth? Many a time did I eat late, not in accordance with my will. But what of the treasures inherited by me from my father [*lit.* of my parental heritage]? With their cunning scheming they seized it all, as though it were pay for the boyar children; but from them they took it all for themselves for their own profit, rewarding them [the boyar children] not according to their service and recompensing them not according to their merits; and they appropriated the incalculable treasure of our grandfather and of our father; and so from this treasure did they forge for themselves golden and silver vessels and upon them they inscribed the names of their parents as though they had been the possession of their parents. Now all people know that during the rule of our mother Prince Ivan Shuisky had a marten fur coat [lined] with green mohair and the skins were shabby [*lit.* ancient]; now supposing this was a [genuinely] ancient possession of the Shuiskys, surely it would have been better, rather than to forge those vessels [as they did], to have exchanged the fur coat and with the surplus [money accruing from the sale of the new coat] to have forged the vessels? But what shall I say concerning the treasure of my uncles? They seized it all for themselves and after this they fell upon [*lit.* jumped on] the towns and villages and thus with the bitterest torment in divers ways did they plunder without mercy the properties of those living there. Who can enumerate the attacks [carried out] by them on their neighbours? All my subjects did they make as servants unto themselves; but their own servants did they set up like grandees; and thinking they were ruling and organizing— instead of this they brought to pass much injustice and disorganization, making immeasurable profit from all and doing and saying everything for gain.

III

Reform to Revolution

Peter the Great was born on 30 May 1672 into the world of old Muscovy—its internecine warfare, the claustrophobic ritualism of church and rulers, its palace intrigue and failed foreign policy. The world that surrounded him was hung heavy with the wall icons and frescoes of Christ and saints in the Kremlin, a place with low ceilings, dark rooms, small windows, and religious paintings proclaiming the eternal alliance between God and tsar in the cosmology of rulership. And yet something was beginning to change. Peter's predecessors could no longer ignore Europe and the need to bring Russia into the fold of European modernization. Reforms had already been initiated in the military, and the centuries' long practice of precedence (*mestnichestvo*), according to which one's career was determined by that of one's father and by birthright, had been abolished in favor of ability and merit. Thus when Peter ascended the throne at age seventeen the initial groundwork had already been laid to bring Russia into the modern era. But Peter also inherited a country that since the Kyivan era had been engaged in almost continuous internecine strife and plagued by the infighting of the boyars (councilors) in the fifteenth and sixteenth centuries. The early seventeenth century had witnessed two foreign armies, Polish and Swedish, occupying Russian soil. Peasant uprisings, religious tensions over a growing foreign presence in Russia, and a Church schism all contributed to the destabilization of the country during the Time of Troubles (1598–1613) and well into the middle of the seventeenth century.

Under Peter's predecessors Russia had begun to expand its borders. Ivan III and Ivan IV had pushed Russia's geographical fortunes to the south and the east and in doing so had added an ethnically diverse population of Tatars, Chuvash, and Mordva to the ethnic makeup of the land. Included now within Russia were peoples who spoke languages that belonged to different linguistic families, Turkic and Finn-Ugric, that bore no relation to Russian. But even as Russia pressed east, Peter looked in a different direction, focusing his attentions on what the West could give his country. Only by acquiring Western European know-how, he reasoned, would Russia be able to compete in the modern age and not be swallowed up by European military and technological supremacy. The reforms he instituted were radical and not always well received. He was asking his countrymen, particularly urban dwellers, to change their ways. He lessened the stranglehold of the Church, built a new city that was the incarnation of his dream of Westernization, and pushed his countrymen into a world dominated by Europe. The dictatorial and repressive measures that had been associated with Peter's predecessors still nipped at the heels of Russia, as the man who was the first in Russia to call himself "emperor" strove to modernize his country, by force if necessary.

Peter was the first Russian ruler to spend a significant amount of time abroad, and moreover with the object of learning from the experience. As part of his plan to Europeanize his country he moved the capital from Moscow to the new city of St. Petersburg that he had built on the Neva River near the Gulf of Finland. He dubbed it his "window on Europe." Built on a swamp at an enormous cost in human life and subject to devastating floods, the city became in Pushkin's poem "The Bronze Horseman" (1833) a deathtrap for his protagonist Evgenii, who is symbolic of the little man crushed under the weight of Peter's dreams.

Part of the emperor's fascination with the West was born of his passion for shipbuilding and navigation, both of which were underdeveloped in Russia when he came to the throne. At the age of twenty-four he traveled incognito (a disguise difficult to retain since he was close to seven feet tall) throughout Europe for sixteen months. Under the name Petr Mikhailov and with a group of some thirty volunteers he learned the arts of shipbuilding and navigation. During his time away he forged important political alliances and recruited manpower in engineering, science, and culture that he brought back to Russia with him. John Perry, represented in this section, was among those recruited and became instrumental in building Russia's navy.

The resistance that Peter encountered at home was not simply a function of the divide between those who directly benefited from his reforms and those who did not. Many who were the recipients of Westernization were nevertheless opposed to it. Even those who were not selected to go abroad to study and live were nevertheless forced to adopt certain Western forms and habits. In Russian cities men were ordered to shave off their beards and wear shorter frock coats in the European manner; only peasants and clergy were excused from having to comply. Foreigners populated the cities and the countryside as tutors to educate the children of the upper classes in the languages of Western Europe, primarily French. Tolstoy talks at length about his German tutor in *Childhood, Boyhood and Youth* (1852–57), and at the beginning of *War and Peace* (1865–69) takes his reader inside a Russian soirée, where his characters speak French. Pushkin's female protagonist Tat'iana from *Eugene Onegin* (1833) cannot write a love letter to Onegin in Russian because she has been educated in French.

By the time of Peter's death in 1724 deep divisions had been carved into Russian society as a consequence of the reforms and of their failure to address some of the preexisting inequities in society. Those who supported the reforms were known as Westernizers, while those who felt that Russia's national destiny was to be found in its own people and in its religion were known as Slavophiles. For them Russia's semi-historical, semi-mystical mission, arising partly out of the legacy of the Moscow ideology and Moscow as the Third Rome, was based on Russian identity as incarnate in the land, its people, and above all its Church. For them the West became something akin to the Antichrist, who would undermine Russia's sanctified place in the world. Indeed even Peter the Great was branded by some conservatives during his time as the incarnation of the Antichrist. Dostoyevsky's immortal character Ivan Karamazov in *The Brothers Karamazov* (1881) compares the West to a graveyard, perhaps reflecting those deep Slavophile fears.

Long after Peter had died the debate generated by his reforms provided the backdrop for much of the political and philosophical discourse in the nineteenth century. "Who are we as Russians? To what degree must our national self-worth be tied to the acceptance of foreign forms and cultures?" asked many of Russia's most notable philosophers, writers, and social thinkers. Many of their questions were generated by the fact that over time members of the *dvorianstvo* (nobility) had come to see themselves as more truly European than Russian, and over the decades had became noticeably distant from their country and from their identity as Russians.

The results of Peter's reforms were decidedly mixed. He created a Table of Ranks that, while abolishing one set of hierarchies, created another. Perhaps more important, he neither abolished nor reformed the institution that was the thorn in everyone's side: serfdom. A century after his death serfdom still lingered in Russia, and on the eve of the emancipation of the serfs in 1861 the country found itself the last in Europe to be enchained by the system. Catherine the Great inherited it, along with a growing number of peasant revolts that followed in the wake of the freeing of the nobility from state service. The peasants quite logically thought that they were next in line to be freed. But such was not to be under Catherine nor under her successors until 1861. Indeed for all the philosophy and literature and grand style of the European Enlightenment that made its way into Russia, the country remained mired in an economic and social system that enchained both serf and master. As the number of movements toward reform emerged in the early part of the nineteenth century, much of the nobility and the landowning gentry opposed emancipation, fearing loss of land, loss of income, loss of labor that was formerly theirs for free, and loss of a lifestyle that defined their identity as landowning gentry.

Life under serfdom carried with it repercussions that far outstripped the economic issues. In "The Challenged Gentry" Elizaveta Vodovozova describes the psychological consequences of growing up and living under such a system. In his novel *Dead Souls* (1842) Nikolai Gogol follows the fortunes of a man named Chichikov who travels around provincial Russia, buying up people's dead serfs in order to obtain a favorable mortgage on some property. Gogol spared no ink in revealing the moral and religious sterility of his country through the image of a man whose dream is to be just like everybody else.

Serfdom, Napoleon's invasion of Russia, the movement for constitutional reform, all created a hothouse atmosphere of ideas and of social and political discourse that would ultimately lead to revolution. Plans for reform mixed almost indistinguishably with concepts of national self-identity. A group of military officers pushed hard for constitutional reform and for an end to serfdom and staged a brief rebellion in December 1825, thus giving birth to their name, the Decembrists. Many consider them the initial spark that ignited the Bolshevik Revolution almost one hundred years later. The rebellion was quickly squelched by Nicholas I and the participants executed or exiled. But long after the rebellion had been suppressed, its very failure gave rise to a resurgence of debate over Russian national identity. Peter Chaadaev, a military officer, raised his voice in opposition to the attempts of the Decembrists to impose a foreign mantle of Western institutions and belief practices on Russia rather than inculcate into his countrymen the philosophical core of Western political philosophy.

The debates over Russianness, over relations with Western Europe, and over Russia's mission in the world carried over onto the pages of the "thick journals" of the time, which published both literary and nonliterary works. A new school of literary criticism was born under the leadership of Vissarion Belinsky (1811–48), who called for a socially engaged literature in the manner of Victor Hugo in France and Charles Dickens in England. Literature, said Belinsky, had a social and political obligation to fulfill. It was its duty not only to point out social ills but to point the way to reform. While he admired Dostoyevsky's novel *Poor People* for what he saw as its deep engagement with the lives of the poor and the marginalized, he broke with Dostoyevsky as the latter went on to investigate the religious and moral dimensions of human action. Belinsky died before Dostoyevsky wrote his greatest novels, in which he explored questions regarding the nature of crime and the possible justification of political violence and killing in the name of creating a more just and equitable society.

This often uneasy marriage between art and politics heralded the canons of socialist realism promulgated under Stalin. Indeed this almost messianic quality ascribed to literature in the Soviet period, when seen against the backdrop of the nineteenth-century school of social criticism, becomes no longer an anomaly unique to Soviet literature but a movement with deep roots in the nineteenth century. Not all literati sided with Belinsky, but what they shared with him was a deep engagement with ideas and with contemporary social and political issues that came to be known as the "cursed questions" (*prokliatye voprosy*). The questions revolved around the practical and moral but also the existential issues of the day, and the existence of God was debated with the same passion as were the contemporary social ills of Russia.

By the 1860s the impulse to reform had given way to impatience. The men of the 1840s who had pushed for constitutional reform found that their sons, impatient with the slow pace of change, took up more radical means to achieve their ends. Some became nihilists; others read Marx and became philosophical materialists. The dialectic between the two generations is at the heart of Ivan Turgenev's novel *Fathers and Sons* (1862), which explores the conflict and the possibilities of finding common ground between the reformists and the revolutionaries. The radical impulses of the 1860s began to merge with the unsolved issues of postemancipation Russia that still struggled powerfully with the legacy of serfdom. Emancipation in 1861 did not bring the peasants all they had hoped for. The land that they had used prior to being freed was no longer theirs to farm since the gentry was able to retain by law at least a third of their arable land. Even the plots that the peasants did receive were not theirs per se but instead belonged to the peasant commune. In practical terms this guaranteed that land would be apportioned equally among the peasants, thereby avoiding the almost certain result of peasants being left without land. However, it also tied the peasants to the village and to the commune, making it difficult, if not impossible, to sell or to move.

The peasants in the late nineteenth century were not the only ones to experience the rupture and displacement of change in their economic and social status. Memoirs and the literature of the time attest to the struggles of the landowning gentry to adapt to an economy in which their estates were no longer run by what amounted to free labor. In *Anna Karenina* (1877) Tolstoy's Levin engages in protracted discussions with his brother over the necessity for agricultural reform. Nowhere, however, was the dilemma of the gentry and the aristocracy facing a world that was on the brink of extinction as poignantly articulated as in Anton Chekhov's *The Cherry Orchard* (1904). At the

Mina Moiseyev, Study for Peasant Holding a Bridle, 1882. Painting by Ivan Kramskoy. Courtesy of the Russian Museum.

end of the play one hears the sound of an axe felling a family's beloved orchard (which, in the manner of a Greek tragedy, takes place offstage), as the estate is sold out in parcels to a member of Russia's emerging but still under-developed middle class. It is a play that spells the end of a way of life, the end of an entire world that Chekhov's contemporary Tolstoy took pains to record in detail, undoubtedly sensing its imminent demise.

The selections in this section were written by eyewitnesses to the events and eras they describe, all, that is, except Tolstoy, who in *War and Peace* looks back on the Napoleonic invasion fifty-three years removed from it. They are written by rulers (Catherine II and Nicholas II), by members of the gentry (Vodovozova), by two of the major nineteenth-century literary figures (Push-kin and Tolstoy), by an Englishman who was brought to Russia in connection with Peter the Great's reforms (Perry), by a woman for whom culture re-volved around cooking (Molokhovets), by a revolutionary who witnessed the emancipation of the serfs (Kropotkin), and by a priest who, as a member of the clergy, lived in the very conditions he was describing (Belliustin). Together they provide the perspective rarely allowed us through deeds, documents, and speeches of the texture of Russian life from the time of Peter the Great up through the last days of the Romanov dynasty. Reading Nicholas's letters to his wife one senses quite another divide in Russian history, one perhaps greater than that separating the peasantry from the gentry and the urban intelligentsia. Ultimately that gulf was Nicholas's inability to understand fully the misery and demoralizing poverty in which a large percentage of his countrymen were still living. Thus as Russia moved into the twentieth century, again the country was asked to forge new identities in a revolutionary transformation that may well have been the greatest makeover in the country's history.

The Bronze Horseman (1833)

Aleksandr Pushkin

In 1833 Aleksandr Sergeevich Pushkin wrote a narrative poem titled "The Bronze Horseman" ("Mednyi vsadnik") about a poor clerk named Evgenii who loses his fiancée in the great Petersburg flood of 1824. Evgenii descends into madness and is ultimately found dead at the doorstep of his fiancée's ruined home on an island in the Gulf of Finland.

Evgenii is only one of several protagonists in Pushkin's poem. The bronze statue of Peter the Great, cast by the French artist Étienne-Maurice Falconet in 1782, still stands in Senate Square today. Peter sits atop his steed facing the West and turning away from the old Russia, symbolized by the serpent biting at the heels of his steed. In the poem he descends from its pedestal to chase Evgenii in his mad delirium through the streets of Petersburg. The image of the emperor on horseback bearing down on the homeless civil servant came to suggest not only the enormous divide between Russia's rulers and ruled but the sacrifices made by the common man in forging Peter's empire. One of those sacrifices involved the building of the city itself. Founded on a swamp at the cost of countless lives in an area subject to flooding, damp, and cold, Petersburg was called by Dostoyevsky "the most artificial city in the world." Perhaps in tacit acknowledgment of Pushkin's argument regarding the tragedy of empire building, Tsar Nicholas I forbade the poem's publication.

In nineteenth-century literature the city acquired its own persona in the works of Dostoyevsky and Gogol. In the twentieth century Andrei Belyi and Joseph Brodsky continued the tradition of endowing the city with its own complex personality. Reprinted here is the introduction to the poem, in which Pushkin in classical style provides an initial encomium to the city that Peter built.

The Bronze Horseman
(monument in St.
Petersburg). Courtesy
of Olga Cullinan.

The Bronze Horseman

A TALE OF ST PETERSBURG

INTRODUCTION

On a shore washed by desolate waves, *he* stood,
Full of high *thoughts,* and gazed into the distance.
The broad river rushed before him; a wretched skiff
Sped on it in solitude. Here and there,
Like black specks on the mossy, marshy banks,
Were huts, the shelter of the hapless Finn;
And forest, never visited by rays
Of the mist-shrouded sun, rustled all around.

And he thought: From here we will outface the Swede;
To spite our haughty neighbour I shall found
A city here. By nature we are fated
To cut a window through to Europe,

To stand with a firm foothold on the sea.
Ships of every flag, on waves unknown
To them, will come to visit us, and we
Shall revel in the open sea.

A hundred years have passed, and the young city,
The grace and wonder of the northern lands,
Out of the gloom of forests and the mud
Of marshes splendidly has risen; where once
The Finnish fisherman, the sad stepson
Of nature, standing alone on the low banks,
Cast into unknown waters his worn net,
Now huge harmonious palaces and towers
Crowd on the bustling banks; ships in their throngs
Speed from all ends of the earth to the rich quays;
The Neva is clad in granite; bridges hang
Poised over her waters; her islands are covered
With dark-green gardens, and before the younger
Capital, ancient Moscow has grown pale,
Like a widow in purple before a new empress.

I love you, Peter's creation, I love your stern
Harmonious look, the Neva's majestic flow,
Her granite banks, the iron tracery
Of your railings, the transparent twilight and
The moonless glitter of your pensive nights,
When in my room I write or read without
A lamp, and slumbering masses of deserted
Streets shine clearly, and the Admiralty spire
Is luminous, and, without letting in
The dark of night to golden skies, one dawn
Hastens to relieve another, granting
A mere half-hour to night. I love
The motionless air and frost of your harsh winter,
The sledges coursing along the solid Neva,
Girls' faces brighter than roses, and the sparkle
And noise and sound of voices at the balls,
And, at the hour of the bachelor's feast, the hiss
Of foaming goblets and the pale-blue flame
Of punch. I love the warlike energy
Of Mars' Field, the uniform beauty of the troops

Of infantry and of the horses, tattered
Remnants of those victorious banners in array
Harmoniously swaying, the gleam of those
Bronze helmets, shot through in battle. O martial
Capital, I love the smoke and thunder
Of your fortress, when the empress of the north
Presents a son to the royal house, or when
Russia celebrates another victory
Over the foe, or when the Neva, breaking
Her blue ice, bears it to the seas, exulting,
Scenting spring days.

    Flaunt your beauty, Peter's
City, and stand unshakeable like Russia,
So that even the conquered elements may make
Their peace with you; let the Finnish waves
Forget their enmity and ancient bondage,
And let them not disturb with empty spite
Peter's eternal sleep!

    There was a dreadful time—the memory of it
Is still fresh . . . I will begin my narrative
Of it for you, my friends. My tale will be sad.

Peter's Social Reforms (1716)

John Perry

When Peter the Great traveled to Western Europe between 1697 and 1698, he did so with an eye to learning all he could about everything from naval carpentry and architecture to the latest in military arts. He was a shipbuilder at heart, an expert in the use of his hands, a man of relentless energy with no use for ceremony and pomp. He also had little patience for gradual reform. In his view Westernization was not a choice but something his countrymen were going to have to confront in order to bring Russia up to European standards. When Peter returned to Russia he issued a proclamation inviting artisans, manufacturers, and industrialists from abroad to come to his country on terms that were highly advantageous to them. In turn he sent scores of young Russians to Europe to learn trades, to learn about industry, and to study everything from medicine to philosophy, furnace building, and bed trimming.

Among those who arrived in Russia as part of Peter's reforms was Captain John Perry, a hydraulic engineer from England who went on to spend fourteen years in Russia, not all of them contentedly. One can see from his account of dress and custom how complicated the Russian response was to Peter's forced Westernization. The very class that was specially singled out to receive the benefits of the reforms was not unanimous in its support of Peter's policies. On the other hand, much that Peter brought back with him was accepted, even welcomed by certain segments of the population. More liberal courtship and marriage customs that he ordered put into practice liberated young women from centuries of arranged marriages, although Leo Tolstoy's novels provide ample evidence that the custom of the dynastic marriage continued right up until the October Revolution of 1917.

Perry's account shows how those who never left Russia were required by law to become no less European than those who had traveled to Europe. One of the most controversial of the laws was the forced shaving of long beards. Peter was motivated not only by his desire that his people resemble Europeans in their outward appearance, but by a desire to humiliate the Church, for whose schisms and ceremony he had little tolerance. The new law, however, alienated Orthodox believers for whom the wearing of a beard was a God-fearing act, symbolic of their own religiosity. Thus it is that the carpenter whom Captain Perry meets coming out of a barber shop in

Voronezh decides to hold onto his beard, shaven though it is, so that after he dies he can explain to St. Nicholas what happened and, he hopes, still gain entrance into the next world.

the *Czar* had another political End in it, for he found that, by reducing their Numbers, he might take Part of their Revenue to himself, for a lefs Number of Villages would then ferve to maintain them.

It had been the manner of the *Ruffes*, like the Patriarchs of old, to wear long Beards hanging down upon their Bofoms, which they comb'd out with Pride, and kept fmooth and fine, without one Hair to be diminifhed; they wore even the Upper-Lip of that length, that 'if they drank at any time, their Beard dipp'd into the Cup, fo that they were obliged to wipe it when they had done, altho' they wore the Hair of their Head cut fhort at the fame time; it being the Cuftom only for the Popes or Priefts, to wear the Hair of their Heads hanging down upon their Backs for Diftinction fake. The *Czar* therefore to reform this foolifh Cuftom, and to make them look like other *Europeans*, ordered a Tax to be laid, on all Gentlemen, Merchants, and others of his Subjects (excepting the Priefts and common Peafants, or Slaves) that they fhould each of them pay 100 Rubles *per Annum*, for the wearing of their Beards, and that even the common People fhould pay a Copeck at the Entrance of the Gates of any of the Towns or Cities of *Ruffia*, where a Perfon fhould be deputed at the Gate to receive it as often as they had Occafion to pafs. This was look'd upon to be little lefs than a Sin in the *Czar*, a Breach

O 2   of

"Peter's Social Reforms" by John Perry, in *The State of Russia, under the Present Czar* (London: Benjamin Tooke, 1716), 195–202.

of their Religion, and held to be a great
Grievance for some Time, as more particu-
larly by being brought in by the Strangers.
But the Women liking their Husbands and
Sweet-hearts the better, they are now for
the most part pretty well reconciled to this
Practice.

It is most certain, that the *Russes* had a
kind of religious Respect and Veneration for
their Beards; and so much the more, because
they differed herein from Strangers, which
was back'd by the Humours of the Priests, al-
ledging that the holy Men of old had worn
their Beards acccording to the Model of the
Picture of their Saints, and which nothing
but the absolute Authority of the *Czar*, and
the Terror of having them (in a merry Humour) pull'd out by the Roots, or sometimes
taken so rough off, that some of the Skin
went with them, could ever have prevailed
with the *Russes* to have parted with their
Beards. On this Occasion there were Letters drop'd about the Streets, sealed and directed to his *Czarish* Majesty, which charged him with Tyranny and Heathenism, for
forcing them to part with their Beards.

About this Time the *Czar* came down to
Veronize, where I was then on Service, and
a great many of my Men that had worn their
Beards all their Lives, were now obliged to
part with them, amongst which, one of the
first that I met with just coming from the
Hands of the Barber, was an old *Ruß* Carpenter

penter that had been with me at *Camiſhinka*,
who was a very good Workman with his
Hatchet, and whom I always had a Friend-
ſhip for. I jeſted a little with him on this
Occaſion, telling him that he was become a
young Man, and asked him what he had done
with his Beard? Upon which he put his Hand
in his Boſom and pull'd it out, and ſhew'd it
to me; farther telling me, that when he came
home, he would lay it up to have it put in
his Coffin and buried along with him, that
he might be able to give an Account of it
to St. *Nicholas*, when he came to the other
World; and that all his Brothers (meaning
his Fellow-workmen who had been ſhaved
that Day) had taken the ſame Care.

As to their Cloaths, the general Habit
which the *Ruſſes* uſed to wear, was a long
Veſtment hanging down to the middle of the
Small of their Legs, and was gathered and
laid in Pleats upon their Hips, little differing
from the Habit of Womens Petticoats.

The *Czar* therefore reſolving to have this
Habit changed, firſt gave Orders, that all his
Boyars and People whatſoever, that came
near his Court, and that were in his Pay,
ſhould, upon Penalty of falling under his Diſ-
pleaſure, according to their ſeveral Abilities,
equip themſelves with handſome Cloaths made
after the *Engliſh* Faſhion, and to appear with
Gold and Silver Trimming, thoſe that could
afford it. And next he commanded, that a Pattern of Cloaths of the *Engliſh* Faſhion ſhould

O 3 be

be hung up at all the Gates of the City of *Mof-*
co, and that Publication fhould be made, that
all Perfons (excepting the common Peafants
who brought Goods and Provifions into the
City) fhould make their Cloaths according to
the faid Patterns ; and that whofoever fhould
difobey the faid Orders, and fhould be found
paffing any of the Gates of the City in their
long Habits, fhould either pay 2 *Grevens*
(which is 20 Pence) or be obliged to kneel
down at the Gates of the City, and to have
their Coats cut off juft even with the Ground,
fo much as it was longer than to touch the
Ground when they kneeled down, of which
there were many hundreds of Coats that were
cut accordingly ; and being done with a good
Humour, it occafioned Mirth among the
People, and foon broke the Cuftom of their
wearing long Coats, efpecially in Places near
Mofco, and thofe other Towns wherever the
Czar came.

The Women alfo, but more particularly the
Ladies about Court, were ordered to reform
the Fafhion of their Cloaths too, according to
the *Englifh* Manner, and that which fo much
the more and fooner reconciled them to it,
was this : It had been always the Cuftom
of *Ruffia*, at all Entertainments, for the Women not to be admitted into the Sight or
Converfation with Men ; the very Houfes of
all Men of any Quality or Fafhion, were
built with an Entrance for the Women a-part,
and they ufed to be kept up feparate in an
Apartment

Apartment by themfelves; only it was fometimes the Cuftom for the Mafter of the Houfe,
upon the Arrival of any Gueft whom he had
a Mind to Honour, to bring out his Wife
the Back way from her Apartment, attended
with the Company of her Maids, to be fa-
luted, and to prefent a Dram of Brandy round
to the whole Company; which being done,
they ufed to retire back to their own Apartment, and were to be feen no more. But
the *Czar* being not only willing to introduce
the *Englifh* Habits, but to make them more
particularly pleafing to the *Rufs* Ladies, made
an Order, that from thenceforward, at all
Weddings, and at other publick Entertainments, the Women as well as the Men, fhould
be invited, but in an *Englifh* fafhioned Drefs;
and that they fhould be entertained in the
fame Room with the Men, like as he had
feen in foreign Countries; and that the Evenings fhould be concluded with Mufick and
Dancing, at which he himfelf often ufed to
be prefent with moft of the Noblility and
Ladies about Court. And there was no Wedding of any Diftinction, efpecially amongft
the Foreigners, but the *Czar* had notice of
it, and he himfelf would honour it with his
Prefence, and very often gave a Prefent to
the Bride, fuitable to the extraordinary Ex-
pence that fuch Entertainments coft them,
efpecially when married to the Officers that
were newly come into the Countrey. At
thefe Entertainments, the *Rufs* Ladies foon

O 4   reconciled

reconciled themselves to the *English* Dress, which they found rendred them more agreeable.

There was another thing also which the Women very well liked in these Regulations of the *Czar*. It had been the Custom of *Russia*, in case of Marriages, that the Match used always to be made up between the Parents on each side, without any previous Meeting, Consent or Liking of one another, tho' they marry very young in that Countrey, sometimes when neither the Bride nor the Bridegroom are thirteen Years of Age, and therefore supposed not to be fit Judges for themselves. The Bridegroom on this Occasion was not to see nor to speak to the Bride but once before the Day that the Nuptials was to be performed; at which Meeting, the Friends on both sides were to come together at the Bride's Father's House, and then the Bride was to be brought out between her Maids into the Room where the Bridegroom was; and after a short Complement being made, she was to present the Bridegroom with a Dram of Brandy, or other Liquor, in Token of her Consent and Good-liking of his Person. And afterwards all Care was to be taken that she was not to see the Bridegroom again until the Day of Marriage; and then she was to be carried with a Veil all over her Face, which was not to be uncover'd till she came into the Church. And thus this blind Bargain was made.

But

But the *Czar* taking into his Consideration this unacceptable way of joining young
People together without their own Approba-
tion, which might in a very great meafure
be reckon'd to be the Occafion of that Dif-
cord and little Love which is fhewn to one
another afterwards, it being a thing common
in *Ruffia* to beat their Wives in a moft bar-
barous manner, very often fo inhumanly that
they die with the Blows; and yet they do
not fuffer for the Murther, being a thing interpreted by the Law to be done by way of
Correction, and therefore not culpable. The
Wives on the other hand being thus many
times made defperate, murther their Husbands
in Revenge for the ill Ufage they receive;
on which Occafion there is a Law made, that
when they murther their Husbands, they are
fet alive in the Ground, ftanding upright,
with the Earth fill'd about them, and only
their Heads left juft above the Earth, and a
Watch fet over them, that they fhall not be
relieved till they are ftarved to Death; which
is a common Sight in that Countrey, and I
have known them live fometimes feven or
eight Days in this Pofture. Thefe fad Pro-
fpects made the *Czar* in much Pity to his
People, take away the occafion of thefe Cru-
elties as much as poffible; and the forced
Marriages being fuppofed to be one Caufe
thereof, made an Order that no young Couple
fhould be marry'd together, without their
own free Liking and Confent; and that all

Per-

Persons should be admitted to visit and see each other at least six Weeks before they were married together. This new Order is so well approved of, and so very pleasing to the young People, that they begin to think much better of Foreigners, and to have a better liking of such other new Customs as the *Czar* has introduced, than they ever did before, especially amongst the more knowing and better sort of People.

It had been a very pompous Custom among all the great *Boyars*, to retain in their Service, as a piece of State and Grandeur, a great Number of useless Servants or Attendants, which when they went any where abroad in the Streets of *Mosco*, some went before them bare-headed, and others follow'd after in a long Train, in all sorts of Dresses and Colours; and when their *Boyars* or Lords went either on Horseback, or in a Coach or Sled in *Mosco*, it was a piece of Grandeur to ride softly, though in the coldest Weather, that these People might keep Pace with them on Foot; and the great *Boyars* Ladies also used to have the like numerous Attendance.

But the *Czar*, who always rides swift, had set them another Pattern, for he went only with a few Servants on Horseback, cloath'd in a handsome uniform Livery; his Courtiers did the same; and commanded the Example to be follow'd among all the *Boyars* and Persons of Distinction; and that the same might
be

Love and Conquest (1769–91)

The Correspondence of Catherine II and Grigory Potemkin

Peter the Great died in 1725. For the next thirty-seven years, until Catherine II, known as Catherine the Great, ascended the throne in 1762, the imperial crown passed through seven different rulers. In the words of the Russian historian Michael Florinsky, "The exotic courts of these rulers and the bizarre and sinister cortege of ignorant, licentious women, half-witted German princes, and mere children on whose shoulders in turn descended the imperial purple present a morbidly fascinating picture suggestive of the imaginative and unreal world created by some medieval craftsman and preserved in ancient Italian embroideries and in stained-glass windows." Catherine's rule decisively reversed this trend.

The woman who would become Catherine the Great was in fact not Russian at all but German. She was born Princess Sophia Augusta Frederica of Anhalt-Zerbst in 1729 and was brought to Moscow to marry Emperor Peter I, a distant German relative from Holstein. In 1762 she orchestrated the overthrow of her husband and became empress of all Russia.

It has been said that if Peter the Great bequeathed Russia the practical skills necessary to the building of empire, Catherine the Great gave Russia the intellectual and cultural foundations that solidified ties with Western Europe. During her reign (1762–96) European culture, particularly that of France, flourished among the nobility. Arriving in Russia already fluent in French, she brought French philosophical writing to her new country. She corresponded with Voltaire, who in turn supported many of her foreign policy decisions; she purchased Diderot's library and honored him with the title of His Majesty's Librarian. Russians were sent abroad during her reign to study at European universities. The museum in Petersburg which became known as the Hermitage first took shape as a special room Catherine set aside in her palace for her own personal collection of European art. French became the language at court, so much so that Russia's nobility slowly became divorced from their native Russian, and by extension from their own culture.

Catherine's reign was initially characterized as an era of liberalism, but with a twist. It was her belief that Russia could best emulate European standards by adhering to a philosophy of enlightened absolutism with strict adherence to the law, the only *possible political system for a country as vast as Russia. However, the American and French Revolutions, as well as the Pugachev Rebellion on Russian soil between 1771 and 1774, whose leader mobilized the serfs to rise up against their masters, caused Catherine to rethink the liberal policies that had initially characterized her reign.*

Under Catherine's rule Russia's empire continued to expand significantly. Already in the seventeenth century much of Siberia and Ukraine had been incorporated into Russia, as well as territory in the Baltic. Catherine brought the Crimea, the northern Caucasus, and much of Poland into Russian territory, and with them many non-Russian peoples—Tatars, Jews, Caucasians, and Poles—thus ushering in the complex and often conflictual relations between Russia and the non-Russian populations that exist up to the present.

Much of the expansion and the day-to-day running of the affairs of state were accomplished with the help of Catherine's lover (and perhaps husband) and advisor, the diplomat and military leader Grigory Potemkin. Their correspondence spanned 1769 to 1791, from the first flush of their passion to their mutual governance of Catherine's expanding realm. Under her aegis Potemkin rose to become commander of Russia's armed forces, grand admiral of the Black Sea and Caspian fleets, and viceroy of Russia's southern lands, among other titles. He was no mere favorite but clearly a man of immense talent and vision, devoted to the military, to the state, and above all to Catherine. Their voluminous correspondence is a record of an evolving relationship that charted their most intimate emotions as well as the growth of the Russian Empire.

Catherine to Potemkin

[March–April 1774]

Precious darling, Grishenka, I love you extraordinarily. Be so good as to take note—here is yet another new [letter], though it came about quite by accident. I just came across this sheet, so kindly look at it closely; it was written out crosswise. You'll probably say that this must be Finnish. Fine, search high and low for any cunning in my love for you. Should you find anything but pure love of the foremost sort, I permit you to put all of this into some cannons in place of a charge and to fire it at Silistria or wherever you want. Hmmm, hmmm, I'm muttering to myself—that was foolishly said, but nothing cleverer came to mind. Surely, not everyone is as clever as I know who, but shall not say. God forbid I become so weak as to tell you who I think is cleverer than I and everyone I know. But no, sir, and kindly don't try to find out—for you won't.

I have cheered up. Oh, my God, how foolish one is when he loves extraordinarily. It's an illness. One should cure people of it in hospitals. Il faudroit des calmants, Monsieur, beaucoup d'eau fraîche, quelques saignées, du suc de citron, pointe de vin, peu manger, beaucoup prendre d'air, et faire tant de mouvement qu'on rapporte le corps à la maison,[1] and the devil only knows whether after all that I might still get you out of my head. I think not. Adieu, you five French volumes in folio.

[Before 28 June 1774]

Bonjour, mon coeur. I awoke so cheerful it's frightening. Oh, my love, don't be angry, for you love it when I am cheerful. Today you won't hear a thing but rubbish. There is, however, one serious matter about which I can speak, for it occupies my senses completely. But I shall end this note with it, and now à propos de cela,[2] I very humbly request that you not delay the lieutenant-colonel list with your comments, or I fear Kuzmin will flog me and Chernyshev will once more befoul his room with smoke.

My darling, my dear, my beloved, je n'ai pas le sens commun aujourd'huy.[3] Love, love is the reason. I love you with my heart, mind, soul and body. I love you with all my senses and shall love you eternally. Precious darling, I kindly beg you—do me the favor and love me too. For you are a good and generous person. Do your best to make Grigory Aleksandrovich love me. I tenderly beg you. Also, write me how he is—is he merry and well?

I thought my dog had gone mad today. She came in with Tatiana,[4] jumped up in bed with me, sniffed a bit, and shuffled on the bed, and then began to move about and to snuggle up to me as if she were happy to see someone. She loves you very much, and so is even dearer to me. Everyone on earth, even the dog, confirms your place in my heart and mind. Consider how dear Grishenka is. He doesn't leave my mind for an instant. Truly, my love, it's frightful, frightful how dear you are.

From Tsarskoe Selo. 9 June 1783

I received today from the hands of Aleksandr Dmitrievich your letter from the 28th of last month. I hope, my little Prince, that my letters have now reached your hands, and when you deign to write: "God forbid that you are forgetting me," that is what we call "to write rubbish." Not only do I often remember you, but often regret and grieve as well that you're there and not here with me, for I'm lost without you. I beg you in every possible way: don't tarry over the occupation of the Crimea. I am now frightened by the threat the plague poses to you and everyone else. For God's sake, do be careful and order all possible measures be taken against it. I very much regret that you and Field Marshal Rumiantsev were not able to meet somewhere. All the world's troubles he bears now on his shoulders: he requests the general staff, engineers, more money, and news from Bulgakov. He also fears being forestalled by the Turks and something being overlooked. Seeing this, I've ordered everything possible sent to him. Let's hope this helps, or it'll all prove a waste. I believe that you have many troubles, but know that you and I are not vexed by them. Word that the shipbuilding is proceeding swiftly is very pleasing to my ear. I'll try to send the required number of men. . . .

The Swedish King broke his arm at his camp at Tavastehus, and so our meeting in Fredrikshamn has been postponed till the 20th of this month. Adieu, mon Ami. . . .

Potemkin to Catherine

13 June [1783]. Kherson

Your Majesty! God alone knows how exhausted I am. Every day I hasten to the Admiralty to force the men there to keep working, and I am beset by a multitude of other concerns as well: the fortification of Kinburn, supplying provisions everywhere, keeping the troops in order and stamping out the plague, which didn't fail to appear in Kizikermen, Yelizavetgrad and even in Kherson. Precautions have been taken everywhere, however, and, thanks to God, it has been stopped. The most alarming aspects of this plague are the reports coming out of the Crimea, where it has appeared in different districts and in our hospitals. I rushed there as soon as I learned of this and took measures to separate the sick from the uninfected, and saw to it that all their clothing was fumigated and washed. I divided the sick according to their illnesses; thank God there are only five as of now. I shan't describe the beauty of the Crimea, which would take much time, leaving this for another occasion. I shall only say that Akhtiar is the best harbor in the world. Petersburg, situated upon the Baltic, is Russia's northern capital; Moscow is its central, and may Kherson of Akhtiar be my Sovereign's southern capital. Let them see which Sovereign made the best selection.

Matushka, do not be surprised that I have not yet promulgated the manifestoes. It truly hasn't been possible without first increasing the number of troops, for otherwise there would be no way to use force were it to be necessary. . . .

Back to the subject of shipbuilding. You will see from the list, which I'll submit following this letter, in what state of disorder everything was. In a word, the only honest man in the entire lot was one master shipwright, all the rest were thieves. Admiral Klokachev truly is a solicitous man, but what can he accomplish without helpers? I earlier requested that the following men be sent here to work on the ships. Then we'll have everything we need. . . .

Regarding the Emperor, do not impede him. Let him take what he wants from the Turks. This will help us a good deal. And it would be a great service were he to create a diversion. I received intelligence from the consul in Bucharest that the Austrian pickets have already driven off the Moldavian frontier guards while also declaring that they intend to occupy the land. This has been communicated to the Porte.

The postal boat sent by the Kapudan Pasha to Ochakov, which Bulgakov mentions, really was in Ochakov and has departed for Tsar Grad.[5] My compliments to Aleksandr Dmitrich. Farewell, beloved matushka, I kiss your tender hands.

Your loyal servant

Prince Potemkin

. . . I'm leaving for the Crimea in three days.

Notes

1. "One would need calmatives, sir, a lot of fresh water, some bloodletting, lemon essence, a drop of wine, to eat little, to get lots of fresh air and to move about so much that one comes home exhausted."
2. "with respect to that"; Catherine's secretary Sergei Matveevich Kuzmin (1724–88).
3. "I have lost all common sense today."
4. One of Catherine's chambermaids.
5. Kapudan Pasha was the title given to the grand admiral of the Ottoman navy. The Russians called Constantinople Tsar Grad, "the city of the Caesars."

The War of 1812

Leo N. Tolstoi

In 1812 Napoleon invaded Russia. Tsar Aleksandr I ordered the Russian troops to retreat as Napoleon advanced farther into his country, reasoning that the deeper the French penetrated the more difficulty Napoleon would have extricating his troops from a vast land, imponderable roads, and, of course, the Russian winter. In the Battle of Borodino that took place on 7 September of that year both sides suffered enormous casualties, and both claimed victory. Believing that Moscow could no longer be defended, General Kutuzov ordered his troops to evacuate, and the following day Napoleon entered the city. Later that day a fire was started, in all probability by the Russians themselves as they fled, destroying three-quarters of the city before finally being brought under control days later.

The remainder of the Napoleonic invasion has become legend. In mid-October, too late to escape the onslaught of the Russian winter, Napoleon and his troops began the arduous journey back to France, loaded with booty and their sick and wounded. As they made their way through hostile territory, inhabitants were little inclined to help them with provisions. Numbering 110,000 men when they left Moscow, Napoleon's troops were reduced to 80,000 by late November.

Much of Leo Tolstoi's epic novel War and Peace, written between 1863 and 1869, is concerned with the Napoleonic invasion. Tolstoi looked at history as both an artist and a philosopher. He believed strongly that the course of war was determined not by battle plans or by the design of this or that general but by forces that were larger than either. That history and the course of war were larger than the personality and decisions of any one leader was key to Tolstoi's philosophy of the heroic. In the confrontation between the two generals, Napoleon and Kutuzov, Napoleon believes himself to be heroic insofar as he sees the outcome of battle as a function of his own personality and decision making. Kutuzov knows better and thus lets things unfold as they will without taking any aggressive action against the French. His reliance on will and reason is ultimately Napoleon's undoing. Kutuzov, on the other hand, sees himself as the simple executor of forces greater than himself and in so doing becomes the embodiment of Tolstoi's philosophy that "there is no greatness where simplicity, goodness, and truth are absent."

Chapter 37

The correlation of causes is a thing incomprehensible by the human mind, but the desire to comprehend them is born with it. Hence those who cannot discern the logic of events jump at the first coincidence that strikes them and exclaim: "This is the cause."

But as soon as we have got to the bottom of the smallest historical fact, that is to say of the mass of humanity from which it took its rise, we discern that the will of an individual not only cannot guide those masses, but is itself under the guidance of a superior power. Though historical events have in fact no other cause than the elementary cause, they are nevertheless governed by laws which are unknown to us, or which we can hardly detect, and which we can never discover until we give up all idea of finding behind them the will of any individual man. Thus a knowledge of the law by which the planets move only became possible when men had given up the notion of the fixity of the earth.

After the battle of Borodino and the evacuation and burning of Moscow, the most important episode of the war of 1812, in the opinion of historians, was the march of the Russian army when it left the road to Riazan to proceed towards Kalouga and establish itself in the camp at Taroutino. They attribute this heroic feat to various individuals, and even the French, when speaking of this flank movement, praise the genius displayed by the Russian chiefs at this juncture. We, however, fail to discover, as these historians have done, any deep-laid scheme, evolved by a single brain, to save Russia and ruin Napoleon, or to see in it the faintest trace of military genius. For no stupendous intelligence is needed to perceive that the best position for an army which is not to fight is in a spot where it can ensure supplies. The veriest child might have guessed, in 1812, that the road to Kalouga offered the greatest advantages after the retreat of the army. By what chain of argument have these gentlemen discovered that this manœuvre was such a brilliant scheme? Where do they find that its direct outcome was the salvation of Russia and the destruction of the enemy? In point of fact, to argue from the circumstances which preceded it, which were coincident with it; and which followed it, this flank march might have been the ruin of the Russians and the saving of the French; and it is by no means clear that it had a favourable result on the situation of the army.

But for the co-operation of other circumstances it could have come to no good issue. What would have happened if Moscow had not been burnt, if Murat had not lost sight of the Russian troops, if Napoleon had not sat down in inaction, if the Russian army had forced a battle on quitting Moscow—as Benningsen and Barclay advised, if Napoleon had marched on Taroutino and attacked the Russians with one-tenth of the energy he displayed at Smolensk, if the French had gone on to St. Petersburg? etc., etc. Under any of these conditions safety would have turned to disaster. How is it that those who study history have shut their eyes and ascribed this movement to the decision of some one man? No one had prepared and schemed for this manœuvre beforehand; and at the moment when it was carried out it was simply the inevitable result of circumstances, and its consequences could not be seen until it had gone far into the realm of the past.

At the council held at Fili the Russian commanders generally were in favour of a retreat in a straight line along the road to Nijni-Novgorod. Ample evidence of this fact exists in the numerous votes given in favour of this course, and more especially in the conversation which took place after the council between the commander-in-chief and Lauskoï, the head of the commissariat. Lauskoï announced in his report that the victuals for the troops were, for the most part, collected along the line of the Oka, in the governments of Toula and Kazan; consequently, in case of a retreat on Nijni the transport of provisions would be intercepted by the river, over which they could not be carried when the winter had once begun. This was the first consideration which led to the abandonment of the original, and, on the whole, the more natural plan. Thus the army was kept within reach of supplies. Then, again, the inaction of the French—who had lost all track of the Russians, the need for protecting and defending the manufactories of arms, above all of keeping within reach of food, drove the army southwards.

After getting out on the Toula road by a desperate move, the generals intended to stop at Podolsk; but the sudden appearance of some French troops, with other circumstances—among them the abundance of victuals at Kalouga—led them to proceed still further to the south and to get off the Toula on to the Kalouga road, marching towards Taroutino. Just as it is impossible to specify the precise moment when the desertion of Moscow was decided on, so it is impossible to say exactly when the march on Taroutino was a settled thing; and yet every one believed himself to have gone there in virtue of the decision of the generals in command.

The route thus taken was so self-evidently that which the army must follow that even the pillagers straggled in this direction, and that Koutouzow incurred the czar's censure for having led the army in the first instance towards Riazan instead of setting out at once for Taroutino. Alexander himself had suggested this movement in a letter which the commander-in-chief did not receive till after his arrival there.

In fact, Koutouzow's skill at this juncture lay, not in a stroke of genius, but in a competent apprehension of the accomplished facts. He alone fully appreciated the inaction of the French; he alone understood and maintained that

Borodino had been a victory for the Russians; he alone—though as commander-in-chief he seemed called upon to take the offensive—did all he could, on
the contrary, to prevent an unnecessary waste of strength in futile struggles.
The Wild Beast had in truth been mortally hurt at Borodino, and was still lying
where the hunter had left it. Was it past fighting? Was it still alive even?—The
hunter knew not. But suddenly it gave a cry which betrayed its hopeless plight;
this cry was the letter brought by Lauriston to Koutouzow in his camp.
Napoleon, no less convinced than ever of his own incapacity of doing wrong,
wrote as follows under a sudden impulse:

To Prince Koutouzow.

I am sending one of my aides-de-camp general to discuss various points of
interest with you. I beg your highness to believe all he will tell you; more
particularly when he shall express to you all the sentiments of esteem and
high respect which I have long felt for your highness. This note having no
other object, I pray the Almighty to have your highness in his holy and
gracious keeping.

(Signed) Napoleon

Moscow, October 30th.

"I shall incur the curses of posterity if I am regarded as the first to take any
steps towards a compromise in any form. That is the spirit which at this
moment rules the nation," replied Koutouzow; and he continued to do all in
his power to direct the retreat of the army.

. . . .

Chapter 38

Napoleon marches into Moscow after the splendid victory of Borodino (or
the Moskova, as it is sometimes called)—it must certainly have been a victory,
since his troops remained in possession of the field. The Russians retire and
abandon Moscow full of stores, arms, ammunition, and incalculable riches. A
month elapses before they resume the offensive. Napoleon's position is obviously brilliant and glorious in the highest degree. No exceptional genius is
needed, it would seem, to enable him to throw his superior forces on the
wreck of the enemy's army and crush it, to extort an advantageous peace, to
march on St. Petersburg, if the Russians prove recalcitrant, to return to Smolensk in the event of failure, or at least to remain at Moscow, and to keep the
advantage already won. Nothing can be more simple and easy than to take

measures to secure that. Pillage must be prohibited; the army must be provided with warm clothing—easily procurable at Moscow, the distribution of food must be strictly regulated—the French historians themselves admit that there were provisions for six months. And yet Napoleon, the greatest genius ever known, who could—as these same historians assert—bend the army as he would, takes none of these precautions, but, on the contrary, selects the most absurd and fatal course.

Nothing, in fact, could more surely lead to disaster than a stay in Moscow so late as October, allowing the army to pillage at will; then, to leave Moscow without any well-defined plan, to go within reach of Koutouzow without giving battle, to get as far as Malo-Yaroslavetz, leaving it on the right, and making for Mojaïsk without trying the fortune of war once more; finally, to return to Smolensk, blindly wandering across a devastated country. Any able strategist studying this series of facts, would unhesitatingly pronounce that it could entail no other result than the destruction—intentional or fated—of the army thus governed. Still, to say that Napoleon sacrificed it voluntarily or by sheer incapacity is just as false as it is to say that he led his troops to Moscow by the vigour of his will, or the brilliancy of his genius. In either case his personal action had no more influence than that of the meanest private; it had to bow to certain laws, of which the outcome was the resultant fact.

It is a mistake on the part of historians to suppose that Napoleon's intellect must have failed at Moscow, as the only way of accounting for his disaster. His energy at this time was not a whit less wonderful than it had been in Egypt, in Italy, in Austria, and in Prussia. Russians cannot form a just opinion of what Napoleon's genius may have been in Egypt—where "forty centuries looked down upon his glory"—or in Austria or Prussia, for we must depend on French and German versions of the facts; and the Germans have always cried up his genius, finding no other way for accounting for his triumphs over fortresses that surrendered without striking a blow, and whole regiments that were taken prisoners without attempting to fight.

We Russians, thank God! need not bow down before his genius to screen ourselves from disgrace. We paid dearly for the right to judge him honestly and without subterfuge, and we are, therefore, not bound to any servile concessions. His vigour while at Moscow was no less than it had always been; plans and orders followed each other without interruption all the time he was there; the absence of the inhabitants, the lack of deputations, the conflagration even, never checked him for an instant. He never lost sight of the enemy's movements, of the well-being of his troops, and of the Russian population close at hand, of the management of his empire, of diplomatic complications, or of the conditions to be discussed, with a view to concluding a peace at an early date.

Description of the Clergy in Rural Russia (1858)

I. S. Belliustin

Holy Russia (Sviataia Rus') was the term employed as far back as Muscovite Russia to describe the country's religious mission as leader of the Christian world, the inheritor of Rome and Byzantium, a mission sanctified by God. But after Peter the Great's ecclesiastical reforms in 1721, which attempted to establish centralized administrative control over the numerous local dioceses, historical and literary documents report little about the workings of the Russian Church, particularly at the local level. We meet monks and yurodivy, or "fools in Christ," on the pages of Russian literature, but about the daily life of the parish clergy in rural Russia, most documents remained silent. All that changed in 1858, when a parish priest by the name of I. S. Belliustin set out to describe the world of Russia's rural clergy. Published anonymously in France and banned in Russia, his Description of the Clergy in Rural Russia nevertheless managed to circulate widely.

And for good reason. Belliustin's work was a searing indictment of ecclesiastical life, from elementary through seminary education to the grinding poverty in which priests were forced to live and the drunkenness, corruption, and moral decrepitude that pervaded an entire class of Russian society. He railed against ritualism in the Church, against the educating of parish priests in Latin(!), and against services conducted in Old Church Slavonic. He wanted a religion and a service to which Russians could actually relate and that was fully participatory. While the upper classes sitting in their salons in the capital tended to idolize the religiosity of the Russian peasant, Belliustin described rural Russia as a place where people were blissfully ignorant of the faith and had little idea of what Christianity was all about. As his book began to circulate in Russia, the upper classes and the parish clergy themselves took up the banner of reform, while the ecclesiastical hierarchy refused to admit the need for change. Overcoming this resistance, Belliustin's work ushered in a new era of reform and dialogue in the Russian Church.

Eighteenth-century
wooden church, Suzdal.
Courtesy of Nancy Ries.

In 1855, a month before the final examinations, authorities at school N. sent all the students home with strict orders to return with a certain sum (the inspector himself fixed the amount due), and warned them that anyone who brought less than the designated sum would remain in the same class, and anyone who brought nothing would be expelled. The largest sum (demanded from many priests) was fifty silver rubles, while the smallest sum was five silver rubles (which the poorest sacristans were to pay). What were the fathers to do? The threat of expulsion would doubtless be carried out. Their sons would either be expelled (what is one to do with boys at such an age?) or denied promotion to the next class (what are the effects when a boy must remain an extra two years in the same class, not to mention the problem of the teacher's inevitable vengeance?). Some, primarily the fathers of scoundrels, hastily did as they were told. The majority, especially those who had absolutely no way of sending the designated sum, or who counted on the fact that their sons fully deserved promotion, appeared before the superintendent. Here the hard bargaining commenced, and some concessions were made. Those who dared pay nothing at all, and who even threatened to complain to superior authorities, were ejected from the inspector's office in disgrace. What was the outcome? If the father paid up, the boy was promoted; if he did not pay, the boy was either denied promotion or expelled.

Some of the fathers, in fact, did file a complaint with the executive board of the diocesan seminary. What happened? They summoned the superintendent for an "explanation"—an "explanation," when they should have launched the most rigorous investigation possible! But that's the way it always turns out in the church: if some poor soul gets caught, he is crushed by investigations; if someone of means commits every imaginable abomination, they "summon" him to the provincial capital (you can guess why—for bribes—and that is the end of it). In this instance, no one knows what the superintendent said, but he returned home with consummate equanimity and continued his misdeeds with even more audacity than before.

A word about formal complaints is in order. Why indeed don't people complain? To understand why, let's take the example of the father whose boy was flogged to death. He in fact came to the town and prepared a complaint. But he still had two sons enrolled in the school; if he did file a complaint, then he would have to withdraw them immediately or their fate would be the same. Yet he could hardly provide for them in his home town: what would he do with them if they left school? He thought it over, wept, grieved—and left it to God's judgment. Another example that one might cite occurred about ten years ago in school X, where the brutality of the superintendent and inspector became so intolerable that the pupils began to flee from the school. Subsequently, a complaint was filed with the executive board of the seminary. Given the gravity of the matter, the rector of the seminary himself went to investigate. What did he do? He spent an entire week at the superintendent's residence without leaving the premises—God alone knows what he did. He then appeared at the school, meted out the most brutal birching to the pupils, and reported to the executive board that the pupils had rebelled and that he had suppressed the uprising. . . . Boys—just eight to fourteen years old—"revolted"; even their fathers, in the face of the cruelest tyranny, amidst a million injustices, would not even dare to think of such a thing! . . . It once happened that a seminary professor was dispatched to a certain school, where he conducted an honest investigation and exposed all the base deeds of the superintendent and teachers. What was the result? The superintendent made a hasty visit to the seminary rector and to the bishop's personal secretary. A new investigation was ordered. Predictably, it completely vindicated the guilty; the professor who made the original inspection was pushed out of the seminary with a negative recommendation. After all that, who would dare conduct a strict, just inquiry? So what is the use of formal complaints? After all this, can anyone still ask why people do not complain?

. . . .

Drunkenness is strongly developed among our lower classes; it is the principal cause of their poverty and of most crime. How can the priest protest against this ruinous contagion when he himself—with his own hands—serves liquor to his parishioners until they are drunk? The peasants' vices are many and of the coarsest variety; the priest should use all his strength and means to excoriate them. But the clergy know that if they attack these vices, they will arouse the guilty against them. How can the priest take action when every unmasking and correction is sure to annoy the sinner, who will never come again to work for him? Involuntarily, at first he is tolerant and silent, but then he becomes accustomed to it, and his parishioners' coarsest vices come to seem ordinary and inescapable, something he need not speak and act against. And finally, one deeply rooted custom has survived among our common people to this day: namely, that the guest should not drink without his host. The priest brings the peasants something to drink, but they will not raise their cups until their host does so. If he does not drink, the guest is insulted, an offense he will not soon forget. The same thing happens during *pomoch'* [parish assistance to local clergy in land cultivation]: if the priest will not drink with the peasants, the whole effort is wasted; it takes but one refusal to drink and thereafter no prayers on earth will suffice to persuade the parishioners to return and work. I know well some priests who, at the time of their appointment, not only felt no inclination to drink vodka but positively detested it. What happened? Work begins; at first the parishioners looked upon the sober priest with amazement, but then they all ceased to come and help with his field labor. What was he to do? Somehow he entices two or three of them and "pays his respects," that is, gulps down a few drops; at first it seems disgusting, but the longer he does it, the more tolerable it becomes; so that gradually he is drawn into drunkenness. He begins to drink and everything is just as it should be: the peasants no longer refuse to help. What would you have him do in view of all this? If the priest were provided the main necessities of life, if he had no need of the help of peasants (who, in accordance with an age-old, ineradicable custom, are rewarded with vodka), he would not sink so low. At least he would not fall in the very first years of his service as priest. But, having withstood the first few years (the most difficult ones), especially if he did not develop a fondness for vodka at the seminary, all his life he would remain abstemious and sober. Even if he had acquired this fondness he would not develop it into a passion; he would have fewer occasions, few motives to drink. But now, a Sunday or holiday means *pomoch'*, and that means vodka. How can he abstain? On Sunday he drinks because of his dear guests; on Monday because of a headache; and with each passing year he adds still another day for some reason (in honor of one thing or another).

And so in the end, the day he fails to drink is terribly onerous, and he feels called upon to satisfy this passion on every occasion. He has to hire a worker, carpenter, stovemaker, or the like to do some repairs at his home; the priest begins to bargain, but it ends in vodka. If this work has to be done at the church, the same thing happens. How well do the woodworkers, gilders, and their ilk know how to exploit this situation! Where they foresee work, they first pay two or three visits to the priest to make his acquaintance, and bring an abundance of food and drink. Then they begin negotiations with the priest, now hopelessly inebriated. You can imagine what happens; again, it ends in a two- or three-day drunken binge. Now the work is started; sobered up, the priest realizes that things are going badly, but how can one rise up against a contractor so generous with food and drink? It sometimes happens that the priest does protest; the contractor, however, has the means ready—he calms the priest down with some more alcohol. The work is at last finished and at the time of the final payment the scene that took place at the initial contracting is repeated. The result: an unforgivable amount of money has been spent; the job was done inexcusably poorly (it needs to be redone almost immediately). But what can the priest do now that he has settled his accounts with the contractor and given him a signed certificate that the work was done well and that he is fully satisfied with it? That is the end of it. Nor did such an episode even serve as a lesson for the future; the next time this kind of work is required, the very same thing is repeated. That is the terrible result of this passion, which sometimes begins with the need to satisfy the wish of parishioners coming for *pomoch'*.

Emancipating the Serfs (1861)

Petr Kropotkin

In 1861 Tsar Aleksandr II issued a manifesto proclaiming the end of serfdom in Russia. He had come to power in 1855 with little in the way of liberal inclination to free Russia's peasantry. He viewed the dvoriane, *Russia's landed aristocracy, as "the mainstay of the throne" and was loath to deprive them of the serfs who constituted the bulk of their privilege. But social and economic conditions dictated otherwise, and the tsar gradually came to realize that emancipating the serfs was not a choice but a necessity. Failure to do so was almost certainly a guarantee of revolution from below. In addition to ongoing uprisings, peasants were fleeing their landlords, who responded by tightening the restrictions on those who remained. Conditions were such by the time Aleksandr II ascended the throne that the future social and economic stability of the country was dependent on freeing 80 percent of its population. Thus on 19 February 1861 Russia, the last country in Europe with a system of indentured servitude, liberated its serfs.*

The emancipation brought enormous upheaval to Russia because it involved much more than the granting of freedom and mobility. As thirty million serfs received their freedom, approximately ninety million acres of land were simultaneously transferred from lord to peasant, a transference that was neither immediate nor simple. The peasants were forced to pay for the land they received through a system administered by the peasant commune. Moreover peasants were still under obligation to their landowners since they were forced to pay them rent after a two-year initial hiatus, until the amount equal to the full assessed value of the land they received was paid. The gentry, for their part, attempted to hold onto as much of their arable land as possible and thus ceded to their former serfs less profitable tracts with an artificially high value placed on them, while retaining the pristine forests and fields for themselves.

The Popular Response to the Emancipation, from the
Memoirs of Prince Kropotkin, 1861

We went to the parade; and when all the military performances were over, Alexander II, remaining on horseback, loudly called out, "The officers to me!" They gathered round him, and he began, in a loud voice, a speech about the great event of the day.

"The officers . . . the representatives of the nobility in the army"—these scraps of sentences reached our ears—"an end has been put to centuries of injustice . . . I expect sacrifices from the nobility . . . the loyal nobility will gather round the throne" . . . and so on. Enthusiastic hurrahs resounded amongst the officers as he ended.

We ran rather than marched back on our way to the corps,—hurrying to be in time for the Italian opera, of which the last performance in the season was to be given that afternoon; some manifestation was sure to take place then. Our military attire was flung off with great haste, and several of us dashed, lightfooted, to the sixth-story gallery. The house was crowded.

During the first entr'acte the smoking-room of the opera filled with excited young men, who all talked to one another, whether acquainted or not. We planned at once to return to the hall, and to sing, with the whole public in a mass choir, the hymn "God Save the Tsar."

However, sounds of music reached our ears, and we all hurried back to the hall. The band of the opera was already playing the hymn, which was drowned immediately in enthusiastic hurrahs coming from all parts of the hall. I saw Bavéri, the conductor of the band, waving his stick, but not a sound could be heard from the powerful band. Then Bavéri stopped, but the hurrahs continued. I saw the stick waved again in the air; I saw the fiddle-bows moving, and musicians blowing the brass instruments, but again the sound of voices overwhelmed the band. Bavéri began conducting the hymn once more, and it was only by the end of that third repetition that isolated sounds of the brass instruments pierced through the clamor of human voices.

The same enthusiasm was in the streets. Crowds of peasants and educated men stood in front of the palace, shouting hurrahs, and the Tsar could not appear without being followed by demonstrative crowds running after his carriage. Hérzen was right when, two years later, as Alexander was drowning the Polish insurrection in blood, and "Muravióff the Hanger" was strangling it on the scaffold, he wrote, "Alexander Nikoláevich, why did you not die on that day? Your name would have been transmitted in history as that of a hero."

Where were the uprisings which had been predicted by the champions of slavery? Conditions more indefinite than those which had been created by the Polozhénie (the emancipation law) could not have been invented. If anything could have provoked revolts, it was precisely the perplexing vagueness of the conditions created by the new law. And yet, except in two places where there were insurrections, and a very few other spots where small disturbances entirely due to misunderstandings and immediately appeased took place,

Russia remained quiet,—more quiet than ever. With their usual good sense, the peasants had understood that serfdom was done away with, that "freedom had come," and they accepted the conditions imposed upon them, although these conditions were very heavy.

I was in Nikólskoye [a Kropotkin estate in the Kaluga guberniia] in August, 1861, and again in the summer of 1862, and I was struck with the quiet, intelligent way in which the peasants had accepted the new conditions. They knew perfectly well how difficult it would be to pay the redemption tax for the land, which was in reality an indemnity to the nobles in lieu of the obligations of serfdom. But they so much valued the abolition of their personal enslavement that they accepted the ruinous charges—not without murmuring, but as a hard necessity—the moment that personal freedom was obtained. . . .

When I saw our Nikólskoye peasants, fifteen months after the liberation, I could not but admire them. Their inborn good nature and softness remained with them, but all traces of servility had disappeared. They talked to their masters as equals talk to equals, as if they never had stood in different relations. Besides, such men came out from among them as could make a stand for their rights.

Classic Russian Cooking (1861)

Joyce Toomre and Elena Molokhovets

History has long been studied from the vantage point of rulers and battles, edicts, reforms, and peace treaties. Thus the most popular canons of Russian history tell us the fate of dynasties, invasions, and the Bolshevik Revolution and their historical and political aftermaths. However, if looked at from a slightly different perspective, the texture of everyday life often written out of the grand narratives of Russian history becomes visible. Elena Molokhovets's cookbook A Gift to Young Housewives *(Podarok molodym khoziaikam) first appeared in 1861. It provides us with a key to homemaking, as well as to the observance of feasts and fasts according to the Orthodox calendar, in much the same way that* The Boston Cooking-School Cook Book *(1895) and* The Joy of Cooking *(1931) allow us entry into the dietary habits, mores, and lifestyles of their time. Published the year the serfs were emancipated, Molokhovets's cookbook for half a century was considered de rigueur for young women just learning how to cook. By the time of the Bolshevik Revolution 295,000 copies of the book had been printed; branded bourgeois by revolutionaries the book ceased publication afterward. Families continued to treasure it, however, recognizing that the world it described was one to which there was no returning. As Joyce Toomre, the editor and translator of Molokhovets's cookbook, notes, the book became a kind of horrifying anachronism as Soviets faced constant shortages and few choices in the food stores.*

Produced in the Russian tradition of advice books, A Gift to Young Housewives *includes instruction on how to set up a kitchen and arrange afternoon tea, what utensils to use, and how to cook for children and for servants. Reading it reveals the culture of the everyday among the gentry in the mid- to late nineteenth century. The first excerpt reprinted here is from Toomre's introduction to the volume; the second, "The Arrangement of the Kitchen," is by Molokhovets herself.*

Eastern Influence on Russian Cuisine, by Joyce Toomre (1992)

Russian foodways have been influenced from the East almost since the dawn of recorded history; to this day the cuisines of Central Asia and the Caucasus are still affecting culinary developments in European Russia. Despite the significance of these Eastern influences, they have not received much attention in the scholarly literature. According to the Soviet food historian N. I. Kovalev, the Russians learned the art of making raised bread from the Scythian nomads, who came from Central Asia and who ruled southern Russia for over three hundred years from the seventh century B.C. The Scythians were displaced by the Sarmatians, another nomadic tribe from central Asia, who ruled until the beginning of the third century A.D. It was during the Scytho-Sarmatian period that Greek civilization developed around the Black Sea and in the Russian steppe. Instead of destroying the Greek colonies, the Scythians and the Sarmatians traded vigorously with the Greeks. I suspect that if the Scythians did not discover the secret of leavened bread themselves, they may have learned about it from the Greeks before passing it on to the Russians. Going back one link in the chain, the Greeks had acquired the skill from the Egyptians, who already had professional millers and bakers by about 2000 B.C.

Another Eastern influence on the old Russian diet was *koumiss* or fermented mare's milk. The nutritive value of *koumiss* was known since ancient times to many Asian people, especially the Kazakhs, Kirgiz, and Bashkirs. The Greek historian Herodotus reported in the fifth century B.C. that the Scythian nomads regularly made *koumiss* and carefully guarded the secret of its production. In the old Russian chronicles, *koumiss* was called *mlechnoe vino* (milk wine), a name which corresponded to the old medical term for this drink, *vinum lactis*. Despite the widespread appreciation for the curative properties of mare's milk in early times, as well as more recently, the Orthodox Church forbade the eating of horse flesh or the drinking of mare's milk in the seventh century; at that period, those items, among others, were considered *pogano* or unclean.

The next major contact with the East that affected Russian cuisine occurred nearly a thousand years later with the opening of trade with Constantinople in A.D. 945 and the introduction into Russia of rice and such spices as cloves and pepper. More important for Russian cuisine, however, was the Mongol invasion in 1237. Mostly Turkic in origin, but known generally as Tartars, these invaders subjugated the native population for the next two and a half centuries. Despite their generally destructive impact upon Russian society, the Tartars enriched the Russian cuisine in several important ways, most significantly by reopening the old Silk Road to China which allowed the introduction of new spices; some of them, notably saffron and cinnamon, ultimately became central flavoring elements in Russian cuisine. The Englishman Samuel Collins, who lived in Moscow from 1660 to 1669 as personal physician to Tsar Alexis, the father of Peter the Great, noted that cinnamon was "the Aroma Imperiale" and that the Tsar liked to drink a little cinnamon water at his meals, or "oyl [*sic*] of Cinnamon in his small beer."

Even more important than the spices, the Tartars brought with them from China the art of fermenting cabbage to make sauerkraut. Cabbage, of course, had long been an important vegetable in northern Europe, but the Russians had not developed the skill for preserving it in salt or brine. Once introduced by the Tartars, fermented cabbage or sauerkraut quickly became a dietary staple throughout northern and central Europe. According to the Polish scholar Anna Kowalska-Lewicka, fermented vegetables were so important to the Poles and their Eastern neighbors that the Lithuanians even "worshipped a god of pickled food called Roguszys." The Russians may not have actually worshipped sauerkraut and other pickled vegetables, but their cuisine is unthinkable without them. Indeed, the Russian peasants mostly survived on a diet of kasha and *shchi,* made of sauerkraut, not fresh cabbage.

As historians well know, the subjugation in the sixteenth century of the Mongol khanates of Kazan (1552–57) and Astrakhan (1556), and of Siberia (1582) had far-reaching political and economic consequences for the Muscovite state. Pointing to the impact of these developments on culinary history, Darra Goldstein has suggested that with the annexation of these vast territories "Eastern foods were more substantially integrated into the Russian national cuisine." As the Russian explorers and settlers spread out into these fertile new lands, they had to adapt their diet to local circumstances; in time some of these foods lost their novelty and became fundamental components of the Russian kitchen.

Tea was the most significant of these new foodstuffs, but this beverage caught on very slowly in Russia, partly because of its scarcity and expense, but also because the Russians were suspicious of foreign novelties. In 1638, gifts of tea were sent by the Mongol Khan to the Russian Court, but Tsar Mikhail Fedorovich reputedly "objected that tea was an unknown and superfluous article in Russia" and that he would prefer the equivalent in sables. After its introduction in the mid seventeenth century, tea remained scarce until 1725 when the establishment of Kiakhta as a trading post on the Sino-Russian border boosted Russian imports. The long overland route—which in the 1860s still took one to two hundred days—and the frequent disruptions in trade kept the price high and delayed the spread of tea drinking in Russia for another hundred years. Although imports rose sharply at the beginning of the eighteenth century, prices tumbled significantly only with the opening of the Chinese commercial ports to Russian traders in the late 1860s. Once the Kiakhta monopoly on the tea trade was broken, the demand for the newer, cheaper varieties (the so-called Canton teas) soared, turning tea into a serious rival of *kvass* as the Russian national beverage.

Despite the wider availability of tea, peasants were puzzled enough by the unfamiliar product for the subject to turn up in songs of the period. One such song tells of an unlucky house serf who was ordered to prepare tea by his master, and not knowing what to do with the leaves, seasoned the brew with pepper, onion, and parsley, the traditional Russian seasonings. When he was abused for his concoction, he decided it was because he forgot the salt. Regardless of such incidents, cheap teas began to circulate ever more widely and, after the 1870s, even began to displace spirits among the working classes. According to Smith and Christian, "It was in the late nineteenth century, too, that 'for tea' (*na chai, na chaek*), rather than 'for vodka,' became the set expression for a tip."

The romance of Russian tea drinking is intimately associated with the samovar. After its introduction in the late eighteenth century, the samovar was quickly adopted by the Russian gentry and became an integral part of their tea-drinking ritual. The preparation of the samovar and the sound of its hissing became as culturally laden in Russian literature as the teakettle whistling on the hob in English literature. The origins of the samovar are unclear. In appearance it resembles an English urn for serving tea, but with its internal tube for burning charcoal, its construction is more like a Mongolian hot pot. Some scholars have speculated that the Russian samovar was probably modeled after "the Western European wine fountain which had a similar shape and also a central cylinder which held ice to keep the surrounding wine cool." The samovar became a common motif in nineteenth-century Russian painting; splendid examples can be seen in Vladimir Makovskij's painting "A Gathering of the Nightingale Watchers" (1872–73) and Vasilij Maksimov's "All in the Past" (1889).

"The Arrangement of the Kitchen," by Elena Molokhovets

EVENING TEA

When acquaintances gather for friendly conversation that does not last far beyond midnight, a late evening tea instead of a supper may be served by the housewife. The tea table is arranged as follows.

Spread a clean tablecloth on a long dinner table and set a samovar on a small side table at one end. In the middle of the long table place a tall vase filled with fruit, such as apples, pears, oranges, mandarin oranges, and grapes; on each side, place stacks of dessert plates and next to them silver or bone dessert knives.

On either side of the bowl arrange serving dishes (*sukharnitsa*), covered by napkins and filled with tea pastries: buns and babas made of egg whites, saffron, wheat flour, or almonds; English biscuits and small baked goods, either purchased or homemade.

Nearby set out small crystal plates with lemon slices, small carafes of rum, red wine, and cherry syrup, and bowls of sherbet, cream, and sugar. On both sides of the table, place small stemmed crystal bowls of jam, to be added to the tea or eaten separately; on either side of the bowls, set out teaspoons and small crystal saucers for jam.

One of the bowls of jam may be replaced by orange slices; these bowls should be placed symmetrically at either end of the table, the jam at one end, the orange slices at the other. The oranges are prepared as follows. With a knife, carefully cut and remove the peel in 4 sections, reserving it to make candied orange peel. Using a sharp knife, slice the oranges so that they are slightly thicker than lemon slices; sprinkle the oranges with very fine sieved sugar. All this may be done in the morning to give the oranges time to absorb sugar.

Near the bowls of jam and oranges, place butter in crystal butter dishes and, next to them, crystal plates or butter dishes filled with flavored butters.

TO CULTIVATE FIELD MUSHROOMS
(*RAZVEDENIE SHAMPIN'ONOV*)

Dig a ditch ¾ *arshin* [one arshin = 28 inches] deep and as wide as is convenient. Fill the ditch with horse manure, sprinkle ½ *arshin* of black earth on top, and level it thoroughly. Coarsely chop field mushrooms, including the roots and any earth that adheres to them, sow them on this bed, and cover with earth to a depth of 3 fingers. After 3 weeks, the earth will begin to rise in small lumps along the top of this bed, a sign that the mushrooms are growing. Planted in this manner, they will last a long time, especially if, when gathering them, you resow the bed each time with chopped roots and cover them up with earth.

SALTED CUCUMBERS (*OGURTSY SOLENYE*)

To have solid rather than hollow cucumbers, they must be salted immediately after they have been gathered, or at the latest, on the next day. To prevent them from drying out, it is best to drop them into cold water with ice as soon as they have been gathered.

Cover the bottom of a small barrel with oak, cherry, currant, and dill leaves and quartered garlic cloves. If not using garlic, add the leaves and shavings of horseradish roots. Stand the cucumbers upright one next to another on the bottom of the barrel and spread a handful of each of the above-mentioned greens on each layer of cucumbers. After filling the barrel in this manner, cover it immediately with another barrel bottom, in which two small holes must be drilled. One hole is to allow gasses to escape; insert a funnel in the other hole and pour in salted water as follows: Use 6 glasses salt and 1 spoon saltpeter for 2½ pails, or for 10 *garnets* [Russian dry measure = 3.28 liters], of river or well water. Mix the water and salts together and pour as is [without heating] over the cucumbers. Immediately cork and tar the barrel. It is good to intersperse the cucumbers with small watermelons, which are abundant in the southern provinces of Russia.

The Challenged Gentry (1887–1911)

Elizaveta Vodovozova

Elizaveta Nikolaevna Vodovozova came of age at a time of political and social ferment in Russia. She was born in 1844 and was seventeen years old when the serfs were emancipated. She lived to see the Revolution and its immediate aftermath and died in 1923. As a young girl she attended the prestigious Smolny Institute in St. Petersburg and subsequently traveled to Europe, where she studied early childhood education. She was convinced that young women in Russia during her time were brought up in a way that not only failed to prepare them for an independent life, but in fact killed any desire for it on their part. After returning to Russia she began to develop her own ideas on educational reform precisely at the time when radical circles in Russia were deeply engaged in debating the ideas that would lead to revolution. Vodovozova organized Tuesday evening gatherings where the progressive intelligentsia of Petersburg, united in their opposition to tsarist autocracy, would assemble regularly to debate how best to overthrow it.

The excerpt that appears here is taken from Vodovozova's two-volume memoir Na zare zhizni *(At the Dawn of Life), written between 1887 and 1911. In addition to her critique of accepted child-rearing practices, she casts a critical eye upon the system of serfdom in the 1840s and 1850s. In her view its corrosive effects on human behavior impacted all who were fated to live during this time and ate away at the very fabric of social and familial relations.*

In that time long ago, that is at the end of the 1840s and in the 1850s, our local nobles, at least those I knew, were not spoiled by comfort. They had quite a simple lifestyle, and the furnishings of their homes were distinguished neither by luxury nor elegance. As a child I had the chance to see how even the richest and most distinguished people lived at that time. Perhaps that is why we children listened with the greatest interest to older people's stories about how these or those land-owners were living with such royal grandeur, how luxuriously their enormous houses were furnished, like palaces, what brilliant feasts they gave, how they arranged hunting parties with huge packs of hounds, how whole regiments of huntsmen and other servants came behind them, and so on. There was nothing of the kind on the estates for at least two hundred versts around us. Never mind the small-scale landowners who were especially numerous in the vicinity in which we lived; even the landowners who had seventy-five or one hundred male souls lived in small wooden houses, equipped with none of the elementary comforts and necessary additions. A landowner's house was most often divided with simple partitions into several rooms or, more exactly, little cells. Four or five such tiny rooms, with the addition of one or two rooms in a wing, would shelter an enormous family which included, in addition to six or seven children, the nannies, wet-nurses, maids, hangers-on, a governess, and female relations of various kinds, unmarried sisters of the master or mistress of the house, and aunties who were left without a crust of bread after falling into financial ruin on account of their husbands. You would come to visit, and members of the house would start to crawl out. You would simply marvel at how and where they could all fit in the small house's tiny rooms.

Things were not at all like that for us, on our estate in Pogoreloe: compared with the neighbors we had a large, high-ceilinged, well-lit and comfortable house with two entrances, seven large rooms, with side rooms, corridors, sections for the male and female servants, and a separate wing in the courtyard. But our house's measurements were impressive only in comparison with the very humble homes of our neighbors. My father built it soon after his marriage and, like everything he built, it testified to his love of a lifestyle higher than what his means permitted.

You could marvel at the fact that only four children in our enormous family had died in the first year of life, and cholera alone managed to reduce the number of its members by more than half. In other landowners' families a multitude of children died off even without contracting cholera. There is still a high infant mortality today, but incomparably more children died in that distant epoch. I knew more than a few families among the nobility with many children, only an insignificant percentage of whom made it to adulthood. It could not have been otherwise: landowners at that time lacked any understanding at all of hygiene and the physical care of children. There were no window vents, even in well-off landowners' houses, and the stale air of the rooms in the winter was purified only by stoking the stoves. Children had to breathe the spoiled air most of the year, since at that time people had no idea that daily walks in fresh air were essential for proper physical development. Even rich landowners set aside the darkest and least attractive rooms, which the grown-up members of the family could not use for anything, as bedrooms for the children. The children slept on piles of featherbeds, which were never aired out or dried. The side a child lay on would overheat from the down in the featherbed, while the other side would stay cold, especially if the blanket slipped off. The stuffiness in the children's rooms was indescribable. They would try to fit all the small children into one or two rooms, and the wet-nurses, nannies, and maids slept there beside them on benches, trunks, or simply the floor, making a bed with whatever junk they had handy.

Prejudices and superstitions went hand in hand with insufficient physical cleanliness. Many families with young ladies of marriageable age held the belief that black cockroaches were an omen of happiness and a quick marriage, so a great many landowning women would breed them on purpose. They would put pieces of sugar and black bread behind the molding in their rooms. In those families the cockroaches would fall onto the sleeping children at night like little pebbles from the walls and beams. As far as other parasites are concerned, roaches, bedbugs and fleas would bite the children so much that many of them always had some kind of rash on their faces.

The food also had little correspondence to the needs of a child's organism. Infants were offered the breast the moment they cried, even if they had just nursed. If a child did not stop crying and refused the breast, they would rock it until it was dizzy in a cradle or carry it around. Rocking made it even harder for the child's body to digest the food just consumed, and it would spit up. Vomiting is exhausting even for a grown-up; how much harder it is for the weaker organism of a child. For all these reasons children rarely slept calmly in landowners' houses. Usually one could hear them crying all night, accompanied by the squeak and creak of the rocker or cradle.

The deeply immoral landowners' habit of a healthy mother handing over her own children to a wet-nurse rather than nursing them herself also had very negative consequences for physical development. The wet-nurse, even more careless, dirty and ignorant than her mistress, would take the child to bed with her in order to sleep better. She knew perfectly well that no one would check on her at that time, and besides, it was not considered harmful for a child to sleep in bed with its wet-nurse, attached all night to the breast. If the infant cried nonetheless, the wet-nurse would give it a pacifier made of bread, sometimes soaked in vodka or with ground poppy-seed added. In most cases children nursed for two, sometimes even three years. Women were chosen as wet-nurses not because they were young and healthy, with no illnesses that might be dangerous for an infant, but out of various domestic considerations. Jealous lady landowners avoided taking young and pretty women as wet nurses, so as not to lead their husbands into temptation.

The ubiquitous habit of swaddling also had a harmful influence: tightly wrapped in swaddling clothes by the midwives from its neck right down to its heels, the unfortunate newborn lay motionless for hours at a time, stretched out like a string, until all its limbs were numb. The position interfered with proper blood circulation and digestion. At the same time, the constant rubbing of diapers against the child's tender skin caused copious perspiration, making the child more likely to get a chill the moment it was unwrapped.

A child moved into its next stage of development with exactly the same lack of healthy concepts. Growing bigger, he would most often try to get into the servants' quarters—it was more fun there than in the nursery. Here the maids, lackeys, coachmen, and cooks, eating lunch, would tell each other all the news they had just heard about other landowners' families, about the romantic adventures of the child's own parents. The servants' quarters also attracted a child because it functioned as a kitchen for the masters at the same time. There were usually leftover turnips lying around, and in the autumn all kinds of cabbage-stalks, since they were chopping cabbage, preparing enormous quantities of it for the winter. The landowners' children would stuff themselves with this raw food even at times when surrounding villages were ravaged by dysentery.

The main pedagogical rule, observed both by families of the highest classes of society and by the lower gentry, consisted of the idea that only the strongest, that is, parents and elders, could claim the best things in the house—a comfortable room, a less bumpy place in the carriage, a tastier morsel. Children were creatures without rights, just like serfs. The parents' interactions with the children were fairly clearly defined: children came to kiss their parents' hands in the morning, when the latter greeted them, they thanked them for lunch and dinner, and they said good-night to them before bed in the evening. Every governess's task consisted first and foremost in watching the children so they would pester the parents as little as possible. At meals together in decent households children were not supposed to interfere in the conversations of their elders, who discussed things without restraint that were not at all suitable for children's ears: the need to whip this or that peasant, whom they called a scoundrel, a rascal, or worse, or they would tell the most scabrous stories about their neighbors. They punished children, just like the serfs, for every misdeed: they smacked them on the head, pulled their hair or ears, shoved, pounded, whipped them with a switch, beat them with rods, and in a great many families flogged and thrashed them mercilessly.

Thanks to my late father, who loved his children passionately, thanks to his natural gentleness, the whip and other pedagogical instruments of the serf-keeping type had no currency in our family. It is true that mama was not averse to smacking someone on the head, giving a shove in the back or pulling a child's hair, but even after father's death she did this fairly rarely. In any case, I can say that the members of my family hardly suffered from corporal punishment, except in cases when mama was obliged to teach one of us a lesson: then she was completely unable to restrain her hot-tempered and impatient character.

Be that as it may, our family stood out sharply among the landowners' families in our area both in its greater mental and moral development, and in its humane attitude towards serfs and other people, both near and far. Even after my father's death I never heard the moans of serfs who had been whipped, and in our house the maids never received slaps in the face or punches in the jaw. I don't mean to suggest by this that my mother was completely untouched by the pathology of serfdom. On the contrary, it may seem strange, but, regardless of spending twenty years of her life married to a man whom she ardently loved and deeply respected, the poison of serfdom had strongly infected mother's blood and from time to time would show itself in the arbitrariness common to those who kept serfs, particularly the arbitrariness with which she wielded her parental power.

Except on holidays, mama would go out every day at dawn into the fields, and we would see her for the first time before lunch, when she came back extremely tired. One after another we would come up to kiss her hand, and she would hastily return our kisses and always ask the same questions: "So, are you well? Did you have a good walk?" My sisters often simply kept quiet at these stereotypical questions, since they often weren't able to go outside because of bad weather, but mama did not notice this or gave no weight to their silence. She was completely absorbed in running the house, had entered totally into a business that was new to her, and in the first years of our country life she didn't have a free minute even to think about her own children. Perhaps in part her lack of worry about us came from the fact that she was well aware of our nanny's passionate love and devotion and sure that we would be properly dressed and fed. Be that as it may, our mother's lack of attention to us quickly destroyed the family element in our home, which we had felt so strongly during the life of our late father, who was always surrounded by children. Now little by little every member of our family began to live a separate life; only our nanny's passionate devotion to us and our common love for her maintained the link between us. In the house she alone knew what concerned each of us at a certain moment, our characters and our desires, our virtues and our flaws, and she devoted her whole soul to us.

If my brothers never sat at home, then my sisters hardly ever went out of the house. As for me, I would not let our nanny take a step away from me: she would go into the barn to scatter flour, grouts or grain, and I would drag along behind her, tossing on my big kerchief. My older sister Nyuta was always embroidering ruffles and collars with satin-stitch (the most common

Cathedral and Riverside
in Pskov, ca. 1900. From
*Pamiatniki starinnoi
arkhitektury Rossii*, edited
by G. K. Lukomskii
(Petrograd: Shipovnik,
1916), 52.

kind of handwork at that time), she recopied various pictures, put together
patterns for women's handwork, ran into the kitchen to cook up some kind of
dish or dug in the garden and the front yard, planting flowers, digging up
bushes; my sister Sasha sat over a book, never lifting her head.

Translated by Sibelan Forrester

Dear Nicky, Dear Sunny (1916)

The Correspondence of Nicholas II
and Empress Aleksandra

He called her by her nickname, Sunny. She called him Nicky. Her mother was English, her father German. Christened Alix Victoria Helena Louise Beatrice, Princess of Hesse-Darmstadt, the young woman who would become the empress of Russia grew up speaking English, French, and German. Nicholas II was conversant in all three of these languages in addition to his native Russian. When the future tsar of Russia met and married Alix, they chose English as the language in which they would converse. In a marriage that lasted twenty-four years (1894–1918), Nicholas II, last tsar of Russia, and his consort, Alix, who changed her name to the Russian Aleksandra upon her marriage, exchanged over seventeen hundred letters and telegrams, most of them during World War I and all of them in English. Their letters bespoke a marriage of intense loyalty, physical passion, and devotion to family. But they also tell us much more, partly because the last days of the Romanov dynasty and the tragic fate of the royal family have been the subject of much imaginative speculation and, indeed, falsification.

Through archaeological evidence we now know that Nicholas's and Aleksandra's youngest daughter, Anastasia, did not survive, as some supposed, but was executed along with the rest of the family in Yekaterinburg in July 1918. What still remains a subject of debate, however, is the character of the tsar himself and his role in the demise of the Romanov dynasty. Do the letters exchanged between the tsar and tsarina point to his deep passivity in the face of the stronger personality of his wife, who interfered in government matters and who was guided in her own decision making by the mystic Rasputin? The man labeled "our friend" who appears in their letters is clearly Rasputin (1872–1916), a holy man, or starets', who heralded from Tobol'sk and acquired enormous influence over the royal family because of his presumed ability to stop Crown Prince Alexis's bleeding from hemophilia. With his almost macabre influence at court Rasputin was an extreme version of the yurodivyi, or "fool in Christ," the beggar or pilgrim of peasant origin. By times cunning and even brilliant in his political strategies, he presented the face of someone who might equally have been thought of as simple-minded. The very simplicity of the fools in Christ was seen by Russians as evidence of their spiritual purity and godliness. Believed to have special healing powers, they were seen by Dostoyevsky, Tolstoy, and Turgenev as the spiritual salvation of the Russian people. Understanding the almost religious venera- tion they were accorded helps explain why Rasputin was embraced by the tsar's family to the degree he was.

Yet Nicholas was a more complex, even paradoxical figure than the presence of Rasputin in his court might suggest. He was a man who reveled in hard work yet hated the endless detail and paperwork of being a monarch; he possessed deep and abiding moral and religious values and yet acted in ways not always in the best interests of his country. Reading the letters of Nicholas and Aleksandra one cannot help but be struck by the deep commitment of husband and wife to family, to each other, and to a set of beliefs clearly at odds with the needs of a nation beset by war and an incipient revolution.

Aleksandra to Nicholas

Tsarskoje-Selo, 8 April 1916

Christ has risen!

My own sweet Nicky love,

On this our engagement day all my tenderest thoughts are with you, filling my heart with boundless gratitude for the intense love & happiness you have given me ever since that memorable day, 22 years ago. May God help me to repay you hundredfold for all your sweetness.

Yes, verily, I doubt there being such happy wives as I am—such love, trust & devotion as you have shown me these long years with happiness & sorrow. All the anguish, suffering & indecision have been well worth what I received from you, my precious bridegroom & husband. Now-a-days one rarely sees such marriages. Your wonderful patience & forgiveness are untold—I can only ask God Almighty on my knees to bless & repay you for everything—He alone can. Thank you, Sweetheart & feel my longing to be held in your arms tightly clasped & to relive our beautiful bridal days, wh. daily brought new tokens of love & sweetness. That dear brooch will be worn to-day. I feel still your grey suite, the smell of it by the window in the Coburg Schloss. How vivid I remember everything; those sweet kisses wh. I had dreamed of & yearned after so many years & wh. I thought, I should never get. You see, as even then, faith & religion play such a strong part in my life. I cannot take this simply—& when make up for sure mind, then its already for always—the same in my love & affections. A far too big heart wh. eats me up. And the love for Christ too—& it has always been so

Aleksandra and Nicholas,
Russia's last monarchs, ca.
1890s. Copyright CORBIS.
Used by permission of
CORBIS.

closely linked with our lives these 22 years. First the question of taking the orthodox faith & then our two Friends sent to us by God. Last night gospels made one think so vividly of *Gregory* & His persecution for Christ & our sakes—everything had a double meaning & I was so sad not to have you standing by me.

Last year I was in the afternoon near Ania's bed in her house (our Friend too), listening to the 12 *Gospels*—a part of them.

To-day at 2 *the carrying out of the winding-sheet* & at 6 *the burial. Loman* begged upstairs instead of the night, as then none of the soldiers can go.

And you alone at the *Headquarters*—ah Sweet One, I cry over yr. solitude!

Baby slept well, woke up only 3 times &, I hope, will be up to-day, as he badly wishes to come to the *morning*-mass but without you I cannot imagine that great and holy feast. Think its Wify kissing you 3 times in Church, I shall feel yr. kisses too & blessings.—

I send you the petition of one of Aunt Olga's wounded men. He is a Jew, has lived since 10 years in America. He was wounded & lost his left arm on the Carpathians. The wound had healed well, but he suffers fearfully morally as in August he must leave, & looses the right of living in either of the capitals or other big towns. He is living in town only on the strength of a special permit, wh. a previous minister of the Interior gave him for one year. And he could find work in a big town. His English is wonderfully good, I read a letter of his to little Vera's English governess & Aunt Olga says he is a man with good education, so to speak. 10 years ago he left for the United States to find the opportunity to become a useful member of human society to the fullest extent of his capabilities, as here it is difficult for a Jew who is always hampered by legislative restrictions. Tho' in America, he never forgot Russia & suffered much from homesickness & the moment war broke out he flew here to enlist as soldier to defend his country. Now that he lost his arm serving in our army, got the St. George's medal, he longs to remain here & have the right to live wherever he pleases in Russia, a right the Jews don't possess. As soon as discharged fr. the army, as a cripple, he finds things have remained the same as before, & his headlong rush home to fight, & loss of his arm has brought him no gain. One sees the bitterness, & I fully grasp it—surely such a man ought to be treated the same as any other soldier who received such a wound. He was not obliged to fly over here at once. Tho' he is a Jew, one would like him to be justly treated & not different to the others with similar losses of a limb. With his knowledge of English & learning he could easier gain his bread in a big town of course; & one ought not to let him become more bitter & feel the cruelty of his old country. To me it seems one ought always to choose between the good & bad jews & not be equally hard upon all—its so cruel to my mind. The bad ones can be severely punished.—Can you tell me what decision you write on the petition; as Aunt Olga wanted to know.—

4 big eggs are for:

1. *Father Shavelsky*, 2. *General Ivanov*, 3. *General Alexeiev*, 4. *Admiral Nilov* (*Fredericks* already has one).

12 small eggs:

1. *Voyeikov*, 2. *Grabbe*, 3. *Dolgorukov*, 4. *D. Sheremetiev*, 5. Silaiev, 6. *Mordvinov*, 7. *Kira*, 8. *Feodorov*, 9. *Zamoi*, 10. *Pustov.*, as he works with you always.

Our Friend wired to me *"Christ has risen, is a holiday and a day of joy, in trials joy is brighter, I am convinced the church is invincible and we, its children, are joyous with the resurrection of Christ."*

My head goes round, & during my writing one interrupts me & I have to choose eggs & write cards, so as to send off most things to-day—after all lots have to get things—& now must get up for luncheon at 12½, & after that shall finish my letter.—I send you my little Eastergifts—the book-marker for the novels you read.—We lunched near Baby's bed in the big room, he feels rather giddy fr. his medicines—but will get up later.—The Image I thought you would perhaps all kiss in Church & then it will be a double remembrance. The egg is *hand-made,* can hang with yr. war Images in Church if you don't know where to put it. Its grey & now raining.—Your sweet blue flowers are too nice, thanks awfully for them, the Children & I love them & I gave some bunches to the ladies, who were quite delighted. —Baby fears he cant go to-morrow night & that worries him.

1000 thanks, Lovebird, for yr. sweet letter—I shall at once let Aunt Olga know about the Jew. *Sturmer* comes to me this evening.—

Yes, he loves oo, my little Boy Blue & already 31 years & belong to you 22.— Now I must end.

3 Easter-kisses, blessings without end, my own lonely Angel, whom I love so endlessly—oh, your sad Easternight—shall miss you more than words.—

Ever yr. very own old Wify.

Nicholas to Aleksandra

Ts.[arist] Stavka. Oct. 30th 1916.

My own sweet Treasure,

Many many fond thanks for your dear letter, that I found on arriving here, on my table. It was a great comfort to get the two letters today because I felt rather low coming to this place. Kiev seems like a nice dream, every-thing went so well there & all the people were so warm! Now I must tell you the events in good order as they followed. On my hasty letter fr. the train in Kiev I stopped at the lunch à trois. At 2.30 one of the shkoly praporshchikov [naval ensigns' academy] came into the courtyard & were promoted. Motherdear [Maria Fedorovna] looked out of the window and was very pleased with the sight, especially by the way Babykins held himself behind me! Then we drove to [my sister] Olga's hospital & spent nearly an hour with her. She was lying on a straw sopha, a favorite one uses in the garden. I saw several sisters [i.e., nurses] of hers I knew previously & two doctors.

From Olga Motherdear took us back to tea & after that I went to the train. He [Aleksei] had his dinner & I wrote & read. At 8.0['clock] I dined with Mama & spent a cosy evening. The next day 29th from 9.30 till 12.0 I visited the four military schools—of which three are quite new and I began by inspecting them. First the Nikolaevskoe voennoe uch. I Nikolaevskoe artiller. uchil. [the Nicholaevsky Military Ac.(ademy) and the Nicholaev-sky Artillery Acad.]—both completely outside the town, near each other. Enormous splendid new buildings, not quite finished in some parts. Then I had to drive right through the town to the Alekseevskoe inzhenernoe uch. [the Alekseev Engineering Ac.,] also a colossal house very well situated & with a grand view down on the Dnepr. Coming back to the palace I played a flying visit to the old milit.[ary] school now called after [i.e., named in memory of] Costia. Luckily I arrived in time for luncheon at 12.30. Mama invited all my gentlemen & hers and Ignatev (gov.[ernor]) with his wife (Jules Urusov['s] daughter). Babykins had walked the whole morning in the garden & had pink cheeks & astonished those at table with his appetite. He talked well with Zina Mengden & behaved alright.

In the afternoon Mama took us for a charming drive on the other side of the river. The view from down there onto the town was lovely—only alas! without any sun. We came back across another bridge & passed by Olga's hospital, got out there, were glad to see her up. But she felt rather gesa-nische [weak]. Then to Mama for tea with Paul and M. P. [, his wife, Miechen]. She gave Motherdear a very pretty image [icon] fr. the whole family, with all the names written behind. Only our's & the children's of course are not on it. She was lukewarm with me & did not say a word about Livadia! Which Mama found strange. Paul was in an excellent mood, he had just seen all of the guard & was delighted. I left Kiev after dinner with Mama, in pouring rain.

Oct 31. I got your dear letter & thank you fr. all my heart for your good advice. Thinking about the prodovol'stv [i.e., supply] question I also found it preferable to settle the affair at once, only I had to wait for that paper to reach me. Now it is done: God help us! I feel it is right. The weather is warm. It rained heavily yesterday. Now I must end. God bless you my angel & the girlies! Ever so many loving kisses from your own Nicky. Love to A[nna Vyrubova].

Aleksandra to Nicholas

Tsarskoje Selo, Dec. 4th 1916

My very precious One,

Goodbye, sweet Lovy!

Its great pain to let you go—worse than ever after the hard times we have been living & fighting through. But God who is all love & mercy has let the things take a change for the better,—just a little more patience & deepest faith in the prayers & help of our Friend—then all will go well. I am fully convinced that great & beautiful times are coming for yr. reign & Russia. Only keep up your spirits, let no talks or letters pull you down—let them pass by as something unclean & quickly to be forgotten. Show to all, that you are the Master & your will shall be obeyed—the time of great indulgence & gentleness is over—now comes your reign of will & power, & they shall be made to bow down before you & listen your orders & to work how & with whom you wish—obedience they must be taught, they do not know the meaning of that word, you have spoilt them by yr. kindness & all forgivingness. Why do people hate me? Because they know I have a strong will & when am convinced of a thing being right (when besides blessed by *Gregory*), do not change my mind & that they can't bear.

But soon all this things will blow over, its getting clearer & the weather too, which is a good sign, remember.

And our dear Friend is praying so hard for you—a man of God's near one gives the strength, faith & hope one needs so sorely. And others cannot understand this great calm of yours & therefore think you dont understand & try to ennervate, frighten & prick at you. But they will soon tire of it. Should Motherdear write, remember the Michels are behind her.—Don't heed & take to heart—thank God, she is not here, but kind people find means of writing & doing harm.—All is turning to the good—our Friends dreams means so much. Sweety, go to the *Moghilev* Virgin & find peace & strenght there—look in after tea, before you receive, take Baby with you, quietly—its so calm there—& you can place yr. candels. Let the people see you are a christian Sovereign & dont be shy—even such an example will help others.—

How will the lonely nights be? I cannot imagine it. The consolation to hold you tightly clasped in my arms—it lulled the pain of soul & heart & I tried to put all my endless love, prayers & faith & strenght into my caresses. So inexpressibly dear you are to me, husband of my heart. God bless you & my Baby treasure—I cover you with kisses; when sad, go to Baby's room & sit a bit quietly there with his nice people. Kiss the beloved child & you will feel warmed & calm. All my love I pour out to you, Sun of my life.—

Sleep well, heart & soul with you, my prayers around you—God & the holy Virgin will never forsake you—.

Ever your very, very

Own.

IV

Far Pavilions: Siberia

Few parts of the world seem to need so little introduction. Siberia is known to everyone everywhere, and at the same time is far enough from most people's experience to be hardly known at all. By dint of its sheer mythic status in the Russian imagination, Siberia has long been a site of heaven and hell, a place for the making and a place for the breaking of human aspirations. It has been cast as a place of divine mystery for its perceived untrammeled purity. Or sometimes just mystery. In 1908, some five hundred miles north of Irkutsk, an extraordinary midair explosion occurred over the Tunguska River basin with a force a thousand times greater than of the bomb dropped on Hiroshima, leaving behind hundreds of kilometers of scorched earth. To this day the causes of the Tunguska event are unsolved.

According to most sources, Siberia was one of Russia's earliest and foremost colonies. But did it remain a colony for long? The contiguity of the Siberian landmass to the east of European Russia made it unlike the faraway island possessions of the rival Dutch, Portuguese, and British Empires (in the eyes of those who sought to defend Russia's claims to the territory as a natural extension of sovereign right). To its possessors Siberia became the very hearth of the Russian soul, and its burden.

Any chance at better grasping the Siberian experience begins with its sheer size and scope. Were contemporary Siberia to be cleaved from Russia at the site of the most commonly recognized natural boundary, the Ural Mountains, it would still constitute the world's largest country, stretching across eight time zones. In Russian parlance, the region is divided into three parts: Western Siberia, reaching from the Urals and stopping short of Lake Baikal; Eastern Siberia, foremost embracing the vast territories around Baikal; and the Far East, taking in the considerable Primor'e and coastal regions from the Bering Strait in the north to Kamchatka, Sakhalin, and Vladivostok in the south. (Russians referring to Siberia today intend only the first two parts, while nineteenth-century imperial documents and long-standing English convention embraces all three.) The effort to simply traverse, let alone unite a space so vast was so great that in the late nineteenth century the Russian government found it more financially efficient to ship exiles headed to the Pacific coast by sea rather than over land, taking them out via the corridors of the Black Sea, through the Bosporus and the Mediterranean, across the Indian Ocean, and back up north again beyond Ceylon. The doctor and playwright Anton Chekhov, who trekked eastward to study the exiles' fate, took the more expensive land route. In diplomatic terms, he insisted that on his journey he saw "prose before Lake Baikal and poetry afterwards," but to friends he confided in the extraordinary tedium of weeks spent in his railway and horse-drawn carriages passing village after village inhabited by people "who manufactured clouds, boredom, wet fences, and garbage."

Geographically Siberia demonstrates extremes of temperature and landscape alongside vast swaths of arable territory and one of the world's greatest concentrations of natural resources. To the east Chinese and Japanese have historically jostled for preeminence, later joined by Americans attracted to the wealth generated in fisheries, mines, forests, and oil fields, all while the region was putatively under the control of a Russian administration alternately more and less able to supervise and conquer such a vast space. Centuries of migration across and between empires have left sizable populations of Turkic peoples, most notably among contemporary Sakha (numbering over 400,000), who occupy the diamond-rich regions north of Baikal. Buryats, in turn (also more than 400,000), share close links with Mongolian language and culture that endure to this day. Another quarter-million Siberians are from the region's forty-one indigenous groups, many of whom once learned Russian only after they had taken up Japanese, Chinese, Mongolian, or Turkish. Throughout the Soviet period, when they enjoyed greater constitutional protections and relatively less pressure from resource developers, nomadic reindeer-herding Evenki covered such a wide territory that many Evenki found it difficult to believe that they could not adapt to any area in the world. Others, such as Chukchi on the Bering Strait, enjoyed the reputation (until the establishment of the Soviet Union) of being the only non-Russian people in the empire that successfully fended off invading imperial armies.

In the Soviet period the legendary status of Siberia could cut both ways. It became the site of extraordinary feats of engineering, as in the founding of the nickel production city of Noril'sk, which went on to become one of the world's first urban centers of more than a million people north of the Arctic Circle; the establishment of one of the world's leading research centers, Akademgorodok, in Novosibirsk; the powerful water dams at Bratsk; and the building of the Baikal-Amur Mainline railways (better known in Russian by its acronym, вам). Millions of Russians responded to government calls to resettle there, inspired by the flush of patriotism and the promise of better pay. Yet the land famous as a site of exile from imperial centers, epitomized in Dostoyevsky's novel *The House of the Dead*, lost none of its capacity to strike fear among those who landed in the labor camps rapidly revived under Soviet rule, or among the even greater numbers well aware of their existence. Less common is an appreciation for the amphitheatric views overlooking the Pacific from the windowsills of a cosmopolitan Vladivostok, or the spectacular wooden architecture still prominent in the cities of Tomsk, Tobol'sk, and Irkutsk.

In the unsteady nationalist climates of post-Soviet Russia, Siberia takes on yet another dimension. Non-Russian migrants from former Soviet republics who head there to earn a better living than they can at home speak of two Russias—the Russia of Moscow and St. Petersburg, where non-Russians are not always welcome, and the Russia of Siberia and the Far East, where new arrivals are relatively freer, if nothing else, to be themselves.

Russia's Conquest of Siberia
(sixteenth and seventeenth century)

Edited and translated by Basil Dmytryshyn,

E. A. P. Crownhart-Vaughan, and Thomas Vaughan

This mid-sixteenth-century text comes from the pen of Ivan IV (1530–84), better known as Ivan the Terrible, the first of the Russian leaders of the growing Muscovy to take the name of tsar, a Russian derivation of caesar, thus marking the state's growing confidence and the claim to empire. With this act he extended hundreds of acres of prime real estate along the Kama River, adjacent to what is the thriving contemporary city of Perm in the Ural Mountain region, to Grigorii Stroganov. The text is a rich example of the nature of conquest. Ivan's chancellery scribes stress that the land has been "uninhabited from time immemorial." The statement is then qualified: "To the present time no one has worked this land nor established homesteads there." An earlier editor of this piece, the distinguished Slavist Basil Dmytryshyn, clarified that "no one" meant "no Russian." Over time the lands around Perm were very much in use by a mix of Tatars, Bashkirs, Komi-Permiaks, Udmurts, and their lesser known predecessors. But how one formally recognized the presence of others was another question. Simply occupying the land was not enough. As in so much of Europe then and since, land use by nomadic or semi-nomadic peoples was not recognized as a claim to sovereignty; one settled permanently or not at all. Hunting, gathering, and trading also did not count as valid claims; one farmed or one didn't. Most of all, one had to pay taxes, yet the scribes wrote, "The uninhabited lands have hitherto paid us no tribute and presently pay none." The lands under question, like so much of broader Siberia to the east, were very much inhabited; it was another matter whether the inhabitants had fixed addresses, farmed, or paid tribute to the tsar.

Among those who lived on or near the lands being deeded were some who had intermarried with the Nogai peoples, then known as the Turkic Mongols, descendants of the Golden Horde who were in retreat by Ivan's time but still feared by many. Thus, as Ivan's decree indicates, upon receipt of his new properties Stroganov must pledge to build forts to protect his uninhabited land from its noninhabitants.

Ermak the Explorer. Courtesy of the Print Collection, Miriam and Ira D. Wallach Division of Art, Prints, and Photographs, New York Public Library, Astor, Lenox and Tilden Foundations.

A Letter Patent [Zhalovannaia Gramota] from Tsar Ivan Vasilevich to Grigorii Stroganov Granting Financial, Judicial, and Trade Privileges on Uninhabited Lands along the Kama River

4 April 1558

I, the Tsar and Grand Prince Ivan Vasilevich of all Russia, have been asked to grant to Grigorii Anikievich Stroganov that for which he has petitioned, namely: the uninhabited lands, black [coniferous] forests, wild rivers and lakes and uninhabited islands and marshlands in our patrimony which extend for some 88 versts [one verst = 3500 feet], along the right bank of the Kama from the mouth of the Lysvaia, and along the left bank of the Kama opposite Pyznovskaia backwaters, and along both banks of the Kama to the Chusovaia River. These uninhabited lands extend for 146 versts. To the present time no one [no Russian] has worked this land nor established homesteads here. To date no tax revenue has been received from this area into the Treasury I hold as Tsar and Grand Prince. At present the land has not been granted to anyone, nor has it been entered in the census books, nor in the books of purchase, nor in legal records.

In his petition Grigorii Stroganov has also asked permission to build a small town there where he will place cannon and defense guns; he will station cannoneers and gunners, and post guards at the gates to protect the town from the Nogai people and from other hordes. He will cut timber along the rivers up to their headwaters and around the lakes, put the land into fields, and establish farmsteads. He will invite persons to settle who are unregistered elsewhere and do not pay taxes. He will search for salt deposits, and wherever he finds these, he will set up saltworks and evaporate salt.

Here in Moscow our Treasury officials have inquired about this area from a man from Perm named Kodaul, who has come from Perm to bring *dan* [tribute] from all the Perm people. This man from Perm, Kodaul, has told our Treasury officials that the region for which Grigorii petitions us has been uninhabited from time immemorial, that it has brought no revenues into our Treasury. Kodaul from Perm has affirmed, that these uninhabited lands have hitherto paid us no tribute and presently pay none, that the Perm people pay no taxes from this region nor do they pay any *iasak* [tribute in furs] from it to Kazan, nor have they done so in the past; and if this patent will present no hardship either to the Perm people or to travelers, then I, the Tsar and Grand Prince Ivan Vasilevich of all Russia do grant this petition of Grigorii Anikievich Stroganov, and authorize him to build a small town in the uninhabited lands some 88 versts below Great Perm, along the Kama River, on the right bank of the Kama from the Lysvaia River and on the left bank of the Kama opposite Pyznovskaia backwaters, and down both banks of the Kama to the Chusovaia. He may build a small town in the black forest, in a secure and well protected location, and emplace cannon and defense guns in that town, and I authorize him, at his own expense, to station cannoneers and gunners and gate guards there to protect the town against the Nogai people and other hordes. He may cut timber around that small town along the rivers and lakes and up to the headwaters, and plough arable lands, and establish farmsteads, and invite unregistered, non-tax-paying persons to settle in that small town.

But Grigorii is neither to invite nor accept registered taxpayers from Perm or from other towns into our Empire, nor is he to accept lawbreakers or persons who have run off from *boiars* with their possessions. If taxpayers from other towns within our Empire should come to Grigorii with their

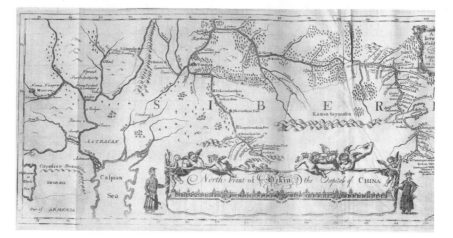

Siberia in the eighteenth century. From John Bell, *Travels from St. Petersburg, in Russia, to Diverse Parts of Asia* (Glasgow: Foulis, 1763). Source: University of Arizona, Special Collections.

wives and children, and the *namestniks* [administrators] or *volostels* [supervisors] or the elected officials object to this, then Grigorii is to send such taxpayers and their wives and children back to the towns from which written objections have come. He is not to accept or hold such persons.

Persons who come to this town from our Empire or from other lands with money or with goods who wish to purchase salt or fish or other things are free to sell their goods and to purchase other items without paying duty.

Grigorii may accept persons who move from Perm to settle in his town, provided they are unregistered and have no tax obligations.

Report to Tsar Mikhail Fedorovich from the Streltsy Sotnik Petr Beketov Concerning His Expedition on the Lena River

6 September 1633

To the Sovereign Tsar and Grand Prince Mikhail Fedorovich of all Russia, a report, Sovereign, from your distant Sovereign patrimony in Eniseisk ostrog, from your humble servants, streltsy sotnik [lieutenant of Cossack troops] Petr Beketov and his servitors, and from your Sovereign's orphan, the promyshlennik[1] Iakov Zarubeevich Semenov.

On May 30, 1631, Sovereign, in accordance with your ukaz, Sovereign Tsar and Grand Prince Mikhail Fedorovich of all Russia, and in accordance with the instruction of your Sovereign Tsar's voevoda Semen Shekhovskii,

I, your humble servant, was sent out from Eniseisk ostrog with servitors on your distant assignment, Sovereign, to the Lena River for one year. Your Sovereign salary and rations were given to me for one year. I, your humble servant, with these servitors and with the promyshlenniks served you, Sovereign Tsar and Grand Prince Mikhail Fedorovich of all Russia, on your distant service on the Lena River, Sire, for two and a half years.

During those two and a half years, while on your distant service, Sovereign, I your humble servant suffered every deprivation. We were starving to death and ate every wretched thing including grass, roots and bark from fir and silver fir trees. I, your humble servant, Petr Beketov, together with the servitors and the promyshlennik, thanks to God's mercy and your luck, Sovereign, brought under your Sovereign Tsarist mighty hand on the Lena River many diverse Tungus and Iakut lands for you, great Sovereign Tsar and Grand Prince Mikhail Fedorovich of all Russia. I, your humble servant, collected iasak from these many diverse Tungus and Iakut lands for you, great Sovereign Tsar and Grand Prince Mikhail Fedorovich of all Russia. And I, your humble servant, collected iasak from many Tungus and Iakut people, using the threat of your Sovereign's might. Sovereign, I, your humble servant, with servitors and the promyshlennik, collected iasak for the year 1632 which consisted of 18 forties of sables.

In the year 1633, from these same Iakuts and Tungus, I, your humble servant, with the servitors and the promyshlennik, added 41 forties and 15 sables to your Sovereign iasak treasury from the Iakuts and the Tungus plus the tithe paid by servitors and by promyshlenniks.

Furthermore, Sovereign, I, your humble servant, collected two forties and 16 sables on the Lena River in your name for your Sovereign Treasury from servitors and the promyshlennik as fees for settling legal disputes. In Eniseisk ostrog these were valued at 130 rubles.

Sovereign, in two and a half years of service on the Lena River I, your humble servant, with the servitors and the promyshlennik, collected a total of 61 forties and 31 sables, 25 Iakut sable shubas [fur coats], 10 sable *plastinas* [pelts sewed together], 2 beavers, 7 red fox, and one red fox pup. Sovereign, prior to this no one had collected your Sovereign taxes from legal judgments on the Lena River. Moreover my men and I have brought back under your mighty Tsarist hand many of your previously rebellious subjects who defied your Sovereign Majesty during this two and a half year period. The names of these princes are listed in the official record, and also the names of the hostages I took from them.

I, your humble servant, with the servitors and with the promyshlennik, came to Eniseisk ostrog on September 6, 1634, with your Sovereign iasak

and tithe Treasury, from your distant Sovereign service on the Lena River. I
submitted my service report in Eniseisk ostrog, in the Prikaz office, to your
Sovereign voevoda, Andrei Andreevich Plemiannikov. . . .

The Oath of Allegiance Which Russians Administered to Bratsk Native Leaders

1642–45

I, Bului, a man of the Bratsk tribe, hereby give my firm oath of allegiance
to my Sovereign Tsar and Grand Prince Mikhail Fedorovich, Autocrat of all
Russia, and to his Sovereign Lordship, the Tsarevich and Grand Prince
Aleksei Mikhailovich. I, Bului, and my brother Bura and our other brothers and tribesmen, and all my ulus² people, swear on our faith, by the sun,
by the earth, by fire, by the Russian sword and by guns, that we will come
under His Tsarist Majesty's mighty authority, in eternal servitude, without
treason, undeviatingly, for all time. I will serve my Sovereign in every way,
loyally and gladly.

I will not commit any treason against his Sovereign servitors or against
any other Russians or against his Sovereign people in the Verkholensk
ostrozhek, or against agricultural settlers, in any places where the Sovereign's servitors and Russians may be working, nor will I come in war or
in secret to kill them or harm them or commit treason against them.
Neither I, Bului, personally, nor my brother nor any of my ulus people will
incite other hostile Bratsk people to commit treason against the Sovereign's people, nor incite them or guide them to come to kill.

Likewise I, Bului, will encourage other Bratsk leaders and their ulus
people to come under His Tsarist Majesty's mighty hand in eternal servitude and to pay iasak and pominki³ to the Sovereign, in large amounts and
in full every year, for themselves and for their brothers, and in every way to
be in complete concord with the Sovereign's people.

When the Sovereign's men come to collect iasak in my ulus, I will
protect them, and will not allow them to be killed. If any Bratsk leaders
and their ulus people become disloyal to the Sovereign, then I, Bului, will
report about these disloyal persons to the Sovereign's prikashchiks [official
of the central government] in Verkholensk ostrog, and I will join the
Sovereign's forces in war against these disloyal people, and will try to
pacify them by means of war and bring them back under your Sovereign
Tsarist mighty hand, and will collect iasak from them for the Sovereign.

Notes

1. During the period of Russian expansion, *promyshlennik* referred to a Russian hunter, trader, or trapper who worked for himself or in a group or who was employed by merchants or government officials for exploration, conquest, and pacification of the natives.

2. *Ulus* is a Mongol term that referred either to a settlement, an area inhabited by a native Siberian tribe, or a domain or realm belonging to a Tatar, Mongol, Kalmyk, or Uzbek ruler.

3. In pre-1700 Russian and particularly in Siberia, *pominki* referred either to a "gift" Russian officials exacted often by force from Siberian natives or a bribe Russian officials received from Siberian natives.

Sibiriaks (1916)

Marie Czaplicka

One of the first female scholars of the Russian North, and by all means one of the best of her generation, the young Polish anthropologist Marie Czaplicka (1886–1921) captured an aspect of Siberian life that still speaks volumes today. Trained at a Russian university in Poland, she left for the London School of Economics to study ethnography with the renowned early fieldworker, Bronislaw Malinowski. Soon becoming an authority on Siberian shamanism and traveling extensively through aboriginal Siberia on her own on the eve of the First World War, she chronicled a simple but long overlooked fact of life across the newly conquered lands of eastern Russia: its remarkable social mixing. "For ages . . . Siberia . . . has been a veritable crucible of race-fusion," she writes, "in which to the basic Finnish[-speaking of the indigenous Finno-Ugric peoples] have been added various Turkic and Mongolic elements, the alloy being completed by the addition of a Slavonic, chiefly Great Russian, ingredient." Of this mix came the Sibiriak. In the more dominantly Russian areas Sibiriaks distinguished themselves as claiming neither Old Believer status (from the Russian Orthodox sect that relocated eastward to gain religious freedoms) nor an exile-prisoner lineage. The Sibiriak was not quite Russian, not quite Finnish, not quite Turkic, and yet all of the above.

If the development of the material resources of Siberia raises problems of absorbing interest for the economist and provides a profitable field of activity for the capitalist, the growth of a new Russian nation in Siberia is no less interesting for the ethnographer and the sociologist. It is hardly too much to say that no other colonial nation presents so curious a mixture of racial elements, and that in no other colony in the world have the physical and social problems arising out of the contact of "lower" and "higher" races so happily adjusted themselves.

It is, indeed, only natural that this should be the case. For ages the region which includes eastern Russia and western Siberia, between the Volga and the Ob, has been a veritable crucible of race-fusion, in which to the basic Finnish stock have been added various Turkic and Mongolic elements, the alloy being completed by the addition of a Slavonic, chiefly Great Russian, ingredient. All this was going on for centuries before the Russian annexation of Siberia, which has merely had the effect of quickening and facilitating the process. What is especially curious is that even educated Sibiriaks, drawn in many cases from western Russia, from Poland, or from Finland, do not seem to preserve, in Siberia, any strong traces of racial prejudice. If, in fact, they do intermarry but rarely with the natives, this appears to be due rather to a consciousness of social superiority than to any racial antipathy.

The Sibiriak—that is, broadly speaking, the colonial whose ancestors have been settling in Siberia, voluntarily or involuntarily, since, say, the end of the Middle Ages—is a man in whose veins there may run the blood of the Little Russian, the Great Russian, the Pole, the German, the Jew, and the aborigine, who is himself the representative of much mixed Finno-Turko-Mongoloid and other strains. The above order represents roughly the relative quantitative importance of the different racial elements which have gone to the making of a modern Sibiriak. This name does not apply to temporary or recent importations from Russia, or to the aboriginal inhabitants of Siberia, the Siberians properly so called. Some colonials would confine the application of the name "Sibiriak" to the *starojily* ("old settlers") who, or whose ancestors, came to live in Siberia before, say, 1885; while the numerous *novosioly* ("new-comers") they would call rather *Rossiyanye,* using the Polish word for "Russians."

In western Siberia the numbers of the sexes almost balance, with a slight superiority in favour of the men. Eastern Siberia has still many more men than women. The rapid growth of population is due chiefly to immigration, although the birth-rate is also very high. Immigration is chiefly to western Siberia, and the pressure of new population tends to drive the *starojily* eastwards. Thus the Sibiriaks of the east, having been longer in contact with native races, have acquired a distinctly Asiatic physical type, as compared with the western Sibiriaks.

There is, of course, no such thing as a Sibiriak language, any more than there is a Canadian or an "American." The educated, that is to say, broadly speaking, the town-dwelling Sibiriak of the "upper classes," speaks the language of Great Russia with a Little Russian accent. But even they have their own style of expression and a large vocabulary of words not used, or used in a different sense, in Russia. Many Polish words, or corruptions of Polish words, are in use; this is significant in the same way as the fact that many Orthodox churches in Siberia which date from the eighteenth century are strongly reminiscent in their structure, and especially in the altars and statues they contain, of the churches of Catholic Poland. The uneducated Sibiriaks, especially those of the northern Yenisei and Lena, speak a dialect of Russian strongly affected by native words pronounced in a Russian manner, and their vocabulary of both kinds is quite poor. Their degeneration in this and other respects is shown also in the kindred fact that they have almost lost their folklore and the capacity for artistic expression in handicrafts which is a characteristic of the Slav peasant in Europe. In both these respects they are poorer also than the Asiatic peoples they live among.

One racial trait, at least, associated with their European origin persists strongly in the Sibiriak: the love of singing and of the making of songs. An anthology of Sibiriak songs, quite apart from their tunefulness, would provide an illuminating document for the student of Siberian life. Among the most popular is the "Tramp Song," "Through the desert steppe, by the bitter lake," which tells of the wanderings of the *brodyaga*, "bare soul and body," in the dismal southern wastes. These *brodyagi*, though many of them are criminals, include no small proportion of men who, brought to trial in Russia for some political offence, and refusing, for fear of incriminating their friends, to acknowledge their identity in court, have been sent, as "nameless men," to the wildest parts of Siberia without any means of support—"bare body and soul." Then there is the song of the imprisoned exile, "Lone in the four-square cell," listening in his solitude to "the tread of the gaoler, the only sound." Or there is the beautiful conscript song, to which now the streets of Moscow not less than those of Krasnoyarsk often echo as the new levies swing by, "To-day's day is the last I spend with you, my friends." Some are gay with the ebullient gaiety of a new nation which feels its chains less than do its brothers who live in the land where the chains are forged; others are gay with the ironic gaiety of brave souls who smile grimly at their own pains; all are racy of the land and the people whose expression they are. True folk-songs they can hardly be called, most of them seem to have originated in more sophisticated circles; but they have a very widespread popular vogue.

What was said above about the "happy adjustment" of problems arising out of the contact of different races in Siberia requires some qualification. In the south, Kirgis, "Tatars," Buryat, and Amur Tungus intermarry with the Sibiriaks and adapt themselves readily to the conditions of agricultural life. In the north the European population is infinitely smaller, and the conditions of life for Europeans, especially for the newer immigrants, who are, moreover, for the most part "undesirables," are too abnormal to permit of a healthy social development. Here contact with the natives is marked by the spread of syphilis and other imported diseases, and the unions of Europeans and natives are either barren or result in physically degenerate offspring. Only decadent and feckless natives will come to live in the settlements; but it is not, as might be supposed, simply the lack of women of their own race which causes the

European settlers to cohabit with native women. Among the Sibiriaks of the north, polygyny might almost be said to be the general rule. The rougher sort, that is the majority, conform to the custom of their native neighbours, and even when already married to Sibiriak women, take one or more native wives also.

The official division of society into classes, so strictly adhered to up to the present time in Russia, has little real significance in Siberia. Although officially 90 per cent of the Sibiriaks are classed as "peasants," this arbitrary distinction has no real relation in many cases to the actual constitution of Sibiriak society. A man of title, for instance, whose opinions on the established order of things have made it unsafe for him to live in Russia, and who has emigrated to Siberia and taken to farming or started a fishing station, would be classed as a "peasant." A student at a Russian university, if not "gentle" by birth, becomes so on graduation. Perhaps he is sent to Siberia as the outcome of a trial for some political offence. He is ipso facto *déclassé*, deprived of all civil rights. On the expiry of a certain term of years in exile, he may seek election as a member of a village community. If the community elects him, he may now reside there, with the status of a "peasant." This is the lowest of the Russian "classes." He can never, except by a special act of grace, recover his former official social standing. Thus the word "peasant" for the Sibiriak does not call up the associations that it does in Russia—the recollection of serfdom, of subjection to landowners and clergy, of a position of humility at the very foot of a social ladder whose rungs are not so much steps as barriers.

The "peasant" in Siberia feels himself a citizen rather. He knows that he is the owner of the country. For, with the exception of the population of the towns—only 6 per cent of the whole—who form a class of "burghers," the clergy and the civil servants, most of whom are new-comers to Siberia, the Sibiriaks are all "peasants."

Exile by Administrative Process (1891)

George Kennan

Long before Dostoyevsky immortalized Siberia as a land of suffering in The House of the Dead, Russians across the empire were well aware of the risks in displeasing authorities. One could be exiled from the empire entirely, sent south to the Caucasus, banished from desirable urban centers such as Moscow or Petersburg, or held in local prisons for indeterminate amounts of time. But few punishments held quite the same punch as exile beyond the Ural Mountains. This is not to say that all Siberian residents were uniformly in straits: the region had many thriving cities, its own local Russian elites, hundreds of thousands of indigenous people, active immigration overland from China and Central Asia, and a relatively cosmopolitan social structure. But the burden of exile status, often accompanied by deep privation and the assignment of hard labor, made entry and adaptation into Siberian life a crushing event.

George F. Kennan (1845–1924), the distinguished explorer, journalist, historian, and diplomat, published one of the best known documentary accounts of this world in his book Siberia and the Exile System, based on his travels throughout Russia in the second half of the nineteenth century. (He is not to be confused with his relative, the later American historian and diplomat, George F. Kennan [1904–2005], who was named after him.) Political tensions in Petersburg ran high in the years Kennan conducted the interviews for the book: young revolutionaries had assassinated Tsar Aleksandr II in 1881—it was the second killing of a Russian emperor in that century, since Pavel I had been killed in 1801—and the never permissive secret police stepped up all measures against antistatist elements. This included the vast number of students who had been involved in Russia's Narodnik, or Populist movement, when members of the intelligentsia swept across the countryside promoting education and political participation among the peasantry. Any manner of suspicious activity, or the most indirect ties to such activity, could become cause for grievous punishment.

Kennan rightly speculates on how much damage the empire did to its own integrity by generating so much ill will among what became largely a sea of innocents sent to painful fates and often death. In a telling gesture, Russian imperial officials declared Kennan himself persona non grata in 1891 for his support of antitsarist *causes abroad. He became one of the Russian Revolution's earliest and most ardent foreign supporters.*

The colony of political exiles in Ust Kámenogórsk was the last one that we saw in the steppe territories, and it seems to me desirable, to describe more fully and carefully the particular form of punishment that these offenders were undergoing—a form of punishment that is known in Russia as "exile by administrative process."

Exile by administrative process means the banishment of an obnoxious person from one part of the empire to another without the observance of any of the legal formalities that, in most civilized countries, precede the deprivation of rights and the restriction of personal liberty. The obnoxious person may not be guilty of any crime, and may not have rendered himself amenable in any way to the laws of the state, but if, in the opinion of the local authorities, his presence in a particular place is "prejudicial to public order," or "incompatible with public tranquillity," he may be arrested without a warrant, may be held from two weeks to two years in prison, and may then be removed by force to any other place within the limits of the empire and there be put under police surveillance for a period of from one year to ten years. He may or may not be informed of the reasons for this summary proceeding, but in either case he is perfectly helpless. He cannot examine the witnesses upon whose testimony his presence is declared to be "prejudicial to public order." He cannot summon friends to prove his loyalty and good character without great risk of bringing upon them the same calamity that has befallen him. He has no right to demand a trial or even a hearing. He cannot sue out a writ of habeas corpus. He cannot appeal to his fellow-citizens through the press. His communications with the world are so suddenly severed that sometimes even his own relatives do not know what has happened to him. He is literally and absolutely without any means whatever of self-defense. To show the nature of the evidence upon which certain classes of Russians are banished to Siberia, and to illustrate the working of the system generally, I will give a few cases of administrative exile from the large number recorded in my note-books.

. . . .

In the year 1880 the well-known and gifted Russian novelist Vladimir Korolénko, two of whose books have recently been translated into English and published in Boston, was exiled to Eastern Siberia as a result of what the Government itself finally admitted to be an official mistake. Through the influence of Prince Imeretínski, Mr. Korolénko succeeded in getting this mistake corrected before he reached his ultimate destination and was released in the West Siberian city of Tomsk. Hardly had he returned, however, to European Russia, when he was called upon to take the oath of allegiance to Alexander III, and to swear that he would betray every one of his friends or acquaintances whom he knew to be engaged in revolutionary or anti-Government work. No honorable and self-respecting man could take such an oath as that, and of course Mr. Korolénko declined to do so. He was thereupon exiled by administrative process to the East Siberian territory of Yakútsk, where, in a wretched native *ulús,* he lived for about three years.

Mr. Boródin, another Russian author and a well-known contributor to the Russian magazine *Annals of the Fatherland,* was banished to the territory of Yakútsk on account of the alleged "dangerous" and "pernicious" character of a certain manuscript found in his house by the police during a search. This manuscript was a spare copy of an article upon the economic condition of the province of Viátka, which Mr. Boródin had written and sent to the above-named magazine, but which, up to that time, had not been published. The author went to Eastern Siberia in a convict's gray overcoat with a yellow ace of diamonds on his back, and three or four months after his arrival in Yakútsk he had the pleasure of reading in the *Annals of the Fatherland* the very same article for which he had been exiled. The Minister of the Interior had sent him to Siberia merely for having in his possession what the police called a "dangerous" and "pernicious" manuscript, and then the St. Petersburg committee of censorship had certified that another copy of that same manuscript was perfectly harmless, and had allowed it to be published, without the change of a line, in one of the most popular and widely circulated magazines in the empire.

A gentleman named Achkín, in Moscow, was exiled to Siberia by administrative process in 1885 merely because, to adopt the language of the order that was issued for his arrest, he was "suspected of an intention to put himself into an illegal situation." The high crime which Mr. Achkín was "suspected of an intention" to commit was the taking of a fictitious name in the place of his own. Upon what ground he was "suspected of an intention" to do this terrible thing he never knew.

Another exile of my acquaintance, Mr. Y—, was banished merely because he was a friend of Mr. Z—, who was awaiting trial on the charge of political conspiracy. When Mr. Z—'s case came to a judicial investigation he was found to be innocent and was acquitted; but in the meantime Mr. Y—, merely for being a friend of this innocent man, had gone to Siberia by administrative process.

In another case a young student, called Vladímir Sidórski (I use a fictitious name), was arrested by mistake instead of another and a different Sidórski named Victor, whose presence in Moscow was regarded by somebody as "prejudicial to public order." Vladímir protested that he was not Victor, that he did not know Victor, and that his arrest in the place of Victor was the result of a stupid blunder; but his protestations were of no avail. The police were too much occupied in unearthing what they called "conspiracies" and looking after "untrustworthy" people to devote any time to a troublesome verification of an insignificant student's identity. There must have been something wrong about him, they argued, or he would not have been arrested, and the safest thing to do with him was to send him to Siberia, whoever he might be— and to Siberia he was sent. When the convoy officer called the roll of the outgoing exile party, Vladímir Sidórski failed to answer to Victor Sidórski's name, and the officer, with a curse, cried "Victor Sidórski! Why don't you answer to your name?"

"It is not my name," replied Vladímir, "and I won't answer to it. It's another Sidórski who ought to be going to Siberia."

"What is your name, then?"

Vladímir told him. The officer coolly erased the name "Victor" in the roll of the party, inserted the name "Vladímir," and remarked cynically, "It doesn't make a—bit of difference!"

In the years 1877, 1878, and 1879, no attempt was made, apparently, by the Government to ascertain whether an arrested person was deserving of exile or not, nor even to ascertain whether the man or woman exiled was the identical person for whom the order of banishment had been issued. The whole system was a chaos of injustice, accident, and caprice. Up to November, 1878, as appears from an official circular to provincial governors, the local authorities did not even take the trouble to make a report of political arrests to the Minister of the Interior. If a man was taken into custody as a political offender, that, in many cases, was the end of it so far as an investigation was concerned. The fact that he had been arrested by mistake, or in the place of some other person, did not necessarily insure his release. The local authorities reversed the human rule of Catherine II and acted, in political cases, upon the principle that it is better to punish ten innocent persons than to allow one criminal to escape.

. . . .

Exile by administrative process is not a new thing in Russia, nor was it first resorted to by the Russian Government as an extraordinary and exceptional measure of self-defense in the struggle with the revolutionists. It is older than nihilism, it is older than the modern revolutionary movement, it is older than the imperial house of Románof. It has been practised for centuries as a short and easy method of dealing with people who happen to be obnoxious or in the way, but who cannot conveniently be tried or convicted in a court of justice. If the "Russian Resident of Eastern Siberia" [an unnamed writer writing in a German periodical about the exile system] will read attentively the works of Tarásof, Sergéyefski, Maxímof, and Anúchin, he will find that administrative exile has been not only a recognized, but a well established, method of dealing with certain classes of offenders ever since the seventeenth century. In the reign of the Emperor Nicholas, for example, nihilism had not been so much as heard of,—the very word was unknown,—and yet men and women were being exiled to Siberia by administrative process, not in hundreds merely, but in thousands, and not only by order of the Tsar, but by order of the administrative authorities, by order of the ecclesiastical authorities, by order of the village communes, and even by order of private landowners. Most of them, it is true, were not political offenders; but they were none the less entitled to a trial, and they were all victims of the system that the "Russian Resident" says was brought into existence half a century later, "in a time of terrible necessity, as the only possible means to counteract the nefarious doings of those dark conspirators," the nihilists.

The careful and exhaustive researches of Anúchin in the archives of the chief exile bureau [*Prikáz o Sílnikh*] at Tobólsk, show that between 1827 and 1846 there was not a year in which the number of persons sent to Siberia by administrative process fell below three thousand, and that it reached a maximum, for a single year, of more than six thousand. The aggregate number for the twenty-year period is 79,909. It can hardly be contended, I think, that the nihilists or the terrorists are responsible for a system that had sent eighty thousand persons to Siberia without judicial trial, long before such a thing as a nihilist or a terrorist was known, and before most of the modern Russian revolutionists were born. The "Russian Resident of Eastern Siberia" has simply put the cart before the horse. It was administrative exile, administrative caprice, and the absence of orderly and legal methods in political cases generally, that caused terrorism, and not terrorism that necessitated official lawlessness. The wolf always contends, with a show of virtuous indignation, that while he was peacefully drinking as usual, the lamb muddied the brook, and thus compelled him to "take exceptional measures for the reëstablishment of public tranquillity"; but his statement is very properly discredited when it appears that he was above the lamb on the brook, and that, for years, he had been taking "exceptional measures" of the same kind with other lambs that had not been near the brook. To defend or to justify the crimes of the terrorists is not the object of my work; but when the history of the nineteenth

View of Zlatoust', in the Cheliabinsk Oblast', Siberia, ca. 1910. Source:
Library of Congress, Prints and Photographs Division, Prokudin-Gorskii
Collection, LC-DIG-prpok-00522. Courtesy of Jean Swetchine.

century in Russia shall have been written by some one having access to the
secret archives of the Ministry of the Interior and the Third Section of the
Tsar's Chancellery, it will appear, I think, to the satisfaction of all men, that
most of the so-called terroristic crimes in Russia were committed, not, as the
"Russian Resident" asserts, by "bloodthirsty tigers in human form at the
prompting of presumptuous fancies," but by ordinary men and women exas-
perated to the pitch of desperation by administrative suppression of free
speech and free thought, administrative arrest without warrant, administrative imprisonment for years upon suspicion, administrative banishment to the
arctic regions without trial, and, to crown all, administrative denial of every
legal remedy and every peaceful means of redress.

Science Everywhere (1997)

Ol'ga Marchuk

The Soviet Union was an ambitiously modernizing state, and few undertakings reflected socialist ideology more than the founding of Akademgorodok (literally, "small academic city" or "Academy Town") in the 1950s. Located on the banks of the Novosibirsk reservoir known as the Ob Sea in Siberia, some twenty kilometers from central Novosibirsk (today Russia's third largest city), Akademgorodok called on the best and the brightest of postwar Russian scientists. On the heels of victory in the Second World War and with greater confidence in a stable future, many Russian scholars heeded the invitation.

In her excellent memoir Ol'ga Marchuk gives us a sense of daily life in the growing Siberian research colossus. The sheer number of institutes rising out of the forest evokes the breadth and the depth of the undertaking. Many were attracted by the chance to start anew in a research setting favored by the government; others noted the range of privileges extended to those who committed early, such as better housing and greater access to elusive grocery staples. Following the collapse of the Soviet Union, many of Akademgorodok's residents became "shuttle scientists," relocating for a semester or more each year to Western universities to teach or do research at a higher salary. In recent years, with its highly educated population, Akademgorodok has begun to thrive again on its own as a center of international research and development.

My husband and I gave almost a third of our lives to the development of science in Siberia. We witnessed the beginning of this unique phenomenon, which the building of the small city of Akademgorodok near Novosibirsk meant for our country, and perhaps for the entire world at that time. Several thousand scientists left their research institutes and their cozy apartments and moved with their families to Western Siberia in order to bring science and culture to a region of rapidly developing resources and industry. They succeeded in building a unique scientific town, a place of exuberant creative energy. In the world press, Akademgorodok was called a scientific miracle.

Other countries of course also wanted to build similar science centers. France developed the research town of Orsay on the outskirts of Paris, as well as Aux-Marseille, outside Marseille. The Japanese developed the town of Tsukuba approximately 100 kilometers from Tokyo. Towns such as these were comprised of dozens of scientific institutions. They probably surpassed Akademgorodok in comfort. And still these towns were missing what we had in our Akademgorodok, namely that special creative atmosphere and the sense of unity of scientists from different institutes working as one body, one organism.

The Academician Mikhail Alekseevich Lavrent'ev had a distinguished, sharp intellect, broad views, and boundless energy. In the 1950s he worked at the Moscow Institute for Precision Mechanics and Computing Technology. Lavrent'ev saw the shortcomings in the way Soviet science was organized. At that time, almost all scientific research was concentrated in several large cities in the European part of the Soviet Union. These institutes, the main centers of research, were for the most part old, following old traditions, with older scientists and obsolete research topics that no longer corresponded to the needs of the state. Mikhail Alekseevich thought that it would be beneficial to relocate some of the scientists to a region with rapidly unfolding life and industrial development. The most promising place in this regard was Siberia. Of course, at that time Siberia was not sufficiently explored and poorly developed, but it was obvious that it was very rich in natural resources and in broad opportunities for developing industry. And there was no shortage of challenges for science there.

In conversations with his colleagues, Lavrent'ev discovered that Academicians Sergei Alekseevich Khristianovich, Sergei L'vovich Sobolev, and several others shared his views. In their discussions, they came to the conclusion that a special town should be founded in Siberia, consisting of several physical, mathematical, and technical research institutes. One would have to find scientists who were not old but who had an established reputation and would be willing to move to Siberia with their research assistants. It was for such scientists that these institutes should be built.

After the idea of creating a scientific town was hatched, Lavrent'ev, Khristianovich, and Sobolev presented their vision to the government. The proposal was considered, the scientists invited, and their ideas heard. They were given the green light. The Presidium of the Academy of Sciences created a committee to organize a Siberian branch of the Academy of Sciences, whose members included, beside Lavrent'ev, Khristianovich, and Sobolev, several other prominent Academicians, namely A. P. Vinogradov, L. A. Artsymovich, V. A. Kotel'nikov and others.

Alongside everything else, the location of this scientific town had to be decided. At first, a place near Irkutsk was proposed. Several committee members, led by Lavrent'ev, went there, looked at the place, but rejected it for various reasons. Then Timofei Fedorovich Gorbachev, head of the West Siberian Branch of the Academy of Sciences, said that there was a suitable plot of land a short distance from Novosibirsk. They traveled there. Indeed, not far from a dam under construction on the River Ob, was a rather flat plain, partially covered with birch and pine trees and partially planted with wheat. The plain belonged to a collective farm. Everybody liked the location: It was not far from the future reservoir, 30 kilometers away from the large industrial city of Novosibirsk, and a four-hour flight from Moscow. The leadership of the collective farm agreed to give up this land for construction of the town in exchange for another territory. For the loss of the already planted wheat in the fields, they received monetary compensation.

On May 18, 1957, the Council of Ministers of the USSR issued a decree, "On the Creation of the Siberian Branch of the Academy of Sciences of the USSR." The edict presaged the creation of a number of scientific institutes of various profiles. Besides the new institutions to be built, the plan envisaged the inclusion of the already existing Western Siberian, Yakut, and Far Eastern branches of the Academy of Sciences, as well as all scientific institutions east of the Urals, into the Siberian Branch of the Academy of Sciences.

The decision was that the Siberian Branch of the Academy of Sciences would build a scientific town near Novosibirsk, with research institutes, apartment houses with all conveniences, and the necessary support structure for everyday life. The Council of Ministers decided to create an Organizational Committee and appointed Lavrent'ev as Chief, and Khristianovich as his deputy.

But what kind of a science center could there be in Siberia? What kind of institutes should it include? First of all, it should be comprehensive. It should include institutes addressing major questions in mathematics, physics, technology, and the humanities. Moreover, these institutes should not focus exclusively on fundamental research but on the practical problems of the region as well.

In June 1957, several executive meetings of the Presidium of the Academy of Sciences of the USSR were held, where the creation of ten scientific research institutes and the appointment of their directors were approved.... Somewhat later the formation of four institutes of chemistry was approved....

The Council of Ministers also decided to build a university in Akademgorodok, to transfer the State Scientific Research Library to the Siberian Branch, and to give the Siberian Branch of the Academy of Sciences priority in selecting graduates from higher educational institutions. Responsibility for designing the scientific town was divided between the planning department of the

Academy and several Moscow and Leningrad design institutes. The construction of Akademgorodok was entrusted to Novosibirskgasstroi.

The talented engineer Chkheidze, who was the model for the hero of Azhaev's novel, *Far from Moscow*, engineer Beridze, was appointed director of construction.

Construction did not begin in an ordinary way. As the blueprints for the institutes were still being drafted in Moscow and Leningrad, construction workers were already at work on a town for themselves, building not only barracks but also four-story brick apartment houses, a school, shops, and a club named "Youth."

In the meantime in Moscow, vigorous efforts were underway to invite scientists to the future research institutes. It was no simple matter to agree to give up a research institute and an apartment in Moscow and move one's whole family far away to Siberia, to a town that did not even exist yet. Many scientists who were satisfied with their work and life in Moscow refused to go. Others understood right away the prospects of developing science in Siberia and agreed to move. Young people full of romantic expectations and ready to overcome all kinds of unimaginable obstacles enthusiastically accepted our invitations. All the young scientists from Lavrent'ev's department at the Moscow Physics and Technology Institute decided to follow him. A large group of graduates from the institute waited impatiently to receive their diplomas so that they could go to Siberia to develop science there.

And so began our new life in Siberia. With the help of our neighbor, Ivan Borisovich, we found a daily household maid. Her name was Grusha. She lived in the neighboring village of Kirovskoe and was single. She was a Siberian woman of small stature but extraordinarily strong. She wore the gray woolen shawl and black plush cardigan typical for rural women at the time. Grusha cleaned our apartment, did the dishes and the laundry. Once a week she made *pelmeni*. She was amazingly good at this. She mixed the dough, covered it on the board with a plate and set it aside to rest. In the meantime, she made her own mixture of beef and pork with a hand grinder. Then she rolled the dough into thin strands, cut them with a knife into small disks, rolled them out into thin sheets and wrapped the ground meat into them, pinching their edges together with lightning speed. After this she pressed the edges of the stuffed, semicircular *pelmeni* together in such a way that they looked like puffy, neatly shaped little ears. Piling the *pelmeni* on a thin board, she put it out onto the balcony in cold weather and continued to shape the next board full of *pelmeni*. After two or three hours the *pelmeni* had turned as hard as pebbles. Grusha poured them into a linen bag, tied it up, and left it on the balcony. Whenever we wanted *pelmeni*, we simply poured from the bag the amount we wanted and boiled them. We loved these Siberian *pelmeni* and consumed them in huge quantities. But regardless, the *pelmeni* in that bag never ran out.

Shortly after our arrival in Akademgorodok, something strange happened. Sasha returned home from school (he was in fourth grade), and as he was taking off his school uniform, I noticed that his arm had been bandaged at the elbow.

—What have you got here? What's going on? Did they give you a vaccination at school? I asked.

—No, no vaccination; they took blood at school, answered my son.

—What for?

—I don't know. They told me they did it for science.

I didn't question Sasha any further, but the next day I went to school to find out why they were taking children's blood from their veins. In the teachers' lounge I was told that there was no doctor at school, only a nurse and that I should talk to her. The nurse listened to me with amazement and said that nobody was drawing anybody's blood.

—What do you mean they didn't draw blood? When my boy comes home and says that they took blood. And I saw myself that his vein had been tapped!

—I believe you, but we didn't do any vaccinations or any kind of blood tests with the children yesterday. Maybe he went to the polyclinic and they did something to him there?

I hurried to the polyclinic and found the children's ward. But there, too, no one knew anything about blood work. When Sasha came home from school, I subjected him to a full interrogation. It turned out that a girl from his class had come up to him and approached him to give her some blood for an analysis, saying that this was for science. After school they went to her apartment and there her mother drew some of his blood with a syringe. He said that it didn't hurt him at all and that I was upset over nothing.

But after this discussion I became even more upset. Just imagine: in an unfamiliar town someone taking a boy to an apartment and doing some kind of injection! Who knows what they could have injected! In one word, when my husband came home from work I was beside myself with despair. I measured Sasha's temperature and didn't allow him to go outside, and Gury told me, in order to calm me down, that he would clear up everything tomorrow.

The next day he found out the name of the girl, where her parents worked, and why they drew Sasha's blood. It turned out that at the Institute for Cytology and Genetics they were carrying out a study on heredity. For this they drew blood from random people and analyzed their chromosomes. Of course, they were interested not only in adult chromosomes but in those from children as well. The girl (evidently the daughter of I. I. Kiknadze) had given blood herself and asked all her classmates to do the same. But nobody agreed. And at that moment, this new boy comes to class, and goes home with her to have his blood drawn!

The next day I got a phone call from the supervisor of the project. He apologized for the scare they had given me and admitted that they hadn't done this right and should have, of course, asked the parents' permission before drawing the children's blood. After a few days, as a token of goodwill, they sent me a photograph of my son's chromosomes. It showed some kind of worm-like squiggles. Now I think that I should have kept that photograph, but at the time I was so angry that I tore it up. Well, that's the kind of adventure that happens when people get carried away by science.

Translated by Hans Jürg Rindisbacher

The Big Problems of Little Peoples (1988)

Aleksandr Pika and Boris Prokhorov

Today some forty-one indigenous groups in Russia comprise approximately a quarter of a million people. As of the 2002 census, Evenki of the central Siberia plain are the largest at forty-one thousand, while there are exactly eight Kereki on the Chukotka Peninsula. Historically these peoples were hunters, gatherers, herders, fishermen, and traders. Sedentary, nomadic, and seminomadic, they were often multilingual given the demands of mobility and trade across vast spaces.

For all the stereotypes of aboriginal peoples cut off from modern life, the mal-ochislennye narody (in Russian, literally, "the numerically small peoples"; more commonly, malye narody, "the little peoples") of Siberia and the Russian Far East show just how central indigenous culture could be to socialist ideology. Marx and Engels each, but especially Engels, took avid interest in these peoples for what they took as evidence of "primitive communism," an instinctive sharing of resources that they believed could be leveraged in the new workers' state. At the outset of the Soviet period, indigenous peoples thus occupied two radically opposed slots: as "primitive communists" they were already the truest proletarians to be celebrated; as garden-variety primitives they were the poster children for education and elevation under the new socialist banner, set to make the "stride across a thousand years" from primitive to communist modes of production.

Across the Soviet period the numerically small peoples of Siberia and the Far East bore these fates fully. In certain respects they enjoyed greater educational freedoms than their indigenous counterparts in the nearby market economies of Scandinavia, Canada, Alaska, and Japan. Yet on most fronts they were fully in the mix of the best and worst of Soviet history. Local Russian elites viewed them as among the most prominent local candidates for persecution during the Stalinist purges, and they were subject to elaborate, sometimes devastating relocation programs as economic policy changed from one political generation to the next. In 1988, with perestroika under way, two Russian demographers, Aleksandr Pika and Boris Prokhorov, shook up indigenous politics by publishing this scorching report on what had become of some of socialism's once most promising citizens.

A Soviet agitational poster aimed against electing shamans to native councils, ca. 1931. Courtesy of www.plakat.ru.

Their ancestors came here thousands of years ago, examined these severe lands and made them their home. They pooled all their knowledge of nature, worked out special ways to survive under extreme conditions and managed to create lively and original cultures. Their roots, their hopes for the future are linked with this area and no other. These are the peoples of the North and, at the present time, their life is not easy.

For many years and decades, a lot was said in our country about the unprecedented progress of the indigenous peoples of the Soviet North who had perfected a gigantic leap from a primitive communal structure to socialism. But this vision of reality was often distorted and embroidered. Because serious economic, social, and demographic studies had not been done for a long time, acute and full-blown problems were either silenced or put aside. This has contributed to the fact that today the northern environment and its closely integrated indigenous inhabitants have almost reached a danger zone beyond which their further existence cannot be guaranteed. Many things could change irreversibly and disappear.

In recent years, disturbing signals from the area, honest and caring scientific reports, which might have once languished in desk drawers or in various archives, began to appear on the pages of newspapers and journals, were being openly discussed at conferences or were broadcast on television. Dozens of commissions of high state and party organizations visited the far North to investigate the facts.

So, what is really happening to the small ethnic groups of the North at the present time?

The national populations of the North occupy about half the territory of the USSR—from the Kola Peninsula to the Lower Amur and Sakhalin. In 1925, by a special decree of the Central Executive Committee and the Soviet of Peoples Commissars, the Saami, Nentsy, Khanty, Mansi, Entsy, Nganasany, Sel'kupy, Kety, Evenki, Eveny, Dolgany, Yukaghiry, Chukchi, Koriaki, Eskimosy, Aleuty, Itel'meny, Tofalary, Ulchi, Nanaitsy, Nivkhi, Udegeitsy, Negidal'tsy, Oroki, Orochi, and Chuvantsy were distinguished as a special group of small ethnic nations of the North. Their total population is now greater than 160,000 people. An important historical stage was reached in 1930 with the creation of national (now autonomous) *okrugs* [territorial administrative division] of peoples of the North. In the years after the War, industrial development in the area of the indigenous inhabitants of the North grew quickly. Owing to migration from other regions of the country, the population here increased many times over, whereas the population of the indigenous inhabitants increased insignificantly. Indeed, their proportion has sharply decreased, and today ranges from 23 percent in the Koriak Okrug to three percent in the Khanty-Mansi Okrug. In the economic balance of the region, the production generated by the indigenous northerners, mainly trade and farming, has become almost unnoticeable against the huge industrial capacity.

The autonomous *okrugs* where the nationalities of the North are living can have their interests defended constitutionally. But the figures for the standards of living of the indigenous northerners are significantly worse than those for the newly arrived population. It is possible to state with complete certainty that their social and living conditions are most unfavorable in comparison to all the other nationalities and small ethnic groups of the USSR. The ethnic settlements have a marked deficit of housing: provisions do not exceed, on average, four square meters per person. There is a lack of facilities in the majority of inhabited centers: only three percent of the houses have gas, 0.4 percent have water and 0.1 percent have central heating. There is no sewage nor water reservoirs to satisfy sanitary and ecological demands. The housing fund is largely run down: buildings were built at the end of the 1950s and beginning of the 1960s. The social infrastructure of the settlements is not developed. The supply of food products and industrial goods is meager.

The situation in the Khanty-Mansi Autonomous Okrug is quite typical for all the North. The Khanty and Mansi are now living in 72 national settlements. In many there is still no electricity and people use kerosene and oil lamps as in the old days. Furthermore, in those places where there are electricity stations, their power is often inadequate, with electricity being provided for only limited hours of the day. In many settlements, there are no hospitals, schools, clubs, bakeries or saunas, and sometimes not even a single shop. There are also certain settlements which are officially considered "liquidated" or non-existent; yet people continue to live in them. They completely lack amenities and the inhabitants have only themselves or their neighbors on whom to rely.

Since the end of the 1930s in the North, a state policy of converting the population to a settled way of life has been carried out (although even up to the present day, more than 15,000 people—almost 10 percent of the indigenous inhabitants—continue to migrate throughout the year and have no permanent home). This policy of conversion has no basis in science, and leads to the destruction of a traditional economy as well as to the dissolution of the indigenous population, to their disappearance as a unit of original ethnic formation, and to the loss of national and cultural distinctiveness. Precisely because of ideas of "cultural inferiority" ascribed to the nomadic way of life, native cultural identification itself has for several decades been officially considered a sort of "temporary existence" which ought to be abolished. Hence, the installation of modern living comforts for nomadic families was never arranged, for it was assumed that the reindeer farming population would be using such amenities in permanent settlements.

The traditional branches of the economy are the basis of the national and cultural individuality of the indigenous peoples of the North. At the present time, less than 43 percent of the working population of the indigenous northerners are involved in deer farming, fishing and hunting (whereas only three decades ago it was more than 70 percent). All these occupations are in a state of crisis because of the unbalanced economy, non-rational methods of trade and deterioration of pastures and natural areas because of the influence of the industry. But mainly it is a crisis in the leadership of the economy. This has a social origin.

The commercial wealth of the northern rivers, forests and tundra, and also of the domesticated reindeer and almost all means of production, have for a long time stopped being the collective property of the indigenous people. These means of production have reached the state where they have actually become the "departmental" property of Gosagroprom, Minrybkhoz, Rospotrebsoiuz, Glavokhota, and so on. These organizations are ruled only by considerations of narrow, departmental, immediate interests. They cannot link their activities to the essential requirements of northern peoples and to their perspectives for development. The results of their leadership of the economy are well expressed in the verses:

> *Ekonomiki osatenela, i u dal'nei severnoi reki*
> *iuzhnuiu rybeshku sardinellu pokupaiut khanty-rybaki.*
> The economy became saturnine,
> and yet by the distant northern river,
> Khanty fisherman purchase southern sardines.

One could not put it better: fish are brought thousands of kilometers by airplane from the Atlantic and Pacific Oceans to be processed at the Surgut and Salekhard fish factories. For feeding the animals on the fur farms in southern Yakutia, meat is being brought from Moscow and fish from the Far East. Almost all commercial agricultural production in the North is expected to make a deficit. In the *sovkhoz Udarnik* [Shock Worker State Farm] in Chukotka, the cost of one polar fox skin is 150 rubles, but it is sold for 65 rubles 13 kopecks. It is not difficult to calculate the loss knowing that the *sovkhoz* produces 5,000 fur skins per year. As a result of the uncontrolled activity of government departments, the number of domesticated reindeer in the country now totals only 1.8 million head—the lowest in the entire history of reindeer farming in this century (in 1965 there were 2.4 million). The intensity of the development of hunting areas and the production of the "northern" wild furs are also decreasing. The fishing resources in many internal waterways of the North are close to exhaustion, and in rich commercial areas of Kamchatka and Sakhalin the indigenous population is being squeezed out from the local fishing by more active newcomers who, in their haste for quick profits, mercilessly undermine the natural potential.

Plans for the industrial development of the Arctic and sub-Arctic regions of the world have always been greeted with great unease. Social and governmental organizations demand reliable guarantees from companies for the conservation of the interests of the local inhabitants. These demands are fixed in an international "Indigenous and Tribal Populations Convention." The experience of foreign countries shows that there exist real possibilities to combine the interests of the indigenous, ethnic groups with industrial development but for this it is necessary to study the possibilities carefully.

How are the interests of the population of the North of our country being defended? The answer to this question can only be: "depressingly badly." Northern native interests were not taken into consideration when the atomic explosions in the Arctic were carried out in the 1950s; they have never been consulted in the search for mineral deposits in the taiga and tundra, nor during the extraction of oil and gas and the construction of gigantic pipelines on their pastures and hunting grounds.

We have been conducting field research in the northern regions for many years. It is therefore painful to see how the few improvements in the lives of northern people that have been achieved, which technology and all the processes of industrial development have brought, are continually canceled out by the damages from organizations developing these regions. Over many years, day and night, the gas-burning flames around Nizhnevartovsk have been lighting everything in a crimson glow. Oil has been floating on the tributaries of the Ob, the forest has been cut down on the shores of the Taz, and the Iceland moss in the reindeer pastures of the Yamal has been perishing under the tracks of all-terrain vehicles. All this is because of endless haste, indifference and obvious neglect of the very land providing the wealth.

In a rare exception, the construction project for the gas pipeline corridor on the Yamal peninsula, which was expected to remove 36,000 hectares of reindeer pastures, was rejected on the advice of Gosplan USSR [c. 1988]. In fact, had this project gone ahead, the area of lost pasture could have been three to four times bigger. It is a sad paradox that the Yamal-Nenets and Khanty-Mansi Autonomous Okrugs are world fuel suppliers. But the inhabitants not only received nothing from the common "energy-fuel pie," they suffer constantly from the invasion of the oil and gas giants.

Through their unskillful work, the Magadan specialists in land reclamation destroyed the plankton in many rivers of Chukotka—the feeding base for Siberian salmon, hump-backed salmon, char, white salmon, and other delicacy fish. When Yermak came to Siberia on the shores of the Sob, the left tributary of the great Ob, the nomadic camp of the Khanty had already existed for a long time and was gradually turned into the Khanty settlement Katrovozh. The local people fished here, trapping animals and birds. Many places in the river valley were always considered "sacred" and it was categorically forbidden to catch fish, go hunting, log the forest or make fires. It was sometimes forbidden to even take water from these places. In such a way, the fish-spawning periods, hibernation quarters and the nests of waterfowl were preserved. What surprise, indignation and confusion there was among the Khanty several years ago when powerful equipment began to excavate the bed of the Sob! Local builders were in need of sand and gravel, but as a result of their digging, the sig [freshwater fish-inhabited lakes in winter and rivers in summer] and salmon disappeared from the river, and people who had been fishermen all their lives lost the natural basis of their livelihood.

There is no end to the list of crimes against nature and therefore, against the indigenous population itself. The Evenk author, Alitet Nemtushkin, who was a delegate at the Nineteenth Communist Party Congress, writes about the building of the Turukhansk Hydroelectric Station, which includes plans to build on his homeland:

> Whole ethnic groups could find themselves on the edge of extinction when, under the guise of benevolence, [developers] want to flood the best commercial grounds and reindeer pastures, depriving us the basis for our life. . . . Any extinction is a catastrophe. But here, unique features of national character, ethnic appearance, language and lifestyle could disappear forever from the culture of mankind and from its genetic stocks.

During the development of the regions where indigenous peoples are living, there appear problems, not only of scarred earth, destroyed pastures and poisoned fish but of two cultures colliding over the vast spaces of the taiga and tundra: one, an ancient culture—unique and, one might even say, fragile; and another modern culture—assertive, self-satisfied and technocratic. The people who are developing this severe region are well known to us through common activities on boreholes, long conversations around the taiga firesides and through meetings concerning the construction of new cities and railways. Some of their characteristics—stamina, devotion to their profession, courage, mutual help and modesty—we admire. Only such people could live and work in the North. But the problem is that they are never, or extremely rarely, reminded about the ecology or the necessity to respect other customs and other lifestyles. The processes which are taking place in the North, especially negative ones, are reflected in the young generation of indigenous inhabitants. When indigenous northerners move into non-traditional occupations, they generally have to be satisfied with low-paid, low-prestige jobs. The percentage of the indigenous population occupied in unskilled physical work (as cleaners, porters, auxiliary workers, and so on) in the employment structure is constantly growing, already comprising more than 30 percent (compared to 13 percent in 1959). This process of the "lumpenization" of these small ethnic groups is interpreted by some scientists ("optimists") as a "new progressive phenomenon, the growth of the working class," whereas the deep social alienation, passivity and pessimism produced by this situation are judged as "the remnants of a tribal, patriarchal past."

Socio-economic changes in districts inhabited by the small ethnic groups of the North are visibly reflected in the most important social indices, in health and demographics. They signal a warning. Indigenous people are turning for medical help and are being hospitalized due to circulatory and oncological diseases. Illnesses of the ear, nose and throat are significantly more common among northern indigenous peoples than among newcomers living in the same districts but under significantly better living conditions. The number of indigenous deaths from these illnesses are also higher. Infant mortality is high. The mental health of northerners is under threat. The level of their social-psychological adaptation to the quickly changing conditions of life is decreasing; the growth of drunkenness and aggressiveness testify to this process. From 1970–1980, one in two deaths among the indigenous population was caused by injuries in the home, accidents at work or murders and suicides (approximately 70–90 cases per 100,000 people which is 3–4 times higher than the national average).

From the middle of the 1960s, the small ethnic groups of the North entered a period of so-called demographic transition, during which high levels of birth and mortality should supposedly have replaced the low ones. But today the birth rate is still decreasing. All this is caused by a special crisis in family relationships, and is very closely related to the general process of cultural assimilation. Incomplete families are growing up in the settlements, mainly single mothers and widows with children.

Overall mortality among the peoples of the North has not decreased over several decades, remaining at an extremely high level, two to three times the prevailing index for the Russian Federation. The life expectancy of the indigenous population of the northern regions is 45 years for men and 55 years for women. This is 18 years less than the average for the whole USSR. The industrially developed countries and many of the developing countries in the world do not have such low indices. Because of this high mortality, the population growth of the small ethnic groups of the North between the censuses of 1970 and 1979 decreased by a factor of five—in 7 out of 26 ethnic groups the numbers of people actually decreased.

Among the problems which are especially alarming for the small ethnic groups of the Soviet North is the absence of work in the national settlements for indigenous people, a poor knowledge of the mother tongue or even a total ignorance of it among the youth, and their alienation from their families and from the traditional economic activities as a result of their long residence in boarding schools. Other phenomena are also alarmingly negative, such as the psychology of "parasitic dependence" which has been produced as a result of the defective system of relationships between offices of local power (which consist primarily of persons of non-indigenous nationality) and indigenous northerners. There is a widespread desire among local administrators to solve problems which are far removed from the interests of the indigenous population, while maintaining an outward show of caring for the people.

The Nivkh author Vladimir Sangi has told us how the resolution of the

Central Committee of the Communist Party of the USSR "On the measures for further economic and social development of the areas occupied by small peoples of the North" (1980) was being fulfilled on Sakhalin Island. In one county seat, Nogliki, there are about 700 Nivkhi (this is almost 65 percent of the total indigenous population of the county) who in their time were forcibly settled here from the small areas. Using the money issued for their economic and cultural development, the local authorities are offering, besides oil pipes, graders and cars—which indigenous northerners are unlikely to benefit from —a thousand pairs of plastic skis with titanium stocks, 200 typewriters, 500 pocket calculators and the same number of "Kompakt" toilets.

Academician A. P. Okladnikov once wrote,

> The present hunting-fishing ethnic groups of the North, whose creativity goes back thousands of years, contribute to the cultural achievements of the world in the same way as other nations on the planet. . . . For us, the problem is not whether to save the original culture of the northern people but how to save it in the best way under the pressures on one side, from the technological revolution and, on the other, from the tendency to internationalize cultures.

In order to save a culture it is necessary at first to save the people themselves.

All these problems have common roots, closely linked with the policies (or precisely the absence of any scientifically-based policies) in operation with the indigenous population. These problems can only be solved as a whole, and the main role in their solution no doubt belongs to true northern natives. All attempts to put into practice measures (however valuable) from above, from Moscow or from Tiumen, from Magadan or Krasnoiarsk, are destined to fail. This has already been demonstrated by previous experience. In the capital of our country, in the provincial, regional and district centers, we have first of all to stop the expansion of the ministries to the North and force them to respect and consider the interest of indigenous peoples. So far, regretfully, they have not done this themselves.

The Nineteenth All-Union Conference of the Communist Party of the USSR affirmed the right of every nation of the USSR to the revival and development of national cultures and the speeding of progress in previously backward regions. In the resolution "On relationships between nations," it was said:

> It is important that, in every national region, economic and social progress be accompanied by spiritual progress with emphasis on the cultural individuality of nations and small ethnic groups. This is entirely appropriate to

the situation existing in the regions of the smaller ethnic groups of the North. Built onto the basis of their social-economic and cultural progress in recent decades must be ideas for preserving national-cultural individuality and the "independent character of their development." First this implies special socio-economic and cultural forms of state national policy directed towards the northern small ethnic groups with the aim of supplying support, not only for the people living in the far, cold North but for all nations with a desire to ensure their survival and preserve their ethnic distinctiveness.

This means somewhat more than simply supplying "equal rights" and "equal opportunities" for all the population of the North so that, under equal conditions, those who "know the rules of the game" always win. Unfortunately so far, northern peoples on native lands are not in this position. The only possible means and way for their survival is through independent development, because if the hurdle of social passiveness and alienation cannot be overcome by indigenous people themselves, they will find no support from the outside. The necessary participation of northerners in all regional and local programs of development at all stages—from ideas and discussion to realization—must be considered as the premier political principle. It seems to us that the foundations of "new thinking" in this area are held in these two ideas.

At the present time, plans for economic and cultural development in the North are being worked out. Scientists who were invited to give their recommendations, as well as representatives of state power, are taking part. Co-operation between government institutions and research collectives in solving complicated national-cultural and social problems can only be welcomed. This is a step forward, but even so, it only reflects the needs of yesterday. Moreover, the concept of "state care" for indigenous peoples of the North leaves no room for the political will or the national-cultural aspirations of these people themselves. At the moment, it is not foreseeable that serious discussion of planning measures will include their direct participation. It is possible that all the legal, financial and socio-economic levers of development of their "small motherland" will once again be put into the hands of the ministries and departments, to those who have already been demonstrating their disinterest for decades.

Decisions about complicated ethnopolitical questions must certainly not be made quickly or be resolved simplistically by disinterested people. By contrast, they should be made by people who are active and who enjoy the respect and trust of people from far northern settlements and nomadic camps: the national creative intelligentsia, doctors, teachers, workers of the Soviet and Party organizations, deputies of local and regional Soviets, and representatives from the northern autonomous regions in the Supreme Soviet of the USSR. Their participation must be integral, not merely in the form of an invitation for the "final conference" to acquaint them with, and get their approval on predrafted resolutions. The time has come to create real representation for northern nationalities. They need living social institutions to be at work permanently on current problems. One proposal to create such an institution, an association of northern nationalities, was put forward by Vladimir Sangi at a meeting of the Secretariat of the Union of Writers of the RSFSR [Russian Soviet Federative Socialist Republic]. It received approval from scientists.

International experience from various northern communities around the world show that, in cases where local peoples were not consulted about forthcoming reorganizations, planned sociocultural changes brought feelings of resentment and helplessness. People were converted into passive executives of an alien will and consumers of "handed down" goods. By contrast, people themselves should decide what is best for them: traditional ways or industrial development, reindeer or oil, state bonuses or economic perspectives.

Awakening the self-awareness of northern indigenous peoples is possible only against a background of social-economic prosperity. Under the present conditions, it is difficult to expect positive changes in the consciousness of people whose interests have been ignored. Governmental departments which exploited the natural treasures of the North and significantly undermined the natural basis of the traditional occupations of the indigenous population must compensate for the damage caused. They must compensate, not simply with money, but by creating modern, comfortable settlements, as well as by building schools, hospitals, clubs, industrial workplaces and transport systems. The leadership of government departments and the indigenous population must clearly understand that this is not a good deed but fair, if far from complete, compensation. This side of the question is very important.

Undoubtedly, the most pressing problem in the organization of normal life in the North is to bring the economies of the indigenous inhabitants themselves into proper order. It is clear that the main aim of economic activity must be aimed at supplying the local population rather than that of distant cities. Production which is unprofitable and unsuited to the North such as dairy farming, Arctic pig breeding and so on, must be downplayed. The independent character of northern firms and family contract work must be encouraged, especially in reindeer farming, tenancy agreements and other forms of co-operation.

Indigenous inhabitants must again consider themselves responsible masters of the taiga and its rivers, tundra pastures and reindeer herds, rather than day-laborers for the visiting "comrade with a briefcase." We must strive so that genuine socialist co-operative ownership of the means of production takes the place of the "departmental" ownership. Such departmental fiefdoms only serve as the feeding ground for a northern bureaucracy and for the overpopulation of the northern settlements by large numbers of newly arrived "specialists and administrators." Only economic self-government and the potential for again becoming independent masters of co-operative property in northern communities can bring a personal and social sense of purpose back to the local people.

At the Source (1981)

Vladimir Sangi

The Nivkhgu (here Nyvkhs; in prerevolutionary times, Giliaki; in modern Russian, Nivkhi) number some five thousand people living on Sakhalin Island and the shores of the Amur River delta on the Russian mainland. Although they were highly mobile, sometimes trilingual fishermen, hunters, and traders during the Russian imperial period, their relative lack of formal education made them subjects of considerable derision. Their reluctance to farm (before the Soviet period, most considered it a sin to pierce the land) meant that even the more sympathetic Russian overseers were unable to recognize any other of their achievements in economic production or social life.

The Nivkh writer Vladimir Sangi's short story "At the Source" captures some of the syncretisms of Nivkh life during the Soviet era. The protagonist, Poloun, is fully integrated into the state economy and yet possesses a knowledge of winds, seasons, and wildlife invisible to most recruits from the Russian mainland who arrived on Sakhalin in search of higher wages and better pensions. As a product of the Soviet educational system, Sangi enjoyed the heights of its privileges; a widely published, celebrated fiction writer, he lived in a large, comfortable apartment in central Moscow and lectured widely to his many readers. In 1996, however, he returned to his native Sakhalin and since then has campaigned tirelessly for the rights of all indigenous peoples of the Russian Far East. He spends his time in his native village of Chaivo on the Pacific coast, officially shut down in the 1960s during the creation of regional agrocenters to concentrate local populations and resources. Today Chaivo is at the center of one of Russia's (and the world's) largest oil development projects.

Poloun got up early. He walked out on the porch and noticed smoke streaming over several houses. It spiraled upward like the smoke from his pipe, isolated from the rest of the world. Thoughts drifted into his head, jammed up and drowned him. Ah, Poloun has missed something important, something that hovers nearby but can't fit into the loop of his thoughts. What is it that depresses the oldest survivor from the Kevongun tribe, the one who has outlived all his relatives? Sometimes this or that ancient event keeps Poloun's mind busy for a long time. He considers his own behavior, and concludes events could have turned out another way if only he had acted differently. Poloun sighed, "Why bother when it happened so long ago."

After the black disease and the raiding, only Poloun and several women were left from his once powerful tribe. He had a bride, but she was taken with most of the other women to a village on the West Coast. Poloun looked for another wife but there were none left. He remained unmarried and over the last sixty-seven winters bitter thoughts piled heavily on his shoulders, bending his back more each year.

Streams of smoke slowly floated up. The sun was stuck somewhere between the mountains but its glow informed the world it was about to appear. A draft broke through the old man's warm chest invigorating his flabby body. As was his habit, he threw his rifle behind his back and cautiously approached the river. Keeping a hunting pace, Poloun came out through the ancient, twisted birch. He had known this place for a long time.

Holding its breath, nature anticipated sunrise, the sky wrapped in an orange shawl. From the damp and silent forest, an autumn scarlet rowan tree and a wrinkled brown alder stared at the dreaming river inlet. They would not admire their fall apparel much longer. Soon the burning frost would sear their leaves; they would stand naked and chilled and tremble all winter in angry winds. From the dense forest pine trees rose. Sullen, reticent, they grumbled and guarded the silence.

On the other bank of the river the lower branches of a rowan tree twitched. A squirrel pulled at drooping bunches of berries. "It knows when to pick berries—rowan berry is sweetest after a light frost," the old man thought. Summer-orange fur still spotted the squirrel's smoke-colored back. "You're so ugly," the old man smiled. As if embarrassed by being caught looking undignified, the squirrel scampered into the bushes.

Deep in the grove of alder trees and birch shrubs on the other bank of the river, a lonely titmouse twittered persistently. Two pink hazel grouses sat on a naked cherry tree branch over the old man's head. They fell as quiet as fungus-growth. Poloun's soul felt like the surface of a wide inlet during silent weather. A slight wind is enough to cause ripples to run and ruffle the mirror-smooth surface.

Poloun quietly stepped down to the river to refresh his tearing eyes with icy water. From the sky at his feet, up looked an old man with white hair sticking out in every direction. Fright and surprise registered in his wrinkled old larch tree-bark face and in his pale lusterless eyes. His chapped lips remained half opened as if something hard and invisible had stuck in his mouth.

Tif, the Season of the Road, was coming. The old man thought of the soft dents left by sable paws on fresh snow. Soon Poloun would go to the *taiga*. He would set up traps and ask Kurig to be generous. Poloun would ask for black sables only. He was never greedy, even when he fished with a crew. How many fish did they catch? No one could count.

A long time ago, Poloun's ancestors crossed Sakhalin following the *Kongre* (west) wind towards sunrise across the high mountain range, Arkvoval. They came out into a sunny valley, densely crowded with mighty poplars. Fast and icy streams of water united here and turned into a great river. Thousands of salmon spawned in numerous *taiga* stretches. They called the newfound river *Tymi*—spawning river. Poloun's ancestors stayed at the Tymi because it was rich with fish. Nowadays, fish decreased with each year—that worried the old man of the Kevongun tribe.

The Russians taught Nyvkhs to dig the ground and to put potatoes in holes. Many Nyvkhs in the village slowly got accustomed to agriculture but Poloun remained a fisherman and a hunter. Like other Tymi Nyvkhs, he was reluctant to learn new skills. Only sometimes would he work on his small piece of land. It was always a surprise when he threw a potato in a hole in the beginning of summer and pulled out eighteen in the fall!

The older Poloun got, the more he meditated on his life. Lately, an incomprehensible tenderness towards any living thing grew in him. He stopped burying live puppies in snow. Now, after raising them, he gave them to his neighbors. Let there be more dogs.

During the spawning of salmon he came out to the river before sunrise and sat stooped over the shore for a long time. No one knew what pulled him down there or what occupied his mind; he couldn't explain to himself why he came to the spawning ground. Tenderly and sadly he looked at the fish and beams of that characteristic smile that all good souls share spread over his face.

In these times he was burnt by a thought that never left him: *Salmon might come no more!* It lifted him from the bench in his house where he spent most of his time. It pushed him outside where he wandered at loose ends. He was probably not the only one bothered by this thought. Not far from the old Nyvkh settlement Tlavo, Russians were putting together strange buildings. Somebody said that they hatched salmon eggs. Poloun never went there.

That summer, right before the salmon spawning season, the rumor spread through the village like fire in a dry forest: the most ancient Kevong had joined the Fisheries Patrol. It was incomprehensible! Why should a Nyvkh become a Fish Control Inspector? Is it his business what others fish? Nobody prohibits Nyvkhs to fish during *Iukola*. His relatives teased him. "Poloun probably cut up both his nets," they said, sucking on their pipes. But Poloun filled his scorched pipe with rough tobacco, inhaled and pretended not to hear. At first poachers tried everything to cajole the old man, but he hunted them coldly. They began to threaten to catch him somewhere and drown him. Poloun grinned only slightly in response.

Since the new Fisheries Patrol began scaring poachers off, fining them and bringing others to court, the spawning grounds calmed down and Poloun's soul felt more at ease. Even his walk became more buoyant.

This morning he was alert to something. He looked into the water and saw a pair of salmon. Every time Poloun saw fish spawning it transformed him. Even when his spirit was down he found himself squinting into a smile. He enjoyed the thought that he, an ancient Kevong, was guarding salmon offspring from bad people. Poloun walked a little up the river and stopped at a shallow stretch—a spawning ground. It boiled with salmon.

The old man bent over the water. Here was a huge swollen-belly female. Her left fin looked worn out. And the male had a crimson paunch on his side. How long did it take for them to come from the far ocean to Tymi's upper reaches? Nobody knew. All along the way walls of iron hooks, nets in the ocean and predator's teeth waited for them. Many of their brothers and sisters never made it to the furthest grounds but these had managed. Battered and wounded, they reached the place where they had to leave life after themselves. Poloun felt like petting each fish with his stiff hand. He had enough tenderness for all of them.

The female salmon barely floated, looking for a place to lay her eggs. From one side a long male salmon swam close but the one with the scarred belly grabbed at him with his huge mouth. Like an arrow, the long one stretched up stream. The scarred male returned to his female. Slowly she looked for the proper place. The male hurried her, poked her with his hook nose and tried to bite her. The female slipped away from his sharp teeth.

There she stopped, pressed herself against the pebbles and pumped the bottom with her fins. *She likes this place.* She hit the bottom with her tail. The stream pulled silt like dust. She dug a small hole, stopped and froze in place, her tail quivering nervously. And then the golden thread streamed into the hole! There were hundreds of eggs and the sun played in each of them. The water was saturated with resilient sunlight—the fish swimming in the sun.

Poloun's heart trembled—he could see the beginning of life! Here they were, thousands of future salmon! The male curled around impatiently, opening his mouth, warning and threatening other males. Finally, the female wagged her tail listlessly and moved aside. The male rapidly took her position. White and murky clouds covered the sparkling eggs. Then the male began to hit the bottom with his tail, carefully hiding the hole, the cradle of his offspring.

All around, hundreds of similar pairs committed this act of continuing their kind. Afterwards, they floated over the hills of pebbles, guarding them, falling apart and dying. The stream carried their flaccid bodies to shore.

Poloun backed up, quietly moved away from the spawning ground and headed further up. A kilometer from here was another spawning ground. How are things going there?

From far away, his experienced ear caught the sounds of splashing water. Who was that? A bear? Poloun loaded his rifle. Fast but soft steps brought him to the bushes at the river's edge. He looked out cautiously.

A man in high rubber boots was standing in the water. Deftly, he hit salmon with a spear and threw them on the shore. There were a few dozen fish already lying there. Some of them had their bellies slit. Nearby stood a barrel.

"He's stocking eggs,"—this thought pierced Poloun's heart.

The man threw a spear into the fish floating by and lifted it trembling over the water. From a wound sparkling with bleeding tears, elastic eggs streamed down into the water.

Poloun recognized the poacher as Serioga, who once lived on the Tymi River. The man had been recruited to Sakhalin as a tractor driver. From Nyvkhs he learned how to salt salmon eggs. During the day Serioga worked in the field and at night he fished salmon and sold his game.

Poloun had already experienced an unpleasant stand-off with him. Last fall the old hunter was coming back from inspecting his area, and at this very spawning ground he unexpectedly ran into Serioga, who was stocking caviar the same way he did now. That time Serioga gave him a glass of vodka and made him promise not to tell anyone.

Feeling somebody staring at him Serioga suddenly turned around with fear in his eyes. He saw a stranger standing behind leaning on a rifle. His fear vanished in recognition and his eyes began to shine. "Ah, that is you, Poloun! Why are you staring at me?" Poloun didn't move and Serioga stopped smiling. Holding his attention, the poacher slowly came to shore.

"Come over here," Serioga's voice broke. Poloun did not move. "Come on, come over here, come to me! Morning is cold . . . but I have something to warm us up." The poacher smiled rapaciously and put his long knife covered with salmon blood in front of him.

"Here's what," Poloun spoke carefully. "Get out of here! And don't think of coming back! If I see you stepping on this ground, I will kill you! I will track you like a bear and kill you. No thieves get away from me. Leave!"

That was the last case of poachers that year. It became quiet at every spawning ground.

When the spawning season ended, Poloun's relatives couldn't recognize the old Kevong. He became sociable. He visited his neighbors. Poloun looked younger and even his back straightened. It seemed like his gnawing thoughts were forgotten.

The Season of the Road passed. Winter stepped into its rights. Many hunters had already turned in their fur. Poloun had just finished his preparations for hunting. He wanted to hurry to the *taiga!* There, ancient centuries-old pine trees with snow collars withstand the strong winds which scarcely penetrate the dense forest. There, cautious sables leave soft paw prints on the fresh snow.

The old man's wide, flexible hunter's skis with ringed seal fur on the bottoms slid easily over the crumbly snow. Poloun came to a large lake, connected to the Tymi River by a channel. To avoid a long detour, the hunter decided to cross the lake. He took his skis off, tied them with a rope and dragged them behind. At the shore frozen water formed several layers of ice. Further out the ice was clear. One could see islands of algae on the yellow bottom.

Suddenly something wiggled under the ice. It was alive and frightening. A tremor ran through Poloun's body. His hair reared and lifted his hat. Who was that, moving at the bottom like a shadow? Was it a water ghost who watched for him? The old man squinted his little round eyes intensely in an effort to see who was there.

Large and dark, it came closer and closer. Soon it gained the shape of a fish. It was a huge hunchback male salmon with crimson-brown stripes on his sides. Slowly, in deep meditation, he floated right under the old man's feet. Poloun bent down on his knees and began to examine the fish.

Strange! All the salmon finished laying eggs a long time ago and died. But this one was alive. His scarred sides were evidence of a difficult route from the ocean to the upper reaches of the river. His gills had faded, worn out. Like a shaggy beard, green algae clung to them.

"Salmon didn't shoot his milt," the old man thought. "He didn't leave offspring after him, and *Kowrne* punished him with a long and lonely useless life. And with his scary look he will startle the other fish of the lake."

Poloun felt sorry for the salmon. He would stop this poor fish from suffering. But how to do it? There was a thick layer of ice between the man and the fish. The old man's eyes clouded; all his life he lived alone.

"So why have you remained unmarried?" the old man asked the salmon.

The motionless eyes of the fish refracted through water and ice, growing bigger and bigger. Now the old man clearly saw the two huge fish eyes and in them—a ghostly reproach.

V

A Changing Countryside

Russia is comprised by and large of its countryside, the *derevnia*. Formed of the southern steppes, the central and northern forest zone, and the endless stretches of Siberian taiga that begin east of the Urals, the land has been seen for centuries as the repository of Russia's spiritual values, a place with enormous emotional resonance for those who live on it. The excerpts that appear in this section have been chosen to give the reader a sense of some of the complex and divergent responses Russians and foreigners alike have had to the land and its changing political and social vistas in the nineteenth and twentieth centuries.

What does the countryside mean for Russians? Because so much of Russian life has traditionally centered on agriculture, the land occupied a special place not only in the culture of the everyday but in people's belief systems. From earliest times the land that Russians cultivated was seen as the *mat' syra zemlia*, "the damp mother earth," a term evocative of fertility. And yet the early Russians who lived on the edge of the steppe in the area that is now Ukraine and southern Russia also saw the land outside their walled cities as a place unknown and forbidding. Intersected by rivers, it was a vast, undulating plain with no natural system of defense to protect those who lived on it from the periodic incursions of the nomads, and thus became virtually synonymous with the faceless, unknown people who swept across it. Even as the center of Russian life moved north with Moscow's ascendancy, the steppe and the open field (*chistoe pole*) became sustaining images for Russians over the centuries. As the threat from the nomadic hordes subsided, the spaces of the steppe acquired a different symbolic hue. The nineteenth-century poet Fyodor Tiutchev and the twentieth-century philosopher Nikolai Berdiaev both compared Russia's soul to its limitless geographical expanse, difficult to contain. Berdiaev even went so far as to suggest that the broad expanse of the steppe had formed the essence of Russian philosophical thought, more adept at tackling religious and existential questions than the pure logic of the Greeks and Western rationalism. The Russian writer Ivan Bunin wrote, "I

Suzdal', Russia, 1991. Courtesy of Nancy Ries.

was born and grew up in an open field," underscoring the steppe as a place of unfettered freedom that acquired even deeper symbolic and emotional resonance as the controls and constraints tightened in periods of despotism in Russian history. Others, such as Anton Chekhov, saw it differently. His story "The Steppe" recounts a journey across the terrain that reverberates with the endless boredom of the land and the lives of those destined to live upon it.

Over the centuries the attention of writers and reformers increasingly became focused on the daily lives of those in Russia's countryside. By the second half of the seventeenth century serfdom had become fully entrenched as an economic and social institution. It was the culmination of mounting peasant indebtedness and impoverishment and arose alongside the growth of political absolutism and the restrictions placed on the free movement of the peasantry. It was a system that sat uneasily on Russia's shoulders. Discontent on the part of the peasantry was such that peasants, both individually and collectively, had begun fleeing their lords' estates already in the seventeenth century. Some fled to neighboring estates where life was sometimes marginally better, sometimes worse; some fled much farther, to the Ural Mountains, to Siberia, and in some cases west to Poland. Discontent also took the form of sporadic uprisings throughout the seventeenth and eighteenth centuries. Two of the most spectacular were those led by Stenka Razin in 1670–71 and later, under Catherine II, by Emelian Pugachev in 1773–74. A Don Cossack, Pugachev staged a mass uprising in which he promised the peasants complete emancipation and their own land and incited them to put to death the nobles who had so destroyed their livelihood. The uprising was finally quelled, but not without consequences. Catherine vowed that she would never allow anything like it to happen again and recanted on many of the liberal reforms that had initially characterized her reign. But even as she reinstated the more restrictive laws, the push toward reform increased from other directions. In 1790 Aleksandr Radishchev, born into nobility and having studied in Germany, published his *Journey from St. Petersburg to Moscow*. Deeply influenced by the European Enlightenment, Radishchev was unsparing in his criticism of the institution of serfdom and argued that it was not only morally indefensible but economically unprofitable. Incensed over the book, Catherine II had him sentenced to ten years in Siberia, a sentence reduced once her successor assumed power.

Radishchev's *Journey* presaged the growing respect of the educated classes for the peasantry. The gulf dividing the classes was enormous: land and privilege on the one hand, destitution and ignorance on the other. Partly in reaction to the Enlightenment and partly to the Slavophiles who saw the strength of Russia in its religion and its peasantry, Russia's educated classes gradually began to view the peasantry as something more than faceless masses. In literature and memoirs of nineteenth-century Russia we read of peasant women used as wet nurses by the gentry, and estate owners hunting with their serfs, as Turgenev's narrator does in *Sportsman's Sketches*. Both were images through which the gentry attempted to purge their own guilt over the economic institution they had inherited and to bridge the gulf that divided them from the people whose lives they controlled. But was that gulf bridgeable? Was it possible for the nobility and the gentry to know the peasants? Attempts were made in a variety of venues. In the early nineteenth century the painter Aleksei Venetsianov began to paint the peasants in Tver'. He focused on those features that underscored their life of hardship and toil and was the first artist to force the Russian public to look directly at the peasant as a human being. Overly idealized, perhaps overly sentimental, Venetsianov's paintings nevertheless opened a window onto peasant life that would influence the group of artists known as the *Peredvizhniki*, or Wanderers, formed in 1870, nine years after Aleksandr II signed the declaration emancipating the serfs. Unlike Venetsianov they saw their art as having a moral mission. Painters such as Il'ia Repin traveled from St. Petersburg out to the Volga, where he painted his famous *Volga Barge Haulers* in 1873. Who are these men in the painting? A former priest, a soldier, an icon painter—all had been arrested on various charges and were now doing the work of animals. The men were influenced by local superstition, which had it that once a person's image was represented on paper one's soul was no longer one's own and became the property of the devil,[1] so before painting them Repin spent time with them and got to know them a bit in order to ease their suspicions about what he was doing. On Repin's canvas the barge haulers become something more than beasts of burden or downtrodden figures miserably used by others. Along with an image of impossible suffering, Repin painted into these men a strength and nobility of character mixed with the potential to throw off the chains of their own enslavement.

In the sphere of music as well, composers were turning to traditional Russian rural life for their themes and in some cases for their melodies. In Petersburg the group of composers known as the Mighty Five or the Mighty Handful (*Moguchaia kuchka*) was formed under the leadership of Mily Balakirev in the 1860s. Among its members Aleksandr Borodin, Nikolai Rimsky-Korsakov, and Modest Musorgsky reached for Russian themes and incorporated into their compositions the melodies of the people and the stories from folklore. They attempted to preserve the tonal aspects of the Russian folk song, the Orthodox chants, and the rhythms of the dances they had heard. Musorgsky in particular was deeply committed to the national theme in music, but for him the act of reaching back into Russia's history and into Russia's countryside was less politically motivated than it was a function of his aesthetic drive. In this he differed enormously from the Peredvizhniki, who saw in art a moral and a social commitment to the lives of those they depicted on their canvases.

By the time the serfs were freed, the reformist movement in Russia that had characterized the first half of the century gave way to more radical leanings that manifested in Russia's Populist movement. Made up of young, educated classes from the cities, many were driven by the guilt of privilege and the desire to separate themselves from their parents' generation to go out into the countryside and live among the peasantry. Their motivations were mixed; some went to help improve the lot of the people; others were driven by a spiritual yearning to find value in their life by living among a group of people who seemed to have an authentic grasp of what was truly meaningful. They believed moreover that the peasant commune represented an egalitarian way of life that would form the basis of socialism in Russia. They were convinced that the answer to many of Russia's social and economic problems lay in the commune, the *obshchina* and the *mir,* a form of collective enterprise that they hoped would lead Russia to a more egalitarian social system. They were firm in their conviction that Russia should not follow the lead of the industrialized West, where peasants had become urbanized and slaves to machines. For them this was nothing more than the substitution of one form of enslavement for another. Instead they wanted to improve the material lot of the peasantry by rescuing them from the humiliation of poverty, disease, and starvation. They wanted to do it, however, in a way that would capitalize on the social organization of the village commune and the village way of life. Their philosophy was basically a balance between two forces: reliance on knowledge from the outside as a way of ameliorating conditions, and reliance on what the peasants themselves could teach the more privileged classes about values and learning how to live. Among those who went to the people during this time was the economist and journalist V. V. Bervi, who wrote this about Russia's peasantry:

> I have carried out experiments and communicated great ideas formulated by European science to people from the peasantry and the gentry and to my no small surprise, the peasants repeatedly grasped what was expressed in language they could understand more profoundly and quickly. Such an observation may seem partial and paradoxical, but it is confirmed by very significant data; most of what has been done in Siberia to make it a better place to live has been done by people from the peasantry, people who are not only uneducated but even illiterate; people who were considered the most advanced in Russia have been unable to compete with the illiterate intelligentsia of the region. The majority of the most adventurous and famous owners of gold-mines and factory-owners in Siberia belong to the peasantry and have emanated from the lower strata of society; the people who are the spirit of the shipping companies, which have again been set up in Siberia, include in their number people of the lowest origin who have received no education; the most famous mechanic and builder of distilleries in Siberia is a person who cannot read or write Russian.[2]

Many of these populist ideals were reflected in the life and works of Leo Tolstoy, for whom the peasant was the incarnation of the values of simplicity and truth that one loses as one leaves the land for the city. Tolstoy founded schools on his estate in an effort to educate the peasants. Much of his work to improve their conditions was grounded in the philosophy that he spent much of his life working through in his novels. "Become who you are" was one of his most famous moral dictums. We are born good, and can reconnect with that goodness only by leaving behind the false values of the city, of man's political, ecclesiastical, and social institutions, and returning to the land and the values held by the peasantry. There was a part of Tolstoy that wanted to be a peasant, and later in life he took to wearing peasant dress on his estate,

Tolstoy at his country estate, Yasnaia Poliana. Courtesy of Adele Barker, personal collection.

walking around in bast (rope) shoes and a peasant cassock and wearing a long beard. But as much as he derided the life of privilege from which he came (he was able to trace his family's noble lineage back to the thirteenth century), his inability entirely to separate himself from his roots formed one of the conflicts that lies at the heart of his writing, as it did of his life.

Russia's revolutionaries were not impervious to populist dreams. For the early Bolsheviks, the state, in line with Marx's vision, was the embodiment of evil, coercion, and inequality. Eliminating it would allow those who made the revolution to tap into a way of life that had remained stable and uncorrupted for centuries. The utopian dream for the revolutionaries was that Russia's peasantry would march into the future hand in hand with the newly created proletariat. History, as we now know, had something else in store. However, throughout the twentieth century the countryside and the people who lived on it continued to tug at the moral imagination of Soviet writers. Aleksandr Solzhenitsyn as well as the country school of writers (*derevenshchiki*) popular in the 1960s were powerfully drawn to rural Russia and those who lived close to the land. Like Vladimir Soloukhin, a member of this group, they looked with romantic longing at a life that had remained spiritually authentic in the face of increasing urbanization and industrialization. Their search was also the classic search for the Russian soul at a time of increasing and constricting Sovietization. It was there in the countryside among its people that the soul of the real Russia lay.

Notes

1. Elizabeth Kridl Valkenier, *Ilya Repin and the World of Russian Art* (New York: Columbia University Press, 1990), 39.
2. Quoted in *A Documentary History of Russian Thought from the Enlightenment to Marxism*, translated and edited by W. J. Leatherbarrow and D. C. Offord (Dana Point, Calif.: Ardis, 1987), 253.

The Dacha (1837)

Faddei Bulgarin

To the Westerner the word "dacha" conjures up images of splendid country homes to which Russia's prerevolutionary nobility repaired. To some extent the history of the dacha, from the Russian verb dat', "to give," bears this out. Dachas first came into being in the eighteenth century under Catherine the Great as a reward for services rendered to the state. However, over the centuries the summer house, the place to which one could retreat, came to be enjoyed by Russians of all classes. While the elite still retained their luxurious country dwellings, families with more modest means built simple wooden structures, often resembling huts, from whatever they could scrounge together. The point for Russians has traditionally been not so much the dacha itself as the fact of being in the country, tilling the soil, planting one's garden, and hunting mushrooms in the nearby forest. The countryside and one's dacha, no matter how modest, became a place of repose and, increasingly in Soviet times, of retreat from the polluted cities, where most Russians were consigned to live in standardized, cramped, high-rise housing.

During the Soviet era, in an odd reflection of prerevolutionary life, dachas continued to be given as a sinecure to those who served the state. Sometimes workers would receive the land free of charge and then build their own dachas from whatever materials they could find. Others, such as the state's official writers, who ground out literature faithful to the Party line, were rewarded for their loyalty with the gift outright of these country homes. It was in this way that dacha settlements came into being. Some, such as Peredelkino outside of Moscow, were designed specifically for writers and artists. Notable also is the Test Pilots dacha village twenty-five miles north of Moscow that was built after the Second World War, when Stalin asked three Soviet airmen who had been shot down by the Nazis outside of Moscow what he could do for them. They asked to be able to build dachas on the spot where they fell and survived.

These days the qualification for having one's own dacha is no longer Party loyalty but wealth. Since the collapse of the Soviet Union in 1991, the class of people known as New Russians who have become fabulously wealthy almost overnight have built palatial dachas, replacing the traditional wood construction with multistory brick *edifices secluded behind high walls. The older residents of the dacha settlements, who live in modest dachas resembling small cabins, view these new arrivals with their fancy cars and freewheeling spending as both an aberration and an insult to the original intent behind their communities. Once a place of retreat to the simple rural life, the dacha has become, in the eyes of these older residents, an insidious status symbol for those with money to flaunt. Yet some things have changed little since the nineteenth century. Just as Faddei Bulgarin notes the impossibility of finding anyone at work in the cities in the summer months, Russians during July and August are still* na dache, *at the dacha.*

Out-of-town houses, or *dachas,* are barometers of a nation's strength, its prosperity, its enlightenment, its civilization and its communal life. I mean it, I'm not joking! Lofty towers, enormous chambers, and magnificent works of art very often indicate the opposite. The ancient Romans began building their out-of-town houses, or *villas,* after Rome had made itself master of the known world and no longer feared its enemies. Out-of-town houses disappeared during the migration of peoples and the period of chivalry, when town-dwellers shut themselves away behind high walls and embrasures. The commanders of the victorious tribes locked themselves up in their castles. For as long as brute physical force ruled in Europe, until such time as there was security for trade, industry, and the liberal arts, there were no out-of-town houses. The savage comrades-in-arms of Odoacer, Gaiseric, Theodoric, and Attila burned down and pillaged out-of-town houses. The flowering hedges of gardens would not have protected a fair maiden from the knights of the middle ages. Eventually, when the invention of gunpowder and printing disarmed the turbulent barbarians and affirmed the idea of property rights, town-dwellers once more began to move out from behind their moats and crenellated walls. Villas, or dachas, began once again to enhance the delightful vicinities of Italian towns. The Italian taste for out-of-town houses was taken over by the sovereigns and wealthy nobility of Germany and France. Later on it crossed into England. But before the end of the eighteenth century it was only rulers, sovereign princes, grandees and wealthy men of the first order who lived in dachas or out-of-town houses. The nobility would leave town to spend the summer on their estates; civil servants would promenade in the public gardens or drive out of town with their families for a breath of fresh air; merchants and tradesman did not dare to move out of their shops, offices, or workshops. In short, town-dwellers spent winter and summer inside their town, within the limits, and would only take a jaunt outside town on holidays in good weather. We can still remember the last of when it used to be like this!

In Russia the building of dachas began to expand during the reign of

The diver at his
dacha. Courtesy
of Rick Hibberd.

The nineteenth-century dacha. Courtesy of the Hoover Institution, Boris Konstantinovich
Shebeko photographs [91054, Envelope A, Shebeko 215], Hoover Institution Archives.

Empress Catherine the Great, along with the upsurge of enlightenment. The fashionable place was the Peterhof road. The islands were empty; every one of them belonged to a particular person and there was only one dacha apiece. Where now there are dachas in their thousands, there used to be only four: one on Elagin Island, one on Krestovskii Island, one on Kamennyi Island, and the Stroganov dacha on the Petersburg Side. On the Peterhof road too there used to be very few dachas, and those that there were belonged to the premier grandees of Catherine's court or to the premier bankers. In Strelnaia and from Strelna Estate to Peterhof there was not a single dacha even in my time. To say of someone that *they live at their dacha* meant the same as saying that they were *rich, powerful, and eminent.* Some people who had acquired wealth or risen in rank preferred not to live at a dacha so as to avoid giving rise to gossip, slander, or envy. I can remember all this very well! At a dinner once I heard a Privy Councilor who had an income of something like forty thousand say (this was about thirty-five years ago): "What kind of grandee am I to go and live at a dacha?" And these days? These days, a friend of mine who is the Assistant Head of a government department lives at his dacha, and so does my tailor! On holidays almost all the stallholders in the city trading arcades take the air at the dachas of their owners. You can die a dozen times before finding your doctor somewhere at a dacha or getting him to drive in from his dacha. In summer don't even try looking for a merchant in his store, a chemist in his shop, a German tradesman in his workshop, a stationer in his office! They'll all be at the dacha!

What does this mean? The same as it does everywhere and in everything— much that is good but a bit that is bad. It's nice, cheerful, pleasant, and healthy to breathe fresh air, to get away from the choking fumes of the city, the dust, and the sun's glare on paved roads. For children especially, to live at a dacha is the same as a health cure, and for those at the age of gout in the hand and foot it's the same as taking a trip to the waters. A love of nature, trees, and flowers indicates a certain degree of cultivation, but the possibility of having *two* houses or apartments is an indication of prosperity. That is all true, with minor exceptions. But apart from that, the taste for dachas has brought into being a new city: *summer Petersburg.* Waste land and marshes have been settled and beautified with the most charming little houses and gardens. As a result the climate has become healthier, and a large number of workers and crafts-men have made money. The number of cabdrivers and carriers has grown improbably large. Whole legions of gardeners and caretakers have sprung into being, and consequently the population has increased.

All this is no bad thing for the *winter city* either, because while the masters are living at their dachas, the courtyards and apartments are being aired out and cleaned, and the male and female servants who stay on in the city can have a sit in their masters' armchairs and on their sofas, take a peek in the lady's pier-glass, drink coffee in their sitting room and play childish card games on malachite tables. All this at least is harmless. What's bad is that when people move to the dacha not for their health and not for the air, but in order not to be left behind in the empty city, that is, when out of bright, dry, and clean rooms they move into a cramped little house in the middle of a swamp for no other reason than to see people and be seen themselves. In the middle of the day it's too hot, in the morning you feel sleepy and can't be bothered getting dressed, and consequently you can only go out in the evening. It would be absurd if *without extreme need* you were to wrap yourself up in a cloak and hide the extremely charming cut of your dress and your fashionable sleeves, or ruin your hairstyle with a hat, and so it's much better to take your stroll just in your frock, with a parasol in your hand and bareheaded. But by this time the sun is setting and casting over *summer Petersburg* a dense canopy woven from mist and damp—the residue of spring and the harbinger of autumn. Take a look at the barometer and the thermometer. The mercury in them has risen high and is holding, because the metal or wood has not yet cooled! How warm it is—according to the thermometer! Meanwhile, though, you've got the shivers, the dampness gets on your chest, and the delicate sole of your shoe cannot withstand the moisture rising invisibly from the earth. Eventually you put on a summer jerkin or mantle. This suits you well—even very well, but then again it won't protect you from catching cold! Even in our frock-coats of stout cloth and our capes, we men can feel it. Esteemed Mr. Imzen, put up more of your Iceland moss in various appropriate guises! Good Mr. Wallenstein, sharpen your dental instruments and brew up your dental tinctures! And you, exemplar of William Tell's contemporaries, Mr. Kunz the honest Swiss, prepare your chocolate with acorns and powdered egg! For the pleasures of the dacha one will have to pay with one's health—or with one's teeth. But who worries about their health these days? Let us instead take a look at what's bad in respect of morals, and begin with the main thing.

I bow my head before medicine and medical men! The premier world science is Medicine; the most important personage in civil society is the medical man or doctor. But what kind of doctor? One who is skillful, loves his fellow man, and sacrifices himself for the good of mankind and the consolation of families. I remain silent about the living, but from among the dead I cite as my example Loder of Moscow. My question is: should a doctor, who has taken upon himself an extensive practice, live at a dacha many miles away from the city? No, a hundred times no! If you have dedicated yourself to humanity, then be a sentry, and do not abandon your post! Everyone who consults you should know where you spend every hour of your twenty-four, where you take lunch, where dinner, where you do business and where you play whist. But no running away to the woods, no hiding away at dachas! When you began your studies of Medicine, you knew what was in store for you! Eternal labor, eternal work—and the blessings of humanity. You may not, like the office worker, take Sundays off. There is work for you even on Easter Day, and the higher the holiday, the more diligent you should be *for Him who was crucified for our sake.* And as for you, highly esteemed Mr. Civil Servant, confess—does not your dacha take up a great deal of your time? Just think how many benefits fate has granted you in return for *your time!* You have them all before you! What's more, if you have no substance and your salary is insufficient, how will you pay for your dacha? Here my tongue cleaves to my throat! My dear highly re-spected Merchants, and you, esteemed German caretakers of dachas, I humbly implore your pardon, but if I should happen to wander into your dacha, please do not chase me out of your garden and your park. I am not a rich man, but I live in a rented apartment, I wear a tail coat and high boots, I drink the wine of the grape, tea, and coffee, and therefore I am your *hireling.* You do not read my books, but I must pay you for everything in ready cash, and I am acutely aware of the reasons why your prices for accommodation, for all items of luxury and products of the skilled trades keep on rising incessantly! You people need to *live at the dacha,* set yourself up at the dacha, maintain the dacha, travel to the dacha, and receive your friends at the dacha, and for this it is I who must pay, I and all of us mortals, your *hirelings!*

The dachas of St Petersburg have added at least one quarter to the price of all goods, apartments, and the labor of tradesmen, and have taken at least *two months* off our business calendar. At the dacha one eats more, sleeps more, relaxes more—and works less. This is as true as twice two makes four. Dachas have made it so the book trade is completely inactive from spring to autumn. When is there time to read at the dacha? You sleep in the morning, and in the heat of mid-day and the cold of evening there is whist. The ladies converse, because at the dacha one makes friends easily and often visits neighbors. In the winter one may not necessarily continue *a summer acquaintance,* for the two cities, the *summer* and the *winter,* have their own rights and customs. There can be no argument that dachas put several million extra rubles into circulation, but not everyone profits from this! Ask the people who live off money earned by heavy labor, and they will tell you what these dachas cost them, these dachas in which they don't live but for which they do pay. But after calculating the advantages and disadvantages, I declare myself *in favor of dachas*—and I wish you happiness at yours!

Translated by G. S. Smith

Work Done "Out of Respect" (1872–87)

Aleksandr Engelgardt

In 1871 a prominent chemist at St. Petersburg University, Aleksandr Engelgardt, relocated to the country. He had no choice: the government had sentenced him to internal exile for a period of fifteen years for political activity at his institute. He settled on his family's estate in Smolensk province, set about the meticulous recording of agricultural and landholding practices, and sent his notes in the form of letters to one of the major journals of the day, Notes of the Fatherland.

Engelgardt's arrival in the provinces turned out to be fortuitous. Russia's peasants had been emancipated in 1861, an event that created a new yet fragile economic and social order in the countryside. While the peasants received land as part of the emancipation proclamation, the gentry simultaneously lost much of theirs as well as their centuries-old source of free labor. The question that was uppermost in everyone's mind, particularly in the cities, was how the Russian peasant and Russian agriculture in general would weather the transition. The gulf separating city and country had for centuries created and perpetuated images of the peasant as ennobled by his simplicity and his closeness to the land, or alternatively as representative of a Russia that was backward and ignorant. To his credit Engelgardt arrived with neither of these preconceptions but with a steady, scientific eye focused on recording what he saw with a view toward improving conditions among the rural population.

In "Work Done 'Out of Respect' " Engelgardt describes the labor peasants performed from time to time for the local gentry in the form of volunteering their services in the garden and the kitchen with no expectation of being compensated. The peasant economy in postemancipation Russia was still a subsistence economy, necessitating that this type of free labor be performed as a kind of insurance policy in the event of a poor harvest or damage to the gentry's property by peasant livestock. Thus if the need arose and the peasants had to count on the help or goodwill of the landowner, they already had insurance in place in the form of the work they had done voluntarily. It functioned as a form of payment up front in an economy not based on the exchange of money for work performed.

September. The Indian summer has arrived. The forest has blossomed into many colors. The leaves on the trees have become brittle and sound like autumn, though they have not yet fallen, as there has been no frost. The sky is gray, a light fall drizzle has set in, and if you catch a glimpse of the sun, it is masked by fog. It shines and warms poorly. It's damp out. Yet thank God for this, because if "the Indian summer is inclement—the fall will be dry." From day to day we wait for the frost. Here in the country we are always waiting for something; we wait for the first warm shower of spring and the first frost of fall and the first snowfall. Though we do not need the frost at all, without it there can be no fall. It is somehow unsettling without the frost; all think that fall cannot come without this evil. This year too much has gone well. Spring started during the first days of April, fall has not yet begun in September, and for five months there has been no frost. "Is this for the better?" grumbles "the old woman." "Now there is no frost, but later there will be enough! All according to God's will," she adds, remembering that it does no good to grumble. "All according to God's will, God is not without mercy, he is merciful, he knows better than us what it is all about."

But now the Indian summer has ended. The "rains have begun." Though fall has arrived according to the calendar, a genuine one has still not come. It is even rather boring. Finally at the Exaltation of the Cross a real frost arrived. Everything was battered during the night. I got up early. It was light, bright and cheerful. I looked out the window and everything was white. The sunflowers were drooping their heads in fatigue.

The leaves on the Indian cress, beans, and morning glories have blackened. Only the green peas and lupine still stand. After the frost the forest quickly shed its leaves: the linden and the aspen have been nipped by frost. It has even gotten the birch; the leaves have thus fallen. With every day the groves become brighter and brighter. The fallen leaf crunches underfoot. The summer birds have flown away and the winter ones have gathered together into flocks. The hare has begun to whiten. Around the house the first winter guests have appeared—titmice.

Once you get used to it, it's nice in the country even in the fall. The main thing is that everything is at ease.

The cattle have been brought in from the fields for the duration. The horses are at peace, as they can wander unencumbered wherever they want. The people are in a festive mood; the grain has grown well, and the hard field work is finished. The peasant is even now not without work, though the day is short and the night is long. He doesn't wear himself out as much with day work and has time to rest at night. The bread is fresh and familiar. From the kitchen gardens and barns come the notes of the joyful autumn wedding songs. The old women have already decided which bachelor is going to marry whom, and in their songs, according to their view, they yoke the names of the boy and girl whose time has come to be married this fall.

In the living quarters one senses that special smell that tells you it is fall, and when you enter a coach inn or a plain hut of a well-to-do peasant, priest or merchant—the smell of onions, peas and dill—permeates everything. One corner is heaped with onions and in the other, beans and Indian cress are ripening on frames. The whole floor is covered with corn and sunflowers. This past year we managed to grow all this. In the windows, on the tables and shelves flower and vegetable seeds and samples of hay, flax and grain are strewn about. On the walls hang fascicles of dill, caraway and parsley.

The vegetable gardens are now being harvested. Avdotya has completely forgotten about me. She is so occupied with the kitchen garden work and the flax (it is her responsibility to deseed, soak and ret the flax properly) that she has been remiss in serving me lunch. Each morning she rushes past me.

"Today, Aleksandr Nikolaevich, I will serve you cabbage soup with mutton."

"Anything else?"

"I will roast the mutton."

"Avdotya, if only you could prepare duck with mushrooms. All it is now is mutton and more mutton."

"As you wish," Avdotya begins to get angry, "you always ask for it at the wrong time. Today the women have gone to chop the cabbage, and you want duck. . . . The choice is yours, as you wish, only don't ask me about the gardening. Just as you wish, I will make the duck, only we will waste the cabbage. Only they baked the pies for nothing."

"All right, all right, roast the mutton! But don't forget to stuff it with garlic."

"I won't forget," Avdotya cheerfully replies and runs out into the dining hall, from where in a minute her resonant voice cries out, "You, girls, get the cabbage and I will turn the flax."

After about half an hour Avdotya runs up to me with two handfuls of flax.

"What kind of flax is that?"

"From Troshchenkovo. Yesterday I deseeded the flax. The fine flax hasn't retted enough, but the lush flax has. Please take a look for yourself."

"Let's take some."

"It is your decision, but in my opinion it is time to take it up. Any longer and it will spoil." Avdotya rushes into the garden, from where her voice can again be heard.

"You, girls, once you have taken in the cabbage, have some breakfast, then begin to cut it. I'm preparing lamb for Aleksandr Nikolaevich's lunch."

Harvesting flax, Perm region, 1910. Source: Library of Congress, Prints and Photographs Division, Prokudin-Gorskii Collection, LC-DIG-prokc-20587. Courtesy of Jean Swetchine.

Avdotya prepares the lunch, but her thoughts are far away in the peasant hut where they are chopping cabbage. When she serves me the meal, it is barely 11 o'clock in the morning. She doesn't wait until I have finished eating, but orders Savelicha to clean up. She rushes into the dining hall to regale the women with vodka and pies, since these women have come to gather the vegetables from the garden "out of respect."

During the harvest, Avdotya completely supplanted me, as though I were not the master. The harvest reached such a point that she brought the cabbage into the house. Once I slept in late and heard some sort of noise from behind the wall. They were dragging something, moving it across the room.

"What's that?" I asked Avdotya.

"We're going to chop the cabbage in the kitchen."

"Which cabbage?"

"The white cabbage. We're going to shred and chop the cabbage for you. Out in the dining room it is dirty; for you we need to do it a bit more cleanly. It occurred to me that we could chop the cabbage in the kitchen."

"And where am I supposed to go?"

"You can go out to the field for now, and in the evening you will be able to sit alone. It will be festive. The old women will play songs, and I invited the very best women singers. We will play 'The Drake.' "

"And will you sing, 'Let the rye stand in circles, then my wife reaps standing, not bending over,' " I laughed.

"We will sing that one, too." Avdotya agreed to everything, only that I not forbid them to shred the cabbage in the house. She so wanted everything to go well with the cabbage, and that it be up to the standards of other estates.

I, of course, allowed them to chop cabbage in the house. Avdotya took over all the rooms, and she even wanted to put some kind of a tub in my office, though I was able to keep her out of there. The evening was festive. In the two clean rooms Avdotya set the girls to shelling the beans and sorting out the onions. On Avdotya's side of the kitchen, they shredded and chopped cabbage. The old women and girls sang songs and finally, having finished with the cabbage, they began to dance. Avdotya gave orders and even her husband, the old-timer Ivan, didn't interfere in anything, since cabbage is women's business. Everything turned out well. They chopped and shredded two whole tubs of cabbage, which they were able to put in the kitchen. The next day I went out visiting and returned after several days. When I entered the room it was horrible; one could not breathe at all.

"Avdotya, why do the living quarters stink so much?"

"Lord have mercy!"

"You must agree, it is impossible to enter the house."

"I know nothing about it. There's nothing of the sort, it hardly smells of cabbage. The cabbage is beginning to sour, and the fermentation has begun. That's nothing."

The cabbage had really begun to sour.

The old women from two neighboring villages gathered all the garden vegetables "out of honor." Only the carrots did they gather "for slops."

Work done "out of respect" is done as a gift, for free. But, of course, you must treat them as guests—before anything you must serve them vodka. Having thought ahead about the cabbage chopping and beet cleaning, Avdotya asked the old women to come "help." No one refuses. Very early in the morning one or two old women come from every homestead. They drink vodka, bake pies, whip up a superior lunch and if there is something to make it from, without fail they produce a beef aspic. That is the first refreshment. These "participants in the work bee" work especially well, particularly the old women, since they won't work for a daily wage. Everyone does their best— they "distinguish" themselves, so to speak. Work is accompanied by laughter, jokes, merriment and songs. They work as though it were a joke, though, I repeat, they do it especially well, just as though they were at home. They don't call it working, but "helping." An old woman from a rich estate, especially now, will take on day work not for money, but "out of respect," "for help," "for a work bee." She will arrive and work hard with a good conscience, just as if she were the landowner. She works better than an old woman from a poor estate, because on a rich estate, under a good landlord, even the old women are orderly—they know how to do everything. They even have more strength since they have plenty to eat. You can't say that they are attracted by the vodka, since old women who do not drink vodka come to work. It happens even that they find out that there is some kind of work to do and come without being summoned. Of course, this all occurs because even now the peasant is dependent on the neighboring lord.[1] The peasant needs a little firewood, some meadow and pasture. Sometimes he needs to borrow a little cash, or perhaps he is forced to, or perhaps he needs to take council about something he will need, because we all walk under God. Suddenly someone may be summoned to court, God protect him! When the occasion presents itself, how is the peasant not to show respect to the lord? After all, in the village the same thing occurs: all come to the rich peasant's work bee "out of respect," for who knows who might need to ask a favor of him. I have noticed that the richer the village, the more prosperous and intelligent the peasants, and the more they try to establish good relations with the lord who is the nearest neighbor. The prosperous peasant is always polite, respectful and ready to perform any kind of petty service. What does it mean to him if he sends over his old woman for a day or two when the fieldwork is done? Of course, he himself won't take on the work cheaply. But if the price is right and the work profitable, then he takes it up, and will work very well.

Translated by Kenny Cargill

Note

1. [Trans.] Serfdom had been abolished by Aleksandr II in 1861, though, as Engelgardt explains, many peasants were far from being independent farmers.

The Mushroom Hunt (1890)

Sofya Kovalevskaya

In the seventeenth century an Englishman traveling in Russia declared of Russia's mushrooms that they were "the poor man's food, and the rich man's dainties." It is an insight often forgotten, as Russians, irrespective of class, both in prerevolutionary times and today, make their de rigueur expeditions into the forest to gather the mushrooms that have been so much a part of their culture and cuisine throughout the centuries. Enjoyed by all, they are also a barometer of class differences.

This excerpt is from Sofya Kovalevskaya's reminiscences of growing up in Russia in the mid-nineteenth century. Having already made a name for herself as one of the major mathematicians of her day, Kovalevskaya (1850–91) set about the task of writing her memoirs with a view to understanding how the events and people from her childhood formed the person she was to become.

Kovalevskaya's parents were wealthy landowners who lived on an estate in western Russia called Palibino. She describes with delight going out to collect mushrooms, an activity in which peasants and landowners alike participated. Poignantly she remarks, "Today was such a special day that class distinctions seemed not to exist," sensing that even this pastime was laced with social divisions. The peasants who were filling their baskets did so because they needed the fungi to survive, marinating, pickling, and storing what they gathered so that they could get through the winter and the next spring. Russia's nineteenth-century gentry, however, engaged in the same pastime less out of need than out of love for the activity.

During the twentieth century mushroom gathering similarly reflected the changing political and historical tides. During the Siege of Leningrad in the Second World War, the gathering of mushrooms and other edible plants saved many from starvation. In better times workers from factories and institutes were organized into mass mushroom-hunting brigades that underscored the Party's insistence on culture for the masses. Finally, in a grim reminder of how the peasantry lived for centuries, many Russians in the immediate aftermath of the Soviet Union's collapse in 1991 resorted to eating what they could collect from the forest or grow on communal plots. At a time of rampant inflation, the one thing that remained affordable was forest mushrooms.

The locale of our estate was very wild but more pictorial than most of the regions of Russia's central zone. Vitebsk province is renowned for its vast conifer forests and its numerous large and beautiful lakes. The last spurs of the Valdai Hills pass through parts of it, so that there are no such immense plains as in central Russia. On the contrary, the entire landscape has a rolling, undulating character.

. . . .

In summer there was no end to the different kinds of berries. First to appear would be the wild strawberries which, it is true, ripen a bit later in the woods than in the fields, but then are much juicier and more fragrant. Almost before the strawberries were gone the bilberries would make their appearance, and then the stone-fruit, the raspberries, the cranberries.

And then, before you realized it, the nuts would be ripening, and after that the mushroom harvest would begin. Even in summer one might find a good many brown-caps and orange-caps, but autumn was the real season for the "milkies," the "rusties," and the prized "whites."

In all the villages round about, a kind of frenzy would come over the women, the young girls and even the children. They couldn't be pried out of the forest by force. They would set off in a throng at daybreak with their bowls, their woven and bast baskets, and not come home until late in the evening.

And how greedy they were! No matter how big a crop they managed to reap from the forest that day, it was never enough. The next day they'd be lured back at the first gleam of light. All their thoughts were focused on gathering mushrooms; for the sake of mushrooms all of them were ready to neglect their work, both at home and in the fields.

Expeditions into the forest were undertaken in our house as well, sometimes in summer at strawberry time, sometimes in fall during the mushroom season. The entire household took part with the sole exception of the master and the mistress, neither of whom cared for rustic pleasures of that sort.

All the arrangements were made the night before. With the first rays of the rising sun the next morning, two or three wagons would already be approaching the porch. Inside the house a merry, festive bustle was beginning. The maids scurried back and forth, rushed about carrying supplies and stowing them inside the wagons: plates, a samovar, various provisions such as tea, sugar, bowls filled with the meat turnovers and cheese tarts called *pirozhki* and *vatrushki,* baked by the cook on the previous day. On the top of the heap they threw the empty baskets and containers intended for the mushroom gathering.

The children, roused from their beds at this unaccustomed hour, with sleepy faces which had just been rubbed bright pink by a wet sponge, were also running about. In their glee they didn't know what to do first, grabbed at everything, interfered with everybody and invariably managed to get under everyone's feet.

The kennel dogs were no less interested in the forthcoming excursion. They had been in a state of nervous excitement since early morning and had been running under people's legs, peering into their faces, yawning long and loud. Finally, exhausted with excitement, they sprawled in the courtyard in front of the porch, but their entire posture expressed strained expectation: they watched the whole to-do with uneasy stares, ready to jump up and tear away at the first signal. Every fiber of their canine being was now concentrated on a single aim—not to let the masters go off and leave them behind!

Now at long last the preparations were finished. Helter-skelter into the carts piled the governess, the tutor, the children, a dozen or so housemaids, the gardener, two or three of the menservants, and also perhaps five or so of the servants' children. The whole servant body was wrought up with excitement. Everyone wanted to take part in the festive outing. At the very last moment, when the carts were on the point of moving off, the scullery maid's little daughter, five-year-old Aksyutka, came running up and raised such a racket when she saw her mother going away and leaving her behind, that she too had to be put into the cart.

. . . .

By now it was about 6 A.M. How strange! On ordinary days we'd be asleep in bed at this hour, but today, just think of all the things that had happened already! No more time to dawdle. Our whole company scattered through the forest, calling back and forth and hallooing from time to time, so as not to separate too widely and get lost.

Which one of us would gather the most mushrooms? This was the question now agitating everyone. Each burned with ambition. It seemed to me at that moment that nothing in the world was more important than filling up my basket as fast as possible. "God!" I thought (involuntarily putting a great deal of fervor into my prayer), "please send me lots and lots of mushrooms!"

Catching a glimpse of an orange or a blackish-brown cap from a distance, I raced to the spot as fast as my legs would carry me, so that no one would snatch my find away. But there were so many disappointments! Now I mistook a dry leaf for a mushroom; then I suddenly spied the firm beige cap of a "white" rising shyly from its bed of moss. I seized it, thrilled. But lo and behold, from underneath it was not solid white, but deeply furrowed gills. So there it was—nothing but an ordinary baby toadstool which from above had assumed the deceitful look of a "white"!

But the most upsetting thing of all to me was walking past a place in complete obliviousness while sharp-eyed Feklusha would snatch up a beautiful mushroom practically from under my nose. That horrid Feklusha—she could sniff out by instinct where the mushrooms were, she simply dug them up from under the earth. Her basket was already heaped to the brim. And what's more, almost all of her mushrooms were "whites" and "rusties." Some orange-caps, perhaps—just a few. But as for the "foxies," the "butters" and the "bitters"—she didn't bother with those at all.

And such lovely mushrooms she had! Choice, every last one: small, clean, pretty—you could eat them raw! Whereas my basket was still only half full, and so many of those were big, shriveled old caps that I was ashamed to show them to anybody.

At three o'clock there was another break. The coachman lit a campfire in the clearing where the unharnessed horses were grazing. A lackey ran to the nearby stream to fill the carafes with water. The maids spread a tablecloth on the grass, started the samovar going, arranged the dishes and plates. The masters sat down in a separate group, while the servants respectfully placed themselves a slight distance away.

But this division lasted no more than the first fifteen minutes. Today was such a special day that class distinctions seemed not to exist. Everybody was possessed by the same all-consuming interest: mushrooms. Therefore the company soon intermingled again. They all wanted to brag about their loot and to see what the rest had turned up. And besides, they had so many things to tell each other now. Each had had his own adventures: one had startled a hare, another discovered a badger's burrow, a third almost stepped on a snake.

After eating and resting for a while, they went back for more mushrooms. But the first ardor had evaporated by then. The tired feet dragged along laboriously. The big basket, even though it now held only a few mushrooms, had suddenly grown so heavy that it weighed on the arm. The inflamed eyes refused to function. Either they imagined mushrooms in places where there were none, or they passed right over a genuine mushroom without seeing it at all.

By now I no longer cared whether I would have a basketful or not. But then I became far more sensitive to other forest impressions. The sun was already close to setting. Its slanting rays glided between the naked trunks and tinted them the color of brick. The little forest lake, set into perfectly flat banks, was so unnaturally calm and motionless that it seemed enchanted. The water in it was very dark, almost black except for one bright crimson spot that glowed like a blood-red stain.

Time to go home. The whole company congregated at the wagons once again. During the day they had all been so engrossed, each in his own affairs, that no one paid attention to the others. But now they looked each other over and burst out laughing. Goodness only knows what they looked like! In the course of this day spent in the open air, they had all felt the effects of the sun. All the faces were windburned and flaming. Their hair was disheveled, their clothes were in indescribable disorder. Both mistresses and maids had put on their oldest dresses, of course (the ones not worth saving), for their excursion into the forest—in the morning all that hadn't seemed to matter.

But now they were a ludicrous sight. One girl had lost her shoes in the woods. On another, what had once been a skirt now hung on her in tatters. The headgear was the most fantastic of all. One of the girls had thrust a big cluster of bright red rowanberries into her unkempt black braids; another had fashioned herself a kind of helmet from fern foliage; a third had pushed a stick through a monstrous death's-cap mushroom and was holding it over herself like an umbrella.

I had wound a flexible branch of forest hops around myself. Its yellow-green cones had become entangled with my tousled brown hair, which tumbled down to my shoulders and gave me the look of a little Bacchante. My cheeks were flaming, my eyes sparkled.

"Hail to Her Majesty, Queen of the Gypsies!" said my brother Fedya, bending his knee before me in mockery.

The governess also had to admit with a sigh that I really did look more like a gypsy girl than a well-brought-up young lady. But if the governess had only known how much I would have given at that moment to be transformed into a real gypsy! That day in the forest had awakened in me so many wild, nomadic instincts. I wanted never to have to go home again; I wanted to spend the rest of my life in that lovely, marvelous forest.

Progress and Prosperity (1912)

Sir Donald Mackenzie Wallace

A British editor and foreign correspondent for The London Times, *Donald Macken-zie Wallace lived in Russia between 1870 and 1876, traveling extensively and making notes on what he saw for his book* Russia, *published in 1877. Subsequently he returned for shorter stays between 1889 and 1896, and served as Tsar Nicholas's chief political officer on his tour of India.*

Wallace was fascinated by Russia and particularly by the situation of the post-emancipation peasantry in the rural areas. He traveled throughout the countryside, observing everything from the quality of the land and agricultural techniques to peasants' work habits. At one point he attached himself to a traveling section of the Agricultural Commission and helped to collect materials on peasant life along the Volga. The excerpt from his book that appears here points to the complicated and sometimes contradictory information regarding the effects of emancipation on peas-ant life in central Russia at the end of the nineteenth century and the beginning of the twentieth.

In beginning my researches in this interesting field of inquiry, I had no ade-quate conception of the difficulties awaiting me. I imagined that I had merely to question intelligent, competent men who had had abundant opportunities of observation, and to criticise and boil down the information collected; but when I put this method of investigation to the test of experience it proved unsatisfactory. Very soon I came to perceive that my authorities were very far from being impartial observers. Most of them were evidently suffering from shattered illusions. They had expected that the Emancipation would produce instantaneously a wonderful improvement in the life and character of the rural population, and that the peasant would become at once a sober, indus-trious, model agriculturist.

These expectations were not realised. One year passed, five years passed, ten years passed, and the expected transformation did not take place. On the contrary, there appeared certain very ugly phenomena which were not at all in the programme. The peasants, it was said, began to drink more and to work less, and the public life which the Communal institutions produced was by no means of a desirable kind. The "bawlers" (*gorlopány*) acquired a prejudicial influence in the Village Assemblies, and in very many Vólosts [administrative unit of several villages] the peasant judges, elected by their fellow-villagers, acquired a bad habit of selling their decisions for vodka. The natural consequence of all this was that those who had indulged in exaggerated expectations sank into a state of inordinate despondency, and imagined things to be much worse than they really were.

For different reasons, those who had not indulged in exaggerated expectations, and had not sympathised with the Emancipation in the form in which it was effected, were equally inclined to take a pessimistic view of the situation. In every ugly phenomenon they found a confirmation of their opinions. The result was precisely what they had foretold. The peasants had used their liberty and their privileges to their own detriment and to the detriment of others!

The extreme "Liberals" were also inclined, for reasons of their own, to join in the doleful chorus. They desired that the condition of the peasantry should be further improved by legislative enactments, and accordingly they painted the evils in as dark colours as possible.

Thus, from various reasons, the majority of the educated classes were unduly disposed to represent to themselves and to others the actual condition of the peasantry in a very unfavourable light, and I felt that from them there was no hope of obtaining the *lumen siccum* which I desired. I determined, therefore, to try the method of questioning the peasants themselves. Surely they must know whether their condition was better or worse than it had been before their Emancipation.

Again I was doomed to disappointment. A few months' experience sufficed to convince me that my new method was by no means so effectual as I had imagined. Uneducated people rarely make generalisations which have no practical utility, and I feel sure that very few Russian peasants ever put to themselves the question: Am I better off now than I or my father was in the time of serfage? When such a question is put to them they feel taken aback. And in truth it is no easy matter to sum up the two sides of the account and draw an accurate balance, save in those exceptional cases in which the proprietor flagrantly abused his authority. The present money-dues and taxes are often more burdensome than the labour-dues in the old times. If the serfs had a great many ill-defined obligations to fulfill—such as the carting of the master's grain to market, the preparing of his firewood, the supplying him with eggs, chickens, homemade linen, and the like—they had, on the other hand, a good many ill-defined privileges. They grazed their cattle during a part of the year on the manor-land; they received firewood and occasionally logs for repairing their huts; sometimes the proprietor lent them or gave them a cow or a horse when they had been visited by the cattle-plague or the horse-stealer; and in times of famine they could look to their master for support. All this has now come to an end. Their burdens and their privileges have been swept away together, and been replaced by clearly defined, unbending, un-elastic legal relations. They have now to pay the market-price for every stick of firewood which they burn, for every log which they require for repairing their houses, and for every rood of land on which to graze their cattle. Nothing is now to be had gratis. The demand to pay is encountered at every step. If a cow dies or a horse is stolen, the owner can no longer go to the proprietor with the hope of receiving a present, or at least a loan without interest, but must, if he has no ready money, apply to the village usurer, who probably considers 20 or 30 percent as a by no means exorbitant rate of interest.

Besides this, from the economic point of view village life has been com-pletely revolutionised. Formerly the members of a peasant family obtained from their ordinary domestic resources nearly all they required. Their food came from their fields, cabbage-garden, and farmyard. Materials for clothing were supplied by their plots of flax and their sheep, and were worked up into linen and cloth by the female members of the household. Fuel, as I have said, and torches wherewith to light the *izbá*—for oil was too expensive and pe-troleum was unknown—were obtained gratis. Their sheep, cattle, and horses were bred at home, and their agricultural implements, except in so far as a little iron was required, could be made by themselves without any pecuniary expenditure. Money was required only for the purchase of a few cheap do-mestic utensils, such as pots, pans, knives, hatchets, wooden dishes and spoons, and for the payment of taxes, which were small in amount and often paid by the proprietor. In these circumstances the quantity of money in circulation among the peasants was infinitesimally small, the few exchanges which took place in a village being generally effected by barter. The taxes and the vodka required for village festivals, weddings, or funerals were the only large items of expenditure for the year, and they were generally covered by the sums brought home by the members of the family who went to work in the towns.

Very different is the present condition of affairs. The spinning, weaving, and other home industries have been killed by the big factories, and the flax and wool have to be sold to raise a little ready money for the numerous new items of expenditure. Everything has to be bought—clothes, firewood, pe-troleum, improved agricultural implements, and many other articles which are now regarded as necessaries of life—whilst comparatively little is earned by working in the towns, because the big families have been broken up, and a household now consists usually of husband and wife, who must both remain at home, and children who are not yet bread-winners. Recalling to mind all these things and the other drawbacks and advantages of his actual position, the old muzhik has naturally much difficulty in striking a balance, and he may well be quite sincere when, on being asked whether things now are on the whole better or worse than in the time of serfage, he scratches the back of his head and replies hesitatingly, with a mystified expression on his wrinkled face: "How shall I say to you? They are both better and worse!" (*"Kak vam skazát'? I lútche i khúdzhe!"*) If, however, you press him further, and ask whether he would himself like to return to the old state of things, he is pretty sure to answer, with a slow shake of the head and a twinkle in his eye, as if some forgotten item in the account had suddenly recurred to him: "Oh, no!"

Svetloyar: In a Wild and Holy Place (1890)

Vladimir Korolenko

A distinct school of nature writing, often identified with particular locales, has been part of American letters since the nineteenth century. In Russia, however, nature writing traditionally emerged from the pens of already established writers of fiction who incorporated their observations on nature into their fiction or wrote separate essays on the natural world.

This lack of a distinct genre of naturalist writing in Russia should in no way suggest that Russia's writers have been heedless of the land. Quite the contrary. Beginning in the nineteenth century writers such as Sergei Aksakov, Andrei Bolotov, Ivan Turgenev, and Leo Tolstoy brought the Russian countryside to the attention of their readership. Sergei Aksakov in Notes of a Hunter of Orenburg Province *(1852) shed the mantle of romanticism and wrote about nature with his own eyes and not as he had been taught to imagine it. But it was Ivan Turgenev (1818–83) whose depictions of Russian nature in* Zapiski okhotnika *(Sportsman's Sketches, 1850–51) remain pivotal in the development of an environmental consciousness in nineteenth-century Russian literature.*

The Russian-Ukrainian writer Vladimir Korolenko (1853–1921) traveled to Lake Svetloyar in 1890 with his backpack and his sketchbook to see how time had left its mark on this place of miracles. The three years he had spent in exile in Siberia beginning in 1881 for his political beliefs had led him increasingly to draw his inspiration from the land and from those whose values were created by it. The lake to which he traveled lies in the district near Nizhnii Novgorod not far from the Uzola, Sanda, and Kerzhenets Rivers. Here in the thirteenth century a town called Bolshoi Kitezh was built under Grigorii II, grand prince of Moscow. According to legend, during the time of the Tatar-Mongol yoke in the mid-thirteenth century, the Mongol horde advanced toward Kitezh only to find the city completely unfortified and its inhabitants engaged in prayer. As they prepared their attack upon the city, the Mongols were stopped in their path by a miraculous sight: fountains of water poured forth from the ground, and the enemy watched as the town slowly disappeared into the lake. Thus was born the legend of the Invisible City of Kitezh. Over the centuries this story has given birth to the belief that in good weather one can hear the sounds of bells and people singing from under the water of the lake. The pure in spirit, so the legend goes, will ultimately find their way to Russia's invisible city.

Beneath the visible surface of Svetloyar, Korolenko discovers the Kitezh of old made permanent through the stories told by the local villagers. In his essay Korolenko finds himself caught between the realities of the present and the tug of the past, with its illusory wonders capable of sustaining Russia's faith over the course of centuries.

1

On my first trip by Svetloyar when the coachman stopped the horses on the broad Semenovsk road, two versts or so from the large village of Vladimir, and pointed with the handle of his whip toward the lake—I was disappointed.[1]

What? This is Svetloyar, woven round with the legend of the "unseen city," where people of varied belief converge—from Perm, sometimes even from the Urals—to set up their icon cases, to pray, to hear the mysterious bells of Kitezh and stand firm for their faith in dispute? From stories, and even from the descriptions of Mel'nikov-Pecherskii [nineteenth-century writer known for his work on provincial Russia] I had expected to see impenetrable forests, narrow paths, places hidden and dark, with the cautious whispering of the "hidden, wild places."

But here, visible from the high road that goes by it, lay a small oval lake with green banks like a saucer, surrounded by a circlet of birches. The trees grow taller and more lush as they run up the small, rounded hills. At the summits birch mix with large oaks, and through the thick greenery the hewn-wood walls and small cupola of a simple chapel peek out.

That's it?

When I came to the lake a second time, my disappointment passed. I felt from Svetloyar its very own, distinctive charm. There was a sort of strangely attractive, almost magical simplicity about it. I tried to remember where I might have seen something similar before. And then I remembered. Bright little lakes like this, and rounded little hummocks and birches like these, show up on old, old icons of unassuming manner. A monk kneels in a round glade. A green oak wood had approached him on the one side, as if listening in on the words of human prayer; and in the background (if there is a foreground and background in such pictures) within green banks as in a chalice, is a tiny lake just like this. The awkward hand of the pious artist knows only simple, naively correct forms: an oval lake, round hills, trees that form a ring, like children for a folk dance. And over it all the air of the maternal wilderness, the very thing these simple-hearted supplicants were seeking.

Not far away, twenty or thirty versts, is the Kerzhenets River with its wild

In wild and holy places. Courtesy of Rick Hibberd.

woods and ruined hermitages, about which the nuns (*skitnitsy*) sing in their ancient voices:

> Here we had houses of prayer. They were like unto heaven.
> The bells we had were a thing of wonder; wonder-filled chiming, like unto thunder . . .

The forests have been cut down now, roads have been cut through the glades, the hermitages have been destroyed, the mystery is breathing its last. Tilled fields have crept up to the "sacred lake," you hear harness bells along the highway, and see cockaded figures in carriages. Kitezh's "mystery" lies exposed at the side of the highway, clutching to the opposite bank, hiding in the shadows round the tall oaks and birches.

It too is quietly breathing its last.

2

The *Chronicle* circulates among the local population in numerous copies. In language that is quite frankly dry and fairly clumsy, with a tasteless mixture of old and more contemporary style, it tells the following story.

Grand Prince Georgii Vsevolodovich, having set out from Yaroslavl' along the Volga, built the city of Lesser Kitezh on the banks of the river. This is present-day Gorodets, a haven of the old faith "with secret clergy." The Prince set off farther by foot along the lower bank, and once he had crossed the quiet, rust-colored rivers of Uzol, Sanda and Kerzhenets, he came to the Liunda River. "He saw that the place was very beautiful and populous," and thus, "due to the supplications of the locals" he decided to build there the city of Greater Kitezh. The legend evidently establishes a kind of spiritual kinship between the two Kitezhes. "Both cities are built with one hand and one axe," the local folk told me. The Prince made the city beautiful, built it round with churches, monasteries, boyars' palaces. Then he encircled it with a trench and raised up walls with embrasures. Having finished all this, he returned to his home on the Volga.

In the meantime a cloud was already hanging over Rus', the "great trembling" was on the move, the Mongol invasion. The vile Batyi made his move: "Like dark clouds in the sky" the evil Tatars moved across Rus', and arrived at Lesser Kitezh (Gorodets). The Grand Prince rode out to meet them, and "struggled mightily with Batyi," but did not conquer him. The Tatars killed his brother, and the Prince himself plunged into the forests, and once he'd passed over the rivers, hid himself in the newly-built city, Kitezh the Great. Batyi lost the Grand Prince's trail and started to "torment" captives, extorting directions from them. One of the captives, Kuter'ma, "not able to withstand torment," showed Batyi the forest tracks to Svetloyar, and the Tatars laid siege to Kitezh.

The chronicle's account of what happened next is obscure. All that is known is that the Prince managed to hide the holy vessels and liturgical accoutrements in the lake, and then died in battle. By God's will the city itself became invisible; in its place was seen water and forest.

And thus there stands to this day the city of Kitezh in the small, round-shaped lake Svetloyar, pure as a tear. Hidden from human eyes are the houses, the streets, the boyars' mansions and the walls with embrasures, the churches and monasteries in which "there are a great multitude of holy fathers, shining forth in their lives like the stars in the heavens or the sands of the sea." And to our sinful, unenlightened gaze it seems there is but forest, and lake, and hills, and boggy ground. But that is only the illusion of our sinful nature. In reality, "in truth," here stand in all their beauty the grand palaces, and gilded chambers, and monasteries. And whosoever is able even partially to see through the veil of deception, will see at the lake's bottom the glittering small flames of processions of the cross, gilded banners held high; and a sweet ringing is carried over the smooth, illusory waters. Then all grows quiet, and again only the oak groves whisper.

Two worlds stand above Lake Svetloyar: one is the real world, but unseen;

the other is seen, but unreal. They flow one into the other, they cover over, and penetrate each other. The false, illusory world is firmer than the true one. Only rarely the latter glimmers through its watery shroud, opens to the pious gaze and then disappears. And once more the crude deception of bodily sensation takes over.

Understandable, how tempting it is. Yearly, "around the feast day of the Vladimir Mother of God," crowds of people come together on the shores of Svetloyar, from Nizhegorod, Vladimir, Vologda *guberniias*, even from Perm and the Urals, eager to throw off if only for a moment the deceptive vanity of vanities and glimpse beyond the mysterious boundaries. Here in the shade of trees, under the open sky, night and day one hears singing, sing-song nasal reading sounds out, and arguments seethe over the true nature of the Russian Orthodox faith. In the dusky twilight and in the blue gloom of a summer evening fires glint among the trees, along the shores and on the water. The faithful creep on their knees three times around the lake, then release bits of wood with candle stubs onto the water; they fall to the ground and listen. Tired, languishing between two worlds, between the fires in the sky and on the water, they give themselves over to the lullaby rocking of the shores, and to the ineffable, distant ringing. Sometimes they fall silent, no longer seeing or hearing anything of what surrounds them. Their eyes have grown blind to our world, but they are ripe for the other world. The face has grown clear, with a "blessed," unsettled smile, and tears. . . . Meanwhile those around them stand and look on in surprise, those who pine but have not been found worthy through lack of faith. . . . And they shake their heads in fear. So this other world does exist, the unseen, but real one. They themselves have not seen it, but have seen the ones who have.

But now it happens less and less frequently, and goes more unnoticed.

Somewhere a tiny little island will flash and grow dim, like a candle burning out, on the mysterious surface of the lake. While all around the deceptive "visible" world sounds on.

3

Once I'd gotten to know the marvelous little lake I came not infrequently, a pack on my back and walking stick in hand, to mingle with the crowd, to watch and listen and try to catch the living stream of folk poetry among the motley flash and noise. The glow of sunset would be dying away as I stood on the hill near the log chapel, in a thick, sweaty crowd of peasants who were following the disputes. And the glow of sunrise would find us all in exactly the same place.

Much naive feeling, little living thought . . . The city of their yearning, Greater Kitezh—is a city of the past. An ancient city with walls, towers and embrasures—naive fortifications that wouldn't stand up to the worst little worldly cannon!—with boyars' palaces, women's quarters in merchants' homes, huts for the simple, "ignoble" folk. There the boyars rule and accept tribute, the merchants place brightly-burning beeswax candles before the icons and give alms to their poor brethren, the rabble obeys with humility and accepts alms with grateful prayers.

There's something touching for us too in this legend. Many of us, who long ago left the paths of old-time Kitezh, who have parted with such faith and prayers. All the same we seek just as passionately our "longed-for city." We even hear, occasionally, sounds of long ago welcoming bells. Coming to our senses, we see ourselves once more in an overgrown forest, surrounded by hills and hummocks, and by bogs.

4

This time I approached Svetloyar not on a holiday but on an ordinary day, and was glad for the chance to look at the marvelous lake in its regular guise, in the quiet of its simple, every-day solitude.

The sun was lowering towards the hilly bank. The birches, alder and oak on the hillsides already stood in shadow, while the young birch on the low eastern bank was still lit through with bright green. The reflected shore with its hills, trees and chapel stood quietly in the mirror-smooth water, barely rippling in straight bands of light. Small fish darted about before the sun set. Occasional figures glimmered among the trees. Two pilgrims with packs, who must have rested from the heat by the lake, laboriously gathered themselves to set off. The chapel was locked. In the pilgrims' guesthouse that the Vladimir village association had built on the shore the shutters were closed tight. Only two years ago an old man of about ninety lived here, hair white as snow, and deaf as a doorpost. The "society" lets whoever wants to live in the small house, so that the sacred place won't be empty. In earlier days there was no need of a house. The initiates—"the laboring folk"—hollowed out the whole hill into dugouts and caves. That's ended now. Partly because in general there's less "devotion," partly because it just doesn't seem to fit with the passport laws. When the police couldn't find any entrances, just "air holes," they routed the zealots with mining rods and smoked them out. The unseen laborers took off. That's when the pious Vladimir elders decided to outfit the chapel and let this old man come. He fit right into the place and lived by the lake for many years, gladdening the Vladimir folk with his pleasant manner.

Hair gone completely white, dressed in a clean shirt and trousers, with new bast shoes tied with bright linden tassels, he brought real grace and beauty to the place during annual gatherings. Leaning on his staff, bare headed so the wind tousled his silver hair, he stood by his *izba*, or hut, and watched the passing crowd with eyes that were at times pure and child-like, at times elderly and stern, as though to make sure that no unclean spirit appeared. He was always surrounded by a crowd, as a man bound by invisible thread to the hidden mystery of the lake.

But there are fewer and fewer such threads linking the two worlds. Many folk press close to the banks to hear the sacred bells of the invisible city from out of the depths. And they hear nothing. But he hears, regardless of the fact that he's completely deaf.

—Shout right into his ear—can't make anything out.

—That means he doesn't need to hear it.

—But he hears the Kitezh bell. And not just on the Vladimir Mother of God's, he hears it without stopping, all the time.

—Out I go, early-early light, to pray to the unseen cross, and it's a-boomin' and a clangin'—I was standing there as he recounted it, smiling with a child's delight, to the astonished crowd.—And the bells, they are like ours, brothers, at Kuzmodemiansk. I left home, left Kuzmo I mean, Demiansk, long ago. A wee bit of a child. But our bell, that I remember. And the one that's here—just like ours did, it sounds at first light.

A happy smile passes over his face.

—The clever are without understanding, and those who have ears to hear do not hear, someone in the crowd remarked severely.—But the Lord gives wisdom to a deaf old man. Woe to those who hear the word and do not accept it.

He cast a fierce glance over everyone with his dry, severe, taunting eyes. Of course he took the "miracle" accomplished in the deaf old man for himself as well, and wanted to see in it the affirmation of his own strict belief, contained in the ancient book. See these particular chapters, Verse Five, and Verses Seven to Ten. And since not all of us, of course, even knew what the fifth and seventh-to-tenth verses said, he had already condemned us to the fires of Hell. Meanwhile the old man smiled at him, too, with his dark blue eyes, pure as the waters of Svetloyar.

This time the old man was no longer there. They found him one morning on the bench, clean, untroubled, and evidently long prepared for the distant journey. His face was happy as a new born's. In all likelihood he had heard once more in the final hour the sounding of his native bell, either from the depths of the sacred lake or from his childhood, which was just as sacred.

Since a sacred place doesn't stay empty, new alms-seekers appeared in his place. Two, in fact. First a lay sister came and moved into the *izba*; then a soldier showed up and asked permission to build a dugout. The elders granted it. But no sooner had the snow gone and grass started to sprout up, the trees to turn green, than shepherds grazing livestock on the "high bank" brought pernicious news, that the elders didn't at first believe—who knows what stupid boys will imagine. It could be the tempter's doing. But one day the shepherds invited the elders to come see for themselves: the lay brother and lay sister were sleeping together on the grass beneath a tree, an empty crock beside them.

They spat and drove off the both of them. Then nailed up the windows. Waited to see if another "real" elder might come again.

Nobody came.

5

I walk round the lake with my companions, listening to the muffled pre-dusk rustling of the trees. From time to time a fish pops out of the lake. A frog grunts in the shallows near the shore where it's warmed during the day. The sparrows chirp about, carefree as children. On the far shore village girls are swimming peaceably together with the boys. Even at a distance the boys' browned bodies stand out from the girls' pallor.

In a secluded spot on the bank, where the forest becomes patchy new growth, an old man stood fishing. He had seen us before we saw him, and now he squinted at his float and kept an attentive eye on us as well. He was barefoot and hatless. His whole demeanor showed a solid, country-style well-being, the kind of look that's typical of a man who respects himself and is used to being respected.

—Good day, granddad!

The intelligent eyes continue to study me for a while from under the mop of grey hair. Then their expression softens.

—May your path be a peaceful one,—he answers.—And who would you be? What kind of folk?

—From Nizhegorod.

—Ayuh. You've come to our hills? Well you should have come for Our Lady of Vladimir. That's when it's fine here.

—I've been for the Vladimir's Feast Day. How is it? What's biting?

—Not so good. Now ten days ago—all you could do to keep casting. Today, you can see, it's not even moving. Carp's all there is—and that doesn't want to mess with worms. . . .

The water really didn't stir. Thin ripples of silver clung to the stems of grasses and held them in brilliant, languid immobility. It was hard to pick out the float among the sparse, thin thistle. . . .

—And are there lots of fish here?

—Oh aye, quite a few. It's a lake full of fish, is ours. Perch, bream, pike, crucian, dace, roach . . . The crucians, they're big healthy ones. Fat, oh my, fat as pigs, every one.

The float shuddered. Two or three ripples rose out from the depths onto the water. The old man started to pull. The hook got tangled in grasses. He pulled it out, looked at it carefully and attached a new worm.

—It's gotten overgrown. For our sins, he said, spitting at the bait.—There was none of that in the old days. Not the tiniest little bit of grass! Like a tear it was, the lake. . . . The main thing is weakness. Now, swimming, that's not forbidden. But then there'll be someone, my friend, who has an unclean body. Women folk again, the girls. . . . It gets even more overgrown from the women.

He cast his rod again and turned to me with an expression of pride:

—But even now, mind you—where are you going to find water like this? Look at it: like a diamond! Toss a needle out there on the bottom, you can see it!

The water really is clear as crystal. Until it gets deep you can see the last little thing on the bottom. It's all littered with "windfall," sprigs and branches, sometimes whole trunks are laid down tight together. They're distinct, as though alive. Nowhere even a shadow of silt, decomposition, rotting.

—But in the middle part, the fisherman says with naive surprise,—It's black as night. It's a wondrous thing, brother, what our lake is like. Near on five years ago we went out in a boat, put down a lead to plumb how deep it is. Near twenty sazhens [1 sazhen = approximately 7 feet] the weight stopped going. I took it like this, shook it off. And what do you think? it went down again, kept going and going. All rope and no bottom. We tied on another one. Seventy sazhens and no bottom.

—And is it true what they say, that there's a current somewhere out there?

—Who knows. Now it is true that there's a small spring lives in the Liunda, come warmer weather. But when they say there's a link-up with the Volga, that's not right. Can't allow as how that could be. Because, see, if that was the case we'd have Volga fish. . . .

—What about you, friend, have you read our chronicle?—he asked, after a brief silence.

—I've read it.

—Not enough tears to cry! Am I right? . . .

—And you, granddad, have you heard the bells?

He stood there silently, as though in uncertainty. Then he began to speak, seriously and with thought:

—Well as for the ringing, I'll tell you an old timers' tale, but you listen now. I was still a boy then, a young one, in my seventeenth year. And now my seventh decade's almost gone. Now is that a lot of time? I was working over there beyond the hills, making bricks for our prince, for Mr. Sibirskii, a landlord, with my mother. An old man used to come to the lake then, Kirill Samoilov. Born in the village of Kovernin. And he had beehives of his own, that was his livelihood. He sold the honey and the wax too. A worthy man he was. And had always wanted to save his soul, didn't want to just die like that, living from his beehives. So he started coming to us "in the hills." He'd wrap up the hives for the winter and come. Make his way into the hill. He'd even come for weeks, to save his soul.

—So there were caves there?

—Oh-ho. Lots of them! Only of course they were secret. Since by that time they'd alrcady started chasing folk out. Well anyway, they'd run you off, but still there was more devotion than nowadays. I still remember it well: the whole hill was dug through. You'd be making your way along in the winter: steam comes out of a little hole or, say, smoke, and the hoarfrost was melted all around. You say "Lord Jesus Christ, son of God, have mercy on us!" And right then out of the hole a hand stretches out for alms.

—How did they get in?

—They'd get in any which way. Over there by the spring stood a birch. It came down not so long ago, ten years maybe. The roots of the birch were all crotched out, and I still remember when you could crawl under those roots on your knees. Not so long ago there was a fellow, had more pluck than the others, crawled ten sazhens in. The way he told it you could have gone further: it went upwards, like a smoke shaft. But, he says, it's fearsome: there's no air. Just look, how this bank is. Take a jump.

In fact, we're standing on a bed of peat-like soil that stretches along the lake. The spot where I jumped was two sazhens from the water—and right away rings rippled out. It was obvious that it wasn't the shore that went off into the water, but the other way around: the water goes under a layer of roots and dense decayed plants.

—And somewhere here they got in too. Must be five years or so ago this one fellow showed up. The last one, probably. Planned to hide out in the hill. Lived there.

—Well, and what then?

—What indeed! The times aren't like they used to be, all due respect. There've gotten to be lots of shenanigans. And he had no need for that. He needs quiet. Folks today don't understand that. Especially the kids, the young folk. What are you going to do with them. They found the air hole, that very one, and started up their pranks. He, dear friend, maybe is standing there praying—for the whole world, for all Christians . . . meanwhile these idiots, from on top of him . . . what a business . . . let's just say they were acting up. . . . Then he'd crawl out into God's creation to go fishing. What of it. No harm in that. It was the Apostles' labor. He put his bag on the bank, went off for a bit. So a soldier made off with the bag. There you are! Just try and live with them, the idiots. We're not worthy! He took off, the poor fellow. . . . The hill's all empty now. . . .

—Well and what of Kirill Samoilov?

—Well, he would come and pray, like I said. But then they started chasing folk out, it became impossible. So he starts to come to us, sleeps in the barn: he's waiting out the hard times. Or he'll stay in my mother's drying barn. We think to ourselves: what of it, no matter. An old man's an old man. No lack of them. But here's what kind of old man he is: starts to hear the bells. It'll be morning and we're sleeping, still not light yet. He wakes us: "Get up, what are you sleeping for. It's a miracle. Listen." We got awake. "Do you hear it?" "No, Kirill Samoilovich, don't hear a thing. Just the wind in the leaves."—"How's that," he says, "you don't hear. Get down on the ground, old woman." Mother went down on the ground. "Well, she says, there's a kind of noise. The trees are trembling, it sounds like bu-u, bu-u . . ."—"That's not trees," he says, "woman of little faith. Your ears are all blocked. I hear it clear as day: it's *them* sounding for matins. All glory to you blessed virgin, holy mother of God, blessed saints. I too, a sinner, have proven worthy." And then it got more and more frequent. So then he started to see as well. There's a mist, he says, on the lake, and he starts pointing in the mist to where the city and the churches are, and the prince's chambers and the great monasteries. He's talking and crying, his little beard's a shaking. And now, he says, I absolutely must go there. It's already clear how it is there: you enter into such blessedness, right into paradise. I'll spare no money. I'll make them an offering.

—So what then?

—Word went out among the people: Kirill Samoilich is hearing bells, the invisible city is opening to him. He went off to his beehives. Then we hear that he's selling the hives, selling his *izba*, all his property—in a word, he's made up his mind. He came back to us. "What's up, Kirill Samoilovich?"

—Keep quiet, he says. Soon they'll come for me. I've come to say goodbye.

—Where are you going? We want to watch.

—You mustn't see how I set off with them. Your eyes are sinful, he says.

We watch: our Kirill Samoilov has become wondrous strange. Bread he won't eat, *kvas* [a fermented drink made from rye bread] he won't drink, wasted away to nothing, but his look is cheerful. One morning early, at first light, I went rushing out, out of the barn toward the wattle fence over there. I look, and Kirill Samoilov is sitting on the shore, there are two people with him, like monks, in cowls, the one's beard looks grey, the other looks black. They're talking. The black one points toward the lake. I got scared, my eyes even clouded over, the water went dark. I ran off. No one's there, just Kirill Samoilov is going up the hill.

—Yes, so that's how it was.—he continued, with much concentration.— Not long after that the old man disappeared without a trace. He was hiding from us too. At the very end he dressed nice and neat, combed his hair, had a wash, said goodbye, and was gone. Like he'd dropped into the water. Our Kirill Samoilov was gone, just gone. We thought: maybe he's gone like before off to his place in Kovernin. It happened I was going in that direction, I called in on purpose. "Now where's your Kirill Samoilov?"—"Kirill Samoilov's not here. He vanished without a trace. Someone else is over at the beehives now." So good friend, that's how you have it. What about it?

—So he didn't turn up later?

—Where would he turn up! There were tales, you might say, all kinds, but if you haven't seen it yourself, what's the point of telling.

—No, go ahead, please, tell me.

—There was an old woman hereabouts. Died long ago. Now just at that time her cow got lost. She thought, well she'll come, but she doesn't come home—it's night, midnight. Her heart got uneasy, she got up in the night-time, went to look for her. Found her in the woods. There, behind the hills, there was a big wood. She was bringing her by the lake and she sees a boat, like it was heading off from the shore, and there were three people in the boat. They're singing a hymn in hushed voices. They went out to the middle of the lake. It sounded like something plopped into the water and let out a cry. But it was dark, a spring night, shadowy. She got scared, drove the cow with all her might. Folks said: that's none other than Kirill Samoilov, setting off for Kitezh.

—Or maybe for the bottom of the lake, granddad?

—Well, if that's so—he said coldly, throwing a confident, unflustered look at me.—The monastery itself is on the bottom. And in the very middle are the main gates. Folks talked like you then, too: Kirill Samoilov drowned, that's all. The authorities came out, hauled us out for questioning. Apparently seized two guys in Semenov. . . .

—And then what?

—What do you think! Nobody knows anything, nobody has any ideas. Go ahead and investigate! Have a look! Town folk, we know their kind. They'll get up to anything.

He stopped talking, and something inexpressible shaded between us. I was town folk too, and with an indignant shudder saw crude, menacing crime where he saw benevolent, sacred mystery. And he sensed that. After a while, though, his eyes softened. He had one more thing he needed to say.

—Now I didn't see it myself, people talked. Peasants were traveling from Semenov, from the fair, in two carts. They were late. It was in early spring. The earth was in a sweat, it was misty. The horses got off the road, went towards the lake. The usual story with livestock: maybe they wanted a drink. The peasants ran out to look for them. The mist was moving in columns over the lake, the sun was barely showing over the hills. And suddenly, brother of mine, what do they see: coming out of the lake on a big cart, can't say if it was monks or not, but something like that. Our peasants start to wondering: what on earth? The monks were strangers. Their horses are big, well-fed, they're fine folk too, with shining faces. And they're coming out of the water right towards them, just as though it was a road. They came up to them, stopped their horses, can you toss some wheat / hay onto our wagon. Then they paid, all honorable like, to the last kopeck, turned the cart around and headed back into the lake. They were the only ones who saw them. And listen to what else. You're a town man. Well, understand it as you will, but apparently they saw Kirill Samoilov with them. But they didn't dare to speak.

We were both quiet for a bit, occupied with our own thoughts. And our thoughts were different. The story teller's were evidently bright and placid. Once again his face took on a kind, benevolent expression.

—Well, my passing friend, I've told you quite a bit. Maybe you're thinking: Everything happens there, what could be left? But our place here isn't just any old place. Oh no. Not just any old place. To you it seems like it's a lake, boggy ground, hills. But in essence it's completely different. On these very hills (he pointed with his finger toward the hills), they say, will be churches. . . . Over there, where the chapel is,—stands their cathedral of the Blessed Savior. And just beside it, on the other hill—the Annunciation. Years ago a birch stood there, just on the church cupola, it turns out.

—How do you know that?

—From the possessed ones, from the shriekers. It would happen that when they were taking one of them by that birch, right then they'd start to shriek: "Oh my mother birch! You've grown up on the cupola. Have mercy on us." That's clear as can be. What else do you need? And their main road went over there where it never dries out. Over there, across from the ravine, between the hillocks there, in the middle of the lake. Sometimes our nets get snagged there. That would be the monastery gates. And they say there are chains on the columns, and there are chests of gold on the chains and different gold vessels left there. Just you think about that. We sinners see bogs and forest and lake. But if you take it for real it's something quite different. Oh what am I doing!

The water where the Tartar thistle grew had been rippling for half a minute or so. My companion came alive and quickly, with an absorbed expression started to "lead" the large fish that was biting.

—Oh, no, you just wait! You'll not get off, my sweet one,—he said, squatting down and alternately pulling the fishing line horizontal, then letting it out, and guiding it from side to side. Then he stood up, pulled on the rod and snatched out a lively, respectable sized perch. The perch flashed in the air and then bent like a bow and fell onto the green grass. He again arched and jumped there, evidently not wanting to part with his illusory existence.

Finally the fisherman took him off the hook and put him in a birch bucket that stood to one side. The old man looked satisfied.

I laughed involuntarily. He looked at me, also smiling a bit, and asked:

—What are you laughing at? Not at me, fool that I am?

—No, granddad. A wonderful thing just came to me.

—And what's that, friend?

—Well, the lake. Is only an illusion?

—Well . . .

—And there's no water there, but a road and the main gates?

—That's the truth.

—Then what about the perch? So it must be that it's only an illusion.

—Go on now. What?—he said with a perplexed, good-natured smile. And then he added:—Now we fools are going to fry it and have it to eat.

He took the perch out again, looked at it, weighed it in his hand and said:

—Not a bad one, just look. A couple more like this—and we've got fish soup!

6

We parted as friends.

The sun was setting lower behind the hills, and a cool shadow extended over the whole lake. Evidently they were starting to bite as it cooled. I'd barely gone a few sazhens from the old man when he had a new catch flashing in the air: a big flat bream made a flying arc and flopped on the grass.

I felt like swimming. I walked a ways away, so as not to disturb the kind man pulling illusory fish from the seeming lake; I undressed near a small stone pier with a boat tied to it and plunged into the water with relish. The high, calm sky was above me. A small golden cloud faded in the dying ruddy light. Beneath me was the enigmatic depth, bottomless and mysterious.

—He-ey! You there, traveler!—I hear someone's voice from the shore. A young peasant, also with a rod and bag, stood right by the water and watched me.

—Hey, swim out a bit . . . A bit more . . . There, right there. Now dive down, dive, just make it real deep. Ready, set . . .

I wanted to do it myself, and once I'd taken a deep breath, went straight down into the depths. It was cold, the water was very dense. There was an involuntary feeling of mystery and awe. I'm quickly carried back to the surface.

Shaking off and opening my eyes, first of all I see the same peasant. Hands clutching the branch of a tree on the shore, he's hanging out right over the water. His eyes are full of a greedy, consuming curiosity.

—That's it . . . once more . . . One more time . . .

I give it a second try. This time is more successful, deeper. The water is colder still and pushes upward like a spring, but I still manage to feel some kind of object with my foot. The branch of a tree. It slips out from under my leg, but there's a second and a third. It's like the tops of a drowned forest. I'm hanging among them in the deeps, dense and dark. More effort. A ringing in the ears. I'm quickly carried up to the surface, and breathe deep chestfuls of air. The young fisherman greets me again with a naive, curious, somewhat frightened look.

—You were under the water for a long time. Well, brother—he said in a friendly way, when I come out onto shore,—you couldn't fill this palm with enough gold to get me to dive into our lake. . . . I wouldn't dive in for anything.

—But you sent me?

—That's your business, he said sheepishly.

The sun had set completely, and on the road to Vladimirskoe village I barely managed to sketch the lake, the hills and the ring of trees in my album. The darkness spread quickly in the valley. Only the quiet Liunda glowed weakly, meandering along the boggy lowlands, and a scrap of lake lazily lit the evening sky with a bluish grey.

Farewell, Svetloyar. Farewell, mysterious lake of wonders, of dark faith in an illusory past.

Translated by Jane Costlow

Note

1. [Author's Note] *Svetloyar* is a volcanic lake on the Liunda River, near the village of Vladimir of the Nizhegorod *guberniia*. The legend of the invisible city of Kitezh is linked with Svetloyar.

Searching for Icons (1969)

Vladimir Soloukhin

In the early 1960s the writer and icon collector Vladimir Soloukhin set out for the Russian countryside in search of icons for his collection. He was a member of the derevenskaia shkola, *Russian village prose writers who came to prominence in the 1960s, and as such, much of his work extols the values of the countryside that these writers believed were being left behind by mainstream Soviet life. Behind the locked doors of churches to which a local Party official had given him the key, in peasant dwellings where the icon corners were still lit with candles, and in restorers' studios, Soloukhin uncovered not only the icons but their role in the social and cultural life of the villages where he traveled.*

With the coming of the Revolution the art of icon painting suffered a fate similar to that of Russia's churches. As the churches were closed down, burned, or turned into museums, icons fell into similar neglect. Some were rescued and subsequently found their way into museums and private collections in the West through Russians who had fled abroad just before and after the October Revolution. Icons, however, were never designed as museum pieces but as objects to be venerated. Russian Orthodox believers pray and confess their sins not to a priest but to the image of the saint depicted on the icon. Even during Soviet times, in villages and hamlets far from the centers of power, Russians quietly retained the tradition of the icon corner or "front corner," where the family placed their icons, lit candles, and continued to worship. An icon collector in Moscow, Pavel Korin, said this to Soloukhin: "A collection of shells or butterflies is just that and no more, but when you collect Old Russian paintings you are collecting the nation's soul." For Soloukhin the collecting, restoring, and display-ing of these religious artifacts were part of the larger process of weaving together memory, cultural identity, and religious tradition in times that discouraged the profession of belief.

We stopped in front of another icon of unusual shape: a narrow horizontal panel, with quarter-length figures of seven sacred personages. The central figure was a full-face one of Christ, and on either side three saints were turned

St. Nicholas the Wonderworker icon. G. I. Vzdornov, *The Russian Icon from Its Origins to the Sixteenth Century*, translated from Italian by Collette Joly Dees (Collegeville, Minn.: Liturgical Press, 1996). Copyright 2009, State Russian Museum, St. Petersburg. Courtesy of State Russian Museum.

towards him: the picture showed not only their faces but their arms, for which there was not much room as they were crowded close together.

"This is what they call a Deesis," my hostess explained. "Usually it consists of several icons, with a saint depicted on each. Notice the full, rich green of the background. The icon was painted in the north of Russia, where the green of the vast forests was the northerners' favourite colour and the one they used most for icons. Even the haloes on this one are not golden, as they would be if it had been painted in Moscow, but a soft, tender green colour.

"Look at the position of the arms too. If you follow the line from left to right across the picture you get a wavy, rhythmic effect, like ducks floating. The whole thing is infused with a sense of softness and entreaty. That is what this type of icon is about."

"Tell me, what are the large black holes at each end of the panel? Are they from nails?"

"Yes. When we found the icon, it was barring up the door to a belfry."

"How do you mean?"

"Just that. There was a door, and to prevent anyone getting in they nailed this to it as a crossbar. But it's nothing to be upset about—the icon was saved by being put to practical use. They must have fastened it to the door when the church was closed, in the early thirties."

"And what about the other icons? I suppose there were several as good as this?"

"We don't know. The church is empty now, anyway. Only this solitary icon survived, having been used to bar up the belfry door. Why are you so surprised? Look at this one now."

I looked at a large panel, some twenty by twenty-eight inches, showing Christ riding on an ass. There were buildings and a tall tree to be seen, and the people welcoming Christ were throwing palm-branches and garments under the ass's feet.

"There you are. This is called the 'Entry into Jerusalem,' but its popular name was 'Palm Sunday.' It belongs to the series of church festivals. It was pure chance that this one survived. We found it in the house of an old woman at Vologda where we put up for the night: she was using it to cover a tub of salted cucumbers."

"But why, for heaven's sake? Even I, who know nothing about painting, let alone icons, can see that it's a fine work."

"Yes, if it had looked as it does now, I dare say it wouldn't have been used as a barrel-lid. But wait till we show you what the icons looked like when they were used to bar up doors or windows in closed churches, or to cover barrels, or when they were simply lying about on the floor somewhere. Take this one here: bring it into the next room and let's put it on the table."

I took the panel, which was quite a weight, and laid it on the table as I was told. It was a mysterious sight: a completely black, impenetrable, unexpressive piece of wood. Here and there it was peeling in tiny whitish flakes, and in one place it looked as if a layer of plaster had come off. White, crumbling holes showed where small nails had held the overlay in place.[1] Some of the nails were still there, and a scrap of metal, the size of a small coin, was attached to one of them: it was jagged at the edge and twisted upward.

My friend the artist had joined us to take part in the operation that now began. His wife took a small piece of cotton wool, dipped it in sunflower-seed oil which she had poured into a saucer, and rubbed it over the surface of the panel, on which the outlines of a picture began to appear through the deep black. It was as though a dull, dirty, flaking expanse of roofing-iron were being transformed before our eyes into a sheet of glass, still black indeed, but allowing something to be discerned beneath. This in itself seemed to me marvellous.

"Can so much dirt really accumulate in the course of centuries?" I asked, thinking that this might really be so.

"It isn't dirt, it's drying oil."

"But then why did they cover the picture with it?"

"The oil was to protect the paint from damp, scratches and the effects of time generally. Besides, when the icon was first covered with the oil it would shine and glitter. It was the early equivalent of varnish. But it had one unforeseen defect: in the course of eighty or a hundred years it goes black and, instead of making the painting bright and radiant, it covers it with a sort of dark curtain. What we are going to do now is to cut a hole in that curtain."

The artist and his wife were now busying themselves with speed but without unnecessary fuss. I could not help being reminded of a surgical operation as they laid the panel on the table, pulled over a bright lamp on a concertina bracket and spread out their instruments: a scalpel, tweezers, a phial containing some chemical or other, cotton wool and a syringe. And now the two surgeons, or the surgeon and nurse, bent over the patient with concentrated attention.

It was all so new and fascinating that I tried not to miss a single movement. With a pair of scissors the "nurse" deftly cut out an oblong piece of flannel about half the size of a man's hand: she trimmed the edges to an exact rectangle and, using the tweezers, dipped it into the saucerful of evil-smelling liquid. This must have been corrosive, as she took care not to wet her fingers.

"Where shall we put it?" she asked her husband, as she turned the flannel this way and that so as to get it thoroughly soaked. "Shall we start with the face?"

"Not on any account."

"What about the city? Or the sword?"

"No, let's be careful and start with the robe. Here will do. Either I'm much mistaken, or this one will be a beauty."

I forgot to say that when they rubbed the icon with the sunflower-seed oil we could see on it, through the black, the full-length figure of a saint. In one hand he was holding at shoulder-level something rather like a town or a monastery, or at any rate a conglomeration of buildings, and in the other hand, at the same level, a short, slightly curving sword.

"It's St Nicholas of Mozhaisk," they explained to me. "A magnificent theme. In one hand he holds a Russian town and in the other a sword to protect it from destruction or any sort of danger. The common people were very fond of this icon. It's still called 'St Nicholas with the Sword and City.' "

I realised now that the surgeons were deciding on which part of the icon to lay the piece of flannel steeped in corrosive liquid. The saint's countenance was too important, the "city" was also too risky, and so they chose the robe. The pale-green flannel, darker now from the liquid, adhered easily and closely to the centre of the panel. They straightened and smoothed out its edges; Nina (my host's wife) did not risk her clever fingers in this operation, as they laid a piece of glass on the flannel and pressed it down.

"Bring the weight!" said the surgeon-in-charge sharply. An old-fashioned two-pound weight was brought, and they laid it on the glass with the flannel beneath. Then we all straightened up, drew breath and stepped back from the table: a few minutes had to elapse for the chemical under the glass to do its work.

I did not intend to waste those minutes: I began asking questions, and although they were very naïve ones my hosts answered willingly, explaining everything as if to a child. Thus I learnt that the icon-painters began by fastening a coarse canvas to the panel and then applied to it a foundation of white gesso, usually composed of alabaster and glue. This, when dry, was polished and resembled smooth, shining ivory. However, even the best surface in the course of time became covered with tiny fissures called *craquelures*. This does not spoil an old icon but, on the contrary, gives it a special fascination and an air of antiquity.

Paints were then applied to the white, shining surface. In the old days these were natural colours, dissolved in yolk of egg. Cinnabar was real cinnabar, ochre was real ochre. The old artists were especially fond of ochre, using it for faces and for the borders of icon, and often for the background. In very old and valuable icons the background is often of pure gold.

To make a large icon, several strips of wood were fastened together by dowels or cleats to make a single panel; these also prevented warping. They showed me the back of a small icon, and here too I could see that two cleats had been fixed across it. The icon being on a single panel, there was nothing to fasten together, and the cleats were only there to prevent warping.

While my hosts were explaining all this, the minutes went by and it was time to return to the operating table. The weight was removed, the glass lifted by one corner and taken off the flannel. The latter, which had been a bright green in colour, was now tinted dark brown from the panel below. The dark stain had seeped right through the flannel and was visible as a sticky, oily perspiration on the glass.

Then they began to peel off the flannel, holding it by one corner. It stuck closely to the board, almost like something that had "caught" in a saucepan, but finally it came off, and I saw that the black surface beneath had, as it were, swollen and loosened. Without a moment's delay Nina took a small piece of cotton wool, compressed it into a wad which she dipped into the same stinking chemical (to me it was by now the pleasantest smell on earth), and moved it to and fro over the loosened varnish. The result was like a conjuring trick. All the black came off on to the cotton wool, and the place where it had been was ablaze with vivid red and deep blue. It took one's breath away. I felt as if I had seen a miracle: it was unbelievable that such intense, radiant colour had lurked beneath the repellent, dull black surface.

"Gently, Nina, treat it lovingly, don't get excited," my host kept urging as his wife reached for the scalpel. With precise but firm, even movements of the razor-sharp instrument she cleaned off the remaining traces of varnish where they had stuck most firmly to the rectangular patch and had not come away with the cotton wool. Now at last we were really looking through an aperture in the dark curtain. On the other side of it everything was bright and festive, red and blue, sunny and lively, while we on this side remained in a dull, drab, gloomy world. It was like looking at a bright screen from the dark of an auditorium—a screen showing a different period of time, a different beauty, a life other than ours.

Note

1. Icons were frequently encased in a metal cover or *riza* in which openings were cut to show the essential sections of the painting.

The Village of Posady (1979 / 82)

Lev Timofeev

"*I am not a peasant, nor have I ever starved,*" begins Lev Timofeev in The Technology of the Black Market or, the Peasants' Art of Starving. *Timofeev set down his observations in 1979, knowing that what he had to say would not pass Soviet censorship. His manuscript circulated in* samizdat *[literally: self publishing] and then made its way abroad, where it was published in the United States, first in Russian in 1982, then in English translation in 1985.*

Timofeev's experience of the Russian countryside was not unlike that of most Russian urban dwellers: he enjoyed outings to the rural areas, went fishing, gathered mushrooms, and rented a small dacha in the summertime. His knowledge of rural Russia took a turn, however, when he went there to write his dissertation on Russian versification and began to view firsthand the demoralizing living conditions of Russian villagers: their isolation, poor roads and inadequate transportation, their lack of access to consumer goods, and a rate of alcohol consumption that had risen at the same rate as conditions had deteriorated. What he saw was a system of collective farms that was both morally and economically bankrupt and whose sole viable element was the private plots that the peasants worked and tilled and whose produce they sold at market. These small, free market relations were, in Timofeev's view, the chief economic phenomenon that kept the Soviet state afloat, though their very existence flew in the face of socialist economic principles.

The question of how much the Soviet economy could tolerate a partial market system became ever more pressing during the Brezhnev years as the system of collective farms faltered and scarcity, deficits, and rationing became the order of the day in many regions. In 1985 Gorbachev inherited these crises and attempted to initiate market reform within a socialist economy. Timofeev argues, however, that there can be no coexistence of the two systems and that improved living conditions for Russia's peasantry are dependent on a healthy market economy.

There is a certain paradox to the situation Timofeev describes. On the one hand, the enormous gulf that had long separated urban and rural Russia contributed to the lack of anything being done about the countryside. Timofeev suggests that it was hard to get the urban intelligentsia to invest intellectually in what was going on in the country. Ironically, however, as the economy stagnated in the transition period of the

1990s, people from the cities began traveling to the outskirts in their free time to work the private plots of land that helped sustain the economy after 1991. Institutes and factories would often buy or rent land for its workers so they could get through the winter and spring on what they had grown. Irrespective of class or background everyone was out there in the fields. Putting food on the table depended on it.

The distance from Gati, the village where Aksinya Yegoryevna lived, to Posady is all of twenty kilometers or so as the crow flies, but if Gati—at first glance—is a poor village in the woods, beneath slate roofs, with a straw one in some places, then in Posady, it seems that not a single wooden hut remains. All the houses are laid with stone, spacious in village terms with two to three rooms, large windows, enormous dacha-style terraces, and, the requisite galvanized roofs. In spring, all of this splendor magically disappears, and makes itself invisible behind the pinkish-white mist of the flower gardens, while in fall, just the opposite happens: the white stone walls and reflecting roofs are visible from as far away as the shores of the river turned black from rain. From where did such resplendence come?

There's no big secret, nor magic about it. In Posady, all income is from the farm plots. There are no potatoes or onions or cabbages planted in the vegetable garden here—only spring cucumbers. In June, the harvest is brought in, and the crops are sent on passing vehicles to the markets of Moscow, Riazan', Penza, and sometimes even farther thanks to the fact that the village is located right beside the road. In autumn, apples are transported to the very same markets. . . .

Even with the smallest plot of land a farmer will always strive not solely for his own food production, but marketable crops, since his family's financial concerns are much greater than the basic produce one can produce on one's own farm.

In good years, one plot of land at Posady produces enough to earn up to 5,000 rubles. With this money people buy potatoes, onions and all the other products they need in the neighboring villages. Five thousand rubles for a family of four to five is not very much, but enough nonetheless that there is something left over after food has been purchased. There are even some communal farms that pay money these days: a good machine-operator gets 1,500 rubles, or 2,000 rubles a year.

Every time our acquaintance Aksinya Yegoryevna came from the city near Posady where her daughter was staying, she was so struck by the difference in income that her imagination carried this difference to a completely unrealistic extreme.

"How do people live! I stopped by one person's place to grab a drink. What did they *not* have?! You could even see through the door. Just think: the television stood in the entrance hall—that means that they don't put any value on it at all. 'That one we watch when the big one breaks.' Their big one is in the nicer part of the house. . . . Where'd they come up with that money? We worked hard there too, and lived our whole lives in a wooden cabin as if we were sitting our lives out by a well."

"I know that house," I started to object. "The farmer there makes money repairing other people's television sets on the side. The TV that stood in the hall was probably someone's broken one, right?"

Aksinya Yegoryevna became quiet. She didn't like to argue, but it was clear that she was sticking to her opinion about how well-off rural farmers are, based on numbers of televisions.

Another time along the road she saw a vegetable garden with cabbages growing from end to end—this amazed her.

"How come there's so much? Or aren't they Russian, eating nothing but cabbage?"

"Maybe the rest is to sell?"

"What're they selling it there for? Cabbage goes for thirty kopecks a head. Let's say there're 2,000 heads—the whole return is 600 rubles. We've gotten a whole lot of potatoes many years with even enough left over for ourselves and the cattle for the whole winter. But those are potatoes! With cabbage you have to take time: you have to water them in the spring, pick worms in the summer . . . no, it doesn't pay."

Although Aksinya Yegoryevna was uneducated, and wasn't trusted with anything other than manual work on the collective farm, I was always surprised at how precisely she reasoned out her day-to-day dealings.

"Wait a second! Maybe they sell it as sauerkraut?" This new idea utterly turned the course of her argument. "Why, yes—they make it into sauerkraut! And you can get fifty to eighty kopeks for sauerkraut in the bazaar. And before a holiday, a ruble a kilo. Yes, it's heavier when made into sauerkraut. There's salt in it, and the salt from the air takes water out of it. So that's how they sell it! That's how they get their money! That way, you're already coming out with a thousand ruble return. And you think it's hard work to make cabbage into sauerkraut? Any old woman can manage it."

All of these revelations troubled her a great deal, and I even wondered whether the idea of producing sauerkraut in order to buy a large television would occupy my neighbor until her old age.

I knew long ago about how she was always ready to use her sole available capital—her own worker's hands. These had more than once given her the means to successfully sell potatoes or take something from the dairy farm for the animals' mash or for some meager cheese for herself. It seemed now as if she was close to doing something. Some sort of idea must have gotten into her head because the next day she was rather sad.

"We were talking about cabbage," she reminded me. "But cabbage would be of no use to us. For one thing, we're far from the road: cabbage sells well in winter, but it gets so frozen around here that you can't even crawl out of the snow banks. Even if some driver agrees to take it, all the profits will go to pay him. Really, even if there were a road it would be bad all the same. You need your own instrument for this kind of thing: you can't shred it all by hand. You need barrels. There should be about nine heads of it per barrel—any less isn't worth it. For the barrels, you need a big cellar. . . . And, well, you have to get used to doing it. Without the experience, you aren't going to grow much cabbage—either the worms will gobble it up or something else will happen. . . . Those aren't things you learn in the first year of planting cabbage."

Some things you get used to, but not others. This explanation is not so naïve as it seems at first glance. Habit, in other words, tradition and experience, the long-term, year-to-year application of the work and knowledge that is a small-time farmer's capital to a repeated farm task, has special meaning: a villager will not take risks and introduce innovations to his farmland—the harvest *of his own* land is too valuable to him.

Nevertheless, I'm sure that Aksinya Yegoryevna is not alone in coming up with the idea of taking sauerkraut or some product more profitable than the traditional potato to market. But under the vigilant control of government authority, that has more than once put harsh controls on small farmers, we need a particularly favorable confluence of circumstances. The peasants will not take needless risks. Although the farmer is persistent once everything is laid out, he is also cautious.

This peasant's life, seemingly incidental to the communal farm but essential to the collective farmer, requires a significantly more responsible approach than the work on the exhausted collective-state farm where everything is mandated from above, where stupidity of all kinds is pardoned—everything fulfilled in an instant, no one troubled by whether it benefits or harms the harvest. But here, the initiative, capital, means of labor, and the entire end product all belong to the peasant. Here, he is master. Here, he is a *person*. Here, he is a kind of micro-model of the master he could become if cattle and land were not taken from him in 1930, leaving him with a miniature version of a farm.

Farmers can make a meager living insofar as they can put part of their working time, part of their strength, into a different economic system, not a socialist command economy, but a market one.

Peasant markets are restricted by the dimensions of market space, weakened by the feudal relationships of personal dependence of the communal farmer on administrative power, and generally have the appearance of an appendage to that central "market" where they sell party posts and demagogic values such as promises of the universal good of the people and the imminent triumph of communism. . . . All the same, it is a market and one that the socialist government cannot do without.

At first glance the numbers are staggering: according to various calculations, private farm plots occupy only *two and a half* or even *one and a half* percent of all area under crop in the country; farms in general possess only *one-tenth* of all the industrial resources of village economies, while they put out *one-third* of all agricultural products. Such is the data according to official statistics.

But official statistics are silent about the fact that no less than a third of agricultural production in communal and state farms is lost every year either in the field, in transit, in the warehouse, or in initial processing. According to some calculations, for example, up to half of all potatoes go to waste.

Official statistics, estimating the gross product in terms of value, are of course silent about the fact that government purchase prices for grain-crops from communal and state farms are set far too high, while the prices of meat, vegetables, potatoes—that is, groceries, most of which are widely grown in personal farms—are set too low.

Official statistics are silent, for otherwise they would be compelled to admit that in the combined volume of *useable* agricultural production, the share contributed by personally-owned farms with their one-and-a-half to two percent of the arable land is far more than half. Further, in the Baltic republics the share of personally-owned farms in combined agricultural production, according to official statistics, makes up almost half: in Lithuania for example, the number is 43.6 percent. At the same time, "in families of state communal farms of the Lithuanian SSR in 1971, 50.5 percent of the overall earnings came from personal farming on the side."

These numbers speak to the disgrace of the Soviet agricultural system and the misfortune of the farmers whose initiative and talent have been chained by the limitations put on the size of the personal vegetable garden and the enormous quantity of administrative prohibitions. It is the peasants' misfortune, but also their hope.

The production of personal farms feeds all the rural people which is forty percent of the population. But that's not a lot. Even in accordance with official statistics, these farms produce half of all potatoes sold, no less than a third of the sold quantity of eggs, a third of all meat on the market—that is, food that is sold and feeds a significant part of the urban population. Without peasants' farms, the socialist economy would not survive a day.

It seems that it's just not possible to regulate the economy absolutely. The economy is a mechanism in which, without ties to the flywheel of market relations worked out over the entire history of humankind, the cogs of the bureaucratic, planned economic system will lock up and come to a halt. The market—the market is at the heart of economics. To do away with it is to do away with the national economy of the country. Stalin understood this well when he turned peasants out to work in personal gardens: " . . . the commu-nal farm cannot undertake. . . ." While market relations are alive, it is possible to add a socialist economy onto them. This holds true even if the relations are *black market* ones dependent on the government administration. A black market is just exactly what the authorities need. But more about this later. For now let's examine what method farmers use to feed the country with their tiny vegetable gardens.

Why is Posady specifically getting rich off of spring vegetables? First, the village is conveniently located. Formerly a river connected it to the city market, and now a highway links the gardens here to the city market straight-away—from the garden bed to the counter without any needless shipping transfers. Second, this place has rich soil, an island of black earth in a sea of loamy sand and infertile soil. As a result, harvests yield more, vegetables ripen earlier, and the crops need less watering. Who can compete with them? Of all the conveniently located villages, the best land is in Posady.

But at the market, everyone sells goods at the same prices whether from better or worse soils because the prices are fixed by the quality of the goods from the poor soils. Were it not this way, who would plant vegetables in their plot of land, knowing there would be no profit? Thus, of all who grow cucumbers, the small independent farmers have the greatest amount of money—their vegetables come to them cheaper than to others and yet go for the same price as everyone else's. The difference goes into their pockets. All of this is textbook political economy: to some extent the black market passes for a normal, open market and in so doing tempts the peasant.

Farmers—even those unfamiliar with textbook political economics—have long known the mechanisms of the market and how to put them into prac-tice. And, of course, not only in Central Russia or, say, Moldova—where in the past "communal farmers cut back on sowing less intensive grain crops and expanded their production of grapes and other fruit—the most profitable and intensive crops." But this has held true above all in Georgia, in the autono-mous republics of the North Caucasus, in the Baltic republics, and in Belarus', where private farming produces more than half the peasant families' com-bined income.

"Potatoes in Kursk go to markets in Donbass; fruit from Central Asia and the Caucasus to the markets of cities in central Russia; Ukrainian onions to

Moscow, Gorky, Tula, and so on. The Riazan' and Lipetsk regions occupy a special place in supplying the markets in Moscow with goods produced on the side by private farms."

The possibility of doing everything on one's own maximizes the benefit of one's labor and pushes people to achieve truly incredible agricultural feats. For example, there is just one farm that produces strawberries in the areas surrounding large cities on just a few hundredths or thousandths of a hectare, and where yields and profits are the likes of which even our friend Aksinya Yegoryevna has not dreamed in her lively agricultural imagination.

The writer Vladimir Soloukhin saw the driving force of this phenomenon:

Toward the end of our flower tour, I was taken to a place called a hot-house. . . .

"Fourteen square meters," the master explained. "Artificial climate. Harvest on demand, at any time of year. But I time it for the first of January."

"Cucumbers or tomatoes? A fresh cucumber on the table at New Year's is, of course, priceless. But then again so is a tomato."

"What're you thinking?! Cucumbers are coarse and cheap."

"Then what kind of harvest are you talking about for New Year's?"

"Flowers. Tulips. That's the kind of harvest I'm talking about. I get two to three rubles for every flower. These fourteen meters bring me a 5,000 ruble return."

Is two rubles a flower expensive or cheap? What about a ruble-and-a-half for a kilogram of potatoes at the markets in Central Asia? Around two rubles for a lemon at a bazaar in Novosibirsk? Expensive, very expensive! But this is the *market* price, and one would be hard-pressed to find an altruist who would charge just pennies for lemons. When market relations are in place, a good soul and a high sense of morality will not help—the market has its own laws and these laws are objective. As a result, it is naïve to curse about the high prices of peaches and mandarins sold by certain Caucasians. The market dealer has no soul. He is a figure of pure economics and the *entire Soviet* economic system is behind him.

The idea that average people have that in central Russian markets Caucasian and Central Asian farmers become phenomenally rich is false. Market earnings need to be shared in accordance with the number of families on a communal farm. When they are, it turns out, for example, that in "1965, Turkmenia held the top place among Soviet republics in aggregate income per family and ninth place in total overall income. . . . In the same year, Estonia held the top place in total overall income and seventh in aggregate per family."

No, high market prices are not due to greed in farmers' souls. Indeed this shining *five thousand* rubles that from time to time appears to be the maximum possible profit from private agriculture is, in the best case, only the income for a family of four to five—and not even pure income at that—but only market earnings. The costs of running the farm are extremely high. So, as it turns out, the peasant does not become the wealthiest person in society from high market prices. The real monetary income of the farming family is not higher, but in the overwhelming majority of cases lower than the average income of a family of two factory workers bringing in two salaries (294 rubles by official data).

No, it is not the farmer who drives the prices up at the market. Tulips—or spring cucumbers, or the first May tomatoes, or the meat that everyone always needs—are expensive at the market only because they are produced by individuals and in small quantities. The farmer cannot expand his production. The dimensions of his farm are administratively set and no kind of private cooperative is allowed. Large-scale agricultural enterprises (communal and state farms) do not depend upon the satisfaction of straight consumer demand, but on the security of exchange and distribution policies of the government, designed in the interests and comfort of the party bureaucracy, that ruling structure of the government that protects the existing system and itself along with it.

Prices and amount of capital investment are determined precisely by the politics of the ruling structure and ultimately determine the volume of production. Consumer demand barely makes its way through the shadows of bureaucratic relations. What is the point of speaking about tulips when over the course of a decade, agriculture has been financed and supplied so poorly, organized so stupidly that bread, meat, and milk from these large-scale farms do not reach us in high enough quantities.

So, these narrow-minded conversations about conscience and soul must be laid aside at least until the reasons for the high prices, the lack of food products in the country are brought to light—then it will be clear whose conscience it is we're talking about. Generally speaking, nothing good can come of the soul—in the mystical sense in which it is understood—interfering in market relations. In Central Asia, I know of one communal farm where private gardens flourish and bear fruit more abundantly than anywhere else around it, but whose owners live worse than their neighbors. As it turns out, the land there is irrigated with water from a sacred spring, and according to Muslim law, putting anything grown in it up for sale is taboo! And because it is taboo, there's no need to look for the most marketable kinds of apples and grapes, no need to dig trenches for citrus fruits—whatever has grown for ages will grow now, too. Ideological conventions have deadened economic possibilities and slowed down initiative.

Perhaps *ideological conventions* are also hindering the development of the economy of the entire country? Private initiative—taboo! Market relations—taboo! Desire to make a profit—taboo! It's not important that bread is brought over one ocean from America and meat over another, from New Zealand. On the other hand, our economy is washed generously in the sacred ideas of Marx, Engels, Lenin . . . (I almost included Stalin, except that it wouldn't be very pleasant to do so now—although what, at bottom, is there to be ashamed of?).

One can, of course, presume that all the existent prohibitions are sad mistakes, that the conventions are misunderstandings that themselves dissipate depending on the gap between the demands of the population for food products, the low productivity of farmers' work, and the meager possibilities for socialist agriculture to satisfy these demands. But we will not pass off what is hoped-for as reality. These prohibitions are not an accident, nor are they a convention. They are an instrument of the *ruling structure*, an instrument of the party bureaucracy—an instrument that protects the existing government order. And all of these prohibitions are established by the tendency to guard the government of party officials from economic encroachment by firmly established peasants or from a politically conscious techno structure.

Stalin understood this better than others. Although today's upper echelon of the party tries to make it seem like it does not notice his shadows, it is precisely him in the midst of all other scholars of Marxism-Leninism who is closer to the current policies of the ruling class. "Is it true that the central idea of the five-year plan in a *Soviet country* amounts to a rise in productivity?" he asked in his famous speech against Bukharin. "No, it's not true. We do not need rapid growth in productivity. We need *fixed* growth of national productivity, and specifically, that kind of growth that protects the systematic advantage of the *socialist* sector of the economy (that is, the non market sector truly dependent on the party bureaucracy, objectively working on the strengthening of its power) *above the capitalist sector.*"

It is precisely these prohibitions that constitute the essence of power, and that support the activity of the party bureaucracy. It can do without abundance of grains in the country, for it does not need commodity returns, nor does it need a comprehensively and harmoniously well developed economy—it needs only power, a limitless abundance of power, profit in the form of expansion of power, a well developed system of receiving more and new power toward advancement in the party hierarchy.

Insofar as the party bureaucracy, similar in former times to the broken down class of feudal landowners, does not take part in the general production of material and spiritual values known as social progress, there remains for it only one possibility in order not to be washed away by this stream: the establishment of a strict system of prohibitions, restrictions, and "taboos." All "measures taken by the party and the government in the area of the economy" purported every time to be a great gift to the people are nothing but the timid maneuvering by the party bureaucracy in the midst of the dams and barriers it itself set up to avoid drowning completely.

It is precisely the *black market* that does not threaten the stability of the current government. Strictly speaking, it is completely under control, and therefore, advantageous. From the very beginning, the communal farm system was thought to be like the black market system, and its sphere is considerably wider than the marketplace. We see this again immediately when we turn back to Stalin:

> If you have no abundance of food in a workmen's cooperative, and you cannot give each individual communal farmer and their family everything they need, then the communal farm cannot take it upon itself to satisfy both societal and personal needs. It is then better to say straight out that there is a domain of work that is societal and a domain that is personal. It is better to admit straightforwardly, openly and honestly, that the communal farm ought to have its own personal farms—not large, but personal. It is better to proceed from the fact that there is cooperative farming, that operates on a decisively large scale essential to meeting the needs of society, and alongside it smaller, personal farming, essential to meeting the personal needs of the communal farmer.

Kind Stalin who, as we see, allowed farming families to save themselves from starvation—in the 30s—and, Brezhnev, who emphatically encouraged farmers to intensify their work on personal farms—in the 70s—did not specify, of course, what percentage of the day farmers ought to devote to "personal farming." Clearly, they meant only what remained after their work for the communal farm. . . . And that's where the "black market" begins! Here, and not at the gates of the bazaar.

It begins with the fact that the peasant is *forced* to sell to society his *overtime* labor, while his work on the communal farm is unceremoniously taken for nothing or next to nothing, without satisfying the elementary needs of the peasant family. Here is where the most important "buying-selling" on the black market is: it is not carrots that are sold, nor parsley, but the labor and life of the hard working countryside.

And who here is the buyer?

Translated by Ezekiel Pfeifer

VI

Near Pavilions: The Caucasus

The Caucasus region is a diverse landmass of 175,000 square miles stretching from the south of Russia to just north of Iran and wedged in between the Black and Caspian Seas. It has been home to dozens of civilizations over its extended history; some have argued that it demonstrates a shared civilizational structure of its own, one evolved from solidarities forged after years of conquest. The Caucasus area is most commonly divided into North (the area contained within Russia proper)—encompassing the peoples often glossed as Circassian (Cherkess and Adyghe among the most prominent), North Ossetia, Ingushetia, the lands of Daghestan, and more famously today Chechnya—and South, embracing the contemporary post-Soviet republics of Armenia, Azerbaijan, and Georgia. Historically when the Caucasus (in Russian, *Kavkaz*) has been spoken of most pejoratively the reference is most often to *gortsy*, the highland peoples of the northern flanks of the Great Caucasus mountain range, whose allegiances to the Ottomans, the Crimean Khan, or more often simply to themselves made them among the fiercest opponents of Russian annexation and some of the most difficult for the Russians to understand. The South Caucasus polities were at times equally recalcitrant to Russian rule and were met with the same derision. But they were relatively more accessible given the organization of small, centralized, semi-independent khanates that functioned through the decline of Persian rule after the death of Nadir Shah in the mid-eighteenth century and perforce understood by Russian officials as relatively further along on civilizational scales.

Readers looking to understand what has transpired since Ivan the Terrible took the Muslim city-state of Kazan' (capital of the contemporary Russian republic of Tatarstan) in 1552 may be surprised to learn that there is not a great deal about the Caucasus in English beyond the perennial standards of archaeology, linguistics, folklore, and more recently, given events in Chechnya and beyond, conflict studies. Part of this has to do with the simple fact of the region's intense pluralisms.

To know the Caucasus has never been simple, even for those who live

Chokh village in Daghestan, 1933. Courtesy of the American Geographical Library from the University of Wisconsin–Milwaukee Libraries. Photographer William O. Field.

there. Using standards common to any conventionally mapped world area, serious study of Caucasian life up to the nineteenth century requires a command of at least one of the dominant languages—Arabic, Persian, or Turkish—and, under ideal circumstances, more than one. For the twentieth century a knowledge of Russian surges in importance. For all periods the need for essential competence in one of the larger republican or regional languages—Adyghe, Avar, Armenian, or Azerbaijani—only begins to suggest the challenges that scholarly study poses. Historically, few scholars have been up to this task. Yet fragments of all of these knowledges come alive every day. To match the punning vocabulary of almost any street vendor in Yerevan, Tbilisi, or Baku, one has to start with a working knowledge of Greek, Roman, Arab, Mongol, Turkic, Persian, Ottoman, and Russian invasions. Most scholars who are new to the region take refuge under the covers and return to (or stay behind in) London, Moscow, Istanbul, or Tehran.

Like so many parts of the world, the Caucasus marks its earliest histories through conquest. As early as the eighth century BCE Greek ships sailed east to command new lands that would help to feed growing armies; Turks, Ottomans, Arabs, and Persians used the Caucasus as a theater of competition between Sunni and Shi'i military campaigns at the height of empire; Mongols took Caucasian lands as part of one of their final bids to march on Central Europe; and Russians aspired to push south and west to warm seas, using the Caucasus as their launching ground. What do these long lines of conquerors

Man selling swords at a village market in Daghestan, 1933. Courtesy of
the American Geographical Library from the University of Wisconsin–
Milwaukee Libraries. Photographer William O. Field.

and would-be conquerors have in common? In each case their respective
Caucasus campaigns began as little more than a staging ground for broader
ambitions, staking out a crucial territory in a set of geopolitical projects that
relied on this region as an "absent presence." In the post-Soviet world little
seems to have changed; the Caucasus continues to be most widely known as
the crucible of broader Russian sovereignty in the case of Chechnya, or of
NATO designs on Russia and the Middle East aided by new strategic partners.

This long-standing tradition of sovereign ambitions over such a small space
has left a deep imprint on how this part of the world is understood. Greeks
were among the first, but by no means the last, to depict the peoples of the
Caucasus as less than welcoming to would-be foreign overseers. What came
first: resistance to invasion, or naturally occurring belligerence? How one
answers this question often tells more about the observer than the observed,
about which sides in a long, shared history of conquest and colonization one
recognizes, and indeed about the constitution of areal knowledge itself.

The briefest survey of the most prominent ways of knowing the Caucasus
begins to paint a picture of a region famous for all of its cultural, linguistic,
religious, political, and economic pluralisms; its violence, savagery, conflict,
and corruption; its nobility, hospitality, natural beauty, and severity. Already

this presents a paradox since, despite such evident histories of diaspora, migration, conquest, and cohabitation, despite such intense evidence of mobilities and crossings, the Caucasus is most often conjured as a place of closure to those "from outside."

The readings in this section focus foremost on the North Caucasus and look to go beyond these stereotypes of insider / outsider knowledges by focusing on how the Caucasus has been known primarily through Russian eyes and what a number of thinkers in the Caucasus have had to say about this part of the world on their own terms. Those who think the Caucasus might be beyond their own frame of reference need only be reminded of the racially charged term *Caucasian* itself, which has spread far beyond its originally intended borders. For his long ago doctoral dissertation in Germany in 1795, Johann Friedrich Blumenbach insisted that a single Georgian woman's skull that had been shipped to him via the Caucasus and England for examination was the "finest and most perfect by which all others should be judged." It was the perception of perfection (and, by extension, the skull's near match to the best European examples) that gave rise to the extended racial classifications many live with today. If that renders the story of the Caucasus closer to the lives of some readers, this is all the better for a part of the world whose recognition as one of the hearths of modern civilization has long been overlooked.

The Russian Conquest of the Caucasus (1908)

John F. Baddeley

John Baddeley (1854–1940) was the son of a British Royal Cavalry officer. He worked as an aide to the Russian ambassador in the United Kingdom and made his first trip to Russia in 1879. The trip proved fateful. He spent much of his life over the next four decades becoming one of Europe's most eloquent conduits to Russian life, first as a correspondent for The London Standard, and later in a number of private commercial ventures, where he continued to write in his personal diaries and diplomatic dispatches. The records of his travels throughout the Caucasus and Siberia in particular, abetted by the wealth of historical scholarship he invoked, made these works classics.

Russia had ambitions in the Caucasus region from the age of Ivan the Terrible onward. Peter the Great made inroads into Daghestan, and his successor, Catherine II, saw the Caucasus as an amphitheater for her interests in Persia. Formal Russian sovereignty began in the South, when Georgian kings sought protection from invading Persian and Ottoman forces in 1801. In brisk succession many of the semi-independent territories now covering the contemporary republics of Armenia and Azerbaijan, khanates once aggressively ruled by the Ottomans and Persia, also joined a Russian fold that, like the Georgians, they soon found they could not leave.

With the South Caucasus secured, taking the more troublesome North Caucasus that lay in the middle between Russia and its new southern holdings proved far more difficult. Thus began the many battles historians have called "the Caucasus war," lasting through 1864 and the surrender of Imam Shamil, the charismatic North Caucasus leader. In his text Baddeley calls it "the Murid war," drawing on the Arabic term for Sufi disciples, some of whom figured prominently in the anti-Russian ranks of what was otherwise a distinctly political rather than religious movement.

The theme of Baddeley's introduction to the peoples of the Caucasus is the legendary pluralism that so many scholars and travelers have attempted to reconcile in such a compact geographical space. Baddeley's conclusion is that, by dint of its extraordinary location as a crossroads between North and South, East and West, the Caucasus, with its long plains, tall mountains, and countless valleys, offered ample respite for the dozens of peoples, both conquering and conquered, who accreted there over *time, each leaving their mark. With so many would-be conquerors, the story of the Caucasus has not been an easy one. "Egyptian, Mede, Alan, and Scythian; Greek, Roman, Persian, and Arab; Mongol, Tartar, Turk, and Slav," Baddeley writes. "These and more have one after another and times without number surged up against the Caucasus like angry waves on a storm-vexed coast."*

The name Caucasus has been used from the days of Æschylus and Herodotus, at least, to denote the chain of lofty mountains stretching across the isthmus between the Caspian and Black Seas from west-north-west to east-south-east, together with a varying extent of the regions on either side.

It is applied at the present day to the whole of the territories south of the government of Astrakhan and the province of the Don up to the Persian and Turkish frontiers.

To describe even in summary fashion a country so extensive and varied within the limits of one short chapter is clearly impossible. For anything approaching full treatment a volume would be little enough, and the following pages aim only at giving the reader some general idea of the Caucasus and its inhabitants, and of the problems involved in the conquest.

The Caucasus is essentially a mountain country; its inhabitants, with the exception of the Christian population occupying the river valleys of the Rion and Koura, essentially mountaineers; for, just as, thanks to its mass and elevation, the great central range has largely influenced all other physical features, so together with them has it been the determining factor in the matter of population. The peoples of the Caucasus owe to it not only their salient characteristics, but their very existence. It may be said without exaggeration that the mountains made the men; and the men in return fought with passionate courage and energy in defence of their beloved mountains, in whose fastnesses, indeed, they were well-nigh unconquerable. Yet, by one of those strange contradictions that meet us on all sides, strength and weakness went hand in hand. The very height and ruggedness of the great ranges, the profound depth and steepness of the valleys, the vast spread of the primeval forest, made union impossible; and without unity the tribes in the long run were bound to fall before the might of Russia.

The mountain chain, to which, admittedly, the name Caucasus was once restricted, has a total length of some 650 miles, of which the really mountainous part is 400 miles long with skirts stretching out for another 150 and 100 miles respectively, to the neighbourhoods of Baku, on the Caspian, and of Novorosseesk, on the Black Sea. Its width varies considerably, and in estimating it there is room for divergence of opinion, but roughly it may be stated at about 100 miles, save in the middle, where it narrows considerably, and at the tapering extremities.

The triple division thus indicated by Nature corresponds, though roughly and for not very obvious reasons, to the three sections into which during the whole of the long struggle for supremacy the mountain country was divided. To the west, from the neighbourhood of El-brouz to the Black Sea coast, is a forest region wherein the main chain sinks gradually from a height of 10,000 feet to the sea-level; and here the local tribes, the Tcherkess and others, to whom in general the name Circassian is applied, kept up a fierce though desultory warfare against the northern invaders from the close of the eighteenth century down to 1864. To the east the Tchetchens in their hillside forests and the many tribes of Daghestan on their barren mountain plateaus maintained the struggle for independence nearly as long, with greater vigour and with a larger measure of success. But in between, where the mountains are highest, where for 100 miles at a stretch there is no pass under 10,000 feet, and for 400 miles but few, the Russians met with little opposition. The Ossietines, Kabardáns, and Tartar tribes to the west of the Georgian road, the Ingoushee, Galgais, Khevsours, and Pshavs to the east, robbed and raided as their nature was, and more than once rebelled; but on the whole they accepted Russian rule, or sovereignty, for the most part nominal, with much equanimity, and seldom gave any serious trouble. There was thus a great gap between the two main theatres of the mountain war threaded by the one and only convenient line of communication from north to south, the Georgian road—a gap that, in spite of Shamil's desperate effort in 1846, was never bridged over; and this in the history of the conquest is a fact of primary importance never to be forgotten.

On the south side of the main chain dwelt the various divisions of the Georgian race in whose defence the Russians first crossed the mountains, and who, with occasional aberrations, held loyally to the compact in virtue of which they became subjects of the Tsar. Farther south still lay, on the east, the Muhammadan khanates, vassal states of Persia; on the west, the semi-independent pashaliks of Turkey in Asia.

Russia's task should now be clear—in the Caucasus proper to subdue, on the one hand, the western tribes, who looked for support to Turkey; on the other, the peoples of Daghestan and Tchetchnia; in Transcaucasia, to reunite the Georgian race, defend it against Persian and Turk, and enlarge and make safe its boundaries at their expense. How this task was accomplished it is the object of this volume to tell; but in regard to the Russo-Turkish campaigns beyond the Caucasus, it must be remembered that they served also a second purpose, and served it well—to keep, namely, in war-time many thousands of Turkish troops employed in Asia Minor, and thus ease, for Russia, the strain in Europe.

The struggle for the possession of the Caucasus was carried on for a period, roughly speaking, of sixty years continuously against the mountaineers, and, in a succession of wars extending over a still longer period, against the Turks and the Persians. The three areas of conflict (counting Transcaucasia as one) were practically separate, though Persia was at times in contact with Daghestan, Turkey with the country of the western tribes; and as, for reasons set forth in the Preface, the present volume deals hardly at all with the last-named, and as, moreover, the Turkish and Persian borders are sufficiently well known, it will only be necessary here to describe in somewhat greater detail the scene of the Murid war—Daghestan and Tchetchnia— and the peoples there inhabiting. But before doing so it will be as well to say a few words as to the races of the Caucasus in general and as to their origin, at once the most fascinating and the most difficult of the many problems there confronting us.

A well-known passage in Strabo states that Dioscurias, on or near the site of the present Soukhoum-Kalé, was frequented by people speaking seventy different languages. Pliny quotes Timosthenes to the effect that the number was 300, and says "afterwards we Romans conducted our affairs there with the aid of 130 interpreters." And Al-Azizi called the eastern Caucasus "the Mountain of Languages" (Djebal Alsuni) because, according to him, the people inhabiting it spoke 300 different tongues. Allowance must be made for Oriental exuberance of imagination, but even quite recently the number was given by sober Europeans as not less than forty for Daghestan alone, and it was supposed that many if not most of these were totally unconnected one with another. But recent researches have thrown quite a new light on this branch of comparative philology, and, according to F. Müller, the greater part of the languages of the Caucasus form one independent family consisting of three groups, namely, the Kartvel, the western and the eastern Caucasian, all originating in one parent language, and differentiated from it in the course of time in much the same way as the languages of the Hamite-Semitic family from a like common original. In this way the Georgian and cognate languages of the Kartvel group would answer to those Semitic languages which are obviously connected together, while the languages of the mountain tribes would correspond to the Hamitic dialects, the connection between which only becomes apparent on the application of analytical methods proper to comparative philology. However this may be, and the last word on the subject has not yet of course been said, the Caucasus is inhabited probably by a greater number of different tribes, races, and peoples than any similar extent of territory on the surface of the globe, speaking, too, a greater variety of languages; and, as General Kómaroff remarks, the more inaccessible the valleys in which they dwell, the smaller the individual groups and the sharper, apparently, the linguistic and other distinctions between them.

Shamil's explanation of this great variety of population in the Caucasus was, that Alexander the Great took a dislike to the country owing to the barrenness of the soil and severity of the climate, and out of spite made it a place of exile for the criminals of all the world; and with the bitterness of a leader who felt that his failure was due to the defection of his own people rather than to the power of his enemies, the captive chieftain professed to attribute the evil nature of the mountaineers to this vile origin. But Alexander was never within hundreds of miles of the Caucasus, and it is unnecessary to seek elsewhere than in its geographical position and physical configuration for good and sufficient reasons why the mountain range between the Caspian and Black Seas should have become the refuge of many a race conquering and conquered in turn, succumbing at last to fresh waves of invasion from south or from north. Driven into the mountains, where defence was easy and the temptation to follow them slight, they made good their footing amongst those who had preceded them in similar circumstances, or, failing in that, disappeared for ever from amongst the nations of the earth. That those who survived maintained in many cases their individuality, that they even differentiated into still more numerous clans and tribes and peoples, varying more or less in appearance, language, customs and beliefs, if such be really the case, was due, no doubt, to the nature of their new country, and is a phenomenon the less surprising when we consider what Humboldt has to say of the similar results produced on the vast plains of Brazil merely by the density of the forests.

From the dawn of history, and doubtless long ages before, these mountain fastnesses were the refuge of vanquished races, the plains at their feet the camping-ground of conquering hordes. Egyptians, Mede, Alan, and Scythian; Greek, Roman, Persian, and Arab; Mongol, Tartar, Turk, and Slav—these and more have one after another and times without number surged up against the Caucasus like angry waves on a storm-vexed coast; but the wonder is that, while some or all of them contributed their quota, traceably or not, to the population of the Caucasus, the majority of the tribes that now inhabit its recesses, or dwell at its base, to judge from existing philological data, derive ultimately from none of them, but are remnants—so at least Uslar thinks—"of many peoples inhabiting in prehistoric times vast stretches of land in Asia and in Europe, and belonging to one race which has everywhere else disappeared."

. . . .

Such, in brief, was the country; and such were the peoples who, with no outside assistance, with no artillery but what they could capture from the enemy, with no trust but in Allah and His Prophet, their own right hands and flashing blades, defied the might of Russia for more than half a century; defeating her armies, raiding her settlements, and laughing to scorn her wealth, her pride, and her numbers. And the story of their heroic struggle has a special claim on the sympathy of English readers. They fought, it is true, for themselves alone—for Faith, freedom, and country. But they stood too, though all unknowingly, for the security of British rule in India. In the words of Sir Henry Rawlinson, "So long as the mountaineers resisted, they formed an effective barrier to the tide of onward conquest. When once they were swept away there was no military or physical obstacle to the continuous march of Russia from the Araxes to the Indus."

Mtsyri (1839)

Mikhail Lermontov

Though he died at the young age of twenty-seven, Mikhail Lermontov found a place for himself among Russia's best-known writers, leaving behind poems such as "The Demon" and the brilliant novel Hero of Our Time. *Raised in Moscow and a young officer in the Russian Imperial Guards, he began his creative life in poetry. His homage to the fallen Aleksandr Pushkin, written after Pushkin's death in 1837, was openly critical of the Russian noble classes and earned him the opprobrium of Tsar Nicholas I. Like Pushkin, he was exiled to the Caucasus. Exiled yet a second time after a duel in Petersburg with the French ambassador's son, the young Lermontov died in the Caucasus resort town of Piatigorsk, in a gunfight with a former military schoolmate.*

Of all the peoples of the Caucasus who joined the Russian fold in the early nineteenth century, Georgians and Armenians were said to be among the most faithful to the empire, given their shared Christianity. Yet as the politically sympathetic Lermontov demonstrates with a lyrical turn in his famous poem "Mtsyri" (The Novice), the empire was built on an unsteady firmament of competing allegiances to history, myth, and landscape.

While partaking, I have partaken of little honey, and behold: now I am dying.
—1 Kings

1

> Not very many years ago,
> Where two Caucasian rivers flow
> And meet in sisterly embrace
> And, having merged, together race,
> There was a cloister; from that place
> One still can see the ruined gate,
> The pillars, as they stood of late,

Gorge of the Terek River along the Georgian Military Road, 1933. Courtesy of the
American Geographical Library from the University of Wisconsin–Milwaukee Libraries.
Photographer William O. Field.

The vault and turrets spared by fate.
But monks in cassocks never halt
To talk or pray within this vault,
And fragrant incense does not rise
From smoking vessels to the skies.
Today an aged man alone,
The feeble guard of crumbling stone,
By death forgotten and by men,
Will walk 'mid tombstones now and then
And clean their legends, telling when
Some king, in glory and renown,
But sadly burdened by his crown,
Gave up his subjects and his star
To humbly serve the Russian Tsar.

And Georgia after that was blessed;
Her thriving land enjoyed a rest,
Unmuddied stayed her cooling source,
The country quietly ran its course,
Protected by a friendly force.

2

A Russian general one day
Through mountains slowly made his way.
He had a captive boy with him;
The child fell ill; too small and slim
He was to travel, ride, or drive;
The boy was six or even five,
Shy as the mountain chamois's breed
And frail and supple as a reed.
But his disease, his sorry plight
Awakened in him all the might
His tribe possessed. His racking pain
Would never make the child complain;
He never groaned and never cried,
He pushed his food and drink aside,
And, proud and silent, nearly died.
A kindly monk began to tend
The patient; and, indeed, his end
He warded off. Thus, saved by care,
The boy survived and grew up there.
But having never learned to play,
From everyone he'd run away,
Avoid the brothers and the priest
And cast long glances to the East.
It made him deeply, strangely sad
To see the home he could have had.
But he succumbed, for he was young,
And learned to speak the alien tongue.
Baptized, he lived like a recluse;
Life was for him of little use,
And long before its cup was drunk
He knew that he would be a monk.
But suddenly, one autumn night,
The brothers missed him. Filled with fright,
They searched the woody slopes around.
For three long days he was not found,
When, finally, upon the ground
They saw the youngster in a swoon

And to the cloister brought him soon.
He looked so gaunt and pale and tense,
As though he'd done some work immense
Or had been dangerously ill.
He lay indifferent and still,
Devoid of interest and will.
And when they saw how low he'd sunk
There came to him his Father monk
And begged him to disclose the truth.
The weak and almost dying youth
Collected all his ebbing strength
And proudly spoke to him at length.

3

"You've come to hear what I can tell.
I thank you for it: you mean well.
And I believe, if I confess,
My burden will torment me less.
But what's my tale to such as you?
I never harmed the men I knew,
I never killed and never stole . . .
And who can tell the world his soul!
I lived a wretched captive boy.
Two lives like mine I'd give with joy
For one and even shorter life,
If it were only filled with strife.
I knew one passion's mighty surge,
A single but consuming urge;
At first a tiny seed, a germ,
It burned and gnawed me like a worm,
But with it I was strong and firm,
For in my dingy, stuffy cell
It called upon me to rebel,
To seek the world of rock and cloud,
The world of men, like eagles, proud.
This urge would torture me and rend,
But I have fed it to the end;
Let earth and heaven now attend—

I say aloud: The dream was mine,
I loved it, and I don't repine.

4

"Old man! I often heard it said
That you had saved me from the dead.
Why did you? Somber and forlorn,
A tiny leaf by tempests torn,
I've grown behind this cheerless gate,
A child by soul, a monk by fate.
My Father . . . mother . . . neither word
I ever said or even heard.
I know how glad you would have been,
If in the cloister-life routine
I had forgotten, like my games,
Those sweet and stirring sacred names.
Oh, labor lost! I used to roam
And saw that men had kin and home,
That only I was robbed by doom
Of parents' love and parents' tomb.
I saw it all and cried no more,
But to myself an oath I swore
That once, just once, my burning breast
To someone else's would be pressed
And that the man who'd see me bend
Might be a stranger but a friend.
Alas, the dream that fed my oath
Is checked in all its blooming growth,
And in an alien land, my grave
Will hide a wretched, orphaned slave.

5

"I do not fear it; dust to dust . . .
The grave protects from torture's thrust,
Its cold and quiet end our strife,
But I am grieved to part with life.
I am young, so young. . . . Say, did you know

The dreams of youth, their sweeping flow?
Perhaps you didn't—or forgot
How love and hatred tie a knot;
How fast the heart in you would beat,
When from a height your eye would meet
The freshness of a sunlit field
And mountains standing like a shield;
Or when you notice from above
A guest from far away, a dove,
Who in a crevice found a seat
And waits for thunder to retreat.
Of course, today it leaves you cold:
You are decrepit, gray, and old.
Your former yearnings must have ceased;
But what of that? You lived at least!
At least you soared before you fell.
You lived. I could have lived as well."

Man and woman in Daghestan. Source: Library of Congress, Prints and Photographs Division, Prokudin-Gorskii Collection, LC-DIG-prokc-21477. Courtesy of Jean Swetchine.

Sandro of Chegem (1973)

Fazil Iskander

*Fazil Iskander (b. 1929) has been regarded as one of the Soviet Union's most distin-
guished fiction writers. In a prolific series of novels, short stories, and poems he has
delivered a mix of fantasy and memoir, based in part on life in his native Abkhazia on
the Black Sea coast. Few of his characters are as well known as the legendary Sandro
of Chegem, whose life is set in the time of Iskander's childhood in the first half of the
twentieth century. Lover, swordsman, leader, and sometimes (if only cunningly) the
buffoon, "Uncle Sandro" is a larger-than-life character whose exploits deftly interpel-
late real-life historical events from the tumultuous early Soviet period. Sandro is from
Kenguria, a fictitious district of eastern Abkhazia. Kengurians are in regular conflict
with the Endurskies, residents of, as Iskander puts it, "an even more fictitious district
in even more eastern Abkhazia." With these disclaimers in place, there is seemingly
nothing that cannot be said about contemporary Soviet and especially Caucasus life
through the prisms of these conflicts. Endurskies, like so many peoples, Iskander
contends, see no reason to improve themselves as they believe they are already the
paragon of civilizational development. This makes them a comedic but telling flash-
point for reflections on ethnic life in the deeply pluralist Soviet state.*

*In this introduction to the life of Sandro, we find him visiting a wealthy Armenian
merchant under assault from marauding Mensheviks. Mensheviks (literally, "of the
minority") were part of a breakaway socialist group whose initially pragmatic disagreements with Lenin (of the Bolsheviks, or "majoritarians") became more definitive
when Mensheviks sided with the provisional government in 1917 and then were
disbanded altogether with the formation of the Soviet Union. A Georgian Menshevik
leader, Noy Zhordania, led the short-lived Democratic Republic of Georgia (including
Abkhazia in its territory) in the brief hiatus (1918–21) between empire and worker's
state. Among its many features, our tale introduces the complex relations between
host and guest found across the Caucasus, where even foes follow strict codes of honor
in each other's homes and sometimes find that they have more in common than they
realized. To Uncle Sandro the fault of the marauders at hand is not that they are
Mensheviks, or that they might even be Endurskies, but that they are not very
competent at their marauding.*

Uncle Sandro has been around for nearly eighty years, so that even by Abkhazian standards he may confidently be called an old man. Considering the many occasions in his youth—and not only in his youth—when people tried to kill him, we may say that he has been downright lucky.

The first time he took a bullet was from a young reprobate, as he invariably called him. It happened while he was cinching up his saddle girth before leaving a prince's courtyard.

At the time he was the princess's lover and had been hanging around her day and night. Thanks to his extraordinary knightly virtues, he was her foremost, indeed her only, lover.

The young reprobate was in love with the princess and had also been hanging around her day and night, exercising his rights as a neighbor, I believe, or a distant relative on the husband's side. He did not, however, as Uncle Sandro himself used to say, have the extraordinary knightly virtues that Uncle Sandro had. Or maybe he did, but he could find no opportunity to make use of them, because the princess was mad about Uncle Sandro.

Nevertheless, he had hopes, so he never moved a step from the princess's house, or even from her side, as long as she would have him there. Possibly she refrained from banishing him because he spurred Uncle Sandro to ever more inventive feats of love. Or perhaps she kept him around just in case Uncle Sandro suddenly became disabled. Who knows?

The princess was of Svanian extraction. That may explain certain of her erotic eccentricities. Among her good points, in addition to those of her fair exterior (Uncle Sandro used to say that she was as white as milk), I think we should note that she was an excellent rider, not a bad shot, and when the occasion required it, she could even milk a buffalo.

I mention this because milking a buffalo is hard—you have to have very strong fingers to do it. So the question of her being effete, infantile, or physically degenerate simply does not arise, despite the fact that she was a full-blooded descendant of the princes of Svanetia.

I don't think that this statement runs contrary to historical materialism if one considers the specifics of societal development under the alpine conditions of the Caucasus, not to mention the splendid air that she and her forebears had breathed. Uncle Sandro used to say that sometimes this amazon was not averse to pinching her beloved at intimate moments. But he bore it and never once cried out, because he was a truly gallant knight.

I suspect that her husband, a peaceable Abkhazian prince, was forced to bear cruder expressions of her despotic temperament. So, just in case, he tried to keep out of range.

At one time the young reprobate tried to enlist the husband's support (come to think of it, he must have been a relative rather than a neighbor). He had little to gain by this ploy, however. Even though the husband also hung around the house a lot, he was not around so much as Uncle Sandro because he passionately loved to hunt ibex, an avocation that requires a great deal of energy and forays lasting many days.

It may have been that the prince needed someone to stay home during his lengthy hunting trips—some dynamic and brave young man who could amuse the princess, receive guests, and if necessary, defend the honor of the house. Just such a young man, in those days, was Uncle Sandro. According to Uncle Sandro, the princess's husband loved him no less than the princess did. To the importunate young reprobate the prince therefore replied once and for all, "Don't get me mixed up in your intrigues."

This remark, perhaps, was what made the nameless young reprobate feel so lonely and bereft that the only remedy he could find was to shoot Uncle Sandro.

In any case, this was how matters stood that day, when Uncle Sandro was briskly cinching up his saddle girth and his inconsolable rival was loitering mournfully in the middle of the courtyard with a decision ripening in his mind, the decision—frivolous even for those days—to shoot Uncle Sandro.

He had just tightened the front cinch when his rival called his name. Uncle Sandro turned, and the shot rang out.

"F—k your mother," Uncle Sandro screamed furiously, "if you think you can do me in with one bullet! Shoot again!"

But just then the princess's servants came running, and the princess herself flew out to the terrace.

They got Uncle Sandro to his feet. With the bullet in his stomach, he kept on swearing for a while, but finally he collapsed.

At first they put him to bed in the princess's house, but then that began to seem improper, and a few days later his relatives took him home on a stretcher. The princess rode along behind and stayed at his bedside night and day, which was no small honor, since his father was a simple peasant, although fairly well off.

Uncle Sandro had a very bad time because the young reprobate's Turkish pistol had been loaded with something like iron splinters. A celebrated doctor from the city was called in to save his life; he performed an operation and treated him for about two months. For each day of treatment he took one sheep, so that subsequently Uncle Sandro's father used to say of him that this "goat" had cost him sixty sheep.

No one knows how much longer the treatment would have lasted if Uncle Sandro's father had not returned home unexpectedly from the fields one day.

He had broken his hoe and was coming for a new one. As he entered the yard he saw the doctor dozing peacefully in the shade of a walnut tree instead of treating his son or at least brewing herbs for him. He may be asleep, but I daresay his sheep are busy getting fat in the pasture, the old man thought as he went into the house.

He was even more surprised when he went into Uncle Sandro's room, because Uncle Sandro was sleeping, and not alone. This was going too far for any sister of mercy, even if she was of princely lineage. The thing that made the old man maddest was that he didn't know on which of the sixty days she had joined Sandro in bed, she being the first to realize that he was well, or at least that the method of treatment could be revised. Had he known a little sooner, he might have been able to avoid giving that lazybones the last ten sheep. Anyway, he poked the princess.

"Get up, Princess, the prince is at the gate!" he said.

"I guess I must have dozed off shooing the flies away from him," she yawned, stretching and hiking herself up a bit.

"Oh sure, from under the covers," the old man grumped, and he left the room.

At this point, Uncle Sandro, who out of modesty had been pretending to be asleep and wanted to keep on pretending, could not stand it any more. He burst out laughing. The princess started laughing too, because as a true patrician, albeit of alpine lineage, she was not particularly embarrassed.

The doctor was banished to town that very day, along with the sheep that were due him. The princess stayed on for several more days as Uncle Sandro's guest, and when she left, like a true princess, she gave his sisters gifts from among her silks and pearls. Everyone was happy—everyone except the young reprobate. After his ill-fated shot he was utterly bereft because the princess had moved to Uncle Sandro's, and despite his considerable effrontery, he did not dare make an appearance there. More than that, he had to get out of our part of the world altogether. He was not hiding from legal retribution so much as to avoid a bullet from one of Uncle Sandro's relatives. While he might still have had some hope in the princess's house, some occasion to demonstrate his more extraordinary knightly virtues (if he had any, that is), he was now forced to suffer from afar.

Besides this incident there have been many other times in Uncle Sandro's life when he could have been killed, or at least wounded. He could have been killed during the Civil War with the Mensheviks if he had taken part in it. In fact he could have been killed even though he did not take part.

Apropos, I will relate an adventure of his that I consider typical of the troubled time of the Mensheviks.

Uncle Sandro was returning home from a feast of some sort. Before he noticed, he was overtaken by darkness. It was a dangerous period, Menshevik detachments forayed everywhere, and he decided to ask to spend the night under the nearest roof. He recalled that a certain rich Armenian with whom he was slightly acquainted lived somewhere nearby. In his time this Armenian had fled from the massacres in Turkey. Now he raised high-grade tobaccos and sold them to the merchants of Trebizond and Batum, who paid him, Uncle Sandro claims, in pure gold.

Uncle Sandro rode up to the gates of the Armenian's house and shouted in his resonant voice, "Hey! Anyone home?"

There was no answer. But he saw the light go out in the kitchen, and wooden shutters closed over the inside of the windows. He shouted again, but there was no answer. Then he bent down to open the gate himself, and rode into the yard.

"Don't come any closer or I'll shoot!" came the owner's none-too-confident voice. Times are bad, thought Uncle Sandro, if this tobacco grower has taken up arms.

"Since when do you shoot at guests?" Uncle Sandro shouted, using his quirt to fend off the dog that leaped out to meet him. He heard women's voices, and the voice of the owner himself, coming from the kitchen. Apparently they were holding a council of war.

"You're not a Menshevik?" the owner asked finally, his voice imploring Uncle Sandro not to be a Menshevik, or at least to call himself something else.

"No," Uncle Sandro said proudly, "I'm just myself, Sandro of Chegem."

"Then why didn't I recognize your voice?" the owner asked.

"Out of fright," Uncle Sandro explained. The kitchen door opened cautiously, and the old man came out carrying a rifle. He walked up to Uncle Sandro and finally recognized him, only then calling off the dog. Uncle Sandro dismounted, his host tied his horse to an apple tree, and they went into the kitchen. Uncle Sandro noticed immediately that the man and his family were glad to see him, although he did not understand the true reason for their gladness until much later. For the moment he took it at face value, so to speak, as a modest tribute of thanks to him for his feats of gallantry, and it made him feel good. Incidentally, the man's family consisted of his wife, mother-in-law, and two teenage children—a boy and a girl.

In Uncle Sandro's honor the man sent his boy to slaughter a sheep, got out some wine, and although the guest, to be polite, tried to restrain him from the bloodletting, everything was done as it should be. Uncle Sandro was happy that his choice had fixed on this house, that his already sensitive nose for the possibilities of finding hospitality among people he barely knew had not betrayed him. In later years, with continuous practice, he developed this sense to the point of absolute pitch. It was largely responsible for his becoming a celebrated tamada, or toastmaster, in our part of the world—at once the merriest and the saddest star, as it were, in the firmament of marriage and funeral feasts.

When he sampled the wine, Uncle Sandro was convinced that the rich Armenian had already learned how to make good wine, even though he had not yet learned how to defend his house properly. Doesn't matter, Uncle Sandro thought, in our part of the world one learns everything eventually. So they sat past midnight by the fireplace fire at a bounteous fine table; the host constantly directed the conversation to Uncle Sandro's feats, and since Uncle Sandro, not being bashful, moved in this direction with satisfaction, the table was animated and instructive. Among other things, Uncle Sandro recounted for him a famous episode from his life, the time he shell-shocked a certain horseman by the sheer force of his voice, sweeping him from his mount as if with a sound wave.

"In those days," he added, when telling me the story of his adventure with the rich Armenian, "I had such a voice that if I gave a sudden shout in the dark the rider sometimes fell right off his horse, though sometimes he didn't."

"What did it depend on?" I probed.

"His blood," he explained confidently. "Bad blood curdles from fright, just like milk, and the man falls in a dead faint, though he doesn't die."

But to go on with the story. The talk and the wine flowed with a peaceful murmur, the logs crackled in the fireplace, and Uncle Sandro was perfectly content. True, it struck him as a bit strange that his host did not send his mother-in-law and children off to bed, because the wife could have taken care of the table alone. But then he decided that the children would profit by hearing tales of his feats; after all, it wasn't every day that they had a guest like Sandro of Chegem.

But now the dog barked again. The host looked at Uncle Sandro, and Sandro at him.

"Hey! Anyone home?" came a shout from the yard. Uncle Sandro listened intently, and from the way the sound kept shifting around, he determined that the dog was barking at five or six people, at least.

"Mensheviks," his host whispered, looking hopefully to Uncle Sandro. Sandro did not like this, but he was ashamed to retreat.

"I'll try my shout on them," he said. "If that doesn't work, we'll have to defend ourselves."

"Hey in there!" someone's voice called again, over the dog's barking. "Come on out, or it'll be all the worse for you!"

"Get away from the doors," Uncle Sandro ordered. "They'll start shooting through the door in a minute. Mensheviks shoot through the door first," he explained. No sooner had he said it than pow! pow! pow!—bullets struck the door, blasting splinters into the kitchen.

All three of the women burst into tears, and the rich Armenian's mother-in-law even set up a wail, just like our women at funerals.

"Why don't you have a chestnut door?" Uncle Sandro said, surprised to see that the door wasn't holding up worth a damn.

"Oh, Allah," his host cried out, "I know the tobacco business, but I don't know about things like that."

He had completely fallen apart. In Uncle Sandro's words, he was holding his old flintlock like a shepherd's staff. You might at least have brought a decent rifle with you from Turkey, Uncle Sandro thought with irritation. He realized that there was no point in depending on this tobacco grower for help.

"Where does that door lead?" Uncle Sandro asked, nodding at the other kitchen door.

"To the storeroom," his host said.

"I'm going to shout now," Uncle Sandro announced. "Have the women and children hide in the storeroom, or they'll ruin my shout with their bawling."

The owner herded his family into the storeroom and was ready to go in himself, so that no one would be in Uncle Sandro's way, but Uncle Sandro stopped him.

He ordered him to stand by one of the shuttered windows while he went over to the other one himself, his rifle at the ready.

"Open up in there, or it'll be all the worse!" the Mensheviks shouted, and again started shooting up the door. More splinters flew. One of these struck Uncle Sandro's cheek and clung there like a tick. Uncle Sandro ripped it out and turned on the rich Armenian in a rage.

"If the Turks never told you about chestnut doors," he said to him, "you could've at least put in oak."

"I don't know about these things, and I don't want to," the rich Armenian lamented. "All I want to do is sell tobacco to the merchants of Trebizond and Batum."

At this point Uncle Sandro inflated his lungs with air and shouted with his incredible voice.

"Hey you!" he shouted. "I've got a full bandolier, and I'm going to defend the house! Look out!"

With these words he opened the shutter a bit and peered into the yard. The moon was shining, but Uncle Sandro saw nothing at first. Then he stared into the dark shadow of the walnut tree and realized that they were hiding there. He was surprised that they had not walked right into the rich Armenian's house—they could scarcely be afraid of him—but then he surmised that they had noticed a strange horse tethered to the apple tree and had decided to bide their time.

They appeared to be talking things over, discussing his ominous warning. Maybe they'll go away, he thought, and then suddenly, I just hope they don't take my horse. He froze at the window, peering intently at the men standing in the shadow of the walnut tree.

"Well, did they fall off their horses?" the old tobacco grower asked. He was too distrustful of the Mensheviks to open the shutter a crack and look out.

"Where would those ragtag Endurskies get horses?" Uncle Sandro muttered, continuing his surveillance.

In those days he believed all Mensheviks came from Endursk. Of course he knew they had a bunch of local stooges around here, but in his opinion Endursk was the true motherland of Menshevism, its hornet's nest, its ideological queen bee.

Now Uncle Sandro saw one of these scoundrels run quickly across the yard and stop in the shadow of the apple tree near his horse. Uncle Sandro could not make out what he was doing there, because he was on the far side of the horse. All the same he didn't like it.

"Hey," he shouted, "that's my horse!" His voice made it clear that the man who was shouting and the man who owned this house were far from one and the same.

"And who are you—Noy Zhordania?" came the answer from beside the horse, where as Uncle Sandro now guessed the fellow was rummaging through his saddlebag. Although the saddlebag was empty, Uncle Sandro did not like this kind of thing in the slightest. If a man dips into your saddlebag, it means he's not afraid of you, and if he's not afraid of you, he might kill you.

"I am Sandro of Chegem!" Uncle Sandro cried proudly, and his desire to blast the fellow's head off was so great that it was all he could do to restrain himself. He knew that if he shot one or two of the men the rest would flee, but they would come back later with a whole detachment and do their worst.

"We'll kill you and the owner both if you don't open up," the fellow said, continuing his search in the saddlebag.

"If you kill me, Shashiko will swear blood revenge!" Uncle Sandro called out proudly. When they heard this, the men standing in the shadow of the walnut tree talked briefly among themselves and called back the one who was over by the horse. Uncle Sandro surmised that word of the famous Shashiko had spread even to Endursk.

"What's he to you?" they asked.

"He's my cousin," Uncle Sandro replied, although Shashiko was only his neighbor. Shashiko was a well-known Abkhazian abrek, a rebel outlaw, and he was worth any hundred good Mensheviks, as Uncle Sandro explained to me.

"Have him open up—we won't look for his gold," one of them shouted.

The old tobacco grower started nervously. "I don't have any gold anyway," he said.

"What kind of rich tobacco grower are you if you don't have any gold?" Uncle Sandro asked in surprise.

"They already took it!" the old man shrilled, throwing down his flintlock and starting to beat his brow.

"You already took his gold!" Uncle Sandro shouted angrily.

All the Mensheviks started shouting at once, so that it was impossible to make out what they were saying.

"Just one of you do the talking," Uncle Sandro shouted. "We're not at a bazaar."

"It wasn't us, it was another detachment that took the gold," one of the Mensheviks shouted in an injured voice.

"Then what do you want?" Uncle Sandro asked in surprise.

"We'll take a few animals, that's all—since you're Shashiko's cousin," one of them answered.

"So shall I let them in?" Uncle Sandro asked, because he did not feel much like risking his life for the tobacco grower, especially since the door was about as bulletproof as a pumpkin.

"Let them in, let them rob me," the old tobacco grower said in despair. "I'm leaving this place anyway."

Uncle Sandro opened the door and walked out, holding his rifle at the ready. The Mensheviks also came out of the shadows and walked toward him, not taking their eyes off him. There were six of them, and along with them was the village clerk, who shrugged his shoulders faintly when Uncle Sandro glanced at him. His shrug intimated that they had forced him to get involved in this distasteful affair.

Looking around warily, the Mensheviks walked into the kitchen. From the way they stared at the table Uncle Sandro could tell that these ragtags did not have dinner every day, and his contempt for them increased, although he did not let on.

"Where does that door lead?" their senior man asked. He wore an officer's uniform, but without epaulettes.

"That's the storeroom," the owner said.

"There's someone in there," one of the Mensheviks said. He aimed his rifle at the door.

"That's my family," the old Armenian said. His mother-in-law set up a low wail to show that she was a woman.

"Have them come out," the officer said.

The owner stumbled to the storeroom and, in Armenian, began trying to persuade them to come out. But they balked and raised all sorts of objections. Uncle Sandro understood everything they said in Armenian, so he suggested a way for the owner to smoke them out.

"Tell them they have to fix the soldiers some grub. Then they won't be afraid," he prompted in Turkish.

The owner spoke to them about the grub, and they did in fact come out and stand by the door. One of the soldiers took a lamp and peered into the storeroom to discover whether there were any armed men in there. No armed men turned up, and the Mensheviks relaxed a little.

The Armenian's mother-in-law threw some fresh logs on the fire and began washing a kettle in which to boil the remains of the sheep. As soon as she started cooking she ceased to fear the soldiers and began reviling them, albeit in Armenian.

"Let's sit down at the table," Uncle Sandro said. "Pile the rifles in the corner."

The Mensheviks very much wanted to sit down at the table but did not want to let go of their rifles. Although they were not afraid of the owner, they realized that Uncle Sandro was not to be trifled with.

"You put yours down too," the officer said.

"You're guests, you have to go first," Uncle Sandro said, explaining basic etiquette to the soldiers' ignorant leader.

"But you're a guest too," he protested. However, it was pointless to argue with Uncle Sandro in such matters, even then.

"I arrived first, so I'm a guest in relation to the owner, and you arrived after me, so you're guests in relation to me," he said with finality, instructing this upstart how to behave before sitting down to a good table in a decent house. Vanquished, the officer understood once and for all that Uncle Sandro was no ordinary man, and he stood his rifle in the corner first. The others followed suit, except for the clerk, who had none. Uncle Sandro stood his rifle separately in another corner of the kitchen. The owner's flintlock lay by the window. No one paid any attention to it.

They all sat down facing Uncle Sandro across the table, each ready at any moment to dash for his rifle, realizing that the main thing was not to let the other get ahead of him. Actually, Uncle Sandro still had a pistol in his pocket, but he pretended that he was now unarmed.

"Usually," Uncle Sandro said to me at this point, interrupting his story, "before I went into a house where there might be danger, I hid a rifle or a spare pistol somewhere nearby. But I hadn't hidden anything here because this was a peaceable Armenian."

"Why would you hide a gun?" I asked, knowing that he was waiting for the question.

He smiled slyly. "If someone suddenly attacks you and disarms you," he said, "there's no better method. He goes off with your gun, he's exulting, he's lost control over himself, and now you catch up with him and take away your gun and everything he's got. Do you understand?"

"I do," I said. "But what if he's hidden a gun too, and now he catches up with you and takes away his gun, your gun, and everything you've got?"

"That couldn't happen," Uncle Sandro said confidently.

"Why not?" I asked.

"Because this was my secret." He smoothed his silver mustache haughtily. "I reveal it to you because you not only have no use for my secrets, you can't even use your own."

After this small lyric digression he went on with his story.

In brief, they sat at the table the rest of the night—drank wine and finished up the sheep. They raised toasts to the happy old age of their host, to the future of his children. They drank, with sidelong looks at the rifles, to the flowering of Abkhazia, Georgia, Armenia, and to a free Federation of Transcaucasian Republics, led, of course, by Noy Zhordania.

Chechnya—A Brief Explanation (2003)

Georgi Derluguian

The motor force of history most often suggests a clear path of conqueror and conquest, yet the case of Chechnya is a telling exception. With the formal arrival of the imperial armies into the North Caucasus in the early nineteenth century, Chechens were among the most consistent in simply saying no to Russian sovereignty. The harsh tactics of some of the more belligerent early Russian generals, such as the notorious Aleksei Yermolov, did little to earn the favor of skeptical Chechen clansmen. Nor did the surrender of Imam Shamil to the Russians in 1859 bring definitive peace. Chechens did, however, join with Bolsheviks in their struggle against tsarist forces, lending considerable aid to the socialist cause just when help was needed. Their leaders were rewarded with the status of an autonomous republic within the Russian Soviet Federated Socialist Republic [RSFSR]. As across the Soviet Union, early hopes were dashed when collectivization was under way. Stalinist purges across the region were everywhere complicated by the genuine support for socialism and what it had offered wide swaths of the Chechen community. In their darkest hour, February 1944, an event bitterly recalled by many still alive today, virtually the entire Chechen population was deported to the steppes of Central Asia and Siberia in return for perceived collaboration with invading German troops during the Second World War.

In his remarkably lucid review of Chechen experiences under empire and socialism, Georgi Derluguian suggests how the repeated collisions of event, chance, and ideology brought Chechnya to its unsteady circumstances today. An initial post-Soviet independence drive, inspired by movements in the Baltics and elsewhere, rapidly buckled under the weight of its own ambitions, followed by what came to be known as the First Chechen War (1994–96) and the Second (1999–). Depending on whom you ask, for all of the stabilities that returned to Russia under Putin, the Second War still goes on.

The place is tiny, especially when compared to the immensity of Russia. Most of the fighting today is taking place in an area of forty by seventy miles. But this area contains a very varied landscape, from the snow-capped mountain peaks of the Caucasus ridge, across the numerous densely populated valleys in the foothills, to the fertile steppe plains that eventually turn into arid semidesert. Mountains offer nooks and crannies where many different communities can coexist without mixing and preserve their own identities and traditions. Chechen and many other languages of the Caucasus, like the Basque language in Spain, have no surviving relatives in the modern world. The likely explanation is that in the past the Caucasus provided refuge for small peoples that otherwise would have been conquered and absorbed either by the ancient civilizations of the Middle East just to the south of the Caucasus or by the nomadic invaders from Inner Asia who dominated the open steppe lying to the north. Squeezed between these two grinding wheels of world history, the peoples of the Caucasus could survive because they successfully adapted to its difficult but protective environment.

Their social and economic adaptations were akin to what we commonly observe among such mountain peoples as the old-time Swiss, the Basques, the Albanians, and the Scots of Europe and the Kurds and the Pashtuns of Asia. The highlanders must be resourceful, tough, and economical because their environments are poor. The men are usually good fighters and their most prized possession would be a weapon: a dagger, a sword, and later in history a gun. Hospitality, friendship, loyalty, and family honor are as sacred to the highlander as is blood revenge. In the mountains a reputation as a valued friend, a generous host, and a fearsome foe is the precarious guarantee of one's life. After the first war, Chechen propaganda featured a leaflet with the photograph of a wolf (Chechens' favorite self-representation to their enemies) and the caption "Think twice before messing with me!" This bravado, no doubt supported by many genuine examples of ferocious valor, nonetheless betrays profound insecurity. Mountain peoples tend to be small because mountainous terrain cannot support large populations. Similarly, they have no states of their own because state organization cannot take root in such terrain, among pervasively armed populations, and with such small economic surpluses to appropriate through taxes. The typical social organization of highlanders is stateless clan society. Clans serve as the collective repository of reputation that plays a key role in structuring the social interactions and creating trust among the people. Clan reputations are assiduously cultivated and transmitted in legends from generation to generation. And these legends motivate people to perform great deeds, above all deeds of courage and honor.

A warning: all this pertains to what sociologists call the ideal type. The highlanders are complex and contradictory human beings like the rest of the human race. I am only suggesting here some elements toward a rational explanation of the ethnic and cultural traits that invariably captivate the imagination of outsiders: the highlanders' sense of pride, independence, toughness, and violence.

Now, imagine what happens when in the early 1800s the Russian Empire descends on the clan societies of the North Caucasus region. From imperial Saint Petersburg, Chechnya looked like a small rock on the road to the riches of Persia and India that all European conquerors so coveted at the time. From its standpoint the demands placed on the natives of the Caucasus seemed natural. The natives were expected to provide the manpower to build the imperial outposts, roads, and bridges to make their lands accessible, pay taxes, supply auxiliary troops, and generally to display subservience to the European masters. In case the natives thought of some "treachery," hostages were taken from locally prominent families. These were typical colonial practices of the epoch: the British in India and the French in Algeria did much the same. And as in so many other territories subjected to European imperial domination, the native peoples revolted.

In 1818 the Russian general Aleksei Yermolov built a fortress in the foothills of Chechnya and called it Grozny, literally Fort Terrifying. By preventing the natives from taking their herds to the winter pasturage, the new fortress threatened the highlanders with starvation—just as General Yermolov expected. When the Chechens tried to burn the hated fortress, they were met with artillery fire, and in the common practice of the time the rebellion was followed by a punitive expedition against a nearby village. To the astonishment of Russian troops, the villagers, even the women and children, preferred to die fighting. The fate of that village endures in Chechen folk ballads. Insisting that the "Asiatic savages" respected only the arguments of superior violence, General Yermolov proceeded to methodically burn the Chechen villages (reportedly while reading Julius Caesar's *Gallic Wars* for inspiration).

Yermolov's toughness achieved the opposite: instead of submission, the numerous small peoples of the North Caucasus began to unite against the common enemy. Since the Russian Empire espoused the official Orthodox Christianity, the resistance found inspiration in the Islamic teaching of holy war against infidels, or jihad. It was a simple yet vigorous faith of independent peasants who rose in a tremendous movement of resistance to empire. Islam provided two crucial mechanisms required by a rebellion: first, a powerfully unifying ideology for the disparate and often feuding mountain clans and, second, the flexible but robust network of Sufi preachers who inspired and coordinated the struggle.

In the 1830s an energetic and capable preacher called Shamil started building a centralized state in the neighboring Dagestan and proclaimed himself its leader, or imam. Shamil's imamate lasted twenty-five years, during which it acquired its own government, built strategic roads, and even developed its own armaments industry. Chechnya provided perhaps the majority of fighters for Shamil's rebellious state.

What started for the Russian Empire as a minor frontier operation unexpectedly grew into its longest and costliest war up to that time. The Caucasus war left an indelible imprint on Russian classical literature, from Alexander Pushkin and Mikhail Lermontov to Leo Tolstoy, who wrote such moving stories as "Prisoner of the Caucasus" and "Haji Murat." Among the peoples of the Caucasus the cultural imprint of that war, of course, is even stronger.

Having said that, I hasten to warn against the extremely common pitfall of viewing the Caucasus war of yesteryear through the prism of romantic literature. To a considerable extent, today's war in Chechnya seems a replay of Imam Shamil's jihad of 150 years ago only because both sides read Tolstoy at school and built their expectations on imagery from the past. Yeltsin and Putin, along with their generals, consider Yermolov a wise and tough patriot of great power (as I tried to show, calling Yermolov tough is an understatement, and wise is sheer nonsense). Today's Chechen fighters, a majority of whom would otherwise be unemployed and without a purpose in life, launched themselves from obscurity to military glory by the conscious emulation of the legendary warriors of Imam Shamil. Since I resolutely protest against this sort of historical memory propagated by the belligerents, I am going to focus on the less heroic side of history that is not preserved in legends but still can be excavated by historical sociology.

The truth regarding Imam Shamil is that he surrendered in 1859 because the Russian side finally realized the futility of Yermolov's terroristic strategy and offered very comfortable terms to Shamil and his circle to end the hostilities. Shamil was taken to Saint Petersburg and introduced to the tsar, who magnanimously gave him a generous pension. Many of Shamil's local officials received equivalent ranks in the Russian colonial administration. By this time the common people were worn out by the decades-long destructive fighting. In Chechnya, Dagestan, and Circassia the war produced bands of professional warriors who fought mostly for personal glory and gain: raiding for booty and trading hostages for ransom eventually became more important than protecting their villages. In this sense the destructive dynamic of the war today is indeed comparable to that of the past.

The Bolshevik revolution of 1917 gave the peoples of the Caucasus another opportunity to rise against imperial domination. Many Chechens joined the Reds, who promised to restore land to the peasants and liberate the oppressed colonial peoples. Quite possibly, the Chechen partisans saved the Reds when in 1919 they dealt a strong blow to the rear of General Denikin's White army, stopping his advance on Bolshevik-held Moscow. After victory in the civil war, the Bolsheviks created for the Chechens an autonomous republic within the framework of the Union of Soviet Socialist Republics. A few dozen such republics were created in the former colonial peripheries of the Russian Empire. Each one was endowed with its ethnic schools, theaters, publishing houses, and eventually universities, and official policy gave preference in admissions and hiring to the native nationalities. The early Bolshevik transformation produced the new group of modern-educated native specialists and brought considerable improvements to the quality of life through public works, free health care and education, and modern cultural amenities.

Here we encounter a major contradiction of Soviet history. On the one hand, the Soviet state promoted urbanization, education, industrialization, equality between the sexes and ethnic groups, and generally all that was regarded as progressive. On the other hand, it was a harshly dictatorial state, born in a brutal civil war and committed to survival through militarization: beginning with Lenin, the Soviet leaders deeply envied the effectiveness of German bureaucracy, and thus their inspiration was Bismarck perhaps even more than Karl Marx.

The Chechen peasants resisted the state expropriation of their livelihood during the collectivization of 1929–32 just like the Russian and Ukrainian peasants. But the Chechen peasants, being highlanders, traditionally possessed weapons, which resulted in a bloody cycle of rebellion and state repression. This is a grim and obscure period of modern history. Evidently many Chechens still believed in the promise of the modern socialist project and felt tragically at a loss trying to reconcile the progressive and the brutal dictatorial sides of the Stalinist regime. As happened elsewhere in the Soviet bloc during the Stalinist purges of the 1930s–1940s, most victims either were taken at random or else were true believers who considered Stalin's policies a deviation from the original idea. This may help to explain the tragically contradictory reaction of the Chechens to World War II.

In 1942, when the German armies surprised the Soviet command by forcefully advancing simultaneously on the Caucasus and on Stalingrad, tens of thousands of Chechens and other North Caucasians enlisted in the Red Army and fought bravely. But we also know that during spring and summer of 1942, the Soviet command was in disarray, and many units at the battlefront were sacrificed senselessly. Only later in the midst of the battle of Stalingrad did Stalin realize that instead of issuing draconian orders he should let the soldiers do their job of defending the country. For the Russian soldiers the survival of their country was clearly at stake.

Many North Caucasians, however, could not feel as patriotic, especially the

An appeal to the peoples of the Caucasus, 1920 poster, color lithograph by I. M. Mashistova after drawing by D. Moor. Courtesy of the Library of Congress, Prints and Photographs Division, LC-USZC4–1158.

peasants from small mountain villages, many of whom barely spoke any Russian and regarded the Germans as just another European invader. Some escaped back into their villages with stories of mayhem reigning near the battlefront, which the Soviet authorities considered desertion and spreading panic. On the German side, a few senior officers who had served in the African colonies used the familiar strategy of fomenting "tribal sentiments" to recruit native scouts and police for the Nazi-occupied territories. Their efforts were successful to some extent before the German advance was rolled back a few months later. On balance, a majority of Chechen soldiers fought in the Soviet army, a minority probably evaded the draft or deserted, and a few joined the Germans either for opportunistic reasons or to take revenge on the Soviets.

The events of this dark period come to us distorted by old rumors and wild accusations. In February 1944, an entire year after the Germans retreated from the North Caucasus, Stalin ordered the wholesale deportation of the Chechens and several neighboring peoples from their homelands. Close to half a million people were crammed into freight trains and, in brutal cold, sent on a long journey to Central Asia. Between a quarter and a third of them did not survive the trip. Stalin's motives remain as murky as ever. After all, many times more Ukrainians and Russians also had joined the enemy during the early disastrous period of Nazi invasion. Likely, the typically small size of the Caucasus peoples made feasible their wholesale forced relocation. It's possible too that Stalin and his chief of secret police Lavrenty Beria, who were both ethnic Georgians from the other side of the Caucasus, shared the stereotype portraying the Chechens as dangerous bandits from the highlands. Stalin, who came to believe that historical accomplishments required a ruthlessness of equally gigantic proportions, seemed little troubled that there were many more women, children, engineers, teachers, and decorated veterans of the Soviet army than traitors and bandits among the deportees.

Importantly, almost every Chechen family has a story of how during the deportation some Soviet soldier or railwayman shared a piece of bread with them. Minutka Square in Grozny, the site of fierce fighting during recent wars, officially bears the name of Khrushchev—a token of Chechen gratitude to the Soviet leader who in 1957 allowed them to return from exile. This kind of popular memory served to reconcile the Chechens to the acute contradiction of their situation under Soviet rule. On the one hand, they suffered from Stalinist terror as immensely as any group in the USSR. But on the other hand, they joined the modern world through the Soviet institutions of education and industrialization in which a great many Chechens achieved considerable success. Key figures of the Chechen revolution in 1991 were a military pilot, a writer, a journalist, industrial managers, engineers, professors, policemen, a few inevitably shady businessmen—but there was not a single traditional peasant, clan elder, or Islamic preacher among them.

The Chechen revolution of 1991 above all sought to eradicate the humiliations and injustices of the Soviet period. Its original promise was a secular and democratic national state that, in a typical hope of the times, would develop a modern market economy and, in a particular Chechen apprehension borne by their history, would secure the survival of the nation. The Chechen revolution was directly inspired by the analogous pro-independence movements in the Baltic republics. General Dzhokhar Dudayev, who until March 1991 served as the commander of a Soviet Strategic Air Force wing of nuclear bombers near Tartu, Estonia, left his military career and became the revolutionary leader and soon the Chechen president by popular acclamation. At innumerable revolutionary rallies and political meetings he impressed his countrymen by arguing that Estonia and Chechnya were roughly the same size, had distinct ethnic characters, and suffered terribly from the Stalinist outrages. What then prevented Chechnya from becoming an internationally recognized democratic state like Estonia? Similarly, just as Estonia could benefit from her location on the Baltic Sea close to Scandinavia, so could Chechnya benefit from its oil reserves and proximity to the Caspian Sea.

Like all politicians carried away by their populist rhetoric, Dudayev wildly exaggerated Chechnya's potential wealth and geopolitical importance. But the sudden collapse of communist rule bred similarly high hopes across the entire Soviet bloc, including within Russia itself. Moreover, in the weeks after the defeat of the reactionary coup attempt of August 1991, Moscow was embroiled in its own revolution. At the time, Yeltsin was busy consolidating his presidency and preparing the dissolution of the Soviet Union. Only when Dudayev declared Chechnya's independence from Russia did Yeltsin realize that this could start the chain reaction of further declarations of independence.

The old Soviet Union was structured like a matryoshka doll. It contained the fifteen republics, like Estonia, Ukraine, and Russia, which theoretically enjoyed the constitutional right to leave the union—which they all took advantage of by the end of 1991. But Russia itself contained a number of lesser-status ethnic autonomous republics and provinces like Chechnya that had been created by the Bolshevik founders back in the early 1920s. In Moscow they now feared that the example of Chechnya would be followed by the more important provinces like Tatarstan or Yakutia. Considering that more than half of Russia's trucks were made in Tatarstan and virtually all diamonds were mined in Yakutia, their independence could spell an end to both the Russian state and the economy.

The nightmare of the domino effect rarely materializes in real life, but it is always a potent argument for military hawks and political hardliners. Moscow rushed to proclaim the independence of Chechnya unconstitutional, imposed a blockade on the separatist province, and called on the international community not to recognize it. However, Russia was not in a position to dislodge Dudayev from his self-declared presidential palace in Grozny (formerly the communist party headquarters). In 1992–93 Russia's main preoccupation was the economic shock therapy conducted by Gaidar's neoliberal government, which for two years left Dudayev's regime in a limbo: neither truly independent nor subordinate to Moscow's policies.

In Chechnya the revolution went sour even faster than in Russia and for largely the same reasons. The economy and public order fell apart, forcing many educated Chechens and Russians who had lived in Chechnya before 1991 to seek a safer and better place to live elsewhere. Just like Yeltsin, Dudayev quarreled with his parliament, elected in the wake of the Chechen revolution. A few months earlier than Yeltsin, Dudayev disbanded the parliament, also with tank fire and bloodshed. Afterward, Dudayev surrounded himself with a coterie of personal loyalists, many of whom proceeded to loot the state coffers even more brazenly than did Yeltsin's cronies. Just as Yeltsin did, Dudayev grew tougher in his pronouncements, blaming all the problems of

Chechnya on enemy forces and calling his nation to prepare for war. Dudayev, always a general, relished military parades.

Many political analysts believed, with good reason, that Dudayev was on his last legs and would sacrifice the unrecognized independence of Chechnya in exchange for a legal and economic deal of the kind that Moscow offered to many other ethnic republics within Russia, such as Tatarstan. But Yeltsin, after all his failures and humiliations in the previous two years, desired a decisive victory. His minister of defense, General Pavel Grachev, was delighted to be useful and famously promised to win with "one paratroop regiment in two hours," while Yeltsin's legal and diplomatic advisers predicted that a small war would not cause objections from Western governments because Chechnya was a Russian internal matter. Unfortunately, Yeltsin's diplomats were and still remain correct in their assessment of the official Western reaction, but the eager General Grachev went badly wrong and started the cycle of warfare that seems to have no end.

Shamil Basayev, the most daring and uncannily lucky among the Chechen rebel commanders, admitted to a Russian journalist that to him the most difficult moment of the war was the first three days, when nobody knew whether the Chechens would be able to resist the invading regular army. Then volunteers began pouring into Grozny, many of them with their own weapons bought at the town market. (In Dudayev's Chechnya, the weapons looted from the former Soviet arsenals were bought and sold as easily as used cars.) The volunteers were organized into small mobile units and assigned defense positions all around the town according to the brilliantly simple plan devised by Aslan Maskhadov, who until 1992 was an artillery colonel in the same Russian army that he was now set to defeat in the streets of Grozny. This spectacular slaughter of the Russian forces has been described by many journalists and military analysts. Let me concentrate on the sociological side of this war and especially on why the Chechen fighters didn't stop fighting even after their incredible victory.

The first generation of Chechen fighters consisted of volunteers who rose in the patriotic defense of their homeland. They fought not only for themselves and their families but also for the ancestors who perished in the deportation of 1944 and in the Caucasus war of the nineteenth century. There is perhaps a special emotional state known only to the peoples that have been subjected to genocide in the past—the "never again!" sentiment that reduces the whole world to the dilemma of survival. It provided the extraordinary determination and moral edge to the Chechen fighters in the first war. In August 1996 they recaptured their ruined capital of Grozny from the badly disorganized and demoralized Russian troops.

It is necessary to mention that Russian society was overwhelmingly opposed to the first war, not to a small degree because Russian journalists in their last moment of professional glory exposed, with great passion, the war's senselessness and ghastly reality. The resulting popular indignation nearly cost Yeltsin his presidency. He proved his inordinate survival skills by firing his hawkish advisers and "buddies" like General Korzhakov and suing for peace.

With the withdrawal of Russian troops in the fall of 1996, the first round of war came to an end, and a durable peace looked possible. Chechnya in effect became an independent state though its formal status vis-à-vis Russia was to be decided in 2001 after a five-year cooling-off period. The chief guerrilla commander, Aslan Maskhadov, whose judiciousness and discipline earned him wide respect, was elected Chechnya's second president (the flamboyant General Dudayev was killed by a Russian rocket during the war).

As the new Chechen leader, Maskhadov faced two problems. First, he had to reestablish decent relations with Yeltsin's Russia, which remained the primary provider of goods and money to the devastated Chechnya. Maskhadov tried earnestly but failed, apparently because many officials in Moscow could not forgive him the humiliation of the lost war. But perhaps there was a dirtier reason: maybe many more Russian officials expected kickbacks that Maskhadov would not provide. The guerrilla hero turned president proved insufficiently pliable.

His second task was to demobilize the Chechen fighters who, after two years of war ending in an astonishing victory over Russia, remained euphoric with little thought to what they were going to do in the future. As part of his demobilization policy, Maskhadov asked the National University of Chechnya (which was in fact a group of surviving professors and students meeting in the gutted wreck of a building) to admit the former fighters without exams and retrain them for civilian professions.

As part of this same effort, President Maskhadov offered the portfolio of prime minister to his younger competitor in the presidential race, Shamil Basayev, whose wartime exploits had become legendary. To the Russians, Basayev was the arch-terrorist who in 1995 seized over a thousand hostages, mostly the patients, nurses, and doctors, in a town hospital in Budennovsk, in southern Russia. It was his way of demanding immediate peace talks. (The same Basayev took responsibility for planning the seizure of a Moscow theater in October 2002.) But in 1997 even in Moscow they grudgingly agreed that by promoting the former terrorist to lead the government, President Maskhadov was neutralizing a serious internal opponent. For a while Basayev earnestly tried to act like a statesman. He even donned a business suit and mused about Internet ventures. However, Basayev's incompetence in the civilian job soon became embarrassingly obvious.

Basayev quit the Chechen government in utter frustration and reverted to his warrior image and lifestyle. Basayev's move into the self-proclaimed opposition attracted many former fighters to him, especially the young men who during the war had become, in effect, professional warriors. They insisted that the struggle with Russia was not yet over and refused to demobilize. Seeking an ideological banner, Basayev and his band of unemployed veterans turned to religion and began propagating the world Islamic revolution as the only true way of overcoming foreign domination and establishing moral order. Russian officials and some journalists citing CIA sources suggest that Osama bin Laden provided inspiration and funding for these activities. As the above should make clear, however, the situation in Chechnya cannot be ascribed so much to Islamic traditions as to Islam becoming the last resort of desperate politicians and society when the promises of the 1991 revolution were replaced by grim reality.

Instead of enjoying peace, by the end of 1997 Chechnya was plunged into violent chaos as various private armies sought the sources of income in a totally ruined small country. The few remaining rackets included oil refineries, gun running, and increasingly the abduction of hostages for ransom. Maskhadov desperately sought to counter Basayev's accusations of betraying the national character of Chechnya by invoking Islamic sharia law and instilling order by dispatching his own small army against the unruly warlords. Failure to restore peace and order weighed heavily on Maskhadov, whose public pronouncements grew sullen and strangely incoherent.

By spring 1999 Chechnya was effectively in a state of internecine war. In August Basayev, operating from his native stronghold in the mountains, invaded neighboring Dagestan, ostensibly to spread his Islamic revolution to this republic that had remained part of Russia. But Shamil Basayev, who was emulating the legendary imam Shamil of the nineteenth century, failed to unite Chechnya and Dagestan by force—the local Dagestani militias resisted the unwelcome Islamic liberators with unexpected determination and, with the help of Russia's regular army, soon forced Basayev to retreat. The Dagestanis clearly wanted to avoid what they saw happening across the border in Chechnya.

The campaign seemed to be over in a matter of days. But in September a series of apartment block bombings in Dagestan and Moscow and other Russian towns brought Russian society to a state of shock and indignation akin to what Americans experienced on September 11, 2001. Shortly before the bombings, President Yeltsin, to everyone's surprise, anointed as his successor the little-known former KGB officer Vladimir Putin. The new leader unleashed a ferocious war on the purported Chechen terrorists (although the Moscow bombings remain unsolved to this day) and promised to return Russia back to normalcy.

Putin's tough, sober, and businesslike image appealed to a great many Russians. The paradox is that now, three years later, Putin has achieved remarkably little, yet his popularity remains very high. Apparently part of the explanation is the much tighter control exercised by the Putin regime over the Russian mass media. The fortunes of Putin and his associates seem secure as long as the Russian economy is not collapsing into another crisis and the war in Chechnya is kept at a low profile. Yet both pillars of Putin's stability seem shaky: the high energy prices that benefited Russia cannot last forever, and the "antiterrorist campaign" in Chechnya is still far from over after three years. If anything, the war in Chechnya has degenerated into a quagmire.

Evening Prayers (1963)

Idris Bazorkin

One of the ironies of life in the Caucasus, even during the Soviet period, is that it was removed enough from mainstream state life to allow for greater creative experiment. An excellent example is the work of Idris Bazorkin (1910–91), whom many consider to be the founder of modern Ingush literature. The Ingush, like their close neighbors the Chechens, were among those brutally deported from their homeland under Stalin following the Second World War. Returning from Central Asia in 1957, in the wake of Khrushchev's short-lived period of liberalization, when many of those deported were able to return home, Bazorkin began work on his best-known novel, Dark Ages, *published in 1963. In this extract from the book, he offers a deeply human portrait of Ingush life, far from the standard Party approach on topics such as Islam, sex, and indigenous Ingush experience that socialist realism had long enforced. On the one hand, the rhythms which fill the days of Bazorkin's characters are profoundly distinct from the Soviet scripts so characteristic of other novels published around the same time. On the other hand, Bazorkin refuses to idealize Ingush village life, as so many of the Russian nationalist* derevenshchiki, *or village prose writers, were doing to the north of him.*

The title of the novel is an ironic reading of the presumption that any Caucasus village must be somehow frozen in medieval social structures. Bazorkin's point was of a different nature: darkness could fall even during enlightened times and was an artifact of timeless struggles among men and women acting in a world made by themselves and by others.

Khassan, the mullah of the village of Egi, arrived when it was still light outside. Goitemir greeted him like an old friend and escorted him into the guest room. They talked about their health and the weather. It seemed like autumn would last forever. Neither snow nor frost was anywhere to be seen. This was bad for the earth, and they were worried about their crops. Then Goitemir told Khassan about how they had sacrificed a ram in honor of his mother-in-law, who was ill. Now they wanted him to read a *movlad*, a prayer they always said for the dead, according to the teachings of Islam.

"Excellent," Khassan said. "God is always pleased by a sacrifice. Let us pray."

Khassan raised his hands. Goitemir and his wife Nasi followed his example. It was a short prayer. Then the mullah took the small Koran that he had purchased in Mecca out of his pocket, opened it, put on his glasses, and began to recite.

Khassan's voice was calm. He seemed entirely sure of himself. His austere, pale face was covered with the chestnut-hued shadow of overgrown stubble. He sat on the tall chair and scratched his chin as he read, turning the brittle pages at rare moments. Nasi stared at Khassan as he read the Koran. She was frowning and seemed to be nursing a secret sorrow. Finally, she forced herself to stand up and go to the kitchen, to finish the chores that awaited her there. Her eyes were full of tears. No one could tell whether she had been touched by the guest's voice, whether she was thinking of her sick mother, or whether the tears had another source, known to her alone.

Goitemir sat across from Khassan and remained piously quiet. From time to time he poured oil into the kerosene lamp, to keep the room illuminated with light for Khassan to read by.

A female voice called for Nasi from a neighbor's yard. When she found out that her neighbor wanted to borrow a comb for wool, Nasi found hers and left to give it to her neighbor. As she was returning to her home, she saw Goitemir on the terrace and pretended to wipe away the tears with her sleeve.

"What's wrong?" Goitemir asked her tenderly.

"Nothing," Nasi turned her head away. She was not in the mood for an intimate conversation with her husband.

But Goitemir was concerned, and he repeated his question.

"When I gave my neighbor the comb, she told me that a man had arrived not long ago from Tsori and said that mother had become worse," Nasi lifted the tips of her fingers to her face, as if to wipe away more tears. Her shoulders were trembling.

"Calm down," Goitemir told her. "You saw yourself how healthy she was when we left!"

"Of course. But she's old. One minute she's better, but the next minute she might be worse. But maybe the man from Tsori had heard an old rumor about her being sick, the same one we heard which made us visit her? Now I'm going to suffer until morning. My poor mother!" Then, as though consumed by thoughts about her mother, she turned her head and glanced out the window which looked onto their guest room. Khassan was sitting there, still reading from the Koran. "How much that man reads!" she exclaimed, hardly hearing her own words. Then she turned her face back to Goitemir and said, "I don't need anything. I don't want anyone to keep me from doing my duty to my mother. Listen, maybe our neighbor can take care of you in my absence? Everything is ready. Nothing needs to be done here. I'm going to see my mother tonight. It's all the same to me where I am. I'm not going to be able to sleep tonight anyway."

"Have you lost your mind?" Goitemir exclaimed. "How do you plan to cross the gorge by night? If you're that worried, I should probably go myself and find out how your mother is doing. I'll return before tomorrow morning."

"Now you're the one who's crazy! You're not so young that you can just traipse around the mountains like that." Nasi's voice was full of fear. She knew well how sensitive her husband was about his age, and that any allusion to it could push him to do something drastic to prove that he was still young and strong. When he heard Nasi's words of caution, Goitemir's face did indeed change. He stepped backwards and stiffened his shoulders as he harshly intoned, "I'm going, whether you like it or not!" Then he added, "Don't disturb our guest. Let him read as long as he wants."

"But what should I tell him?"

"What do you mean what? Just feed him. Then make his bed and you can go to sleep."

"But that's the last thing I need, a man in the house when you're not home. Maybe he should go home to sleep tonight. It's not that far, after all," Nasi said. "What would happen if someone found out that you left your wife alone with another man?"

"We can't make a guest return home!" Goitemir said firmly. "We must observe the laws of hospitality. We told him to come here, and now we have to take care of him, at least until tomorrow. He's not a child after all! No one will know that I left you alone with him. Just tell Khassan that I was called away on business. I'm the village elder, after all. Such things happen all the time. I'll return tomorrow and escort him home."

Nasi wiped the tears from her eyes again. "But don't forget about the headaches that you get sometimes. What if you get a headache on your journey? And your heart is weak! You never know what might happen. God honored me by giving you to me as a husband. Go if you have to, just return as quickly as you can! And I beg you to avoid all the dangerous places! Be careful! I won't shut my eyes until you step across the threshold of this house again, alive and well."

Nasi brought Goitemir his saddle, riding gear, and weapons. Goitemir jumped into the stirrups and proudly hoisted his legs onto the horse's back. When he reached the gate, Nasi called to him to stop, ran inside, and brought out a stack of pancakes stuffed with meat wrapped inside a cloth.

Goitemir began to protest. He didn't want to take the pancakes with him, but Nasi continued to hold the package high in the air, for her husband to take. "You haven't eaten anything!" she protested. "No one will see you, don't worry."

Finally, Goitemir left, holding the reins for his horse in one hand and the cloth package of pancakes and meat in the other.

"May Allah watch over you on your journey!" Goitemir heard his wife call out from a distance.

When Goitemir disappeared behind the last tower in the village and she could hear his horse's trampling on the asphalt path, Nasi unlocked her hands and laughed. Then she ran inside. Khassan's chanting still resounded from the guest room. When she reached the guest room, she paused in front of the door. Khassan stopped reading and rested his eyes on her. An ascetic fire glowed in his hard glance. He ended the prayer in a whisper, shifted the beads on his prayer rope so that they were all bunched together, and then kissed them. Then he stuffed the prayer rope in his chest pocket.

"If you want to eat, I'll bring the food. It's time to think not only about the soul, but about the body as well." Nasi lowered her eyes to the floor. The faint trace of a smile lingered on her face.

Khassan was impressed by the pearly whiteness of her teeth, which clashed against her full red lips. He continued to pray, but nodded with his head, to indicate that she could bring in the food. Nasi went into the kitchen, where her neighbor was waiting for her.

Khassan's dinner was one of the most elaborate Nasi had ever prepared: the meat of a young ram, marinated in a sauce of herbs and cabbage leaves, a cow's head, ram testicles on a separate wooden plate, pancakes fried in butter, and stuffed meat. Each dish served separately would have been sufficient for ten people. As a grand finale to a luxurious meal, she brought out a huge turkey on a platter, which was then followed by dessert: halva and sugared tea.

Khassan was touched by Nasi's solicitude, but he couldn't bring himself to eat.

"So the guest is afraid of getting fat!" Nasi teased as she carried the un-touched plates loaded with food back into the kitchen. Her neighbor commented that restraint in eating was the mark of a cultivated man.

"Of course! What does a bachelor need with food?" Nasi shot back, never one to let a sarcastic comment pass unsaid. "What else does he have to expend his energy on when there are no women around? Books? But for a real man to live without meat, that's like a horse that doesn't eat oats. He won't be able to drive a cart, that's for sure!"

Nasi's neighbor laughed so hard that she couldn't control herself for a long time.

When her neighbor finally stopped laughing, Nasi invited her to eat with her, as decorum required. She then explained that she was alone in the house with a man because her husband had to leave on urgent business concerning her poor, dying mother. They didn't like to violate tradition, Nasi explained, but Goitemir loved her so much that he couldn't stand to see her worry about her mother and insisted therefore on making sure she was all right, even though that meant leaving his wife alone with their male guest.

The neighbor finally got the hint and left. Nasi then went to sit by the window in the guest room where Khassan had finished eating. He sat there motionless, apparently frozen by the passage of time. Then she explained why Goitemir had asked him to pay a visit.

Khassan listened attentively, his eyes open wide and his lips slightly curved. He was surprised by her words. When Nasi finished speaking, he said:

"If they love each other, you don't stand much chance of stopping them from getting married. We all know what will come of this." Khassan stared at Nasi intensely. She noticed the sadness in his eyes, and lowered her head. "There are people who fall in love only once in their lives. If they lose the chance to be happy with their beloved, they will be tormented forever. Such a person cannot bring happiness to anyone. We both know this quite well. That's why I advise you to think carefully before you act. It's not for nothing that they say: get married in the day, and make sure to light a lamp!"

"You're a wise man," Nasi said. She had heard quiet steps behind the door and guessed that her neighbor was eavesdropping on the conversation. "That's why we decided to approach you about this. We wanted to take advantage of your wisdom and seek counsel from you. But my husband hesitates to act, and time is passing quickly. If you'll excuse me, I'll go make your bed and in the morning you can discuss this further with him, after you've slept and eaten."

Nasi brought in a towel. Khassan went outside while she made his bed on the bench with the most luxurious blankets she had in the house. Khassan returned and recited his nightly prayers. Nasi pushed a large chest against the edge of the wall, and walked away into the other room, loudly wishing her guest a good night. The light was soon extinguished in the guest room. Nasi and her neighbor gossiped for the better part of an hour as they washed the dishes.

Then her neighbor went home, carrying a bag full of pancakes for her children. Nasi had been generous and given her as much food as she could carry. She escorted her neighbor to the gate, released the dog from his cage, fed him and went to her room. Her shadow trembled for a few minutes in the window, and then the dim light was replaced by pitch blackness. Sleep swept over the mountains and the village. There was nothing to interrupt the silence.

Group of children in Daghestan, 1933. Courtesy of the American Geographical Library from the University of Wisconsin–Milwaukee Libraries. Photographer William O. Field.

But no one was sleeping inside. Khassan stared out the dimly illuminated window and listened to every movement of her steps. He tried to mull over what Nasi had told him. But his thoughts disappeared as soon as they appeared, though the image of her face remained imprinted upon his imagination. He saw her blossoming body and her deep, tender eyes near the window where she had sat that night. He tried to free himself from her image by reading a prayer. But then he would remember how Nasi had smiled at him, revealing her fresh, full lips, and gleaming teeth, how she lowered her eyes to breathe more freely, and how he noticed the outline of her breasts. He was tortured by the limitlessness of his desire and cursed himself for agreeing to sleep in the same house with her.

He soon realized that he would never fall asleep that night.

While Khassan was immersed in fantasies, Nasi locked her door, and pulled the curtain over her window. She undressed near her bed and washed herself with the sweet-smelling Persian soap that her husband had bought for her on his pilgrimage to Mecca. She looked at herself in the weak light which still burned in the corner of her room and hurriedly covered her otherwise naked body with a silk nightgown. Then she left her room and tiptoed to the basement, where the animals lived during the winter.

She froze after closing the basement door behind her. She was thinking deeply about something, but probably she herself could not even have articulated her thoughts if she had been asked. Then she ascended to the upper floor along a different set of stairs, entered the living room, and extinguished the light in the stove. When the fire went out, she returned to the basement.

Nasi inspected all corners of the basement in the dim light that flickered above her. She extinguished that light as well and then climbed up a third staircase, which led into the guest room. When she reached the top step, she stood still for several minutes and listened, unable to hear anything other than the beating of her own heart.

Khassan had been listening to the movement below with great excitement for a long time already. Was it sheep or a dog? But then he noticed the trunk shift suddenly away from the edge of the wall, where Nasi had placed it a few hours before. His whole body trembled. He dug his hand beneath his pillow and gripped his dagger.

"Maybe Goitemir suspected something and placed a trap for me?" Khassan wondered. His entire body grew tense with listening. A wooden panel, which led to the staircase, levitated for a moment above the floor, and a woman jumped out of the hole. Even though it was completely dark, Khassan recognized Nasi. His first impulse was to jump up, but she tore off her dress, flung it on the floor and jumped into bed with him before he had time to move.

"You're crazy!" Khassan whispered.

"Look what's going on here," Nasi answered just as quietly, and pressed his hand against her heart. But Khassan couldn't hear any beating. He could barely breathe, so excited was he by her proximity. The night began. It was one of the longest—and at the same time one of the shortest—nights in both of their lives.

Khassan had been born to a poor family who sent him away to a *madrasah*, or religious school, to become a mullah when he was still a child. He received an excellent education there, both in the things of the world and the things of Allah. By the time he left the *madrasah*, he was already a grown man. His head was full of sayings from the *hadith* and other treasuries of Islamic learning, but his pockets were empty. Only much later in life was he able to provide for himself. While he was still poor, his beloved, whom he adored for her beautiful manner of speaking and her graceful gait had been given away in marriage to a rich and influential old man. His name was Goitemir, and he was a village elder.

The old man knew that someone else planned to marry her first, but he was determined to stop him. The old man had no idea how deep Khassan's love was for his betrothed. Goitemir didn't notice anything strange even after the marriage took place. But this didn't make things any easier for Khassan. He had to accept his bitter fate because he understood that there was no point in fighting a hopeless battle. Khassan had the chance to get married many times after he lost his beloved to the old man. The families of many rich girls hinted to him that they wanted to make him part of their clan. But he turned them all down. Of all the women in the world only Nasi existed for him. He took an oath that he would have his revenge on Goitemir, for lusting after his beloved, for ruining his life.

No one knew about Khassan's secret love. He concealed the insult which life had dealt him from everyone. Many times he had found himself in Goitemir's presence, engaged in one kind of business or another. But he couldn't make up his mind to kill Goitemir. It wasn't cowardice that stayed his thirst for revenge, but rather his practical sense. He knew it was impossible to kill without being discovered, and that anyone who sheds blood must, according to the customs of their people, be avenged. If he killed Goitemir, Khassan would have had to explain to the villagers that Goitemir had stolen the woman he loved. He was afraid of this more than anything else, because admitting that would mean admitting that he had failed, that he had been defeated by a man richer than he.

Khassan dreamed of committing the kind of murder that would place him beyond suspicion. He wanted to feast his eyes on the spectacle of his enemy's death, to make him feel his failure, in the hope that in some way it would alleviate the intensity of his own pain. Several times, Khassan had felt himself close to achieving his goal. But at the last moment, some obstacle always appeared to stand in the way of his happiness.

Khassan and Nasi met rarely. Sometimes they waited for years to be together. The longer they waited, the more they felt themselves driven insane by the intensity of their desire.

The first time Khassan slept with Nasi after her marriage to Goitemir, Khassan laughed at the old man. He felt proud of his victory, and gloried in the fact that Nasi had never stopped loving him, even though she had agreed to marry another man. But then he began to look at it from another perspective: it was not he who was living with someone else's wife, but Goitemir who was living with his bride. And Goitemir was living with her openly, unlike Khassan who was doomed to experience the most significant moments of his existence in secret. And then Khassan suffered all over again from the insult of seeing his beloved possessed by another man. His sense of helplessness was as powerful as it had been at the beginning. Rage against Goitemir, along with the desire to avenge him, filled him once again.

Years passed. Goitemir luxuriated over his riches, his women, his domestic bliss, and his children, while Khassan had nothing he could call his own with which to fill his life with joy. He would have gladly given up all his scholarly achievements and all the respect of society just to experience one evening with a family he could call his own! So many hours, so many sleepless nights, so much yearning, and what did it all add up to? It allowed him to run as fast as he could to the top of the mountain, to smash his naked chest against the rocks and to howl, to become an animal and to let himself be eaten alive by the pain that was consuming him. But the problem was that such displays of emotion made no difference in the end. Life remained the same. He gradually learned to grit his teeth and suffer silently.

And now fate had dropped another crumb of happiness onto his plate. He, Khassan, was lying on another person's bed, under another person's roof, with another person's wife. He, a mullah, and a *haji* who had completed the pilgrimage to Mecca, and therefore ought to have been regarded as one of the holiest men in the village of Egi, was a thief, though all he was doing was reclaiming the happiness which someone else had so wrongfully stolen from him.

Nasi knew that he loved her more than anyone else in the world, that in fact he loved her and no one else. But she was unable to understand the depth of his suffering, because they had different kinds of souls, and because of the many years dividing them. Nasi loved Khassan. He was the first man she had ever slept with. He was strong even though he was old, and he loved her alone. All these facts made her care about him. She knew nothing about him, really, nor did she have any desire to know more. She understood at some level perhaps that the very thing that divided them—their inability to understand each other—was what enabled them to make each other happy.

On the rare occasions when he met Nasi, Khassan didn't say anything about his suffering. It was easier for both of them that way. She was satisfied with having him for the moment and with the transient joy she was able to offer him.

Suddenly, the first rooster crowed. Nasi spoke again about their plans for their son's marriage.

Khassan thought to himself of what had happened between them. How could Nasi wish to inflict such suffering on someone else?

"The person who divides lovers will burn in hell," he said quietly.

"What about the person who sleeps with another man's wife?" Nasi laughed. "Both of us are going to burn in hell. So let's take advantage of all the pleasures for which we have sacrificed our chances of paradise."

Khassan laughed. "You get wiser with the years!" he said.

Nasi was so absorbed by the excitement of the moment that she didn't hear her husband unlock the gate leading into the yard and bring his horse into the stable. She trembled when the horse snorted not far from the window. Then she jumped up and embraced Khassan.

"Save me from his grimy hands!" Nasi whispered into Khassan's ears and then disappeared though the trap door leading to the basement. As she lowered the wooden panel over herself, Nasi whispered to Khassan to move the chest back against the wall, to cover the hole beneath it, which opened onto the staircase leading into the basement.

Khassan did as she asked and then lay back down. At that very moment, a knock resounded on the door. Nasi had not yet made it back to her bedroom. But she wasn't afraid. She closed the cellar door and ran into the yard. Goitemir stood a few feet away, on the terrace.

"Who is it?" she cried out tenderly.

"It's me, Goitemir," he said, though they both knew perfectly well that there was no one else it could be at that time of night. Nasi went inside and opened the door.

"How is mother?" Nasi asked, her voice trembling with simulated fear.

"She's just the same as she was when we left her," Goitemir said. "The man who scared us with his news must have heard an old rumor." Then he sniffed at his wife's skin. "You smell different today. Your skin looks somehow younger and fresher."

"Compared to you, I'm just a little girl," Nasi said, trying to suppress the bitterness that was surging unexpectedly inside her. "I washed myself in the Persian soap you bought me. But you're imagining things if you think my skin has changed."

Goitemir was annoyed by his wife's words. He rolled his eyes in the darkness. Dawn had not yet reached the valley, and Nasi couldn't see, though she felt, the way in which she had annoyed her husband. Goitemir remained silent. He knew that words wouldn't help him, wouldn't make his wife love him more, or even accept a compliment. Then Nasi suddenly clutched his hand and placed it on her heart.

"Listen to it beat!" she whispered passionately. "You see how desperately I've been waiting for you?"

Goitemir kept his hand pressed on his wife's chest and silently called upon Allah to help him. Allah had not been very diligent lately, and had ignored his pleas for help, specifically with reference to the needs of the body.

Translated by Rebecca Gould

VII

Revolution

For those following global events at the outset of the twentieth century, it is hard to underestimate the force of the tectonic shifts that reorganized loyalties and polities. After the collapse of the Manchu Dynasty in China in 1911, the onset of the First World War only a few years later set in motion the collapse of four more world powers presumed to be eternal: the Austro-Hungarian Empire, the German Empire, the Ottoman Empire, and, last but not least, the Russian Empire. It was an age, to recall Marx and Engels, when common men could "cut history off at the pass," carving out their own destinies. In the case of Russia, by 1921 millions found themselves without a monarch, in the avant-garde of socialist revolution, and in the throes of a civil war that seemed to know no end.

At the time of the empire's folding in 1917, the population was more than 80 percent rural. Ironically this made Russia a far from ideal candidate for Communist reform. As Marx stressed in his landmark work, *Capital*, Communism was to spread in only those countries where the majority of the population comprised advanced industrial urban wage laborers whose experiences would have taught them the exploitive powers of capitalism and the ready need for its dissolution. Russia was in no such position in 1917. Yet that did not stop the surprising inability of the monarchy to respond to social unrest, or the impressive ingenuity of a small group of socialist activists who seized on a moment they knew might never come again.

Loss of faith in imperial rule was a growing concern from the beginning of the new century. On 9 January 1905 imperial guardsmen fired into a peaceful crowd of two hundred thousand striking workers and their families who had come to St. Petersburg's Winter Palace with a petition to improve labor conditions. Tsar Nicholas failed to appear to receive the petition addressed to him, and after several hundred lay dead or wounded public opinion began to turn against the tsar. What soon became known as "Bloody Sunday" was followed that same year by the armed suppression of sailors and civilians on the Odessa Steps, a scene recreated to stunning effect in Sergei Eisenstein's film *Battleship Potemkin* (1925). Regardless of political stripe, almost all citizens shared in the alarm of the empire's defeat in the Russo-Japanese War, a battle pitting the Russian behemoth against a far smaller Japanese enemy at the close of a long year. It was a humiliating public defeat for an increasingly overstretched and slow-moving imperial project.

The march of the First World War further strained the Russian military command, by that time active on the home front to restrain waves of labor strikes and antiwar demonstrations as Russia slid into economic and political crisis. Inflation and food shortages tortured the general population, while urban workers faced long workdays, poor housing, and often even poorer sanitary conditions. City and countryside alike lobbied heavily for reform, and by 2 March 1917, after the first of the two revolutions that year that would change the face of Russia forever, Tsar Nicholas II agreed to abdicate.

In Nicholas's absence a provisional government led by the charismatic politician Aleksandr Kerenskii worked with an array of locally supported councils, or soviets, in a partnership known as the "dual powers" (*dvoevlastie*). The idea behind the alliance was to allow the provisional government leaders to reform state structures, while the smaller councils would channel unrest and build political energy for democratic rule. Russia's vast rural population, meanwhile, only partially engaged by debates in Petersburg and the industrial centers, began seizing land amid the uncertainty over state property and usage rights. Appreciating the unrest all around them, members of the Communist International, many of whom, such as Vladimir Lenin (born Vladimir Ulianov), had taken refuge abroad under threat from tsarist police, savvily leveraged these days of uncertainty and exhaustion with war to call for even deeper social changes.

Lenin's personal task on the eve of revolution, however, was to return from Switzerland across German enemy territory. German officials gave their approval for Lenin's rail passage in anticipation that his return would destabilize their weakened Russian foes. They took their own precautions by sealing the train while it traveled across German territory, foreclosing the possibility that the Russian leader might be tempted to stay a while and concentrate his energies in a Germany whose revolutionary potential Marx greatly preferred to that of Russia. Those same German officials did not remain in power long enough to consider the consequences of the fateful itinerary they laid before one of Russia's key undoers. Then again, in the world's first socialist state, the Union of Soviet Socialist Republics that rose out of the ashes of the monarchy, the complete works of Marx—which is to say, including the famous notebooks in which he railed against the adoption of revolution in Russia—were, tellingly, never released for just this reason.

The Communist Manifesto (1848)

Karl Marx and Friedrich Engels

One of the most famous political works in modern European history, The Communist Manifesto *(1848) was originally intended to be distributed as a pamphlet for the industrial working classes to guide them in their struggles. The* Manifesto *is known for its inspired brio and its clarion call to overthrow a capitalist system built on bourgeois control of the means of production. This does not mean that Marx and Engels were without appreciation for the bourgeoisie. They admired the restless ambition of this new class, with accomplishments "far surpassing Egyptian pyramids, Roman aqueducts, and Gothic cathedrals." Indeed the breathtaking skill of the bourgeoisie was part of the problem. In a world understood by Marx and Engels to have graduated from primitivism, through slaveholding, to feudalism, and in some places by the mid-nineteenth century to capitalism, these new holders of the means of production were among the savviest at masking their exploitation of the poor in all manner of respectable camouflage. Their offer of paltry wages to an increasingly impoverished industrial workforce, as Marx and Engels saw it, represented the work of an only seemingly free market, one that was abetted by the Church and exalted in countless elections organized by and for leading social forces. "The Communists turn their attention chiefly to Germany," Marx and Engels wrote, because in Germany, more so than in France, England, Switzerland, or even Poland (among the other countries where talk of revolution was at its height), urban, industrial working conditions were at their most advanced for the full realization of the need for change among the broadest swaths of the population. Nowhere in the* Manifesto *is largely agrarian Russia, whose industrial potential and thus its class consciousness was still largely unrealized, once mentioned.*

The history of all hitherto existing society is the history of class struggles.

Freeman and slave, patrician and plebeian, lord and serf, guild-master and journeyman, in a word, oppressor and oppressed, stood in constant opposition to one another, carried on an uninterrupted, now hidden, now open fight, a fight that each time ended, either in a revolutionary reconstitution of society at large, or in the common ruin of the contending classes.

In the earlier epochs of history, we find almost everywhere a complicated arrangement of society into various orders, a manifold gradation of social rank. In ancient Rome we have patricians, knights, plebeians, slaves; in the Middle Ages, feudal lords, vassals, guild-masters, journeymen, apprentices, serfs; in almost all of these classes, again, subordinate gradations.

The modern bourgeois society that has sprouted from the ruins of feudal society, has not done away with class antagonisms. It has but established new classes, new conditions of oppression, new forms of struggle in place of the old ones.

Our epoch, the epoch of the bourgeoisie, possesses, however, this distinctive feature: It has simplified the class antagonisms. Society as a whole is more and more splitting up into two great hostile camps, into two great classes directly facing each other—bourgeoisie and proletariat.

. . . .

The bourgeoisie has played a most revolutionary role in history.

The bourgeoisie, wherever it has got the upper hand, has put an end to all feudal, patriarchal, idyllic relations. It has pitilessly torn asunder the motley feudal ties that bound man to his "natural superiors," and has left no other bond between man and man than naked self-interest, than callous "cash payment." It has drowned the most heavenly ecstasies of religious fervor, of chivalrous enthusiasm, of philistine sentimentalism, in the icy water of egotistical calculation. It has resolved personal worth into exchange value, and in place of the numberless indefeasible chartered freedoms, has set up that single, unconscionable freedom—Free Trade. In one word, for exploitation, veiled by religious and political illusions, it has substituted naked, shameless, direct, brutal exploitation.

The bourgeoisie has stripped of its halo every occupation hitherto honored and looked up to with reverent awe. It has converted the physician, the lawyer, the priest, the poet, the man of science, into its paid wage-laborers.

The bourgeoisie has torn away from the family its sentimental veil, and has reduced the family relation to a mere money relation.

The bourgeoisie has disclosed how it came to pass that the brutal display of vigor in the Middle Ages, which reactionaries so much admire, found its fitting complement in the most slothful indolence. It has been the first to show what man's activity can bring about. It has accomplished wonders far surpassing Egyptian pyramids, Roman aqueducts, and Gothic cathedrals; it has conducted expeditions that put in the shade all former migrations of nations and crusades.

The bourgeoisie cannot exist without constantly revolutionizing the instruments of production, and thereby the relations of production, and with them the whole relations of society. Conservation of the old modes of production in unaltered form, was, on the contrary, the first condition of existence for all earlier industrial classes. Constant revolutionizing of production, uninterrupted disturbance of all social conditions, everlasting uncertainty and agitation distinguish the bourgeois epoch from all earlier ones. All fixed, fast-frozen relations, with their train of ancient and venerable prejudices and opinions, are swept away, all new-formed ones become antiquated before they can ossify. All that is solid melts into air, all that is holy is profaned, and man is at last compelled to face with sober senses his real conditions of life and his relations with his kind.

The need of a constantly expanding market for its products chases the bourgeoisie over the whole surface of the globe. It must nestle everywhere, settle everywhere, establish connections everywhere.

. . . .

You are horrified at our intending to do away with private property. But in your existing society, private property is already done away with for nine-tenths of the population; its existence for the few is solely due to its non-existence in the hands of those nine-tenths. You reproach us, therefore, with intending to do away with a form of property, the necessary condition for whose existence is the non-existence of any property for the immense majority of society.

In a word, you reproach us with intending to do away with your property. Precisely so; that is just what we intend.

From the moment when labor can no longer be converted into capital, money, or rent, into a social power capable of being monopolized, i.e., from the moment when individual property can no longer be transformed into bourgeois property, into capital, from that moment, you say, individuality vanishes.

You must, therefore, confess that by "individual" you mean no other person than the bourgeois, than the middle-class owner of property. This person must, indeed, be swept out of the way, and made impossible.

Communism deprives no man of the power to appropriate the products of society; all that it does is to deprive him of the power to subjugate the labor of others by means of such appropriation.

It has been objected, that upon the abolition of private property all work will cease, and universal laziness will overtake us.

According to this, bourgeois society ought long ago to have gone to the dogs through sheer idleness; for those of its members who work, acquire nothing, and those who acquire anything, do not work. The whole of this objection is but another expression of the tautology: There can no longer be any wage-labor when there is no longer any capital.

All objections urged against the Communist mode of producing and appropriating material products, have, in the same way, been urged against the Communist modes of producing and appropriating intellectual products. Just as, to the bourgeois, the disappearance of class property is the disappearance of production itself, so the disappearance of class culture is to him identical with the disappearance of all culture.

That culture, the loss of which he laments, is, for the enormous majority, a mere training to act as a machine.

. . . .

The Communists fight for the attainment of the immediate aims, for the enforcement of the momentary interests of the working class; but in the movement of the present, they also represent and take care of the future of that movement. In France the Communists ally themselves with the Social-Democrats, against the conservative and radical bourgeoisie, reserving, however, the right to take up a critical position in regard to phrases and illusions traditionally handed down from the great Revolution.

In Switzerland they support the Radicals, without losing sight of the fact that this party consists of antagonistic elements, partly of Democratic Socialists, in the French sense, partly of radical bourgeois.

In Poland they support the party that insists on an agrarian revolution as the prime condition for national emancipation, that party which fomented the insurrection of Cracow in 1846.

In Germany they fight with the bourgeoisie whenever it acts in a revolutionary way, against the absolute monarchy, the feudal squirearchy, and the petty bourgeoisie.

But they never cease, for a single instant, to instill into the working class the clearest possible recognition of the hostile antagonism between bourgeoisie and proletariat, in order that the German workers may straightway use, as so many weapons against the bourgeoisie, the social and political conditions that the bourgeoisie must necessarily introduce along with its supremacy, and in order that, after the fall of the reactionary classes in Germany, the fight against the bourgeoisie itself may immediately begin.

The Communists turn their attention chiefly to Germany, because that country is on the eve of a bourgeois revolution that is bound to be carried out under more advanced conditions of European civilization and with a much more developed proletariat than what existed in England in the 17th and in

France in the 18th century, and because the bourgeois revolution in Germany will be but the prelude to an immediately following proletarian revolution.

In short, the Communists everywhere support every revolutionary movement against the existing social and political order of things.

In all these movements they bring to the front, as the leading question in each case, the property question, no matter what its degree of development at the time.

Finally, they labor everywhere for the union and agreement of the democratic parties of all countries.

The Communists disdain to conceal their views and aims. They openly declare that their ends can be attained only by the forcible overthrow of all existing social conditions. Let the ruling classes tremble at a Communist revolution. The proletarians have nothing to lose but their chains. They have a world to win.

Workingmen of all countries, unite!

The Background of Revolution (1953)

Edward Hallett Carr

To understand the October Revolution requires a firm sense of what Russian losses to the Japanese meant to the empire at the outset of the twentieth century. They were followed by the many debilitating public protests, the peculiar interregnum of the "two powers," and the uneasy truce between the provisional government and the Petrograd Soviet on the heels of the abdication of Nicholas II. But as the British diplomat and historian E. H. Carr has noted, one should go back fifty years earlier, to the fateful emancipation of the serfs, organized under the watch of Aleksandr II in 1861. In the mid-nineteenth century roughly half of Russia's peasantry qualified as serfs, whose rights and future lay in the hands of the private landowners to whom they belonged from birth. Yet the long toll of difficult working conditions led to widespread peasant revolts across the Russian countryside. Emancipation's compromise was to implement mass agrarian reforms that financially compensated landowners for the loss of their indentured laborers, while transferring the burden of payment onto peasants, who received new land allocations. (See Mackenzie Wallace in part V.) The government in effect charged rural workers for their freedom, a significant burden that lasted through 1907. Unevenly implemented, the emancipation reforms were a significant way of stemming popular discontent but did little to alleviate the actual stresses mounting from one year to the next among rural communities. Meanwhile in cities the "hot-house development of Russian industry," as Carr refers to it, created little solidarity between workers and management. In much of Western Europe managers often had risen from within worker ranks and thus could draw on relatively deep ties across enterprises, Carr argues. In Russia the almost overnight appearance of giant factories offered few circumstances under which workers and management might appreciate each other's conditions. Widespread discontent in the countryside and alienation on the factory floor were but two of the significant factors setting the stage for transformation.

The Bolshevik revolution of October, 1917, did not come like a thunderclap out of a clear sky. It had been preceded eight months earlier by the February revolution which overthrew the Czar and set up a liberal republican government. The February revolution was not only the product of two-and-a-half years of frustration and disorganization in the first world war; it was also an echo of the short-lived revolution of 1905 which had followed defeat in the Russo-Japanese War, and which now seemed in retrospect like a dress rehearsal for the major event of 12 years later.

The 1905 revolution had behind it a long trail of incipient or abortive revolutionary movements, beginning with the so-called "December" conspiracy of 1825—an officers' mutiny aiming at a palace revolution. The distant, faintly heard rumble of revolution had been the background of Russian history and, still more, of Russian literature and thought, all through the Nineteenth Century.

If, however, one seeks a convenient and arbitrary starting point for the story of 1917, the best landmark to take is the emancipation of the serfs by Czar Alexander II in 1861. The emancipation was an attempt to break up the feudal structure of Russian society, and to introduce into the primitive peasant economy the beginnings of industrial development on modern Western lines. In Marxist terminology, it was the first stage of the Russian bourgeois revolution—the same process set on foot in Western Europe by the French Revolution and its economic concomitant, the Industrial Revolution.

It was, like one previous important attempt to transform and modernize the basis of Russian life under Peter the Great, a revolution from above. The impulse came from within the ruling class, from a group of courtiers who had the ear of the Czar. Its motive was to remedy the chronic inefficiency and backwardness revealed by the Crimean War, and, by bringing the Russian administrative, military and economic machine up to date, to enable Russia once more to hold her own among the European powers.

But it was also a revolution from above designed, as Alexander II confessed, to forestall a revolution from below. In this respect it enjoyed a real, though equivocal, success. Short though it fell of meeting the needs and demands of the peasants, it went far enough to put an end to the long series of peasant revolts which had marked the course of Russian history.

But in so doing, it made certain that the Russian Revolution, when it came, would be infinitely more profound and more far-reaching. The emancipation and its consequences, direct and indirect, determined the course and character of the revolution of 1917.

By breaking the legal fetters which riveted the peasant to the land, the emancipation created the raw material of an industrial proletariat, and made possible the development of a "free" labor market. In other words, it played the same role in Russian history as the enclosures played in the early stages of the industrialization of Great Britain. The process developed slowly, and gathered momentum only in the 1890's, when the international conjunction of forces gave birth to a Franco-Russian alliance, and stimulated an abundant flow of French capital investment to Russia for the purpose of building up Russia's industrial and military strength.

Peculiar Development

Under these impulses Russian industry, and especially heavy industry, developed in the 20 years before 1914 at an astonishingly rapid rate. But the same impulses gave a peculiar twist to the industrialization of the Russian economy. First of all, large scale Russian industry almost from the moment of its birth was geared to the production of "war potential," including railway construction, rather than to the needs of a consumer market. It was "planned" in the sense that it depended primarily on government orders, not on spontaneous market demand; it was financed by loans accorded for political reasons rather than for the traditional "capitalist" motive of earning commercial profits. In these respects it anticipated much that was to happen in Russia under the Five Year Plans 30 years later.

Secondly, the tardy arrival of industrialization in Russia meant that it skipped over many of the earlier stages through which the much slower growth of industrialization had passed in Western Europe—the gradual transformation from the single-handed craftsman to the small workshop, and from the first primitive factory to the giant agglomeration employing hundreds and thousands of workers.

When modern Russian industry was born at the end of the Nineteenth Century, it immediately assumed the characteristic modern shape of the large-scale factory. Already before 1914, one quarter of all Russian industrial workers worked in factories employing more than one thousand persons each. In Germany the corresponding proportion was only eight percent; in Great Britain it was lower still. Russian industry, the youngest in Europe and in other respects the most backward, was the most advanced in respect of the concentration of production in large-scale units.

This hot-house development of Russian industry produced a social structure sharply differentiated from that of the older industrial communities of Western Europe, and falsified the prognostications of those Marxists who assumed that Russia would imitate, at a long interval of time, but without substantial modifications, the experience of the West and travel the Western democratic and capitalist road.

History, as commonly happens, failed to repeat itself. The rapidity and belatedness of Russian industrial development shaped the human factor on

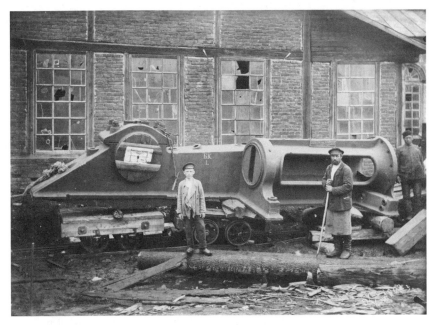

Steam engines, Lyssva iron-mining district east of Perm, in the Ural Mountains, pre-1917. Courtesy of the Hoover Institution, Fedor F. Foss Collection, Envelope E, Hoover Institution Archives.

both sides of industry on distinctive lines of its own. In the West, something of the spirit of the earlier entrepreneur, attentive to the changing conditions of the market and in close personal contact with his workers, survived even in the manager of modern industry. In Russia, the industrial manager was from the first the administrator, the organizer, the bureaucrat. In the West, the industrial worker contrived to retain, even in the age of mass production, something of the personal skills and independent spirit of the artisan. In Russia, the vast majority of the new generation of industrial workers were still peasants in factory clothes.

A "grey mass" of peasants had been transformed overnight into a gray mass of factory workers. But to drive the peasant into the factories and force on him the rigors of factory routine required—before, as after, the revolution of 1917—a harsh and relentless discipline which shaped relations between industrial management and industrial worker on lines of a sharply defined class hostility. Weak and backward as it was, the Russian proletariat provided a far more fertile soil than the advanced proletariats of the West for the proletarian revolution.

The factories had, however, touched only the fringes of the Russian peasantry. When the revolution took place, more than 80 percent of the population still lived on the land. The emancipation had freed the peasant from a legal status which had become an intolerable anachronism. But it had not solved the agrarian problem.

The peasant commune as a collective organ of cultivation was less, rather than more, efficient when the rights of the landowner had been abrogated; and the annuities now payable by the peasant proved not less onerous in practice than the obligation formerly owed by him to the landowner. What the emancipation did was to give the exceptionally capable, industrious or fortunate peasant the opportunity to rise out of the ruck and prosper at the expense of his less provident fellows, to acquire livestock and implements, to hire a worker or two, and set up as a petty landowner on his own—in a word, to become a *kulak*.

To encourage the *kulak* was the purpose of the Stolypin reform of 1908 in the system of land tenure, described by its author as a "wager on the strong." But, once again, too little was done and the time was too short. The prosperity of a few was enhanced at the expense of the increasing misery of many. The emancipation seemed to have staved off the revolution by lifting the burdens of serfdom from the shoulders of the peasant. But, in liberating him, it had destroyed the traditional structure of society and created no other. The peasant, cast adrift, could not make a revolution for himself. But he could, as the sequel showed, easily be harnessed to a revolution made by others.

Belated Reform

The political history of the Russian autocracy in the half century before 1914 reveals the same insecure and transitional character. Just as the emancipation of the serfs was a belated attempt to modernize the Russian economy on Western lines, so the political reforms which accompanied it were an attempt to bring an obsolete system of government up to date by borrowing and adapting Western liberal and democratic institutions. The courts were reformed, rudimentary social services were established, and an enlightened—though scarcely democratic—machinery of local self-government was grafted on to the rigid age-old trunk of autocratic power.

But, just as the Russian economy developed in a forcing house at a temperature maintained by pressures from without, so the political reforms grew not from the strength of their own indigenous roots, but under alien impulses from the West. They were accepted, reluctantly and with suspicion, by the rulers of Russia. Rarely has there been so striking a confirmation of Tocqueville's dictum that the foundations of revolution are laid when a ruling class loses confidence in its own right to rule.

It would be foolish to argue that Russia was inherently incapable of developing an industrial capitalist economy, or liberal democratic institutions, or of producing a commercially and democratically minded middle class and a thrifty and responsible "labor aristocracy" (to borrow Engel's convenient phrase). All these things had happened in the West. But, for history to repeat itself in Russia, it would have been necessary to isolate Russia from the external pressures of the West, so that events there could follow their own natural course of development.

What was not possible was to telescope into a period of 50 years the evolution of Russia from a primitive feudal society into a modern industrial democracy. Yet this is what was required if Russia was to catch up the time-lag and confront the Western Powers as their peer. Hence, in the ding dong battle waged throughout this period of Russian history between the traditionalists and the reformers (or revolutionaries), between those who thought that things were moving too fast for stability and those who thought they were not moving fast enough to catch up with the modern world, both sides were right.

Things were not moving nearly fast enough to put Russia on terms of material equality with the Western Powers. But the traditional supports of autocracy were being hacked away far too rapidly and ruthlessly for the halting efforts of those who were trying to raise pillars of society and government to replace them.

The story of the 50 years before 1914 explains why, when the revolution came, the whole edifice collapsed with a startling suddenness, leaving behind it a void of chaos and anarchy with hardly any constructive forces in sight. In 1905 defeat in the Japanese war almost gave the autocracy its *coup de grace*. The proletariat of Petrograd revolted and tasted a brief moment of power in the first Petrograd Soviet. The liberals reiterated their demand for constitutional reform, and obtained promises which were not kept. The army hesitated, and stood firm.

A naval mutiny did not spread. Smoldering peasant discontents broke out, but too sporadically and too late to affect the issue. It was a trial of strength. But, once more, the concessions made, the reforms undertaken or promised, while they did not go far enough to allay the revolutionary ferment, went more than far enough to complete the discrediting of autocratic government. After 1905 the autocracy was a self-confessed failure.

When the storm broke in Petrograd in February, 1917, friend and foe alike were overwhelmed by the suddenness and completeness. The old order collapsed, not because new claimants for power were pushing it aside, but through its own inherent rottenness. No intermediate period of compromise with the decaying monarchy, such as occurred at the beginning of the French Revolution, was possible. Abdication was from the first the all but universal demand; attempts to secure continuity by substituting the brother or young son of the fallen Czar failed through lack of any broad basis of support.

Out of this void two potential governments emerged; the Provisional Government of the liberal intelligentsia, pledged to some form of constitutional government and using the watchwords of democracy, and the Petrograd Soviet, a revival of 1905, claiming to speak in the mystic name of "the revolution."

Dual Power

But neither of these forces was united or determined enough to govern a nation at war in the throes of an inextricable economic and military crisis. From February to October, 1917, in conditions of ever-increasing chaos, Russia lived under the so-called "dual power"—an uneasy compromise of mutual and grudging toleration between the Provisional Government and the regime of the Soviets (for these had sprung up, spontaneously and anarchically, all over Russia).

The Bolsheviks were at the outset a tiny majority in the Soviets. These were everywhere dominated by the peasant party of the Social Revolutionaries; in Petrograd and Moscow the Bolsheviks were, at first, outnumbered even by the Mensheviks. It was not till September that the Bolsheviks obtained a majority in the Petrograd and Moscow Soviets; almost everywhere else they remained in a minority till after the revolution.

Nor at the start were the Bolsheviks themselves united. Like everyone else, they had underestimated the breakneck spread of events in Russia, and assumed that the revolution there, having overthrown the Czar, would pass through its constitutional and capitalist phase. Only Trotsky, who had seen the revolution of 1905 at closer quarters than any of the other leaders, clearly realized that the basis for the intermediate stage, corresponding to the liberal democracy of the Western world, was lacking in Russia.

By the time Lenin returned from exile to Petrograd in April, 1917, he had come round independently to the same view, and forced it on his at first wavering colleagues. The record of events between the February and October revolutions of 1917 reveals that the Bolsheviks seized power, not because this was part of their original intention, and not because they had at first any large measure of support for such a policy. They seized power because the intermediate democratic regime which they, in common with all the other revolutionaries, had expected to see established, proved impotent.

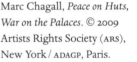

Marc Chagall, *Peace on Huts, War on the Palaces.* © 2009 Artists Rights Society (ARS), New York / ADAGP, Paris.

This was the situation that Trotsky had foreseen, and which Lenin diagnosed from Switzerland in the first days after the February revolution. It is, of course, true that the Bolsheviks played their part in discrediting the Provisional Government and the parties in the Soviet which later joined the government coalition. But their power and their following were at first extremely small; and they could have made little headway against a government of even moderate strength and determination.

Like the February revolution, the October revolution was almost bloodless. In Petrograd there was no resistance worth the name. The Bolsheviks won because, once the Czar was overthrown, they were the only group who consistently showed confidence in their ability to seize and maintain power. Every middle road seemed to be blocked.

The dilemma which had opened the road to power for the Bolsheviks continued to beset the new regime when power had fallen into its hands. The feverish attempt to catch up the time-lag which separated the Russian economy from that of the West had proved fatal to the Russian autocracy. It had frustrated the ambitions of Russian liberals. The attempt had now to be made once more in the new conditions. No Marxist had hitherto believed that it was possible to make the transition, politically or economically, to socialism except in a community which had already passed through the stages of developed democracy and capitalism.

If Lenin and the early Bolsheviks now believed this possible, if they believed that backward Russia could catch up and surpass the rest of Europe, it was because they also believed that the proletarian revolution was imminent in Europe, and that the advanced worker could come to the aid of his more backward Russian colleagues.

When the hope of European revolution faded, the Bolshevik regime was faced once more with the old unsolved dilemma. How could the gap between autocracy and socialism be bridged in a country which had never had time to learn the lessons of bourgeois democracy? How could an advanced socialist order be built in a predominantly peasant country which had never possessed the resources in capital equipment and trained workers proper to a fully fledged capitalist economy? What would be the fate of the attempt of a socialist economy in Russia to catch up and overtake the economic development of the Western world—an attempt which had already proved incompatible with the survival of Russian autocracy and with the hopes of Russian democracy? The answer to these questions was to provide the central theme of the history of the Soviet period.

Revolution and the Front (1923)

Viktor Shklovsky

Viktor Shklovsky (1893–1984) was one of the founding figures of Russian formalism, an influential school of literary criticism during the first three decades of the twentieth century that argued for the primacy of the text itself in literary analysis. Many readers of his popular memoir, Sentimental Journey, *were therefore not surprised to see considered reflections on revolution coming from a man who would go on to found the Society for the Study of Poetic Language. The commander of an armored-car division in the Russian army in the First World War, Shklovsky offers a palpable feel for daily life in the changing cityscape of St. Petersburg, where "average" soldiers could not be found, almost all having perished on the front. In their absence military barracks "became simply brick pens to which more and more red and green draft notices drove ever-increasing herds of raw humanity." Among the political protesters of the day, soldiers could be considered victims of autocratic war policy, in whom solidarities could be found. It was less so with the police forces and Imperial Guards who might have otherwise been the soldiers' allies. Shklovsky's touchstones in this first-person account range from the rumors circulating around the city of the killing of Grigorii Rasputin, the religious healer and counselor to the tsar's family, whose body had been pitched by offended nobles into the Neva River in December 1916; the revolt of the elite Volhynian Regiment in March 1917, when subordinates murdered their own officers; and the famous note penned a month later by Pavel Milyukov, minister of foreign affairs in the provisional government, causing local uproar when he pledged that Russia would stay in the unpopular war as long as the Allies needed them. It was a time when hunger was widespread, gunfire was regularly heard in the streets, and all waited in doorways to see what would come next.*

Before the revolution, I worked as an instructor in a reserve armored division, which made me one of the more privileged soldiers.

I'll never forget the terrible sense of oppression that weighed on me and my brother, who was serving as a headquarters clerk.

I remember running furtively down the streets after eight o'clock at night

The Battle of the Red Knight with Dark Forces, 1919 poster based on color lithograph by B. Zverykin. Courtesy of the Library of Congress, Prints and Photographs Division, LC-USZC4–1160.

and being restricted to the barracks for three months, but most of all I remember the streetcars.

The whole city had been turned into a military camp. The military police were called "semishniki," because they apparently got two kopeks for every man they arrested; they regularly hunted us down, cornered us in courtyards and threw us in the guardhouse. The reason for this "war" was that the soldiers crowded the streetcars and refused to pay for the ride.

The officers considered this a question of honor. We, the common soldiers, answered them with mute, vindictive sabotage.

This may be childish, but I'm convinced that restriction to the barracks, where men torn from their duties rotted on bunks with nothing to do, the dreariness of the barracks, the dull despair and resentment of the soldiers at being hunted down in the streets—all this stirred up the Petersburg garrison more than the constant reversals in the war and the persistent rumors of "treason."

A special folklore, pitiful and characteristic, developed around streetcar themes. For example: a nurse is riding with some wounded men; a general starts bothering the wounded men and insults the nurse; she throws off her cape and stands before him in the uniform of a grand duchess. That's how they told it—"in the uniform." The general gets down on his knees and begs forgiveness, but she doesn't forgive him. As you see, the folklore was still completely monarchistic.

This story is sometimes set in Warsaw, sometimes in Petersburg.

They used to tell how a Cossack once killed a general. The general had tried to throw him off a streetcar and, in the process, ripped off his military decorations. Apparently such a streetcar killing really did happen in St. Pete, but I think the general was added for an epic effect: in those days, generals weren't riding streetcars yet—except the poor, retired ones.

No one was disseminating propaganda in the units—at least no one in my unit, where I was with the soldiers from five or six in the morning until late at night. I'm speaking about party propaganda. But even in its absence, the revolution was somehow an established fact. Everyone knew it would come, only it was expected after the war.

There was no one to disseminate propaganda in the units; there were few party members and those few were workers, who had almost no contact with the soldiers. Intellectuals, in the most primitive sense of the word—that is, anyone with some sort of education, even two years of secondary school— were promoted to officers and behaved, at least in the Petersburg garrison, no better and perhaps worse than the career officers. The second lieutenants weren't popular—especially those in the rear, who fought tooth and nail to stay in the reserve battalion. The soldiers used to sing about them:

Before he spaded in a garden.
Now we bow and beg his pardon.

Many of these men were guilty only of having too easily succumbed to the well-entrenched discipline of their military training. Later on, many of them sincerely devoted themselves to the cause of the revolution—indeed, they succumbed to its influence just as easily as they had previously toed the mark.

The story about Rasputin was widely circulated. I don't like this story. The manner in which it was told exposed the moral decay of the people. Later, the revolutionary pamphlets—all those "Adventures of Grishka"—and the success of this type of literature proved to me that, for large numbers of the common people, Rasputin had become a peculiar sort of folk hero—something like Vanka the Steward.

But for various reasons—some of which simply frayed nerves and created the occasion for an outburst, while others acted internally, slowly changing the psyche of the people—the rusty iron hoops binding the masses of Russia grew taut.

The food supplies of the city continued to dwindle. By the standards of that time, the situation was bad. A shortage of bread made itself felt; lines appeared at the bakeries. At the Obvodny Canal, people had already begun to break into the shops. Those lucky enough to get bread carried it home, holding it tightly in their hands and looking at it lovingly.

Bread was bought from the soldiers. The crusts and scraps which, along with the sour smell of servitude, had been the trademark of the barracks now disappeared.

The cry for bread rang out under the windows and at the gates of the barracks, already carelessly guarded by the sentries, who let their comrades go out whenever they wanted to.

The barracks had lost faith in the old order. Pressed by the cruel, but already wavering, hand of the authorities, they began to ferment. At this time, a regular soldier—in fact, any soldier from the age of twenty-two to twenty-five —was a rarity. They had been savagely and senselessly slaughtered in the war.

Regular noncommissioned officers had been poured into the front lines as common soldiers and had perished in Prussia near Lvov and during the famous "strategic withdrawal," when the Russian army paved the whole countryside with its corpses. The Petersburg soldier of those days was either a dissatisfied peasant or a dissatisfied city-dweller.

These men were not even dressed in their new gray overcoats, but just hastily wrapped in them, then lumped into crowds, bands and gangs and called reserve battalions.

In essence, the barracks became simply brick pens to which more and more red and green draft notices drove ever-increasing herds of raw humanity.

The numerical proportion of officers to rank-and-file soldiers was in all probability no higher than that of overseers to slaves on the old-time galleys.

And outside the walls of the barracks, rumors circulated that the workers were "getting ready to demonstrate," that on February 18 workers from Kolpino "would march on the State Duma."

There were few ties between the workers and the rank-and-file soldiers, who were recruited either from the peasants or the petty bourgeoisie, but all these circumstances were conspiring to make some kind of explosion possible.

I remember the days before that explosion. The far-fetched conversations of the instructor-drivers about how nice it would be to steal an armored car, fire at the police and then ditch the armored car somewhere at the edge of town and leave a note on it: "Deliver to the Mikhailovsky Riding School." One very characteristic detail: concern about the vehicle remained. Evidently the men still lacked confidence in their ability to overthrow the old order. They only wanted to stir up a little trouble. But they had resented the police for a long time—mainly because the police were exempt from duty at the front.

I remember about two weeks before the revolution, our unit (about two hundred men) was marching along, hooting at a squad of policemen and shouting, "Dirty cops, dirty cops."

In the last days of February, people were literally hurling themselves at the police. The squads of Cossacks that were sent out into the street touched no one: they rode along laughing good-naturedly. This greatly heightened the rebellious mood of the crowd. On Nevsky Prospekt there was some shooting; several people were killed. A dead horse lay for a long time not far from the corner of Liteiny Prospekt. I still remember it. It was unusual then.

On Znamenskaya Square, a Cossack killed a police officer who had struck a woman demonstrator with his saber.

Indecisive patrols stood around in the streets. I remember an embarrassed machine-gun detachment with small machine guns on wheels (manufactured by Sokolov), with machine-gun belts in the packs of the horses—evidently some kind of equestrian machine-gun brigade. They stationed themselves at the corner of Basseinaya Street and Baskovaya Street. The machine gun, equally embarrassed, hugged the pavement like some little animal. The crowd clustered around it, not attacking or using their hands, but somehow pressing with their shoulders.

. . . .

Despite scattered gunfire, many people stood around in doorways—even women and children. They looked as if they were waiting for a wedding or a magnificent funeral.

Three or four days before this, we had been ordered to render our vehicles inoperable. In our garage the volunteer engineer Belinkin gave the removed parts to the soldiers who worked in his garage. But the armored cars of our garage were transferred to the Mikhailovsky Riding School. I went to the riding school, which was already full of people making off with automobiles. There were not enough parts for the armored cars. It seemed to me of primary importance to get the Lanchester cannon car back in operation. We had spare parts at the drivers' school, so I went there. Despite the commotion the men on duty were still at their posts. That surprised me at the time. Later on in Kiev, at the end of 1918, when I incited an armored division against the hetman, I noticed that almost all the soldiers claimed they were "on duty" and I was no longer surprised.

They liked me very much at the school. A soldier who opened the door for me asked, "You, Viktor Borisovich, are you for the people?" Getting a positive answer, he began to kiss me. We all kissed a lot in those days. They gave me the parts and even promised not to say who took them. I went back to my unit. To this day, I don't know if someone came to get the men or if they broke up and dispersed of their own accord. Men were milling around in the barracks. I took two experienced foremen from the garage, Gnutov and Bliznyakov, got some tools and went with them to repair the car. All this was in the afternoon, two or three hours after the revolt of the Volhynians—the first day.

I don't understand how so many events could have been packed into that day.

We towed the armored car to a garage on Kovenskaya Street, where we occupied the building, tore out the telephones and began to repair the car. We worked on it until evening. It turned out that water had been poured into the gas tank and had frozen. We had to chop out the ice and dry the tank with rags.

During a break, I ran over to see a writer I knew.

It was crowded and hot in his rooms; the table was piled high with food; the tobacco smoke was like a wall. Some people were playing cards and they played for two more days without setting foot outside the door.

Later this same man very quickly and very sincerely became a staunch Bolshevik. Almost everyone who had been sitting around that table became a Communist.

And even now I remember so clearly their supercilious irony toward the "disturbance in the streets!"

Even before all this, a strike had been called in the city. The streetcars weren't running. All the cab-drivers who didn't join the strike were prevented from working. On the corner of Sadovaya Street and Nevsky Prospekt, I ran into an assistant professor I knew—an extremely talented and extremely foolish man formerly associated with the "academicians"—largely, it seems, at drinking bouts. He was shouting and commanding a group which was stopping cars. He was sober, but completely beside himself.

The uprising had already enveloped the area around the State Duma. The proximity of the various barracks to the Tauride Palace and, to a lesser extent, the memory of the speeches given there made the Duma the center of the uprising.

Apparently the first detachment was led to the Duma by Comrade Linde, later killed by the soldiers of the Special Army, in which he was a commissar. This is the same Linde who would lead the demonstration of the Finland

Regiment in April and try to arrest the Provisional Government after Milyukov's famous note.

Our armored car rushed pellmell through the city. The dark streets were alive with people, standing around in small groups. They said that the police were shooting here and there.

They had been standing on the Sampsonievsky Bridge, had seen some policemen, but the police hadn't succeeded in shooting at them: they had all scattered. In some places people were already breaking into wine cellars. My group wanted to take some of the wine that was being handed out, but when I said that they shouldn't, they didn't argue.

At the same time, the armored cars from Dvoryanskaya Street had also sallied forth with Comrades Anardovich and Ogonians in charge. They immediately occupied the Petersburg side of town and headed toward the Duma. I don't know who told us that we should go to the Duma too.

An armored car, apparently a Garford, was already stationed at the approach to the Duma.

At the entrance to the Duma, I ran into an old army comrade, L., a volunteer—then already a second lieutenant in the artillery. We exchanged kisses. Everything was fine. We were all being swept along by a river and the whole of wisdom consisted in yielding to its current.

Letters from the Front (1917)

Edited by Ol'ga Chaadaeva

The First World War on Russian soil coincided with the decline and fall of Russia's last monarch, Nicholas II. When Germany invaded in 1914 Nicholas vowed, as had Aleksandr I during Napoleon's campaign into Russia in 1812, that he would not rest as long as there was a single enemy in his country. While the words initially united a population otherwise badly divided, the reality of the social, economic, and political situation was such that the country was ill prepared for war. Artillery ammunition was in short supply, civilians were hastily recruited and poorly trained, and the transportation system was underdeveloped and thus unable to handle the transfer of people and supplies to and from the front. Industrial production suffered enormously, as poorly trained personnel were hired to replace those who had been conscripted. Initially, however, agricultural production remained steady, as the peasants who had been called up were replaced at home by women and men who were either too old or too young to serve.

The letters that appear here were all written to the Petrograd Assembly by soldiers at the front between March and November 1917. They are part of a larger collection of 129 letters written primarily by men with minimal education from the peasant and working classes. The time period within which they were written is all-important. Nicholas abdicated on 2 March 1917; prior to this date government censorship prevented these kinds of letters from reaching their intended destination. Even as conditions continued to deteriorate at the front, Nicholas, despite his own best intentions, seemed unable to comprehend the gravity of the situation. Mired in the corruption and intrigue that centered around Grigorii Rasputin, Nicholas's court suffered from a combination of constitutional and psychological paralysis. Oblivious to the riots over food at home and the demoralization at the front, he wrote to Aleksandra on his way home that he wanted "to take up dominoes again in [his] spare time." The very hardships to which Nicholas seemed impervious would create the social and economic conditions that fostered the coming revolution.

*To the Executive Committee of Workers and Soldiers Deputies in Petrograd
from your Comrades at the Front [undated]*

Petition

Comrades, you have forgotten us. You forget that we, your brothers, fathers, and sons are in the trenches. We are experiencing the final horrible events of war, and you do not see the terrible things going on in Russia, the famine and the high prices. Where will it all lead if you do not take the most radical and extreme measures to conclude peace immediately? Now the most urgent moment has come because, as you know, a plan which is the most advantageous for all of the Great Powers has been developed in Bern. Comrades, you have forgotten about us. To think that you are living well there and having your fill! But what about the terrible hunger tearing apart our wives and children? I write to you, and in general all of the comrades here earnestly request that if peace is not made, no matter what, by the fall, it seems to me that probably everyone will desert and go home with weapons in hand. . . .

By winter everyone will be on board because the weak already have long ago agreed to this, and the strong are fed up with the situation. There is, for example, the one who has been wounded five times, while others are the ones who are all decorated with medals. The former is especially interested in how life will develop after the war. This is just a miserable headache for all of us except for those who dream about a return to the old regime.

Letter from the 3rd Infantry, Russian Division, 9th Regiment, Machine Gun Unit

(16 September 1917)

Comrades!

Do you still intend to continue fighting in the winter, comrades? We don't have anything to make tea with, and we don't have vodka either. We can't stand it any more and have no strength left. Comrade soldiers and peasants, we have had enough of this bloodshed. Comrades, we have a favor to ask of you. Just give us peace. We beg you. We can't take this any longer. The Romanian cornmeal is killing us.

Comrade soldiers and peasants, we don't have the strength to hold up under this damn slaughter. Please, comrades, make peace before winter, and if there's no peace before then all of us are gonna go home anyway. We just can't take it any more. Comrades, remember, you guys who spent the winter here in these damp trenches. You all know very well what life's like here. There's nothing left to write, you yourselves know full well that the soldiers will stay at the front only until October. [Please reply to the 9th Rostov Division, Machine Gun Unit]

To the Committee of Soldiers' Deputies

(11 March 1917)

Comrades, I bring to your attention the following information: Our comrades at the front, sitting in the trenches, know nothing of what has been happening or about the overthrow of the Old Power because the officers of the regiment named below, beginning with the Ensign and ending with the Colonel, did not explain anything about the events and have even been spreading rumors that just don't correspond to reality. They are explaining to the soldiers that the Tsar has left, like he has gone on vacation or something for a little while, and that Mikhail [the Tsar's younger brother] is taking over his duties, and they say that everything will be just like it was before. Also, the Commander of the Regiment, Colonel Ivanov, is forbidding the soldiers from spreading rumors which they have gotten from somewhere or other, about the activities of the new government and its Executive Committee. We, as you see, having signed our names below, are a group of soldiers touched by feelings of freedom and equality, and we are in a hurry to let you know that we do not dare remain indifferent and cold-blooded, and we want to tell you this in time so that you will let those people know who are supposed to know that it is high time to stop all of this propaganda and provocation of our officers and people in favor of the Old Order. You know, we as a group are touched that you share our feelings, and we are still faithful, just like we were before, to the victory of our people.

Signed

Soldiers of the 13th Finland Infantry Regiment:
Senior Non-Commissioned Officer I. Parvenov
Lance Corporal I. Tkachev
Rifleman N. Pratasov

20 March 1917

I write in the trenches a few steps away from the enemy, every minute fearing for my life, working day and night in trenches that are flooded up to the knee and sometimes even higher in places. Of course, it is impossible to describe in detail the entire life of an infantry soldier, far from the Motherland, who seems to be at the mercy of fate in these circumstances, and who has already forgotten that people can live without fear of being killed or buried alive or blown to pieces every minute, a soldier who has even forgotten his own previous existence, and cannot even picture how all of this could end, and how he might be able to begin living the life he lived in the past. Some think that this war should be unending. This is what they say: most likely we are fated to be here forever, and sooner or later we must certainly perish; we will never succeed at seeing freedom or joy which they write about in the newspapers. Of course, we cherish all that our brothers did within Russia. We thank them from the bottom of our hearts and will always be grateful and will pass this on to our children so that if we will no longer be here, our children will also glorify the names of those who won our freedom with their blood. Let those very people who gave us this opportunity to take a breath of freedom, may those very people see this. It depends on you, our glorious conquerors of freedom. You can make it happen so that hundreds of thousands more will be able to see this joy and make use of it. If there are among you, people who were in these dirty trenches and who endured the burden of being an infantry soldier, then most likely they will say that these are the sufferers, who, like moles, live in the ground and are afraid to raise their heads, risking being killed, they would also say that it is necessary and even imperative to try and let them see freedom and put it to work. Then we will all raise a great hurrah, which will ring out from the Caucasus to the Baltic Sea. It will be a real hurrah in every way, which Russia has never heard. All of these millions who are in the trenches can say only one thing: let there be peace as soon as possible. Only that can make us happy, and only then will we feel the freedom and liberation that our fallen brothers gave us. We talk only of peace and that's all. In the active army, nothing has changed except officers are now addressed informally as Mr. Lieutenant or Mr. Ensign, etc. and even in the familiar form of "you." But the army expects everything new. Soldiers say this: they call us citizens, but what kind of citizens are we when our wages are 75 kopecks, and we sit here without any tobacco? Tobacco is our entertainment, yet there's no place to even get it. Let them give us a little bit of our pay in advance. Do we, defenders of the country, not deserve a free trip on the railroad? And where are we supposed to get the money to pay a fare of one third of a kopeck when our wages only cover what we need for a single day? You know not everyone has parents who are capable of sending money to their son or whomever, and should they do that when he is no longer working for them? They have lost hope of any real support from him. Of course, some receive an allowance for their sons and husbands, but it is nothing and not everyone receives it who should. The soldiers demand that their leave should not be held up by anybody since at present every hour is precious to them. Leave lasts only twenty to twenty-five days, of which seven to eight are spent on the road, and there are still various dangers on the way. They demand some sort of payment for passage, and in order to ride, you have to run around to various commanders, and sometimes you still wind up in the wrong car.

Among the soldiers there is growing suspicion. They say: Why don't they write clearly and exactly why they are sending out police to the front? All of us soldiers want the police to be sent immediately to the field and assigned to the trenches. Let them find out and get acquainted with life in the trenches; those bloodsuckers did not love our brother soldiers—let them have their just reward. Let the machine guns that we need so badly show up here. We also don't want to have our leave interrupted even during the war and that at least five people out of every hundred be sent on leave. Five out of a hundred won't make a big difference; there are people who have been here more than a year in the same unit and all that time in the trenches. Do these people not deserve leave? Should these people perish without seeing their loved ones? We also request that the people elected as committee members should not just be from the field but from the front line trenches, not people located in various headquarters as non-combatants who, during the entire war saw nothing of it, and don't know what the trenches are and how to live in them. These people are always ready to say that the war needs to be waged to the end. They don't suffer from it and it is not terrifying for them when the enemy opens fire. If these non-combatants and staff officers were put in the trenches, then all would shout out: Down with the war!

Now all of us soldiers count only on you, only you can imagine our life and improve it. You need to support the army. The army is a mighty force which can overcome anything. We hope for improvement.

P.S. Written from the south-west front. Maybe nonsensical, so please forgive me—it is impossible to make sense when you write from here.

[Unsigned]

Translated by Kelly Kozik

The Withering Away of the State (1917)

Vladimir Lenin

Vladimir Il'ich Lenin (born Ulianov, 1870–1924) wrote his famous State and Revolution *in the summer of 1917 before the storming of the Winter Palace that marked the formal beginning of the Soviet government. Much of the book is devoted to reclaiming Marx from the Marxists, as it were, or better put, reasserting a reading of both Marx and Engels better disposed to the situation in contemporary Russia. One of Lenin's concerns was that a new socialist state should not fall into the service of an oppressing class, as had so many states before it. Across Western Europe, Lenin suggested, "the advanced countries are becoming military convict prisons for the workers."*

Like Marx, Lenin believed that world history had known four central modes of production—primitivism, slaveholding, feudalism, and capitalism—and would soon know a fifth, communism, via the intermediary stage of socialism. The difference between socialism and communism, at its core, was that socialism would have a state and communism would not. The key pivot in the transition was a transformed labor market. "From each according to his ability, to each according to his needs!" is the famous line by Marx. As workers were free to maximize their skills, society would become so prosperous that workers would have all their needs met. The state's central role as a coercive redistributive organism would no longer be needed. "The whole of society will have become a single office and a single factory, with equality of labour and pay," Lenin wrote. Average citizens would regulate themselves, in effect administering their own lives. The state would wither away, and true communism would be reached.

Lenin presaged some of the reactions of unsympathetic readers. "From the bourgeois point of view," he wrote, "it is easy to declare that such a social order is 'sheer utopia' and to sneer." Nor did he deny his own pragmatism. Even a tarnished bourgeois state, such as Russia was left with in 1918, would be needed to maintain stability as reorganization got under way. Indeed until such time as the "higher" phase of communism was in place, Russian society was to be placed under lockdown. The property of capitalists would be expropriated, and the state would be run by cadres of armed workers. Lenin's text offers not only an ideological platform for the events of autumn 1917; it offers a taste of what would go on to become standard reading for generations of Soviet youth trained in the canons of Soviet political economy.

Lenin speaking to the crowds. Courtesy of the Hoover Institution, Russian Pictorial Collection, 764, Envelope AO, Item I, Hoover Institution Archives.

The State will be able to wither away completely when Society has realized the formula: "From each according to his ability; to each according to his needs"; that is, when people have become accustomed to observe the fundamental principles of social life, and their labor is so productive, that they will voluntarily work *according to their abilities.* "The narrow horizon of bourgeois law," which compels one to calculate, with the pitilessness of a Shylock, whether one has not worked half an hour more than another, whether one is not getting less pay than another—this narrow horizon will then be left behind. There will then be no need for any exact calculation by Society of the quantity of products to be distributed to each of its members; each will take freely "according to his needs."

From the capitalist point of view, it is easy to declare such a social order a "pure Utopia," and to sneer at the Socialists for promising each the right to receive from society, without any control of the labor of the individual citizens, any quantity of truffles, motor cars, pianos, and so forth. Even now, most bourgeois *"savants"* deliver themselves of such sneers, but thereby they only display at once their ignorance and their material interest in defending Capitalism. Ignorance—for it has never entered the head of any Socialist "to promise" that the highest phase of Communism will actually arrive, while the *anticipation* of the great Socialists that it *will* arrive, assumes *neither the present* productive powers of labor, *nor the present* unthinking "man in the street" capable of spoiling, without reflection, the stores of social wealth and of demanding the impossible. As long as the "highest" phase of Communism has not arrived, the Socialists demand the *strictest* control, *by Society and by the State*, of the quantity of labor and the quantity of consumption; only this control must *start* with the expropriation of the capitalists, with the control of the workers over the capitalists, and must be carried out, not by a Government of bureaucrats, but by a Government of the *armed workers*.

. . . .

In its first phase or first stage Communism *cannot* as yet be economically mature and quite free of all tradition and of all taint of Capitalism. Hence we see the interesting phenomenon of the first phase of Communism retaining "the narrow horizon of bourgeois law." Bourgeois law, in respect of the distribution of articles of consumption, presupposes inevitably the capitalist State, for law is nothing without the organization for *forcing* people to obey it. Consequently, for a certain time not only bourgeois law, but even the capitalist State may remain under Communism without the capitalist class.

This may appear to some a paradox, a piece of intellectual subtlety, of which Marxism is often accused by people who would not put themselves out to study its extraordinarily profound teachings. But, as a matter of fact, the Old surviving in the New confronts us in life at every step in nature as well as in Society. It is not Marx's own sweet will which smuggled a scrap of bourgeois law into Communism; he simply indicated what is economically and politically inevitable in a society issuing from the *womb of Capitalism*.

Democracy is of great importance in the working-class struggle for freedom against the capitalists. But Democracy is not a limit one may not overstep; it is merely one of the stages in the course of development from Feudalism to Capitalism, and from Capitalism to Communism.

Democracy implies equality. The immense significance of the struggle of the proletariat for equality and the power of attraction of such a battle-cry are obvious, if we but rightly interpret it as meaning the *annihilation of classes*. But the equality of Democracy is *formal* equality—no more; and immediately after the attainment of the equality of all members of society in respect to the ownership of the means of production, that is, of equality of labor and equality of wages, there will inevitably arise before humanity the question of going further from equality which is formal to equality which is real, and of realizing in life the formula "From each according to his ability; to each according to his needs." By what stages, by means of what practical measures humanity will proceed to this higher aim—this we do not and cannot know. But it is important that one should realize how infinitely mendacious is the usual capitalist representation of Socialism as something lifeless, petrified, fixed once for all. In reality, it is *only* with Socialism that there will commence a rapid, genuine, real mass advance, in which first the majority and then the *whole* of the population will take part—an advance in all domains of social and individual life.

Democracy is a form of the State—one of the varieties of the State; and, consequently, like every State, it stands as an organized, systematic application of force against mankind. That is its one aspect. But, on the other hand, it is the formal recognition of the equality of all citizens, the equal right of all to determine the structure and administration of the State. Out of this formal recognition there arises, in its turn, a stage in the development of Democracy, when it first rallies the proletariat as a revolutionary class against Capitalism, and gives it an opportunity to crush, to break to atoms, to wipe off the face of the earth the capitalist government machine—even the republican variety: the standing army, police, and bureaucracy. Second, it enables it to substitute for all this a more democratic, but still a *State* machinery in the shape of armed masses of the working class, which then become transformed into a universal participation of the people in a militia.

Here "quantity passes into quality." Such a degree of Democracy carries with it the abandonment of the framework of capitalist society, and the beginning of its Socialist reconstruction. If *everyone really* takes part in the administration of the State, Capitalism cannot retain its hold. As a matter of fact, Capitalism, as it develops, itself prepares the ground for everyone to be able really to take part in the administration of the State.

We may class as part of this preparation of the ground the universal literacy of the population, already realized in most of the more progressive capitalist countries; then the education and discipline inculcated upon millions of workers by the huge, complex, and socialized apparatus of the post, railways, big factories, large-scale commerce, banking, and so on, and so forth.

With such an *economic* groundwork it is quite possible, immediately, within twenty-four hours, to pass to the overthrow of the capitalists and bureaucrats, and to replace them, in the control of production and distribution, in the business of apportioning labor and products, by the armed workers, or the people in arms. The question of control and book-keeping must not be confused with the question of the scientifically educated staff of engineers, agriculturists, and so on. These gentlemen work today owing allegiance to the capitalists: they will work even better tomorrow, owing it to the armed workers. Book-keeping and control—these are the chief things necessary for the smooth and correct functioning of the *first phase* of Communist society. *All* the citizens are here transformed into the hired employees of the State, which then is the armed workers. All citizens become the employees and workers of *one* national State "syndicate." It simply resolves itself into a question of all working to an equal extent, of all carrying out regularly the measure of work apportioned to them, and of all receiving equal pay.

The book-keeping and control necessary for this have been simplified by capitalism to the utmost, till they have become the extraordinarily simple operations of watching, recording, and issuing receipts, within the reach of anybody who can read and write and knows the first four arithmetical rules. When the majority of the citizens themselves begin everywhere to keep such accounts and maintain such control over the capitalists, now converted into employees, and over the intellectual gentry, who still retain capitalist habits, this control will, indeed, become universal, pervading, rational: it will be ubiquitous, and there will be no way of escaping it.

The whole of society will have become one office and one factory, with equal work and equal pay. But this "factory" discipline, which the proletariat will extend to the whole of society on the defeat of Capitalism and the overthrow of the exploiters, is by no means our ideal, and is far from our final aim. It is but a foothold as we press on to the radical cleansing of society from all the brutality and foulness of capitalist exploitation: we leave it behind as we move on.

When all, or be it even only the greater part of society, have learnt how to govern the State, have taken this business into their own hands, have established a control over the insignificant minority of capitalists, over the gentry with capitalist leanings, and workers thoroughly demoralized by capitalism— from this moment the need for any government begins to vanish. The more complete the Democracy, the nearer the moment when it ceases to be necessary. The more democratic the "State" consisting of armed workers, which is "no longer really a State in the ordinary sense of the term," the more rapidly does every form of the State begin to decay. For when all have learnt to manage, and really do manage, socialized production, when all really do keep account and control of the idlers, gentlefolk, swindlers, and suchlike "guardians of capitalist traditions," the escape from such general registration and control will inevitably become so increasingly difficult, so much the exception, and will probably be accompanied by such swift and severe punishment (for the armed workers are very practical people, not sentimental intellectuals, and they will scarcely allow anyone to trifle with them), that very soon the *necessity* of observing the simple, fundamental rules of any kind of social life will become a habit. The door will then be wide open for the transition from the first phase of Communist society to its second and higher phase, and along with it to the complete withering away of the State.

Voices of Revolution, 1917

Edited by Mark Steinberg

All too often history is studied from the top down, from its leaders and laws, and from the point of view of what happened rather than the average person's response to the events at hand. The three letters that appear here were written by ordinary Russians in the city and the countryside and are less an account of what happened than an account of how people were reacting to the events that were changing their lives.

The October Revolution brought chaos in its wake. Crowds took to the streets, some with joy at having deposed the old order, others with uncertainty about the future. People's lives changed almost instantly. In addition to the months of economic and social upheaval, average Russians found that the very language had changed and that they were now expected to know Bolshevikese, the language of the new revolutionary order, used by many, yet often imperfectly understood; we see, for example, in the second letter that the author misuses the word provocateur. *One can also sense that Russians saw the Revolution as having a moral imperative to bring about a spiritual cleansing of the country as a whole. Thus the Committee of Elders at the Atlas Factory asks for help in rooting out the "vile drunkenness" that threatens the purity of the Revolution. A letter from a soldier in Poltava province is suggestive of some of the chaos that was at work at the local level, where people were still not receiving basic information about the progress of the Revolution. And a letter written some ten months later from Rostov-on-Don is suffused with anger at the Bolsheviks for failing to deliver on their promise to bring about true peace and improve economic conditions.*

Appeal to workers from the Committee of Elders of the Atlas Metal and Machine Factory, Petrograd, printed in the Menshevik newspaper Rabochaia gazeta, *11 June 1917*

Comrade workers! We must report to you that a sad phenomenon has continued and intensified at the Atlas Factory: heavy drinking is flourishing. Men are drinking denatured alcohol, varnish, and other such substitutes. They are drunk on the job, speak out of turn at meetings, shout inappropriate phrases, prevent politically conscious comrades from speaking, and paralyze their organizational work. There is total disarray in the shops. Owing to all the alcoholism, politically conscious workers are suffocating in this kind of atmosphere. You have no strength left to work when barriers go up at every step you take, but what is even more offensive is that politically conscious, advanced workers are participating in this vile business. Comrade workers, if you are alcoholics, isn't it about time you changed your thinking? You're ruining yourselves, you're wrecking production, you're destroying what has been purchased at such a high price: at the price of many lives. Comrade workers! Change your thinking and admit your guilt. You're putting a barrier in front of us, but know that we will not stop for anything or any kind of barrier. Conscious that we are right, we will fight to our last breath. Comrade workers! We ask you to come to our aid, to root out the vile drunkenness—we appeal to you with good intentions; otherwise, you will ruin the freedom bought at such a high price, specifically, many lives. Comrade workers! Remember that you will have to answer to the politically conscious proletariat. We are asking our politically conscious comrade workers from other factories to come to our aid in the fight against alcoholism. Write protests. Work out effective measures in the fight.

Committee of Workers' Elders

Atlas Factory

Letter to Izvestiia *from a peasant and former soldier, Nikifor Tatianenko, Poltava Province, 12 May 1917*

Letter to the editor!

Comrade soldiers and workers,

I categorically declare that in our the village of Belogorenka in Poltava Prov., Lofitsk Uezd, Luksk Volost, we do not have any provocateurs. The people here are ignorant and not united. Half the population of the village sticks to the old order—things with them are still done strictly according to the old way. There is a committee, but they elected its members from those people who do not care about the people but only about their own pocket: the priest and the volost elder who even before used to say that we would live better when the German conquered us. Measures need to be taken with them now.

Comrade soldiers, I beg you to send provocateurs here because I can't deal with this alone and I don't know what's going on there in Petrograd because the newspapers do not reach here from Petrograd.

Send a newspaper here from your offices free of charge, unite the ignorant people. If you don't have an account for sending it out for free, then we will take up a collection for *Zemlia i volia* [Land and Freedom, an organization designed to spread revolution into the countryside].

The peasants gather for meetings, but they don't decide anything or resolve any problems, because they don't know and no one has explained to them what a democratic republic or a nation means, what annexations and indemnities are, and so forth, and even if someone started to explain it, they still wouldn't understand. Comrade soldiers and workers, send a newspaper here so that we could at least take issues from the newspapers and tell people what's going on in Petrograd.

Comrade soldiers and workers, do not forsake my request, send newspapers. From here I will inform you in writing what is going on in the provinces.

Address: Lofitsk Uezd, Poltava Prov., Luksk Volost, to the village Belogorenka

Nikifor Danilovich Tatianenko

To Comrade V. I. Lenin

Chairman of the Council of People's Commissars!

I will be brief. At first I believed in you because you promised good things for us—real peace, bread, and freedom. I thought you wouldn't destroy the homeland. But instead of what you promised, you sold Russia out, gave us no bread, and established a Nicholas kind of freedom. May you be thrice cursed and know that the wave of popular vengeance will reach you and you who have destroyed Russia will perish. Don't think I'm one of those so-called "patriots." No, you'd better tell us what we workers are going to do when there is unemployment and the Germans or someone else brings in cheap goods. We are going to turn into Chinamen, aren't we? May you be cursed once more because soon I'm going to be starving. You sold Russia to the Germans and are spilling our brothers' blood all over the country under the command of German officers.

I curse you and all your comrades in the Council of Usurpers and Betrayers of our native land.

Rostov-on-Don, 19 December 1917

A former Bolshevik

PLATE 1 The Trinity, by Andrei Rublev, about 1411. From G. I. Vzdornov, ed., *The Russian Icon from Its Origins to the Sixteenth Century*, translated from the Italian by Colette Joly Dees (Collegeville, Minn.: Liturgical Press, 1996), 101. Courtesy of the State Tret'iakov Gallery.

PLATE 2 Side portrait of Ivan the Terrible. *Ivan IV, Tsar of Russia.* Courtesy of the Slavic and Baltic Division, New York Public Library, as well as the Astor, Lenox and Tilden Foundations.

PLATE 3 Princess
Zinaida Yusupova
(1900–1902). Painting
by Valentin Serov.
Courtesy of State
Russian Museum,
St. Petersburg.

PLATE 4 Barge haulers on the Volga, 1870. Painting by Ilya Repin. *Repin* by Grigory
Sternin, published, Leningrad 1985 (Khudozhnik RSFSR). Copyright 2009, State Russian
Museum, St. Petersburg. Courtesy of State Russian Museum.

PLATE 5 Harvesting the potato crop in Kamchatka. Courtesy of Nelson Hancock, www.nelsonhancock.com.

PLATE 6 Sergei and Natasha Firun with their sons in the closed village of Liugi, Sakhalin Island, 1990. Courtesy of Douglas Vogt.

PLATE 7 Eternal rest, detail (Levitan, 1894). From *Isaac Levitan: The Mystery of Nature*, by Alexei Feodorov-Davydov (St. Petersburg: Aurora Art Publishers, 1995). Courtesy of the State Tret'iakov Gallery.

PLATE 8 Soviet poster, "Rabotat' nado." Vladimir Lebedev, 1920.

PLATE 9 "Glory to the Great Stalin, Best Friend to Children." Courtesy of the Library of Congress, Prints and Photographs Division, LC-USZC4–9529.

PLATE 10 Moscow Metro. Courtesy of the photographer, Alexander Savin.

PLATES IIA, IIB,
IIC Mass graves at
Levashovo. Photos
by Adele Barker.

PLATE 12 Young Pioneers of the Communist Party. Source: The Library of Congress, *Look* Magazine Photograph Collection, Prints and Photographs Division, LC-L9–54–66-0, #21. Photographer Paul Fusco. Copyright Paul Fusco/Magnum Photos. Courtesy of Paul Fusco/Magnum Photos.

PLATE 13 An afternoon by the river. Courtesy of Donald Weber, www.donaldweber.com.

PLATE 14 Men by river bank with steam from bucket. Courtesy of Nelson Hancock, www.nelsonhancock.com.

PLATE 15 The funeral of the Romanovs. Courtesy of Liza Malott Pohle and the Hoover Institution.

Gedali (1926)

Isaac Babel

In the 1920s a Russian Jewish writer by the name of Isaac Babel (1894–1940) wrote a series of stories about a young Jewish intellectual serving in a Cossack regiment during the Russian campaigns into Poland. He himself had served as a war correspondent for the newspaper of the Red Cossack Army under General Budennyi during the Russo-Polish campaign, partly in response to the writer Maxim Gorky's advice that if he wanted to be a writer, he had best experience the world. Born into a middle-class Jewish family in the southern port of Odessa in Ukraine and given a traditional Jewish education, Babel set about following Gorky's advice and published Konarmiya (The Red Cavalry) in 1926.

The stories that comprise The Red Cavalry are one of the great literary paradoxes of the revolutionary era. In them Babel's narrator is serving alongside the very group that attacked Jewish settlements during the tsarist era in what were called pogroms, looting, burning, raping, and leaving havoc in their wake. There is recognition on both sides as Babel's narrator nevertheless tries to conceal his Jewishness. Most paradoxically the narrator finds much to admire in these Cossack horsemen, in particular their physical grace, their freedom, their sense of passion. Babel's Jewish intellectual wants to become one of them . . . almost. He wants to slough off his intellectual side, his passivity, his glasses and gain acceptance, even if it means acquiring the Cossack ethos. Interestingly the Cossacks are less affected by the narrator's Jewish identity than by his intellect; he can read, and they can't. But his Jewish identity continues to tug at him at odd moments.

In "Gedali" he leaves his unit one Sabbath eve to wander around the Polish town of Zhitomir. The short sketch narrates his encounter with an old Jew named Gedali, a vignette infused with the paradoxes of the Revolution. If the Jews welcomed the Revolution as liberation from tsarist oppression, how then, wonders Gedali, were they to make sense of the violence brought by the Revolution? How is one to distinguish the Revolution from the counterrevolution?

In later years much of the terror under Stalin bore a distinctly anti-Semitic caste. Like many writers of conscience during his time, Babel refused to comply with the artistic credo of socialist realism. In 1934, in fact, he declared himself the "great *master of the genre of silence." Arrested in 1939 by the* NKVD, *he was forced under pressure, and possibly torture, to confess to crimes he never committed. In January 1940 he was executed for espionage on Stalin's order. Fourteen years after his death he was rehabilitated and cleared of all charges.*

On Sabbath eves I am oppressed by the dense melancholy of memories. In bygone days on these occasions my grandfather would stroke the volumes of Ibn Ezra with his yellow beard. His old woman in her lace cap would trace fortunes with her knotty fingers over the Sabbath candles, and sob softly to herself. On those evenings my child's heart was rocked like a little ship upon enchanted waves. O the rotted Talmuds of my childhood! O the dense melancholy of memories!

I roam through Zhitomir in search of a shy star. By the ancient synagogue, by its yellow and indifferent walls, old Jews with prophets' beards and passionate rags on their sunken chests sell chalk and wicks and bluing.

Here before me is the market, and the death of the market. Gone is the fat soul of plenty. Dumb padlocks hang upon the booths, and the granite paving is as clean as a skull. My shy star blinks, and fades from sight.

Success came to me later on; success came just before sunset. Gedali's little shop was hidden away in a row of others, all hermetically closed. Where was your kindly shade that evening, Dickens? In that little old curiosity shop you would have seen gilt slippers, ship's cables, an ancient compass, a stuffed eagle, a Winchester with the date 1810 engraved upon it, a broken saucepan.

Old Gedali, the little proprietor in smoked glasses and a green frock coat down to the ground, meandered around his treasures in the roseate void of evening. He rubbed his small white hands, plucked at his little gray beard, and listened, head bent, to the mysterious voices wafting down to him.

The shop was like the box of an important and knowledge-loving little boy who will grow up to be a professor of botany. There were buttons in it, and a dead butterfly, and its small owner went by the name of Gedali. All had abandoned the market; but Gedali had remained. He wound in and out of a labyrinth of globes, skulls, and dead flowers, waving a bright feather duster of cock's plumes and blowing dust from the dead flowers.

And so we sat upon small beer-barrels, Gedali twisting and untwisting his narrow beard. Like a little black tower, his hat swayed above us. Warm air flowed past. The sky changed color. Blood, delicate-hued, poured down from an overturned bottle up there, and a vague odor of corruption enfolded me.

"The Revolution—we will say 'yes' to it, but are we to say 'no' to the Sabbath?" began Gedali, winding about me the straps of his smoke-hidden

Krasnaia Konnitsa [Red Cavalry], by Kazimir Malevich. Courtesy of the Russian Museum, St. Petersburg. © 2008, State Russian Museum, St. Petersburg.

eyes. "Yes, I cry to the Revolution. Yes, I cry to it, but it hides its face from Gedali and sends out on front nought but shooting . . ."

"The sunlight doesn't enter eyes that are closed," I answered the old man. "But we will cut open those closed eyes . . ."

"A Pole closed my eyes," whispered the old man, in a voice that was barely audible. "The Poles are bad-tempered dogs. They take the Jew and pluck out his beard, the curs! And now they are being beaten, the bad-tempered dogs. That is splendid, that is the Revolution. And then those who have beaten the Poles say to me: 'Hand your phonograph over to the State, Gedali . . .' 'I am fond of music, Pani,' I say to the Revolution. 'You don't know what you are fond of, Gedali. I'll shoot you and then you'll know. I cannot do without shooting, because I am the Revolution.'"

"She cannot do without shooting, Gedali," I told the old man, "because she is the Revolution."

"But the Poles, kind sir, shot because they were the Counter-Revolution. You shoot because you are the Revolution. But surely the Revolution means joy. And joy does not like orphans in the house. Good men do good deeds. The Revolution is the good deed of good men. But good men do not kill. So it is bad people that are making the Revolution. But the Poles are bad people too. Then how is Gedali to tell which is Revolution and which is Counter-

Revolution? I used to study the Talmud, I love Rashi's Commentaries and the books of Maimonides. And there are yet other understanding folk in Zhitomir. And here we are, all of us learned people, falling on our faces and crying out in a loud voice: 'Woe unto us, where is the joy-giving Revolution?'"

The old man fell silent. And we saw the first star pierce through the Milky Way.

"The Sabbath has begun," Gedali stated solemnly; "Jews should be going to the synagogue. Pan comrade," he said, rising, his top hat like a little black tower swaying on his head, "bring a few good people to Zhitomir. Oh, there's a scarcity of good people in our town. Oh, what a scarcity! Bring them along and we will hand over all our phonographs to them. We are not ignoramuses. The International—we know what the International is. And I want an International of good people. I would like every soul to be listed and given first-category rations. There, soul, please eat and enjoy life's pleasures. Pan comrade, you don't know what the International is eaten with . . ."

"It is eaten with gunpowder," I answered the old man, "and spiced with best-quality blood."

And then, from out of the blue gloom, the young Sabbath came to take her seat of honor.

"Gedali," I said, "today is Friday, and it's already evening. Where are Jewish biscuits to be got, and a Jewish glass of tea, and a little of that pensioned-off God in a glass of tea?"

"Not to be had," Gedali replied, hanging the padlock on his little booth. "Not to be had. Next door is a tavern, and they were good people who served in it; but nobody eats there now, people weep there."

He buttoned his green frock coat on three bone buttons, flicked himself with the cock's feathers, sprinkled a little water on his soft palms, and departed, a tiny, lonely visionary in a black top hat, carrying a big prayerbook under his arm.

The Sabbath is coming. Gedali, the founder of an impossible International, has gone to the synagogue to pray.

Two Years among the Peasants in Tambov Province (1924)

A. Okninsky

"I am a native Peterburzhets" (Petersburg resident). So begins the brief introduction to the notes made by Anton Leontevich Okninsky during the two years he lived in the Tambov guberniia of Russia between 1918 and 1920. We know little about Okninsky other than what he tells us in that introduction. By his own account he ultimately ended up in Tambov due to an initial problem with finding a livable apartment in Petrograd, as refugees fleeing the western part of the country had taken up all available apartment space. Initially Okninsky packed up his bags and moved slightly north of Petrograd to Levashovo. In 1918 he headed south to Tambov guberniia, on the northern fringe of the black-earth region, where he decided to wait out the civil war. At the beginning of November 1920 he left the village of Podgornyi, where he had lived for most of those two years, and traveled to Latvia, where he wrote down all that he had seen and heard.

Initially Okninsky had no thoughts of publishing his notes, but after he arrived in Riga and began reading various accounts of the Revolution, he saw that not one of them was written from the perspective of someone living in the countryside. Thus he had his notes published. Given the volatile situation in Soviet Russia at that time, however, he chose to change the names of some of the people in the villages where he lived.

Okninsky's account provides extraordinary insight into what village life in central Russia was like in the days immediately following the Revolution. He was witness to the ongoing Revolution as it spread out into the countryside in the form of grain requisitioning. The area where Okninsky settled was flooded with displaced persons, with deserters and people generally fleeing famine. The Bolsheviks were repeatedly extracting grain from the local population, which was sometimes sold to speculators and sometimes left to rot. Okninsky reports that local villagers often joined the Party to avoid having their own grain taken from them. His account paints a sobering picture of how the new Bolshevik order was introduced by force into the countryside. In Tambov guberniia the result was a series of peasant uprisings "against senseless cruelty and exorbitant hypocrisy" that rocked the area between 1918 and 1921.

Father Gleb's home was near the *volost'* office. I caught him just as he returned from church and had sat down to tea. On the table, besides the big shining copper samovar was a teapot with dried apple leaves instead of tea, a small saucer with pieces of boiled beets instead of sugar and a plate with sliced rye bread and a saltcellar. His wife was sitting there.

After exchanging greetings, Father Gleb invited me to join his tea party. He said to me, "Forgive me, Anton Leont'ich, that I am going to talk somewhat about farming matters in front of my old woman. There's all sorts of things that I forget [to mention] for lack of time." After that, obviously resuming a conversation he had had with his wife before I arrived, he said to his wife:

"Well then: will there be anything to break our fast with?"

"May God will it," answered his wife, "I've saved up four dozen eggs. Mitrevna's brought three pounds butter, an' Stepan Ivanych's son's wife's brought ten pounds cottage cheese and two pounds sour cream. 'At's how we'll provide for them, just as Pestrukha [a country name for a cow] provided calves. We'll paint eggs tomorrow. There's still some paint from the year before last. We'll have ourselves an Easter. I'll bake Easter cakes from sifted flour. But the main thing is that Moisei Nikolaich has promised go and slaughter the hog."

"Couldn't we wait on the hog until the fall?" said Father Gleb. "We could fatten him up after the harvest and potato picking. That way we could add an extra *pud* to him. Right now he wouldn't come out to more than six *puds* [one *pud* = approximately 36 pounds—Trans.]. If it's possible to get by without him, then it would be better to wait. These are not the times to indulge in luxuries. At the fast-breaking there will be enough eggs and other things which you've managed to get hold of."

"That's just the point; it's forbidden [to eat pork on feast days]," his wife objected. "Remember how I told you about all the things we need to buy? Lidia needs a dress for Ascension. Masha also needs a little dress and maybe some boots. Mitia also needs boots, and look at me: all my clothes are worn through. If I said it once, I'll say it again: we'll save the gammon and head for ourselves and exchange the rest in Moscow for what we need. They say that right now in Moscow for a pound of pig lard they'll give you 2,000 rubles. Ivan Pavlych is ready to go and barter for us in Moscow. He'll arrange everything for the best: he's reliable and a smart one too, he is.

"Well, besides that, God only knows what comes next. We'll hold onto the hog; we don't want it taken away from us, just like what happened to Father Sergii. They just took his hog and had a good laugh over it: 'For you, as a priest, to eat so much pork is sinful. It's forbidden food for feast days. A piglet would be plenty for you.'"

"That's the first time I've heard of Father Sergii," Father Gleb said. "When did this happen? How do you know about it?"

"This happened on Palm Sunday. The school teacher Mar'ia Vasil'evna told me about it. She traveled to their village on business."

I was deeply taken aback by their bad news, which put an end to their hope of attaining their goals, modest though they were and at that time attainable. However, I considered it necessary to warn them about the upcoming raid by local robbers, which is partly why I came to see them, and explained to them what I had overheard.

Father Gleb looked at me frightened and then, looking at the icon, crossed himself. His wife burst out crying and in tears began to regret that they'd let slip the opportunity to sell the hog and that they should have sold him last week. But Father Gleb interrupted her:

"Your screaming and yelling will get you nowhere. . . . There's nothing you can do. It's easy to see that it was preordained that we should suffer raids. . . ."

At this moment their son, Mitya, ran into the room and said hurriedly, catching his breath:

"Pappy, the Soviets are coming for us."

His mother rushed to the window.

"Yes, for us," she said in a lowered voice, choked by tears. "We live here alone, they couldn't be coming for anyone else."

Father Gleb also looked through the window and frowned.

"Husband, you should go out to meet them. Maybe they . . ." she began.

"What do they want?" he interrupted her with nervous agitation. "Do you think that if I go out to meet them, I'll be able to appease them? Imagine what a great honor it would be for them, in these times no less, to meet a priest! Even before they didn't exactly respect our brother, but now there is nothing to be said about it. No, it's all the same now. What will be will be," and he decisively waved his hand.

At this time a police officer came to the door.

"The plenipotentiary for taxation in kind and [members of] the soviet are waiting for you by the porch," [said the policeman].

When Father Gleb and the rest of us went out onto the porch, besides the plenipotentiary, Butiakov, and another police officer (the friend of the *volost'* chairman, Beliaev, did not come because he did not like these kinds of affairs), stood the chairman of the local village soviet, a middle-aged man with thinning hair and small, sly, wandering eyes, who said something quietly to Butiakov, and one police deputy.

"You have a large bread deficit," began the plenipotentiary, addressing Father Gleb. "You still haven't handed over twenty *puds* of rye. I can't wait any longer. I was sent here to oversee that all is done in a fair and timely manner. You are no poorer than anyone else. You use the land like everyone else, and yet you have bigger yields. Thus I demand that you make up the deficit in short order."

"How am I supposed to give you twenty *puds*? I don't have them—just go and search for them. I sow the grain, and if I can [pay the deficit], then I'll do it before next harvest," Father Gleb answered.

"But you do have yields. You can buy seed and distribute it."

"What kind of income am I supposed to have anyway? It was just a misunderstanding. Before, when you went to see a sick person you'd take a whole loaf of bread with you and you'd even put two loaves in your cart, either that or eggs, butter, maybe even a chicken, depending on what you could get hold of. But now there's nothing. And it's not because [farmers] give nothing, or that they don't want to give, but it is because these people themselves have very little. All that we could possibly give back to you we've already given. And if you take money from what has been reserved for the occasional religious ritual, say three thousand a month, then what do you think that means in these times of costly living, when a pound of salt costs 500 rubles? I have a family, after all, and quite a handful, seven of us, [to provide for]."

"You are assessed not only for bread, but for butter and eggs."

"I ask that our village soviet postpone this assessment. My cow has yet to calve, so how am I to get butter? I have children who have no milk. We only have three chickens; they've already taken all the other ones. And I have two small children: they need eggs. It's impossible to feed all of them on one potato and watery *shchi* [cabbage soup]."

"Look at how many deficits you have. But besides that there is one other important thing. You have committed, as they say, a crime against the working people," Butiakov continued in an emotionally strained voice. "While our comrade workers in Moscow and Petrograd are starving, here you are, just like a genuine bourgeois, thinking only about yourself! If only everyone acted like you, thinking only about themselves, then everyone in the capitals would have already died of hunger."

. . . .

Towards the spring of 1920 the local population was left without any salt whatsoever. It is a necessity that has been promised but has not been distributed to the population. It can only be obtained from railroad workers, mainly from conductors, through barter: one pound of salt can be had for a *pud* of flour or ten pounds of millet, though that's not always certain. Peasants say this about the situation:

"We can live without sugar, we can also get by without tobacco—after all, we can smoke blades of grass. Without salt we can't make do: there is no desire to eat, and without food—how are we supposed to work!"

And so, as soon as the spring season of impassable, muddy roads was over, "pilgrims" started to pass by our windows, heading south east . . . in search of salt. I call them "pilgrims" because they resembled wandering *bogomols:* thin, emaciated, blackened, with knapsacks over their shoulders and staffs in their hands. They were mostly middle-aged and old women as well as young people. They went by in groups of three and four, though some came in pairs or even by themselves. The last were those who lagged behind and were eventually separated from their parties because of physical weakness. They came from the Tambov, Kozlov, and other *uezds* even farther away. They would pass by at all times of the day and night. And we saw them even up to the date of our departure from Podgornyi at the end of September of that same year.

Translated by Kenny Cargill

VIII

Building a New World from Old

Inheritors of a revolution that careened between destiny and chance, the peoples of Soviet Russia of the 1920s and early 1930s lived through years of staggering trial, upheaval, and exhilarating experiment. Writers such as Maxim Gorky and Vladimir Mayakovsky and filmmakers such as Sergei Eisenstein and Dziga Vertov perhaps most famously captured the tumults and the ideological exhilarations of that first decade of Soviet power. But the country itself was far from a fully fledged entity waiting to emerge after years of planning. It was instead a deeply challenged work in progress, forged under the duress of a World War still in progress on the heels of 1917, and with equally great upheavals to come.

Eager to withdraw from an unpopular war, Lenin conceded considerable territories of the defunct Russian empire—Finland, the Baltics, and eastern Poland, most prominently—with the signing of the Treaty of Brest-Litovsk in March 1918. With that tentative step toward peace behind them, however, the country plunged into three years of Civil War, with "Reds," or supporters of the leading Bolshevik forces, in deep struggle with "Whites," who counted among them a diverse array of Menshevik, monarchist, liberal democrat, and counterrevolutionary forces, to speak only of those in active combat. It would be more accurate to describe the entire country as locked in a struggle of epic proportions, as the privations of battle spurred Lenin to declare a period of "war communism" (1918–21) in which the long-term goals of economic centralization and nationalization were rushed into effect to provide for the Red Army and to create some semblance of regularized supply in the cities. In layman's terms "nationalization of the means of production" meant that among the many fronts on which war communism was waged, citizens could expect compulsory labor in country and city, the abolition of private property, and the forced requisition of grain supplies. The resulting chaos led in late 1918 to the "Red Terror," the first of many waves of repression that the struggling government would soon declare a necessity. When asked what one eats to the sounds of revolution, Isaac Babel's famous character, Gedali, answers, "It is eaten with gunpowder, and spiced with the best-quality blood."

The peoples of the former empire went through periods of unprecedented famine across the 1920s. Between 1921 and 1923 alone over seven million are thought to have perished from hunger.

To speak of the Soviet Union immediately after 1917 is premature. By early 1918 wide swaths of the former empire had declared themselves independent countries, adding to the multiple fronts across which the socialist leadership stretched itself: to defend themselves from the Whites, to quell unrest against harsh new policies in city and countryside, and to set about recapturing breakaway states. Only in 1922 was the USSR as such founded. It transformed Soviet Russia into the Russian Soviet Federated Socialist Republic, a "leader among equals" alongside Ukraine, Belorussia, and the three states of the Transcaucasus Federation (who would be recognized years later as the Soviet Republics of Armenia, Azerbaijan, and Georgia). Uzbekistan, Turkmenistan, Tajikistan, Kazakhstan, and Kirgizia (contemporary Kyrgyzstan) joined in the late 1920s and 1930s. The Baltics and Moldavia (contemporary Moldova) were incorporated in the early 1940s, and Ukraine expanded considerably with the return of eastern Polish territory in the twilight of the Second World War.

Few might have imagined such an expansive future for the young socialist state at the outset of the Soviet period. In the 1920s, isolated by the newly formed League of Nations (who would concede recognition of the Soviet Union in 1934), Russia sought to assuage internal revolt and build greater international ties with the "New Economic Policy," when small entrepreneurship flourished and limited private property was permitted. For the country to truly advance, government leaders recognized the need for an active economic infrastructure, however it might be acquired. A wide spectrum of the population sought emigration abroad, and peasants flocked from the impoverished countryside to the cities, carried by newly affordable mass transportation in search of employment and led by promises of free health care and higher education in a worker's paradise.

Adding suspense to surely sufficient drama, Vladimir Il'ich Lenin, the architect of it all, was diminished by a series of strokes in 1922, only five years into the great socialist experiment. He died two years later, in 1924. His widow, Nadezhda Krupskaia, asked for his final will and testament—which included a brief but searing dismissal of Joseph Stalin's capacity for leadership—to be read aloud at the thirteenth party Congress of Soviets. The testament was read at a closed session of party elders who rejected Stalin's offer to resign, reasoning that Lenin had been ill at the time he wrote the testament. The ensuing power struggle, and Stalin's rise to power in 1929, set the stage for a country whose commitment to rapid modernization at any cost would impress as much as it would terrify the people of the new socialist Leviathan.

Make Way for Winged Eros (1923)

Aleksandra Kollontai

[handwritten margin note: she was first ambassador, after quietly removed from women's dept.]

In his landmark study, The Origin of the Family, Private Property, and the State (1884), Friedrich Engels remarked on the rise of monogamy. The celebration of the nuclear family, he wrote, was little more than a means of legalizing private property among males, much in the same way that states privatized property in the hands of the oppressors. If one were really concerned about tracking inheritance, Engels asked, why would society not follow a matrilineal line, since parentage could surely be affirmed more directly through women than through men? This story of property, patriarchy, and oppression was one more brick in an edifice of inequality that young socialist writers such as Aleksandra Kollontai (1872–1952) sought to overturn.

In the 1920s sex was a key player in Soviet Russia. The Revolution was a purge, a cleansing of the old moral order, and in its first years its adherents, reflecting the practices of religious ascetics, repudiated sexual relations and in some cases food as part of the new ideological chastity of the Soviet state. The state and its body politic would, in their view, be uncorrupted by contact with both the West and those who threatened to subvert it from within. In the heady first months of the Revolution, as Lenin declared the death of the personal life, personal desires were redirected to a world where life was public and communal. Ideas such as vigilance, purity, and noncontamination filled the air. But sex and its ideological position in the new order were never actually settled and remained an ongoing topic of debate as they increasingly clashed with issues of Party control.

Kollontai's novels and essays were part of that debate. "Winged Eros" follows Marx and Engels in calling for a fundamental rethinking of family relations at the outset of the twentieth century. In many families, rich and poor, European women were in a position of unrewarded indentured labor, she reasoned, little more than prostitutes to their husband's needs and nannies to children they struggled to raise (often on their own). Under socialism, by contrast, Kollontai saw an opportunity to merge political and sexual liberation. She advocates a new kind of "love-comradeship," as beautiful and complex as the love familiar to her bourgeois readership, but one which would be free of the exclusive, "all-consuming," possessive character that drained social energies away from collective causes. At her most ambitious, Kollontai *predicts a time when all children will be raised by the government, liberating parents and ensuring the proper ideological formation of future generations. Yet even as Kollontai calls for an end to bourgeois sexual mores that tie sexuality to procreation and the family, she seems to step back from her own radical stance. Increasingly she begs the question of sex itself and redirects it, not to the family, but to the cause of the greater good of the collective. In "Winged Eros" sex becomes less corporeal and is seen instead as "woven of delicate strands of every kind of emotion."*

Kollontai's early rise after the October Revolution, first being named as the People's Commissar for Social Welfare and later as the founder of the Zhenotdel, or the Women's Department, in 1919, did not last long. Despite its embrace of women's suffrage in 1917, a shocked public declared itself unwilling to surrender its children to state hands, and a predominantly male Soviet leadership quietly sidelined her through a series of diplomatic posts. Though she became the world's first female ambassador in 1923, to Norway, she found herself effectively in exile, a diminished voice in the affairs of her country.

Love as a Socio-psychological Factor

You ask me, my young friend, what place proletarian ideology gives to love? You are concerned by the fact that at the present time young workers are occupied more with love and related questions than with the tremendous tasks of construction which face the workers' republic. It is difficult for me to judge events from a distance, but let us try to find an explanation for this situation, and then it will be easier to answer the first question about the place of love in proletarian ideology.

There can be no doubt that Soviet Russia has entered a new phase of the civil war. The main theatre of struggle is now the front where the two ideologies, the two cultures—the bourgeois and the proletarian—do battle. The incompatibility of these two ideologies is becoming increasingly obvious, and the contradictions between these two fundamentally different cultures are growing more acute. Alongside the victory of communist principles and ideals in the sphere of politics and economics, a revolution in the outlook, emotions and the inner world of working people is inevitably taking place. A new attitude to life, society, work, art and to the rules of living (i.e. morality) can already be observed. The arrangement of sexual relationships is one aspect of these rules of living. Over the five years of the existence of our labour republic, the revolution on this non-military front has been accomplishing a great shift in the way men and women think. The fiercer the battle between the two ideologies, the greater the significance it assumes and the more inevitably it raises new "riddles of life" and new problems to which only the ideology of the working class can give a satisfactory answer.

The "riddle of love" that interests us here is one such problem. This question of the relationships between the sexes is a mystery as old as human society itself. At different levels of historical development mankind has approached the solution of this problem in different ways. The problem remains the same; the keys to its solution change. The keys are fashioned by the different epochs, by the classes in power and by the "spirit" of a particular age (in other words by its culture).

In Russia over the recent years of intense civil war and general dislocation there has been little interest in the nature of the riddle. The men and women of the working classes were in the grip of other emotions, passions and experiences. In those years everyone walked in the shadow of death, and it was being decided whether victory would belong to the revolution and progress or to counter-revolution and reaction. In face of the revolutionary threat, tender-winged Eros fled from the surface of life. There was neither time nor a surplus of inner strength for love's "joys and pains." Such is the law of the preservation of humanity's social and psychological energy. As a whole, this energy is always directed to the most urgent aims of the historical moment. And in Russia, for a time, the biological instinct of reproduction, the natural voice of nature dominated the situation. Men and women came together and men and woman parted much more easily and much more simply than before. They came together without great commitment and parted without tears or regret.

Prostitution disappeared, and the number of sexual relationships where the partners were under no obligation to each other and which were based on the instinct of reproduction unadorned by any emotions of love increased. This fact frightened some. But such a development was, in those years, inevitable. Either pre-existing relationships continued to exist and unite men and women through comradeship and long-standing friendship, which was rendered more precious by the seriousness of the moment, or new relationships were begun for the satisfaction of purely biological needs, both partners treating the affair as incidental and avoiding any commitment that might hinder their work for the revolution.

The unadorned sexual drive is easily aroused but is soon spent; thus "wingless Eros" consumes less inner strength than "winged Eros," whose love is woven of delicate strands of every kind of emotion. "Wingless Eros" does not make one suffer from sleepless nights, does not sap one's will, and does not entangle the rational workings of the mind. The fighting class could not have

Women at the wheels of industry. Courtesy of the Library of Congress, Prints and Photographs Division, *Look* Magazine Photograph Collection, LC-USZ6–2416.

fallen under the power of "winged Eros" at a time when the clarion call of revolution was sounding. It would not have been expedient at such a time to waste the inner strength of the members of the collective on experiences that did not directly serve the revolution. Individual sex love, which lies at the heart of the pair marriage, demands a great expenditure of inner energy. The working class was interested not only in economising in terms of material wealth but also in preserving the intellectual and emotional energy of each person. For this reason, at a time of heightened revolutionary struggle, the undemanding instinct of reproduction spontaneously replaced the all-embracing "winged Eros."

But now the picture changes. The Soviet republic and the whole of toiling humanity are entering a period of temporary and comparative calm. The complex task of understanding and assimilating the achievements and gains that have been made is beginning. The proletariat, the creator of new forms of life, must be able to learn from all social and psychological phenomena, grasp the significance of these phenomena and fashion weapons from them for the self-defence of the class. Only when the proletariat has appropriated the laws not only of the creation of material wealth but also of inner, psychological life is it able to advance fully armed to fight the decaying bourgeois world. Only then will toiling humanity prove itself to be the victor, not only on the military and labour front but also on the psychological-cultural front.

Now that the revolution has proved victorious and is in a stronger position, and now that the atmosphere of revolutionary élan has ceased to absorb men and women completely, tender-winged Eros has emerged from the shadows and begun to demand his rightful place. "Wingless Eros" has ceased to satisfy psychological needs. Emotional energy has accumulated and men and women, even of the working class, have not yet learned to use it for the inner life of the collective. This extra energy seeks an outlet in the love-experience. The many-stringed lyre of the god of love drowns the monotonous voice of "wingless Eros." Men and women are now not only united by the momentary satisfaction of the sex instinct but are beginning to experience "love affairs" again, and to know all the sufferings and all the exaltations of love's happiness.

In the life of the Soviet republic an undoubted growth of intellectual and emotional needs, a desire for knowledge, an interest in scientific questions and in art and the theatre can be observed. This movement towards transformation inevitably embraces the sphere of love experiences too. Interest is aroused in the question of the psychology of sex, the mystery of love. Everyone to some extent is having to face up to questions of personal life. One notes with surprise that party workers who in previous years had time only for *Pravda* editorials and minutes and reports are reading fiction books in which winged Eros is lauded.

What does this mean? Is this a reactionary step? A symptom of the beginning of the decline of revolutionary creativity? Nothing of the sort! It is time we separated ourselves from the hypocrisy of bourgeois thought. It is time to recognise openly that love is not only a powerful natural factor, a biological force, but also a social factor. Essentially love is a profoundly social emotion. At all stages of human development love has (in different forms, it is true) been an integral part of culture. Even the bourgeoisie, who saw love as a "private matter," was able to channel the expression of love in its class interests. The ideology of the working class must pay even greater attention to the significance of love as a factor which can, like any other psychological or social phenomenon, be channelled to the advantage of the collective. Love is not in the least a "private" matter concerning only the two loving persons: love possesses a uniting element which is valuable to the collective. This is clear from the fact that at all stages of historical development society has established norms defining when and under what conditions love is "legal" (i.e. corresponds to the interests of the given social collective), and when and under what conditions love is sinful and criminal (i.e. contradicts the tasks of the given society).

. . . .

But though bourgeois morality defended the rights of two "loving hearts" to conclude a union even in defiance of tradition, and though it criticised "spiritual love" and asceticism, proclaiming love as the basis of marriage, it nevertheless defined love in a very narrow way. Love is permissible only when it is within marriage. Love outside legal marriage is considered immoral. Such ideas were often dictated, of course, by economic considerations, by the desire to prevent the distribution of capital among illegitimate children. The entire morality of the bourgeoisie was directed towards the concentration of capital. The ideal was the married couple, working together to improve their welfare and to increase the wealth of their particular family unit, divorced as it was from society. Where the interests of the family and society were in conflict, bourgeois morality decided in the interests of the family (cf. the sympathetic attitude of bourgeois morality—though not the law—to deserters and to those who, for the sake of their families, cause the bankruptcy of their fellow shareholders). This morality, with a utilitarianism typical of the bourgeoisie, tried to use love to its advantage, making it the main ingredient of marriage, and thereby strengthening the family.

Love, of course, could not be contained within the limits set down by bourgeois ideologists. Emotional conflicts grew and multiplied, and found their expression in the new form of literature—the novel—which the bourgeois class developed. Love constantly escaped from the narrow framework of legal marriage relations set for it, into free relationships and adultery, which were condemned but which were practised. The bourgeois ideal of love does not correspond to the needs of the largest section of the population—the working class. Nor is it relevant to the life-style of the working intelligentsia. This is why in highly developed capitalist countries one finds such an interest in the problems of sex and love and in the search for the key to its mysteries. How, it is asked, can relations between the sexes be developed in order to increase the sum of both individual and social happiness?

The working youth of Soviet Russia is confronting this question at this very moment. This brief survey of the evolution of the ideal of love-marriage relationships will help you, my young friend, to realise and understand that love is not the private matter it might seem to be at first glance. Love is an important psychological and social factor, which society has always instinctively organised in its interests. Working men and women, armed with the science of marxism and using the experience of the past, must seek to discover the place love ought to occupy in the new social order and determine the ideal of love that corresponds to their class interests.

Love-comradeship

The new, communist society is being built on the principle of comradeship and solidarity. Solidarity is not only an awareness of common interests; it depends also on the intellectual and emotional ties linking the members of the collective. For a social system to be built on solidarity and co-operation it is essential that people should be capable of love and warm emotions. The proletarian ideology, therefore, attempts to educate and encourage every member of the working class to be capable of responding to the distress and needs of other members of the class, of a sensitive understanding of others and a penetrating consciousness of the individual's relationship to the collective. All these "warm emotions"—sensitivity, compassion, sympathy and responsiveness—derive from one source: they are aspects of love, not in the narrow, sexual sense but in the broad meaning of the word. Love is an emotion that unites and is consequently of an organising character. The bourgeoisie was well aware of this, and in the attempt to create a stable family bourgeois ideology erected "married love" as a moral virtue; to be a "good family man" was, in the eyes of the bourgeoisie, an important and valuable quality. The proletariat should also take into account the psychological and social role that love, both in the broad sense and in the sense of relationships between the sexes, can and must play, not in strengthening family-marriage ties, but in the development of collective solidarity.

What is the proletariat's ideal of love? We have already seen that each epoch has its ideal; each class strives to fill the conception of love with a moral content that suits its own interests. Each stage of cultural development, with its richer intellectual and emotional experiences, redefines the image of Eros. With the successive stages in the development of the economy and social life, ideas of love have changed; shades of emotion have assumed greater significance or, on the other hand, have ceased to exist.

In the course of the thousand-year history of human society, love has developed from the simple biological instinct—the urge to reproduce which is inherent in all creatures from the highest to the lowest—into a most complex emotion that is constantly acquiring new intellectual and emotional aspects. Love has become a psychological and social factor. Under the impact of economic and social forces, the biological instinct for reproduction has been transformed in two diametrically opposed directions. On the one hand the healthy sexual instinct has been turned by monstrous social and economic relations, particularly those of capitalism, into unhealthy carnality. The sexual act has become an aim in itself—just another way of obtaining pleasure, through lust sharpened with excesses and through distorted, harmful titillations of the flesh. A man does not have sex in response to healthy instincts which have drawn him to a particular woman; a man approaches any woman, though he feels no sexual need for her in particular, with the aim of gaining his sexual satisfaction and pleasure through her. Prostitution is the organised expression of this distortion of the sex drive. If intercourse with a woman does not prompt the expected excitement, the man will turn to every kind of perversion.

This deviation towards unhealthy carnality takes relationships far from their source in the biological instinct. On the other hand, over the centuries and with the changes in human social life and culture, a web of emotional and intellectual experiences has come to surround the physical attraction of the sexes. Love in its present form is a complex state of mind and body; it has long been separated from its primary source, the biological instinct for reproduction, and in fact it is frequently in sharp contradiction with it. Love is intricately woven from friendship, passion, maternal tenderness, infatuation, mutual compatibility, sympathy, admiration, familiarity and many other shades of emotion. With such a range of emotions involved, it becomes increasingly difficult to distinguish direct connection between the natural drive of "wingless Eros" and "winged Eros," where physical attraction and emotional warmth are fused. The existence of love-friendship where the element of physical attraction is absent, of love for one's work or for a cause, and of love for the collective, testify to the extent to which love has become "spiritualised" and separated from its biological base.

. . . .

The hypocritical morality of bourgeois culture resolutely restricted the freedom of Eros, obliging him to visit only the "legally married couple." Outside marriage there was room only for the "wingless Eros" of momentary and joyless sexual relations which were bought (in the case of prostitution) or stolen (in the case of adultery). The morality of the working class, on the other hand, in so far as it has already been formulated, definitely rejects the external forms of sexual relations. The social aims of the working class are not affected one bit by whether love takes the form of a long and official union or is expressed in a temporary relationship. The ideology of the working class does not place any formal limits on love. But at the same time the ideology of the working class is already beginning to take a thoughtful attitude to the content of love and shades of emotional experience. In this sense the proletarian ideology will persecute "wingless Eros" in a much more strict and severe way than bourgeois morality. "Wingless Eros" contradicts the interests of the working class. In the first place it inevitably involves excesses and therefore physical exhaustion, which lower the resources of labour energy available to society. In the second place it impoverishes the soul, hindering the development and strengthening of inner bonds and positive emotions. And in the third place it usually rests on an inequality of rights in relationships between the sexes, on the dependence of the woman on the man and on male complacency and insensitivity, which undoubtedly hinder the development of comradely feelings. "Winged Eros" is quite different.

Obviously sexual attraction lies at the base of "winged Eros" too, but the difference is that the person experiencing love acquires the inner qualities necessary to the builders of a new culture—sensitivity, responsiveness and the desire to help others. Bourgeois ideology demanded that a person should only display such qualities in their relationship with one partner. The aim of proletarian ideology is that men and women should develop these qualities not only in relation to the chosen one but in relation to all the members of the collective. The proletarian class is not concerned as to which shades and nuances of feeling predominate in winged Eros. The only stipulation is that these emotions facilitate the development and strengthening of comradeship. The ideal of love-comradeship, which is being forged by proletarian ideology to replace the all-embracing and exclusive marital love of bourgeois culture, involves the recognition of the rights and integrity of the other's personality, a steadfast mutual support and sensitive sympathy, and responsiveness to the other's needs.

The ideal of love-comradeship is necessary to the proletariat in the important and difficult period of the struggle for and the consolidation of the dictatorship. But there is no doubt that with the realisation of communist society love will acquire a transformed and unprecedented aspect. By that time the "sympathetic ties" between all the members of the new society will have grown and strengthened. Love potential will have increased, and love-solidarity will become the lever that competition and self-love were in the bourgeois system. Collectivism of spirit can then defeat individualist self-sufficiency, and the "cold of inner loneliness," from which people in bourgeois culture have attempted to escape through love and marriage, will disappear. The many threads bringing men and women into close emotional and intellectual contact will develop, and feelings will emerge from the private into the public sphere. Inequality between the sexes and the dependence of women on men will disappear without trace, leaving only a fading memory of past ages.

In the new and collective society, where interpersonal relations develop against a background of joyful unity and comradeship, Eros will occupy an honourable place as an emotional experience multiplying human happiness.

1918 in Petrograd, by Kuzma Petrov-Vodkin (1878–1939). Source: The State Tret'iakov Gallery.

What will be the nature of this transformed Eros? Not even the boldest fantasy is capable of providing the answer to this question. But one thing is clear: the stronger the intellectual and emotional bonds of the new humanity, the less the room for love in the present sense of the word. Modern love always sins, because it absorbs the thoughts and feelings of "loving hearts" and isolates the loving pair from the collective. In the future society, such a separation will not only become superfluous but also psychologically inconceivable. In the new world the accepted norm of sexual relations will probably be based on free, healthy and natural attraction (without distortions and excesses) and on "transformed Eros."

But at the present moment we stand between two cultures. And at this turning-point, with the attendant struggles of the two worlds on all fronts, including the ideological one, the proletariat's interest is to do its best to ensure the quickest possible accumulation of "sympathetic feelings." In this period the moral ideal defining relationships is not the unadorned sexual instinct but the many-faceted love experience of love-comradeship. In order to answer the demands formulated by the new proletarian morality, these experiences must conform to three basic principles: 1. Equality in relationships (an

end to masculine egoism and the slavish suppression of the female personality). 2. Mutual recognition of the rights of the other, of the fact that one does
not own the heart and soul of the other (the sense of property, encouraged by
bourgeois culture). 3. Comradely sensitivity, the ability to listen and understand the inner workings of the loved person (bourgeois culture demanded
this only from the woman). But in proclaiming the rights of "winged Eros,"
the ideal of the working class at the same time subordinates this love to the
more powerful emotion of love-duty to the collective. However great the love
between two members of the collective, the ties binding the two persons to
the collective will always take precedence, will be firmer, more complex and
organic. Bourgeois morality demanded all for the loved one. The morality of
this proletariat demands all for the collective. ✳

The Bathhouse (1924)

Mikhail Zoshchenko

cultural

The October Revolution of 1917 is generally studied from the point of view of the sea change it brought to the political and economic system of Russia. Yet this historical shift also had enormous impact on private life. Property became de-privatized. Well-to-do Russians who formerly were living in large apartments or houses found their living quarters subdivided in accordance with the revolutionary order to communalize in an effort to gradually eliminate class distinctions. Perhaps because of the enormity of the events themselves, it is easy to overlook how the daily life of the average Russian was turned completely upside down during the early years of the Bolshevik order. Orthography and language changed. Political and revolutionary slogans filled the newspapers. Revolutionary posters and banners hung in public places and were exported to the countryside to announce the Revolution. Suddenly one was meant to call one's neighbor or colleague at work "comrade" (tovarishch) instead of "sir" or "madam." Prerevolutionary street names were replaced by Marx, Lenin, and Revolution Avenues, while others were named after prominent revolutionary writers.

The writer Mikhail Zoshchenko (1895–1958) was there, recording in his satirical stories the response of the average Soviet who bumbles through the new political order, having little understanding of the world into which he or she has been deposited. In the following story Zoshchenko's narrator, semi-educated and no doubt from the provinces, attempts to go to a public bathhouse. This fact alone is not extraordinary, as bathhouses existed in Russia well before the Revolution. The problem is that Zoshchenko's unwitting hero runs head-on into the new Soviet bureaucracy, and his attempts to negotiate it meet with failure. Zoshchenko's satire, however, is directed not only at his narrator but at a fledgling system already awash in its own mind-numbing red tape.

By the 1930s Zoshchenko's brilliant satires no longer found favor with the Party, as the artistic canon of socialist realism became the order of the day. In 1946, along with the Leningrad poet Anna Akhmatova, he was singled out for vicious attack by Stalin's right-hand man, Andrei Zhdanov, in what became known as the Leningrad Affair. Although Akhmatova and Zoshchenko were rehabilitated after Stalin's death, Zoshchenko never again wrote the quality of satire that distinguished his work in the 1920s.

I hear tell, citizens, they have some excellent bathhouses in America.

For example, a citizen just drives in, drops his linen in a special box, then off he'll go to wash himself. He won't even worry, they say, about loss or theft. He doesn't even need a ticket.

Well, let's suppose it's some other, nervous-type American, and he'll say to the attendant, "Goot-bye," so to speak, "keep an eye out."

And that's all there is to it.

This American will wash himself, come back, and they'll give him clean linen—washed and pressed. Foot-wrappings, no doubt, whiter than snow. Underdrawers mended and sewed. That's the life!

Well, we have bathhouses, too. But not as a good. Though it's possible to wash yourself.

Only in ours, there's trouble with the tickets. Last Saturday I went to one of our bathhouses (after all, I can't go all the way to America), and they give me two tickets. One for my linen, the other for my hat and coat.

But where is a naked man going to put tickets? To say it straight—no place. No pockets. Look around—all stomach and legs. The only trouble's with the tickets. Can't tie them to your beard.

Well, I tied a ticket to each leg so as not to lose them both at once. I went into the bath.

The tickets are flapping about on my legs now. Annoying to walk like that. But you've got to walk. Because you've got to have a bucket. Without a bucket, how can you wash? That's the only trouble.

I look for a bucket. I see one citizen washing himself with three buckets. He is standing in one, washing his head in another, and holding the third with his left hand so no one would take it away.

I pulled at the third bucket; among other things, I wanted to take it for myself. But the citizen won't let go.

"What are you up to," says he, "stealing other people's buckets?" As I pull, he says, "I'll give you a bucket between the eyes, then you won't be so damn happy."

I say: "This isn't the tsarist regime," I say, "to go around hitting people with buckets. Egotism," I say, "sheer egotism. Other people," I say, "have to wash themselves too. You're not in a theater," I say.

But he turned his back and starts washing himself again.

"I can't just stand around," think I, "waiting his pleasure. He's likely to go on washing himself," think I, "for another three days."

I moved along.

After an hour I see some old joker gaping around, no hands on his bucket. Looking for soap or just dreaming, I don't know. I just lifted his bucket and made off with it.

So now there's a bucket, but no place to sit down. And to wash standing— what kind of washing is that? That's the only trouble.

[handwritten: nude staff, his clothes get swapped, dirty bathhouse.]

All right. So I'm standing. I'm holding the bucket in my hand and I'm washing myself.

But all around me everyone's scrubbing clothes like mad. One is washing his trousers, another's rubbing his drawers, a third's wringing something out. You no sooner get yourself all washed up than you're dirty again. They're splattering me, the bastards. And such a noise from all the scrubbing—it takes all the joy out of washing. You can't even hear where the soap squeaks. That's the only trouble.

"To hell with them," I think. "I'll finish washing at home."

I go back to the locker room. I give them one ticket, they give me my linen. I look. Everything's mine, but the trousers aren't mine.

"Citizens," I say, "mine didn't have a hole here. Mine had a hole over there."

But the attendant says: "We aren't here," he says, "just to watch for your holes. You're not in a theater," he says.

All right. I put these pants on, and I'm about to go get my coat. They won't give me my coat. They want the ticket. I'd forgotten the ticket on my leg. I had to undress. I took off my pants. I look for the ticket. No ticket. There's the string tied around my leg, but no ticket. The ticket had been washed away.

I give the attendant the string. He doesn't want it.

"You don't get anything for a string," he says. "Anybody can cut off a bit of string," he says. "Wouldn't be enough coats to go around. Wait," he says, "till everyone leaves. We'll give you what's left over."

I say: "Look here, brother, suppose there's nothing left but crud? This isn't a theater," I say. "I'll identify it for you. One pocket," I say, "is torn, and there's no other. As for the buttons," I say, "the top one's there, the rest are not to be seen."

Anyhow, he gave it to me. But he wouldn't take the string.

I dressed and went out on the street. Suddenly I remembered: I forgot my soap.

I went back again. They won't let me in, in my coat.

"Undress," they say.

I say, "Look, citizens. I can't undress for the third time. This isn't a theater," I say. "At least give me what the soap costs."

Nothing doing.

Nothing doing—all right. I went without the soap.

Of course, the reader who is accustomed to formalities might be curious to know: what kind of a bathhouse was this? Where was it located? What was the address?

What kind of a bathhouse? The usual kind. Where it costs ten kopecks to get in.

We: Variant of a Manifesto (1922) *propaganda*

Dziga Vertov *filmmaker made propaganda 2) documentary*

Film and revolution were nearly synonymous in the new Soviet state. The problem of how to export the news of the Revolution to Russia's rural areas was neatly solved in the first years by agitators who traveled on trains and ships with projectors onboard, stopping at local villages to show short propaganda pieces to the local population. These agitki, as the short newsreels were called, enjoyed tremendous popularity, by all reports. The peasantry flocked to see them not just for informational purposes but because they had never seen anything on film before. The film historian Peter Kenez estimates that by the end of the Civil War, more peasants knew what Lenin and Trotsky looked like than they did Tsar Nicholas II, whose portrait few had ever seen.

Among those who worked on the agitki was a young filmmaker named Dziga Vertov (1896–1954). He got his start in newsreels and went on to become a revolutionary filmmaker par excellence. Born Denis Kaufmann in the Polish wing of the late Russian Empire, he changed his name to reflect socialism's embrace of the Enlightenment mission of human perfection. "Dziga" comes from the sound that chugging sprockets make in film projectors, "Vertov" from the Russian word for helicopter, vertolet. Man-the-machine had found a new body.

Vertov knew that the Revolution demanded a revolutionary cinema, one that would depart from traditional narrative structure, traditional plot, traditional camera angles. He sneered at conventional narrative cinema, especially the popular Pinkerton detective films coming from abroad. For him there was only one genre of filmmaking, and that was documentary cinema. He aimed to liberate the camera from the human eye and give it an independent existence. We cannot see everything that surrounds us, he claimed, and thus the function of the camera is to give us a view and a vision of reality not ordinarily accessible to the human eye. Moreover cinema needed to reflect the powerful surge toward industrialization, the marriage of man and machine, the liberation of people from the senseless, meaningless labor that Marx had decried as a function of capitalism. "Saws dancing at a sawmill convey to us a joy more intimate and intelligible than that on human dance floors," he writes in his famous manifesto. Until communism could remake humanity in its own image, only the camera could suggest "the perfect electric man."

Like Sergei Eisenstein, Vertov proved himself a master of new technologies, star-
tling the world with his use of montage, freeze frames, acceleration, split screens, and
reverse motion. Both were not only directors but also theoreticians who wrote volu-
minously about film and the techniques of filming in the new Soviet state. But where
Eisenstein, relatively speaking, was the practiced dean of Soviet art circles, Vertov, in
the words of one critic, was cinema's Trotsky. *Unyielding in his idealisms, he found*
his extraordinary talents at first embraced and then increasingly out of step with the
conservative Stalinist climate of the late 1920s and early 1930s.

Vertov's feature-length experimental documentary masterpieces include Kino-
Pravda *(1925),* One Sixth of the World *(1926),* Man with a Movie Camera *(1929),*
and Enthusiasm *(1931). He called for revolution long after the Revolution itself had*
ended. Under Stalin he spent his last years working on precisely the kind of newsreel
cinema that his own philosophy had so strongly rejected.

We call ourselves *kinoks*—as opposed to "cinematographers," a herd of junk-
men doing rather well peddling their rags.

We see no connection between true *kinochestvo* and the cunning and calculation of the profiteers.

We consider the psychological Russo-German film-drama—weighed down
with apparitions and childhood memories—an absurdity.

To the American adventure film with its showy dynamism and to the
dramatizations of the American Pinkertons the kinoks say thanks for the
rapid shot changes and the close-ups. Good . . . but disorderly, not based on a
precise study of movement. A cut above the psychological drama, but still
lacking in foundation. A cliché. A copy of a copy.

WE proclaim the old films, based on the romance, theatrical films and the
like, to be leprous.

—Keep away from them!

—Keep your eyes off them!

—They're mortally dangerous!

—Contagious!

WE affirm the future of cinema art by denying its present.

"Cinematography" must die so that the art of cinema may live. WE *call for*
its death to be hastened.

We protest against that mixing of the arts which many call synthesis. The
mixture of bad colors, even those ideally selected from the spectrum, produces not white, but mud.

Synthesis should come at the summit of each art's achievement and not
before.

WE are cleansing *kinochestvo* of foreign matter—of music, literature, and

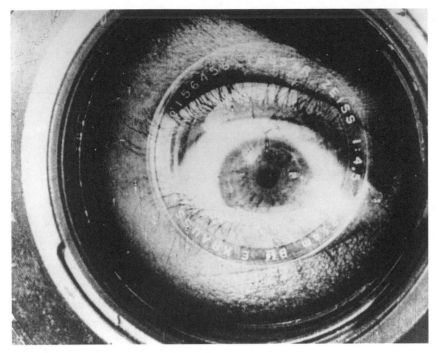

Kino-Eye. Courtesy of the MOMA Film Stills Archive.

theater; we seek our own rhythm, one lifted from nowhere else, and we find it in the movements of things.

WE invite you:

—to flee—

the sweet embraces of the romance,

the poison of the psychological novel,

the clutches of the theater of adultery;

to turn your back on music,

—to flee—

out into the open, into four-dimensions (three + time), in search of our own material, our meter and rhythm.

The "psychological" prevents man from being as precise as a stopwatch; it interferes with his desire for kinship with the machine.

In an art of movement we have no reason to devote our particular attention to contemporary man.

The machine makes us ashamed of man's inability to control himself, but what are we to do if electricity's unerring ways are more exciting to us than the disorderly haste of active men and the corrupting inertia of passive ones?

Saws dancing at a sawmill convey to us a joy more intimate and intelligible than that on human dance floors.

For his inability to control his movements, WE *temporarily exclude man as a subject for film.*

Our path leads through the poetry of machines, from the bungling citizen to the perfect electric man.

In revealing the machine's soul, in causing the worker to love his workbench, the peasant his tractor, the engineer his engine—

we introduce creative joy into all mechanical labor,

we bring people into closer kinship with machines,

we foster new people.

The new man, free of unwieldiness and clumsiness, will have the light, precise movements of machines, and he will be the gratifying subject of our films.

Openly recognizing the rhythm of machines, the delight of mechanical labor, the perception of the beauty of chemical processes, WE sing of earthquakes, we compose film epics of electric power plants and flame, we delight in the movements of comets and meteors and the gestures of searchlights that dazzle the stars.

Everyone who cares for his art seeks the essence of his own technique.

Cinema's unstrung nerves need a rigorous system of precise movement.

The meter, tempo, and type of movement, as well as its precise location with respect to the axes of a shot's coordinates and perhaps to the axes of universal coordinates (the three dimensions + the fourth—time), should be studied and taken into account by each creator in the field of cinema.

Radical necessity, precision, and speed are the three components of movement worth filming and screening.

The geometrical extract of movement through an exciting succession of images is what's required of montage.

Kinochestvo is the art of organizing the necessary movements of objects in space as a rhythmical artistic whole, in harmony with the properties of the material and the internal rhythm of each object.

Intervals (the transitions from one movement to another) are the material, the elements of the art of movement, and by no means the movements themselves. It is they (the intervals) which draw the movement to a kinetic resolution.

The organization of movement is the organization of its elements, or its intervals, into phrases.

In each phrase there is a rise, a high point, and a falling off (expressed in varying degrees) of movement.

A composition is made of phrases, just as a phrase is made of intervals of movement.

A kinok who has conceived a film epic or fragment should be able to jot it down with precision so as to give it life on the screen, should favorable technical conditions be present.

The most complete scenario cannot, of course, replace these notes, just as a libretto does not replace pantomime, just as literary accounts of Scriabin's compositions do not convey any notion of his music.

To represent a dynamic study on a sheet of paper, we need graphic symbols of movement.

WE *are in search of the film scale.*

WE fall, we rise . . . together with the rhythm of movements—slowed and accelerated,

running from us, past us, toward us,

in a circle, or straight line, or ellipse,

to the right and left, with plus and minus signs;

movements bend, straighten, divide, break apart,

multiply, shooting noiselessly through space.

Cinema is, as well, the *art of inventing movements* of things in space in response to the demands of science; it embodies the inventor's dream—be he scholar, artist, engineer, or carpenter; it is the realization of kinochestvo of that which cannot be realized in life.

Drawings in motion. Blueprints in motion. Plans for the future. The theory of relativity on the screen.

WE greet the ordered fantasy of movement.

Our eyes, spinning like propellers, take off into the future on the wings of hypothesis.

WE believe that the time is at hand when we shall be able to hurl into space the hurricanes of movement, reined in by our tactical lassoes.

Hurrah for *dynamic geometry,* the race of points, lines, planes, volumes.

Hurrah for the poetry of machines, propelled and driving; the poetry of levers, wheels, and wings of steel; the iron cry of movements; the blinding grimaces of red-hot streams.

The Travels of My Brother Aleksei
to the Land of Peasant Utopia (1920)

Aleksandr Chaianov

[handwritten marginalia: fictional short story about the future.]

Aleksandr Chaianov (1888–1937) is best known for his landmark work in economic sociology. His study of small rural collectives gave rise to what he called the "theory of peasant economy," an approach that eschewed grand abstractions about rural life on the one hand, while attributing complex reasoning to peasant households on the other. Running counter to Marx's (among others') view of the "idiocy of rural life," Chaianov argued that Russian peasant farmers flexibly worked to maximize both their input and their output, efficiently scaling back efforts by season and by opportunity when necessary. Translated into English for the first time in 1966, his Theory of Peasant Economy *revolutionized development economics and continues to be influential in comparative rural studies today.*

Few know that Chaianov, like so many educated scholars of his day, was also a man of letters, a master of the short story genre. In this first translation of "The Travels of My Brother Aleksei," a young Muscovite, Aleksei Kremnev, finds himself transported to the Moscow of 1984. Russia of the future is a true Renaissance world, where economic logic and the pursuit of beauty are as seamlessly matched in the world of dreams as they are in Chaianov's own mind. Despite his general support of Soviet socialism, his early criticisms of Marx and Soviet state policy earned him little favor. He was arrested in 1930, put on show trial, and eventually perished in a labor camp in 1937.

Part 1,
in which the gracious reader
becomes acquainted with the triumph of socialism
and with the hero of our novel, Aleksei Kremnev

It was already long past midnight when the owner of labor record No. 37413, who in the bourgeois world had once been called Aleksei Vasil'evich Kremnev, left the stuffy, badly overcrowded large lecture hall of the Polytechnic Museum.

The foggy haze of an autumn night spread over the sleeping streets. Occa-

Street market in Russia. Courtesy of the American Geographical Library, University of Wisconsin–Milwaukee Libraries. Photographer William O. Field.

sional electric streetlights seemed lost in the departing distances of intersecting alleys. The wind tossed the yellow leaves on the trees of the boulevard, and the walls of Moscow's small Chinatown, next to the Kremlin, stood white in the darkness like some massive thing in a fairytale.

Kremnev turned onto Nikol'skaia Street. In the foggy haze it seemed to have taken on the outlines of a long-ago past. Wrapping himself vainly in his raincoat against the raw night, Kremnev looked with sadness at St. Vladimir's Church, at the chapel of Panteleimon. He remembered how many years ago, as a first-year law student, with a sinking heart, he had bought Flerovskii's *ABCs of the Social Sciences* right here in Nikolaev's used book shop. Three years later he had laid the foundations of his icon collection when he found the Novgorod Savior at Elisei Silin's, and for many long hours he had rooted, eyes burning with proselytic fervor, through the handwritten and printed treasures of Shibanov's antiquarian bookstore—there, where now in the dim light of the streetlamp you could make out the short sign "Chief Administration of Paper Industry."

Chasing away his criminal recollections, Aleksei turned towards Iverskii, passed the First House of the Soviets and plunged into the shadows of the Moscow alleys.

But the words, phrases, fragments of phrases he had just heard at the meeting in the Polytechnic Museum burned in his mind:

"By destroying the family hearth, we will deal the final blow to the bourgeois system!"

"Our decree, which forbids nourishment at home, casts the joyous poison of the bourgeois family out of our way of life and stabilizes the socialist principle until the end of all time."

"Family comfort gives birth to proprietary desires; the joy of the small-time property owner conceals the seeds of capitalism."

His exhausted head ached, and he had started to form thoughts by habit, without thinking, to realize without making conclusions. His feet moved mechanically towards his half-destroyed family home, condemned to complete destruction in one week's time, according to the decree of October 27, 1921 just-published.

Part 2,
which tells about the influence of Herzen
on the inflamed imagination
of a Soviet civil servant

Aleksei spread butter on a large piece of bread, blessed gift of the Sukharevka open-air food market, which God had spared. He poured himself a glass of boiled coffee and sat down in his working chair.

Through the panes of the large window, the city was visible. Down below in the foggy haze of night a chain of streetlights stretched out in milky patches of light. Here and there windows where lights still burned showed dim yellow in the black masses of the buildings.

"And so, it's come to pass," thought Aleksei, looking hard at nocturnal Moscow. "Old Maurice, virtuous Thomas, Bellamy, Blanchfort, and you others, kind and lovable utopians. Your solitary daydreams have turned into universal conviction, your greatest daring is now an official program and the most everyday, ordinary way of life! In the fourth year of the revolution, socialism may consider itself the undivided ruler of the earth's globe. Are you satisfied, you pioneering utopians?"

And Kremnev looked at the portrait of Fourier which hung over one of the shelves in his library.

However, for *him*—an old socialist, an important Soviet functionary who ran one of the departments in the World Council of National Economy, somehow all was not well in this incarnation. He felt a kind of unfocused regret for what was departing. Some cobweb of bourgeois psychology still darkened his socialist consciousness.

He paced across the rug of his office, ran his eyes along the bindings of books, and unwittingly noticed a series of small volumes on a half-forgotten shelf. The names of Chernyshevskii, Herzen, and Plekhanov gazed at him from the leather bindings of the solid volumes. He smiled, the way children smile at a recollection, and took Pavlenkov's edition of Herzen from the shelf.

It was two o'clock. The clock struck with a drawn-out hiss and then fell back into silence.

Good, noble and childishly naïve words opened before Kremnev's eyes. The reading lifted him up, excited him, the way one feels excited by memories of first youthful love, the first youthful vow.

It was as if his mind freed itself from the hypnosis of Soviet everyday life. New thoughts that were not banal stirred in his consciousness, it turned out to be possible to think in new variants.

Kremnev excitedly read a prophetic page that he had long forgotten:

"The weak, puny, stupid generations," Herzen wrote, "will drag along somehow until the explosion, until this or that eruption of lava, which will cover them with a stone blanket and give their chronicles over to oblivion. And after that? After that, spring will begin, young life will boil up on their gravestone, the barbarism of infancy, full of incompletely constructed but healthy forces, will replace the old barbarism, a wild fresh strength will burst open in the young breast of the youthful peoples, and a new circle of events will begin—a third volume of world history.

"Its fundamental tone can already be understood. It will belong to the societal ideas. Socialism will develop through all its phases to extreme consequences, to absurdity. Then a cry of negation will tear once more from the titanic breast of the revolutionary minority, and the mortal struggle will begin again, in which socialism will take the place of the current conservatism and will be conquered by a future revolution, one as yet unknown to us."

"A new uprising. Where is it? And in the name of what ideals?" wondered Kremnev. "Alas, the liberal doctrine was always weak in its inability to create an ideology and in having no utopias." He smiled with regret. "Oh, you Miliukovs and Novgorodtsevs, Kuskovas and Makarovas, what sort of utopia can you trace on your banners?! What do you have as a replacement for the socialist system, besides the obscurantism of reactionary capitalism?! I agree . . . we are far from living in a socialist paradise, but what will you give us in its place?"

Herzen's book suddenly closed by itself with a snap, and a packet of documents *in octo* and *in folio* fell from the shelf.

Kremnev jumped.

The room smelled chokingly of sulfur. The hands of the large wall clock began to turn faster and faster, and their mad movement blurred into invisibility. The pages of the desk calendar loudly tore themselves off and spun upward, filling the room with a whirlwind of paper. The walls shook and were somehow distorted.

Kremnev's head was spinning, and a cold sweat dampened his forehead. He twitched, ran in panicked horror for the door which led to the dining room, and the door slammed behind him with a crash like a falling tree. He looked in vain for the light switch. There was nothing in the place where it had been. Moving in the darkness, he bumped into unfamiliar objects. His head was spinning, and his consciousness grew hazy, as if he were seasick.

Exhausted by his efforts, Aleksei sank onto some kind of couch that had not been there before, and consciousness left him.

Part 3,

depicting Kremnev's arrival
to the land of Utopia, and his pleasant conversations
with a utopian Muscovite woman
about the history of art in the twentieth century

A silvery ringing awoke Kremnev.

"Hello, yes, it's me," he could hear a woman's voice. "Yes, he's arrived . . . late at night, it seems . . . He's still asleep . . . Very tired, he fell asleep without undressing. Good. I'll call."

The voice fell silent, and the swish of a skirt indicated that its wearer had left the room.

Kremnev raised himself on the couch and rubbed his eyes in amazement.

He was lying in a large yellow room, flooded with rays of morning sun. He was surrounded by yellow-upholstered mahogany furniture of a style strange and unfamiliar to Aleksei, half-open yellow curtains on the windows, a table covered with the oddest metallic objects. In the next room he could hear light feminine steps. The door creaked, and everything fell silent.

Kremnev jumped to his feet, wanting to figure out what had happened, and walked quickly to the window.

Thick autumn clouds were sailing like ships through the blue sky. Along with them, somewhat below them and just above the ground, slipped several airplanes, some small, some large, of peculiar shape, with turning metal parts that glistened in the sun.

The city spread below . . . Without a doubt, it was Moscow.

To the left rose the mass of the Kremlin towers, on the right the red of Sukharevka, and there in the distance Kadashi stood proudly.

A familiar view for many, many years.

But everything around was changed in some way. The stone giants that once blocked the horizon had disappeared, whole architectural groups were missing, familiar buildings were not in their place . . . But everything was swimming in gardens. The spreading cupolas of trees flooded all the space almost up to the Kremlin itself, leaving isolated islands of architectural groups. Streets and alleys intersected a green, already yellowing sea. Along them pedestrians, automobiles, carriages flowed in a living stream. Everything breathed some kind of precise freshness, a confident cheerfulness.

Without a doubt, this was Moscow, but a new Moscow, changed in appearance and illuminated.

"Surely I haven't become the hero of a utopian novel!?" exclaimed Kremnev. "I have to admit, it's a pretty stupid position!"

In order to get his bearings, he began to look around, counting on finding some starting point to get to know this new world that surrounded him.

"What awaits me outside these walls? A beneficent kingdom of socialism, enlightened and stabilized? The marvelous anarchy of Prince Petr Alekseevich? Renewed capitalism? Or perhaps some new, formerly unknown social system?"

As far as he could judge from the window, one thing was clear: the people were living at a fairly high level of well-being and culture, and they lived in harmony. But this was still not enough to understand the essence of his surroundings.

Aleksei greedily began to look over the things that surrounded him, but they told him extremely little.

Most of these were everyday things, standing out only in their painstaking finish, some kind of emphasized exactness and elegance of execution and the strange style of their forms, which recalled partly Russian antiques, partly the ornaments of Ninevah. In a word, it was a strongly Russified Babylon.

Above the couch where Kremnev had awakened, which was very deep and soft, hung a large picture which attracted his attention.

At first glance he could say with certainty that this was a classical piece by Pieter Breughel the Elder. The same composition with a high horizon, the same bright and precious paints, the same short little figures, but . . . the board was painted with people in colored frock-coats, women with umbrellas, automobiles. Without a doubt, the subject was something like airplanes taking off. Several reproductions that lay on the neighboring table had the same character.

Kremnev went over to the large working desk, made of something like very firm cork, and hopefully began to look over the books scattered on the desk. These were the fifth volume of B. Sher's *Practice of Socialism,* as well as *The Renaissance of the Crinoline: An Experiment in the Study of Contemporary Fashion,* two volumes of Riazanov's *From Communism to Idealism*, a wonderful edition of Pushkin's *Bronze Horseman,* the brochure *The Transformation of B-Energy*. Finally, trembling with excitement, he reached to pick up a fresh newspaper.

Worrying, Kremnev opened the smallish page. At the top stood the date: 23:00 p.m., September 5, 1984. He had passed through more than sixty years.

There could be no doubt that Kremnev had awoken in the land of the future, and he settled into reading the newspaper.

"The peasantry," "The previous epoch of urban culture," "State collectivism, of unfortunate memory . . . ." "This was in capitalist times, that is, almost prehistoric . . . ," "The isolated Anglo-French system . . ."—all these phrases and dozens of others penetrated Kremnev's brain, filling his soul with amazement and a great desire to know.

The sound of a telephone broke his cogitation. He heard steps in the room next door. The door flew open, and a young woman entered along with a flood of sunlight.

"Ah, you've already gotten up," she said merrily. "I slept through your arrival yesterday."

The telephone rang again.

"Excuse me, that must be my brother, worrying about you . . . hello . . . yes, he's already up . . . I don't know, really. I'll ask him now . . . You speak Russian, Mr. Charlie . . . Mann, if I am not mistaken."

"Of course, of course," Aleksei cried out unexpectedly and very loudly.

"He does, and even with a Moscow accent . . . good, I'll pass him the receiver."

Kremnev, at a loss, took something that recalled an old-fashioned telephone receiver; he heard a greeting, uttered in a soft bass voice, a promise to drive over and get him in three hours, an assurance that his sister would take care of him in every way. Hanging up the receiver, he realized with absolute clarity that they were taking him for someone else, someone named Charlie Mann.

The young woman had already left the room. With the decisiveness of despair Aleksei leaped toward the desk, counting on finding amid the papers and packets of telegrams at least some hint about the secret that surrounded him.

Luck was with him. The first letter that he picked up was signed by Charlie Mann. It laid out in a few phrases that person's desire to visit Russia and get acquainted with the country's engineering constructions in the area of agriculture.

Part 4,
continuing the third
and separated from it only so that
the third part be not too long

The door opened, and the young hostess entered the room, carrying a tray over her head with steaming cups of morning breakfast.

Aleksei was charmed by this utopian woman, her almost classical head, ideally placed on a strong neck, broad shoulders and full breast, which lifted the collar of her blouse with every breath.

A minute's silence upon first acquaintance soon gave way to lively conversation. Kremnev, avoiding the role of narrator, drew the conversation to the sphere of art, presuming that this would cause no difficulty for a young woman who lived in rooms with marvelous pieces of art hanging on the walls.

The woman, whose name was Paraskeva, spoke with the flush of youthful interest about her favorite masters: old Breughel, Van Gogh, old man Rybnikov and wonderful Ladonov. An admirer of neo-realism, she sought in art the secret of things, something either divine or diabolical, but surpassing human power.

Recognizing the higher value of everything essential, she demanded from the artist a congeniality with the creator of the universe, valued the power of enchantment in a picture, the spark of Prometheus, which conveyed a new essence, close to the realism of the old Flemish masters.

From her words Kremnev understood that the art of the epoch of the great Revolution, characterized by futurism and the extreme decadence of old traditions, had been followed by a period of baroque futurism, futurism that was tamed and sweetened.

Thereafter, as a reaction, like a sunny day after a thunderstorm, a thirst for mastery came to the fore; the artists of Bologna began to come into fashion, the primitivists were somehow forgotten immediately, and museum halls with pictures of Memling, Fra Beato, Botticelli and Cranach had hardly any visitors. However, obeying the circle of time and not declining from its height, mastery gradually took on a decorative tendency and created the monumental canvases and frescoes of the epoch of a barbaric conspiracy, the epoch of the still life and the blue scale passed in a stormy wave; then the twelfth-century Suzdal' fresco mastered the thoughts of the world, and the rule of realism began, with Pieter Breughel as its idol.

Two hours had passed unnoticeably, and Aleksei did not know whether he should listen to the deep contralto of his interlocutor or look at the heavy braids coiled on her head.

Her wide-open eyes and the mole on her neck spoke to him better than any proof of the superiority of neo-realism.

Translated by Sibelan Forrester

Learning to Labor (1932)

Anastasiia Bushueva

Anastasiia Evstaf'evna Bushueva was thirteen when the Revolution took place. Her family was semiliterate, impoverished, and barely able to clothe or feed themselves. Over time Bushueva managed to obtain a modest education and gradually rose to become a manager at the Trekhgorka Manufacturing Plant in Moscow.

Autobiography has long held a special place in Russian and Soviet letters. The personal narratives of writers from Alexander Herzen to Maxim Gorky have always been written with a view to understanding the larger canvas of Russia itself at the time these autobiographies were produced. Bushueva's short, straightforward narrative was typical of autobiographical writing in her era. Workers, peasants, managers, writers, Party figures—all were exhorted to write their life stories for Party archives, factory archives, and institute archives. And every ten years they were exhorted to write them again so as to update, delete, or amend anything that was not in line with changing Party ideology. These autobiographies were meant to be models for the political and moral upbringing of the ideal socialist worker and Party member. Precisely because the stories had a strong ideological underpinning, many were subjected to the censor's red pen before being recorded in the archives or published.

Not everyone during the autobiographic heyday from the 1920s through the 1950s had what was considered a good biography. Those from the prerevolutionary middle class could not claim the fortuitous, impoverished conditions that became the hallmark of the Soviet hero as worker. The poet and novelist Vera Inber, who came from a bourgeois background, lamented in the 1920s that she was not lucky with her biography and spent her life trying to reclaim the heroic life story she never had. Bushueva's story, on the other hand, contains all the ingredients for the perfect Soviet biography: a background of grinding poverty and harsh circumstances, obstacles to be overcome, access to education, and the requisite enthusiasm with which the new revolutionary order was embraced.

Much in this short autobiography is glossed over. There is less about her private life and feelings in Bushueva's account than about the times in which she lived. One can read between the lines to sense the trauma felt by Orthodox Russians in the newly proclaimed atheistic state. Similarly we hear almost nothing about the birth of

Bushueva's second child or the obviously difficult relations with her husband, whom she subsequently left. What was important for her to stress at the time was her life as a worker and as a member of the kollektiv.

There are particular moments in Bushueva's account that would have resonated with the Soviet worker in the 1920s and 1930s. Chief among them is her access to education. When Lenin assumed power in 1917 it was estimated that 75 percent of Russia's rural population were illiterate. By 1927 70 percent of males were judged to be literate. Many who were writing and reading these autobiographies originally came from illiterate or semiliterate backgrounds. The push for education was a product of the Bolshevik belief that the economic, political, and cultural improvements in the country were predicated on bringing education to the people. Bushueva also speaks movingly about announcing her intention of becoming a shock worker (udarnik [male] or udarnitsa [female]). This term originated in the First Five-Year Plan (1928– 32) to describe a campaign that was set in motion to increase industrial production by establishing competition between work brigades. By declaring herself a shock worker, Bushueva throws herself into the movement toward rapid industrialization to fill and overfulfill the production quotas set by her factory, thereby becoming a model socialist worker.

Her autobiography was collected along with those of other women workers from Trekhgorka and published in 1932.

I was born in 1904 in Bronnitsa Station in the village of Orovo. Father spent all of his life working as a switchman on the railroad. He began working when he was thirteen years old. Mother stayed at home—there were thirteen in our family, later only eight of us were left. At first we had a little parcel of land, just enough for half a soul. There was no house. When grandfather died, god-father gave father his house but we didn't live there long. When I was five years old we were already living in a state apartment at Bronnitsa. During the revolution they provided us with some land, and godfather gave his old house back to us. They gave him a new place, and he built himself a new house. We planted only potatoes on the homestead, but our land was under public management. In 1919 when father was getting on in years, he stopped working, and began to do some farming; at first there were no horses, and we worked the land with hired workers, but in 1922 we bought a horse. Our house was old; it was more like a bathhouse than a house. In 1924 when I was working at the Red Banner Factory, they gave me a prize of twenty rubles, later at the factory they found out that my father had consumption and that we were really hard up, so the factory committee collected fifty-five rubles for me. At that time my brother was working, and we built a new house. Father died that year and we had to sell the horse.

Children on the street with food bowls during the Famine of 1921. Courtesy of the Library of Congress, Prints and Photographs Division, LC-USZ62–96998.

My father was semi-literate; he had about two years of schooling, and mother was also semi-literate. Father wasn't religious, he was actually quite opposed to religion, from birth he never went to church and never had priests over to his house. But conditions compelled mother to go to church, but now she lives in a kolkhoz and says that she will take down the icons with pleasure. She is on the board of the kolkhoz, she is actively engaged in public life and attends the kolkhoz congress. It's been three years now that she's been involved with this work.

In 1910 they transferred father from Bronnitsa to Bykovo Station. Our family had lived in Bronnitsa for about fourteen or fifteen years. Father moved to Bykovo because he got a promotion and was then earning fifteen rubles. They gave him a room measuring eight square meters.

We arrived barefoot in Bykovo with almost nothing on. Mother began to help the wife of the station manager, she washed her linen, herded the cows, and the lady gave us some used clothes. Mother also washed for the holiday visitors. We had to get up at three in the morning with "go rinse the linen." We washed for Von Mekka, and for a count, and this helped father. The lady manager was extremely capricious. "Don't wash the shirt like that," she said, giving it back to us. All the women in Bykovo washed for the vacationers.

We shared a communal kitchen, everybody there did washing, racing

Five women standing outside of a log house. Courtesy of the Library of Congress, Prints and Photographs Division, LC-USZ62–119082, J228128 U.S. Copyright office.

about from morning till night. Father worked for twelve hours as a switchman and came back to unload the firewood. Boy our life was hard. Our grandmother gathered us up. There was no place to go. We had to eat something.

Manager Von Genike said to father: "Give us Nastia, let her work for us, and we'll school her." He wasn't a bad German, he even worked with me, but the lady was capricious and didn't want me to study. I went to work for them when I was nine and lived there three years. I helped the servant, washed clothes, and milked the cow. They didn't pay me anything, I lived for bread, father was glad that there was one less mouth to feed. But sometimes you cry and beg. "Take me home," I pleaded. But my mother said, "What am I going to do with you?"

I enrolled in the Ministry Railroad School; they give priority to workers' children and then if there are any places left, those go to the children of the switchmen if there were no bad marks against them. Father worked like an ox.

I did well in all my subjects except scripture because father said "God does not send manna, it would be enough if he would dress you and give you shoes." Sometimes it happened that he would start crying. In school they drummed religion into our heads, and I sang in the choir. I used to ask father "Why do rich people live well?" Grandma read the gospels to us. You say to her "Grandma, tomorrow is Sunday, and we don't have anything to eat or even enough food to make vegetable pies," and she says "To make up for it, everything's going to be fine in the next world." You say "This is miserable," but even so, you believe and you pray.

This is what I believed until I was fifteen years old when the first jolt took place. They beat father and arrested him, and he sat in prison for three months. Then even mother said that there was no god. This is how it happened: an express train with important people on it was coming through, they chased everyone away from the track, and not far from the station a track came dislodged and the watchman noticed this in time. So they started to look for father and couldn't find him at his post. For this they arrested four men. What to do? They said that we had to pay 100 rubles to release him on bail, then we sold the cow, mother took money from the savings book (she saved for us) and they let father go. He got his freedom back, but they tried the other three for negligence on the job and chased them away. Among them was a Bolshevik named Sokolov; he had a hot temper and said at his trial, "No matter, we'll strangle all of you." Father I suppose also took part, but they couldn't prove anything against him though this was probably their intent. Father said nothing to us about this.

I lived at the German's for about three years. Then I started to try and get away from them. They fired the servant, but had two cows, a heifer and a pig, and I was all of twelve years old and it got to be hard for me. During this time my older brother Sergei began working as a platform guard. Mother bought a cow and sold milk, and I kept coming to father, telling him that the German was making fun of me. And so I came home. I studied and finished school in 1916. In all I studied for five years.

I love to read novels. I've read Tolstoy, I read *Dead Souls* and was entranced: somehow they tug at my heart.

In 1917 I stopped believing in God altogether. I went to demonstrations in Ramenskoe, understood nothing, but kept going and singing. In Ramenskoe all the workers went to vote, only they tell me "You're still young, you don't have the right to vote."

In 1917 they made father head switchman, and I enrolled in the Ramenskoe seven year school; but as it turned out I didn't get the chance to study. In 1918 father came down with typhus, my brother was at the front, both mother and grandmother were sick and I was going back and forth for bread. For nine months father lay in the hospital, he got gangrene. He wasn't able to work like he used to, so they made him a watchman, and so he worked until he fell under one of the train cars in a train wreck. Soon after the accident they discovered that he had tuberculosis and gave him a disability pension. We left for Yurovo where we had neither house nor home. We bought a cow and began selling milk.

I lived in Yurovo until 1921 and took milk and potatoes to sell.

In 1921 I started to work in an office as a courier and later worked as a kind of clerk at Bronnitsa in the dried fruit workshop. But in 1923 the workshop burned down and I had nowhere to go, so I went directly to Ramenskoe to the Red Banner Factory. They hired the poverty-stricken there and taught me machine tooling.

I didn't study much. I turned out to have ability and found my way to a good woman weaver. At first no one took me in to train me. I would go around the factory crying and the head of the factory committee asked me about everything and set me up with the teacher Niusha. During week number three she spoke to the head foreman Malinkin (a Party member) and told him: "The girl works hard, place her as soon as possible at a loom." Within two weeks I had started working at two machine stations: the one next to me stood empty. Then the foreman put me at both of them. They saw that I was working without ever taking a rest and began to get me involved in community work. At first I was afraid, then it was okay. I worked in the cultural council, was a delegate to the factory section, conducted meetings with the women and for this massive work was awarded a prize of twenty rubles. I was also on the jury of the Comrade's Court. Later I was chosen from the factory to the All-Union Conference of Textile Workers, in all only eleven were chosen.

Within a month and a half I had begun to do well on two looms facing each other and began earning sixty to seventy rubles. I had a good relief worker, an old worker who had been on the job since 1905, and she would come early in order to show me how to do things. I worked like this until 1925.

In 1925 they transferred me to three looms. Uncle Misha, the old Bolshevik says: "Let's go to three," but at first no one went, the naughty weavers used foul language at the meeting, they screamed and hollered but then the majority decided to go. I went too, but at first I couldn't work the loom, and left, but Uncle Misha kept pestering me, and again I went for three, got used to it and began doing first-rate work. My relief worker, Aunt Dasha, didn't like the young workers and found fault with every little thing. She frequently arrived slightly drunk, didn't do a good job and had pieces of material all over the place. I began complaining to Malinkin, and they gave me a good relief worker, Malinkin's sister.

Uncle Misha left us. So then he came back and said: "Let's go to four looms, we'll give it a try." At first I was scared, then I went ahead and did it. The women were cursing me in the bathroom. But Uncle Misha, a muzhik with soul says, "You have to do this for the sake of the government." So twelve of us were put on four looms, and later half the factory converted over to four. So we were all working on four. And when I left the Red Banner, I cried.

In 1927 I got married; my husband said "Let's go to Moscow, we'll work there." He wasn't a Party member, he worked as a stoker on the Moscow Hydroelectric Station tram station.

When we arrived in Moscow, he didn't let me work: I had given birth to a baby, a little girl. I didn't baptize her, but his parents believed in God and he himself prayed and wanted to baptize her, and my mother was telling me the same thing. But our little girl had something wrong with her eyes, and later when she was already two months old, it was already too late to baptize her. In our apartment they used to say "Nastia is the first Bolshevik to show the Bolshevik spirit." And when out little girl died that summer, I buried her without a priest. Her coffin was covered in red.

For two years I didn't work and then decided to go back to work.

From the labor exchange I started work at Trekhgorka in October 1929. My life with my husband was not going well. I was in torment. At the factory committee they told me to go to a Health Resort. I went on holiday with the baby to the Kalinin Health Resort at Tarasovka Station. From there I took the baby to my mother's. I went to my husband, and he chased me out. He had come home drunk.

I went to see Surin, the Secretary of the Party Committee of the Trekhgorka manufacturers. He told me "We'll help you." This cheered me up. On September 4th when the meeting was held, I announced that I was a shock worker, and I submitted my application for Party membership. It didn't go well. I was supposed to give a rousing speech and instead I cried.

Shock Worker Day was at the beginning of September 1930. For us this was the first enrollment of shock workers. I told Nikadorova: "I can't talk at the meeting, my nerves are bad." At the meeting a lot of people began to proclaim themselves shock workers, but I held back. I was afraid of my husband, I had bad thoughts, but then I thought to myself, "I have to help. What am I," I thought, "worse than everyone else?" They gave me the floor, and I spoke, "Before us lie huge tasks and responsibilities," and I burst into tears there. But then I said "The conditions of life compelled me to reflect deeply, and I join the Party as a shock worker." Everyone applauded. The next day they called me into the office, and found some people who would vouch for me, and the head, Popugin, put in a good word for me. He said "She's a good worker." I was given community work to do.

But my husband took all of my money. One time he beat me so badly that I was unable to work. I came to my cell and told them "If you can, help me." Surin says "We've got to get things settled for you." And Ukolova called me in and I stayed with her for two days. Otherwise I would have ended up spending the night at the railway station. After that I stayed longer at Nikadorova's, I lived at her place from September to January. And so I made do . . . they gave

New mass production. Courtesy of the Library of Congress, Prints and Photographs Division, *Look* Magazine Photograph Collection LC-USZ6–2417P.

me a room. I've been living there now for a year, and my husband gave me nothing. Now I've become so much a part of Trekhgorka that nothing could make me to go back to my former life.

Seven people now remained of our family. From the time he was thirty-one my oldest brother has been working on the rails at Perovo Station. One sister is twenty-one years old. She works at a cotton fiber producing machine at the Red Banner Factory. A brigade leader of the cost-accounting brigade, she joined the Komsomol this autumn. Another sister is married to a kolkhoznik in Yurovo. I also have a little sister, fifteen years old who is studying at the Technical School for Fabric Production at the Red Banner to become a worker on a cotton machine. And the two others, my little brother and sister, are still in school, both at the top of their class.

Before I entered into shock work I worked on two machines making furniture upholstery and earned sixty-five rubles. As to how I became a shock worker, they transferred me onto a fourth machine where I began to earn eighty-five to ninety rubles and was given a prize—The Order of Textiles.

Here I began to conduct civic work in the co-op bureau. At meetings held to discuss the Factory Workers' Committee, I explained things. In January 1931 they selected me to be on the board of the committee, they chose me at a general meeting and not one voice was raised in opposition. I've served on the board up to the present. Earlier I was responsible for the agricultural sector. I wasn't that successful at it, but I tried and managed it. Now they've trans-ferred me over to the fulfillment sector.

When the youth brigade was organized in 1931, they suggested that I enter it. At first I wasn't up to it and couldn't work the exterior machines very well. Then the boys helped me and I did a good job. During the first month we fulfilled 101 percent of our quota and later 104 and 105 percent.

In April the regional committee took me off the loom and told me to start working on the campaign against illiteracy. The place was in complete disar-ray when I arrived. There were no word lists, nothing. I set up an inventory, got attendance in hand. People studied with us all spring and in the summer we had 60 percent attendance.

During this time I took a course for propagandists and completed it with a good grade.

In August, Solov'ev, the head of cultural and educational propaganda, sent me to head the Soviet Party School base where I took inventory, got it in hand, and introduced a monitoring system. Our task was to organize 31 groups, but we organized 37, and gave a push to the local sector. This was technical work. I wasn't trained for it and didn't do a good job at it. I began to tell them that I wasn't cut out for this kind of work.

They decided to use me as a propaganda worker, and I took to this work. They wanted to send me to do charity work for those who had fought in the revolution, but the regional committee wanted me to work locally as a propagandist but the Party committee wouldn't release me.

They gave me the main sector of the Workers' Finance Division. It took me a long time to agree to do this, I was scared that I wasn't going to do a good job of it, but they helped me and I began to do the job. I got the socialist emulation up and running, I make sure that the brigades have an understand-ing of cost accounting so that the inventory is posted on time, and not two months late. I keep in touch with the brigadiers, teach the workers, and take note of any suggestions they might make on the inventory.

Last year I studied for an entire year in the Soviet Party School, then for a month and a half in the course for propagandists from April 20th through June. For now my working conditions don't allow me to study, but for a couple of days I'm going to the Factory Academy or possibly to the local committee institute of higher learning. I'll definitely go somewhere to study: I have great desire to do this.

I read the newspaper *Pravda* although it's considered difficult. When I was at the propagandist course, I read *The Handbook for Agitators*. I wrote for *The Propagandist* and *The Trekhgorka Banner* about our enterprise and wrote about the Soviet party school and the campaign against illiteracy.

At first I would only read the leading article, the one that's the most essential. Of course, I don't read the entire paper. I also read the telegrams about what is going on abroad, I read about the conflict between Japan and China, and I read Litvinov's diplomatic note. In *Izvestiia* I always look for the decrees on textile industries since this is my area.

I read much of Lenin: *What the "Friends of the People" Are* and *What is to be Done?* When work calls, I always look to Lenin.

In the Soviet Party School we studied the history of the Party, the history of 1905 and 1917 and examined the history of the Party during the NEP [New Economic Policy] period. We also studied serfdom and imperialism.

At first I didn't read fiction but later read *The Quiet Don*, *Mutiny* and read about Stenka Razin, and all that was revolutionary.

In December we had to do storm-work, pushing extra hard to fulfill an urgent plan by the twentieth of the month. As it happened I had a leave until the 11th of December, but the storm work began on the first. I didn't leave Moscow and started working during the storm. I talked with the weavers about why we had to fulfill this plan. I worked at the machines several times, I specifically requested this even though it was my vacation period.

Now we are checking the agreement with both sides. You come to the factory shop, you wonder how is it going with this one and the other one. I'm interested in the fulfillment of the industrial and financial plan, not only in weaving.

Translated by Adele Barker

Stalin's Forgotten Zion (1998)

Robert Weinberg

In the late eighteenth century the Russian Empire inherited nearly one million Jewish inhabitants after the partitions of Poland. In response to concerns that Jews were exploiting peasants and acquiring too much influence in municipal affairs, Empress Catherine the Great restricted the Jewish population to the areas in which they had lived before the partitions. Known as the cherta osedlosti, *or Pale of Settlement, this region embraced the western borderlands of the empire, including approximately 20 percent of contemporary Russia and much of present-day Lithuania, Belarus, Poland, and Ukraine. Jews tended to reside in small market towns known as shtetls (from the German root noun,* Stadt*), where they served as tax farmers, engaged in a variety of small retail ventures, and worked as tailors and cobblers and in other handicrafts. By the late nineteenth century the Pale contained almost five million inhabitants, roughly 40 percent of the world's reported population of Jews at the time. The bulk of the empire's Jews lived in poverty, due in large part to the pressures of overpopulation caused by residential restrictions.*

Jews in the Pale faced an extraordinary number of obstacles, including double rates of taxation, highly restricted access to higher education, and an edifice of laws and regulations designed to persecute them as a parasitic minority intent on undermining the social, economic, and political fabric of the Russian Empire. Official anti-Jewish policies combined with popular anti-Semitism to create a volatile situation for Russian Jewry. Few threats to Jewish survival in the empire were as sharp as the pogrom, *from the Russian root word for "thunder," the sudden attacks and rioting periodically visited upon Jewish communities in the late tsarist period and throughout the Russian Civil War that followed the October Revolution. The Bolshevik regime granted Jews full civil and political freedoms and promised to put an end to all forms of anti-Semitism by integrating Jews into socialist society. The founding of the Jewish Autonomous Region, Birobidzhan, in 1934, the first official Jewish territory since antiquity, spoke to the Kremlin's paradoxical efforts to resolve the "Jewish Question." Located in the Russian Far East, thousands of miles away from the centers of Jewish culture, Birobidzhan was designated as the site where the Jews would be resettled, partly to provide the Soviet Union a buffer zone against Chinese and Japanese expansionism and partly to help the state tap the natural resources to be found there.*

In May 1934 the Soviet government established the Jewish Autonomous Region (J.A.R.) in a remote, sparsely populated region of the Soviet Far East. Located along the Sino-Soviet border some five thousand miles east of Moscow, the J.A.R.—popularly known as Birobidzhan, the region's capital city—was designated the national homeland of Soviet Jewry. The Birobidzhan project met with great fanfare both in the Soviet Union and abroad and marked the culmination of an effort begun in the 1920s. The creation of the J.A.R. was part of the Communist Party's effort to set up a territorial enclave where a secular Jewish culture rooted in Yiddish and socialist principles could serve as an alternative to Palestine and resolve a variety of perceived problems besetting Soviet Jewry. The notion of a Jewish homeland appealed to many Soviet Jews, and the Birobidzhan project was intended to undercut the Zionist focus on Palestine.

The J.A.R. still exists today; there one can still buy a Yiddish newspaper, study Yiddish at the local teachers' college, and listen to a weekly Yiddish radio program. However, Jews always have been a small minority of the inhabitants of the J.A.R. and by no means has the region ever embodied the national or cultural aspirations of Soviet Jews. In 1939, for example, on the eve of World War II, Jews constituted just under 20 percent of the region's population; by 1989 the proportion of Jews had dropped precipitously to under 5 percent. The Jews of Birobidzhan have lived the fiction that they inhabited the national homeland of Soviet Jewry. But with the dissolution of the Soviet Union, they now find themselves confronted with the challenge of transforming this fiction into a reality. Like Jews all over the former Soviet Union, they are wrestling with the problem of Jewish identity on both an individual and a communal level and are engaged in a renaissance of Jewish cultural and religious life, despite the fact that decades of Soviet power and, in the past twenty years, emigration have vitiated Jewish life.

Besides examining the reasons behind the Soviet leadership's decision to establish the J.A.R., we seek a glimpse into the lives of those Jews who chose to settle in Birobidzhan. What was (and is) specifically Jewish about the J.A.R., and how did the Soviet leadership set about to transplant Russian Jewish culture and society to the region? How was Jewish life promoted in a stridently secular and militantly antireligious setting, and how did the Soviet government promote the Birobidzhan project to both the Soviet public and the international community? What elements of Jewish culture survived under Soviet power, and how have they provided the foundation for the current Jewish cultural and religious activism in the J.A.R.?

The story of the Soviet Zion provides an unusual point of entry for examining the Kremlin's shifting policies toward Jews and the fate of Soviet Jewry under Communist rule. This perspective also permits us to assess the response of world Jewry to the novel experiment undertaken in the J.A.R. Given the persistence of the "Jewish question" in Russia for the last two hundred years, the study of the J.A.R. has several implications. First, it sheds light on a host of important historical and contemporary issues regarding the Jewish identity, community, and culture. Second, the history of Birobidzhan illuminates the larger issue of Soviet policies toward ethnic and national minorities and illustrates how such policies have left a lasting legacy during the challenging transition from communism to democracy in the former Soviet Union.

The collapse of the tsarist regime in the wake of World War I and the consolidation of Bolshevik rule by 1921 ushered in an age of unprecedented freedom for Russia's Jews. The nearly two and a half million Jews then living under Soviet power enjoyed the same civil and political liberties as other citizens. Despite the militant atheism of the Communist Party, many Jews welcomed Bolshevik rule because the new masters in the Kremlin promised an end to social and economic inequality, offered new employment opportunities, and took a strong public stance against anti-Semitism. The Bolsheviks professed a commitment to the rights of national and ethnoreligious minorities, and Soviet nationality policy in the 1920s—the era of the New Economic Policy—was relatively open: all national and ethnic cultures were tolerated, though some of their specific features, such as religion, were combatted. Cultural diversity was allowed if it was "national in form and socialist in content."

However, the reality of ruling a multinational empire with well over one hundred national and ethnoreligious groups left the fledgling Soviet leadership with no choice but to acknowledge the diversity of the Soviet Union's populace. Vladimir Lenin and Joseph Stalin, the Bolsheviks' leading theorists on nationality policy, believed that socialism would doom to extinction all religious and nationalist sentiments and loyalties. In the long run, all cultures would fuse with each other to form a common socialist Soviet culture. Until that time, each national and ethnoreligious minority would be permitted to maintain its cultural and linguistic traditions and continue to reside in its territory of traditional settlement. According to Lenin and Stalin, the Jewish question would ultimately be solved by facilitating the integration of Jews into Soviet society. With the disappearance of religion under socialism, the secularization of Soviet Jewish society would proceed smoothly and weaken obstacles to Jewish acculturation and integration.

The Kremlin was also concerned about the Jews' grinding poverty, unrelenting unemployment, and overpopulation, as well as the resurgent popular anti-Semitism and vicious pogroms in the years after the Soviet seizure of power. The overwhelming majority of Soviet Jews lived in small towns and cities, and made livings from petty commerce, retail sales, small-scale handicraft production, and unskilled labor. They were particularly hard hit by the collapse of the economy due to the combined impact of world war, revolution, civil war, and pogroms between 1914 and 1921.

The number of Jews out of work reached startling proportions in the early 1920s. In the area around the city of Gomel in Belarus, Jews constituted some 70 percent of the unemployed. Moreover, despite the fact that private trade was tolerated in the 1920s in an attempt to revive the wrecked economy and restore social peace, the government continued its policy of nationalizing private property. By the early 1920s, then, many Soviet Jews occupying traditional trades and crafts were suffering from the impact of political unrest, civil strife, and economic breakdown.

Backed by the Jewish Sections, the arm of the Communist Party that conducted propaganda among Jews, the government was concerned about the dire economic straits of the Jewish masses and encouraged their settlement on the land. As defined by Communist officials, one aspect of the Jewish question was the ideologically suspect nature of Jewish economic life. Thus, the government hoped to resolve the Jewish question in the 1920s by refashioning the occupational profile of the Jews and transforming them into farmers.

Tsarist attitudes and policies helped to shape certain features of the Communists' approach to the Jews. The Bolshevik conviction to alter the socioeconomic structure of Jewish society had its roots in the late eighteenth century, when, as a result of the partitions of Poland, the Russian Empire absorbed a substantial Jewish population. Tsarist policy toward the Jews was contradictory, since it combined efforts to integrate Jews into Russian society with attempts to keep them segregated from the mainstream. These policies, enacted through such measures as enforced Jewish residence within the Pale of Settlement and enrollment in secular schools, worked at cross purposes and characterized tsarist treatment of the Jews until the collapse of the Romanov dynasty in 1917.

One aspect of the Jewish question, as defined by tsarist officials, was the perceived unproductive nature of Jewish economic life. Because the Jews were heavily involved in leaseholding, commerce, moneylending, and the sale of vodka, tsarist officials regarded them as parasites who exploited the defenseless peasantry. Thus, some tsars such as Alexander I tried to "normalize" the socioeconomic profile of Russian Jewry by encouraging Jews to till the land or become small-scale manufacturers. The solution to the Jewish question, therefore, depended on transforming the Jews from a harmful and retrograde community to one incapable of causing social and economic damage. Such thinking had also characterized the Jewish policies pursued by some other European states in the eighteenth and nineteenth centuries.

This experiment in social engineering never achieved its desired ends, in part because Russian Jews resisted changing livelihoods, preferring instead work with which they had experience and familiarity. In addition, the government's commitment to agricultural resettlement was halfhearted and never received serious financial and other material support. More important, other policies designed to isolate the Jews countered the policy of land resettlement and dominated the autocracy's Jewish policy at the end of the imperial era. Indeed, Jews were prohibited from settling on the land in the wake of the assassination of Tsar Alexander II in 1881. Nevertheless, on the eve of World War I slightly more than fifty thousand Jews (or 3 percent of the total Jewish population in the Russian Empire), including the family of Leon Trotsky, tilled land as agricultural settlers. The overwhelming number of Jews remained engaged in commerce, manufacturing, and the service sector by the end of the nineteenth century.

. . . .

Mystery shrouds the 1928 decision to designate the Biro-Bidzhanskii District as the official territory for Jewish land resettlement. The region, approximately the size of Belgium, had been annexed by Russia in 1858 and derived its name from two tributaries of the Amur River, the Bira and the Bidzhan, that flowed through the territory. Summers in the area are hot and rainy; winters are dry and cold. Rich in natural resources, particularly in the north, where mountains and thick forests punctuate the landscape, the Biro-Bidzhanskii District then had large tracts of swampland and marshes. Along with several hundred indigenous Siberian peoples who subsisted on hunting and gathering, the twenty-seven thousand or so inhabitants residing there on the eve of Jewish settlement were primarily Great Russians, Cossacks, Koreans, and Ukrainians who had gone to the region in the late nineteenth and early twentieth centuries. Placement was concentrated in the south, along the Amur River, and in the north, around the Trans-Siberian Railway.

Attracting Jews to the Soviet Far East was an integral part of a plan to lure Soviet Jewry to the land as early as the beginning of 1924. Though a contingent of leading Jewish activists in KOMZET [Committee for the Settlement of Working Jews on the Land] and the Jewish Sections of the Communist Party vociferously opposed the Birobidzhan experiment because they thought the region too far from the pocket of Jewish population to be viable, they were overridden by Stalin and other proponents of the project. The government intended to vitiate the movement of Jews to the land in Ukraine, Belarus, and the Crimea to appease the native populace, which was resisting plans to settle more Jews in these regions. In addition, officials in the Commissariats of

Defense and Agriculture also had an eye toward establishing a strong presence in the Soviet Far East. The area possessed untapped economic resources and had geostrategic significance given fears of possible Chinese and Japanese expansionism in the 1920s.

Furthermore, many in the Kremlin were interested in creating a Jewish national territory within the borders of the Soviet Union. Soviet Jewry, like several other extraterritorial minorities such as the Volga Germans, occupied an anomalous position because they lacked a national territory. Soviet policy in the 1920s aimed at normalizing the status of nonterritorial minorities by establishing official enclaves for them. However, what made granting Soviet Jews their own territory a special case was that the place selected for them was not one in which they had roots. The obvious comparison with Palestine was not ignored by advocates of Birobidzhan, and many interested observers, such as I. Sudarskii in his book *Birobidzhan and Palestine* (Yiddish version in 1929, Russian in 1930), argued that Birobidzhan was more suitable for Jewish settlement than Palestine.

Proponents of the Birobidzhan project believed that the establishment of a territorial homeland for Soviet Jews would facilitate the development of a secular, Yiddishist culture rooted in socialist principles, while at the same time ensuring the national and cultural consolidation of Soviet Jewry. The president of the Soviet Union, Mikhail Kalinin, had adopted the creation of Jewish territory as a pet project in order to preserve Jewish culture. In 1926 Kalinin declared:

> [I]t is completely natural that the Jewish population . . . strives to find its place in the Soviet Union. . . . The Jewish people faces the great task of preserving its own nationality, and to this end a large part of the Jewish population must be transformed into an economically stable, agriculturally compact group which should number at least hundreds of thousands. Only under such conditions can the Jewish masses hope for the future existence of their nationality.

The settlement of Jews in the J.A.R. would transform the shtetl Jew from petit-bourgeois shopkeepers and unskilled laborers into productive Soviet citizens contributing to the building of socialism.

The government began encouraging Jews to move to the J.A.R. soon after the publication of a March 1928 decree reserving the Biro-Bidzhanskii District for the settlement of Jews who would work the land. The decree banned agricultural settlement by non-Jews and stated that if Jewish settlement were successful, "a Jewish national, administrative-territorial entity" might be set up. This dream was realized in 1934, when the district was designated as the

АЗИМОВ МОРДХЭ –
ПОЧТАЛЬОН, ОДИН ИЗ ПЕРВЫХ ПЕРЕСЕЛЕНЦЕВ.

Postman Mordecai Azimov, one of Birobidzhan's first settlers. Courtesy of Robert Weinberg.

Jewish Autonomous Region, with Birobidzhan as its capital city, thereby establishing it as the national territory of Soviet Jewry. As stated above, the guiding principle behind Jewish land resettlement in the J.A.R. was to make Soviet Jews more productive by attracting unskilled, poverty-stricken Jews to agricultural work in the region. No less an authority than Semen Dimanshtein, chairman of OZET [Society for Settling Working Jews on the Land] and a prominent party official in charge of Jewish affairs, wrote that the organized settlement of the J.A.R. would "strengthen the tempo of the productivization of the Jewish poor." Another supporter of attracting Jews to agricultural labor noted that it would lead to the "physical rebirth and renewal" of Soviet Jewry. As one of the first Jews to move to the region stated, "I thank you, comrades, for sending me here. Here I am getting settled and will stop living life like a 'Jew,' that is, as a *luftmentsh*" (literally, a person who lives on air, that is, with no visible means of support, a common way to refer to poor Jews). As one Jewish migrant to a rice plantation in the southern part of the J.A.R. stressed soon after his arrival in 1928, perhaps speaking for others who saw themselves as pioneers, "We came here to become peasants!"

IX

Rising Stalinism

In the 1989 documentary *Is Stalin with Us?* the director Tofik Shakhverdiev introduces us to a Moscow schoolteacher, a taxi driver and a factory foreman from Tbilisi, Georgia, and a public prosecutor from Kharkov, all of whom are staunch Stalinists. The director asks the schoolteacher about her family. She tells him the reason she never married: "My family is this one man [Stalin] for whom I live. Every year I go to the places connected with his life, to see those houses that he might have seen, to walk the streets he might have walked. This is a thread that ties me to the man who is now gone. He is my happiness. I love Stalin." Extreme? Rather, and yet this allegiance, bordering on worship, to a dead dictator, has not been an unfamiliar phenomenon in late socialist and even in post-Soviet society. To many, scenes of a late middle-aged school-teacher brushing away dead leaves from the stone bust of her beloved leader are impossible to fathom, impossible to absorb. How can a man who was directly or indirectly responsible for the deaths of more than twenty million in the Gulag, under whom the Soviet Union sustained almost unprecedented losses in the Second World War, and whose policies of forced collectivization, induced famine, and starvation call forth such emotion? How ultimately do we assess this man, once called by Lenin the "wonderful Georgian," the revolutionary who followed in Lenin's footsteps yet created a society very different from the one Lenin had envisioned? Was Stalin an aberration, corrupting a system that, without his presence, would have led the Soviet Union on the successful path to socialism? Or was his rule the natural and inevitable culmination of Leninist policies? Both leaders, after all, advocated the strong state, the mass mobilization of peasants and proletarians, the sweeping away of capitalism, and the use of terror to eliminate enemies of the state, and both exhibited complete intolerance of opposing political views. There are those who believe that Stalin was an uninspired leader who happened to get caught up in industrialization and other forces that were bound to take place irrespective of the Revolution. The historian Isaac Deutscher believes that Stalin was neither a great leader nor the inevitable result of Leninist policies. What all of these views suggest is the startling complexity of the image of Stalin as leader that has gravitated between savior of the nation, demigod, and mass murderer.

If one takes the view that Stalin was the natural culmination of Leninist ideology, it is also true that he deviated markedly from the platforms that Lenin initially set forth. Both shared a utopian vision for Russia, but their experiences and backgrounds led them down divergent paths. Like many of his generation, Lenin was a Marxist in that he had not only read Marx but had lived abroad and was conversant with the European culture that Marx had studied. Marx failed to predict the revolution in Russia, but Lenin turned toward Europe as Marx had and felt that the only way the revolution was going to work in Russia was by igniting a similar revolution in one of the European industrial countries. Stalin had a very different take on where the revolution was heading. For one thing, he did not have the European orientation that Lenin did. Stalin was Georgian. Born Iosif Vissarionovich Djugashvili (literally, "son of Djugash") in Gori, a small town northwest of Tbilisi, his revolutionary activity was confined to Russia.

The milieu within which the two leaders developed and tested their ideas may ultimately have accounted for the different directions in which their ideologies developed. Closer to a classical Marxist, Lenin saw that the revolution needed to be made by an intellectual elite who would continue to remain at the helm until the dictatorship of the proletariat was achieved. Stalin relied much less on Marxist theory as such and looked to practical administrative solutions to the problems of a fledgling state. Instead of staffing the Soviet state with the educated elite who had made the Revolution, he relied on apparatchik-managers and functionaries who controlled goods and the economy. Some of this was undoubtedly due to his suspicion that the educated classes were the source from which political dissent traditionally arose. To his critics it seemed that Stalinist society gradually became overrun by bureaucrats, and indeed in the 1930s the state burgeoned into a colossus, drowning in its own red tape and bureaucracy. In Soviet literature of the 1930s, one can sense the growing bureaucratic behemoth, as the new literary heroes, in a far cry from Marx's utopian prediction of the gradual withering away of the state, became the commissars, the managers, and the Party functionaries.

If Stalin deviated from strict Marxism and Leninism, he was also engaged in fashioning his own ideology that, from the late 1920s on, increasingly molded Soviet society. Stalin created a new *Homo sovieticus* who would lead the country into its radiant future. The new Soviet physique would be strong and healthy, mirroring the health of the Stalinist state. Sports competitions, an emphasis on physical culture, mass parades, and spectacles became the order of the day, celebrating the new body politic. However, fashioning the body was the least of what Stalinism was about. Its greater goal was the reengineering of the minds and hearts of the Soviet Union's people.

Stalin's vision was bold and deliberate, and might even have earned him a slightly different place in history had the casualty list from his vision not been as large as it was. On the cultural front new state writers had to be created. They came from the peasantry and the workers, often with minimal education, and were trained in the art (if one could call it such) of grinding out the requisite production novels that would provide models for the new Soviet citizen to emulate. We hear in their writing the noise of the factory as their characters are engaged in fulfilling and overfufilling the Five-Year Plans. The new heroes were shock workers who would forge this new industrialized state. They operated machines, went into the mines, and shoveled coal both on the pages of fiction and in their workaday lives that aspired to the literature that was being written about them. When Bushueva ("Learning to Labor" in part VIII) talks about working at three or four looms in the factory and taking pride in it, she is reflecting not only the ideology at the time but also the enthusiasm felt by Soviet workers in the first years of the Revolution.

Lenin had wrestled with what to do with prerevolutionary Russian culture in the new revolutionary idiom. He wanted to raise the educational level of the people so that they could appreciate the great masters of literature, art, and music. Stalin, however, wanted culture to be accessible to the people (*narod*), which meant producing art that was on a level that the people could comprehend. By 1929 all private publishing houses had been closed down as well as non-Party journals, and by 1934 all the arts had been brought under state control. All culture had become official culture. Workers and peasants became not only the consumers of this culture but its producers as well. Writers and readers clubs were introduced at factories, as workers were encouraged to write for local journals and newspapers. People needed to be brought into the production process not only in the factories but in the arts, as the latter were simply seen as part of production goals.

Mythmaking was the oil that made the Stalinist machine run. People were educated into believing that things were getting better even as they were starving or watching their neighbors and family members disappear into the camps. "Life has become better, life has become more cheerful" was a refrain originally enunciated by Stalin in 1935 and repeated over the years. Sometimes this belief in how good things were took wicked and paradoxical form. The historian Sheila Fitzpatrick notes that the one honestly good year in the Five-Year Plans and the harvest was 1937, the first year of the purges and the show trials.

Pioneers and young children with their "physculturist" mothers on a float on Red Square. From *A Pageant of Youth* (Moscow: State Art Publishers, 1939).

Another myth was that there were saboteurs everywhere. Posters showing a woman with her finger over her lips could be found with the caption "Ne boltai" (Don't gossip). Originally the poster referred to the need to remain silent during wartime since rumors were said to aid the enemy. But the worker with her finger over her lips pointed to the enemy within as well. If there were traitors within the Party and the state, there could just as easily be saboteurs in one's collective apartment or at work. The word of the day was *vigilance,* as Soviet citizens were instructed to inform on anyone who was suspect. Perhaps the greatest fear that the state encouraged was the fear of imminent war with the capitalist nations, even early in the 1930s. There were Soviet citizens still very much alive then who remembered the debacle of the Russo-Japanese War in 1904–5 and the First World War that had been brought to an artificial halt by the Revolution. Hitler's rise simply reinstilled old fears, and with the help of Soviet propaganda in the 1930s created the belief among Soviet citizens that there were enemies everywhere.

As the Soviet citizen became a pawn in the reengineering scheme, the image of Stalin himself underwent certain modifications. Short in stature

Marriage registration in Moscow. Courtesy of the Hoover Institution, Russian Pictorial Collection, Envelope FBY, Item 1, Hoover Institution Archives.

with a pockmarked face, Stalin rarely went out. There was much of the Soviet Union he never saw, perhaps because of a certain timidity and social reluctance, which by the late 1930s developed into an increasing fear of his enemies. Nevertheless, his image changed profoundly beginning in 1929 on the occasion of his fiftieth birthday. This is the date generally given for the beginning of the personality cult and Stalin's appropriation of almost demigod status. By 1936 that cult was firmly in place. Cities and towns were named after him. Streets were lined with larger-than-life banners of his image, extolling him both as a strong leader and as the father of his people and friend to children. Casting this image of the stern leader who was also benevolent to his people (even as he exterminated them!) became an important part of the propaganda of the time. The Soviet family had been decimated by war, famine, industrialization, and now the purges, with the most devastating losses of all still to come in 1941. Stalin as pater familias, head of the Great Soviet Family, became integral to his image as the country staggered under the blows of families torn apart.

One of the persistent questions about Stalinism, and one to which we may perhaps never have the answer, is to what degree people believed the propaganda and to what degree the goal of reengineering an entire population was successful. One can take the cynical view that people believed the myths when it was in their interest to do so. Several of the essays in this volume written by Russians themselves who lived through this period attempt to come to terms with the propaganda and ideology. In "The Paradox of Nostalgia for the Front" (part XI) Viacheslav Kondrat'ev notes that it was not ideology but patriotism that got Russians through the Second World War and that the ideological veneer by that time was too thin to sustain any form of loyalty to Stalin himself. Natal'ia Il'ina's narrative "From Harbin, Home" (part XIII) provides a different take altogether on Stalinist ideology, one that suggests that utopian visions are inevitably larger than the realities to which they give birth.

Lenin's "Last Testament" (1923)

Vladimir Lenin

In May 1922 Lenin suffered a major stroke. He was still able, however, to stay in contact with Kremlin and Party leaders on an almost daily basis. With his approval Stalin had been appointed interim First Party Secretary and continued to keep Lenin informed of Kremlin politics and policies. Lenin, however, was beginning to entertain serious doubts over whether Stalin was the right person to take over the reins of leadership once he was gone. While there were points of disagreement between the two over how the federation should be constituted, the deeper issue that worried Lenin was Stalin's tendency toward authoritarianism. With this in mind, Lenin, knowing that his health was deteriorating, set about dictating his political testament. In it he argued for the continuation of a collective leadership at the top, hoping that Stalin and Trotsky would reach a modus vivendi. He drew portraits in his testament, some more critical than others, of the leading Bolsheviks of the time, including Stalin. In January 1923 he dictated an all-out attack on Stalin, whom he viewed as too crude to be retained as Party Secretary. He also took Stalin to task for his verbal abuse of Lenin's wife, Nadezhda Krupskaia. But he had little time to do more. On 6 March Lenin suffered another major stroke and remained incapacitated until his death on 21 January 1924.

Lenin had written "Open only after my death" on the outside of the envelope containing his testament. Krupskaia respected his wishes, and after opening it she decided to have it read aloud at the Thirteenth Party Congress. Stalin sat there as the testament was read, knowing that his fate would be decided that day. Grigorii Zinov'ev, a member of the Politburo, uttered a brilliant lie, claiming that there was no rift between Stalin and Trotsky and that the Congress was therefore free to disregard Lenin's wishes on the matter of succession. By a show of hands, the Congress moved to retain Stalin in office, a vote that sealed the fate of the Soviet Union for the next thirty years, some would argue more.

By the stability of the Central Committee, of which I spoke before, I mean measures to prevent a split, so far as such measures can be taken. For, of course, the White Guard in Russkaya Mysl (I think it was S. E. Oldenburg) was right when, in the first place, in his play against Soviet Russia he banked on the hope of a split in our party, and when, in the second place, he banked for that split on serious disagreements in our party.

Our party rests upon two classes, and for that reason its instability is possible, and if there cannot exist an agreement between those classes its fall is inevitable. In such an event it would be useless to take any measures, or in general to discuss the stability of our Central Committee. In such an event no measures would prove capable of preventing a split. But I trust that is too remote a future, and too improbable an event, to talk about.

I have in mind stability as a guarantee against a split in the near future, and I intend to examine here a series of considerations of a purely personal character.

I think that the fundamental factor in the matter of stability—from this point of view—is such members of the Central Committee as Stalin and Trotsky. The relation between them constitutes, in my opinion, a big half of the danger of that split, which might be avoided, and the avoidance of which might be promoted, in my opinion, by raising the number of members of the Central Committee to fifty or one hundred.

Comrade Stalin, having become General Secretary, has concentrated an enormous power in his hands; and I am not sure that he always knows how to use that power with sufficient caution. On the other hand Comrade Trotsky, as was proved by his struggle against the Central Committee in connection with the question of the People's Commissariat of Ways of Communications, is distinguished not only by his exceptional abilities—personally he is, to be sure, the most able man in the present Central Committee; but also by his too far-reaching self-confidence and a disposition to be too much attracted by the purely administrative side of affairs.

These two qualities of the two most able leaders of the present Central Committee might, quite innocently, lead to a split; if our party does not take measures to prevent it, a split might arise unexpectedly.

I will not further characterize the other members of the Central Committee as to their personal qualities. I will only remind you that the October episode of Zinovieff and Kameneff was not, of course, accidental, but that it ought as little to be used against them personally as the non-Bolshevism of Trotsky. [The fact is that Trotsky stood outside the Bolshevik party until the Summer of 1917.—M. E.]

Estimate of Younger Leaders

Of the younger members of the Central Committee I want to say a few words about Bukharin and Piatakoff. They are, in my opinion, the most able forces

Trotsky in Mexico. Courtesy of the Hoover Institution, Russian Pictorial Collection, 764, Envelope BA, Item 221, Hoover Institution Archives.

(among the youngest), and in regard to them it is necessary to bear in mind the following: Bukharin is not only the most valuable and biggest theoretician of the party, but also may legitimately be considered the favorite of the whole party; but his theoretical views can only with the very greatest doubt be regarded as fully Marxist, for there is something scholastic in him (he never has learned, and I think never has fully understood, the dialectic).

And then Piatakoff—a man undoubtedly distinguished in will and ability, but too much given over to administration and the administrative side of things to be relied on in a serious political question.

Of course, both these remarks are made by me merely with a view to the present time, in the assumption that these two able and loyal workers may not find an occasion to supplement their knowledge and correct their onesidedness.

25 / XII / 22

A Significant Postscript

Postscript: Stalin is too rough, and this fault, entirely supportable in relations among us Communists, becomes insupportable in the office of General Secretary. Therefore, I *propose to the comrades to find* a way to remove Stalin from that position and appoint to it another man who in all regards differs from Stalin in one superiority—namely, more patient, more loyal, more polite and more attentive to comrades, less capriciousness, &c. This circumstance may seem an insignificant trifle, but I think that from the point of view of preventing a split and from the point of view of the relation between Stalin and Trotsky which I discussed above, it is not a trifle, or it is such a trifle as may acquire a decisive significance.

Lenin
Jan. 4th, 1923

The Body and the Shrine (1983)

Nina Tumarkin

One of the preponderant images to come out of Soviet history has been that of endless lines of Soviet citizens waiting patiently for hours in subzero temperatures to pay homage to the embalmed body of the leader who founded the Soviet state, Vladimir Il'ich Lenin. Today the mausoleum that contains what is purported to be Lenin's body attracts fewer visitors. The lines that once reached down from Red Square and around the Aleksandrov Garden are a thing of the past. A tourist now and then snaps a digital picture of the structure that once symbolized the Soviet Union's past, present, and future.

It may seem odd today that the question of what to do with Lenin's body was an issue of national concern in the Soviet Union in 1924. In Russian tradition the bodies of the deceased had always been buried according to Christian tradition. Yet Lenin had acquired nearly sanctified status as the maker of the Revolution that had over-turned tsarist autocracy and forged a state that promised a new future for millions of Russians. That all he had promised had not yet come to pass was immaterial when it came to memorializing him and, indeed, keeping him alive. As the architect of the Revolution he had created an atheistic state that, in the tradition of Marx, viewed religion as the "opiate of the people." Even as Lenin rejected religion's preeminent role in the lives of Russia's people, many transferred their religious yearnings onto the leader himself, deifying him in a way that Lenin and his widow, Nadezhda Krup-skaia, had actively discouraged. After Lenin's death a movement took shape to preserve his body intact in much the same way the early Russian monks had been mummified and put on display for the faithful to see in the Monastery of the Caves in Kyiv, Ukraine. In medieval Russia an entire lore had arisen around those monks, whose bodies in death emitted a fragrant odor, hinting both at their incorruptibility and at their candidacy for sainthood.

As Nina Tumarkin illustrates, what began as a desire to keep not only the memory but the leader himself alive became linked with the all-important goal of establishing Soviet science's preeminent role in the world. What better place to start than suc-cessfully embalming the leader who for many would live forever.

How long the Lenin cult survived is a matter of speculation. Throughout the

Soviet era posters and placards still proudly proclaimed, "Lenin Lived, Lenin Lives, Lenin Will Live." By the late 1920s and early 1930s Stalin began to establish his own cult, raising himself to the nearly deified status of father of the nation and invincibly wise leader, even as he proceeded to decimate the Soviet population. Decades later Leonid Brezhnev would attempt to resuscitate the cult of personality that Stalin constructed around his own rule. By Brezhnev's time, however, there were no more Great Fatherland Wars to fight, and the platitudes about the radiant future and the all-knowing leader were increasingly falling on deaf ears.

A regime that derives its legitimacy from a single ruler risks instability upon his death. But if after death that ruler becomes the object of a cult predicated on his continuing living power, then that cult can serve as a stabilizing force. This is precisely what happened with Lenin. The cult established nationwide upon his death was based on one theme: Lenin lives! Lenin's death was not to interfere with his continuing leadership of Soviet Russia. In the words of the All-Russian Soviet of Trade Unions, "Healthy or sick, living or dead . . . Lenin remains our eternal leader."

A declaration of Lenin's immortality was a pledge of faith and loyalty to the party and government. This gesture was made over and over again during mourning week in many of the slogans, poems, and eulogies that filled the press. It was a political act in that it implied a desire to perpetuate the system of rule personified by Lenin. "He has not died and will never die!" read one slogan. "He lives. He lives. He has not died. He will not die," was the opening line of a poem published shortly after Lenin's death. Another elegiac poem denied that any death could kill Ilich. Some responses to Lenin's death were more expansive, explaining how or why Lenin continued to live: "Lenin has died, but Leninism, which has become rooted in me, in all the working class, lives! It lives, comrades! For us Lenin has not died." Many statements stressed the immortality of Lenin's cause. The headline in *Izvestiia*'s first regular issue published after Lenin's death read: "That which was mortal in Lenin has died, but his cause and his legacy will abide forever."

There were also slogans and statements suggesting that Lenin was eternal and omnipresent, a true spiritual entity. One eulogy described Lenin as a life force that cannot be killed: "Lenin and death—these concepts are mutually exclusive of each other. . . . Lenin—like nature and the world surrounding us—lives outside of our subjective ideas." The last phrase mixes Marxism and mysticism: Lenin, an omnipresent spirit, is part of the objective world as an immortal life force) The first theme, that Lenin and death cannot coexist, is also stressed in Vladimir Maiakovsky's poem, "Komsomolskaia."

"Lenin" and "Death"—
> these words are enemies.

"Lenin" and "Life"—
> are comrades . . .

Lenin—
> lived.

Lenin—
> lives.

Lenin—
> will live.

Some eulogies spoke of the special relationship between Lenin and the people.

> . . . Lenin has not died.
>
> Lenin lives.
>
> Lenin has ceased to be an individual—Lenin belongs to the millions.
>
> Lenin—has for a long time already been the revolution itself, . . . the great wisdom of proletarian tactics, the great will of the proletariat, will and confidence in history. . . .
>
> Lenin has not died. Lenin lives. There is not a corner in the world where there are working people, oppressed [people], exploited [people], where Lenin is absent.

. . . .

From the moment of his death, the remains of the leader were invested with life and power: "And he is pale-yellow, calm, great even in his coffin; even in silence he continues to do that with which he was busy his entire life: he organizes, rallies, calls people to the struggle again and again." Lenin's body was to become the focal point for the cult that followed his death. Leninism would communicate his political vision to future generations, Lenin Corners would serve as local shrines for the veneration of his memory, but the body made him simultaneously a proven saint with visibly incorruptible remains and an immortal.

The Autopsy Report

Before Lenin's body was taken from Gorki to Moscow, it underwent a complete autopsy. The operation was performed by a large team of physicians supervised by Dr. A. I. Abrikosov. The autopsy lasted four hours and forty minutes and was carried out in the villa where the body was kept until the morning of January 23. Approximately halfway through the process Lenin's brain was opened, and the direct cause of death was ascertained. He had suffered a brain hemorrhage. Due to severe sclerosis of the arteries leading to the brain, the blood vessels of that organ had been seriously impaired. The sclerosis meant that fatty deposits in the arteries had calcified and prevented a normal flow of blood, and with it a necessary amount of oxygen, from reaching the brain. The cerebral blood vessels were in an extraordinarily weakened state, and when Lenin suffered a stroke on January 21, 1924, a large amount of blood rushed into his brain, much more blood than the sclerotic arteries had been transmitting. This pressure was too great for the brain's damaged vessels, and the walls of those vessels broke down, flooding the brain with blood. The blood vessels immediately destroyed were in that section of the brain controlling the respiratory function, and for that reason Lenin's breathing stopped.

A brief mention of the direct cause of death was the only autopsy result included in the medical bulletin circulated in Moscow not long after the operation. Nothing more detailed was published until three days after the autopsy had been performed. The most striking feature of the official autopsy report published in all newspapers on January 25 is the great detail in which Lenin's corpse was described. In the report, the doctors discussed Lenin's brain, noting that symptoms from which Lenin suffered during his protracted illness—paralysis and aphasia—were explained by the extreme sclerotic condition of his cerebral arteries. The report also detailed the condition of his skin, including scars and lesions, described his heart, with exact measurements, and provided information on his stomach, kidneys, and other organs.

In his newspaper story, Walter Duranty observed that the sanguine Russian reaction to this report was yet another proof of the difference between East and West: "To a Western country, such detail as the publication of the extraordinarily minute report of the autopsy may seem rather horrible, but the Russians have a different outlook, and the fact is, the dead leader was the object of such interest that the public wants to know everything." If Valentinov [Nikolai Valentinov, a professional revolutionary from the provinces] and his friends were at all representative of the contemporary nonparty Moscow intelligentsia, the autopsy report evoked a good deal of surprise and shock. "It seems to me," Valentinov wrote, "at no time before this and nowhere in the world were dead leaders, tsars, kings, etc., presented in such a way, naked, down to the tiniest anatomical detail. There were no anatomical secrets kept; everything was revealed." Valentinov's associate, E. L. Smirnov, felt that the report was an expression of the Bolsheviks' crude materialistic conception of human nature. Another colleague added: Lenin was known as a revolutionary, a leader, a dictator, if you will. One could sympathize with him or not. But he was a person, a soul (*psikhika*). Yet the report conveyed the message: "Lenin is only *matter,* nothing more than a combination of a cranial hemisphere, intestines, an abdominal cavity, a heart, kidneys, a spleen, with such and such characteristics. In this there is something quite shocking." Valentinov points out that his Communist friends were impressed not as much by the detailed character of the autopsy report as by one piece of information it contained. The weight of Lenin's brain was 1340 grams. One of Valentinov's Communist colleagues who seemed genuinely grieved at Lenin's passing, assured him that Lenin's genius was directly connected with the large size of his brain.

. . . .

The Decision To Embalm

There is no direct evidence on how the commission reached the decision to preserve the corpse. In its official report it claimed to have responded to thousands of letters and telegrams from the public, expressing the wish to be able to see their deceased leader. A few such letters appeared in the press before Lenin's funeral. On January 25, 1925, the Moscow daily *Rabochaia Moskva* published three under the headline, "Lenin's Body Must Be Preserved!" One letter said: "Under no circumstances can we give to the earth such a great and intensely beloved leader as Ilich. We suggest his remains be embalmed and left under glass for hundreds of years. . . . Let him be with us always." Another letter pointed out that future generations would need to see the body of the man who had brought about the world revolution. The letters all ask for the same thing, that Lenin be preserved and exhibited under glass. It would appear their authors had been coached, but by whom? Valentinov indicates that the idea of preserving Lenin's body had been discussed among Politburo members several months before Lenin's death. This would allow time for the idea's supporters to spread the word to selected comrades and mobilize popular backing for it.

. . . .

When Lenin died, the question of his cremation could be only theoretical, since there was at the time no crematorium in Russia. This very fact indicates that Stalin was correct when he warned that the reduction of the body to ashes might shock the Russian people. "Cremation has always been abhorrent to Christian feeling, and though it was contended that the fate of the immortal soul was not affected by the mode of the disposal of the body, there can be little doubt that the real cause of the revolt against the funeral pyre is to be found in the doctrine of the resurrection of the flesh." The resurrection of the body is a most important aspect of Christian eschatology. Eternal life must be life in a body: "The body will rise again, all of the body, the identical body, the entire body."

Immediately after Lenin's death, plans were evidently made to bury him at the end of that week, for on Tuesday, January 22, Dr. Abrikosov, who had performed the autopsy, embalmed the body with the express purpose of preserving it for six days—until the funeral. Within a few days, according to Bonch-Bruevich, a decision was made to embalm the body for forty days. [This is a traditional number in the Russian Orthodox church; prayers for the dead are said for forty days.]

. . . .

Abrikosov was placed in charge of the body. He feared that the autopsy he had performed might have hindered the possibility of a successful preservation. But he nonetheless expressed the hope that Lenin's body would remain unchanged for a long time, "three or four years at least," if the temperature of the crypt were kept at around zero, the humidity very low, and if the coffin were completely airtight. Consequently, on January 26, the Soviet press reported that the temperature inside the crypt would be kept at zero "for the better preservation of the body." On Lenin's funeral day Steklov rhapsodized about the prospect that Lenin's body might be preserved:

> No, he will not go! He will stay with us even physically, at least for a while. Oh, how well we understand the workers' earnest desire to preserve Lenin's body forever, so that all future generations might see him. . . . Unfortunately, until now, science has not found a way of preserving human remains forever. But we know that all possible measures will be taken to preserve Lenin's body from decay as long as possible, and to enable all those who so wish, to venerate his remains.

Steklov was eager to reassure those who mistakenly and "sorrowfully think that they will not be able to see his face." And two days later he wrote of Lenin: "The whole populace hopes that his remains can be preserved forever, so that they might be able to gaze on him."

Despite this publicity, as late as the day after the funeral Krupskaia was apparently unaware of the planned preservation of her husband's remains. She wrote to I. A. Armand on January 28: "Right now they have not closed up his grave yet, and it will still be possible to look upon Ilich." Obviously,

Russians pay homage to the memory of Lenin, 1925. Courtesy of the Library of Congress, Prints and Photographs Division, LC-USZ62–101129, No. 27, 384 F.C.

explains her biographer Robert McNeal, she assumed that Lenin would soon receive a decent burial. But about that time the decision was made to exhibit Lenin's body not for forty days, but for as long a time as possible.

It appears likely that Krupskaia learned of the decision to preserve the body indefinitely on January 29. The following day she published in *Pravda* a "veiled protest."

COMRADES WORKERS AND PEASANTS!

I have a great request to make of you: do not allow your grief for Ilich to express itself in the external veneration of his person. Do not build memorials to him, palaces named after him, [do not hold] magnificent celebrations in his memory, etc. All of this meant so little to him in his lifetime; he found it all so trying. [Remember how much poverty and disorder we still have in our country. If you want to honor the name of Vladimir Ilich—build day care centers, kindergartens, homes, schools . . . etc., and most importantly—try in all things to fulfill his legacy.]

. . . .

The means by which the party leaders made the decision to preserve Lenin has never been revealed; nor have Soviet authorities published the minutes of any deliberations that explain why Lenin was fated to meet this (to date) unique end. The only publicly stated reason appeared in the press in mid-June 1924, when the embalming of Lenin was nearly complete:

> On the first night after the death of Vladimir Ilich, his body was submitted to an embalming and an autopsy, the results of which were immediately thereafter published in the press.
>
> The embalming was performed by A. I. Abrikosov, professor at Moscow University; he was charged with the task of preserving the body of V. I. for a short time, until it would be committed to the earth. . . .
>
> We all remember the days when hundreds of thousands of people stood for hours in 28 degrees of frost, attempting to see and engrave in their memories the physical features of [their] beloved leader.
>
> During three days and nights access to the Trade Union House was continuous, and this period of time turned out to be not big enough for a significant proportion of Moscow's population.
>
> For this reason, the government made the decision to not commit Vladimir Ilich's body to the earth, but to put it in a mausoleum and to allow those who wished to, to visit it.

Certainly the overwhelming popular response to Lenin's lying-in-state must have played a significant role in prompting the decision to preserve and display Lenin's corpse. [As a relic, he was to continue to legitimize Soviet power and mobilize the population.]

Soviet Literature: The Richest in Ideas (1934)

Andrei Zhdanov

In 1932 at the Soviet Writers' Congress, the Party proclaimed that all Soviet literature was to conform to a single artistic method as part of the goal of building a new socialist state. The term socialist realism *was coined to describe this new relationship of literature to the state. The term was a misnomer, as the literary works produced under its aegis were anything but realistic. Writers were exhorted to portray Soviet life moving toward what Stalin termed the "radiant future" (svetloe budushchee), a mandate that led literature to lose contact with the actual tenor of life lived at that time. Stalin's radiant future translated into happy endings on the pages of fiction. He called the writers who produced this prescriptive literature "engineers of human souls." They were engaged in constructing the new Soviet man and woman and inculcating socialist values in their readers. Their works were nothing if not tendentious. Simple master plots with clearly defined positive and negative characters were readily accessible to readers from the worker and peasant classes, many of whom had only recently acquired basic literacy. Moreover, these readers found themselves the subjects of the novels and stories that were frequently written by authors who came from backgrounds similar to their own. Personal psychology and exploration into the inner lives of characters that had characterized Russia's nineteenth-century literature gave way to the spirit of the collective, in which the concept of the personal life was subsumed into the greater goals of the state. Writers were exhorted to hold firm to the principles of partiinost' (party-mindedness), narodnost' (populism), and ideinost' (ideological correctness). What these principles generated were production novels that took as their themes industrialization, factory work, shock work, the new collective farms, and the "enthusiasts" who sacrificed everything for the greater glory of the new socialist state.*

There was something deeply reminiscent in these new artistic credos of the nineteenth-century world with which the Soviet state was so intent on severing its ties. Socialist realism possessed more than a passing resemblance to the school of social criticism led by Belinsky, Chernyshevsky, and Dobroliubov, who viewed the role of literature as the model and instigator of social change. The resulting tensions between art and politics were no less reminiscent. Belinsky had broken with Dostoyevsky over the latter's perceived failure to write the kind of socially engaged literature Belinsky advocated. Dostoyevsky had responded by telling him, "I am a realist in a higher sense." Similarly, the intelligentsia during Stalin's time balked at the kind of prescriptive literature they were being mandated to write. Writers such as Anna Akhmatova, Mikhail Bulgakov, Osip Mandel'shtam, and Boris Pasternak were unable to get their works published because they refused to conform to the new canon. The writer Isaac Babel announced that henceforth he would practice the genre of silence.

In theory socialist realism remained the official method to which all artistic works were supposed to adhere during the Soviet era. Gorbachev, however, paved the way for its demise through his enunciation of glasnost, or openness, at the Writers' Congress in 1986. It is also true that adherence to this method waxed and waned depending on the political winds over the sixty years that it was enforced. Paradoxically, during the Second World War the artistic controls eased since the Party's attentions were less focused on policing its writers than on defeating Hitler's army. During the Thaw after Stalin's death, much became possible in art that formerly had been prohibited. After Khrushchev's ouster, however, the reins once again tightened. But throughout it all, the challenge for many artists was how to adhere to socialist realist doctrine while simultaneously writing open and honest prose.

The selection that appears below is excerpted from the speech given by Andrei Zhdanov, chief of the Leningrad Party Organization and spokesperson for cultural affairs, at the Soviet Writers' Congress in 1934.

In our country the main heroes of works of literature are the active builders of a new life—working men and women, men and women collective farmers, Party members, business managers, engineers, members of the Young Communist League, Pioneers. Such are the chief types and the chief heroes of our Soviet literature. Our literature is impregnated with enthusiasm and the spirit of heroic deeds. It is optimistic, but not optimistic in accordance with any "inward," animal instinct. It is optimistic in essence, because it is the literature of the rising class of the proletariat, the only progressive and advanced class. Our Soviet literature is strong by virtue of the fact that it is serving a new cause—the cause of socialist construction.

Comrade Stalin has called our writers engineers of human souls. What does this mean? What duties does the title confer upon you?

In the first place, it means knowing life so as to be able to depict it truthfully in works of art, not to depict it in a dead, scholastic way, not simply as "objective reality," but to depict reality in its revolutionary development.

In addition to this, the truthfulness and historical concreteness of the artistic portrayal should be combined with the ideological remoulding and education of the toiling people in the spirit of socialism. This method in *belles lettres* and literary criticism is what we call the method of socialist realism.

Our Soviet literature is not afraid of the charge of being "tendencious." Yes, Soviet literature is tendencious, for in an epoch of class struggle there is not and cannot be a literature which is not class literature, not tendencious, allegedly nonpolitical.

And I think that every one of our Soviet writers can say to any dull-witted bourgeois, to any philistine, to any bourgeois writer who may talk about our literature being tendencious: "Yes, our Soviet literature is tendencious, and we are proud of this fact, because the aim of our tendency is to liberate the toilers, to free all mankind from the yoke of capitalist slavery."

To be an engineer of human souls means standing with both feet firmly planted on the basis of real life. And this in its turn denotes a rupture with romanticism of the old type, which depicted a non-existent life and non-existent heroes, leading the reader away from the antagonisms and oppression of real life into a world of the impossible, into a world of utopian dreams. Our literature, which stands with both feet firmly planted on a materialist basis, cannot be hostile to romanticism, but it must be a romanticism of a new type, revolutionary romanticism. We say that socialist realism is the basic method of Soviet *belles lettres* and literary criticism, and this presupposes that revolutionary romanticism should enter into literary creation as a component part, for the whole life of our Party, the whole life of the working class and its struggle consist in a combination of the most stern and sober practical work with a supreme spirit of heroic deeds and magnificent future prospects. Our Party has always been strong by virtue of the fact that it has united and continues to unite a thoroughly business-like and practical spirit with a broad vision, with a constant urge forward, with a struggle for the building of communist society. Soviet literature should be able to portray our heroes; it should be able to glimpse our tomorrow. This will be no utopian dream, for our tomorrow is already being prepared for today by dint of conscious planned work.

One cannot be an engineer of human souls without knowing the technique of literary work, and it must be noted that the technique of the writer's work possesses a large number of specific peculiarities.

You have many different types of weapons. Soviet literature has every opportunity of employing these types of weapons (genres, styles, forms and methods of literary creation) in their diversity and fullness, selecting all the best that has been created in this sphere by all previous epochs. From this point of view, the mastery of the technique of writing, the critical assimilation of the literary heritage of all epochs, represents a task which you must fulfill without fail, if you wish to become engineers of human souls.

Comrades, the proletariat, just as in other provinces of material and spiritual culture, is the sole heir of all that is best in the treasury of world literature. The bourgeoisie has squandered its literary heritage; it is our duty to gather it up carefully, to study it and, having critically assimilated it, to advance further.

To be engineers of human souls means to fight actively for the culture of language, for quality of production. Our literature does not as yet come up to the requirements of our era. The weaknesses of our literature are a reflection of the fact that people's consciousness lags behind economic life—a defect from which even our writers are not, of course, free. That is why untiring work directed towards self-education and towards improving their ideological equipment in the spirit of socialism represents an indispensable condition without which Soviet writers cannot remould the mentality of their readers and thereby become engineers of human souls.

We require a high mastery of artistic production, and in this connection it is impossible to overrate the help that Maxim Gorky is rendering the Party and the proletariat in the struggle for quality in literature, for the culture of language.

And so our Soviet writers have all the conditions necessary for them to produce works which will be, as we say, consonant with our era, works from which the people of our times can learn and which will be the pride of future generations.

All the necessary conditions have been created to enable Soviet literature to produce works answering to the requirements of the masses, who have grown in culture. Only our literature has the chance to be so closely connected with the readers, with the whole life of the working population, as is the case in the Union of Soviet Socialist Republics. The present congress is in itself peculiarly significant. The preparations for the congress were conducted not only by the writers but by the whole country together with them. In the course of these preparations one could clearly see the love and attention with which Soviet writers are surrounded by the Party, the workers and the collective farm peasantry, the consideration and at the same time the exacting demands which characterize the attitude of our working class and collective farmers to Soviet writers. Only in our country is such enhanced importance given to literature and to writers.

Organize the work of your congress and that of the Union of Soviet Writers in the future in such a way that the creative work of our writers may conform to the victories that socialism has won.

Create works of high attainment, of high ideological and artistic content.

Actively help to remould the mentality of people in the spirit of socialism.

Be in the front ranks of those who are fighting for a classless socialist society.

Swell the Harvest (1930)

Shock Brigade of Composers and Poets

As the Soviet Union embarked on the road to industrialization and collectivization, folklore, music, posters, and film were all commandeered in support of everything from the Five-Year Plans to bringing in the harvest. Here a five-stanza rhymed ditty called a chastushka *is used to urge the peasants to employ the more mechanized tools that the* kolkhoz *was providing.* Chastushki *came into being in the second half of the nineteenth century and were particularly popular in those areas of Russia where rural and urban life met on the outskirts of cities. Frequently accompanied by dancing and sung to the accompaniment of a balalaika or accordion, the* chastushki *were popular forms of folk entertainment covering everything from courtship to political satire. During the Stalin era they acquired the decidedly ideological tone presented here.*

Hey, Fyodor and Malania,
And Avdotia and Pakhom,
Let's strike up a merry song
About the sowing season.

Hey you, Vanya, best stretch out
That accordion past your ears.
Why should you be sowing from
Your grandpa's basket in these years.

Take a gander in the barn—
Ain't it mighty nifty
How that newfangled machine
Sorts the grain so swiftly.

Hey you, basket, blow away,
Like some measly weevil,
Cuz we got ourselves a drill—
A fancy city seed-drill.

It ain't nothing like you are,—
It'll dance a pretty dance,
Each seed drops out where it should,
Not a single one askance.

Dizzy with Success (1930)

Joseph Stalin

The rapid movement toward industrialization in Stalin's Russia was closely tied to the move to collectivize agriculture beginning in 1930, in the hope that this would increase productivity. New towns sprang up to serve new factories and industrial plants. The demographic shift from the countryside to the towns and the resulting need to feed the growing worker population provided much of the momentum for the First Five-Year Plan in 1929. The problem, however, was that not everyone wanted to be collectivized. Kulaks (successful, independent farmers) in particular wanted nothing to do with the system of collective farms, and many of Russia's middle- and lower-level peasants similarly resisted being collectivized. The initial months of collectivization were focused not only on setting up collective farms but on de-kulakization, under which the kulaks were forbidden not only to own land but to work on collective farms. The movement of de-kulakization inadvertently undermined the economic basis of Soviet agriculture since kulak holdings had accounted for the lion's share of the harvests.

Precisely how people were supposed to be collectivized was not made entirely clear. In 1930 roughly twenty-five thousand men, some from factories, some from the militia, and the requisite Party workers were sent out to the villages to strong-arm Russia's recalcitrant peasant population. Goals had been set for grain production and for collectivization. What had not been set, however, was the limit on what means could be used to accomplish these two goals. Resistance was met with violence, often excessive, directed at the peasantry irrespective of whether or not they were kulaks. Faced with chaos in the countryside and sporadic peasant uprisings, Stalin called a temporary halt to collectivization in an article written for Pravda entitled "Dizzy with Success." In it he attacked local officials for their excesses, though the mandate for those excesses had its origins in Moscow. Hearing that Stalin had ordered a temporary halt in collectivizing Soviet agriculture, peasants raced to leave the kolkhozy. Shortly thereafter Stalin tightened the reins again and collectivization was resumed.

Problems of the Collective Farm Movement

Everybody is now talking about the successes achieved by the Soviet government in the sphere of the collective farm movement. Even our enemies are compelled to admit that important successes have been achieved. And these successes are great indeed.

It is a fact that by February 20, this year, 50 percent of the peasant farms of the U.S.S.R. had been collectivized. This means that by February 20, 1930, we had *fulfilled* the estimates of the Five-Year Plan *more than twice over*.

It is a fact that by February 28, this year, the collective farms had *already* stored more than 3,600,000 tons of seed for the spring sowing, *i.e.,* more than 90 percent of the plan, or about 220,000,000 poods [one pood is just over 36 pounds]. It cannot but be admitted that the storing of 220,000,000 poods of seed by the collective farms alone—after the grain-purchasing plan had been successfully fulfilled—is a tremendous achievement.

What does all this show?

It shows that *the radical turn of the rural districts towards socialism may already be regarded as guaranteed.*

There is no need to prove that these successes are of tremendous importance for the fate of our country, for the whole working class as the leading force of our country, and, finally, for the party itself. Apart from the direct practical results, these successes are of tremendous importance for the internal life of the party itself, for the education of our party. They imbue the party with a spirit of cheerfulness and confidence in its strength. They arm the working class with confidence in the triumph of our cause. They bring to our party new millions of reserves.

Hence the task of our party: to *consolidate* the successes achieved and to *utilize* them systematically for the purpose of advancing further.

But successes also have their seamy side; especially when they are achieved with comparative "ease," "unexpectedly," so to speak. Such successes sometimes induce a spirit of conceit and arrogance: "We can do anything!" "We can win hands down!" People are often intoxicated by such successes, they become dizzy with success, they lose all sense of proportion, they lose the faculty of understanding realities, they reveal a tendency to overestimate their own strength and to underestimate the strength of the enemy; reckless attempts are made to settle all the problems of socialist construction "in two ticks." In such cases care is not taken to *consolidate* the successes achieved and systematically to *utilize* them for the purpose of advancing further. Why should we consolidate successes? We shall anyhow reach the complete victory of socialism in "two ticks." "We can do anything!" "We can win hands down!"

Hence the task of the party: to wage a determined struggle against this

At the harvest, 1947. Courtesy of the Hoover Institution, Peter Christoff Collection.

frame of mind, which is dangerous and harmful to the cause, and to drive it out of the party.

It cannot be said that this dangerous and harmful frame of mind is really widespread in the ranks of our party. But this frame of mind nevertheless exists in our party, and, moreover, there are no grounds for asserting that it will not spread. And if this frame of mind acquires the rights of citizenship among us, there can be no doubt that the cause of the collective farm movement will be considerably weakened and the danger of that movement being disrupted may become real.

Hence the task of our press: systematically to expose this, or anything like this, anti-Leninist frame of mind.

The success of our collective farm policy is due, among other things to the fact that this policy rests on the *voluntary* character of the collective farm movement, and that it *allows for the diversity of conditions* existing in the various parts of the U.S.S.R. Collective farms cannot be set up by force. To do so would be stupid and reactionary. The collective farm movement must rely on the active support of the great bulk of the peasantry. Methods of collective farm construction in developed districts cannot be mechanically transplanted to backward districts. To do so would be stupid and reactionary. Such a "policy" would discredit the idea of collectivization at one blow. In determining the speed and methods of collective farm construction we must carefully take into account the diversity of conditions prevailing in the various districts of the U.S.S.R.

The War against the Peasantry
(documents from 1929–30)

Edited by Lynne Viola et al.

Stalin's "Dizzy with Success" speech belied the true state of affairs in the provinces, where collectivization continued to take its toll on the population. Between 1929 and 1932 a drive to increase the supply of bread to Russia's workers in urban areas brought famine to the countryside. Collectivization was Stalin's answer to myriad problems, chief among them grain procurement, kulak recalcitrance, and the perennial problem of Russia's failure to catch up to the rest of the industrialized world. The kulaks dug in their heels and the peasants slaughtered their livestock, creating an initial surplus that was soon followed by severe shortages, famine, and starvation. Foreign trade and private business were both curtailed, inflation soared, and peasants raced to buy anything they could as they watched the value of their money depreciate. It was recommended to Stalin that he increase the production of consumer goods while curtailing the export of food in order to bring economic stability to the countryside. Stalin's goal, however, was to industrialize the country as swiftly as possible. The cost of this strategy: the Russian countryside.

Letter of M. D. Mikhailin, a peasant from the village of Dement'evka, Samara Guberniia, to his son about grain procurements

16 July 1929

A letter from your parents.

Good day dear son, we are sending you greetings from all the family, and from the relatives, and from the acquaintances. We have received your letter and the money, 15 rubles, for which we are very grateful.

You asked about the harvest. From spring till Trinity there was a drought, and since Trinity it has been raining. So now the grains have rested a bit, and we will collect grain for the family. Though we will collect the grain, they will hardly give it to us, for we are having grain procurements here. They have imposed 20 poods on us, and we ourselves have been

People waiting in long queues in Moscow, 1931. Courtesy of the American Geographical Library, University of Wisconsin–Milwaukee Libraries. Photographer William O. Field.

buying since the winter. With [us], they have confiscated a colt and four sheep; they take away everything from everyone in the village on credit. Whoever has two horses and two cows—they take away a horse and a cow and leave one horse and one cow per home. The rest they take away. They take away every single sheep. And whoever lacks a beast—they take whatever goods they have: clothes, furniture, and dishes. In Korolevka, from Uncle Vasia Badinov they took a horse, a cow, a heifer, a year-and-a-half-old bull, seven heads of sheep, a sowing machine, a samovar, a cloth coat, a feather bed, a tow, and even wool; and from Len'ka they will probably take a cow and two year-and-a-half-old bulls. They go from house to house and look for grain everywhere; where they find a pood or half a pood, they take everything away, leaving only one pood per eater. One can't buy grain anywhere, can't find [it], and can't sell [it]. They want to bring the new grain to one threshing-floor and thresh it all together there, and starting in the fall they want to give us a norm of one pood per month per eater, and all the rest they will take away and pour together in a common barn. Thus, Mitiunia, write to us how this whole business should be explained; there are rumors that there will be a big war soon and if not war, that they want to drive everyone into a collective farm, and we will all work together.

Write what is going on with you in the center. The people are greatly frustrated. They even don't want to sow grain. Write to us about all this, and write to us whether this decree has been sent out from the center, or it is the local authorities that manage things so; we know nothing about this.

Vladikavkaz Street, 1931. Courtesy of the American Geographical Library from the University of Wisconsin–Milwaukee Libraries. Photographer William O. Field.

Also this is what happened: they hired us to put up house [*izba*] frames, we wanted to put up the frames 12 arshin long and 7 arshin wide [1 arshin is approximately three-quarters of a yard]. Now that they confiscated our animals we have postponed this, and we want to wait till the autumn; perhaps there will be some change. If they drag us together into one collective farm, then we do not need this. When you receive this, write what rumors you have [heard]. Even though we have no grain, still we do not wander around looking for grain, we have savings from the spring, so that there will be enough till the fresh reap; soon we will reap the new grain. With this, good-bye. Write in response; we are all alive and healthy and wish you the same. We all together send you our greetings. Write as soon as possible what is going on there with you.

OGPU Order on Measures for the Liquidation of the Kulak as a Class

2 February 1930

No. 44 / 21

Moscow

In order to carry out the liquidation of the kulak as a class in the most organized manner and to decisively suppress any attempts by the kulaks to counteract the measures of Soviet power for the socialist reorganization of agriculture—above all in raions of wholesale collectivization—a devastating blow must be delivered to the kulaks as soon as possible, especially the richest and most active counterrevolutionary part. The kulaks' resistance must be and will be decisively broken.

The implementation of this historic task will demand exceptional intensity in every area of party and soviet work. The tasks entrusted by the party to the OGPU organs are especially serious, complex, and responsible.

What will be demanded of our organs more than ever is an exceptionally intense effort, determination, and perseverance, an exceptionally rigorous class line, and efficient and swift action.

The tasks that have been set will be successfully carried out only if there is unconditional support for them from the majority of landless laborers and poor and middle peasants; only when these tasks are organically linked to the process of mass collectivization. The support of the masses of landless laborers and poor and middle peasants will be at its fullest if our measures have a strict class orientation.

The blow must be inflicted solely on the kulaks. A blow at the kulak *aktiv* must disorganize and neutralize all of the kulaks.

The measures of the OGPU organs should develop in two basic directions:

1. Immediate liquidation of the counterrevolutionary kulak *aktiv,* especially the cadre of active counterrevolutionary and insurrectionist organizations and groups and the most inveterate, diehard individuals (category 1).
2. The mass exile (from raions [districts] of wholesale collectivization and the border zone first) of the richest kulaks (former landowners, quasi-landowners, local kulak leaders, and the entire kulak cadre from which the counterrevolutionary *aktiv* is formed, and the antisoviet kulak *aktiv* of clergymen and sectarians) and their families to remote northern areas of the USSR and confiscation of their property (category 2).

In order to carry out the campaign to exile kulaks and their families in the swiftest and most painless manner, it is imperative above all that our organs decisively and immediately liquidate all existing counterrevolutionary kulak–White Guard and bandit cadres, and especially the counterrevolutionary organizations, groups, and bands that they have set up.

The liquidation of such counterrevolutionary entities and the most active individuals is already underway in all of the principal areas of the Union, pursuant to telegraphed OGPU directives.

This operation must be basically completed by the time the campaign to exile the kulaks and their families begins to unfold. Resolute operational actions against such counterrevolutionary elements and especially against manifestations of organized counterrevolution and bandit activity must naturally be carried out as well during the exile campaign and afterward.

Collectivization 1931

Ivan T. Tvardovskii

By 1930 the revolution in Soviet agriculture had resulted in chaos. The kulaks resisted all efforts by the state to forcibly expropriate their land. These were peasants with their own land holdings, who knew how to work productively and who often had a degree of education. Stalin determined that the new system of collective farms was to be made up of middle- and lower-income peasant households and thus set about ridding the countryside of the very sector that knew best how to work the land. Those deemed most dangerous were sent to forced labor in the Gulag or summarily shot; others were sent into internal exile in distant provinces. Some were allowed to remain, but on a significantly smaller parcel of land.

The rural nightmare that spread through Russia's countryside did not spare Ivan Tvardovskii's family. He once said of his life, "Happiness was in no hurry to settle in our house [Ne toropilos' schast'e poselit'sia v nashem dome]." The younger brother of the Soviet poet Aleksandr Tvardovskii, he was the child of a kulak family whose land and even horse had been forcibly seized during collectivization. Dispatched to the Gulag in the Arctic, the family worked in miserable conditions, survived a typhus epidemic, and in 1932 fled from exile into the Ural Mountains. It was here that Tvardovskii attempted to begin life over again, until he was conscripted into the army during the Russo-Finnish War of 1939–40 and subsequently taken prisoner. He escaped and remained in Sweden and Finland during the Second World War. After the war Tvardovskii, like many at the time, returned home only to be arrested at the border. He was sent out to the Gulag and released only in 1952.

On March 19, 1931, our family left Zagor'e forever. Our lives had been disrupted even before that day. Our father, working somewhere in the Donbass, had not been home for almost half a year, and would only rarely visit us or drop us a short letter by post.

Everything began at the moment of collectivization, in the spring of 1930.

I remember well when, returning once from Lobkovo in the spring of that same year, I noticed a change in our home. There was no longer a light smoke coming from the forge, and I didn't hear the familiar sound of the anvil. In the hut there was nothing but silence and sadness. Sitting by the window, father was reading a book. This was at the height of the work day, so it seemed unusual and attracted my attention. It was clear that mother, too, was not herself: her swollen eyes and despondent look immediately communicated something unpleasant to me, some kind of sorrow.

The reason for this lay in the individual property tax that had been levied on my father's farm, an amount which made it clear that there was no sense in trying to pay it—but only to sell everything, and even then we wouldn't be able to make it. Why did this happen? This question, to which I could find no answer, tormented me. I knew how difficult it was for us, and I saw how my father and older brother had to work late every day to feed and somehow clothe our enormous family. . . . It was especially difficult for me that things were turning out this way. "They'll know right away in school," I thought to myself. All of us—my father, [my brother] Konstantin, and the rest—were all trying to figure out what we should do.

We decided to petition the regional powers to rescind this excessive tax. We were assured that the matter would be re-examined. We thought we noticed something promising, and our father brightened up a bit, although his doubts about this being resolved in the appropriate and best way possible never abandoned him. This was why the forge was not working, why the farm was in decline, and why father's earlier energy had been snuffed out. At the time we had a one and only cow, some small livestock, and a horse. But the horse was outstanding—a four or five year old stallion which, although he was not a purebred, was a trotter with good conformance—there were few like him in the region, and he was my father's and Konstantin's pride and joy.

Sometimes my brother would bring the horse out into the churchyard, and we would all run out to watch him dance, rear, and whinny for freedom as we happily ooh-ed and ah-ed. Our father would say, "Well, let him stretch his legs!" And my brother would give the horse free rein. I envied the speed with which he would jump up on the horse, and Shepherd (the horse's totally inappropriate name) would spring into a dance, snorting, splaying his lean, sculpted legs, and bending his shimmering neck as he carried the rider out of the churchyard. Gradually picking up speed, Konstantin would follow a well-marked trail lined in greenery as far as the eye could see as the entire family stood and waited for his return, knowing that he would hit a full trot only on the way back, when the horse would begin to obey the rider. The pace of the trot was wonderful—in his headlong sprint Shepherd demonstrated the full exquisiteness of his nature and would fly into the churchyard like a marvel from a fairy tale.

This horse, as I've already said, was always the object of our special attention. This started with our father. He loved good horses with a passion only comparable to that of a hunter for his hound. This attraction was passed on to Konstantin, who had followed in his father's footsteps since he was a teenager. There were times when the two of them would go to the horse market in El'n just to look at good horses and watch them being broken in as part of the transactions.

And then all the discussions that would follow! Names, the coat colors of specific individuals, and how "The rascal, took off, how he spread himself out: Ay, Ay, Ay! And the shoes themselves: Clang, clang, clang!" father would tell us later.

After Stalin's speech "Dizzy with Success" was published, the campaign to organize collective farms seemed to have calmed down, and everything in Zagor'e remained as it had been in the past. The spring tasks in the fields went on in their own ways, as they had one, two and five years earlier. We did some things on our farm, but now with a kind of hidden speculation: nothing had been heard about rescinding the individual property tax. And father hung a lock on the door of the smithy.

At the beginning of the summer of 1930, there was a rumor that an agricultural co-op was being organized in the village of Liakhovo. There was a proposal to base it on the site of a former gentry estate although nothing other than an old garden, a sleepy park and a few half-standing farm structures remained of it.

Among the still small number of co-op members, there was a close acquaintance, indeed, a man whom I would even call a friend, of my father's, Roman Ivanovich Ignatenkov. He was almost a neighbor of ours, but his farmstead was not part of Zagor'e but of the village of Stoliovo. The fact that Roman Ivanovich had joined the co-op prompted my father to think about it as well. In fact, we might describe this as throwing himself from one extreme to the other. At that moment, father had neither money nor food supplies, and maybe for him joining the co-op meant finding a way out of his predicament. However, the co-op had just gotten organized and had no resources, so it had no way to help him. All of the co-op members were still living on their own farmsteads, and did not do any work in common, coming to the co-op plots only when necessary. Only one man, Roman Ivanovich's son, worked there as a watchman, living in one of the few rooms in the master's ruined outbuilding that had survived. His name was Ruuf. Even as a teenager, he had been a lad with an awful temper, and he became an invalid because of his own foolishness. This happened during threshing, when he was driving the horses without paying attention. The ties on his bast shoes came loose and were caught in the drive gear of the thresher. It proved impossible to bring four highly strung horses to a quick stop, and Ruuf lost a foot. As a result of his handicap, he got trained to be a shoemaker, which did not interfere with his watchman's duties.

There were many conversations and discussions in our family about the possibility that had opened up of becoming members of this co-op, but no firm decisions were made. In the evening we would arrive at a general consensus that we needed to join, that there was no other way out. But in the morning, either mother or father or Konstantin would have their doubts. And the most important question that remained was this: without income from the blacksmith's shop, the family had nothing to live on during this period of organization. But continuing to work in the smithy was also impossible because of the unresolved tax question.

Finally, we wrote an application requesting that our family members be accepted into the "Zaria" agricultural co-op in Liakhovo. We figured that we would continue to live where we had been living, maintain—as others did— ties with the governing board, and do everything necessary on our own farmstead, with the director's approval.

Soon thereafter a meeting was held and our family was accepted into the co-op.

Everything was done with the purest of intentions, but somehow we forgot that, according to regulations and the law, we needed to turn over our stallion to the common livestock, to be used for hauling. And so father gave up the horse. He turned it over himself, reluctantly. But that was when his spirit flagged. He could no longer find a place for himself. A worm crawled into his heart and soul, and gnawed at him night and day. He lost sleep, he lost his appetite, the whole wide world grew dim for him. And either on the third or fifth day, father went to Liakhovo. "Let me, at least, take a peek at him, see how he's doing," was on his mind as he approached the old garden, where the co-op's central farmstead was located. ↵ *lost his will to work*

There had been a time when the side of the garden near the road had been lined with firs to protect it from the wind. For some reason, my father assumed that Shepherd would be standing behind in the garden.

Two or three hours must have passed. The weather was hot, and the whole horde of us sat on the stoop of our new hut (we now had a new hut), on the shady side.

I don't know what each of us was thinking about, but we kept glancing either at the sunrise, or at the trail beside Yellow Hill, which we took to get to school, in Liakhovo. And suddenly we heard Shepherd's neighing—so familiar and so alarming, as can happen when the owner is nearing home after a long trip. Then, from the woods, along the same trail, a rider appeared, and it became clear that it was father who was riding Shepherd, although as a rule he didn't ride. He approached and brought the horse under the roof. And that's when we understood that there was trouble. For some reason, none of the youngest ones ran up to greet father, which was what usually happened when he returned from the market or from some other trip. Father sat down next to us and feeling embarrassed and guilty told us the following:

"I'm walking up to the garden, to that strip of firs, and even though I don't see him, I can hear him neighing furiously. And it's him—Shepherd! And it's as if he's listening, snorting, as if he's waiting for an answer. The voice is his for sure. It's him, I think. And I come up, closer and closer, tearing through the firs. He noticed me, he started to spin around, beating and digging with his hooves at the ground, as if to say, 'Save me! Take me away! And it's burning hot!' It's completely calm there—not even a breath of wind. Flies and horse flies swarming all around him. Tree snags and twigs, and he's tied to a little apple tree. He's all tangled up and fighting it. I see trouble. My heart just goes, tuk-tuk, tuk-tuk, as if it were not inside me but somewhere outside, next to me. I untangled and untied him, attached the belt from my pants, looked around—nobody! I don't believe in God, but still, bless me, Oh Lord . . . and so, that's how it is . . ."

He, father that is, became silent. Lit a cigarette, inhaled deeply, and sighed.

"No, I can't . . . I can't bear it!"

"Well, how did you decide to do this? How can this be? They'll charge you!" said mother, crying, with an expression of complete and utter calamity. "Well, what have you done? What were you thinking?" she continued.

"Let whatever may happen, happen. Maybe I shouldn't have done it, but I couldn't do anything else. And I repeat: What awful thing have I done? I didn't steal him—the horse is mine!" father continued.

"No! That's just it, you did steal him! You did a bad thing! And where will you go with him? They'll come and charge you with stealing. They'll take Shepherd away, and you won't be the man they thought you were! No one will condone this act!"

The next day they took Shepherd back to Liakhovo.

Soon afterwards, father left Zagor'e for the Donbass. We didn't know anything about him for a long time. At that time, the family lived with a certain sense of shame and discomfort because of father's haste and thought-less actions.

Translated by Natasha Kolchevska

Anna's Story (1993)

Edited and translated by James Riordan

The excerpt that appears here is taken from an interview conducted in 1993 by the sociologist Ol'ga Litvinenko in the Kurgan region of Russia, just beyond the Ural Mountains. This area supplies much of the foodstuffs to the cities of Cheliabinsk and Yekaterinburg and beyond, and as such was one of the hardest hit by de-kulakization in the late 1920s early 1930s. Russians could not even officially talk about this period before 1990 and 1991. Even in 1993 the people Litvinenko interviewed—the children, grandchildren, and great-grandchildren of kulak farmers—were reluctant to give their full names during the interview process convinced that, in Litvinenko's words, "fear is the solitary legacy passed on from one generation to the next in peasant families." Below is a segment of her interview with "Anna," born in 1916, the daughter of a kulak.

Childhood

My grandfather arrived in the Transurals from Central Russia in the late nineteenth century. He came with his brothers and sisters of his own volition. They were all keen workers, got married to local girls—and that's how our family started.

Grandfather had a big family and he put them all to work. He couldn't abide slackers: he never ate "unearned" bread and never gave it to others. He even used work as a panacea for all ills. Whenever he felt unwell he used to go out and chop wood!

Our family lived in the village of Tikhonovka, in Kurgan Region. It was a tiny place, with only forty households, yet a pretty spot. We had a stream running past where we all used to swim and catch fish in summer. As for the forest it was full of mushrooms and berries which we used to pick and put by for winter so as to keep ourselves alive through the long winter months.

I was born in 1916 and remember our village having only three well-to-do households; most of us were medium peasant farmers, with a smattering of poor peasants. My parents came from a long line of peasant farmers. There were eight of us children; a ninth was born just before resettlement. We initially lived with Grandfather, but then built our own home, with everyone giving a hand. Our farm stock consisted of four cows and four horses. Mother had all of us to look after as well as the house; she had no time for anything else. Father did what peasant farmers do: he ploughed, sowed and made all our footwear. He even gave us lessons since the village had no school. Naturally, all the children assisted Father in reaping, ploughing and furrowing, as best we could. We also had our own farm tools: a plough, mower and threshing machine, but they were split between the four brothers who took it in turns to use them. Often we didn't come home to eat because our land was a tidy distance away. Although we didn't own much land, the nearby Tatars were selling theirs and father purchased it and ploughed it up. If he hadn't done so, we wouldn't have had enough to feed ourselves. We milled our own flour at the windmill: and we also baked our own bread. In fact, virtually all our food was home grown, so to speak: meat, milk, butter and vegetables.

We dressed very poorly; nothing was bought. Mother made us canvas skirts which we shared; the men had canvas trousers, and our sheets were of canvas too. We sewed our own blankets, matting and table cloths; nothing was purchased. For the bed we had a piece of felt which Father would unfurl each night and we would all lie down upon it, in a row. Our house was quite large. Father had only just built it and not yet divided it into kitchen and living rooms. He didn't have time. Outside we had a barn, stable and several sheds. Our father made them all himself, with help from us.

I cannot say that religion passed us by. Dad was not particularly god-fearing, but he went along with religion since his mother and father were elderly and he respected his father's faith. The village had no church, so we had to travel ten kilometres to go to church in the next village. Mostly, we just didn't have the time and went only for Easter, Epiphany and Shrovetide, for the major festivals. Not that we neglected religion altogether. We had no Old Believers; we were all Russian Orthodox.

Our dekulakization started in 1928. It all happened surreptitiously. Our parents kept mum in front of us, so we knew nothing about it. I just started to notice people disappearing: first one, then another, and another. Exiles took place at night so that nobody would see. I only ever saw one family being carted off; I recall the waggon being full of children. All the rest simply vanished into thin air.

Then some villagers began to set up a commune; it attracted all the poorest and the laziest characters. Though we had no thieves and vagabonds in the village, we did have plenty of idlers. When a person loafs about, he earns nothing and starts to envy others who do. That's why the poor of the village became communist activists. They were in their element, cutting off their beards and plaits, even lopping off the horses' tails, shouting and bawling.

"We are Communards. Down with the kulaks!"

Meanwhile, the people who had to give up their cattle and poultry to the commune just sat and wept. My parents didn't join the commune, remaining single farmers—for which they were to pay dearly.

First they had a massive tax to pay; it was so high they were quite unable to pay it. They just didn't have the grain. After that, activists from the commune descended on us, breaking all the locks on the barns and clearing us out of all our corn. Next time they came to list our property. They noted it all down and carried it off, although there was really nothing left to take. Our furniture was all home-made; father had made all the tables, chairs and bed out of wood himself. It was all confiscated, along with the samovar, clothing and pillows. Incidentally, I later came upon one of those activists at the cemetery; she was begging for charity. Clearly she hadn't made good at others' expense and had remained as poor as when she had started out.

We were woken up in the night in early spring, 1929; we were told, "You're going for good." We didn't even protest, there was no point, since they were ignoramuses scared stiff of the authorities. They didn't even have any guns. It was two Young Communist girls from the commune and some activist or other from town. They knew we had nowhere to run to. How could Dad desert his family? And where would we kids go? Since they knew we wouldn't try to escape they weren't frightened of us. At dawn they lined several families up in the Rural Council building and then sent us off into the unknown.

Exile

First we were taken to some freezing cold barracks; I don't even know where they were. All I know is that we froze and starved a full ten days in those barracks. And then off we went farther in carts to Perm Region. Once there, all able-bodied men were rounded up and sent on foot to a logging camp. They were not even permitted to spend the night with us. We had no idea where they were being taken or for how long. They could even have been shot as far as we knew. We lost Father and our eldest brother who was then 20. Only later did we hear whispers that they were 25 kilometres from our settlements, cutting timber, but they were not allowed to visit us.

Women and children, meanwhile, were billeted in tumbledown shacks that were standing empty. Two families shared one such hovel, commiserating with each other. Mother fell ill straightaway, leaving me as the eldest to take charge. I had to look after my eleven-year-old brother and two younger sisters—but the sisters both died of hunger and disease in the first few months. My elder sisters had remained behind in the village since they had married poor peasants, which had saved their lives.

We knew terrible hunger in that settlement. I saw people drop dead on the street, without a bite to eat for ten days. All we got later was half a loaf of bread to last two weeks; we never set eyes on a whole loaf. Mother would divide our share into five pieces: we would eat for five days and starve for ten. Mother could hardly move from lack of food, my brother could not talk at all, he just lay there. As for me, I too suffered terribly, but I was determined to save them. I went into the forest for mushrooms which we boiled up in a pot and ate. When May arrived, they forced us to dig the soil and gave us chunks of bread for our work. The trouble was that I was the worst worker owing to ill health and my youth; the women were stronger than me and hard workers.

I would work in the daytime and go mushrooming straight after work. That's how we survived the summer. That autumn, father was brought back to us; but he was dying. They had brought him to that state after six months logging. He was only 43 years old. We learned from him that our elder brother had escaped; he wandered around for a long time, documentless, hiding here and there, before finally settling in Kurgan. It was three years before we were to meet up again. Father died that same autumn. He was conscious until the very last day, and he would tell us he could see Death approaching. First she was standing in the doorway, then she entered the room and approached his bed. Soon after, he told us, "Not long now." What with my brother lying there and Mother barely able to walk, there was nothing I could do to save him, even had I been able.

We gave Father a good send-off. We got hold of a coffin, dug a grave and even called a priest—a mighty rare event at that time. We gave him a fine funeral for a long-suffering peasant.

After Father's burial, the woman who shared the house began to nag at Mother about me going to work at the logging camp, to earn some cash; otherwise we'd all perish. I had no idea where the camp was, but was quite prepared to go and find it. Just as I was leaving, my little brother suddenly got up from his bed and started after me. God knows where he found the energy.

Neither of us had any shoes, so we went barefoot and my brother almost immediately cut his foot; it bled so badly, yet there was nothing to bandage it with. I would have taken him back had he not kept hobbling after me. It's here my memory fails me from the sheer misery of it all. I see it all as if through a thick fog. We must have walked about twenty kilometres before we stumbled upon some village or other. There we were given a bun and some money. Again I cannot remember the journey back; I do recall us not touching the bun, we wanted to keep it for Mother. When at last we reached home, all the neighbours came out to gaze at our prize. It was then that the woman we shared the hovel with began to pester Mother again.

"Take them away from here while you've still life in you. If you die, they'll die with you. You have some bread and some money, so go. When your money runs out you can beg."

So Mother took her advice. Although it was a dreadful time, it was clear a mile off that we were frail, tattered exiles, which helped us get by. For the authorities never thought we were capable of escaping even if we had left the settlement. There was a boat station not far away, and we managed to get there by horse. While my brother and I hid in a corner of the boat house, Mother went to buy a ticket for herself on the ferry; she was so afraid she would not have enough money. But as luck would have it she had just enough to get to Kurgan. All of us kept well out of the way until the last moment, for fear of being sent back. But we made it, scrambled on board the ship and spent about two days on the river. When we arrived, we walked from the town to our native village. By now virtually nothing could have frightened us: winter was upon us and we were likely to die anyway, either from hunger or from the communists. At least we would be buried in our native soil.

The Proletariat's Underground Paradise (2002)

Irina Kokkinaki

Alongside the push to collectivize agriculture came a similar push to industrialize the *country. Both took uncompromising form, as the state mandated in 1929 that the* *goals of the First Five-Year Plan be met in four years. The language of the particular* *Soviet brand of industrialization bespoke its goals: words and phrases such as* shock work *and* shock workers, mobilization fronts, overfulfilling the plan, *and* storming of production quotas *became part of the language of the day. The new* *hero of the day was Aleksei Stakhanov, a coal miner in the Don Basin who in 1935, in* *five hours and forty-five minutes, shoveled out 102 tons of coal, a figure fourteen times* *greater than his quota.*

In Stalin's vision industrialization meant monumental. *It meant a ring of* *skyscrapers circling Moscow, more ornate, more baroque than anything Moscow had* *ever seen. It meant the building of new cities such as Magnitogorsk and Komsomol'sk* *on the Amur in the late 1920s. A steel town on the western Siberian steppe, Magni-* *togorsk grew from a population of twenty-five when it was founded in 1929 to 250,000* *in 1931. Donetsk, known then as Stalino, grew similarly, rising to become a major* *Donbas coal and steel town by 1937.*

As part of his plan to industrialize his country through storm and shock work, *Stalin conceived of the idea of Moscow's Metropolitan, the metro system that is still,* *by anyone's reckoning, one of the best underground urban train systems in the world.* *In addition to solving the transportation problem in a city that was swelling with* *new arrivals, the metro was to symbolize the workers' paradise, decorated with* *mosaics, painted, and bejeweled in a way that the historian James Billington likens to* *Muscovy under Ivan the Terrible. What was denied the Soviet worker in the 1930s in* *a country defined by the unlikely combination of "enthusiasts," economic and social* *chaos, and the terror awaited him hundreds of feet below the street, where he could* *briefly pass through the socialist paradise of the future while changing trains. For an* *excellent virtual tour of Moscow's Metropolitan we direct the reader to the system's website. In the selection below art historian and critic Irina Kokkinaki revisits the early days of the metro—its construction, its design, and the place it occupied in the hearts of the workers who built it.*

This structure is for us, workers and peasants; these, are our own Soviet and socialist marble columns. A socialist government can permit itself the building of a structure which gives the best emotional experience and artistic pleasure to the population. Our worker, riding the metro, must feel that he is working for himself, knowing that every nut and bolt is socialist.—From L. M. Kaganovich's speech at the celebratory gathering dedicated to the opening of the L. M. Kaganovich Metropolitan

> Well, just as it always turns out:
> Everything in life has gotten mixed up,
> In order to harness my horse I travel in the morning
> From Sokol'niki to the [Central] Park [of Culture] on the metro.

So sang Leonid Utesov. The contrasts of bustling Moscow under construction play out in the song, in which Model "M" cars and the newly opened metropolitan settle in along with horse-drawn carts. It is no coincidence that the park is mentioned: the first route of the Moscow metro, Sokol'niki to the Central Park of Culture, connected two parks representing the apotheosis of socialist leisure. They are the logical termini of the route. There was nowhere further to go. In London and New York underground transportation has existed since the nineteenth century. The issue of building a metropolitan (the "capital road") in the Fatherland was raised as early as 1901 by the Riazan-Ural Railroad Society. From 1901–10 a series of projects was proposed, according to which each metro line would cross the Moscow River Bridge and would end in the large building of a central station in Red Square. (See A. Lebedev's site www .metro.ru.) However, not one prerevolutionary project ever came to fruition. In 1924 the Directorate of Moscow Roads and Tramways created a subsection for the preparation of a proposal for a Moscow metropolitan. . . . A plenum of the Central Committee of the All-Union Communist Party decided that construction would begin in 1933. They determined that the metro would be laid out as ten radii. Historians are fond of mentioning the strategic functions of the metropolitan, forming a whole underground city with secret passages known to just a few. In 1932 the first workers' project got underway with the participation of invited guests from abroad. In the spring they began the digging. More than five hundred enterprises set about producing the necessary equipment. Young people assembled in the capital from all parts of the country under the banner, "You will make the metro possible!" Miners from the Donbas, builders of the Dnepr Dam—all built the Lazar Kaganovich Metropolitan in order to show the ideological superiority of the USSR over the West. By the spring of 1935, the metro conducted its first test runs. At this time a ticket for a single ride was considered tantamount to a medal for special services to the Motherland. The line was opened for passenger use on 15 May 1935. On opening day a coach car designed according to American specifications was used. The car was lit in a yellow-brown hue by the lighting fixtures, and the seat stuffing was made of horse hair. Throughout its history the metro ran trophy German coach cars along with various other models. And you no doubt noticed the manufacturer's name, "Mytishchinskii Coach-Car Factory," displayed on the end windows. This factory was actually founded by Savva Ivanovich Mamontov. . . .

The architectural achievements of the Moscow Metro station were admired both at home and abroad. The model of the "Komsomol'skaia" Station . . . was put on display at the International Exhibition in Paris in 1937. Among the impure styles is the "Palace of Soviets" station . . . , which we know as Kropotkinskaia Station. This station creates a pleasing illusion of a roof supported by columns of light. Special stylistic achievements distinguish the "Red Gates" Station whose surface entrance hall, where arches seem to flow one into another—a metaphor for a tunnel which seems to become smaller towards the vanishing point—, is an example of the uniqueness of early Soviet architecture. On the second route, the "Kursk–Kievsk" line allowed the Sokol'niki line to function independently. A section of the route from the Arbat radius to the center was added on, and the "Hunters' Row" station absorbed part of the traffic going through "Revolution Square." The radius from "Sverdlov Square" to "Eagle" completed the construction of the second route (1938). The architectural arrangement of these stations is in the form of a fan due to the proximity of Khodynsky Field, where the Central Aerodrome is located. The ribs of the vault of the main hall in "Airport" station fly up like parachute shroud lines . . . , and an ethereal cupola forms the soaring vault of the surface entrance hall of the "Dinamo" station. . . . Sky blue heavens populated by gliders and Zeppelins breeze through the lunettes of "Maiakovskii" Station. . . . A. A. Deineka's mosaics have entered into the history of art as examples of the monumental-decorative style.

The metro became an object of intensive exercise in architectural imagination, a symbol of the future communist paradise. The best stones from the Caucasus and the Altai, from Central Asia and the Ukraine were brought in— granite, red Onega porphyry, onyx, labradorite, Crimean and Ural marble. There are paintings and statues, mosaics, majolicas and stained-glass windows, each complementing the other. Regardless of the individual design decision, each station maintains a high level of performance: split-second punctuality and the uninterrupted flow of trains distinguish the Moscow metro from all other underground [rail]roads in the world. In this transportation environment one can see palaces from the era of eastern despots. The polished surfaces of carpeted floors with intricate ornaments and the inlaid work of wall panels, along with ventilation grates and lighting fixtures are executed with near technical perfection, answering the idea of "luxury for the people." The people are proud of the Metropolitan, and the construction of the metro has been showered with medals. Songs have been composed about it, stories and novels have been written about it; it has been made a subject of statistical comparison with foreign models and has been exhibited within the country and abroad. . . .

The restraint and noble refinement of the design of the metro of the 1930s were replaced by the grotesque magnificence of the style of the post-War years. Increasingly, glazed tile, imitating porcelain, was used. The triumphal, "unconquerable" style became a symbol of the victory of the Soviet system over world fascism. "The Book of Tasty and Healthy Eating" embodies the universal victory over the enemy system; the book came out after the war and destroyed any doubt that it was possible to flourish and improve oneself morally and physically in the country of Soviets. Sheaves of wheat, chalices of plenty from which cascades of fruit spill forth, drawing in like a wind a group of dancing Soviet people—these are the characteristic, decorative motifs of the stations of the Ring Line. The attempt to randomly bring together all the achievements of national architecture from various periods gave birth to a whole series of stylistic curiosities. The red star appeared as a leafy, rococo rosette, supporting the ancient Russian engraved weight. The ceiling of the hall of the Komsomol Station on the Ring Line is decorated with the heroes of Russian history depicted upon molded heraldic shields in imitation of the porcelain figures of later Eclecticism [a movement in nineteenth-century Russian architecture—Translator]. This shows the influence of the post-War retrospective line of art. "I was in a whole series of European capitalist countries, and I can attest that the metro in Paris, London or Vienna resembles our Soviet metro like a barn resembles a palace. Glory to our Soviet people!" wrote an enthusiastic eyewitness of the great upheavals in a review of the construction of the Smolensk station in 1953. According to the testimony of long-time Muscovite residents, who lived in cramped communal apartments, they made it a habit of going for evening rides on the metro, reflecting upon how the palatial stations and beautiful, kaleidoscopic scenes of Russian everyday life succeed each other in sequence. The metro was "Luxury for the people," who were used to thinking in slogans, and perceiving everything from the point of view of the collective. Everyone coped separately with their own personal poverty. "I, woman worker of the metropolitan, am proud that I live in the country of socialism, that I work in the underground palaces of the Soviet country."

Translated by Kenny Cargill

X

The Great Terror

By all accounts the purges instigated under Stalin were the grimmest period in Soviet history. The death toll between the years 1934 and 1953 rivaled that sustained by the country during the Second World War. Statistical reports from Soviet archival documents estimate that the total number of arrests between 1935 and 1940 were 18.8 million. Of those who were arrested at the height of the terror in 1937–38, approximately 85 percent were convicted. Some data suggest that approximately seven million people were executed between 1937 and 1938. The numbers are as staggering as the losses from the war, and equally as unimaginable. If the war brought destruction from without, the purges brought it from within, compounding the tragedy, to say nothing of the senselessness, of the losses.

Robert Conquest, one of the foremost historians of the Great Terror, has correctly noted that Stalin's purges didn't simply "come out of the blue." Throughout Russian history there is a long-standing tradition of imprisoning and sentencing to internal exile (within the country proper) political and religious dissidents. From as far back as the seventeenth century there are accounts of such exiles, such as that by the archpriest Avvakum, who was exiled and tortured by the Orthodox Church for his dissenting religious beliefs. Into the eighteenth and nineteenth centuries administrative or internal exile became a common form of punishment experienced by literary and political figures alike. Among those sentenced to internal exile were a group of army officers known as the Decembrists, who in 1825, in protest against the rule and autocratic policies of Tsar Nicholas I, staged what has been considered the first Russian Revolution. Several were executed; others were exiled to Siberia, the Far East, and Kazakhstan.

While the camps reached their nadir under Stalin, the groundwork for them was laid during the first years of Bolshevik rule. The early Bolsheviks viewed the wholesale elimination of certain groups of people—the bourgeoisie and the nobility, for example—as necessary to the cause of the Revolution. The first camps were set up during the Russian Civil War (1918–21). But it was under Stalin that a system of camps was put into place and expanded to become, in Aleksandr Solzhenitsyn's words, an "archipelago" within the Soviet Union. This was the Gulag, an acronym that originally meant Chief Administration of the Camps but which gradually came to signify the camps themselves and the system of labor within them. Between 1929 and 1953 the Gulag housed approximately eighteen million prisoners. There was an odd paradox about the camps: although few initially knew of their existence or about conditions there, the Gulag nevertheless functioned as part of the economy of the country, reaching deep into the forest zone, into the areas richest in mineral wealth and natural resources that could be tapped to strengthen the new socialist economy. At the height of the Gulag there were 476 separate camp complexes that contained thousands of smaller, separate units.

The year 1934 is usually cited as the beginning of the terror. It marks the assassination of the Leningrad Party boss Sergei Kirov, a murder that to this day has not been solved, although by all accounts it was on Stalin's direct order that Kirov was killed. What at first seemed an isolated event gradually grew into the successive elimination of high-ranking Party cadres whom Stalin suspected of seeking to undermine his authority. By the mid-1930s, as Hitler was expanding his sphere of influence in Eastern Europe, Stalin was in the process of cleansing his own country of some of the best and brightest. Quite apart from ordinary citizens being summarily sent off to the Gulag, a series of public prosecutions, or show trials, took place in 1936–37 during which major Party figures were tried and executed. Some were accused of operating a Trotskyite-Zinovievite terrorist cell. Others, including Nikolai Bukharin and Aleksei Rykov, were accused of belonging to an anti-Soviet right-wing bloc of Trotskyites.

It was no accident that the terror reached new heights just when it did. In the mid-1930s Stalinist society still found itself on very shaky ground. Many of the promises made in the early days of the Revolution had failed to materialize. In many parts of the Soviet Union, people were still living in grinding poverty without basic services. Industrialization, forced collectivization, and famine in 1929–32 had brought in their wake displacement, poverty, and social instability. Identifying greater and greater numbers of enemies inside Soviet society, the terror scapegoated millions of Soviet citizens for policies that had failed at the top. Many of the high-ranking Party officials who were eliminated had a hand in some of the programs and policies that had failed. Others, such as Bukharin, an excerpt from whose interrogation by the Central Committee is included in this volume, took issue with Stalin over which economic policies would put the country on a more stable footing. He was executed.

It was not merely high Party officials who were eliminated during the

Great Terror; no one was immune. People came under suspicion by association, by virtue of the fact that they lived in the same communal apartment or worked in the same institute as someone who had been arrested. One of the multiple tragedies of the era was that one stood a greater chance of being sent off to the camps simply by virtue of who one was than for any kind of overt criminal activity in which one might have engaged. Moreover, the seemingly random nature of the arrests kept people in a constant state of vigilance for themselves and their families and in a permanent state of suspicion of those with whom they came into contact at work and in daily life.

Despite the illogic of many of the arrests, certain groups of people, by definition, came under attack. Soviet citizens whose ethnic origins were non-Russian, who had prerevolutionary connections, or who had foreign-sounding last names, particularly Jewish ones, were seen as potential enemies of the state. Similarly, people who were overtly religious landed in the camps, as did those who had seen the world outside of Stalin's Russia. Soldiers and high-ranking commanders from the Soviet Army who had beaten back Hitler's forces and liberated Berlin were arrested when they returned home victorious from the war. The writer Aleksandr Solzhenitsyn was put into the camps for a line he had written to a friend from the front containing a veiled criticism of Stalin. Émigrés who had settled abroad were invited back only to be arrested and sent to the camps or in some cases simply shot upon their return.

Certain groups were particularly hard hit, among them the Russian intelligentsia. The poet Osip Mandel'shtam was arrested and sent out to the Russian Far East and died in a transit camp in Vladivostok. The writer Eugenia Ginzburg found herself caught up in the purges despite being a loyal member of the Communist Party. Ginzburg gradually awoke to the realities of Stalin's rule; however, many who were arrested and sentenced remained convinced to the end that their arrests and imprisonment had all been a mistake that would be cleared up sooner or later. The professorial ranks at universities were thinned either by virtue of the topic of one's research, a line in an article one had written, or views that were seen as inconsistent with Party ideology. Robert Conquest has noted that unlike other groups of people who simply fell silent in order to avoid saying anything incriminating, professors had to continue to teach and speak, while never being sure how a comment they made in class might be taken.

There is no doubt that Stalin masterminded the extermination of many Party officials, but it is now clear that he also took an active role in the purges. Based on archival documents that have come to light since 1991, we now know that he signed execution orders, chose juries for the trials, and was often present at the trials of high-ranking Party members.

Even with Stalin's direct participation in much of the decision making in the purges, the terror gradually acquired a life of its own and for that reason became even more insidious. Soviet citizens became implicated in the very process that was destroying their society. One of the great paradoxes of the terror is that it came full circle, as its accusers, denouncers, and prosecutors often became victims of the very terror they helped to instigate and perpetuate. Often out of a desire to save their own skin, and sometimes out of their conviction that the Soviet Union was indeed under threat from within, many Soviet citizens took an active role in informing on neighbors, colleagues, and acquaintances. Part of what propelled this insidious network of informing and denouncing was the concept of *krugovaia poruka*, or collective responsibility, the notion advanced during the Stalin era that not only were people's lives inextricably bound together but that one was responsible for the actions of one's colleagues, one's neighbors, and one's family members. Such responsibility included informing on them for the greater good. Many arrests were the result of precisely this motive. Gradually most people simply arrived at a point where they did not know who, if anybody, they could trust. The situation was exacerbated by the fact that a large number of Soviet citizens were living in communal apartments with shared living space. Thus one's own personal space was not immune from the presence of *stukachi*, or informants.

We tend in any study of terror to look more closely at the victims than at the often anonymous accusers. Yet their situation raises interesting questions about the mechanics of the terror. That people became informers suggests the effectiveness of political propaganda among a sizable portion of the population in the 1930s and immediately after the war. In studying the archives from the years of the Great Terror, the historians J. Arch Getty and Oleg Naumov reluctantly came to the conclusion that the terror was very much a collective undertaking and, moreover, one that operated by consensus. The effectiveness of Stalin's propaganda machine not only enjoined people to take part in the unraveling of their own society, but also created a belief system that allowed people to turn in family members for the greater glory of the "real" family: the Great Soviet family, with Stalin as pater familias. One of the more horrifying stories to come out of this warped mindset was that of thirteen-year-old Pavel Morozov, who in 1932 presumably denounced his father as a kulak, or rich peasant, and was subsequently murdered by his own family members. Thereafter he was rewarded with semi-mythological status by a Communist Party that celebrated his allegiance to a family greater than his biological one. Although post-Soviet archival research has suggested that Pavel's story may be totally fictional, at the time it fed elegantly into the myth of loyalty to the state that Stalin was trying to foster.

Stalin's death in March 1953 brought to a halt the worst of the terror. Almost overnight an amnesty was put in place for all prisoners who were serving a sentence of five years or less. By the end of March, over one million people had been granted amnesty from the Gulag. Stalin's successors, Lavrentii Beria, followed by Nikita Khrushchev, understood all too well (partly because they had a hand in them) that the grand construction projects that were meant to be accomplished by the *zeki*, or prisoners, were a drag on the economy and that most of the prisoners incarcerated in the camps were innocent.

The dismantling of the entire Gulag system took much longer than the realization of the injustices perpetuated by it. Special camps were still in place up until the Gorbachev era. Soviet citizens could still find themselves sentenced to administrative exile; the physicist and dissident Andrei Sakharov, for example, was forced to move from Moscow to the city of Gorky, where he resided between 1980 and 1985. But from the day of Stalin's death some practices were halted, never to be reinstated. Soviet citizens were no longer dragged off in the middle of the night in cars known as "Black Marias" for interrogation or worse. Repression still continued but in a different form and in a way that guaranteed that one was not going to be summarily shot for daring to speak out against official policy. In the mid-1950s the Soviet Union began the long, slow process of recovery that included liberal reform and the rehabilitation of those who had been repressed. Questions of collective guilt among those who managed to survive still linger.

Bukharin 1936

J. Arch Getty and Oleg V. Naumov

Nikolai Bukharin, one of the leading Bolshevik theoreticians and editor in chief of the newspaper Izvestiia *from 1934 to 1937, fell victim to Stalin's terror, as did many other high-ranking members of the Party. He was put on trial in 1936 accused of sabotage, terrorism, and various other trumped-up charges, expelled from the Party in 1937, and executed in 1938. In the course of those two years, 750,000 Soviet citizens were executed and many more were sent to the Gulag.*

The document that appears here is the transcript of Bukharin's trial. Such documents became available only in 1991, as Party archives, once closed, were declassified after the Soviet Union collapsed. Prior to this time there was little information on how the terror was instigated from above. Memoirs written by those who had suffered in the purges became available in the West beginning in the 1960s, but the picture they provided was necessarily incomplete, as the authors themselves had no access to the larger questions of how decision making at the top took place nor the degree of Stalin's involvement in the actual arrests, trials, and sentencing. Evidence now suggests that Stalin stood at the helm, masterminding the extermination of millions of people, from the upper echelon of the Party to lower-level bureaucrats and unsuspecting Soviets who happened to stumble into the terror. The archives, sadly, have also revealed that the elimination of millions of people in a spate of violence unprecedented in human history was very much a collective undertaking, operating to a large degree by consensus.

Bukharin's trial provides insight into the means by which the Party devoured its own during the height of the terror, from 1936 to 1939. Guilt was often established through association, a ploy which propelled the purges forward, as the confessions at one trial placed other Party members under suspicion and ultimately created more victims. During the infamous show trials confessions were forced out of high-ranking Party members who had nothing to confess, yet confessed in the belief that by doing so they would be saving family members as well as themselves. In a society that operated according to one master narrative, any deviation came to be viewed as nothing less than treason and sabotage not only by the accusers but, in a deft manipulative turn, by the accused as well. Bukharin himself ultimately confessed after his trial in 1938.

Thus shortly before his death he wrote a personal letter to Stalin recanting his earlier confession and proclaiming his allegiance to the Party, as well as to Stalin himself.

Bukharin's language in these documents is typical of that of Party members of his day. He speaks the language of his accusers, the language of the Party and of Stalin. Bukharin had come of age as a Party member and a political thinker at a time of complete realignment of the political, economic, social, and linguistic structure of the country. To deviate from the new revolutionary language was to enter a region where one's very survival became suspect.

Bukharin was ultimately undone by the very system he had helped create. One year later the same machinery would similarly turn against Nikolai Ivanovich Yezhov, one of his chief accusers, who was executed in 1940 as an enemy of the state. What was left after the purges was the shell of an elite that had willed the new Soviet state into existence.

Bukharin's Speech to the December 1936 Central Committee Plenum, 4 December 1936

BUKHARIN: Comrades, it is very difficult for me to speak here today, because this may well be the last time that I speak before you. I know that it is especially difficult for me to speak now, because, in point of fact, it is necessary for all members of the party from top to bottom to exercise extreme vigilance and to help the appropriate [NKVD] organs utterly destroy those swine who are engaged in acts of sabotage and so on.

It follows quite naturally from all this—and should serve as our point of departure—that this is the main directive, that this is the main task before our party. I am happy that this entire business has been brought to light before war breaks out and that our [NKVD] organs have been in a position to expose all of this rot before the war so that we can come out of war victorious. Because if all of this had not been revealed before the war but during it, it would have brought about absolutely extraordinary and grievous defeats for the cause of socialism.

BERIA: I think you ought rather to tell us what role you played in this whole affair. Tell us, what were you doing?

BUKHARIN: I'll tell you.

A VOICE: Before the war and after it, we shall not ask about it.

BUKHARIN: It is difficult for me now to speak because a whole lot of letters, people, tears, and gestures have passed before your eyes and before the eyes of the investigators who have scrutinized these cases, and all of this has turned out to be false.

But I shall begin with the following. I was present at the death of Vladimir Ilich Lenin, and I swear by the last breath of Vladimir Ilich—and everyone knows how much I loved him—that everything that has been spoken here today, that there is not a word of truth in it, that there is not a single word of truth in any of it. I had one and only one face-to-face confrontation, and that was with Sokolnikov. After this confrontation, Comrade Kaganovich told me that they had the impression that I had nothing to do with this matter. Two days later appeared the statement by the procuracy. Based on the above-mentioned confrontation, it said that the investigation must be discontinued. If you had the impression that I was really involved, that I had something to do with this affair, then why did you make that statement?

KAGANOVICH: We were referring to the juridical aspect of the matter. That's why we said [this to you at the time]. It's one thing to speak of juridical matters, quite another thing to speak of political matters—

BUKHARIN: For God's sake, don't interrupt me. After all, I asked [you] to record the fact that he [Sokolnikov] didn't speak to me about any political matters, that he got this fact from Tomsky, who was already dead at the time. Nikolai Ivanovich Yezhov asked me in particular not to allude in any way to the fact that Tomsky had already been shot, that they have all been shot.

LIUBCHENKO: Tomsky shot himself. He was not executed.

BUKHARIN: But he was no longer alive. What could a confrontation with Sokolnikov yield? After all, Sokolnikov spoke to me about nothing. Not a word about politics was exchanged between me and Sokolnikov. Suddenly, this horrible, monstrous charge was brought against me. On the basis of this, the impression was created that I had participated in this affair—

A VOICE FROM THE PRESIDIUM: I read to you the testimonies of Uglanov and Kulikov.

BUKHARIN: As it pertains to Sosnovsky, comrades, I have written several times. Why could you not have arranged a confrontation for me with Sosnovsky? I never had a single conversation about politics with him and never spoke to him about any Riutin Platform. I myself have never read the Riutin Platform because it had been shown to me once and only once at Comrade Stalin's order. I never saw it. I was never even informed of it.

And suddenly this monstrous charge was brought against me. Why? And why, to make an end of it, if you say that Sosnovsky said this, why do you not arrange a confrontation for me with him? Why do I not have the opportunity to confront him?

STALIN: You were offered a confrontation with Sosnovsky, but you were ill, we were looking for you.

BUKHARIN: But I wrote Yezhov a letter. I really was ill, but I told him in my letter that, though I was ill, I would drag myself to the confrontation. But no one called for me.

MOLOTOV: At any rate, this can be arranged without difficulty.

BUKHARIN: But this is the Plenum of the CC. Is this the way things are done at the Plenum of the CC? I must tell you, comrades, that I have never denied that in the years 1928–29 I was an oppositionist, that I fought against the party. But I don't know how I can assure you that I had not the slightest notion, not an atom, about these general views, these platforms, or about these aims. And the charge has been thrown in my face that I knew about it, that I participated in it, that all this time I was trying to worm my way into the government! Do you really believe that I am that type of person? Do you really believe that I could have anything in common with these subversives, with these saboteurs, with these scum, after 30 years in the party and after all of this? This is nothing but madness.

MOLOTOV: Kamenev and Zinoviev also spent their entire lives in the party.

BUKHARIN: Kamenev and Zinoviev lusted for power, they were reaching for power. So you think that I too aspired to power?! Are you serious? What are you saying, comrades? After all, there are many old comrades who know me well, who not only know my platform, who know not only this or that about me but my very soul, my inner life—

BERIA: It is hard to know someone's soul.

BUKHARIN: All right then, so it is difficult to know someone's soul. But judge me as a human being! I am saying that, before bringing charges against me, you should have settled all this business having to do with the face-to-face confrontations.

BERIA: They'll be settled.

BUKHARIN: Very well, Comrade Beria, but I wasn't asking you. I wasn't referring to you.

. . . .

STALIN: Why should they be lying about you? They may be lying but why would they? Can we conceal this from the plenum? You [informal *ty*] are indignant that we raised this question at the plenum, and now you must accept this as a fait accompli.

BUKHARIN: I am not indignant that the matter has been raised at the plenum, but rather that Nikolai Ivanovich [Yezhov] had drawn the conclusion that I knew about the terror, that I am guilty of terrorist acts, etc.

Concerning Kulikov, it is very easy to do this, to clear up the matter —as to where and when he saw me—and it will become clear that he has not seen me since 1928–29.

STALIN: That's possible.

. . . .

BUKHARIN: In 1928–29, I don't deny that some members of the CC were at my apartment. They were. But should one deduce from this fact that I am affiliated with foreign states, that I have placed my name as a candidate for the government, that I am helping those sons of bitches to kill the workers in the mining shafts? And after all this, you [plural *vy*] brought me into the CC at the 16th Party Congress.

MOLOTOV: Piatakov was a member of the CC. It was his business to do so.

BUKHARIN: Let me appeal to Comrade Sergo Ordzhonikidze. I'd like to tell you about something that happened a long time ago, at the beginning of my party work. I was at Sergo's apartment when he asked me: "What is your opinion of Piatakov?" This is literally what I told him: "My impression of him is that he is the sort of person who is so thoroughly ruined by his tactical approach to things that he doesn't know when he is speaking the truth and when he is speaking from tactical considerations."

ORDZHONIKIDZE: That's true.

BUKHARIN: So here Sergo is confirming what I said. So could I have ever recommended an accomplice and leader in this way?

BERIA: Well, you [formal *vy*] could have said that out of tactical considerations.

BUKHARIN: Well, that's quite simple. There is always a logical way out. If I say that I've met with a certain person, then it's out of tactical considerations. If I say that I didn't meet with him, then it's because of conspiratorial considerations. There is no such dialectic that allows you to say that someone has both met and not met someone else.

KALININ: You must simply help the investigation.

BUKHARIN: Well, it looks like I'm a son of a bitch, no matter what I do. That's all.

If I am to speak from a businesslike, calm—insofar as I can speak calmly—point of view, then, first of all, let's talk about the face-to-face confrontation with Sokolnikov. I assert that, by its very nature, this confrontation could not possibly have yielded anything for the simple reason that, as Sokolnikov himself has admitted, and I asked that this fact be entered by the investigators in their notebooks, he did not so much as once talk to me about politics. He spoke to me about a review of his wife's book.

STALIN: But he had talked with Tomsky, who told you, didn't he?

BERIA: At any rate, he is not an enemy of yours, is he?

BUKHARIN: I am not speaking of Tomsky. I am speaking of myself. When I was asked about Tomsky by Comrades Yezhov and Lazar Moiseevich [Kaganovich], I told them that in my opinion he might have complained that life was going badly for him. But I could never suppose that he would engage in such matters. For me, this whole business with Tomsky remains an enigma because Sokolnikov said that Tomsky had spoken at my instructions. I know that I never talked to Tomsky about such things. I am suspicious of anything said about Tomsky.

KAGANOVICH: Tomsky himself admitted his connections with Zinoviev.

BUKHARIN: He might have admitted his connections [with Zinoviev]. I don't know anything about his connections with Zinoviev. He never said a word about them to me.

Mass Attack on the Watershed (1934)

Edited by Maxim Gorky et al.

In 1931, as part of Stalin's First Five-Year Plan, an enormous construction project was undertaken to link the White Sea and the Baltic by means of a canal. One of the many projects begun at that time as part of the rapid push toward industrialization, the Belomor Canal was unique in that it was built exclusively with Gulag labor. Originally meant to be finished in mid-1932, it took a year longer partly due to the primitive tools used to construct it and the fact that it was built with prison labor. Official documents, as one might expect, report that the prisoners were enthusiastic shock workers who consistently overfulfilled the plan. There may have been some truth to this statement, since many who worked on the project were subsequently pardoned and released after the canal was completed; Solzhenitsyn reported, however, that conditions were so miserable that during the first winter of construction 100,000 workers died.

What, then, of the final product? The canal officially opened in May 1933 with Stalin in attendance, sailing along the canal in a pleasure boat. But no sooner had it begun operation than it was found to be too shallow, and plans were again under way to make it deeper. Was the canal's failure due merely to the fact that it was built by prison labor, or did Stalin's mandate that it be built fast and cheaply factor into the equation?

This excerpt is taken from the volume on the building of the canal written by thirty-four Soviet writers and published in 1934. The writer Maxim Gorky, who spearheaded the volume, called the canal project a "splendidly successful attempt at the transformation of thousands of former enemies of Soviet society" and "one of the most brilliant victories of human energy over the bitterness and wildness of nature." And yet the writers who journeyed north to view the project could not help but see the other side of this so-called socialist success.

All next day snow kept falling and falling. People slept badly in their barracks, and kept looking out through the windows. It snowed all night and next day, and for days and nights it snowed and snowed!

"Will it ever stop, damn it?"

"It's a long time yet to the change of shifts."

A foreman came in. He pulled on a sheepskin jacket, wound a scarf carefully around his hoarse throat, and hurried to the workings. Everything was levelled and heaped up with snow. Extra digging and extra work again, that wouldn't matter so much. But think how much water there will be in the spring. He looked angrily up at a sky the colour of soapsuds.

Morning. A meeting. "Don't conceal the laggers," shouted the brigade leaders. "The first division did 128 percent working on soil. The third division did 130 percent, though it had weak horses and broken picks." "We'd have done more," someone shouted from the third division, "if it hadn't been for Markaryan, the chief of transport!"

In general, the groups complained that they were given bad horses. They were all sick. The picks were broken.

Fifty people had had to stop work in order to repair the steam navvies. They were short of horses—103 horses had not been delivered at all. . . . There were not enough reins or harnesses and the stables weren't ready. The horses spent the night under the open sky. A snowstorm was raging. The stablemen went about slapping their hands and cursing, popping in and out of their tent and having to keep a sharp eye on their charges because "shock-workers" from other brigades came nosing round leading their worst horses, trying to replace them with better ones. Other men also took wheels from the wagons when they got a chance. Shouts and noise and marvelous cursing! "Down with the grabbers," shouted the stablemen. They swore to expose all those who tried to work dishonestly.

The second group, which worked next to the eighth, did only 109 percent on February 14. Of course, they felt bad about it. And they did so little simply because there was not enough rolling-stock to carry the rock away. One man in the group, the record breaker Popov, did 300 percent every day. He strutted around puffing at his pipe, but he was sorry for his unsuccessful phalanx. On the quiet this Popov gave them advice as to how to increase their percentage. Night fell. Popov led his comrades to their neighbors' territory. The neighbors were eating, secure in their victory. The record setter uncoupled a car and pushed it hastily with his shoulder. The car rolled away. A wind blew under the car, and snow flew along the rails. A second car, and then a third rolled down the slope. "Stop," shouted the shock-workers of the eighth brigade. "They've stolen our cars, the devils." Uproar. A short meeting. Once more the grabbers are condemned—these stupid people, who don't understand the right way to work. And the shock-workers of the second brigade, including Popov himself, promised that they would be irreproachable record-setters in the future. We shall see!

In general, there was much that was worth seeing!

The liquidation of illiteracy is spreading. True enough, but the shock-workers of the fourth division complained of the vulgar language used at the club. The wall newspapers still sang out vulgar songs. The string orchestras amused themselves with public-house ditties. "We understand, Moscow wasn't built in a day, but still . . . ," said the shock-workers of the fourth division, which was working on rock. They had found their section in the most chaotic condition. They had immediately set to work to clear away the dirt and rubbish. They built a large production meter in front of the barracks, to show what had been done and what was left to be done. And then they formed an agitation brigade which worked as well as agitating. There was a wall newspaper, and a production bulletin board.

Every evening the brigade discussed the plan for the next day's work.

Take a look at the weekly menu worked out by the record breakers and the chief-of-supplies of the eighth division—the division whose cars were stolen. The menu is decorated at the top with a picture of the construction, and at the bottom are some sort of lilac flowers and the slogan: "Eat, and build as well as you eat!"

DINNER
Cabbage soup—1.2 litres a head.
Kasha with meat—300 grams.
Fish cutlets with sauce—75 grams.
Rolls stuffed with cabbage—100 grams.

"We went to work singing," says Bisse, chairman of the prisoners' commune in Leningrad. "We sang as we marched, like soldiers in very high spirits. We had to drill by hand so that we ate into the rock rather slowly. But we wanted to get the earth out of the trenches as quickly as possible. We loaded it hastily on the derricks, pushed wheelbarrows up and down the planks, and threw it into the boiling rapids of the Vyg. There was a continuous line of wheelbarrows and many banners near them.

"As far as sounds are concerned, the terrific noise of the workings reminded me of a huge factory, where one can't hear the sounds made by individuals, but one feels that this is collective creation. Explosions thundered noisily almost all the time. And the sound of axes on wood, the ringing of hammers on shining steel, and the loud whistle of the electric motors, sucking water out of the wooden chutes echoed everywhere. Piles of sand thrown down from above by the spadeful fell with a dull sound. Horses' hoofs clattered along the bottom of the excavation. There was noise everywhere."

Requiem (1935–49)

Anna Akhmatova

Like millions of other Soviets, the poet Anna Akhmatova got caught up in the purges. In 1935 her son, Lev Gumilev, a historian of Central Asia, and her partner, Nikolai Punin, an art historian, were both arrested on false charges and sent into exile and forced labor. Both were released in 1938, after which Akhmatova's son was again arrested and sent into internal exile. He was released for the final time only in 1956, during the post-Stalinist Thaw.

During the 1930s Akhmatova, like countless others, stood in line in Leningrad every day to learn of Gumilev's and Punin's whereabouts from the authorities. What distinguished her from the thousands of others standing in endless lines, waiting for news, was that she was already a well-known poet in her country. She had begun writing verse well before the Revolution. By 1925, however, it had become increasingly difficult for her to get her work published, as the deeply personal nature of her poetry ran counter to the growing politicization and public nature of literature under Stalin. Only during the war was there a brief reprieve that made publication of her writing possible. Although she had been effectively silenced, someone recognized her in a line in 1935 and asked her if she could describe the scene before her. She answered, "Mogu" (I can), an acknowledgment that the times she and others were forced to live through could be given poetic expression.

Composed between 1935 and 1949, "Requiem" is a dirge both for those who had disappeared and for those who had been left behind to mourn. Akhmatova memorized it, entrusting each one of the seventeen different sections to the memories of different friends, lest the poem be discovered by the authorities. In "Requiem" her personal loss becomes symbolic of the losses sustained by all the women who had lost sons in the purges. The figure of the solitary mother merges with that of Mary, who watches the sacrificial death of Christ, thereby raising the specific and the personal to the level of myth.

Officially "Requiem" was not available in the Soviet Union until 1987, when Gorbachev's policy of glasnost made it possible for formerly forbidden works of literature to be published. However, it was published abroad in Munich in 1963 and subsequently translated into a number of languages. Typical of much of tamizdat literature (literally, works published abroad) at that time, it made its way back into the Soviet Union, where it continued to circulate in the underground.

Anna Akhmatova, 1930s.

Requiem

> No, not under the vault of alien skies,
> · And not under the shelter of alien wings—
> I was with my people then,
> There, where my people, unfortunately, were.
> *1961*

INSTEAD OF A PREFACE

In the terrible years of the Yezhov terror, I spent seventeen months in the prison lines of Leningrad. Once, someone "recognized" me. Then a woman with bluish lips standing behind me, who, of course, had never heard me called by name before, woke up from the stupor to which everyone had succumbed and whispered in my ear (everyone spoke in whispers there):

"Can you describe this?"

And I answered: "Yes, I can."

Then something that looked like a smile passed over what had once been her face.

April 1, 1957
Leningrad

DEDICATION

Mountains bow down to this grief,
Mighty rivers cease to flow,
But the prison gates hold firm,
And behind them are the "prisoners' burrows"
And mortal woe.
For someone a fresh breeze blows,
For someone the sunset luxuriates—
We wouldn't know, we are those who everywhere
Hear only the rasp of the hateful key
And the soldiers' heavy tread.
We rose as if for an early service,
Trudged through the savaged capital
And met there, more lifeless than the dead;
The sun is lower and the Neva mistier,
But hope keeps singing from afar.
The verdict . . . And her tears gush forth,
Already she is cut off from the rest,
As if they painfully wrenched life from her heart,
As if they brutally knocked her flat,
But she goes on . . . Staggering . . . Alone . . .
Where now are my chance friends
Of those two diabolical years?
What do they imagine is in Siberia's storms,
What appears to them dimly in the circle of the moon?
I am sending my farewell greeting to them.

March 1940

PROLOGUE

That was when the ones who smiled
Were the dead, glad to be at rest.
And like a useless appendage, Leningrad
Swung from its prisons.
And when, senseless from torment,

Regiments of convicts marched,
And the short songs of farewell
Were sung by locomotive whistles.
The stars of death stood above us
And innocent Russia writhed
Under bloody boots
And under the tires of the Black Marias.

I

They led you away at dawn,
I followed you, like a mourner,
In the dark front room the children were crying,
By the icon shelf the candle was dying.
On your lips was the icon's chill.
The deathly sweat on your brow . . . Unforgettable!—
I will be like the wives of the Streltsy,
Howling under the Kremlin towers.
1935

II

Quietly flows the quiet Don,
Yellow moon slips into a home.

He slips in with cap askew,
He sees a shadow, yellow moon.

This woman is ill,
This woman is alone,

Husband in the grave, son in prison,
Say a prayer for me.

III

No, it is not I, it is somebody else who is suffering.
I would not have been able to bear what happened,
Let them shroud it in black,
And let them carry off the lanterns . . .
                              Night.
1940

IV

You should have been shown, you mocker,
Minion of all your friends,
Gay little sinner of Tsarskoye Selo,
What would happen in your life—
How three-hundredth in line, with a parcel,
You would stand by the Kresty prison,

Your fiery tears
Burning through the New Year's ice.
Over there the prison poplar bends,
And there's no sound—and over there how many
Innocent lives are ending now . . .

V

For seventeen months I've been crying out,
Calling you home.
I flung myself at the hangman's feet,
You are my son and my horror.
Everything is confused forever,
And it's not clear to me
Who is a beast now, who is a man,
And how long before the execution.
And there are only dusty flowers,
And the chinking of the censer, and tracks
From somewhere to nowhere.
And staring me straight in the eyes,
And threatening impending death,
Is an enormous star.

1939

VI

The light weeks will take flight,
I won't comprehend what happened.
Just as the white nights
Stared at you, dear son, in prison,

So they are staring again,
With the burning eyes of a hawk,
Talking about your lofty cross,
And about death.
1939

VII

THE SENTENCE
And the stone word fell
On my still-living breast.
Never mind, I was ready.
I will manage somehow.

Today I have so much to do:
I must kill memory once and for all,
I must turn my soul to stone,
I must learn to live again—

Unless . . . Summer's ardent rustling
Is like a festival outside my window.
For a long time I've foreseen this
Brilliant day, deserted house.
June 22, 1939
Fountain House

VIII

TO DEATH
You will come in any case—so why not now?
I am waiting for you—I can't stand much more.
I've put out the light and opened the door
For you, so simple and miraculous.
So come in any form you please,
Burst in as a gas shell
Or, like a gangster, steal in with a length of pipe,
Or poison me with typhus fumes.
Or be that fairy tale you've dreamed up,
So sickeningly familiar to everyone—
In which I glimpse the top of a pale blue cap
And the house attendant white with fear.

Now it doesn't matter anymore. The Yenisey swirls,
The North Star shines.
And the final horror dims
The blue luster of beloved eyes.
August 19, 1939
Fountain House

IX

Now madness half shadows
My soul with its wing,
And makes it drunk with fiery wine
And beckons toward the black ravine.

And I've finally realized
That I must give in,
Overhearing myself
Raving as if it were somebody else.

And it does not allow me to take
Anything of mine with me
(No matter how I plead with it,
No matter how I supplicate):

Not the terrible eyes of my son—
Suffering turned to stone,
Not the day of the terror,
Not the hour I met with him in prison,

Not the sweet coolness of his hands,
Not the trembling shadow of the lindens,
Not the far-off, fragile sound—
Of the final words of consolation.
May 4, 1940
Fountain House

X

CRUCIFIXION

"Do not weep for Me, Mother, I am in the grave."

1

A choir of angels sang the praises of that momentous hour,
And the heavens dissolved in fire.
To his Father He said: "Why hast Thou forsaken me!"
And to his Mother: "Oh, do not weep for Me. . . ."
1940
Fountain House

2

Mary Magdalene beat her breast and sobbed,
The beloved disciple turned to stone,
But where the silent Mother stood, there
No one glanced and no one would have dared.
1943
Tashkent

EPILOGUE I
I learned how faces fall,
How terror darts from under eyelids,
How suffering traces lines
Of stiff cuneiform on cheeks,
How locks of ashen-blonde or black
Turn silver suddenly,
Smiles fade on submissive lips
And fear trembles in a dry laugh.
And I pray not for myself alone,
But for all those who stood there with me
In cruel cold, and in July's heat,
At that blind, red wall.

EPILOGUE II
Once more the day of remembrance draws near.
I see, I hear, I feel you:

The one they almost had to drag at the end,
And the one who tramps her native land no more,

And the one who, tossing her beautiful head,
Said: "Coming here's like coming home."

I'd like to name them all by name,
But the list has been confiscated and is nowhere to be found.

I have woven a wide mantle for them
From their meager, overheard words.

I will remember them always and everywhere,
I will never forget them no matter what comes.

And if they gag my exhausted mouth
Through which a hundred million scream,

Then may the people remember me
On the eve of my remembrance day.

And if ever in this country
They decide to erect a monument to me,

I consent to that honor
Under these conditions—that it stand

Neither by the sea, where I was born:
My last tie with the sea is broken,

Nor in the tsar's garden near the cherished pine stump,
Where an inconsolable shade looks for me,

But here, where I stood for three hundred hours,
And where they never unbolted the doors for me.

This, lest in blissful death
I forget the rumbling of the Black Marias,

Forget how that detested door slammed shut
And an old woman howled like a wounded animal.

And may the melting snow stream like tears
From my motionless lids of bronze,

And a prison dove coo in the distance,
And the ships of the Neva sail calmly on.
March 1940

Memories and Biographies
of the Leningrad Terror
Leningrad Martyrology

Between August 1937 and November 1938 approximately forty thousand people from the city of Leningrad and the surrounding territories of Murmansk, Novgorod, Pskov, and Vologda were put to death on trumped-up political charges. Most were buried in mass graves in a secret site north of Leningrad, in an uncultivated area known as Levashovo. Only in 1991 did the process of rehabilitation begin in earnest, as archives and secret documents became open to the public. In some cases the few who had survived initiated the process of their own rehabilitation; in other cases families and loved ones or organizations with which the victim had been affiliated did the necessary paperwork. Organizations such as Memorial and Poisk (Search), the local newspapers, the National Library, and the State Archives of St. Petersburg all supported the idea of publishing a martyrology that would record the names of those from the Leningrad region whose lives had been lost in the terror. The result was a seven-volume collection containing the names, dates of arrest, sentences, and dates of execution of the victims. Relatives who could be located were asked to provide their memories of the deceased. Several appear here.

Fedor Stepanovich Almazov

My father, Fedor Stepanovich Almazov, was arrested in September 1937 right at work. Mama was given no reason for the arrest. She had at that time lost most of her hearing and so they really could not talk to her, and on top of that she was illiterate. And we children (including the eldest daughter who had her own family, three sons, born in 1922, 1924 and 1926, and me, the daughter, born in 1928) did not understand why they arrested papa. Mama went everywhere and asked for a meeting. When they finally said yes, she took me with her to see father. They told us: "Wait here." When they led him out for questioning, they said: "You'll be allowed to talk with him for a little while and see him." (Only afterwards was it explained that he was being led out for his final interrogation, after which no one would be able to recognize him, so horrific was it.) When we saw him he walked calmly, confident of his innocence. He came close and asked mama how the children were and added, "Try and make sure that the children get a complete education." That was the last time we saw papa. Mama was told afterwards that everyone was sentenced to ten years in prison.

Now we had become the children of an enemy of the people. Our life changed dramatically. Mama worried that we would be expelled from school and not be allowed to finish our education. Our teacher assured her that the children would be able to continue to study given how they had done so far in school. Children do not answer for their father. However, it didn't turn out like that. It is true that we finished school. Mama fulfilled father's wish. But all further doors were closed to us. My older brother was forbidden to attend the airplane modeling club even though he dreamed of becoming a pilot. The war began. My brothers were hit with the full onslaught of the war. Only my younger brother returned. I went to work in the engineering department without the right to access secret documentation. I was allowed to work there only because the main engineer of the Svir'-2 factory knew mama from work, when he had been a section head. How much grief and deprivation mama had to endure, how much she had to carry on her own shoulders! A person is not made of iron, however, and she grew ill. This happened in 1953—a slow madness. The burden of all she had endured in life made itself felt in her old age.

In January 1958 I finally received trustworthy information about father. When we told mama that our papa was innocent, she told us that she knew that, of course, and then broke down in bitter tears over all that had happened. In March 1958 she died. All her life she heard already, "Don't forget that your husband is an enemy of the people." And this fear visited itself upon us, the children.

In April 1961 my younger brother perished while rescuing a government vehicle. And I have lived peacefully for almost forty years. No one has of yet accused me of being the daughter of an enemy of the people. My husband fought in the war. Right now we live in his hometown of Anap. There are pensioners and veterans of labor here.

It is difficult to recall all that has happened. I will put an end to this matter because those who have done this evil are either no longer among the living or very old.

I do not have a photograph of my father, and so I am not able to send it, which I regret very much. However, I remember very clearly in my memory what he looked like. He was handsome, not all that old and with a little bit of gray in his forelocks. Even-tempered. He never raised his voice at us, the children, and he never punished us. He loved mama. He was respected. Everyone addressed him by his first name and patronymic. He cared about his family a lot.

Raisa Fedorovna Lushchuk, Anap, Krasnodarskii Krai

Dmitrii Savel'evich Prokof'ev

My father, Dmitrii Savel'evich Prokof'ev, born in 1886, was raised in a large merchant family of modest means in the town of Morshansk, Tambov Province. His father was a merchant of the third guild, a religious man, an Old Believer. He had a small business and lived with his family in his own house, which stood in the center of a large orchard. There were three daughters and three sons in the family, of which my father was the eldest. Father was inclined towards learning, though grandfather Savelii tried with all his might to get him to become the head of household and engage in business. As a young man father ran off to Moscow to his aunt's. He graduated from a technical school there, and later from Moscow University and the Moscow Agricultural Institute.

In 1915 he was mobilized as a militiaman in the fortress battery at Revel', where he commanded cavalry.

After the revolution father worked as an agronomist and livestock specialist. In 1919 he married my mother. In 1922 they had me, their daughter Elena, and in 1925 a son, Nikolai. Due to the nature of his work, my father was forced to move frequently. In 1927 or 1928 we moved from Smolensk, where he had worked on a horse farm, to Leningrad. Up until the day of his arrest, father had continued to work as an agronomist and livestock specialist. His last job was in the Leningrad Pig Raising Trust. He was loyal to the government and had no party affiliation. Close acquaintances and friends said that he was a very interesting, multi-faceted, educated man.

I remember him as being large, wide of girth and in an open coat. He was full of life and high spirits. He was a great gourmand, and ate with huge gusto. He loved entertaining and had many friends. He dressed simply, wore a *kosovorotka* [a Russian shirt with a collar fastening on one side—Translator] and played the *balalaika* (which he gave to his son) and the guitar. He loved us children. He spent his free time with us skating. Father was kind, and often took us children to his mother, grandmother Klavdiia, who lived with her younger son on Krestovskii Island. He regularly gave her money and groceries. In 1935 I lay ill with scarlet fever in the infection ward of the Botkin Hospital. I remember him leaning into the window of my room at the hospital, which is where he often went in order to see me, since no one was allowed inside. I saw him for the last time in the summer of 1937 in the settlement of Siverskaia, where I was staying at the dacha. He visited me after his business trip, and he looked slightly depressed. The next time he had a day off he promised to take me home to Leningrad, saying that he would bring me lots of gifts.

I never saw father again. I know that he worried a lot about the developing situation in the country, and once he told me, "Remember, dearest daughter, that there will be a time when everything that is now happening in the country will come to judgment." After that there was much that was not comprehensible, but I sensed his distress. The consequence of what happened to father fills an enormous place in my life. When I was in school and went to enter the Komsomol in the autumn of 1937, at the first meeting of the Committee of the Komsomol, I was asked if I loved my father. I answered, "Yes." I was blackballed. Later I witnessed how children in the upper grades (9–10) got placed behind bars. I studied in a prestigious school, the first model school of the Petrograd district, where children of the important Leningrad party functionaries studied. The home address for many of them was Kirovskii Prospekt, building 26 / 28.

Elena Dmitrievna Ronginskaia-Prokof'eva, St. Petersburg

Olimp Mitrofanovich Ivanov

My papa was a man who loved his family and job very much. He had to spend much of his time at work, so we barely saw him at home. My younger sister, waking up, would often ask if papa had kissed her when he came home from work or when he had left for it again. In the evening, if he managed to get home from work early, he would read to us wonderful little books. When he finally got some free time, he would try to spend it with us. He would play and take strolls with us. He didn't like being a guest at someone else's home or playing host himself at the table. He once took me to a parade, and I sensed his distress and agitation when the tanks would roll across the square.

The family spent the last summer before his arrest in the Ukraine, in a very picturesque place. We walked a lot in the forest and swam. He would carve us all different kinds of wooden toys. My sister has long treasured a little boat that he carved from the bark of a tree. He often had to go on business trips. He always returned from these trips with a bouquet of flowers for mama. But when he returned from his last trip to Moscow, just before the arrest, he arrived in a very nervous state and without a bouquet.

They arrested him at night, in the fall of 1936. The caretaker led in two NKVD [People's Commissariat for Internal Affairs—Translator] men. Papa was told to sit in the chair in the bedroom. Mama pressed her hands to her chest, and looked with horror first at papa and then at the NKVD men, who unceremoniously walked around the apartment and turned the closet inside out. My sister and I looked out horrified from under the blanket. As they led papa away, mama blurted out, "Is it going to be for long?" They replied mockingly, "We are hospitable. People are usually detained at our place for a long time." Only one letter arrived from papa in prison. He asked that mama protect the children and not worry about him.

From that moment began all our ordeals. During the summer of 1937 mama was sent to Uzbekistan. We were supposed to be sent to an orphanage, but our lot changed: we were taken in by our grandmother and aunt.

We only found out that papa was shot when we received the rehabilitation notice. Before that there was always the hope that he was still alive. In 1988 I read the proceedings against papa. In his last speech he requested that he be given the opportunity to work.

Evgeniia Olimpovna Ishchenko, St. Petersburg

Isaak Moiseevich Rif

In 1932 we moved to Leningrad from Vladivostok, where my stepfather, Isaak Moiseevich Rif, worked at the Dal' Factory as one of its leading engineers. Upon arriving in Leningrad he began to work at the Stalin Metallurgical Factory, also as a leading engineer. It seemed that nothing could disrupt our peaceful life.

But beginning in 1937 my family went into complete shock over the arrest of my uncle, Vladimir Fedorovich Prokhorov. Our close friends began to make comments. All this made it hard to live peacefully. In July 1937 two twin brothers joined the family, Igor' and Vladimir. This event brought great joy into our family. Our stepfather had always dreamed about children, and suddenly he got two sons. By this time we had already given up hope of seeing Uncle Volodya again, and so we named one of the children after him in his memory. Right around this time stepfather was recruited into the cadres of the factory. One disagreeable person summoned everyone and asked a series of questions. Chief among them was "Why did you leave Vladivostok?" And with no small amount of irony this unpleasant person noted that it would not be a bad idea if stepfather took a change of clime. From this day a dark, grim atmosphere settled in over our home. Shura, or so Isaak Moiseevich was called at home, lost all peace of mind. He was convinced that there was some hidden design against him afoot and that he was doomed. We lived on tenterhooks.

Being a twelve-year-old girl, I remember sleepless nights when the screeching of car tires, breaking beneath the windows, summoned fear and panic. We lived on the ground floor and everyone would rush to the windows: was it a black patrol car [NKVD agents often arrived in cars called Black Marias—Translator]? Then on the rainy night of 16 October 1937—I had a terrifying dream, I remember it even now—we were awoken by a knock at the door. Two men in leather jackets and a Red Army soldier with a threatening rifle entered. Their appearance was understandable. Everything became clear. The two in leather jackets set about searching the premises. The only things that they found were technical journals and books. Everything was hurled onto the floor. They took aim at the journals in foreign languages. They asked what he was doing with journals like these, particularly the ones in Japanese. I remember how he answered, "I am an engineer." They confiscated the journals as incriminating evidence. Later on we were told what the sentence was, "Sentenced as a Japanese spy to ten years without right of correspondence." Soon thereafter it was time to say goodbye. He stood quietly, bent over the crib where his two little three-month-old sons were sleeping. My heart burst from the mental anguish, from horror and fear for this exceptional man. They rushed him out of the room and led him away. They led him away forever. My mother signed a statement that she would not leave Leningrad. It is something of a wonder that we remained there and that they did not send us away. At the same time they came to take stock of our things. We had nothing except for a writing desk and a chair which had moved with us from Vladivostok. They confiscated them. These from a family with three destitute children.

We received a document twenty-two years later about his rehabilitation and a description of his death, which said that he died of a heart attack in 1942 in a camp. It was only fifty-nine years later that I read in the newspaper that Isaak Moiseevich Rif was shot in December 1937, that is two months after his arrest. It is painful and difficult to write about this. And it is very, very sad.

Debora Borisovna Veksler, St. Petersburg

Translated by Kenny Cargill

Revelations from the Russian Archives

Edited by Diane P. Koenker and Ronald D. Bachman

These two documents were part of the secret archives of the Central Committee of the Communist Party. In 1991 some seventy million documents became available to researchers both in Russia and the United States, where representative selections were translated by the Library of Congress. They helped throw light upon the Stalinist terror, U.S.–USSR relations, the cold war and the wartime alliance, and the Cuban missile crisis.

The first document is an appeal to the American people written in 1939 by General G. S. Liushkov, former head of the Far East Secret Police and a political refugee in Japan, to put a stop to the crimes of Stalin. The second document is a decree issued in 1949 ordering particularly dangerous state criminals who had completed their sentences in labor camps and prisons to be further exiled to remote places within the Soviet Union. After the war prisoners who were approaching the end of their sentence increasingly were sentenced again to keep them from having any kind of contact with the mass of Soviet citizens back in urban areas. In this way millions were to remain as uninformed as possible of the extent of the Gulag and its workings.

People's Commissar
of Defence of the USSR
Intelligence Department
Worker-Peasant Red Army
Section ___
January 4, 1939
No. 143009
Moscow, 19,
B. Znamenskii, No. 19
tel. 1–03–40, ext.

Top Secret
Copy No. 1

Of Particular Importance.
To People's Commissar of the USSR
Marshal of the Soviet Union
Comrade Voroshilov

Attached I submit a translation of a communiqué from the "Domei" agency
Attachment: 3 Pages
Deputy Chief of the Intelligence Department
of the Worker-Peasant Red Army
Division Commander [signed] A. Orlov

Issued: 3 Copies
[Stamped]
No. 20
5 January 1939
People's Commissar of Defence of the USSR

TOP SECRET

Tokyo

General Genrikh Samoilovich Liushkov, former head of the Far East Unified State Political Directorate [OGPU], who has now become a political emigrant in Japan, has issued the following declaration to the American people:

I wish to tell the democratic people of America of the truly great tragedy that has been taking place in the Soviet Union during the past several years and which, evidently, will not end soon. All the news that you are receiving about the Soviet Union comes from official sources. These sources announce that: Socialism has been constructed in the Soviet Union, that the Soviet Union has the most democratic constitution, that the Soviet people (as one) are now happily united around Stalin's leadership. If these declarations were correct, there would be no need to doubt the happiness of the Soviet people. However, if everything is as blissful as they officially declare, a question inevitably arises: Why has the Soviet government arrested 1,000,000 people during the last two or three years? In the Far East there are 5 concentration camps containing 500,000 persons. In the entire Soviet Union there are around 30 such camps with a population of 1,000,000 people. These numbers do not include those who have been shot and those permanently incarcerated.

If it is true that Iagoda, Pauker, Tkalun (commander of the Kremlin garrison), Kork, Petrovskii (commander of the Moscow Proletarian Division), and Egorov participated in the terrorist plot against Stalin, why did they fail to kill him at a time when they had full power?

The following data are available for the Far East:

From among the 8,000 persons under arrest, without any judicial process, 4,000 have already been shot and about 4,000 have been confined in concentration camps. From among those incarcerated in prisons, 5,000 have already been shot. In 1938 in the Far East, a total of about 10,000 persons were arrested, and of these 8,000 were shot and 2,000 are confined in concentration camps. From among those held in prisons 12,000 have already been shot. Additionally, 11,000 Chinese residents in the Far East have already been arrested. 8,000 Chinese were forced to move from the Far East to other locations. Also 180,000 Koreans were forced out of the Far East, and 2,600 of them were arrested.

About 1,000 Soviet citizens who formerly lived in Harbin and 6,000 who formerly lived in Poland were also arrested, together with several hundred Germans, Latvians, and other foreigners. About 2,500 Communist Party leaders, officers (commanders) of the Red Army, and personnel of the political department were shot in 1938. They are accused of originating or participating in intrigues and were condemned to death as a result of the "open" trials by military tribunal. Masses of people live in constant fear of sharing the same tragic fate. Such horrors are being perpetrated in the Far East, an area with a population of only 2 million. In this manner, Stalin is deceiving the peoples of his own and other lands. I do not have the space here to describe what is going on in other parts of the Soviet Union.

The material presented here is enough to draw your attention to how brutally Stalin is dealing with his opponents.

A bloody nightmare has engulfed millions of people in the Soviet Union. A full light must be cast upon the hypocrisy of Stalin, who cold-bloodedly condemns tens of thousands of people to death.

According to the laws of the Soviet Union, a wife is answerable for her husband. Does this law reflect Stalin's humaneness? Wives rarely lose their husbands, except to death. Yet in the Soviet Union, if husbands are arrested by the Soviet government, wives are also subject to arrest, shooting, incarceration in camps, or change of residence, even when they are totally innocent. Besides, all victims of the bloody putsch, by Stalin's order, are subjected to the confiscation of their property, and their children are placed in concentration camps for juveniles. The blood of tens of thousands of innocent people is being shed. Tears pour from unfortunate wives, mothers and orphans, who demand emancipation.

Americans! Are you deaf to the pathetic call of the unfortunate wives and children? No, I do believe in the humaneness of the American people. They will never fail to react to the shedding of blood and tears.

I call upon you to use all your public organizations, trade unions, and your press to stop the persecutions, despotism, and crimes of Stalin!

Send your protests to the Soviet Embassy!

Publicize your protests in the press!

Press your government to withdraw its support from the Stalin administration—a cabal of butchers and swindlers!

No. 128/11
Not for publication

Decree of the Presidium of the Supreme Soviet of the USSR

On exiling to remote areas of the USSR especially dangerous state criminals upon the completion of their sentences.

1. The Ministry of Internal Affairs of the USSR is ordered to deport all inmates of special camps and prisons, namely, spies, saboteurs, terrorists, Trotskyites, right-wingers, Mensheviks, Socialist Revolutionaries, anarchists, nationalists, White emigrants, and members of other anti-Soviet organizations and groups, as well as persons dangerous by virtue of their anti-Soviet connections and inimical activity—upon the completion of their sentences—as directed by the Ministry of State Security of the USSR to the following exile areas under the supervision of organs of the Ministry of State Security [MGB]:

—the region of Kolyma in the Far North;
—the regions of Krasnoiarsk *krai* and Novosibirsk *oblast'* within 50 kilometers north of the Trans-Siberian Main Line;
—the Kazakh SSR, excluding the *oblasts* of Alma-Ata, Gur'ev, South Kazakhstan, Aktiubinsk, East Kazakhstan, and Semipalatinsk.

2. The Ministry of State Security of the USSR is ordered to exile state criminals as listed in paragraph 1 who have served out their sentences in corrective-labor camps and prisons since the end of the Great Patriotic War.

The deportation of these persons is to be carried out in accordance with the decisions of a Special Conference of the MGB USSR.

Chairman of the Presidium of the Supreme Soviet of the USSR, N. Shvernik
Secretary of the Presidium of the Supreme Soviet of the USSR, A. Gorkin
Chairman of the Council of Ministers of the USSR
[signed] J. Stalin
Manager of the Council of Ministers of the USSR
[signed] IA. Chadaev

Moscow, the Kremlin
February 21, 1948
Doc. No. 111/8

Labor Camp Socialism (2000)

Galina Ivanova

How did Soviet labor camps function? What determined their location? How did their internal economy work, and who served as personnel there? These and other questions could only be guessed at prior to the opening of archives in the Gorbachev years. Even as information became more accessible, most research in the late 1980s focused on the purges rather than on the camps per se. Galina Ivanova set herself the task of looking at the internal workings of the camps and at public and private morality among those who served as personnel there. Ivanova discusses how the camps became economic disaster zones, primarily because those who had designed them had failed to factor in the effect of wasteful and involuntary labor on production. Ivanova quotes one worker:

> *We hollowed out ditches in the frozen ground. We worked with heavy miners' hacks in fifty-degree below zero weather. We tried to fulfill the quota. It was extremely difficult work. The ground was like cement. Our breath froze in mid-air. Our shoulders and backs ached from the strain. But we worked honestly. Then in the spring, when the earth thawed, they sent a tractor out with a ditch digger, and in a single hour it dug a ditch the size of the one that had taken six people two months to dig.*

Increasingly, studies of the Gulag have revealed that the camps were not a separate entity set off from the rest of Soviet society, but were woven into the economic, political, and moral fabric of the country during the Stalin years. Ivanova sees a symbiotic relationship between life on the inside and life on the outside, much as Solzhenitsyn does in his novel One Day in the Life of Ivan Denisovich, *not only in the economic sphere but in the split morality among the camp personnel. Espousing communist principles on the one hand, they lived in a world of institutionalized violence on the other, which they transmitted to the world outside the camps and which became endemic to much of Soviet life during and after this period.*

During the 1930s, the Gulag expanded not only geographically. Its organizational and administrative structures also grew and adapted to cope with large-

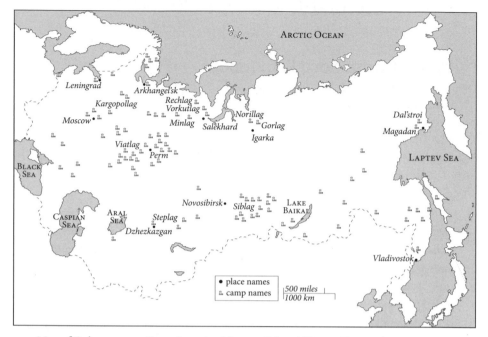

Map of Gulag, 1939–53. From Anne Applebaum, *Gulag: A History* (New York: Doubleday, 2003). Courtesy of Doubleday, a division of Random House, Inc.

scale economic tasks as punitive policies became more severe. Beginning in the second half of the 1930s, the system of crediting workdays was discontinued and parole was abolished. All the camps began to install solitary-confinement punishment cells, whose functions, including the conditions and procedures for holding prisoners in them, were regulated by the Temporary Instruction of 1939 on Procedures for Incarcerating Prisoners in Solitary-Confinement Punishment Cells of Corrective-Labor Camps and Colonies of the NKVD of the USSR. The camp administration turned punishment cells into an ideal instrument of retribution against insubordinates and uncooperative prisoners. The prisoners were kept in solitary cells without any bedding; they were not taken out to work, and they were given hot food—swill (*balanda*)—only once every three days. The maximum term of imprisonment in a solitary cell was set at twenty days, which was beyond the endurance of many prisoners. It is interesting to note that the central Gulag administration was very critical of commandants in whose camps the number of prisoners in solitary exceeded a reasonable limit. Such overzealous prison authorities were often subjected to censure at closed Party meetings, where they were told to find other, more appropriate measures of punishment for offenders. The reason for such "humanitarianism" is absolutely clear—each prisoner in solitary meant one less worker-day, which translated into a loss to the state.

The "social status" of prisoners gradually changed as well. Up until the fall of 1937, propaganda, official correspondence, and even official documents avoided using the word "prisoner." Prisoners of the Gulag were more commonly called "foresters," "shock workers," "Stakhanovites," and so on. The term "Stakhanovite" in general was very widely used in the official lexicon of the camps during the mid-1930s. Productive prisoners were housed in special "Stakhanovite barracks" and served rations from "Stakhanovite kettles" in the camp canteens. In 1936, the following was still a common scene at railroad stations: a prisoner transport train passes through, its cars adorned with Stakhanovite banners and slogans, as well as portraits of the leaders, Stalin and Kaganovich, and a poster saying "Stakhanovite Shock-Work Construction," and right there, for all to see, armed guards and the "Stakhanovite Shock Workers" themselves gazing through the gratings on the train windows at the free world outside. One day a high official in the camp administration witnessed one of these scenes in Petrozavodsk and realized how absurd it was, and only then did things change. In September 1937, the Culture and Education Section (*kul'turno-vospitatel'nyi otdel*) of the Gulag issued detailed orders stating that it was a glaring political error to call prisoners Stakhanovites.

. . . .

By the end of the 1930s, the activities of the Gulag were completely shrouded in secrecy. The country was covered with a network of "post-office boxes," "special facilities," "units," "farms," and "forestry enterprises" with not a word about the camps or their inhabitants. The list of information constituting official state secrets in 1936 totaled 372 circulars, with 300 more added to them a year later. The totalitarian censorship raged behind barbed wire as well as in the country as a whole. Each camp newspaper carried a label saying "Not to be removed from camp territory." Hundreds of censors worked vigilantly to ensure that no information, no matter how indirect, on the geographical location of the camp, the address of the editorial board, or the nature of the camp work projects filtered through to the camp press. The question of secrecy became particularly relevant in 1938–39, during the struggle with the "effects of sabotage in the NKVD system." "All the documents we are dealing with are secret, secret to varying degrees, secret nonetheless," asserted I. I. Pliner, the head of the Gulag, at a Gulag Party meeting in August 1938.

Substantial material expenditures were required to ensure such a high level of secrecy; all secret correspondence was delivered by special couriers. In 1940 alone, 25 million secret packages were delivered by the NKVD field communications division. Of these, 675,000 secret packages and 537 tons in cargo of secret correspondence were delivered by the central apparatus of the communications division, for which 274 NKVD couriers received government awards. Additionally, officials of the people's commissariat who had access to top-secret documents received a special bonus in pay.

"Top-secret" documents in the Gulag consisted primarily of information concerning the Third Section (operations) and the Second Section (accounts and distribution), the work of secret-service agents, sanitation and health issues, and the work of the fuel-industry section, as well as all information concerning secondary railway lines being built by prison labor, primarily in the Far East.

. . . .

The Gulag colonies prepared large quantities of so-called mass-consumption goods: shoes, knit products, aluminum kitchenware, hardware, horse harnesses, furniture, and many others. Here, as in heavy industry, production goals increased significantly. For example, the production plan for furniture increased in 1938 from 30 million rubles to 150 million. The Gulag was the country's primary and practically only supplier of industrial leather goods for the defense industry and the army. At the beginning of 1941, production of special sealing, which was to become one of the chief products of industry during the war years, began in the colonies.

Prisoners worked in agriculture as well as industry. In 1940 a large number of livestock was being raised in the Gulag for meat production: over 60,000 cattle and 290,000 sheep and swine. The country's largest meat-production enterprise was the Karagandinsk (Karlag) State Farm Camp, which contained over 150,000 sheep and some 30,000 cattle and was run using forced labor. Karlag incurred significant losses: twenty to thirty thousand rubles annually, with waste amounting to tens of thousands of livestock. In 1939 the back-breaking labor of starving Gulag prisoners provided the state with 143,000 metric centners of meat (the plan had called for 160,000 centners) and 406,000 centners of fish (compared to a plan of 500,000 centners).

It is virtually impossible to list everything that the Gulag mined and produced. By 1940 the camp economy included 20 branches of the national economy, the most important of which were nonferrous metallurgy (which accounted for 32.1 percent of the overall goods production of the Gulag), forestry (16.3 percent), and the fuel industry (4.5 percent).

. . . .

Vorkuta I. The camps in Vorkuta, Komi Republic, Russia. Courtesy of Bernard Grzywacz / KARTA, the Hoover Institution, and Archiwum Wschodnie.

In spite of the intensive efforts aimed at improving the technical level of Gulag construction sites and facilities, the majority of them failed to fulfill their state planning goals, and not only because there were practically no estimates or designs. In 1939, the Gulag completed only 88 percent of its construction plan, and the productivity level of prisoners' labor came to only 88–89 percent of the target. In 1940, the overall NKVD new-facilities plan was completed only at the level of 82.3 percent, the Gulag timber industry plan at 37.7 percent; Glavpromstroi at 60.6 percent, the Gulag fuel-industry plan at 85 percent, and so on. Only the Chief Administration of the Railroad Construction Administration and Dalstroi met their plan targets in individual areas of production. The daily work productivity for a single prisoner under the Chief Administration of Special Industrial Production in 1940 was set at 46 rubles 27 kopecks, but the actual average level was 41 rubles 80 kopecks. The plan goal in railroad construction was set at 35 rubles 60 kopecks, but the actual productivity of prisoners working on the railroads came to 30 rubles 70 kopecks.

Why was it that the dreams of the state planning officials for a significant increase in labor productivity in the NKVD system did not come true? Of course, the main reason was that no one had factored in the involuntary nature of the labor or the predatory, wasteful nature of the camp economy. Involuntary forced labor was markedly less efficient than the same work done by free workers. According to the data of the Gulag chief V. G. Nasedkin, in January 1941 labor productivity in construction and assembly work in the Gulag was 23 rubles 50 kopecks, whereas labor productivity under the Union People's Commissariats was 44 rubles 98 kopecks; in February the levels were 24 rubles 80 kopecks and 49 rubles and 67 kopecks, respectively. Labor productivity on NKVD construction sites was an average of 50 percent lower than at construction projects under the Union People's Commissariats. Daily productivity per worker in the camps differed greatly from that under the civilian People's Commissariats: in the Chief Administration of Camps for Railroad Construction it was 64 percent lower than in the NKPS; in the Chief Administration of Camps for Industrial Production, 55 percent lower than in Narkomstroi; in the NKVD's Chief Administration of Camps for Hydroelectric Construction, 39 percent lower than the Glavgidrospetsstroi of the People's Commissariat of Construction. A similar situation could be observed in all branches of the camp economy.

The Gulag was also unable to achieve plan goals for lowering the cost of manufacturing. Often the actual cost of camp production was several times more than the planned cost. For example, one cubic meter of land for the construction of the northern route of the Chibiu-Krutai was estimated to cost 1 ruble 6 kopecks, but its actual cost, based on calculations of camp economists, came to a minimum of 6 rubles. In 1940, the Gulag incurred a 22 million-ruble overexpenditure due exclusively to the increased cost of camp production. The camp economy had a predatory effect not only on people but on machinery as well. For example, in the Eastern Siberia Trust of the Chief Administration of Camps for Highway Construction, ninety-four trucks were completely destroyed within three years. The machinery on location at camp facilities and construction projects was seriously underutilized. There were many reasons for this, but the underlying one was that the basic concept of the camp economy was incompatible with qualified, productive, and conscientious labor.

. . . .

Camp mortality reached its peak in 1942, when an average of over 50,000 prisoners died every month. In some camps the death rate was substantially higher than in the Gulag as a whole. In Sevurallag, for example (in what the administration considered to be the worst of the camps), in 1942, 1,615 prisoners died in January alone. Mortality was so high that the Gulag leadership gave official permission to bury the dead in common graves without coffins or clothing. In all, according to our calculations, which are based on official data on the location and transportation of prisoners, over 2 million people

Vorkuta II. Prisoner graves in Vorkuta, Komi Republic, Russia. Courtesy of Bernard Grzywacz / KARTA, the Hoover Institution, and Archiwum Wschodnie.

died in the camps and colonies of the Gulag during the war years; over 10,000 of these were shot based on court verdicts and decisions of the Special Board —generally for refusing to work, for escape attempts, and for anti-Soviet agitation. Our totals do not account for losses among the so-called mobilized contingents, special settlers, residents of children's labor colonies, and several other categories of citizens under the authority of the Gulag, whose mortality rates were also extremely high.

Without insisting on a comparison, we will simply note that, according to a report of the Repatriation Authority of the USSR Council of Ministers for 1946, "On Implementing the Decisions of the Government of the Union of SSR on Repatriation of Citizens of the USSR and Citizens of Foreign States During the Great Patriotic War (1941–45)," the total number of Soviet citizens (civilians and prisoners of war) who died while imprisoned by the Fascists was 1,135,000.

In all, during the war years, over 5 million prisoners passed through Gulag camps and colonies; of these, about 1 million were released early and sent to the front.

As of July 1, 1944, there were 56 camps in the Gulag that reported directly to the center and 69 regional administrations and departments of corrective-labor camps and colonies. These camp complexes included 910 individual camp divisions and 424 colonies.

The war brought significant changes in the prison population. Since prisoners convicted under Article 58 were not eligible for early release and in spite of their frequent requests were not sent to the front after the completion of their terms, their proportion increased from 27 percent in 1941 to 43 percent in 1944. The relative number of female prisoners also shot up. In 1941, they made up 7 percent of the overall prison population; by the summer of 1944, that number had grown to 26 percent.

The overwhelming majority of those remaining in the Gulag were ill, emaciated, and infirm. Many of them had survived purely by chance—some had been given light work, others had encountered a "good" boss or a humane doctor. It was unrealistic to expect a high level of labor productivity from these people; the camp authorities could only meet their production goals by making the working day as long as possible and maximally increasing the number of prisoners. The internally established daily routine gave prisoners three days off a month and eight hours daily for uninterrupted sleep. Prisoners were expected to work for the entire time remaining, and, in practice, were often deprived of even the minimal envisioned rest time.

From the very first days of the conflict, the Gulag contributed to the war effort; all industrial colonies were reprofiled to produce ammunition, special sealings (*spetsukuporki*), uniforms, and other military supplies. On February 18, 1942, a special department of military production was created in the Gulag, charged with the organizational and operational/technical management of all NKVD facilities that produced ammunition and special sealings. By the end of the war, the Gulag was the USSR's second-largest supplier of fragmentation land mines and ammunition sealings.

Spies and Murderers in the Guise of Physicians and Scientists (1953)

V. Minayev

Just months before he died, Stalin began to orchestrate another major purge, this one directed against Kremlin doctors, many of whom were Jewish. Stalin's increasing paranoia was such that in his last years he began eliminating those closest to him and who, in the case of the doctors, could potentially save his life. Stalin died before the Doctors' Plot, as it came to be known, could be carried out, and immediately thereafter the charges against the doctors were dropped.

This last round of purges was a thinly veiled attack against Soviet Jews. Anti-Semitism in the Soviet Union had continued unabated despite the promises of the Revolution. During the Second World War Soviet Jews had been rounded up, arrested, sent to concentration camps, or simply shot, a fact that the Soviet government never properly acknowledged in the postwar collective mourning. With the establishment of the state of Israel in 1948, the persecution of Soviet Jews intensified since a Soviet citizen could not, in Stalin's view, simultaneously bear allegiance to two different homelands. Increasingly, Party propaganda equated Soviet Jews with the West and with the West's desire to undermine Soviet influence in the world. The expression "rootless cosmopolitans," a euphemism for Jews, began to appear in the press and in Party propaganda, helping to fuel the anti-Zionist hysteria that had insinuated its way into postwar Soviet society. The problems experienced by Soviet Jews continued to multiply as Jewish quotas were instituted at universities; they experienced similar setbacks in housing and employment. While Stalin's death brought an end to the anti-Semitic purges, Soviet Jews continued for decades to suffer from the Party's exclusionary policies.

TASS reported today the discovery and apprehension by the state security organs of a terrorist group of doctors who planned through deleterious treatment to shorten the lives of prominent figures in the Soviet Union.

Documentary evidence, investigations, the conclusions of medical experts, and the confessions of those arrested established that the criminals, hidden enemies of the people, have been administering deleterious treatment to their patients, thereby undermining their health. Taking advantage of their position as physicians and abusing the patients' trust, the members of the terrorist group in a deliberately vicious manner undermined their health. Intentionally ignoring the data of an objective examination of the patients, these physicians made incorrect diagnoses and thereby killed their patients through improper treatment.

Among the members of this odious gang of murderers are professors of medicine Vovsi, Vinogradov, M. Kogan, B. Kogan, Yegorov, Feldman, Etinger, and Greenstein, and the physician Mayorov.

Comrades A. A. Zhdanov and A. S. Shcherbakov died at the hands of these cruel monsters disguised as doctors and scientists. The murderers confessed that they had incorrectly diagnosed Comrade A. A. Zhdanov's illness; concealing his myocardial infarction, they had prescribed a regimen that is contraindicated in that serious condition, thereby killing the patient. The criminals also shortened the life of Comrade A. S. Shcherbakov: they improperly administered powerful medication, prescribed a harmful regimen, and thereby drove him to his death.

These villains and wreckers tried their hardest to undermine the health of leading military cadres, to put them out of action and weaken the country's defense. Their arrest thwarted the traitors' criminal plans.

It has been established that all members of the terrorist group of physicians were hired agents of foreign intelligence services. The heinous crimes of these monsters, who had lost every human semblance, were controlled by the American and British intelligence services.

Most members of the terrorist group (Vovsi, B. Kogan, Feldman, Greenstein, Etinger, and others) had sold their body and soul to a branch of American intelligence—the international Jewish bourgeois-nationalist organization, the Joint. Numerous irrefutable facts fully demonstrated the repugnant character of this sordid Zionist espionage organization which operated under a cover of philanthropy.

It has been established that professional spies and killers from the Joint, using corrupt Jewish bourgeois-nationalists as their agents and under the guidance of American intelligence, are conducting far-flung espionage, terrorist, and other subversive activities in a number of countries, including the Soviet Union. The monster Vovsi received directives "to exterminate leading cadres of the USSR" from this international Jewish bourgeois-nationalist organization through the intermediaries, Moscow physician Shimeliovich and the well-known Jewish bourgeois-nationalist Mikhoels.

Other members of the terrorist group (Vinogradov, M. Kogan, Yegorov) turned out to be long-standing agents of the British intelligence service.

Aspiring to achieve world domination, the American monopolists and their British accomplices in the aggressive imperialist camp use all the foulest means and methods in their subversive activities. Frantically preparing to unleash a new world war, the American and British imperialists are striving to accomplish what the Nazis failed to do: to create their own subversive fifth column in the USSR. The incredibly cynical and shameless law adopted by the American government, earmarking $100 million for subversive, terrorist, and espionage activities in the socialist countries, serves as irrefutable proof of this intention.

The case of the exposed spies and murderers who were caught red-handed while hiding behind the masks of scientists and physicians demonstrates once more how far the American and British imperialists have gone in their wicked, inhuman activities, and with renewed force exposes their criminal plans before the entire world. The exposure of the gang of doctor-poisoners deals a crushing blow to these vile schemes.

It is the patriotic duty of Soviet citizens never for one minute to forget about the designs of the warmongers and their agents, indefatigably to increase their vigilance, to strengthen in every way possible our armed forces and the state intelligence organs.

The successes achieved by the Soviet people under the leadership of the party of Lenin and Stalin in Communist construction in the USSR are tremendous indeed. Having gained a historic victory in World War II, and within a brief period of time having eliminated the serious consequences of the war, the Soviet people have achieved remarkable successes in the further development of a socialist economy and culture.

Nevertheless, it would be absolutely wrong to derive the conclusion from these facts that the danger of sabotage, subversion, and espionage has already been eliminated, that the ringleaders of the imperialist camp have given up their attempts at subversive anti-Soviet activity.

Comrade Stalin teaches us not to let success generate careless, self-complacent attitudes. The imperialist intelligence services take advantage of this kind of self-complacent, thoughtless attitude for their subversive activities.

The Communist party, Lenin, and Stalin teach the Soviet people that the class struggle does not die down as we advance successfully toward communism, but rather it intensifies. "The more we forge ahead," Comrade Stalin says, "the more successes we achieve, the more the remnants of the defeated exploiting classes will become embittered. They will turn more quickly to sharper forms of confrontation, they will play dirtier tricks on the Soviet state, they will try the most desperate means, the last hope of the doomed."

After the crushing defeat and liquidation of the remnants of the exploiting classes in our country, the international bourgeois lost all support within the Soviet Union in its fight against the Soviet state. It nevertheless keeps trying to use vestiges of capitalism in the consciousness of Soviet citizens for its own purposes. Agents of the foreign intelligence services are ceaselessly looking for weak, vulnerable spots among certain unstable strata of our intelligentsia, which are plagued by subservience to everything foreign, by cosmopolitanism and bourgeois nationalism. These people, with their bourgeois ideology and belief in private ownership, are secret enemies of our people. They become tools of the foreign intelligence services, they harm us and will continue to do so.

To ignore this fact is to permit criminal gullibility, to leave loopholes for evil imperialist intrigues. The doctor-saboteurs were able for a certain period of time to act with impunity because some of our Soviet organs and their leaders had lost their vigilance and became infected with gullibility. As long as we are gullible, there will be sabotage. In order to eliminate sabotage, we must decisively put an end to gullibility, complacency, and relaxed vigilance.

The state security organs must be particularly vigilant. These organs did not expose the terrorist organization of the doctor-saboteurs right away, even though in the not so distant past there were cases in which enemies of the people operated in the guise of physicians. We are referring to the "doctors" Levin and Pletnev who, by incorrect treatment, murdered the great Russian writer A. M. Gorky, and the prominent Soviet statesmen V. V. Kuybyshev and V. R. Menzhinsky. The leaders of the Soviet Ministry of Health also overlooked the sabotage and terrorist activity of these hirelings of the imperialist intelligence services.

Soviet citizens with anger and indignation condemn the crimes of these monstrous poisoners who, under the cover of the noble medical profession, trampled the sacred banner of science and defiled the honor of scientists. The Soviet people will crush the vile traitors of our homeland, the contemptible hirelings of foreign intelligence services, who sold out for dollars and pounds sterling! Our people with anger and indignation also condemn the foreign masters of the criminal gang of murderers: the American and British imperialists. Let them remember that the long arm of justice will reach them as well!

XI

The War Years

It is known as the Second World War in Europe and the United States. On Soviet soil it is called the Great Fatherland War. It began on Soviet territory on 22 June 1941 as German forces invaded the Soviet Union in what was known as Operation Barbarossa. Partly because of the Nazi Soviet Pact of Non-Aggression signed in 1939, to which Stalin stubbornly adhered even as Soviet intelligence was rife with daily reports of Hitler's advance to the east, Stalin and the Soviet high command itself were unprepared for an invasion on three fronts. The German army advanced into the Soviet Union in the north with the object of surrounding Leningrad, while in central Russia the army focused its sights on Moscow. Its southern flank, whose ultimate goal was the oil wells of the Caspian Sea, took Hitler's forces through Ukraine and across Russia's southern steppe toward the Caucasus and Stalingrad.

By the end of August 1941, the northern flank of attack had surrounded Leningrad, effectively cutting it off from all supply routes. Evacuation of the city prior to the siege had been slow, partly due to what Alexander Werth called "wishful thinking" on the part both of the military and the civilian population, neither of whom believed that the German army would advance as far as Leningrad, to say nothing of blockading it. When the Germans completed their land blockade of the city in early September, three million people were still trapped inside with a one-month supply of meat and grains and two months of sugar. The Siege of Leningrad, the longest blockade of a city in history, took as many civilian casualties as did the war at the front. From August 1941 to January 1944, the city was cut off from supplies except over the thirty-mile stretch of Lake Ladoga, known as the Road of Life—ice in winter and water in spring and summer—that served for two years as the only route that brought food and fuel into the city and the evacuees out. Much that was transported over the ice by truck never reached its destination, as the trucks fell through the ice or were shelled by German aircraft.

In the winter of 1941 people began to die of starvation. The bread ration fell to four and a half ounces for office workers, dependants, and children, while the total daily caloric allotment for dependents and children hovered between 466 and 684 calories. By all accounts even that estimate is high. People were reduced to eating whatever they could get their hands on. A jelly made out of sheep guts became a substitute for meat; people caught and ate birds; soup was made out of carpenter's glue, castor oil, hair oil, and wood shavings. People burned books, furniture, whatever they could get their hands on, to stay warm. Every act, as Lidiya Ginzburg detailed in her *Blockade Diary*, was calculated with reference to the number of calories that one could afford to expend on it. Oil and coal ran out during the first winter of the blockade and were replaced by what timber could be felled in the territory surrounding Leningrad. People were fiercely dependent on their ration cards, their ticket to food allocation, but even the cards could not sustain life; there were five cuts in rations in the fall of 1941 alone. Hence it was not unusual for people to begin forging ration cards, appropriating the cards of those who died, or simply stealing them. Being in possession of two ration cards was often the difference between life and death.

By January 1943 Russian troops were able to break through a portion of the southern section of the German blockade, recapture the city of Schusselburg, and reestablish a rail link with the mainland. But for approximately nine hundred days Leningrad suffered as few other cities have in the history of war. By the blockade's end over six hundred thousand had died of starvation, cold, or disease. Four hundred thousand children had been trapped inside the city; those who survived had become orphans.

Ultimately it was Hitler's intent to take Moscow as well, but the gradual strengthening of Soviet forces and the military expertise of Marshal Georgi Zhukov prevented the capital from being taken. Other cities and areas were not as fortunate. The German army moved across southern Russia and Ukraine, taking with it the cities of Kerch, Kharkov, Sevastopol', and Rostov as it moved on toward Stalingrad. The turning point in the war came in November 1942 as the Soviet Army stopped the German forces at the Battle of Stalingrad, precipitating the beginning of the slow German retreat across the southern steppe, with Hitler's forces seeking to recapture the cities that the Soviet Army had retaken. By 1945 Hitler was in full retreat as the Soviet Army pushed his army back through Poland. In September of that year, with the help of the allied forces moving into Germany from the west, Berlin fell and Germany surrendered.

At war's end the Soviet Union was decimated, its economy in shambles and the demographics of the country shattered for the next forty years. The casualty figures were catastrophic, far outnumbering the losses in the country it had just defeated. Ol'ga Verbitskaia discusses the changing statistics on the number of dead and why, with increased access to records and archives, we are able to calibrate more exactly how many were lost in the war. For decades, however, the numbers hovered in the range of twenty million, not counting those who perished in the camps.

This is a war that has remained with the Soviet people for over half a century. And for good reason. It has persisted in personal memory, as there was scarcely a family in the country that did not sustain losses between 1941 and 1945. In Piskarevskoe Cemetery in St. Petersburg, half a million victims of the siege are buried in graves marked only by the year of their death. Inscribed in the wall are the words of the Leningrad poet Ol'ga Berggol'ts: "No one is forgotten, nothing is forgotten."

The war on Soviet soil has been kept alive not only through personal memory but also through official propaganda and collective memorializing. The official version eulogizes the extraordinary feats of heroism both at the front and at home as well as the sacrifices of the Russian people. Over the decades memory became ritualized as Komsomol members bore wreaths to the eternal flames marking the graves of the Unknown Soldier throughout the Soviet Union. Even now it is de rigueur for newlyweds to make a pilgrimage to the eternal flame, as they did in Soviet times. For decades after the war Soviet children were raised on cartoons exhorting them to write letters to the front to support the soldiers. On Veterans Day (Den' Veteranov, November 11) veterans gathered in city squares, their lapels hung heavy with war medals, and Victory Day (Den' Pobedy, May 9) was the day on which the military hardware was paraded on Red Square.

The origins of the cult of the Second World War on Russian soil have much to do with the mood of the country just prior to the German advance. The Soviet Union had just suffered through the worst spate of the purges, in 1936 to 1939. Friends, colleagues, and family members had disappeared into the camps or were exterminated. The terror had acquired a life of its own, as denunciations and show trials became the order of the day. By the late 1930s over fifty thousand officers from the army and the navy had been purged, among them Marshal Tukhachevskii, the major strategist of the Red Army. Others included the commanders of the Far Eastern Army and the Kiev and Belorussian districts. The purges had virtually decimated the ranks of experienced leadership in the Soviet Army on the eve of the Nazi advance into Russia.

In addition to the trauma experienced by the population during the terror, peasants in the countryside had lived through the bitter aftermath of forced collectivization. Moreover, the country was in the midst of yet another Five-Year Plan to industrialize the nation and put its economy on par with that of other developed nations. Faith in Stalin was wavering to such an extent that when the Nazis advanced into the newly acquired territories in the south-western part of the USSR they were welcomed by the local population, who saw them as liberators. It fell to Stalin to find a way to recommit to the war effort a country that had already been scarred by catastrophes since the 1920s (many of which he had induced). He resurrected many of the symbols and rituals from Russia's religious past to turn the war into not only a patriotic but a religious calling. Prince Aleksandr Nevskii, who in 1242 had pushed back the forces of the Teutonic Knights, was recanonized by the Russian Orthodox Church. Even as Stalinist propaganda looked back to the saints and martyrs of the past, it also created new ones as a way of unifying the Soviet people and providing a modicum of spiritual compensation for the enormous losses sustained during the war. One of the best known of the martyrologies produced during this time told of an eighteen-year-old Komsomol girl, Zoia Kosmodemianskaia, who, according to the official story, in the first winter of the war burned a German stable and was tortured and hanged by German forces in a village not far from Moscow. Her body was found by a *Pravda* reporter several weeks later, and the story of her murder became an icon of self-sacrifice and courage that entered the popular imagination as a modern-day saint's life.

During the war whatever questions the Soviet public may have had about the country's lack of preparedness and Stalin's virtual disappearance from the scene during the crucial first ten days of the German advance were suppressed as the country got on with the business of defending itself. In the immediate postwar years, as long as Stalin was alive any expression remotely resembling criticism was completely forbidden. Even as he instigated another round of purges just after the war, he was also the moving force behind film, literature, and Party propaganda that took on the role of recommitting the Soviet people, victorious yet demoralized, to the greater ideological goals of the state. Films such as *The Fall of Berlin* (1949) portray him as the all-knowing commander, coolly and confidently directing the course of the war from the Kremlin while Hitler sinks deeper into paranoia and madness. Buried in his own paranoia Stalin rarely left the Kremlin and took his entertainment from movies such as these that were made expressly for him.

In the Thaw years, after Stalin's death in 1953, writers and filmmakers were given permission to present a more open and honest view of the war. Personal and more complex, Thaw films allowed questions to be asked and characters to make decisions on behalf of their own personal lives as opposed to the goals of the state. By the Brezhnev years, however, the doors again closed as censorship tightened and Stalin and his policies were partially rehabilitated. Only with the coming of glasnost in 1986 were possibilities re-established for an open and honest appraisal of the war on Russian soil. The questions that Viacheslav Kondrat'ev asks in his essay "The Paradox of Nostalgia for the Front," written in 1990 on the anniversary of the Great Fatherland War, were those that had gone unspoken but surely not unthought of for decades: Were the sacrifices worth it? Were there cases of needless sacrifices? How were the Germans allowed such inroads into the country in the initial days of the war? With the demise of the Soviet Union, these questions have become, if anything, more immediate as the country gradually relinquished the territories, the ideology, and the political state for which it had fought in the war. Even as the veterans disappear and there is no longer the same psychological need to keep the war alive in people's memory, that moment in history still carries enormous emotional weight as it feeds into cultural myths of Russia and Russianness far older than the war itself.

June 1941: The Enemy Will Be Destroyed

Leading editorial in Leningrad pravda

At 5:30 on the morning of 21 June 1941 Viacheslav Molotov, Stalin's commissar of foreign affairs, received the German ambassador, who delivered word that Germany intended to invade the Soviet Union. Later that day Molotov announced the Nazi invasion to the Soviet people.

Molotov had been the Soviet signatory to the 1939 Soviet-German Pact of Non-Aggression, signed for the German side by its foreign minister, Joachim Von Ribbentrop. To this day it is generally acknowledged that the Soviet Union had little recourse but to sign the pact. Despite Russia's strained relations with Hitler's Germany, Stalin was afraid of becoming involved in a war on two fronts, against the Japanese in the east and the Nazis in the west. By signing the non-aggression pact the Soviet government banked on not having to fight in the east since the Japanese were allies of the Nazis. What it did not foresee was the Nazi offensive into Soviet territory two years later. Stalin's belief that the Nazis would abide by the terms of the treaty, despite all intelligence to the contrary in the weeks prior to the invasion, is one of several reasons the Soviet forces were defeated as soundly as they were in the first months of the war.

It is a matter of life . . . and death of the Soviet state. Of the life and death of the peoples of the USSR; of the peoples of the Soviet Union being free or falling into slavery. It is important that the Soviet people understand this, that they cease being carefree, that they mobilize, and reorient their work toward a new military mode that shows no mercy to the enemy. —J. Stalin

The government is calling on you, citizens of the Soviet Union to close ranks ever tighter around our glorious Bolshevik Party, around our Soviet government, around our great leader, Comrade Stalin.

Our cause is righteous. The enemy will be defeated. Victory will be ours.
—V. Molotov

Yesterday, at four o'clock in the morning, German troops attacked our country. It was a bandit attack, unseen in its cynicism and treachery, ordered by the leaders of the unbridled Fascist clique, on whom falls the entire responsibility for this unheard-of evil.

Despite the existence of the Non-Aggression Pact between the USSR and Germany, despite the conscientious adherence to the terms of this treaty by the Soviet Union, German Fascism marched its troops against our country, without provocation, and without declaring war.

Despite the peaceful stance of the Soviet Union, despite the fact that neither our troops, nor our air force violated the border even in one location, German Fascism has unsheathed its bloody sword against the Soviet people, against our great socialist motherland.

War has begun. . . . It has been imposed on us by the bloodthirsty Fascist gang that dreams of world domination, that has enslaved and torments many nations whom they have stripped of their independence. We know full well that neither the German workers and peasants nor the laboring intelligentsia imposed this war on us. It was conceived by the despicable gang of Fascist operators possessed by an insane mania for pillage and conquest. No provocative maneuvers, no documents concocted after the fact, no fabrication will conceal the truth that *Fascist Germany is the attacking side.*

Like thieves in the night, the Fascist vultures attacked Soviet cities—Zhitomir, Kiev, Sevastopol', Kaunas, and others. More than two hundred people have been wounded and killed. Air strikes and artillery fire also came from Romanian and Finnish territories. The Soviet people responded to the news of these bandit attacks firmly and courageously.

Across the entire country, across the whole world, radios broadcast the announcement of this event by Comrade V. M. Molotov, Vice Chairman of the Soviet of People's Commissars and People's Commissar for Foreign Affairs. In his declaration made on behalf of the Soviet Government and its leader, Comrade Stalin, Comrade Molotov said:

"The government of the Soviet Union expresses unshakeable confidence that our courageous Army and Navy, and the brave falcons of the Soviet Air Force, will carry out with honor their duty toward their Motherland and the Soviet people, and will strike a shattering blow at the aggressor."

The history of our country has known many barbaric invasions. Bravely and fiercely the Russian people fought for their native land, and not one conqueror succeeded in dominating Russia. Russian warriors always smashed the enemy and more than once entered their European capitals victoriously. Love of the Motherland, fearlessness, and military valor inspired Suvorov's miraculous *bogatyrs*, wonderful soldiers—sons of the people. The military genius of Napoleon was put to shame in Russia, because the masses arose and took up the sacred fight against him. Nobody will ever see our people in slavery to foreign powers!

After the Great October Socialist Revolution, in the difficult Civil War against fourteen capitalist states, the Soviet country emerged victorious. And in other military tests, forced upon us by the bourgeoisie, the Soviet Union stood up for its rights with honor and dignity.

And now, as Comrade Molotov declared, "The Red Army and our entire people will again go forth into a victorious Patriotic War for their Motherland, for honor, and for freedom."

What can be nearer and dearer to the Soviet patriot than our Motherland—the land of all progressive mankind, a mighty union of sixteen socialist republics, a brotherly commonwealth of many nationalities! The great work of communism, labor, creativity, and the happiness of our children—it all flows together in that one beautiful word "Motherland!"

Every honest worker of our country proudly calls himself a citizen of the USSR. Building a new world, working for the well-being and flourishing of the native, Soviet land, defending it, without sparing one's strength, and if need be, without sparing one's life—this is the highest honor!

Only in the Soviet Union can every worker work freely and hone his physical and spiritual strengths. This right has been won under the guidance of the Bolshevik Party, as well as Lenin and Stalin. This right is called simply and majestically—freedom.

For freedom, for honor, and for the Motherland our entire nation of 193 million people rises, firmly united around our glorious Bolshevik Party, our Soviet government, and our great leader Comrade Stalin.

"Each of us," said Comrade Molotov, "must demand from himself and from others, discipline, organization, and selflessness worthy of true Soviet patriots, so that the needs of the Red Army, Navy, and Air Force can be met and victory over the enemy insured."

This announcement was met with enthusiastic responses from across the nation and brought about a huge surge in patriotism. Everywhere wherever Soviet people live, they are taking a firm, unshakeable oath to do *everything to destroy the enemy.*

A resolution of the shop floor meetings at the Kirov factory states, "Our collective of many thousand workers assures our government that we, the workers of the Putilov-Kirov factory, will remain loyal to our military and revolutionary traditions and will carry out with honor any task assigned by the Party and government and fulfill our duty to the Motherland."

At factories such as Elektrosila, Red Vyborzhets, Svetlana, and others bearing the names of Zhdanov and Anisimov, and at many other factories and enterprises of the city that bears Lenin's name, workers demonstrate their solidarity, unity, and loyalty to the glorious traditions of the Petrograd proletariat.

Moved by the overwhelming love for their Motherland, tens of hundreds of patriots submit their request to be sent to the front. The workers of the Marti factory and others are asking the government to increase their workday, so that they may meet the needs of the Army and Navy better. Working men and women stand ready for Stakhanovite shifts. Ignoring their days off, hundreds of workers of the Voroshilov factory came to work yesterday.

Today, by order of the Decree of the Presidium of the Supreme Soviet of the USSR, is the first day of mobilization for those born between 1905 and 1918. Mobilization is being carried out in many military districts, including Leningrad.

By order of the Decree of the Presidium of the Supreme Soviet of the USSR, certain regions of the country, including Leningrad and the Leningrad region, have been placed under martial law.

All these measures of the Soviet government are dictated by the military situation.

The workers of the city of Lenin have always, at all stages of their heroic struggle for socialism, marched in the vanguard of the Soviet people. There is no doubt that even now, in days of this threatening war, the citizens of our glorious city will become models of determination, patriotism, and loyalty to the great cause of Communism.

Iron organization, discipline, and selflessness is what is demanded from every Soviet patriot. The serious situation places on every worker a great responsibility for the fate of the Motherland, requiring him to treat his obligations with dutiful awareness and to tirelessly help the Red Army crush the enemy through selfless labor.

The courage of the warrior, the organization of the citizen, calm, endurance, selfless labor, and heroism of the entire people—herein lies victory.

Our cause is righteous. Our cause will prevail!

Translated by Alexander Rindisbacher

Magnificent Stubbornness (1941–45)

Vasilii Grossman

Vasilii Grossman wrote for the Soviet Army daily newspaper Krasnaia zvezda *(Red Star) during the Second World War and produced over five hundred pages of collected dispatches from the front between 1941 and 1945. With a writer's eye finely developed long before he became a war correspondent, he caught the detail and texture of daily life on the front line. His descriptions of division commanders, snipers, nurses, typists, and ordinary soldiers have an emotional and intellectual range unique among war dispatches. He remained with the Soviet Army from the first days of the invasion to the Battle of Stalingrad, the retreat of the German forces, the Battle of Kursk, and the final surrender of Germany in Berlin in April and May 1945. He wrote about the horrors of Treblinka in July 1944, and at war's end walked through Berlin, speculating, as did many of the Soviet soldiers, why a country with a higher standard of living than the Soviet Union's had felt it incumbent upon itself to attack.*

Grossman was born into a family of Jewish intellectuals in 1905. His literary debut took place before he became a correspondent. Even at the front, while filing dispatches, he wrote one novel, Narod bessmerten *(The People Are Immortal, 1942) and started another,* Za pravoe delo *(For a Just Cause, 1943). Grossman began work on his epic novel* Zhizn' i sud'ba *(Life and Fate) in 1950. As a writer and as a Jew, he wrote not only about the war on Russian soil but about the Nazi atrocities against the Jews and the system of labor camps in the Soviet Union. Over the years he came more and more to identify with his Jewish roots and spoke increasingly on the horrors of totalitarianism as a political system.*

"The Line of the Main Drive" is taken from Grossman's Stalingrad dispatches. In it he describes a Siberian division under the leadership of Colonel Gurtiev. Oddly, Gurtiev's was the only division fighting on the Stalingrad front that was not awarded Guard status or a unit citation after the fighting. It has been suggested that the men whom Grossman described with such empathy were in fact penal battalions that were given assignments that no one was expected to survive. Grossman may have singled them out knowing that the only praise they would receive would be from his pen.

If Gurtiev's division failed to receive the honor it deserved, Grossman's own fate fell on equally hard times. In 1967, under Brezhnev, an enormous memorial was erected in Volgograd (formerly Stalingrad) in honor of the fiftieth anniversary of the Bolshevik Revolution to honor those who had lost their lives in the fierce fighting in and around the city. A quotation taken from "The Line of the Main Drive" was engraved into the wall outside the mausoleum in the memorial complex: "An iron wind struck them in the face and yet they pressed on, and once again a superstitious fear must have seized the enemy: 'Were these men marching to the attack, were they mortal?' " No source was given for the quote. In addition, Grossman's two greatest novels, Life and Fate *and* Forever Flowing, *would have to wait twenty-five years after he died in 1964 to be published in his own country.*

The Line of the Main Drive

The Siberian regiments of which Colonel Gurtiev was Divisional Commander moved into position at night. There had always been something grim and severe about the plant, but nowhere in the world could a grimmer sight have been seen than the sight that met the eyes of the men on that October morning of 1942. The dark towering bulk of the shops, glistening wet rails already touched with rust, a chaos of smashed freight cars, piles of steel girders scattered in confusion over a yard as big as a city square, heaps of coal and reddish slag, huge smokestacks riddled by German shells—such was the zone assigned to the Division. Dark bomb craters yawned in the asphalted square, and fragments of steel rent by the force of the explosions like so many strips of calico were strewn about everywhere.

The Division was ordered to stand fast in front of this plant. Behind it flowed the dark icy waters of the Volga. At night the sappers smashed the asphalt and dug into the stony soil with picks, building trenches. They bored loopholes in the thick walls of the shops, and fixed up shelters in the cellars under the ruined buildings. The regiments under Markelov and Mikhalev were assigned to defend the plant. One of the command posts was set up in the concrete conduit that passed under the structures of the main shops. Sergeyenko's regiment defended the area abutting on a deep ravine running through the workers' hamlets to the Volga. The "Gully of Death" the men and commanders of the regiment called it. Yes, behind them flowed the dark icy waters of the Volga, behind them was the fate of Russia. The Division would have to stand firm to the death.

The last World War had cost Russia great sacrifices and much blood, but at that time the dark force of the enemy had been divided between the Western and Eastern fronts. In this war Russia bore the whole brunt of the German offensive. In 1941 the German regiments were moving from sea to sea. This year, in 1942, the Germans concentrated the entire force of their thrust in a southeasterly direction. The force that had been divided between two fronts of the big powers in World War I, that last year had pressed with all its weight solely on Russia along a front of 3,000 kilometers, this summer and this autumn was brought down like a sledge-hammer on Stalingrad and the Caucasus alone. Even more, here in Stalingrad the Germans intensified the smashing force of their offensive to the utmost. They stabilized their efforts in the southern and central sections of the city, directing the full fire power of innumerable mortar batteries, thousands of guns and aircraft against the northern section of the city and this very plant, the Barricades Plant, that stood in the heart of the industrial district. The Germans assumed that human nature could not stand such a strain, that there were no hearts or nerves but would give way in this frenzied inferno of fire and shrieking metal which shook the earth and rent the air. Here was concentrated the entire diabolical arsenal of German militarism—heavy tanks and flame-throwing tanks, six-barreled mortars, armadas of dive bombers with screaming sirens, shrapnel bombs and high-explosive bombs. Here, tommy-gunners were supplied with explosive bullets, artillerymen and mortar-gunners with thermite shells. Here was concentrated German artillery from small-caliber anti-tank semi-automatics to heavy long-range guns. Here bombs resembling innocent red and green balls were thrown, and air torpedoes that blasted craters the size of a two-storey house were launched. Here, night was as light as day from the glare of fires and flares, and day as dark as night from the smoke of burning buildings and smoke screens. Here, the uproar was as dense as earth, and the brief intervals of silence seemed more terrifying and ominous than the din of battle.

. . . .

"The line of the main drive"—no words are more sinister than these to the ear of a military man; in war there are no words more fraught with menace. Hence it was no matter of chance that it was Colonel Gurtiev's Siberian Division that came to hold the plant on that gloomy autumn morning. Siberians are a sturdy folk, stern, inured to cold, taciturn, sticklers for order and discipline, and blunt of speech. Siberians are a rugged folk, men who can be depended upon. In grim silence they hacked into the stony ground with their picks, cut loopholes in the walls of the shops, and built dugouts, bunkers and communication trenches, preparing to defend themselves to the death.

. . . .

These Siberians who had moved into the great defense line were well prepared. The Division had been thoroughly schooled before it came to the front. Colonel Gurtiev had trained his men assiduously, intelligently, exactingly. He knew that no matter how grueling military training was with its drills in night attacks, tanks driving over men cowering in tiny pits, and long route marches, actual warfare was a hundred times worse. He had confidence in the staunchness and strength of his Siberian regiments. He had tested them en route to the front, and throughout the long journey there had been only one untoward incident, when a man had dropped his rifle from the train. The soldier had jumped out of the car, snatched up the rifle and had run three kilometers to the next station to overtake the front-bound train. Colonel Gurtiev had tested the staunchness of his regiments in the Stalingrad steppe when these men of his, who had not yet been under fire, coolly repulsed a surprise attack of thirty German tanks. He had tested the endurance of his Siberians during their last spurt to Stalingrad, when in two days they had covered two hundred kilometers. Nevertheless, the Colonel peered anxiously into the faces of his men as they took up their position in the main defense zone—in the line of the main drive.

. . . .

Scarcely had the Division dug itself into the rocky Stalingrad soil, scarcely had the Divisional Headquarters installed itself in the deep burrows hollowed into the sand cliffs above the Volga, scarcely had the telephone wires been laid and the keys of the wireless transmitter connecting the command posts with the artillery positions across the Volga begun to tap, scarcely had the murk of night given way to the light of dawn, when the Germans opened fire. For eight hours on end Junkers-87's dived and swooped over the Division's defenses; for eight hours on end, without a minute's pause, wave after wave of German aircraft kept coming over; for eight hours on end sirens shrieked, bombs howled, the earth quaked and the remains of brick buildings crashed; for eight hours on end the air was filled with clouds of smoke and dust, and shell and bomb splinters whined their death song. Anyone who has heard the shriek of air heated to incandescence by bombs, whoever has lived through a harrowing ten minutes' raid of German aircraft, will have some idea of what eight hours of intensive bombing by dive planes mean.

For eight hours on end the Siberians fired from all arms at the German aircraft, and something akin to despair must have seized the Germans when from this burning plant wrapped in a dark pall of dust and smoke, rifle volleys stubbornly continued to crack, machine guns to rattle, anti-tank rifles to send out short bursts, and anti-aircraft guns to keep up their even, wicked fire. It would seem that everything living must have been smashed, destroyed, but the Siberian Division that had dug in neither crumpled up nor went to smash;

it continued to fire stubbornly, deathlessly. The Germans brought their heavy regimental mortars and artillery into action. The monotonous hiss of mortar bombs and the screaming of shells added their note to the wailing of sirens and the roar of bursting air bombs. And so it continued until nightfall. In grim, brooding silence the Red Army men buried their dead. That was the first day—the house-warming. And all night long the German artillery and trench mortar batteries kept up their barrage. Few people slept.

. . . .

All night long the German artillery thundered, and the sun hardly rose again over the battle-scarred earth when forty dive bombers appeared, and again sirens shrieked, and again a dark pall of dust and smoke rose above the plant, covering the ground, the shops and the wrecked railway cars; and even the high factory chimneys were lost in the black cloud. That morning Markelov's regiment came out of its dugouts, shelters and trenches, quit its stone and concrete bunkers, and took the offensive. The battalions moved over mountains of slag, over the ruins of houses, past the granite building of the works office, across the railway track, and through the park in the suburbs. Past thousands of bomb craters they pressed forward, while the German air army released a veritable inferno over their heads. An iron wind struck them in the face and yet they pressed on, and once again a superstitious fear must have seized the enemy: "Were these men marching to the attack, were they mortals?"

Yes, they were mortal men. Markelov's regiment advanced one kilometer, occupied a new position and dug in.

. . . .

Several times a day the German guns and mortars suddenly fell silent, and the shattering action of dive bombers ceased. A tense silence would set in. At such times observers would shout: "Stand by!" and the men in the outposts would reach for incendiary bottles, tank-busters unfastened their canvas cartridge pouches, tommy-gunners wiped their rifles with the palms of their hands, grenade dischargers pulled the grenade boxes closer. These brief moments of silence did not mean a respite. They preceded an attack.

. . . .

In the course of one month, the Germans launched one hundred and seventeen attacks on the regiments of the Siberian Division. There was one awful day when the German tanks and infantry attacked twenty-three times. All twenty-three attacks were repulsed. Every day, except three that month, German aircraft strafed the Division for ten to twelve hours at a stretch.

Three hundred and twenty hours of bombing in one month. The Operations Department arrived at a figure of astronomical proportions in calculating the number of bombs dropped on the division by the Germans, a figure with four noughts. A similar figure gives the number of plane flights made by German bombers over our position. And all this on a front of one and a half to two kilometers long. The roar was enough to deafen all mankind: the squall of fire and metal was enough to set fire to and destroy a whole country. The Germans thought they would break the morale of the Siberian regiments. They thought that they had gone beyond the limit of what human hearts and nerves could stand. But strangely enough the men neither flinched, nor went mad, nor did they lose heart, instead they became even more steadfast and cool. These taciturn rugged Siberians grew even grimmer and more taciturn; their cheeks grew hollow, and their eyes stared gloomily. Here, in the line of the Germans' main drive, even during the brief moments of respite, there was no bantering, no singing or accordion playing. The men here were laboring under a superhuman strain. There were times when they went without sleep for all of three or four days, and it was with a catch at his heart that Colonel Gurtiev, the grey-headed Divisional Commander, heard one soldier say to him softly: "We've got everything we need, Comrade Colonel: 900 grams of bread and hot meals brought up in vacuum containers. regularly twice a day, but somehow I don't feel like eating."

Gurtiev liked and respected his men, and he knew that when a soldier says: "I don't feel like eating," it really must be going hard with him. But now Gurtiev had no misgivings. He knew that there was no power on earth that could dislodge his Siberian regiments.

In the course of this battle, his men and officers had acquired great and cruel experience. The defenses were stronger and more efficient than ever. In front of the factory shops a regular maze of engineering works had sprung up —dugouts, communication trenches, rifle pits. Fortifications had been pushed far forward beyond the shops. The men had learned to maneuver underground swiftly and dexterously—to assemble or disperse, to pass from the shops to the trenches and back by way of the communication trenches, depending on where the enemy aircraft struck their blows or where his tanks and infantry launched their attacks. Underground "whiskers" or "feelers," as the men called them, were set up, and along these the tank-busters got to the German heavy tanks, which had halted some hundred meters from the plant buildings. Sappers mined all the approaches to the plant, carrying the mines under their arms, two at a time. This road from the shore to the plant was six to eight kilometers long and thoroughly raked by German fire. The mines were planted in the darkest hours, just before dawn, and often at a distance of only thirty meters from the fascist lines. In this way approximately two thousand mines were laid under the logs of bombed-out houses, under piles of stones and in shell craters. The men learned how to defend big houses, sending out a solid sheet of fire from the first to the fifth storey. They set up remarkably well-camouflaged observation posts under the very noses of the enemy, made use of craters blasted out by heavy bombs in their defenses and the intricate system of gas mains, oil conduits and sewers under the plant structures. Every day saw an improvement in the contact between the infantry and the artillery, until sometimes it seemed that the Volga no longer lay between the guns and the men, that the all-seeing guns which reacted instantaneously to each movement of the enemy, were right beside the platoons and the command posts.

Together with experience came moral steeling. The Division became a perfected and marvelously co-ordinated body. The men themselves were not aware of the psychological changes that had taken place in them during the month they had spent in this inferno, in the forward positions of the great Stalingrad defense lines. It seemed to them that they were just what they had always been. In their rare free moments, they scrubbed themselves in their underground bathrooms, they were brought their hot meals in thermoses as usual, and bewhiskered Makarevich and Karnaūkhov, looking like peaceful village postmen, continued to bring newspapers and letters from far-off Omsk, Tiumen, Tobolsk and Krasnoyarsk to the forward position in their leather pouches under enemy fire. As before, the men continued to reminisce about their work as carpenters, blacksmiths and peasants. They jeeringly dubbed the German six-barreled mortars "footlers," and dive bombers with their sirens—"screechers" or "musicians." To the German tommy-gunners who threatened them from the neighboring ruins with shouts of: "Hey, Russians, surrender," they replied with loud guffaws saying to one another: "Those Germans must prefer their lousy water to the Volga." It seemed to them that they had not changed and only a newcomer from the opposite bank would look with respectful awe at these men who no longer knew fear, and for whom the words "life" and "death" no longer existed. Only an onlooker could appreciate the iron strength of these Siberians, their indifference to death, their cool determination to bear to the bitter end the stern lot of men holding a defense line to the death.

Heroism had become routine with them, the "style" of this Division and a habit with its men. There was heroism everywhere and in everything—not only in the exploits of the combatants, but also in the work of the cooks peeling potatoes under the blasting fire of thermite shells. Supreme heroism was displayed in the work of the Red Cross nurses—high school girls from

Tobolsk—Tonya Egorova, Zoya Kalganova, Vera Kalyada, Nadya Kasterina, Lyolya Novikova, and many others who dressed wounds and brought water to the wounded men in the height of battle. Yes, if one were to look with the eyes of an onlooker, heroism would be seen in every gesture of the men of this Division. It would be seen in Khamitsky, the commander of the signalers' platoon, as he sat on a slope near the dugout peacefully reading a novel while roaring German dive bombers pounded the ground. It would be seen in Liaison Officer Batrakov as he carefully wiped his spectacles, placed a report in his dispatch case, and set off on a twelve-kilometer tramp through the "Gully of Death" as matter-of-factly and calmly as if he were going for a quiet stroll on a Sunday. It would be seen in tommy-gunner Kolosov who was buried up to his neck in earth and debris when a bomb burst in his dugout and who merely turned his head and winked merrily at Svirin, second in command. It would be seen in Klava Kopylova—the buxom, red-cheeked Siberian Staff typist—who sat down to type an order of the day, was buried under, dug out and moved into another bunker where she continued her typing, but was buried under a second time, dug out again and moved into a third dugout, where she calmly finished typing the order and brought it to the Divisional Commander for his signature. Such were the people who stood in the line of the main drive.

It is the Germans themselves who know their indomitable persistence best of all.

One night a prisoner was brought into Svirin's dugout. His hands and his face with its stubble of grey beard were absolutely black with filth. The woolen muffler around his throat was a tattered rag. He belonged to one of the spearhead crack units of the German army, had been through all the campaigns and was a member of the Nazi party.

After the usual interrogation Svirin asked him:

"What do the Germans think of the resistance in the area of the plant?"

The prisoner was standing with his shoulder against the stone wall of the dugout.

"Oh!" he exclaimed, and suddenly burst into tears.

Yes, the men who stood in the line of the main drive were real men, their nerves and their hearts held out.

At the end of the third week the Germans launched a determined attack on the plant. Preparations for this attack were conducted on a scale the world has never witnessed before. For eighty hours aircraft, heavy mortars and artillery pounded the Division's defenses. Three days and three nights were one long chaos of smoke, fire and thunder. The hissing of bombs, the screeching squall of shells coming from six-barreled mortars, the howling of the heavy shells, and the long-drawn-out shriek of sirens were ear-splitting enough in themselves. But they only preceded the blasts that followed. The jagged flames of explosions stabbed the air while the piercing scream of shattered metal rent the skies. For eighty hours this kept up. Then the barrage was lifted and immediately, at 5 a.m., German heavy and medium tanks, drunken hordes of tommy-gunners, and infantry regiments came over the top. The Germans succeeded in breaking through to the plant; their tanks roared beneath the walls of the shops; they split up our defenses and cut off the divisional and regimental command posts from the forward position. It would seem that deprived of direction the Division was bound to lose its capacity for resistance and that the command posts, having come within direct reach of the enemy's blows, must be destroyed.

But astonishing to relate, every trench, every pillbox, every rifle pit and fortified ruin turned into a stronghold with its own direction and its own system of communication. Sergeants and privates became commanders, and skillfully and efficiently repulsed the attacks. In this dire and perilous hour, commanders and staff officers turned their command posts into forts and themselves beat off attacks like rank-and-file privates. Chamov repulsed ten assaults. The strapping, red-headed tank commander who had been assigned to defend Chamov's command post, having fired his last round, scrambled out of his tank and held the approaching German tommy-gunners at bay with a shower of stones. The Regimental Commander himself manned a mortar gun. Regimental Commander Mikhalev, the Division's favorite, was killed when a bomb hit his command post. "Our father's been killed," mourned the Red Army men. Major Kushnarov, who replaced Mikhalev, transferred his command post to a concrete main that ran beneath the plant. For several hours Kushnarov, Dyatlenko—his Chief of Staff—and six commanders fought at the entrance to this conduit. They had several cases of hand grenades and with these grenades they repulsed every attack of the German tommy-gunners.

This battle, unparalleled in ferocity, lasted several days. The fight now was not for individual buildings and shops, but for each step of a staircase, for a corner in some narrow corridor, for each machine-tool, for the passageway between them, for the gas main. Not a single man in the Division yielded an inch of ground in this battle. If the Germans did succeed in capturing some spot, it meant that not a single Red Army man had survived there to defend it. All fought like the giant, red-headed tank driver whose name Chamov never learnt, like sapper Kossichenko—who pulled the safety rings from the hand grenades with his teeth, since his left hand had been shattered. It was as if the dead had passed on their strength to the survivors, and there were moments when ten resolute bayonets held an area which had been defended by a whole battalion. Time and again the shops passed from the hands of the Siberians to the Germans, only to be recaptured by the Siberians. The Germans captured a number of buildings and shops.

In this battle the German attacks reached their peak. The onslaught in the line of the main drive reached its highest potential. Just as though they had lifted too great a weight, some spring that had brought their battering ram into action seemed to snap.

The curve of the German pressure began to subside. Three German divisions, the 94th, the 305th, the 389th, were pitted against the Siberians. The one hundred and seventeen infantry attacks cost the Germans five thousand lives. The Siberians held out against this superhuman strain. In front of the plant lay two thousand tons of scrap metal that had recently been tanks. Thousands of tons of shells and bombs had fallen on the plant grounds and structures. But the Division withstood the pressure. It did not yield its fatal ground. Not once did it look back. It knew that behind it was the Volga, and the fate of the country.

One cannot help wondering how this magnificent stubbornness was forged. It was, of course, compounded of both national character and the realization of a great responsibility, of both rugged Siberian obstinacy and splendid military and political schooling and stern discipline. But I want to mention one other trait that played no little part in this grand and tragic epic—the astonishing morale, the firm attachment that knit together the men of the Siberian Division, and the spirit of spartan modesty typical of the commanders of this Division. It was revealed in trifles, and in their intelligent, quiet efficiency. I saw this affection that bound together the men of the Division in the grief with which they spoke of their fallen comrades. I heard it in the words of one of the men of Mikhalev's regiment who to my question: "How're things going?" replied: "Ekh, how're things going—we've lost our father."

I detected it in the touching meeting between Colonel Gurtiev and Zoya Kalganova, a battalion nurse, when she returned after having been wounded for a second time. "My dear, dear girl, welcome back," he said warmly as he moved forward swiftly with outstretched arms to meet the girl with her wan face and close-cropped head. It was the way a father would greet his own daughter. This affection and faith performed miracles.

It was this affection and faith in one another that helped Red Army men take the place of commanders in the midst of some terrific battle, that helped commanders and men from Headquarters to get behind a machine gun, to fling hand grenades and bottles of incendiary liquid to repulse German tanks attacking command posts.

Three German soldiers walking down a desolate street, Stalingrad, September 1942. Photo by Rothkopf and Heine. Courtesy of the Library of Congress, Prints and Photographs Division, LC-USZ62–75078.

The women and children will never forget their husbands and fathers who fell on the great Volga sector. These splendid, loyal men can never be forgotten. Our Red Army can honor the sacred memory of those who fell in the line of the enemy's main drive in only one way that will be worthy of the dead, by an offensive that knows no barrier, an offensive that will liberate our occupied territory. We are confident that the hour of this offensive is nigh.

November 20, 1942
Stalingrad Front

Wait for Me (1941)

Konstantin Simonov

Konstantin Simonov (1915–79), like Vasilii Grossman, was a war correspondent. He was also a poet, novelist, and playwright. His poem "Zhdi menia" (Wait for Me) was written in 1941 and was part of a larger collection he wrote for his wife while he was covering the war. Simple, clear, and devoid of metaphor, the poem won the hearts of soldiers at the front and of those whom they had left behind. Circulated in Pravda and in newspapers at the front beginning in 1942, the poem was clipped out by soldiers and carried into battle. They frequently sent it home to their wives and girlfriends who, in turn, wrote answers that were often published in the front line press.

"Wait for Me" and another poem by Simonov, "Kill Him," became classics of the Soviet war years. Both provided the sustaining myths for those at the front and those at home. At a certain point in the war, the necessity to defend the Motherland was transmuted into a level of rage against the Germans that for many Russians justified any act of violence or atrocity committed against the enemy. The rage found expression in "Kill Him," in which Simonov urges, "Kill a German / Kill him soon." The second myth, articulated in "Wait for Me," was that all would be as it once was when the soldiers returned home. The reality, not written about at the time, was that conditions and the stress of war were such that not all the women waited for the men who loved them. It was only during the Thaw under Khrushchev that such topics were finally brought out into the open, notably in films such as Letiat zhuravli (The Cranes Are Flying, 1957) and Ballada o soldate (Ballad of a Soldier, 1959) that depict the complicated circumstances that left spouses unable to bear the waiting. Whatever the ultimate outcome, Russian soldiers advanced and retreated with the poems in their pockets that sustained them in deeply personal ways.

Wait for me, and I'll come back,
Wait and wait, my dear.
Wait, even when yellow rain
makes you feel so sad,
wait when snowstorms rage around,
wait in summer's heat,
wait if other women don't,
forgetting days gone by.
Wait, when from far far away
letters never come,
wait when they've all had enough,
those who also wait.

Wait for me, and I'll come back,
don't think well of all
those who think they know for sure
the time's come to forget.
Let my mother and my son
think I've gone for good,
let the friends who won't still wait
sit down by the fire,
and drink that bitterest of toasts,
for me to rest in peace . . .
Wait. And when they raise that glass,
wait to do the same.

Wait for me, and I'll come back,
every death done down.
Those who didn't wait can say
good luck brought me through.
They will never understand—
when I was under fire,
with your waiting it was you
kept me safe and sound.
Only we will ever know
how I stayed alive:
you knew how to wait, that's why,
more than all the rest.

Translated by G. S. Smith

Smolensk Roads (1941)

Konstantin Simonov

For Russians, poetry has never been a genre simply consigned to the bookshelf. It has always been something living, recited in public, and committed to memory. Poets throughout the Soviet era would recite their verse in public squares and on street corners. And always they commanded an audience.

The Second World War brought with it a veritable groundswell of verse and song that soldiers took with them into battle and that those who were left behind sung, recited, and read to sustain themselves. "Smolensk Roads" by Konstantin Simonov was, along with "Wait for Me," one of the most popular wartime poems. Its popularity undoubtedly stemmed from the fact that Simonov appealed to something that transcended politics and ideology. Soviet soldiers were fighting a war for a leader and a political system that many would argue had failed them miserably in the 1930s, with forced collectivization, the shock work of industrialization, and most spectacularly the purges. "Smolensk Roads" calls forth an image of the Russia of old—Holy Russia, Mother Russia with its fields and forests, and the people who from time immemorial have inhabited it. "The wail of the widow" and the women who wait at home become Simonov's most eloquent incarnation of Mother Russia.

Here Simonov skillfully evokes religious emotionalism and the sacred past of ancient Russia—a theme that fit in later with the official softening of antireligious policy and clearly matched the deeply authentic moods of popular patriotism that the war augmented.

To A. Surkov

You remember, Alyosha, the roads of Smolensk province,
And how the evil rains poured down and gave no rest,
And milk in jars was offered by tired women
Who hugged each jar like a babe against the breast.

How they quietly wiped their tears and whispered to God
"Lord, save them," praying, as we rolled,

And again described themselves as the wives of soldiers
As the custom was in great Russia of old.

Measured by tears rather than versts, and lurching,
The paths wound into the hillocks, lost in space,
Villages, villages, villages, with churchyards,
As if all Russia had met in this huddled place,

As if behind each village-bound, all day,
Protecting the living with the cross of their hands,
Our great-grandfathers in village *mirs* were praying
For the unbelieving heirs of their broad lands.

I see my country—I think you know it, Alyosha—
Not in the townhouses where time idled by,
But in the hamlets with their simple crosses
On Russian graves, where our forefathers lie.

Not vainly, I trust, has war borne me along
These village-ways, to hear with anguished heart
The wail of the widow and the women singing,
And learn for the first time here the country-part.

You remember near Borisov the wooden shack,
The girls lamenting the dead man day and night,
The grey-haired woman in the velvet jacket,
The old man dressed for meeting death, in white.

What could we say to them? How console their tears?
But the old woman knew why we looked so stern,
And read and answered our grief, "Now go my dear ones,
And we'll be waiting here when you return."

Aye, we'll be waiting, all the cornfields rustled,
Waiting for your return, the forests cried.
Alyosha, I heard them in the midnight hush,
The voices always echoing at our side,

And so, as the Russian custom ordered, grimly
The homes were burned and the heavy winds were grey;
Before our very eyes, our comrades, dying
Tore their shirts down the front, the Russian way.

So far we've come in safety through the bullets,
Though thrice I thought I'd seen my last of earth.
How proudly have I come to know in fullness
The loved and bitter country of my birth.

Proud that it's destined for my death-bed,
Proud that a Russian mother gave us to the day,
And proud that Russian women bid us proud farewell
With threefold kisses, in the Russian way.

Kandalaksha, November, 1941

The Blockade Diary of

A. I. Vinokurov (1942–43)

Aleksei Ivanovich Vinokurov was born in 1904 in the Poddorskii region of Leningrad Oblast. He worked as a geography teacher in Middle School No. 5 and No. 72 in the Petrograd section of the city and during the blockade lived on Soviet Street, No. 2, apartment 15. Every day after he came home from work during the blockade he meticulously recorded in his notebook all the day's events that seemed important to him.

On 12 February 1943 Vinokurov was arrested by the Leningrad branch of the NKVD. His diary was produced as evidence that he had systematically engaged in "counterrevolutionary, anti-Soviet agitation in which he had slandered the Soviet system, Soviet life, the Red Army, and the press." He was sentenced to death by firing squad and all his possessions were confiscated.

In March 1999, by order of the procurator of St. Petersburg, Vinokurov was rehabilitated.

Friday. 17 January [1942].
I went down to the Neva for water. Brought back four buckets on a little sled. The distance between Moscow station, near which I live, and Kalashnikov [Sinopskii—Compiler] Embankment is about three kilometers round trip. I got tired not so much from dragging the water as from lifting it from the ice hole onto the shore and up to my third-story apartment. I can imagine how difficult it is for those who live on the sixth or seventh floors. I'm not surprised that those inhabitants of the city who have lost their strength from hunger don't bother themselves with the consequences of using water from the Fontanka, Moika, or Obvodnyi Canals.

18 January.
I wasted the whole day registering for ration cards.

19 January
My neighbor, S. A. B., died. The mortality rate in the city has reached monstrous proportions. During the last week in our apartment house twelve people have died and three have disappeared without a trace, probably be-

Bodies on the street in Leningrad during the blockade. Courtesy of ITAR-TASS.

cause they died somewhere on the street. Relatives have tried but have been unable to find them. In our apartment the number of survivors has decreased by half. Two have perished fighting in regions outside the city, three have died from exhaustion and one is currently in the Red Army.

In certain apartments no one remains.

20 January

Recently Nevskii Prospekt has become a quiet street covered in snow. Buildings which have not been repaired in a long time look even gloomier than usual. They have become disfigured by the defense installations made of boards and sand alongside the windows of the lower floors. The street itself has not suffered much from bombing and fires. Bombing raids partially destroyed two buildings (on the corner of Fontanka and on the corner of Ekaterinskii Canal, respectively). Half of Nevskii's storefronts in the Gostinnyi Dvor have burned down (the ones that are close to the city Duma building). Most of the stores are closed, including the *Passazh*. Not all of the movie theaters are operational due to lack of lighting.

Bakeries and ration stores are open. They are lighted by primitive oil lamps.

It's hard to understand why they keep the ration stores open day after day. The operators have absolutely nothing to do. During January the population has received no rations besides bread. Dining halls and "restaurants" are open. Dishes, consisting usually of a plate of hot water with a little bit of cereal, are given out by ration card to the members of organizations, and to those who work in the dining halls. In certain dining halls it is possible to get bread by ration card, which avoids the necessity of having to go to the bakery.

At the corner of Sadovaia, by the *Passazh*, there is a line for water for days on end. The water they get from a well in the road. Everyone dips in their pail which undoubtedly pollutes the source.

The tram hasn't run since the first days of December. The rails are not visible. They lie under a thick layer of snow. Passers-by move slowly down the sidewalks and roads. There are several times fewer of them than a year ago. Automobiles rarely go by; the ones that do are mainly of the gas-generator variety. Many of the passersby are pulling small sleds. For the most part they pull firewood, water and corpses without coffins. Not everyone can afford a coffin and thus they are limited to wrapping or sewing up the deceased in a bed sheet or blanket. The people who pass by have exhausted, worried faces. You often meet people who are swollen from hunger. Against the grayness of some of their faces the whites of their eyes protrude. These are the ones who haven't washed themselves in a long time.

. . . .

1 March [1942]

The public library is closed. Snow drifts covered in dirt tower above it. There isn't even a path to the vestibule of the reading hall. It is obvious at once that no one has gone there in a long time. I tried to get books at the Central Library on Fontanka. There they told me that the library only serves readers who registered last year, and they advised me to go to the Nekrasov Library on Staro-Nevskii Prospekt.

In the Nekrasov Library I found the same disorder as in the Central Library: they directed me to go to other libraries, including the Central one.

2 March

A man who was about forty years old walked into the dining hall, and after he stood in line for about two hours, received two portions of soup and *kasha* according to his ration card. He was able to eat the soup, but his *kasha* sat untouched. A waitress approached him and realized that he had died sitting at the table. They sent for a policeman. The public did not disperse. Everyone was interested in who would get the *kasha*.

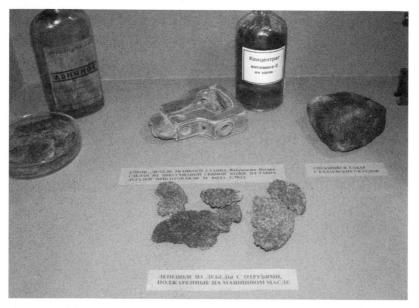

Museum of the Blockade, St. Petersburg. Exhibit showing diaries kept by Leningrad residents during the blockade. Photo courtesy of Adele Barker.

Photograph of food, Museum of the Blockade, St. Petersburg. Clockwise, from top left: linseed oil; part of a loom from the Nogin Factory made from pressed pigskin (from parts like this twenty-two different kinds of food were prepared); Vitamin C concentrate from pine needles; cakes of sugar from Badaevsky storehouses; flat cakes made from swan mixed with bran and fried in car oil; yeast cutlets. Photo courtesy of Adele Barker.

4 March

I went to the bathhouse. There was no line. The temperature in the change room was lower than zero degrees, and in the washroom it wasn't any higher than 10 or 12 degrees. The water was slightly warmer. Visitors didn't linger for long. In the men's bathhouse they now serve women, since all the male bathers have either died off or been drafted into the army.

7 March

In the middle of the day German war planes flew over the city. The anti-aircraft guns fired at them, *but just like always*, they missed [this has to do with the fact that German airplanes flew at a predetermined altitude and the anti-aircraft rounds could not reach them—Compiler]. The air sirens did not go off.

8 March

Many factories, establishments and educational institutions were evacuated into unoccupied territory. Directions are frequently broadcast on the radio on behalf of the administration of the institutes concerning the registration of surviving professors, teachers, and students. Rumors are circulating around the city that more than half of the professors and teachers have died from hunger.

9 March

Recently, after a three-month suspension, several movie theaters have opened and the "Musical Comedy" theater has begun operations anew.

In the building of the Aleksandrinskii Theater "Sil'va," "Maritsa," "Baia-dera" and other films equally as interesting are now being shown. Shows begin at 11:00 in the morning and 4:00 in the afternoon. Tickets are bought up like hot cakes well before the show time. By the entrance to the theater, enterprising young people exchange tickets for cigarettes. For every ticket they get five to ten cigarettes, and sometimes they agree to sell the tickets for money, demanding five times the value of the ticket. Today they showed "Maritsa." The theater was packed. The audience was made up mostly of soldiers, waitresses from the dining halls, women attendants from the food stores, in short, normal folks who in these awful times were supplied not only with a piece of bread but with a lot more as well.

In the hall and on the stage it was so cold that you could see the performers' breath while they were singing, just like you can when you see people chatting on the street in frosty weather. I liked the show. The performers were treated to a nice applause.

Translated by Kenny Cargill

The Diary of a Red Army Soldier (1941–42)

S. F. Putiakov

Semen Fedorovich Putiakov was born in 1905 in the Pustynkinskii region of the Kalinin oblast. He was called up for service in July 1941 and was arrested on 24 January 1942 for "anti-Soviet activity." Throughout the months he spent in the Leningrad region during the blockade he kept a diary that filled four notebooks. They were subsequently seized and produced by a Military Tribunal as evidence of his anti-Soviet agitation. He was shot on 13 March 1942 and posthumously rehabilitated on 6 December 1967.

22 January [1942]. 1:30 P.M. On guard.
Today is the anniversary of Bloody Sunday. The weather is warmer. It snowed. Good, powdery snow. Today they say 100 grams of bread will be added to our rations as well as other kinds of food. Right now there is hope for life. One can wait for the spring and summer. It is simply hard to guess what comes next. At the moment we are completely inoperative.

News from the front is good. They took back Mozhaisk. Things are progressing towards a purging of our territory.

23 January. 1:40 P.M. On guard.
Yesterday evening they brought us clean underwear. There is nowhere to do the washing. We were forced to do it right here, in the dugout. I melted some snow and washed my head, less so the rest of my body. It seems like everything eased up. I hadn't washed myself since 26 December. Yesterday and today I received 400 grams of bread. The rest of the ration stayed the same. In general I can only hope. There is something to hope for. The weather today is strange. The frost melted a little as it got warmer. It was −28 degrees. In general things are fine. Standing is sort of hard, but on the other hand it's good for fighting back fascists. I will live.

The swelling on my face has gone down somewhat, but my legs have swollen up. I can now stand cheerfully. The only trouble is that there are no letters. Why, I don't know. They've made this blockade around me and there is no way out. Today I am going to write Misha and Sapron in Rakh'ia and get after them for not writing me.

24 January. 1:45 P.M. On guard.

There was a harsh frost yesterday. Today there is an even bigger one. It is difficult to keep standing. It's a small thing, though. Today I received joyful news. They dealt a healthy blow to the fascists. They say they've taken back Velikie Luki. Things then are fine. Today they gave us something new in our rations. They've started to give out three meals a day. At breakfast I purchased one portion of meat and I bartered cigarettes for another half portion. I ate everything and I felt a little easier.

The frost is minus 30–35 degrees. Yesterday and today too there was wind. I dreamed about mama. I fell asleep with her. But for some reason she didn't talk to me. She didn't see her child. Life, life—I hope it gets better soon. They're bringing lunch now.

Note of "the detainee."

25 January. 4:35 P.M.

Today I returned from guard duty. I lied down on my plank bed, in the same place that I had occupied before my guard duty. A rival had come upon my spot. They proposed that I leave and cede the place to this person. I wouldn't agree. I demanded they show me another spot. They wouldn't show me to another place and ordered that I leave. I didn't obey the order and for that I was to be arrested for two days. The impudent Zakrutkin carried out this order from the assistant to the platoon commander, Efremov. Tomorrow I am going to get out and I will write a report about this illegal action. Scoundrels. Murderers. *In this company many people have already died, all at the hands of Sergeant Major Orlov, Lieutenant Zakrutkin and others. They uphold the prison-like conditions.*

I am going to take measures. Otherwise I will die. Today my face swelled up. I feel terrible hunger. As ill luck would have it my half-rations of bread were stolen. Scoundrels. *Lord, Lord, when will this torture end? I have become something inhuman.* Until now, until the 38th BAO [Aerodrome Defense Battalion], I resembled a person. And now! I am going to write letters tomorrow evening. The assistant to the platoon commander wouldn't let me have any paper.

They say that tomorrow they will add to the bread ration and probably hand out a ration of other types of food. The sooner the better. The head of food rationing didn't answer me. I can't wait.

Translated by Kenny Cargill

Tragic Numbers: The Lives Taken by the War (1995)

Ol'ga Verbitskaia

Ol'ga Verbitskaia's essay points to the world of nebulous facts that governed history and record-keeping for much of the Soviet era. Varying numbers of war casualties were doled out to the Soviet population depending on the political and ideological needs of the era. The numbers released to the Soviet people immediately after the war were gross underestimates. Under Khrushchev they were increased to twenty million, though it was never made clear how this figure was calculated. By 1991 the official figure was raised to twenty-seven million. Memoirs written during the Thaw period aided in calibrating the figures more exactly. However, those same memoirs were subsequently doctored during the more conservative Brezhnev era by Voenizdat, the military publishing house, or denied publication altogether, resulting in prescriptive works that failed to tell the real story of the early defeats and the effect of the purges on the Soviet military high command. The gradual opening of archives since the mid-1980s and the publication of memoirs since that time have provided a more honest assessment of the war and have enabled demographers to arrive at the tragic figures that Verbitskaia quotes.

The Soviet Union's human losses in the Great Patriotic War remain to this day an open question. Thus far, only the irreplaceable losses of servicemen have been counted with approximate precision. But, as we know, those who were killed on the field of battle and who died in hospitals constitute only a small fraction of the total number of lives lost in the war.

The first "official," generally accepted estimate of the USSR's total losses in the Great Patriotic War was released by Joseph Stalin in February 1946. These figures, published in the journal *Bolshevik*, report that "As a result of the German invasion, the Soviet Union suffered irreplaceable losses of about seven million people in battle, in the occupation, and in the subjection of the Soviet people to hard labor." Why precisely this figure was given is difficult to understand. But initially there was always a tendency to underestimate: The

Cold War had begun, and the Soviet leadership made explicit efforts to conceal from its watchful former allies the true scale of the losses sustained by the country.

At the beginning of 1961, Nikita Khrushchev announced a different figure to the international community, indicating that, "The war took the lives of twenty million Soviet citizens." Although this does not hold up to scholarly scrutiny either, it became the accepted number for almost a quarter-century, making its way into all scholarly and literary works. This, of course, did not mean that the scholarly research on losses ended once and for all. Even in the Brezhnev years of stagnation, attempts were made to come up with more precise numbers. By that time, Russian historical demographers had already worked out a specific methodology that allowed for the correction of falsified figures.

After the war—and primarily at the beginning of the 1950s—almost every country that had taken part in the war organized a census to gather rough estimates of the scale of their losses. The USSR deferred such a census for a good length of time, carrying it out only in 1959. Factoring in the demographic changes of thirteen and a half years, from May of 1945 to 1959, this was a significant period of time. Specialists had to use a wide variety of historical sources, such as voter lists in the elections of the Supreme Soviet of the USSR from 1946 through 1954.

According to these data, as of the middle of 1941, the population of the USSR (including territories incorporated after the beginning of the Second World War, from 1939–40) was 196.7 million people. In the beginning of 1946, the population totaled 170.5 million—that is, 26.2 million less than before the war.

On the basis of strategic dispatches from the front, the materials of the General Staff, and reports from military medical headquarters, the total number of losses among registered members of the Armed Forces, along with border and internal security forces, was determined as 8,668,000 people. The remaining losses—about eighteen million—were among the civilian population of occupied territories and those adjacent to the front.

At an international research conference, which took place in March 1995 at the Moscow Institute of Russian History in the Russian Academy of Sciences (RAN), the majority of experts agreed on the following numbers. Of eighteen million civilians approximately 8,500,000 people died of famine, bombings, artillery cross-fires, unlivable conditions, and back-breaking labor in occupied territories and those bordering the front. 2,165,000 more perished as a result of forced labor in Germany. The number of those deliberately annihilated as a consequence of Hitler's genocidal politics (those shot or killed in ghettos, jails, and concentration camps) totaled approximately 7,420,000 people.

In sum, as we see, the losses among the civilian population were twice as high as the battle casualties of the USSR Armed Forces.

Alongside direct losses, demographers also account for indirect losses from increased mortality during wartime; that is, premature death from deteriorating quality of life, unsatisfactory medical care, and extraordinary stress. Losses are also associated with declining birth rates, which during wartime dropped to 30–50 percent of their prewar levels. These losses total twenty-two to twenty-three million people.

Thus, based on the data we have, the USSR's direct and indirect population losses in the years of the Great Patriotic War can be estimated at forty-eight to fifty million people. In the future these numbers will undoubtedly become more exact.

Translated by Larissa Rudova and Rebecca Holz

The Paradox of Nostalgia for the Front (1990)

Viacheslav Kondrat'ev

Trauma and its aftereffects are memorialized and dealt with differently throughout the world. In the sixty-plus years since the end of the Great Fatherland War, Soviets have been remembering victims, celebrating the victories, watching films dealing with the war years, and visiting monuments erected in memory of the war. The act of remembering has continued to be a very public activity across the former Soviet Union. Monuments, popular culture, and orchestrated national holidays have all served as constant reminders of the sacrifices Russians made on behalf of their rodina, *or Motherland. That today these holidays are still celebrated, but on a more muted scale than in the past, is due in part to simple demography; fewer are alive who remember the war years. But just as important is the resculpting of memory that has taken place, as Party mandate has been largely replaced by an altogether different order of reconstituting the past.*

This essay by Viacheslav Kondrat'ev (1920–93) illustrates the new face of an old war, no longer filtered through public and official discourse. Written in 1990, a year before the collapse of the Soviet Union, it appeared in the major literary newspaper Literaturnaia gazeta *(Literary Gazette). Kondrat'ev spoke out about those aspects of the war that lay outside the parameters of the officially sanctioned myth. He spoke openly about the ill-advised actions of those in command who threw their soldiers into battle at any cost; about the stripping of Soviet corpses by their fellow countrymen, presumably due to lack of supplies and equipment during the war; and of the discernible improvement in living conditions after the war. For Kondrat'ev the lessons to be learned from these years were not those that Soviet children were taught in school but those garnered in the brief interlude of freedom from ideology and censorship that the war brought and peacetime took away.*

The war, as this piece articulately illustrates, was a complicated moment in Soviet history. It became even more so in 1990 as the Soviet Union was unraveling and the political system and ideology for which millions fought stood on the brink of its own demise. The question "What did we fight for?" was uppermost in the minds of many who had lived through the Soviet years. Soldiers were exhorted to fight "for the Motherland, for Stalin," but like soldiers everywhere, Soviet soldiers fought in the

*war for different reasons. Kondrat'ev suggests that Communist ideology played a
negligible role in what motivated the army. And yet just as telling is the fact that
although card-carrying members of the Communist Party were arrested and sent to
the Gulag, to the end of their days they retained their belief in the Party and in the
system. From the beginning of the war in 1941, Communist Party membership grew
from 3.8 million to 5.7 million in 1945 despite the decimation of the population and the
high command of the Red Army in the purges. Whether it was ideology or belief in
something that transcended ideology that incited soldiers on the battlefield may
ultimately be unanswerable. Kondrat'ev's essay only complicates the argument.*

The poet Yuri Belash who served at the front in World War II has a poem
entitled, "What Is Most Terrifying in War." One soldier says tanks; another,
bombings; a third, artillery fire; and a fourth, "smoking a cigarette off to the
side, suddenly comes to a firm conclusion: 'Why're you arguing senselessly?
After all, the most terrifying thing in war, brothers, is when there's no more
tobacco . . .'" To me, having experienced everything the soldiers of Belash's
poem are arguing about, the most terrifying aspect of war seemed to be what
I saw at the break of day on the front lines—corpses of our soldiers stripped
down to their very undergarments. Their underwear blended in with the
snow, making only their heads, hands, and feet clearly visible. As though
stripped of their very bodies, they appeared to us through the gray pre-dawn
haze with frightful dark blotches—the picture struck me like a knife through
the heart, with a pain that has yet to pass.

All the dead on the front lines were undressed—on the battlefield, only
those closest to the front were stripped, while those who were further inside
enemy lines, those whom our "trophy teams" could not quite reach, remained clothed, looking like they were not quite so pitiful, not quite so
expendable. As a result, I thought it would be better to be killed closer to the
German lines because our trophy hunters would be afraid to crawl there. At
the very least, one would not be lying there humiliated by being stripped of
one's clothes. Although I understood in my head that there was not enough
of what the army needed—even uniforms already pierced with bullets, covered in grit, and washed in blood—my heart could not take it: death had not
become so ordinary or commonplace, something that was always nearby—it
was still in some way mysterious—and a dead person was somehow holy. To
undress him and drag him into a communal grave seemed like sacrilege. I
must say that even having seen a lot in war, I never got used to that.

The war ended forty-five years ago, and I dream of it less frequently at
night now, though earlier I dreamt of it often—especially before I took a trip
outside of Rzhev to my former front line. There in the forest, twenty years

Young soldiers at war memorial, Moscow, 1978. Courtesy of Adele Barker.

following the battles, lay remains, just skulls now of those who were with me, of those with whom, perhaps, I ate out of the same mess kit, with whom I smoked one of my hand-rolleds from dry, two-year-old paper since the "most terrifying thing in war," by conclusion of the fourth soldier of Belash's poem, also happened to us—there was no tobacco, just like there was practically no bread, usually only a dried crust each per day, just like there was no good, thick soup—only half a mess kit of thin porridge for two men. Then, in the 1960s, nostalgia for the front lines imposed itself upon me, forcing me to go to the battle grounds, to make my way almost twenty versts in the dirt and slush of the road from the station in Chertolino to the former front. Yes—it was nostalgia and dreams that made me go, because I dreamed most often exactly of a return trip to those places where I began the war. In my dreams, I did not recognize the former front, though while I was awake, it appeared to me just as it was. In the forest every step of the way, I was met with helmets, mess kits, soldiers' boots, zinc casings from gun cartridges, ammunition shells, rusted grenade casings, and, here and there, jutting up out of the ground, rusted, unexploded German mines.

It is inexplicable, the phenomenon of nostalgia for the front that torments us all, waning for a time, then grabbing hold of us again as though there were something good or bright in the war, something worth longing for. Viktor Astaf'ev who served as a private wrote somewhere that he knew nothing but unbearable work and perpetual exhaustion in the war. I would add a few things in describing that burdensome existence at the front—the cold at some times; the dusty, stuffy heat at others; the hunger, the grit, the endless middle-of-the-night camp movements, the forced marches and the endless sleep deprivation, when German mortar served as an early wake-up call, and at night the unexpected bombings would never let one sleep. The hourly expectation of death or some terrible wound was somehow not so bad—let it be, you think, you're not afraid of those things, you'd even be happy to have a little break, to be on the mend in the not-too-distant rear flank or in one of the front-line hospitals, to get a good night's sleep, and, perhaps, to get a few decent meals in you.

So what is there to recall, what to miss? The fraternity of the frontlines, the friendship that came with being a soldier? Such friendship commonly seemed all too brief. One only had time to meet someone, get close to him, when he would be wounded or killed—the soldier's life at the front is indeed short, making two weeks in battle alright but something like two months "too much." You get through that time with only one small thought: be killed or wounded sooner rather than later to stop the torture—there is a limit, after all, to human patience and strength. . . . It depressed us no less on the very edge of the front lines that our commanders did not spare us, abandoning us to our own rashness, to being deliberately doomed to failed attacks, as we engaged in battle in order to achieve victory "at any cost" without thought to losses. . . . Now one thinks about how many were sacrificed for nothing—because of inability, because of ambition, because we were ordered to take back a city for every Soviet holiday. And always, always—at any cost! But how many lives could have been saved fighting slightly more intelligently, slightly more prudently, with slightly more pity for human beings. No, people were not pitied, just like they were not pitied in 1917, 1921, 1929, or 1937—in war, not even God orders that people be pitied—victory is more important. Some kind of results are always more important to us, not people. People are piled up in Russia—we have more than enough.

So where does this nostalgia come from, why does it torment our souls? Perhaps, because the war came at the very beginning of our youth? The war certainly did deprive us of our youth, tore it to pieces, ripped out the best years of our lives, not to mention the fact that, hopefully five still remain alive out of every hundred born in our generation. After all, in the first months of the war, the regular army—made up of those born in 1919, 1920, 1921, and 1922—took the entire blow of the German forces. To this very day, no one knows how many of them were killed. Millions were taken prisoner. How many does that leave? No—the point is not, most likely, our youth. Perhaps it helped us endure, to get through this savagely waged war. It was not so much the physical strength that came with it as our youthful idealism, so cruelly wasted by Stalin, our belief in the legitimacy of the war, whose truth we had no knowledge of at all. Had we known, maybe we could have avoided it or taken it on under more favorable conditions for ourselves. We knew nothing at all, then, although we felt it deep inside: something about that pact with Germany was not right, did not fit. We did not know that collectivization in Russia, having frightened the German farmer, would contribute to Hitler's ascent to power, that Stalin had done Nazism a good turn by splitting the social-democratic movement and destroying its ties with the parties of the left, and even weakening the Communist Party itself. There was a lot we did not know as it turned out, and our ignorance helped us fight because everything was clear and simple to us—fascism has attacked our country, we have to fight it, we have to defeat it.

Maybe, after Victory, we could begin to live normally again? Alas, no. Our hopes that after the war a beautiful life would begin were not realized. We hoped that Stalin, convinced of the loyalty of the people—what greater proof could he need than victory in the war?—would end the repressions, especially since they abated during the war. Those who came back disabled, especially those who were already working prior to the war, received such miserable pensions that they weren't enough even to redeem their ration cards. I've come across a copy of *Literary Gazette* from 1948 with an article about the poor quality of prosthetic limbs. Today almost half a century has passed and yet the same conversations are taking place for a new generation of injured—Afghans. A friend of mine from grade school, because he broke his prosthetic leg, fell and broke his other leg and was thus bed-ridden for a number of months—but what would have happened had the bone not healed? The currency reform of 1947 raised the price of groceries to twice what they had been before the war, while salaries stayed the same. True, stores were well-stocked, but no one had the money to buy anything.

At the end of 1948 and 1949, there began a round-up of political prisoners who were freed in 1947, those few who did not have a sentence in a labor camp tacked on, and those who were labeled incapable due to illness. Once again many were arrested, searched, and then taken away in cattle-cars to the Krasnoyarsk region, groups being unloaded at Siberian stations and smaller substations for eternal exile. In those years, former prisoners of war who received clearance in 1945 began to be imprisoned and sent off to the camps. I do not think even Stalin believed in the treason of those people—he just felt the need to rid society of those who knew a lot: political prisoners could talk about how investigations were carried out, about life in the labor camps; former prisoners of war studied the handling of propaganda from both the

German side and that of the recruiters for the Russian Liberation Army, who explained a lot to them about collectivization and the year 1937. In addition, in those years, a wave of arrests swept through the ranks of institutions of higher education, especially targeting veterans. All of our hopes that something would change collapsed. There was nothing bright about our post-war lives, nothing to recall with nostalgic sorrow—we were considered the "lost generation," though we were not supposed to talk about it. For us in the Soviet Union, so to speak, this phenomenon could not exist. Thus, there was much that, not surprisingly, remained utterly beyond our understanding, for we were born in this regime, we knew no other life if you do not count the hazy memories of the final years of the New Economic Policy, when the counters of the stalls on Okhotnyi Riad in Moscow were crammed with every imaginable kind of product. But we remember more clearly the ration cards, the waiting in lines, the tiny pieces of bluish rabbit meat, called by the people, "Stalin's Oxen."

We really knew practically nothing then, and how could we know when so much of the richness of human thought was closed to us? What if we had read, for example, the lines from Gorky's poem "Untimely Thoughts" about how "the people's commissars treat Russia as material for experiments; for them, the Russian people are a horse inoculated with typhus by bacteriologists so that it will produce an anti-typhoid serum in its own blood." Perhaps we would have understood something in life. I don't know if it would've been better had everyone known or remained in the dark. Incidentally, we see now that that "serum" produced by the "cruel experiments," as Gorky put it, experiments that were doomed in advance, produced the strong immunity to the fantastical notion of a "paradise on earth," world "happiness" that we must "drive humanity into with an iron fist." It is painful and bitter that that experience cost so much, so many human lives, and that now in the midst of almost three hundred million people, we cannot find an alternative leader for our government.

And so, finding ourselves in utter ignorance, we quickly submitted ourselves to post-war life. What was important was that the war was behind us, we stayed alive, and in front of us lay the alluring expanses of communism, where everything would be "according to one's needs." To say that we believed in it without hesitation is, of course, not true. But everyone hoped for something better.

Now we are hoping again, though not to the same degree, for something better, considering the sad paradox of our time, which leaves us little to hope for. This paradox lies in the fact that the Communist Party (its better part), having proclaimed perestroika, is itself putting the brakes on it in the face of the other, say, not-so-good part, which is incapable of giving up its monopoly on uncontrolled power and therefore cannot or does not want to renounce those communist myths that gave it the power the Party has used for more than seventy years, having brought the country to ruin while holding itself accountable for nothing. And if the Party doesn't dissociate itself from its own relics that pull the entire Party backwards, then it seems inevitable to me that given free elections and the availability of other, more radical parties now, it will suffer as crushing a defeat as the communist parties of Western Europe have. But I would not want that to happen—not because I hold tender feelings toward my "close and beloved Party," but because I see real and fresh intellectual vigor in the modern Party, the ability to bring the country authentic democracy and radical economic reforms. It goes without saying, however, that this would only hold true assuming a complete repudiation of the now decrepit ideology that has proven to be so disastrous for the country.

However, things are not so simple. Letters I have received from readers concerning my article "Let's Talk about Ideals" show that the belief in communist ideals has still not left the consciousness of many people. No matter how much we wrote or spoke of the utopianism of these ideals, it must be acknowledged that they gave a degree of spirituality to the meager and gray life of the common man. After all, a consciousness in which the postulate that "We live not for ourselves but for the future" is an altruistic one similar to a religion that undoubtedly somehow comprehends the lives of human beings and therefore one that we cannot disregard completely.

Almost all of us understand today that a free market is inevitable, that it is necessary to draw nearer to real life, to disavow schemes and abstractions. But how can one persuade that a considerable portion of the population who, despite having lived and who continue to live with a poor standard of living, experienced some degree of psychological comfort, and had clear and comprehensible goals?

But I have digressed from the war. Despite the fact that I can't recall the warfare itself very well, because my memory was somehow wiped clean of all the terrible and distressing physical aspects of it, there still remains the spiritual side, those bright and clean surges of spirit peculiar to a war of justice, a war of liberation. There was one strange thing in the war—we felt ourselves to be freer than in peacetime. Should the freedom of a soldier seem that way, even though everyone is above him, beginning with corporal all the way to commander? Of course, when "driven" to attack, you stomp around the field, exposing yourself to bullets and debris, there and then you become "cannon fodder," there and then little depends on you. But if you are lucky and make it to the enemy trenches, there, you can show yourself—there, you yourself are master. There, no one commands you; there, you hold a lot in your hands, if not everything. But, when defending, you also need a sharp mind, a keen intellect. I have a story called "A Memorable Day." The hero of the story, a former soldier in the Great Patriotic War, says to his drinking buddies, also veterans,

> Well, take me for example—I'm a lathe operator now—nothing to brag about but not a bad gig—but suppose I leave my factory and nothing comes of it, nothing changes, another drone just takes my place and works hard there; and then in the war. . . . If I'm not there on the left flank with my machine-gun, what'll happen? And when a German breaks through in that place! I'll stop the rat! He's not passing, the bastard! In the war, I was absolutely indispensable. And not just anyone could replace me. Look, suppose that there was a different soldier in place of me on that left flank with the exact same machine-gun. And already, no confidence that he'll stop that German—and the eyes, and the wit, and the character, could all be a little weaker. . . . There was that feeling that precisely you alone hold the fate of Russia in your hands. . . . It's true, after all. . . . But now . . . whether I exist or not, everything still runs as usual.

Yes—in peacetime life in our society, that's how it was. "Whether I exist or not, everything still runs as usual," since nothing depends on a single individual in the government of our homeland. But in the war, it was different: there, every single one of us felt our personal contribution toward victory.

There was yet another level of personal freedom in the war, though—freedom from ideology. Although the war was carried out under the usual Soviet slogans and appeals, and even though soldiers shouted out every now and then at the urging of political leaders "For the Fatherland, for Stalin!" it was not for Stalin, of course, that we fought. Once again Yuri Belash says it well in one of his poems:

> If I were to speak truthfully—
> we thought least of all in the trenches
> of Stalin.
> God, we recalled more often.
> Stalin
> played no part at all
> in our soldiers' war
> and to speak of him—
> there was simply no reason.
> And if it weren't for the newspapers,
> honestly, we would have forgotten
> that name that one does not come across
> in the Russian language.

It is fitting to say here that prior to the war, Stalin had begun to remember "the great forefathers"—on the threshold of the war, he was completely justified in placing more hope in Russian patriotism than in ideology.

It is true that the ideological veneer was too thin in people's minds; it was only twenty years old, compared to the age-old love for the Fatherland and the age-old desire to defend one's homeland. Therefore, Soviet ideology, in my view, played virtually no role in the Great Patriotic War, appropriately named because at its core, that's what it came to be. Whether Stalin had been there or not, the Russian soldiers would have fought selflessly, courageously, just like they've fought in all wars that have been brought upon our country.

And thus "that feeling that precisely you alone hold the fate of Russia in your hands" was nothing other than the sincere and authentic feeling of a citizen responsible for the Fatherland. It seems to me that nostalgia for the front can be explained by this, for the war took place at a time when a person reached for more than he thought was in him, aware that he was "absolutely indispensable" to his Homeland, feeling a personal responsibility for its fate.

But once we defeated fascism and liberated Europe from its clutches, we all returned as victors. More accurately, we saw ourselves as such for only a short time while we were hoping for something. When hopes were not fated to be realized, disappointment and apathy descended upon us, which we explained to ourselves as coming from the slump and exhaustion following the inhuman exertions of the war years. Did we understand, then, that in saving our Homeland, in saving Russia, we had also saved the Stalinist regime? Probably not. But even if we had understood everything during the war, we would have fought all the same, preferring our home-bred totalitarianism to Hitler's foreign version, because it's easier to endure violence from one's own than from others.

And so the liberation of Europe that we were so proud of in 1948 and 1949 turned into anything but liberation—the hand of Stalin extended over many countries of the so-called people's democracy. We understood that then, in spite of songs like Virta's "Conspiracy of the Doomed" or Simonov's "Under the Chestnuts of Prague."

The war has almost stopped haunting my dreams, but the bitter yet nonetheless bright memories of it have not quite deserted me. The war has come to be the most important thing of our generation, no more, no less. That pure surge of love for the Fatherland, sacrificial incandescence, and readiness to give up one's life for one's country are unforgettable—nothing like it has ever happened since. Recently, when I was going through my archive, I came upon the letters I wrote to my mother that she had saved from my time in the Urals where my infantry brigade was formed. I had absolutely no memory of what I wrote to her then, and so I began to read them with interest. And what do you know—I saw in them that I had quite calmly prepared both myself and my mother for my possible death; I wrote that I was not afraid to die at the walls of my native city, that what was most important was not to let the Germans get all the way to Moscow. On these letters went, in the same romantic but more or less sober tone, because, having served already for two years in the army, I knew what infantry was—I knew what little chance there was of coming back alive. So I readied myself and my mother. And I was surprised by the kind of reconciliation to death there was in the letters, the preparedness for it. I was all of twenty-one years old then. Could one really forget all that?

There were millions of similar letters, from the front to the rear and from the rear to the front, and in all of them there was a belief in victory and a readiness to lay down one's life for it. No one swore his love for Russia, nor beat his own chest—but many died for the country. There, in those letters, was the modesty and calmness felt by those newly-proclaimed patriots, the majority of whom had done nothing substantive yet for Russia, and in whom after all the incantations, one sees a love not for Russia as such but for themselves as Russians, as though being Russian was not some accident of birth, but some kind of special service. . . .

I am not saddened by the fact that no monuments were erected in honor of the 45th anniversary of Victory, that none were dedicated to any of the military commanders—not even to Zhukov himself, who, by the way, was known by every Russian soldier as the "Maker of Victory." I am depressed by the fact that in honor of that day, we've done so little to ensure that those "Makers of Victory"—the disabled and veterans of the War, who gave so much of their strength and blood to rescue their motherland, of whom no more than five million now remain—can live out the last years of their brutal, utterly deprived lives like real human beings.

I for one will not forget to the end of my days the thing that was "most terrifying" in the war, and that I saw on my very first day at the front—my fellow soldiers, dead, stripped down to virtually nothing, and scattered everywhere; the sharp pain and pity that pierced my heart; and then, after a week or two, the unnatural, listless indifference to the daily losses, to the moans of the wounded; the horrible adaptation to the slaughter of people by people that had become commonplace, as though it were the usual mode of life of a person at the front.

God forbid such horror ever repeats itself.

Translated by Larissa Rudova and Ezekiel Pfeifer

XII

The Thaw

Stalin died on 5 March 1953. His death, as Yevgeny Yevtushenko makes poignantly clear in the excerpt from *A Precocious Autobiography* that appears here, left a nation in mourning and, in some sense, directionless. As the Soviet Union began to struggle with Stalin's legacy, it did so in an atmosphere of gradual liberalization that became known as the Thaw (*ottepel'*), taken from the title of the novel by Il'ia Erenburg that dealt with the intelligentsia in the period immediately following Stalin's death. While the Thaw period is generally associated with Khrushchev's rule (1953–64), it both outlasted him in some respects and waxed and waned during his time in power. Like most thaws in Russia, it was accompanied by periodic freezes.

The initial months after Stalin's death jump-started the era of liberalization, as a general amnesty was declared for all prisoners in the Gulag. People who had been incarcerated in the Gulag on various trumped-up charges arrived back home with stories of camp life, stories that until then had remained locked with them inside the camps. Articles began to appear in the press on the need for greater sincerity and freedom of expression in literature. But there were limits. How far could one go? Did freer expression mean outright condemnation of the Party, of the system, and of Stalinism as a whole? What about Stalin's conduct of the war? That line was never explicitly drawn, perhaps in a paradoxical way echoing the system of terror that Stalin himself had put into place during the worst years of the terror. The line of permissibility constantly shifted, as doors were open at certain moments only to be closed again.

By 1956 Khrushchev had consolidated his power. On 25 February he gave his "Secret Speech," which was in fact a semipublic address to a select audience at the Twentieth Party Congress. In it he denounced Stalin's excesses and his cult of personality while stopping short of unilateral condemnation of the Politburo, many of whom, including himself, had been in office under Stalin. One of the immediate results of the speech was an increase in the number of prisoners released and rehabilitated from the Gulag. Within several months after the speech, between seven and nine million people were rehabilitated, many of them posthumously.

The Twentieth Party Congress also opened the door for freer expression of opinion in the press, on screen, and in literature. There was a sense of hope among the Soviet people that things were changing and that henceforth it would be possible to speak one's mind without sacrificing one's life. That same year one of the major works of the Thaw period was published, the novel *Ne khlebom edinym* (Not by Bread Alone) by Vladimir Dudintsev, who raged against Soviet bureaucrats who abused power for their own ends. Paradoxically, however, much of official policy toward openness in literature and in the press during the Thaw years turned on events outside the country. In 1956 Khrushchev responded to the uprising in Hungary by sending in Soviet troops, an act that precipitated the tightening of controls at home and a retreat from much of the promised liberal reform. The Eastern European countries as well as the Baltic states of Estonia, Latvia, and Lithuania had been brought under Soviet control under Stalin, and in their view Khrushchev's denunciation of Stalin signaled the possibility of their own liberation from Soviet control. Just months after the uprising in Hungary was quelled, the infamous Pasternak Affair took place, causing many to question the promises of the Thaw. The Russian writer Boris Pasternak came under fire by the Party for publishing his novel *Doctor Zhivago* abroad in 1957, before it was released in his own country. Whether Pasternak expressly gave permission for the Italian publisher Feltrinelli to go ahead and publish the novel or whether the publisher did so independently remains a moot point today. Pasternak fell afoul of the Party and was forced to reject the Nobel Prize awarded him in 1958. He died in 1960, hounded and broken by the events of the last three years of his life.

The very year the Pasternak Affair erupted, however, films were being made and literary works appeared that wrote the individual, his thoughts, feelings, and doubts back into Soviet art. One of the hallmark films of the era, *Letiat zhuravli* (The Cranes Are Flying, 1957), whose action is set during and immediately after the Second World War, depicted a world not of cookie-cutter Soviet men and women marching toward Stalin's *svetloe budushchee*, or radiant future, but of people who crumbled under the stress of war, who debated whether they should even fight, and who persistently struggled for a personal life at a time when such things were meant to be put aside for the greater glory of the Party and the state. *The Cranes Are Flying* was followed swiftly by another film that became a Soviet classic, *Ballada o soldate* (The Ballad of a Soldier, 1959), which told the story of a simple Russian soldier whose real heroism was manifested not on the battlefield but in his own personal sense of morality as he journeyed back into Russia's heartland to briefly visit his mother.

By the early 1960s the process of de-Stalinization which Khrushchev had set in motion was felt keenly throughout Soviet society. A new generation of poets—among them Yevgeny Yevtushenko, Andrei Voznesenskii, and Bella Akhmadulina—recited their poetry to packed houses and on street corners. Their poetry was personal, it took risks, and it criticized Stalinism. But the poets were not the only ones who dared speak out. Editors of journals began publishing works that formerly would have had no place in the ideological canon. One in particular, Aleksandr Tvardovskii, editor in chief of the leading literary journal of the day, *Novyi mir* (New World), received a manuscript in 1961 from an obscure teacher of mathematics in the city of Riazan', a man named Aleksandr Solzhenitsyn. It was the story of a twenty-four-hour period in a labor camp in the Gulag told from the point of view of a simple Russian man who was arrested as a Nazi spy after escaping from a German prisoner of war camp and returning to his country. Tvardovskii read the manuscript and knew it had to be published. Given the sensitive nature of the topic, he went to Khrushchev directly. Khrushchev gave the go-ahead, and indeed placed a special resolution with the Central Committee, allowing the book to be published. When *One Day in the Life of Ivan Denisovich* made its appearance in *Novyi mir* in 1962, it was for many Soviets their first exposure to life in the camps, a day which the protagonist declares to have been a good one. Further, Solzhenitsyn drew suggestive parallels in the novel between life inside the camp and Soviet society writ large, thus implicitly turning the camp into a microcosm of the Soviet state.

Whatever the strides made toward more openness, cultural life in the Soviet Union continued to serve as the handmaiden of politics. Even as Solzhenitsyn decried the Soviet system in 1962, that same year Khrushchev was forced to back down over the Cuban missile crisis, an event that proved to be one of the major turning points in his political fortunes. As he sought to protect his power by aligning himself with the more conservative forces in the Party, warning the Writers' Union the next year of pernicious bourgeois elements seeping into Soviet literature, his political fortunes took a downward slide. The initial achievements from the late 1950s and his initial agricultural successes suffered reversals. The promises he had made to bolster the consumer sector could not be fulfilled as long as the cold war continued. Overplanting as part of the virgin lands campaign had resulted in a series of disastrous harvests. What popularity remained to him was further undermined at home by the Cuban missile crisis in October 1962, when Khrushchev was forced to back down after American intelligence discovered missile sites being constructed in Castro's Cuba. Two years later he was forced out of office and replaced by Leonid Brezhnev as First Secretary of the Communist Party of the Soviet Union.

The Thaw did not end abruptly with Khrushchev's ouster. Faced with a leadership that represented a clear conservative backlash, writers and editors hastened to publish before the lid was clamped down on liberal publication venues. If there was a moment when the literary community knew that their fate had been sealed, it was perhaps the Sinyavsky-Daniel Trial in 1965. The two writers, Andrei Sinyavsky and Yulii Daniel, were sentenced to prison for publishing their works abroad under pseudonyms before the works were released in the USSR. In some ways the fate of these two writers signaled the end of an era. Henceforth, in the opinion of many writers and members of the intelligentsia, open honest literature could find a venue only in the underground through samizdat, or self-publishing, where writers would circulate carbon copies of their works among those who shared their views. When Tvardovskii was forced to resign as editor of *Novyi mir* in 1970, with him went the last vestiges of the Thaw and any hope of publishing the many manuscripts languishing in writers' and editors' desk drawers.

In a sense Khrushchev was a paradoxical and perhaps tragic figure. Had he not come to power, major improvements that took place, in the arts in particular and in Soviet society as a whole, might not have occurred, or would have been much delayed. During his time in office Soviet citizens were no longer taken away in the middle of the night and sent to the Gulag for unspecified periods. The state security apparatus was brought more strictly under Party control in an effort to ameliorate the conditions that had allowed the purges to continue unchecked during the Stalin era. Despite whatever censorship controls still remained in place by the time he was forced out, it was undeniable that the atmosphere had changed for writers and for artists. Moreover, the Soviet Union had begun to open its doors to the West. While it was still extraordinarily difficult for Soviet citizens to travel outside their own borders, save for professional conferences and in groups at that, the first academic exchanges between the United States and the USSR were initiated under Khrushchev in 1958. Ultimately, however, for whatever reforms he put into place Khrushchev was still beholden to the policies and the system that had been deeply etched into Soviet society under Stalin. Yet what began under Khrushchev set in motion something that could never entirely be reversed.

March 5th, 1953 (1963)

Yevgeny Yevtushenko

Yevgeny Yevtushenko is one of the group of younger Thaw poets whose work swung between official acceptance and dissent. Born in 1933 in Zima Junction near Lake Baikal in Siberia, he published his first book of poems in 1952. Along with "The Heirs of Stalin" (1962), a poem in which he suggests that the ideology of Stalinism survived the death of Stalin, Yevtushenko is best known for his poem "Babyi Yar" (1961). In it he condemned the mass killings of Soviet Jews during the Second World War that went both unacknowledged and unmemorialized in his country. The poem struck a sensitive chord in Soviet society, as Yevtushenko accused his countrymen of the same anti-Semitism that had fueled Hitler's policies.

The excerpt that follows is from Yevtushenko's Precocious Autobiography. *His decision to have the book published initially in France in 1963 caused him to come under fire at home. In the section that appears here, Yevtushenko paints a picture of the ravages of Stalin and Stalinism in a description of the crowd that had come to see Stalin's coffin. The last line sums up the searing complexity of the man and the country he had ruled.*

On March 5, 1953, an event took place which shattered Russia—Stalin died. I found it almost impossible to imagine him dead, so much had he been an indispensable part of life.

A sort of general paralysis came over the country. Trained to believe that they were all in Stalin's care, people were lost and bewildered without him. All Russia wept. And so did I. We wept sincerely, tears of grief—and perhaps also tears of fear for the future.

At a meeting of the Writers' Union poets read their poems in honor of Stalin, their voices broken by sobs. Tvardovsky, a big and powerful man, recited in a trembling voice.

I will never forget going to see Stalin's coffin. I was in the crowd in Trubnaya Square. The breath of the tens of thousands of people jammed against one another rose up in a white cloud so thick that on it could be seen the swaying

Funeral of Joseph Stalin, 9 March 1953. Photograph by Vasilii Egorov. Courtesy of and copyright held by ITAR-TASS, Image 100855.

shadows of the bare March trees. It was a terrifying and a fantastic sight. New streams poured into this human flood from behind, increasing the pressure. The crowd turned into a monstrous whirlpool. I realized that I was being carried straight toward a traffic light. The post was coming relentlessly closer. Suddenly I saw that a young girl was being pushed against the post. Her face was distorted and she was screaming. But her screams were inaudible among all the other cries and groans. A movement of the crowd drove me against the girl; I did not hear but felt with my body the cracking of her brittle bones as they were broken on the traffic light. I closed my eyes in horror, the sight of her insanely bulging, childish blue eyes more than I could bear, and I was swept past. When I looked again the girl was no longer to be seen. The crowd must have sucked her under. Pressed against the traffic light was someone else, his body twisted and his arm outflung as on a cross. At that moment I felt I was treading on something soft. It was a human body. I picked my feet up under me and was carried along by the crowd. For a long time I was afraid to put my feet down again. The crowd closed tighter and tighter. I was saved by my height. Short people were smothered alive, falling and perishing. We were caught between the walls of houses on one side and a row of army trucks on the other.

"Get those trucks out of the way!" people howled. "Get them out of here!"

"I can't do it! I have no instructions," a very young, tow-headed police officer shouted back from one of the trucks, almost crying with helplessness.

And people were being hurtled against the trucks by the crowd, and their heads smashed. The sides of the trucks were splashed with blood. All at once I felt a savage hatred for everything that had given birth to that "I have no instructions," shouted at a moment when people were dying because of someone's stupidity. For the first time in my life I thought with hatred of the man we were burying. He could not be innocent of the disaster. It was the "No instructions" that had caused the chaos and bloodshed at his funeral. Now I was certain, once and for all, that you must never wait for instructions if human lives are at stake—you must act. I don't know how I did it, but working energetically with my elbows and fists, I found myself thrusting people aside and shouting: "Form chains! Form chains!"

They didn't understand me. Then I started to join neighboring hands together by force, all the while spitting out the foulest swearwords of my geological days. Some tough young men were now helping me. And now people understood. They joined hands and formed chains. The strong men and I continued to work at it. The whirlpool was slowing down. The crowd was ceasing to be a savage beast. "Women and children into the trucks!" yelled one of the young men. And women and children, passed from hand to hand, sailed over our heads into the trucks. One of the women who were being handed on was struggling hysterically and whimpering. The young police officer who received her at his end stroked her hair, clumsily trying to calm her down. She shivered a few times and suddenly froze into stillness. The officer took the cap off his straw-colored head, covered her face with it, and burst out crying.

There was another violent whirlpool further ahead. We worked our way over, the tough boys and I, and again with the help of the roughest curses and fists, made people form chains in order to save them.

The police too finally began to help us.

Everything quieted down.

"You ought to join the police, Comrade. We could use fellows like you," a police sergeant said to me, wiping his face with his handkerchief after a bout of hard work.

"Right. I'll think it over," I said grimly.

Somehow, I no longer felt like going to see Stalin's remains. Instead, I left with one of the boys who had been organizing chains. We bought a bottle of vodka and walked to our place.

"Did you see Stalin?" my mother asked me.

"Yes," I said coldly, as I clinked glasses with the boy.

I hadn't really lied to my mother. I had seen Stalin. Because everything that had just happened—that was Stalin.

The Secret Speech (1956)

Nikita Khrushchev

When Nikita Khrushchev made his now famous "Secret Speech" to the Twentieth Party Congress on 25 February 1956 behind closed doors to a small group of Party delegates and other Presidium members, his audience sat stunned. For years people had spoken cautiously and in private about Stalin's crimes, but this was the first time Stalin's excesses had been vented even in a semipublic format. In front of a selected audience Khrushchev spoke for four hours about Stalin's crimes, the mass arrests, deportations, and executions of Soviet citizens, from highly placed Party figures to average collective farm workers. He attacked Stalin for incompetent wartime leadership, for the cult of personality that resulted in self-deification, and for the failure of Soviet agriculture. In Khrushchev's view, Stalin had betrayed the values of Lenin, and it was to Leninism that Khrushchev promised to return the country.

In the words of his biographer William Taubman, Khrushchev's speech was the "bravest and most reckless thing he ever did," brave because even after Stalin's death people still feared the repercussions of truth telling, and reckless because those who owed their career to Stalin were still alive and working in the Politburo. Khrushchev stopped short of unilaterally condemning all of Stalin's policies and all those who worked under him. His explanation as to why the Politburo had failed to put a stop to these crimes was essentially that these were complicated times; moreover, once high-ranking Party members understood what was taking place, the terror had reached a point where it was impossible to curtail it.

If Khrushchev's speech ushered in the Thaw, it also ignited the Hungarian Revolt against the Soviet regime in October of that year. Whether Khrushchev understood when he wrote his speech how it would affect Soviet strategic interests in Eastern Europe is not clear. What is clear is that in suppressing the Hungarian Revolt he used the same strong-arm techniques with which Soviet society was all too familiar from Stalinist days.

Comrades! In the Party Central Committee report to the 20th Congress, in a number of speeches by delegates to the Congress, and earlier at plenary sessions of the Party Central Committee, quite a lot has been said about the cult of the individual leader and its harmful consequences.

Khrushchev greeting the crowds. Photography by Patty Ratliff. Courtesy of the Hoover Institution.

After Stalin's death the Party Central Committee began to implement a policy of explaining concisely and consistently that it is impermissible and foreign to the spirit of Marxism-Leninism to elevate one person, to transform him into a superman possessing supernatural characteristics akin to those of a god. Such a man supposedly knows everything, sees everything, thinks for everyone, can do anything, is infallible in his behavior.

Such a belief about a man—specifically about Stalin—was cultivated among us for many years.

The objective of the present report is not a thorough evaluation of Stalin's life and work. Concerning Stalin's merits, an entirely sufficient number of books, pamphlets and studies had already been written in his lifetime. Stalin's role in the preparation and execution of the socialist revolution, in the Civil War, and in the fight for the construction of socialism in our country is universally known. Everyone knows this well. At present we are concerned with a question which has immense importance for the Party now and in the future—[we are concerned] with how the Stalin cult gradually grew, the cult which became at a certain specific stage the source of a whole series of exceedingly serious and grave perversions of Party principles, of Party democracy, of revolutionary legality.

Because not all as yet realize fully the practical consequences resulting from the cult of the individual leader, the great harm caused by the violation of the principle of collective direction of the Party, and because immense and limitless power was gathered in the hands of one person, the Party Central Committee considers it absolutely necessary to make the material pertaining to this matter available to the 20th Congress of the Communist Party of the Soviet Union. . . .

We have to consider this matter seriously and analyze it correctly in order that we may preclude any possibility of a repetition, in any form whatever, of what took place during the life of Stalin, who absolutely did not tolerate collegiality in leadership and in work and who practiced brutal violence not only toward everything which opposed him, but also toward what seemed, to his capricious and despotic character, contrary to his concepts.

Stalin acted not through persuasion, explanation and patient cooperation with people, but by imposing his concepts and demanding absolute submission to his opinion. Whoever opposed this concept or tried to prove his viewpoint and the correctness of his position was doomed to removal from the leading collective and to subsequent moral and physical annihilation. This was especially true during the period following the 17th Party Congress, when many prominent Party leaders and rank-and-file Party workers, honest and dedicated to the cause of communism, fell victim to Stalin's despotism.

We must affirm that the Party fought a serious fight against the Trotsky-ites, rightists and bourgeois nationalists, and that it disarmed ideologically all the enemies of Leninism. This ideological fight was carried on successfully, and as a result the Party was strengthened and tempered. Here Stalin played a positive role.

The Party led a great political ideological struggle against those in its own ranks who proposed anti-Leninist theses, who represented a political line hostile to the Party and to the cause of socialism. This was a stubborn and a difficult fight but a necessary one, because the political line of both the Trotskyite-Zinovievite bloc and of the Bukharinites led actually toward the restoration of capitalism and capitulation to the world bourgeoisie. Let us consider for a moment what would have happened if in 1928–29 the political line of right deviation had prevailed among us, or orientation toward "cotton-dress industrialization," or toward the kulak, etc. We would not now have a powerful heavy industry, we would not have the collective farms, we would find ourselves disarmed and weak in a capitalist encirclement.

It was for this reason that the Party led an inexorable ideological fight and explained to all Party members and to the non-Party masses the harm and the danger of the anti-Leninist proposals of the Trotskyite opposition and the rightist opportunists. And this great work of explaining the Party line bore fruit; both the Trotskyites and the rightist opportunists were politically iso-lated; the overwhelming Party majority supported the Leninist line and the Party was able to awaken and organize the working masses to apply the Leninist Party line and to build socialism.

Worth noting is the fact that even during the progress of the furious ideological fight against the Trotskyites, the Zinovievites, the Bukharinites and others, extreme repressive measures were not used against them. The fight was on ideological grounds. But some years later, when socialism in our country had been fundamentally established, when the exploiting classes had been generally liquidated, when the Soviet social structure had radically changed, when the social base for political movements and groups hostile to the Party had shrunk sharply, when the ideological opponents of the Party had long since been defeated politically, then the repression directed against them began.

It was precisely during this period (1935–37–38) that the practice of mass repression through the state apparatus was born, first against the enemies of Leninism—Trotskyites, Zinovievites, Bukharinites, long since politically defeated by the Party—and subsequently also against many honest Communists, against those Party cadres which had borne the heavy burden of the Civil War and the first and most difficult years of industrialization and collectivization, which had fought actively against the Trotskyites and the rightists for the Leninist party line.

Stalin originated the concept "enemy of the people." This term automatically rendered it unnecessary that the ideological errors of a man or men engaged in a controversy be proved; this term made possible the use of the most cruel repression, violating all norms of revolutionary legality, against anyone who in any way disagreed with Stalin, against those who were only suspected of hostile intent, against those who had bad reputations. This concept, "enemy of the people," actually eliminated the possibility of any kind of ideological fight or the making of one's views known on this or that issue, even issues of a practical nature. In the main, and in actuality, the only proof of guilt used, contrary to all norms of current law, was the "confession" of the accused himself; and, as subsequent investigation has proved, "confessions" were obtained through physical pressures against the accused.

This led to glaring violations of revolutionary legality, and to the fact that many entirely innocent persons, who in the past had defended the Party line, became victims.

We must assert that, in regard to those persons who in their time had opposed the Party line, there were often no sufficiently serious reasons for their physical annihilation. The formula "enemy of the people" was specifically introduced for the purpose of physically annihilating such individuals.

It is a fact that many persons who were later annihilated as enemies of the Party and people had worked with Lenin during his life. Some of these persons had made mistakes during Lenin's life, but, despite this, Lenin benefited by their work, he corrected them and he did everything possible to retain them in the ranks of the Party; he induced them to follow him. . . .

Everyone knows how irreconcilable Lenin was with the ideological enemies of Marxism, with those who deviated from the correct Party line. At the same time, however, Lenin, as is evident from the given document, in his practice of directing the Party demanded the most intimate Party contact with people who had shown indecision or temporary nonconformity with the Party line, but whom it was possible to return to the Party path. Lenin advised that such people should be patiently educated without the application of extreme methods.

Lenin's wisdom in dealing with people was evident in his work with cadres.

An entirely different relationship with people characterized Stalin. Lenin's traits—patient work with people; stubborn and painstaking education of them; the ability to induce people to follow him without using compulsion, but rather through the ideological influence on them of the whole collective— were entirely foreign to Stalin. He [Stalin] discarded the Leninist method of persuading and educating; he abandoned the method of ideological struggle for that of administrative violence, mass repressions and terror. He acted on an increasingly larger scale and more stubbornly through punitive organs, at the same time often violating all existing standards of morality and of Soviet law.

Arbitrary behavior by one person encouraged and permitted arbitrariness in others. Mass arrests and deportations of many thousands of people, execution without trial and without normal investigation created conditions of insecurity, fear and even desperation.

This, of course, did not contribute toward unity of the Party ranks and of all strata of the working people, but, on the contrary, brought about annihilation and the expulsion from the Party of workers who were loyal but inconvenient to Stalin. . . .

Lenin used severe methods only in the most necessary cases, when the exploiting classes were still in existence and were vigorously opposing the revolution, when the struggle for survival was decidedly assuming the sharpest forms, even including a civil war.

Stalin, on the other hand, used extreme methods and mass repressions at a time when the revolution was already victorious, when the Soviet state was strengthened, when the exploiting classes were already liquidated and socialist relations were rooted solidly in all phases of national economy, when our party was politically consolidated and had strengthened itself both numerically and ideologically. It is clear that here Stalin showed in a whole series of cases his intolerance, his brutality and his abuse of power. Instead of proving his political correctness and mobilizing the masses, he often chose the path of repression and physical annihilation, not only against actual enemies, but also against individuals who had not committed any crimes against the Party and the Soviet government. Here we see no wisdom but only a demonstration of the brutal force which had once so alarmed V. I. Lenin.

The Defense of a
Prison-Camp Official (1964)

Anna Zakharova

One of the most vexing questions that arose in the post-Stalinist era was how far down the line culpability went for the crimes committed under Stalin. While issues of guilt and responsibility were addressed by Khrushchev at the Twentieth Party Congress and again in 1961 when high-ranking Party members such as Molotov, Kaganovich, Voroshilov, and Malenkov were directly implicated in the purges, many questions remained that were not directly addressed in the official press about the role played by lower level functionaries.

The letter that appears here was written to the editor in chief of the newspaper Izvestiia *by Anna Zakharova, who had worked as a minor official in the camps for fourteen years. She was prompted to write it by the appearance of Aleksandr Solzhenitsyn's novel,* One Day in the Life of Ivan Denisovich *in 1962 and Boris Diakov's memoir,* A Tale of Survival, *in 1964. While the two authors were of very different political persuasions, both described in chilling, often understated detail the dehumanizing and brutal treatment of political prisoners in the Gulag. Zakharova defends the camp system in general and those who worked there, explaining that in essence they had no other choice when faced with the presence of what she terms "the dregs of society."*

Zakharova's letter was never published. It was obtained by the dissident historian Roy Medvedev, who circulated it in the underground samizdat magazine Political Diary, *which he compiled and edited between 1964 and 1971. In his introduction to Zakharova's letter, Medvedev described the complex nature of guilt and responsibility within the camps, citing the fact that many of the camp officials had limited education and moreover were convinced of the correctness of their actions. One of the more difficult aspects of Khrushchev's revelations in 1956 was that official Soviet citizens of all ranks were suddenly faced with the knowledge that the work they had performed during the Stalin years might well have been to no good end, hurting the very country they hoped to help. Such is the tragedy of the letter that appears here.*

To the Editor in Chief of Izvestiia:

I, Anna Filippovna Zakharova, have worked for the Ministry for the Preservation of Public Order [Russian initials, MOOP] since 1950. I was a member of the Komsomol and have been a Communist since 1956. Having read *One Day in the Life of Ivan Denisovich* by Aleksandr Solzhenitsyn, I was angered to the depths of my soul, as I am sure all MOOP employees who read the book also were. I intended to write immediately to the publisher but somehow never had the free time. But now that I have read another work of the same kind, *A Tale of Survival* by Boris Dyakov, I decided to write even though time is precious. In discussing this article, or rather these works, with MOOP employees who had read them, what I heard universally was anger, rage, and indignation.

Please try to understand our question. What were the officers and guards guilty of, these people who are painted in such dark colors by the former prisoners (although granted they were unjustly condemned)? Are they to blame because the Party and the people called on them to shoulder the most difficult burden of our time—working with the criminal world? We practical workers, who lived in the outlying areas, were deprived of the most elementary conditions for a human existence, unlike the inhabitants of cities and urban districts. Sometimes there was not enough food or housing for us, not to mention apartments with all the modern conveniences. Or real schools and libraries. And there's no need to even go into the question of the theater or various sports facilities. For us those were luxuries.

We work with what actually are the dregs of society—criminals. Just imagine. A person is working as part of the collective at one place or other. He gets drunk, he is a debaucher and a thief, he steals, he kills, and so on. The collective goes to great pains over this person, worries about him, and finally hands him over to the courts as the very worst of the worst, who prevents others from living and working normally. And here we have this "cream of society" all together in a camp. Can you imagine what it's like to work with them? But we have to. And what are we? Aren't we also Soviet citizens who should be able to live and work normally? Are we people of such a kind that we should not be able to enjoy the gains achieved by our fathers and children? We, too, wish to live quiet and pleasant lives in normal conditions among normal Soviet citizens. But the Party and the people have called upon us and have entrusted us with the most difficult lot in life, and we shoulder this burden for the good of all the people, for the sake of their tranquillity. So why are we blackened and discredited? And why do our organs of the press allow MOOP workers to be made fun of, and all the services they rendered be trampled into the mud? It's disgraceful! Among us there are many officers who are veteran Communists, who served their time and have retired on pensions as invalids because of the terrible and difficult work. And here this noble work is being mocked at, work in which a person's health has been ruined and in which some people even laid down their lives, and for what?

And what do the camp guards have to do with it all anyway, may we ask? They were only carrying out what was required of them by the regulations, orders, instructions, and so on, as people do in any office, factory, or plant. They didn't make up things on their own on the spot, taking advantage of the absence of control over them, or the personality cult. It's not our fault that such policies were followed. That's not the fault of the rank-and-file guards, the camp officers, Communists, and so on. So why abuse and insult them? Because every year it was harder for us to work with this criminal element? [Nowadays] the prisoners, taking advantage of the humanness of our policies, try in every way to taunt and mock the prison staff in the camps and labor colonies. At any time, they can insult any employee, and right to their face in front of everyone. And nothing will be done to them for that, except that certain possibilities, not very large, are available to the chief of a prison unit. The prisoners can call any of us Beria-ites freely, and say this to Communists, and this can't be reported. And no measures are taken against them. We have to operate by methods of explanation and clarification. And their errors are explained to them. But is a hardened criminal going to listen? Of course, there are some among the convicts who conduct themselves in a model fashion. But, for the most part, they are all hostilely disposed.

In this letter, I can't tell everything about how difficult it is for us to work with them. And we get no thanks. On the contrary, one of the prisoners will write a letter and make up such things against the administration and put in such details about this or that incident that the higher authorities take it as absolutely true. They send commissions, representatives from the procurator's office, and so forth. This makes the staff members nervous, and after things have been investigated, it turns out that the facts were not confirmed. Imagine. How can you work normally here? There are a lot of letter writers like that. And so we have to work in this kind of feverish atmosphere almost all the time. Is it possible, do you think, to describe and explain everything?

For thirteen and a half years, I have been working with these prisoners, as has my husband, Major Zakharov. His health has already been ruined working with the criminal world, because all the work here wears on your nerves. We would be happy to move on, because my husband has already served his time, but they won't let him go. He is a Communist and an officer, and he is bound by the duty of his position. But don't we have the right to live and work among positively oriented Soviet people? Don't we have the right to give our children a good education, since we have known no such thing? But here we are being blackened for all the misfortunes we have known, and the possibility of working any more is taken out of our hands. How unjust this is!

Let me go directly now to Solzhenitsyn's story.

Solzhenitsyn calls the security officer a "godfather." What does that mean? Who gave him the right to heap insults upon an official position that was established under the regulations of the MOOP of the Russian Republic? Or is that the customary practice among writers, to distort things? A person in this position has to be an officer and usually is a Communist. And they are at the present time also. And in regard to this "godfather," he certainly does use foul language; the writer says so himself. Also, according to Solzhenitsyn, if one of the prisoners is more conscientious, realizes his duty to the motherland, and does what his conscience calls upon him to do—that is, tells the security officer that one of the criminals is planning a murder or an escape or some other crime—Solzhenitsyn says that this is "self-preservation at someone else's expense." Some patriot, I must say.

I myself worked with a contingent of Article 58 [counterrevolutionary] prisoners, and there was nothing like what Solzhenitsyn writes about. The only thing was that some prisoners, as I have written, were more conscientious and revealed to the security officer a number of additional crimes against the motherland—committed by murderers, traitors, German collaborators, and the like. And for this, the Soviet people should only say thank you to these prisoners who came to a proper understanding. But Solzhenitsyn isn't pleased with this, you see.

Now about reveille and bedtime. This is part of the daily routine. You can't do without this in a camp. If there's no daily routine, there'll be no order in the camp. There are, in fact, particular regulations providing for such routine, and this continues to be the case now as it was before. There isn't any other way. But apparently Solzhenitsyn would like to have chaos in the camp and to have no order at all. But that cannot be.

And how Solzhenitsyn carries on about the guards. "Having stripped to their grubby tunics." One might think that they weren't wearing uniforms provided for in the MOOP regulations, but that these were tramps of some sort living on an uninhabited island without any higher ranking leadership, commanding officers, and so on.

And what is the implication, that the guards are fools? They are doing their duty, and they are obliged to carry out what is required of them.

And what does the hero of this story represent? One can guess right away what he was. When he had washed the floor in the camp supervisor's office, he tossed the unsqueezed cloth behind the stove and poured the dirty water out onto the path, the very one the authorities used. This shows how much he respects Soviet people—Communists—and how he takes care of socialist property. If every prisoner sloshed water around in the barracks the way he did, what would be left of them after five years? Everything would rot away, and the state would have to build again and the people would have to pay. But that's all right with Solzhenitsyn.

We can see why the hero of this story, having such an attitude toward the Soviet people, hopes for nothing but the sick bay in order somehow to get out of redeeming his guilt, the wrong he did to his motherland, through toil. After all, he is in a corrective-labor camp, even if he is innocent, and so he ought to set an example for the others, as a real Soviet citizen, as a Communist, to inspire others and not to get demoralized and demoralize others. And why exactly should a person try to avoid physical labor and show scorn for it? After all, for us labor is the foundation of the Soviet system, and it is only in labor that man becomes cognizant of his true powers. But here, as we see, the heroes of these stories are afraid of work, have a fearful attitude toward it; they seem to be afraid to go out felling timber. Millions of our Soviet people, however, fell timber for a living and praise this kind of work, and they don't march out to work at rifle point; they undertake this difficult and noble labor following the dictates of the heart.

Now, as for the "frisking"—or the body searches, to use the proper expression—they still exist today; there is no other way. The prisoners, you know, try to take anything they can outside the camp and sell it or exchange it for tea, vodka, and so on. There are free workers of all kinds around us, most often former prisoners of the same type, and they try by any means possible to interfere with the camp administration's attempt to organize the workings of the camp in a proper way. That is why the prisoners try to carry off camp property—and it is state property—and they try to smuggle out various letters of a slanderous nature against the Communist Party and Soviet government, and to engage in various kinds of criminal contacts, and so on. The administration is obliged to protect itself against this; otherwise, it cannot fulfill its mission and cannot follow the instructions outlined in the regulations on operating procedures and treatment of prisoners. If this kind of thing were permitted, if searches were not carried out, the prisoners would commit such crimes that the people would long remember their mistake in allowing prisoners to do just anything they wanted. These authors themselves write that there were real criminals in the camps—robbers, killers, counterrevolutionaries—as well as innocent people, and how is the administration to distinguish between who is guilty and who is not?

. . . .

My understanding of things is this: it is necessary and indispensable to criticize the personality cult, and we all are doing that now; but it is not necessary to drag in people who had absolutely nothing to do with it. All Soviet citizens experienced this period the same way, so why should a certain section of the people be blamed for it? It's quite clear that this period was the result of the policies of a certain category of people and not of all the people, and so there's no reason to let such writers as Solzhenitsyn and Dyakov discredit and smear the MOOP.

I somehow feel certain that all employees of MOOP feel the same way I do; I am convinced of this from my conversations with a great many of them. And all of them that I have had a chance to talk with are of the same opinion—the authority of MOOP has been undermined decisively in the eyes of the people and cannot now be restored.

Who Lives Better? (1959)

Giuseppe Boffa

In December 1953, just nine months after Stalin died, Giuseppe Boffa arrived in Moscow as chief correspondent for L'Unita, the newspaper of the Italian Communist Party. Boffa lived with his family for five years in the Soviet Union during the period of de-Stalinization and the Thaw. As a Communist Boffa viewed the unprecedented changes that were taking place in the USSR from a very different perspective than most in the West were wont to see them. He arrived full of excitement, knowing that the country whose life had been so closed off to foreigners was now beginning to reveal itself. With so little information about the internal workings of Soviet society leaking out under Stalin, anything a journalist wrote about the country in the aftermath of Stalin's death grabbed the headlines. "There were people," he writes, "who had seriously stated that lovers no longer existed in Soviet life; that love had been nationalized like the trees and the leaves, that the Anna Kareninas and the Natasha Rostovas were dead and the gentle girls of Turgenev overwhelmed." People in Italy referred to this country as Planet Russia, and to the Russian people as Martians. For Boffa's readers the great revelation was that these people were human. He writes with delight that all he had to do to be an effective journalist was walk the streets, watch people eating ice cream in fifteen degrees below zero, or look at the queues for books and records.

Much of Boffa's writing about the Soviet Union in those years was informed by his own changing vision. He arrived with a view of the Soviet Union as the Promised Land, the land of utopian brotherhood that would teach the rest of humanity how to live. With the years the myth that he and other Communists had constructed was replaced by a real country with real people living in it with real problems. But even as Boffa confronted the reality, he never let go of the dream, believing in its promise even as he wrote of its failures.

Millions of people throughout the world see in Socialism the promise of a better life, a life easier and more serene, freer and more civilized. Is this faith justified? By a series of historical circumstances the Soviet standard of living is temporarily inferior to that of leading capitalist nations. Hence the facile demagogy of capitalist apologists, who, isolating a few factors, attempt to assert the superiority of their system. Hence, also, the diffidence of people who are convinced of the superiority of socialism. A frank discussion is needed, for here, too, Soviet socialism has amply demonstrated its superiority to capitalism.

There are people who maintain that capitalism is superior simply because the American standard of life is still clearly higher than the Soviet. But all comparisons between these two countries must be historical, must begin with the points of departure of the two countries. It is possible that in forty years the standard of life in China or India may still be inferior to that of the British, but one can only pity the individual who maintains that the Chinese Revolution or Indian independence are failures. The Chinese and the Indians have another criteria—their internal progress. For the USSR the first comparison to be made is not between them and the United States, but between the USSR of today and tsarist Russia. From the day of the Revolution to today, life has improved enormously. The real wages of workers and peasants have multiplied from four to six times in forty years. But not only has the standard of living improved; the very way of living has changed to the point where it is totally unrecognizable. The progress has been continuous. I saw myself a steady improvement in the five years I lived in the USSR; from year to year people ate better, dressed better, had more fun. Since victory there have been several considerable price reductions on consumer goods which have cut in half the cost of living. Between the First and Second World War the benefits were more elementary but equally important.

The internal comparison is the significant one, but it is also useful to compare the USSR with a Western country, if only to provide a frame of reference in which to measure the accomplishments. I will compare, therefore, the Soviet standard of living with the Italian, though I know that Italy is not the most advanced Western country. However, forty years ago Italy was 'way ahead of the USSR. I shall use my personal impressions over a five-year period, as well as some statistics. The comparison is more valid if one fact is kept in mind—the Soviet side is in rapid forward movement, while the Italian is practically stagnant. Italian consumption is static; that of the Soviets increases year by year.

The dominating item in all family budgets is food. There is no question whatever that the Soviet citizen eats better than the Italian, though not better than the Frenchman. I am speaking of the northern Italian rather than of the poorer southerner. Like the Italian, the Russian eats a lot of starch. He eats less vegetables. Above all, however, he consumes more meat, fats, milk, and butter. Statistics confirm my observations. I use Soviet production figures, but as the exports and imports are small and tend to balance, the figures will do roughly for consumption. In 1957—and things have improved since then in the USSR—the Soviet average per person was seventy-nine pounds of meat per year, while the Italian didn't reach forty-four pounds. For butter the figures are eight pounds for the Soviet, three and a third pounds for the Italian. As for sugar, the figures for 1958 are fifty-seven pounds for the Soviet and thirty-five pounds for the Italian. Statistics on milk are lacking, but here the disparity is far greater because the Russians use a lot more milk and milk products than do the Italians. We must not think that such consumption is traditional in Russia. People eat much better today than forty years ago, or even twenty years ago. Studies made in 1940 on families of workers and farmers show that while consumption of bread and other starches has gone down slightly, the consumption of milk, meat, eggs, and sugar has doubled. Increased consumption is restrained by insufficient production. Sugar, for example, is scarce in villages, but for 1960 the plan calls for a production and consumption of seventy pounds per person per year.

If the Soviet citizen eats better, he dresses worse than the Italian. Actually, the Italians who arrive and see the bundled-up Russian think he dresses worse than he really does. The English, the Germans, and the Americans are less scandalized by Russian clothes than the Italians are. Of course, if the truth be told, the Italians consider that the English, the Germans, and the Americans don't dress very well either. However, if you go to Tiflis, in Georgia, you will find among the Georgians a much higher level of clothes, for the Georgian has an elegance comparable to that of the Neapolitan. The climate, of course, constrains the Russian; for the greater part of the year he has to wear an overcoat three times heavier than one wears in Milan, a fur hat, heavy shoes, and woolen underclothes. However, it is true that his clothes look shabby; all clothes are scarce, of inferior quality, and very expensive. Production in this area has to increase in quantity and quality, and prices need to be lowered.

The Soviet level of education and culture is higher not only than the Italian but higher than that of any other country in the world, without excepting the American. I doubt that anyone would argue that education and culture are not part of a civilized standard of living. The Soviet citizen not only has greater opportunities for education, but he uses them to the full. Furthermore, he has easier access to all cultural areas. There are no fees whatever in any schools, including universities and institutes. Stipends are paid to the great majority of university students. There is a great variety and relative abundance of schools, libraries, laboratories, museums, and other facilities for students. Studying is one of the habits of the country. There are factories where the majority of the youth, and not only the youth, is studying while

Young ballerinas. Courtesy of the Hoover Institution, Russian Pictorial Collection, Envelope ʙᴋ, Item 21, Hoover Institution Archives.

holding down a job. Within a family, small personal libraries are very common. I don't believe there is a country in the world where the instruments of culture are available as easily and as cheaply as in the USSR. A good high-fidelity record of a Beethoven symphony is the same price as two packs of cigarettes. Books cost about the same. Tickets to the theater, the cinema, and the ballet are cheaper than in other countries and there is talk of making them even cheaper.

The greatest lack in the Soviet standard of living is housing. To understand the seriousness of this problem we must go back to the beginning. The young Soviet state inherited from tsarist Russia a collection of houses and living quarters totally insufficient and unhealthy, moth-eaten, as it were, during the First World War. These were ruined during the Civil War. In the old Russian cities, eighty-eight percent of the houses were wood. When we justly note the poor quality of Soviet building, we must remember that brick construction, which has centuries of tradition in the West, is still in its infancy in the USSR. As soon as they could, the Soviets began to build houses, but the needs of the first Five Year Plans took precedence and they never built as much housing as was necessary. At the same time, the strong industrial development created one of the most massive examples of urbanization the world has ever seen. Enormous numbers of peasants swamped the cities. Then came the war, and its devastation vastly worsened the housing problem. The first years of reconstruction were limited to rebuilding prewar housing, yet the population continued to rise. From 1950 on construction began to regain some ground, but it is only in the last few years that an enormous effort is being made on a huge scale. From 1913 to 1956 housing increased from one and a half billion square feet to six billion, a not inconsiderable increase. Yet the urban population went up from twenty-five million individuals to eighty-seven million.

The Soviet citizen is still badly housed. Everyone in the USSR is conscious of this and Khrushchev said plainly that here "we are still reduced to a system of rationing." True, there are no rationing cards, but the scarcity is obvious. People live on top of each other. Generally only one room is assigned to a household. An apartment is still rare. In general, the scarcity is felt equally by everybody. The academician, the well-known artist, or the scholar, who need privacy for their work, still live in small quarters. In part compensation for this situation, rents are ridiculously low—around four or five percent of wages. These are beyond doubt the lowest rents in the world, for they don't even pay maintenance costs. But there is no question of raising them unless and until there are better housing facilities.

I have compared only the chief material elements which make up a standard of living, things which are more easily measured. I could make comparisons in lesser areas—there is a scarcity of modern appliances and products (automobiles, for example, though not radios or TV's), of places of entertainment (cinemas and cafes, but not clubs or sports facilities). If I stopped here, the comparison would not be correct because not complete. There are three more factors to consider, factors which are decisive although not always included in the concept "standard of living."

The first factor is that of justice in distribution. Not that all people live at the same level; there are differences and they are necessary. But at the same time the USSR is a country where the extremes are, for the most part, not excessive. It is a country where, if somebody tells you that the average consumption is half a chicken a person, the statistic is not the result of my having eaten a whole chicken while you fasted. Averages have a more realistic content in the Soviet Union. The cities show little difference between the capital and the outlying regions, and if there is a difference it is not always in favor of the first. Just as there has been justice in the sacrifices required, there has been justice in the distribution of the good things. However small, a benefit is made generally available both socially and geographically. To realize how important this is, think for a moment of the great Western countries and their colonies. What would be the Western standard of living if the misery of the colonies, whose riches they exploited, were entered into the scale?

The second factor is perhaps even more important and illuminates the first. I refer to full employment, for women as well as for men. It has always been said that there is no unemployment in the USSR. This is correct. Unemployment has been eliminated for many years; it doesn't exist today and there is no possibility of its ever existing, not even as a remote or latent threat. But there is something more. No one *thinks* about unemployment, literally no one. It has vanished from the psychology of the worker. In this regard his security and tranquillity are complete. Moreover, the great majority of women work and rare is the family where there is only one income. Wages are not particularly high, except for certain categories (miners, oil workers, a few difficult and key skills) and for certain areas (because of the many drawbacks of the East and the North, workers are given some extra compensation). A table of comparative wages would mean very little, because of its complexity, because of different criteria of value (a coal miner gets more in the USSR than in any other country in the world, while this is far from true for a typographer), and because the differences in prices (high for clothes, low for rent, minimal for medicines) make the money values difficult to compare. However, in Moscow and elsewhere I had the clear impression that money was not lacking, and the widespread increase in savings confirms my impression. Full employment is behind this phenomenon.

It is misleading, therefore, to talk only of the fact that unemployment has disappeared. The Soviet citizen, particularly the young man, not only has no fears for his future; he is, so to speak, tempted by it. The work opportunities before him are numerous and varied, full of surprising possibilities. Whoever travels in the Soviet Union is struck by the extraordinarily adventurous life that people have. The mentality of man is being transformed; a totally new concept of life is evolving, of life as exciting, challenging, intensely interesting. This is an aspect which cannot be measured in a "standard of living" analysis, yet it seems to me equally as important as the statistics we have covered.

Finally, a third factor is found in that ensemble of rights, social achievements, and insurances (pensions, free medical care, canteens, rest homes, asylums) which have always been one of the most important areas of progress for Soviet workers. Many of these social achievements exist in other countries today, but the Soviet Union is the country where many of them first appeared, even when it was far behind other capitalist states. This is a fact which exists in the consciousness of Soviet workers and will not be erased, however much other countries copy them. Some of these benefits haven't even appeared in a country like the United States. Take pensions as an example. Their value had been considerably reduced by the war and its aftermath. In 1956 they were increased and they are now at a level that few countries can match. (Already promises of further increases have been made.) These pensions are paid entirely by the state, with no contributions from the citizens. Analogous observations can be made about sanitariums run by unions, where workers can spend their vacations. Not all people who want to can use them yet, but a lot do and more will. The same is true of canteens and restaurants, of which there are very many, serving meals at very low prices. These too will increase in number and in quality.

A special place must be given to free medical care. I don't mean to imply that it is perfect. The number of hospital beds per capita is inferior to German, English, French, and American levels. Although the number of beds has been multiplied eight times since 1913, it is still only at the Italian level. On the other hand, the proportion of doctors is greater than in any other country, including the USA. But the great fact about Soviet medical care is that it is absolutely free and the results are there for all to see. The mortality rate of the Soviet Union, which was four times greater than that of Western countries at the time of the Revolution, is today the lowest. The average expectation of life for a man has gone from 32 years to 67 years. The figure of a doctor has changed. The doctor is usually a woman and is a much less "important" personage than in the West, more familiar and democratic. Finally, in one aspect of medical care—childbirth—the USSR has no peer. The care given to pregnant women is methodical, rigorous, vigilant in the extreme. Ways have been found to minimize the pains of childbirth. This care given to pregnant women is matched by the other great aspect of Soviet life—the care given to infants and children. Children do have a privileged position in Soviet society, sheltered from sacrifices to the greatest possible extent. Kindergartens, youth hostels, camps are among the best institutions in the USSR and, though not fully sufficient, are enough to assure every city child three months in the country.

A full picture of life in the USSR is quite different from the images made up by people who stress its deficiencies. There are great achievements there, and more are on the way. There are gaps which are far from insignificant, but these are, in part, an important spur to Soviet production. The reasons for the deficiencies are worth examining; they are as instructive as the reasons for the successes.

For years the Soviet people have made sacrifices. Often in the West I've come across people who, unable to deny the achievements, lower their eyes virtuously and murmur that they cannot approve of the "human sacrifices" involved. There is, of course, a good dose of hypocrisy in such statements. The Soviet people, on the contrary, speak of their sacrifices with simple pride. It is true, they say, that for years we have dressed badly and renounced other goods, not because we discount their value but because we had no alternative. Khrushchev declared that in the peaceful construction of the country, his fellow citizens had shown the same spirit as they had fighting at the front in the Civil War. "We understood that we had no other road; either we tightened our belts, cut down on everything, and through a tenacious labor built the strength of our country, or we would be again smashed by the enemy, be dragged through the abyss of a lost war, and see ourselves condemned to a miserable existence under the heels of the capitalists and the landowners."

We should be clear, however, about what the Russians sacrificed. They sacrificed an abstraction—the consumer goods they could have had in place of some of the heavy industry. In the last analysis they sacrificed what they had never had before anyway. And, in the long run, without the heavy industry, they could never have had a chance of raising their standard of living substantially. What they have today they built with their hands. No one ever helped them; even the American machinery of the first Five Year Plans had to be handsomely paid for. In the mythology of the rising bourgeoisie, the individual who "builds himself" a fortune through ceaseless hard work and scrimping is considered a "hero," the incarnation of a capitalist, a Horatio Alger. The ideal is Ford, the man who started with nothing, the protagonist of the American legend. What shall we say then of an entire people who worked this way to create not individual wealth but social wealth?

When Did You Open Your Eyes? (2000)

Boris I. Shragin

Boris Shragin began his career as a Marxist and a member of the Communist Party. He was a teacher at the Surikov Art Institute in Moscow and a fellow of the Institute of the History of Arts in the USSR. In 1968 he was stripped of both his academic position and his Party membership as a result of his involvement with the human rights movement and his role as a signatory to a letter of protest against political prisoners held in Soviet psychiatric hospitals. Shragin emigrated with his family to the United States via Italy in 1974 and went to work for Radio Liberty, a subsidiary of Radio Free Europe. He taught and continued to write about Soviet intellectual dissent until his death at the age of sixty-three in 1990.

"When Did You Open Your Eyes?" re-creates those moments in the post-Stalin era when Soviet society had not completely shed the residue of Stalinism. As a young researcher Shragin is asked to accompany a group of foreigners to the studio of the Soviet painter Aleksandr Gerasimov, who created monumental murals of Stalin and socialist life strictly along the lines of socialist realism. Contact between Soviets and foreigners was highly circumscribed in the immediate post-Stalin era and continued as such up through the 1970s. Foreigners were confined to groups in order to keep better track of them; too many excursions and too little opportunity to get to know the country and its people were the usual complaints voiced by those who came to visit the USSR. There is a moment, however, when Shragin tries to break through and communicate his feelings to a Japanese tourist. He knows only the French word merde *(shit) to describe Gerasimov's paintings. For his part, the Japanese tourist understands that the art is bad, yet does not understand the context. Strangely, for all that they cannot communicate, it is the foreigner's question "When did you open your eyes?" that Shragin remembers years later. He sees it distilled in a moment of madness when his friend scaled a statue of a famous botanist on the day of Stalin's death and went with Shragin to finish off half a liter of vodka—in short, that moment when he finally stepped out of line.*

It was in 1957, during the All-World Youth Festival in Moscow, that I was given the task of accompanying a group of young foreign artists to the studio of

From left: Iosif Bogoraz, Elena Bonner, Viktor Nekrasov, Lev Kopelev, and Boris Shragin, 1969. Courtesy of Natal'ia Sadomskaia.

Aleksandr Gerasimov (at that time I was a researcher at the Institute for the History and Theory of Fine Arts). The choice put before our visitors, it must be said, was not a commanding one: either Aleksandr Gerasimov, or Nikolai Tomskii. The first offered painting; the second, sculpture. But apart from this technicality they were both paragons of socialist realism, typical representatives of Soviet pseudo-classicism devoted to the glorification of Stalin. Around this time both were equally derided in professional circles. Yet the fact that they could be chosen to represent the height of our artistic achievements was consistent with the aesthetic tastes of the government.

A few buses pulled up to the building that housed Gerasimov's apartment and studio on the day of the tour, and released some eighty visitors—Brits, Dutch, Japanese, Finns, Mongolians, and who knows who else—no matter. Gerasimov's home was in the Sokol district, an area much less built up than other parts of the city and very green—as close as the city might have gotten to an American suburb. By Moscow standards it was very posh.

They led us through several rooms to an enormous gallery. The rooms were laid out in Old World style, just as one might imagine the homes of wealthy merchants from Ostrovskii's plays: stuffed armchairs, tassels and fringes everywhere, green cloth lampshades, and the inevitable samovar. The museum feeling was cemented by the presence of two elderly ladies wrapped in shawls. And yet in spite of the grandeur of the space, it still felt cramped, dark, and musty.

At the time I had become an advocate of the modern rationalist style, a disciple of Bauhaus. The grand layout of Gerasimov's apartment did little to allay my already deeply rooted feelings against him. Though looking back today, when I am no longer such a worshipper of glass, metal, and concrete, the world of this omnipotent art world dictator leaves me less agitated. In his youth, before the Revolution, Aleksandr Gerasimov demonstrated all the signs of a great painter, with a talent for rich and joyful styles. He had more than one picture hanging in the Tret'iakov Gallery that were fine evidence of this. But when time came to adapt to the new era, there was clearly something in his character that resonated with the vulgar naturalism and pomposity of Stalinist taste. A more thoughtful visitor to his apartment at the time might have done better than me to understand this kind of double life—that there was something in his work that kept government regulators at bay, and yet saved something private for himself.

Gerasimov's studio gave pride of place to an enormous canvas featuring the usual scene from the life of Lenin. Gerasimov offered his interpretation in English with such an impenetrable accent that my foreign wards stood on in polite stupefaction. "*Zees iz . . .*" and so forth. They asked the ancient statesman of fine art to speak in Russian instead, with a translator, but he pressed on.

Out of boredom, the visitors drifted about the studio, looking in all corners, digging under piles of jetsam, and flipping over canvases that had long been turned to the wall. I was surprised to discover an enormous number of sketches on one and the same theme—the women's bathhouse. Our host fashioned himself a connoisseur of women so full-figured, large-breasted, and wide-hipped that they were almost formless. These steamy bodies suggested that our President of the Academy of Arts, of whom all had long tired, our foremost charlatan of the cults of Lenin and Stalin had been, at least artistically, quietly casting for forbidden fruit.

However one chose to see it, it was clearly all quite awful. Pools of oil ran across canvases like rouge on the face of an old woman who had lost her touch. Paint colors had faded and begun to meld into a brownish dirt. I could not begin to understand how it all had come to this.

I found my way to a small bench and resolved to patiently sit out the tour, the way one waits in a notary's office. A young Japanese man sat down next to me, to rest a moment and catch his breath. This was, after all, how they treated foreigners in our showcase Moscow, running them like horses around a track until they could no longer tell up from down.

We tried to make conversation but it was not easy. Through trial and error I explained that I was a better reader than speaker of English, but could manage a few phrases in French.

"*Merde*," I carefully pronounced, pointing to an unfinished canvas by the Great Master. There concluded my powers of speech.

"This person did not understand what Cezanne was about," commented my companion. He turned out to be an art historian from Tokyo.

I tried as best I could to explain that, nonetheless, the very same Aleksandr Gerasimov had served as the President of the Academy of Arts under Stalin. Obviously, I was not fulfilling the role for which I had been recruited. By all patriotic standards, I was betraying the Motherland.

"What was it that opened your eyes?" asked my companion.

I could not bring myself to answer, but not because I did not have the words. Open my eyes—to what? Aleksandr Gerasimov had never been my ideal.

On leaving, Gerasimov handed all the guests an autographed postcard of one of his works from the Tret'iakov collection. Even one for me. Only the Mongolian artists, unfortunate graduates of our Surikov Art Institute, looked grateful.

As our host waved us goodbye and the visitors returned to the bus, they began to cluck in all possible languages, "Gerasimov is a Picasso! He's a Picasso!"

My heart smiled. I envied them a certain bourgeois openness.

"When did you open your eyes?" I heard this question countless times after my own emigration.

Or the simpler variation:

"When did you become a dissident?"

The question is impossible to answer because the answer can only cast reality in its own image. Ancient Sophists reminded us of this when they asked, "When did you stop beating your parents?" If you have stopped, that means you used to beat them. If you haven't stopped, you beat them still. And I never beat them. Never.

In the spring of 1968, when I was excluded from the party and lost my job, I was a hero. My wife and I socialized a good deal. Friends tried to console us, support us, express their appreciations, and extend help when needed. Our social circle did not so much change as get significantly wider.

One day, at the height of my brief celebrity, I went to see Leonid Efimovich Pinskii. When I was a student, I had attended his lectures on European Literature, as no one taught the subject at the Institute of Philosophy. Later he was arrested, and at Komsomol meetings it was common to hear people refer to him as "Pinskii—that enemy of the people." But our friendship, or at least, a warm collegiality developed over time. We were both smokers and loved to talk as Muscovites do, that is, on all possible subjects. Sometimes, not often, we saw each other in Reading Room No. 3 at the Lenin Library and headed for the unforgettable smokers' corner downstairs for a chat, every hour on the hour.

I must admit that it was Leonid Efimovich who was the talker. He was an incomparable orator. To hold a conversation with him was to be sure to listen, never to interrupt and, optimally, to interject encouraging phrases periodically to enable him to keep going. Pinskii was a fountain of words. His eyes flashed with joy, then sarcasm, then irony (he was also prone to drooling slightly at moments of high narrative drama).

I never tired of listening to him. Jumping from one topic to the next he never lost the thread. Entire monologues spontaneously poured forth from his lips, replete with smart turns of phrase and unexpected quotations. His talent had nothing to do with chatting or passing the time, but was found in a genuine art of conversation. I would even call this a Russian art. Later in my life, in New York, I never found the Pinskii I so needed. My friend Geoffrey Hosking once wrote me after one of his trips to the USSR, "I basked in the art of Moscow conversation." Leonid Efimovich was a leading light of the genre.

I learned a great deal from him as well. One day I commented on how everyone I knew could not bear Marxism, could not hear a single word about Marx, or read him for even a moment. Leonid Efimovich began to share his thoughts on Marx but then interrupted himself. "In the house of a hanged man," he said, "it is not appropriate to speak of the rope." The moment was like a projector flash onto the night sky.

On March 5th, 1968, Leonid Efimovich invited me to take part in an unusual celebration. In an apartment in one of the writers' buildings on Krasnoarmeiskaia Street, there was a gathering of former political prisoners to mark the 15th anniversary of the death of Stalin. It was strange to me to celebrate the death of anyone, even a tyrant. But this kind of thing had gradually come into fashion. Whenever it started, 1968 or before, I can hardly recall a year when this day was not met with much food, drink, and laughter. But back then it was my first time. Moreover, it was the first time when I found myself the only one in a room who had not had the distinction of having served in prison. The invitation was a gesture of recognition for my political views. And, I have to admit, I was proud to be asked.

The event began exactly as if the men were still in camp. The women were energetically at work handing out regulation portions of black bread, with each man carefully measuring his slice against the length of a match so as not to lose out. Meanwhile, the conversation flowed. One fellow, an actor in the Moscow Theatre recounted how he had recently received a mysterious summons to appear at the KGB building on Lubianka Square. He went there in such fear and trembling that he was drenched in a cold sweat. Although he had no special cause for concern, he was convinced that his earlier rehabilitation would be revoked, that they would put him back in a prisoner's uniform and send him to the camps on the spot. His legs refused to move, but somehow he got there anyway, because it was unthinkable not to go. It turns out that they had merely invited him to their club, and wanted to ask if he would organize an amateur drama circle for them. The truly great thing was that he said no.

I knew many former prisoners, older ones from the time of Stalin's "cult of personality" and younger ones fresh from their release. There was not much in common between these two generations. Returning to freedom, prisoners of the Khrushchev and Brezhnev eras were often assumed by their superiors to be taking part in dissident activities, and were naturally terrified of being sent back to the camps. But they never had that mystical, unconscious, almost inhuman look of fear that you saw on the faces of Stalin's victims. Sergo Lominadze, son of the famous Bolshevik, whom students knew from the *Short Course on the History of the Party* and as an "immoral monster" once said to me flinchingly: "Anything goes, but just not *that*," while his face seemed to slowly twist in pain. Sergo, as the "son of an enemy of the people," first went to the camps as a child and spent his youth there.

It's not that I think physical conditions in the camps had improved any since Stalin's time. It wasn't that. The difference was that during Stalin's time, people landed in camps without the slightest awareness of any conflict with the government. And yet, there they were, on the wrong side of the fences and barbed wire. Prison came to them blindly and cruelly in the way that a flying brick lands on your head in the middle of the street on a bright day. Along with their hope, they lost all perspective; they became slaves, waiting only to die in loneliness and oblivion. They were not fighters.

The bread rations went around the table as symbols of the past. Soon appeared an array of more appealing delicacies and, of course, vodka and, of course, cognac—far from the life of the camps. The actor found a guitar and began to sing from a wide repertoire. Galich's "Ave Maria" is one I can not forget: the common, almost banal story of the death of a nameless prisoner told in the cynical and dry jargon of the setting, but mixed in with the pure music of the Holy Mother. The refrain would catch you by the soul, "And

Madonna went through Judea . . ." again and again and again. For those who had lived through the camps, it was not a song about humiliation but about the mortal encounter between good and evil, between kindnesses and monstrosities. Some listeners wept. I, too, did not hurry to wipe away my tears.

It was decided that all present should recount where they were and what they did on the day of the death of the notorious Georgian, Stalin. We were reminded that the names of prisons and camps were changed. Those who were kept in "general" detention were now in "minimum security facilities"; those who had been working in the fields were moved to lighter clerical and commercial tasks. But the picture was the same among everyone. For my companions, the death of Stalin was the first sign of hope. These memories lifted everyone's spirits, as much as the act of remembering itself.

And me? There's no way out now. Time to confess.

On March 5th, 1953, I was to give lessons at school. In the tram I took to get there, there was a heavy silence. If passengers spoke at all, it was in whispers. I looked out the window and thought, everything looks the same. But, of course, everything was different, because *he* no longer existed. As long as I could remember he was always there. Without him the future was a complete unknown.

En route I improvised for my lessons and lectures. I decided to not worry about the usual classroom drills since this was a day, if there ever was one, when students had every right to come to class unprepared. It would almost be blasphemous for them to study as usual. I planned instead to launch into a story, but to make sure that it was all somehow about Stalin.

I worked in a girls' school and, though I had only just turned twenty-six, I had become a bit shy, or perhaps better said, a bit earnest before my students. How could you not lose your composure before a room of sixteen and seventeen year-old girls, in their black pinafores with white collars and their modest hairdos? It's very probable that on that particular morning, amidst the flurry of emotions, I was also looking to make an impression.

The lesson was in psychology and by the schedule I was to hold forth on "the life of the mind"—on the values of a wide erudition, originality, self-criticism, and I don't remember what else. I punctuated the lecture with events from the life of Stalin, what I could recall at least, along the way. My young maidens wept. At the sharper moments, they looked almost as if to be silently begging, "Please! Enough!" But I, flush with inspiration, pressed on ahead.

Before the bell rang, I sat behind the teacher's desk and said practically in a whisper, "The most important thing for us all now is to maintain our reserve, and to work." Thus was a Soviet teacher to speak to his Komsomol flock.

Ha! You don't take the words out of the song [*iz pesni slova ne vykinesh*]. That's just the way it was.

After teaching, I called my friend Eval'd Il'enkov and arranged to meet him in our usual spot at the Nikita Gates. Around then we saw each other almost every day.

All over the city there were mourning banners, and advertising placards were covered over with blank paper.

When I reached the Timiriazev monument on Nikitskii Boulevard, I understood that Eval'd had not yet arrived. Getting ready to patiently wait it out, I sat down on a bench, lit a cigarette, and saw the most extraordinary sight. Eval'd had climbed up on the pedestal and, sidling up to Timiriazev in some kind of grotesque embrace, pulled back his head and was looking up to the cloudy sky. He was clearly having a good time.

"Eval'd, get down! How could you do this on a day like today?"

"Borik, come on, *he's* the one who keeled over!"

Indeed, it struck me. He had died, really, after all.

And so in high moods we went to finish off the half litre of vodka that Eval'd had set aside for a special occasion.

So maybe that was it, at 6 p.m. Moscow time, on March 5th, 1953, when I opened my eyes?

The very question presumes a sharp, momentary break. As if someone who has marched in strict file suddenly hears *"Abooouuut face!"* and turns to march in the opposite direction. This can happen to individuals and their personal development, but not with whole societies, and not with history. In history there is no one to give the commands to, because the passengers and commanders are all on the same train.

The person who lives through several decades and experiences such dramatic events still remains the same person, if not someone who ages prematurely. Turns of event in every biography are inevitable. Perhaps what stays constant are the philosophies we preach, our theoretical foundations, that which builds intelligence. The life of the mind is made strong by this consistency, and for the ability to reject that which doesn't agree with established sensibilities. But man does not live by prudence alone, for experience changes him little by little, quietly but constantly. He, for his part, projects his character onto a world each day refashioned. And history moves forward as far as the sum of human wills can carry it.

Translated by Bruce Grant

The Last Trolley (1957)

Bulat Okudzhava

The atmosphere of the Thaw period spilled out onto the streets. Poets recited their poetry on city squares and street corners. The names of Yevgeny Yevtushenko and Andrei Voznesenskii became widely known for the poetry that dared to speak about what was unspeakable during the Stalin years. As artistic life and public performance awoke from the stalemate of the past, a new genre of music appeared: guitar poetry. In one sense the genre had existed for centuries, its roots reaching deep into Russia's oral folk tradition. But in the late 1950s and 1960s this unique blending of poetry and song became associated with specific performers, especially Aleksandr Galich, Novella Matveeva, and Vladimir Vysotskii. It was Bulat Okudzhava, however, who was the undisputed leader of the group. In the 1960s the availability of the tape recorder meant that the songs of the guitar poets made their way across the Soviet Union into millions of homes. Soviet audiences loved the songs both because they were often poetry set to music and because, while the songs were not always expressly dissident, the poets took ample advantage of the new freedoms allowed during the Khrushchev era.

Born in Moscow to Armenian and Georgian parents, Okudzhava (1924–97) composed lyrics that resonated deeply with his audience and caught the spirit of the times. Many of his early songs came in for official condemnation partly for their pacifist leanings, but by the 1970s his repertoire was readily available through official channels. A melancholic strain runs through many of his songs, whether he wanders through the streets of Moscow or sits on the last trolley at night. Live recordings of his performances are widely available on the Internet.

When I haven't the strength to overcome my troubles,
When despair's creeping up,
I get on a blue trolleybus as it passes,
The last one, a chance one.

Midnight trolleybus, sweep through the streets,
Make your circuits round the boulevards,

Picking up everyone who in the night has suffered
Disaster, disaster.

Midnight trolleybus, open your door for me!
For I know that this freezing midnight
Your passengers, your crew,
Will come to my aid.

It's not the first time I've left trouble behind
Riding shoulder to shoulder with them . . .
You wouldn't think there is so much goodness
In silence, in silence.

The midnight trolleybus sails through Moscow,
The roadway flows away into dawn . . .
And the pain that pecked like a starling in my temple
Grows quiet.

Translated by G. S. Smith

XIII

Russians Abroad, Near and Far

Even before Peter the Great opened his famous window on the West in the early eighteenth century, Russians had been traveling abroad as pilgrims, diplomats, and merchants. Beginning with Peter's mandate that the doors to the West be forcibly opened, Russians of a certain class began traveling abroad, most often to Western Europe. Some were sent on government missions, others to be educated. Some traveled there for medical treatment, as did Dostoyevsky, or went and stayed for love, as did another nineteenth-century Russian writer, Ivan Turgenev. So long did Turgenev stay in Europe that Dostoyevsky advised him to get himself a telescope to see Russia better if he remained intent on writing about it from afar. Among the well-to-do it was fashionable to take the waters in Germany; we read in Tolstoy's *Anna Karenina* of the Shcherbatskii family traveling to Baden-Baden for several months in an effort to restore their daughter Kitty's health after her disappointment in love. While the Shcherbatskiis strolled among the spas, other Russians in the 1850s and 1860s were using Europe, and in particular Switzerland, as an intellectual staging area for the radical ideas that would culminate in the Bolshevik Revolution. In the early twentieth century Lenin, Trotsky, and Lunacharskii, among others, all spent time abroad, where they worked out the strategies for the coming revolution. Indeed, it has been said that the Bolshevik Revolution would most probably have never taken place had the revolutionaries not been able to live and plan their strategies in the very Western European countries whose economic and political systems Marxist doctrine was most intent on overthrowing.

By the late 1920s the whole notion of moving across borders acquired a different tone. For most of the twentieth century, it is not of the Russian traveler we speak, but of the Russian émigré or the exile, as Russians, motivated by political, religious, economic, and artistic considerations, left their country for Europe, China, South America, Australia, and the United States. Indeed, the Russian emigrations of the twentieth century were mostly a response to political rupture at home, causing the voluntary or forced displacement of millions. The emigrations from Russia and the Soviet Union are generally spoken of in terms of waves, each one placing its own particular stamp on the émigré experience.

Although there had been a substantial Jewish exodus from Russia in the late nineteenth century and another just prior to the First World War, the first wave of emigration generally dates from the Bolshevik takeover in 1917, more specifically from the defeat of the White Army in the Civil War (1918–21). Those who fled were primarily White Army officers and members of the nobility, the bourgeoisie, and the landed gentry. Many made their way to Western Europe, primarily Berlin and Paris, the latter of which increasingly became the center for émigré life. Others, many of whom had fought in the White Army in Siberia, fled to Harbin in Manchuria, an area that had already been settled by Russians involved in the building of the Russian-Chinese Eastern Railway in the 1880s. By the 1930s much of the émigré community in China had shifted south to Shanghai in response to Japanese incursions into Manchuria and greater opportunities in Shanghai among a large international community. In 1945 the first wave of emigration that had brought Russians to China came to an end as Mao rose to power. Some émigrés, as Natal'ia Il'ina poignantly recounts in this section, chose to return to their homeland, while others pulled up roots yet again and left for South America or the United States, where many settled in San Francisco.

Although the cultural geography of the two émigré communities in Western Europe and China was very different, the two groups shared one thing in common: both were convinced that their displacement would be short-lived and that return to their homeland was imminent. The realization that such was not to be hit Russia's émigrés hard, as they set about the business of making their way in a world that was essentially alien to them. This first wave of emigration had been educated in prerevolutionary Russia and carried that culture abroad with them, where they attempted to perpetuate it and transmit it to their children born in emigration and to the foreign cultures where they were now living.

These two primary cultural environments within which the first wave of emigration found itself each molded the émigré in different ways. In some ways, the émigré communities in Paris and Berlin had an easier time of it because the European world was less alien to them than the Chinese society of Harbin. But to say that there was no cultural assimilation among the Russian community of Harbin is as inaccurate as to say that there was complete cultural assimilation between the Russian émigré community in Paris and French life. Some argue that the cultural proximity that allowed a degree of assimilation in Europe unavailable to the Russians in Manchuria led to a watering-down of Russian culture in Western Europe that Harbin émigré culture never experienced. On the other hand, much that was written by the émigré community in Western Europe became more readily accessible to the Western reader than did literary output from the Harbin emigration, whose publication venues gave them less access to the West.

With the 1940s came the second wave of Russian emigration, which consisted mainly of those who had gotten caught up in various ways in the German invasion. By the time the Soviet Union entered the Second World War in 1941, Russians had lived through forced collectivization and forced industrialization. They had gone through the purges that would gather momentum again after the war, and as a consequence there were those who were all too willing to go over to the German side. Others were forcibly recruited by the Germans to work for them; still others were taken prisoner during the war and remained in Europe when released. This wave of emigration distinguished itself from the first in that it did not form itself into a well-defined community with a defined response to the political situation at home. It did not produce the writers or thinkers that the first and third waves did, but what it did produce was a complicated response from those Russians who were already living in émigré communities abroad. Those who were still alive from the first wave viewed the new arrivals as less educated and socially refined than those who had made their way to Western Europe after the Civil War. The relations between the two waves were further complicated by the fact that while many first-wave émigrés had supported the Soviet Union in the war against the Nazis (although even that decision was fraught with complexities), they tended to identify the second-wave émigrés with the Soviet system. Thus much of the anger they felt against the system that had caused their displacement to begin with was redirected against their own countrymen who arrived in the 1940s.

The third wave of emigration from the Soviet Union began in the 1970s and consisted primarily of Soviet Jews. Anti-Semitism has deep roots in Russia that predate by centuries the establishment of the Soviet state. Soviet Jews, however, had more than religious reasons for wishing to emigrate, reasons that were shared by more than the Jewish community. After Stalin's death many Jews had sought to stay in the Soviet Union, hoping for an improvement in their situation in view of the fact that Moscow had reestablished relations with Israel. Many saw themselves as Russians first and Jews second. But as the economy stagnated and promises of liberal reform disappointed, increasingly Soviet Jews sought reunification with their families abroad; they wanted a better standard of living, and they wanted to live where they could breathe freely. However, up until the 1970s, the number of Jews allowed to emigrate remained minuscule.

Soviet emigration policy in regard to third-wave emigration became entangled in the 1970s with international affairs, in particular with the Jackson-Vanik Amendment passed by the U.S. Congress in 1974, which tied the granting of "most favored nation" trade status to the Soviet Union's willingness to allow Jews to emigrate. The Soviet government, however, repeatedly dug in its heels, resulting in an emigration process that became both arbitrary and uncertain. Once they applied to emigrate, many Soviet Jews found that their personal situation became intolerable, resulting in loss of jobs and apartments and being constantly subject to harassment or worse.

The third wave of emigration associated with the Brezhnev era in the late 1960s and the 1970s was in many ways closer in spirit to the first wave in that it consisted of artists, writers, and people who were highly educated. Many were dissidents; some, such as Aleksandr Solzhenitsyn, were forcibly exiled. Many had already made their career in the Soviet Union, among them the writers Vasilii Aksenov, Joseph Brodsky, Lev Kopelev, Andrei Sinyavskii, Aleksandr Solzhenitsyn, and Aleksandr Zinov'ev and the cellist and conductor Mstislav Rostropovich and his wife, the opera singer Galina Vishnevskaia. While the United States had received members of both the first and second waves, it was the third wave that flocked specifically to U.S. shores. Unlike the first wave that was centered in Paris, Berlin, and Harbin, the third wave fanned out across the United States, settling where their professions took them, most notably Brighton Beach, known as Little Odessa, in Brooklyn, New York. By and large, Russian émigrés from the Brezhnev years did not form the kind of close-knit émigré communities that characterized the early years of emigration.

The new freedoms and the initial economic and political uncertainties in post-Soviet Russia have given birth to yet a fourth wave of emigration, this one socioeconomic in nature. When Russians emigrate today they are no longer obliged to leave behind their culture, family members, and professional relationships. Increasingly the two worlds, once so far apart, have again found each other through travel, the Internet, and an increasingly globalized world. And yet ultimately the émigré experience, whatever else it has brought those who have taken part in it, has not lost the fundamental anomie and dislocation that any new life in foreign lands brings with it. Even as more and more Russians today make themselves part of a broader international community, that sense of displacement still tugs at the heart of many.

Russian Harbin (1998)

Elena Taskina

Elena Petrovna Taskina was part of the Harbin emigration. Born there in 1927, she left for the Soviet Union in 1954, the year after Stalin's death. Almost forty years passed between the time she returned to the Soviet Union and the publication of her memoirs in 1994, for the Soviets forbid the publication of works extolling the virtues of émigré life. The openness that glasnost brought with it in 1986 kindled a renewed interest on the part of many Russians in first-wave emigration, about which they knew very little.

Taskina paints a picture of Harbin at a complicated moment in its history. Although the city predated the arrival in 1898 of the Russians who came to help build the Chinese Eastern Railway, the Russian émigrés who settled there claimed Harbin for themselves and viewed it as having been founded by Russians. By the 1920s Russian émigré life in China was concentrated almost exclusively in Harbin. Taskina describes a city increasingly destabilized, as the Soviet government, long a partner in the joint Sino-Soviet administration of the Chinese Eastern Railway, was forced to sell its holdings to the Chinese puppet state of Manchukuo that was under Japanese control. As the Japanese government made further inroads into Manchukuo, creating both political and economic instability for the local Russian émigré community, the Russians began to move to Shanghai, Beijing, and Tianjin to escape Japanese control.

Not surprisingly, much of what Taskina writes is a nostalgic evocation of a place whose day-to-day struggles had dimmed with the years. The reality of the Harbin emigration was that many Russians, among them nobility, suffered a stunning decline in their living standards. It is also unclear what the effect was of the lack of true contact between the two cultures, each so foreign to the other yet occupying the same city. There are those who argue that it was precisely the lack of assimilation that kept Russian culture alive and undiluted in the Harbin emigration. Others maintain that these same forces created a climate wherein émigré culture was deprived of the very influences from the outside that might have enabled it to develop more than it did.

Sometimes I see this in my dreams: a train comes into the Harbin station. I leave the car, go out to the square, turn right and go up Station Boulevard directly to the Church of St. Nicholas. On the right are the Moscow Rows and on the left the "lace" house of Gibello Socco. Here's Bolshoi Boulevard. I go in the direction of the Churin complex, and then beyond, past the Church of the Feast of the Protection of the Mother of God. Soon I'll get a glimpse of the spire of the Lutheran church, but I keep going, past the Catholic Church, the Buddhist shrine and Paradise Temple, to Assumption Cemetery, where my ancestors are buried.

I have not been there in over forty years.

In reality, practically none of this remains, neither the churches, nor the cemetery, nor the old railway station. The city's inhabitants who attended these churches have been scattered in different directions. The wind of history has blown them around the world, and many have passed away, but the memory of how representatives of many ethnic groups and religions lived for almost half a century in China is still alive. Their invisible traces are guarded by sections of Bolshoi Boulevard, and by other parts of Harbin, with their synagogues, mosques, an Armenian church and a Confucian shrine.

In spite of its Russian features, Harbin developed from its earliest years as a multi-national city. The major ethnic groups created national-cultural societies, thereby preserving a historical dedication to their peoples. Since my early years I can remember how, in addition to mentioning the usual notable dates from Russian history and culture, the local press would also publish announcements from the various colonies about their own events. The Latvians are inviting their countrymen to a bonfire on the left bank of the Sungari River in honor of Ligo, their national holiday. The Georgian colony was observing its annual national holiday—the creation of a monarchy in Georgia. The "Brit-Trumpeldor" and "Maccabee" unions of Jewish Youth propose commemorating several important dates: the thirtieth anniversary of the death of the famous Jewish writer I. Perets, one hundred years since the birth of the historian Shaefer. The "Polish Lords" invite you to a concert. Or, "The Muslims are observing a month of fasting, Ramadan, which has begun with the evening prayers 'Taravikh Namazy' in the mosque." And there were other announcements—many more than I can remember.

From the distance of the decades I've lived through since, I would say that religion had the strongest effect on the national consciousness of people who had been torn away from their traditional homes. And let me add to that: religious tolerance, which distinguished life in Harbin in those years. As I've already mentioned, in Harbin alone, by 1940, there were twenty Orthodox churches for the thirty to forty thousand Russian émigrés, but there were also mosques, synagogues, a Catholic church, a Protestant church and an Armenian church. It is also worth noting this fact: the "Three Russian Heroes" desk calendar that was published in Harbin for twenty-three years contained, in addition to the complete Orthodox calendar, several less comprehensive ones: Roman Catholic, Protestant (Lutheran), Armenian Apostolic (Gregorian), Jewish and Muslim.

I remember that in addition to the Russians in my class there was a Czech girl, several Jews, Koreans and Chinese. Our group at the college included Tatar and Greek girls and a Jewish boy. In her memoir, the former Harbin resident Dvorzhinskaia writes, "In our apartment building there was an old Chinese man from the steppes who owned two houses connected by a court-yard; a Japanese man with a Russian wife; a large Indian family that owned a silk fabric store; a Turk and his wife, who was half-German and half-Russian; a Polish family; a young Jewish couple; and the Chinese caretaker, who also had a large family. What a conglomeration!"

However, the most important thing was that this multi-cultural fellowship existed under an alien, although very hospitable, sky against the background of the unique world that was old China, the life and reality of which were on an altogether different order than that of the other nationalities.

I should mention that Harbin and, for that matter, the entire territory alongside all the branches of the railway line, had been almost unpopulated not very long before this and was growing incredibly fast, attracting as it did a great number of Chinese residents. Even on the eve of World War Two, these seemingly incompatible realities were closely intertwined: alongside the rick-shaws and two-wheeled Chinese vehicles called "maches" there were Russian cabbies and later, Russian taxis. Sometimes in the winter, a bit of northern exoticism—horse-drawn sleighs—would appear on the snowy streets.

Kvartalov's butcher shop and the Ter-Akopov kebab shop were neighbors with a Chinese shop, and the Vorontsov Brothers Dairy adjoined an Asian textile shop. The famous Toon Faloon Company survived happily, in spite of the powerful network of factories and departments of I. Ia. Churin and Co., and the many foreign firms in Harbin in the 1930s.

The dynamic Chinese traders eagerly carried goods and rendered various services to their buyers, so that there was constant bustling on the street. The Chinese, who quickly adopted Russian customs and the church calendar to create considerable profit for themselves, invariably appeared on the streets with pussy willows and flowers on the eve of Easter, with fir trees for New Year's and Christmas, and with bunches of fragrant grass for the Trinity.

Before Epiphany, the Harbin diocese would place an order with skillful Chinese and Russian craftsmen to erect a cross and pulpit out of ice on the Sungari, and they would carve a christening font in the thick part of the icy crust. The huge ice cross, rising above the open space of the frozen river and the railroad bridge spanning it, glistened in the sunlight. Imagine for yourselves: there's a holiday procession, and in the distance comes a "push-push" —an unprecedented form of sleigh transport (actually, the only one of its kind)—driven by Chinese "gondoliers" in winter caps with ear flaps and quilted coats. "Jordan" on the Sungari River, the festive crowd of Russians and Chinese noisily celebrating in the crackling January frost. Bathing in the ice font. And in the winters, sometimes in the intolerable January wind, we would go to Modiagou (*Ch.* Majiagou) to the churchyard of the charity home to see the next marvel: church objects and utensils all made out of ice. Illuminated from the inside by electric light, they produced an indelible impression. And they were created jointly, by Chinese and Russian craftsmen.

How did we all understand each other? In general, unless we are talking about individual specialists, the local Russian population did not study Chinese very seriously. Nevertheless, Russians and Chinese understood each other very well in their everyday lives, using a completely inimitable "Far Eastern" method of discourse.

In his short story, "A Portrait," A. Nesmelov has a dialogue between a Russian and a Chinese about someone who has disappeared without a trace. He gives us an idea about this distinctive Far Eastern "pidgin."

> "Him, my thinks, already isn't live."
> "What? What do you mean? Explain to me what might have happened to him."
> "Him say, that him wants 'contras' for self."
> "What are you saying? For what reason?"
> "Him say, my live now don't want . . . Him say, my go Fujiadian, little little khanshin drink and in Sungari is drown."
> "But why didn't you say anything earlier."
> "My don't know. No my business."

Russians, especially the young ones, could make themselves understood in Chinese, limiting themselves to the words necessary for getting around every day. Many Russian orientalists, who studied original texts, had a high level of knowledge, not just of conversational but also of literary and written Chinese.

I should note that the administration of the Chinese Eastern Railway (CER) tried to institute a reasonable language policy in Harbin during those years. The directorate organized permanent Chinese language courses for its Russian workers, and Russian for Chinese specialists. Textbooks, instructional materials and dictionaries were published.

Beginning in 1924, about the time that the CER began its joint operation by

ЛУЧ АЗІИ

НА СУНГАРИ У ІОРДАНИ.
Снято г. Д. Л. Невилль камерой „Лейка".

Январь 1938 г.   Харбин. № 41-1.

At the annual ice festival, Harbin, 1938. Cover image from the journal *Luch Azii* 41, no. 1 (1938). Courtesy of Patricia Polansky, University of Hawai'i, Hamilton Library Collection of Chinese Imprints.

the USSR and China, the entire life of the city was lived under, as we now say, pluralism. Religious music and church services existed alongside celebrations of May 1 and November 7. There were Soviet foreign trade organizations (Dal'gostorg, Dal'bank and other agencies) along with foreign consulates and foreign companies. There were Soviet style professional unions in the roads department of the CER. A Refugee Committee, supported by voluntary contributions, worked to provide necessary aid to refugees who found themselves in difficult straits. Performers from the Soviet Union as well as local artists gave performances in Zhelsob [Harbin's theater], and both Soviet and émigré poets and writers vied with one another in the literary-artistic associations. Wonderful Soviet and imported goods from various countries were sold in the Moscow Rows on Cathedral Square [meant as a "trade museum" to showcase new Russian goods to Chinese consumers] where, alongside other institutions, the CER workers' cooperative was located. The newspaper stands sold newspapers with different political views. CER workers would go home to Russia on business trips and write about their impressions in the press.

For many, a new and difficult life began, testing their endurance and stability in the struggle for existence. After all, the political changes in Manchuria were followed by complications caused by the global economic crisis. Exports of agricultural products—the foundation of Manchurian trade—declined considerably. Representatives of various procurement firms and brokerages, as well as foreign companies, began to close their doors. A similar fate awaited many local trading enterprises, all of which resulted in unemployment. Owners not only reduced the numbers of workers, but also cut their salaries.

At that time there were no professional unions other than the Soviet ones at the Chinese Eastern Railway. For this reason, there were no pensions or other forms of social security. A man would work and receive his salary, but if he got sick—sorry! Only the larger respectable firms, including I. Ia. Churin and Co., gave workers who could not continue to work because of old age a so-called "discharge benefit."

Yet we had to pay for everything. If there was no well in the courtyard, we had to bring water home ourselves from a water distribution pipe (or we hired water carriers, whom we had to pay monthly for their services). It was expensive to bring a water line to a private home. We bought firewood at the lumberyard for heating and then brought it home and unloaded it. . . . For our secondary, and especially our university educations—money was required everywhere for "proper instruction." Rent for an apartment or room (and not necessarily in a brick building with plumbing but even in an adobe house with no conveniences) took up a large portion of one's salary. It was under these conditions—and they became common for Russian émigrés in those years—that we had to feed our families and raise and educate our children.

Of course, there was social stratification depending on one's property, profession or education. Owners of stores, income producing buildings, or enterprises, or simply entrepreneurs with resources were the classes that were the best off in Harbin society. (There were Soviet citizens among them during those years.) Qualified and enterprising engineers and managers of large-scale enterprises constituted their own "sub-class."

The region's long-term residents—Soviet railway workers and foreigners—these constituted vertical slices, as it were. I should note that all of them, living abroad as they were, endeavored to understand one another. If we ignore the attitudes of the political "top," most of the population did not have strongly expressed antagonisms, although occasionally you did see individual manifestations of this.

Nonetheless, the émigrés probably had it hardest under those complex conditions. Understandably, the emigration—the more than 100,000 Russian speakers of Harbin and Manchuria—was not and could not be a uniform group in those years. It represented all classes of pre-revolutionary Russia with their own habits, customs and hierarchical social relationships, although it is true that for many, the struggle for existence "leveled" out earlier affectations.

These people, who had come to Manchuria over the ice of Lake Baikal, or who had suffered through the ordeals of maritime escapes through Korea, or had simply crossed the Chinese border with only the things they could carry in their arms (for various reasons few could leave the USSR on ordinary passenger itineraries)—struggled both materially and psychologically. "Their" Russia no longer existed. They, and even their children, had been declared enemies in their own country. They all hoped for the possibility of return, but the oldest generation died on alien soil with the bitter taste of loss and ruin, having survived all kinds of political upheavals in a country that was not their own.

The next major political event that took place was the Japanese occupation of Manchuria. It started in 1931, and at daybreak on February 6, 1932, Japanese units entered Harbin. This was the beginning of a new and difficult page in the life of the city, a collision of eras that would play out over the next fifteen years.

Did this happen unexpectedly? After all, Japan had long been attempting to expand its influence in Manchuria and China, and its relations with Russia in the Far East region after the Russo-Japanese War and the signing of the Portsmouth Agreement were determined by expansionist policies imposed on the country by militaristic circles. The aggressive goals of these policies, which were carried out against the Soviet Union as well, have now been thoroughly examined by historians from a distance of several decades. However, for most of the Russian population in Harbin, these events seemed unexpected at the time.

Since the Japanese military did not encounter any resistance, they acted very energetically. By the end of February of that year, Pu Yi, the former emperor of the Tsin dynasty, was declared the "temporary ruler-regent," and on March 1, 1932, the independent state of Manchukuo was declared set up, transformed two years later into the Manchurian Empire, with Pu Yi as Emperor. Even a new way of counting years, Kan-de, was introduced, according to which time was counted from the year of "Emperor Pu Yi's ascension to the throne." In official documents in Russian, all dates were written in an expanded fashion, for example, "1936, third year of Kan-de."

The new regime imposed countless burdens on the peoples of Manchuria. The Chinese in particular suffered, although thousands of Russians fell under its well-organized oppression as well. This did not, however, happen immediately. The appearance of Japanese units in Harbin occurred rather quietly, and was hardly felt at first. Dressed in khaki-colored uniforms, wearing fur caps (most of the Japanese in Manchuria were not used to heavy frosts), short, disciplined, they smiled and went about their business quietly, patting children on the head and generally behaving neutrally.

The mostly Chinese police were responsible for keeping order in the city, although sometimes there were Russians among them. The Emigrants' Office, which took care of the Russian residents, continued to operate. However, as is well known, the Japanese military missions played a role behind the scenes in social and political matters.

In the 1930s, the population of Harbin began to grow slowly as a result of Japanese civilian emigrants. A government office, Mantaku, was established to build Japanese settlements on agricultural lands that brought some economic changes. Japanese stores and businesses began to appear. Japan continued to tread across Manchuria with increasing confidence, and it expanded its influence in this region. The economy of the region gradually turned out to be fully dependent on Japanese business concerns and banks.

There remained one last bastion of independence—the CER, which was controlled, as I mentioned before, jointly by the Soviet Union and China. However, beginning in the middle of 1931, Japanese authorities used various excuses to restrict the USSR's rights over the CER: they began to seize railyard right-of-ways and forcibly closed its commercial offices. There were groundless arrests of Soviet citizens.

Under these circumstances, the Soviet side decided to sell its rights-of-way to the Manchurian government of Manchukuo, though in fact, this was a sale to the Japanese powers. In 1935, after a two-year long negotiation, the Soviet Union sold the CER for the very modest sum of 140 million yen, although the check it received was for only 23 million yen.

Thus, for a short period of time (about ten years), the railway received a new name, assigned it by history, the Northern-Manchurian Railway (NMR). People began to leave. The first to set out for their homeland were the Soviet rail workers. Emotions, gatherings, partings, separations. Friends and acquaintances left. Ties were broken, as a rule, forever.

I remember how our family twice prepared to depart, but because of a confluence of family circumstances, we remained in Harbin. Only father had left for the USSR. Grandfather received a one-time discharge benefit from the CER, while for mother, who had worked until then in one of the foreign trade organizations, a difficult life began.

The courtyards of the railway workers' apartments became empty. For a long time we children would walk around the little summer houses and kitchens without supervision, looking into the empty or half-empty open sheds.

The railway workers lived in single-storied, brick or stone company houses

Chinese boy and Russian boy at play, Harbin, 1930s. Courtesy of F. E. Fuhrman III. Source: The Hoover Institution, Frederick E. Fuhrman Collection, Envelope D, Item 1, Hoover Institution Archives.

with little gardens and yards. I spent my childhood in such a house, not far from Cathedral Square in New Town. The large garden in front of the house was a wondrous place, a secluded corner, surrounded by Manchurian elms and acacia bushes. Children from neighboring houses would invariably gather here to compete to play Russian baseball (*lapta*), "Cossacks and Robbers," or the eternal hide-and-seek (it was a blessing that we had many places to hide — the yard was filled with a variety of empty buildings). Games such as "pictures" and "marbles," the owner of which was the winner of the game, were irresistibly attractive. (I must say that Chinese merchants could respond instantly to the possibility of making some money from this adolescent passion and, using American marbles as models, they produced them somewhere and then sold the glass balls, which enticed us with their color combinations and intricate incrustations, everywhere.)

Every place has its own games and its own heroes. Harbin, at the intersection of many roads, borrowed some unsophisticated lore from children of other countries. Not only heroes from Russian folk tales penetrated our world, but those from Disney cartoons and American comic books as well. (I should mention, as an aside that in those years Western heroes were kinder than those of the present and didn't resemble today's aggressive supermen.) We would cut out the images from the comics we particularly liked and save them. We were also fascinated by miniature portraits of movie stars that were included in packs of American cigarettes.

These and others were the trophies we hunted in the empty yards. It would happen that we would find other things as well that reminded us of the people who had lived here: buttons, scraps of fabric, fragments of photographs and letters, remnants of old household utensils that their "competitors" from neighboring blocks had not managed to pick up. Was there something romantic about those naughty childish expeditions to neighboring yards?

While this was going on, the previous residents of these places, full of enthusiasm and hope, were approaching or crossing the border of that "wondrous land of Five-Year Plans and achievements." No one knew then, that two years later, in the fateful year of 1937, many of them would become victims of the repressions and would share their homeland's tragic fate.

And what about Harbin itself? It did not empty out, although the Russian inhabitants were leaving in small, steady streams for Shanghai and other cities in China. Soon afterwards, their vacated homes were occupied by Japanese transplants. The problem of living space became even more acute. In our family, too, the question of where to live intensified. Farewell to the well-equipped railway residences! We began our ordeal of looking for private apartments.

With the sale of the CER, the face of Harbin began to change drastically. At first, the changes had to do with the railway itself: there were no longer Russian conductors or switchmen, and the Russian porters disappeared. There were fewer Russian cabbies. Many private Russian enterprises shut down. On the other hand, all the new signs of a Japanese presence started to appear: on holidays Japanese flags flew together with the flags of Manchukuo, and there were men's and women's kimonos, which Japanese civilians still wore.

"How can they stand our thirty degree below temperatures with wind in that light clothing?" the Russians would wonder as they watched the Japanese walk in their kimonos, bravely and steadily along the city's snow-covered streets. Indeed, the Japanese settlers tried to acclimatize with enviable tenacity. Many, although they did not change the style of their dress, tried to overcome the severity of the Manchurian winter by wearing woolen belly warmers and respirators, both of which were advertised. Russians, who were used to wearing fur hats and coats and warm felt footwear in the winter, initially found the settlers' appearance quite intriguing, but then they got used to it and stopped paying attention. Nonetheless, they respected their ability to adapt. During the winter, the military dressed according to the weather—in cloth, partially fur-lined jackets, fur hats with flaps, and warm footwear. At other times of the year, they wore a khaki-colored cloth uniform and leather boots.

In their everyday conversations, Russians began to master a new language: "konichiwa," for hello, "sayonara" for good-bye, "arigato godzaimas" for thank-you. Japanese politeness is known world-wide but, as we observed, in men it seemed to co-exist with rudeness in everyday life and with cruelty in the military. The cruelty soon became apparent to everyone, especially to those residents of Harbin who, unfortunately, had to come into contact with the police and the gendarmerie.

As in any society, there were various kinds of people among the civilian Japanese population: some regarded the "lesser" population, consisting of the tens of thousands of Russians in Manchukuo, condescendingly, while others hardly even noticed them, and a third group were neighborly, polite and friendly.

There were some Japanese traditions that evoked admiration. We took particular note of their landscaped gardens and ability to arrange flowers in their homes, that is, the art of ikebana, which is now widely known in many countries of the world, including Russia. This art form, imported into Japan from India at the beginning of the seventh century, and which then developed within various schools and movements essentially became, as is well known, the symbol of Japanese material culture.

It was impossible to remain indifferent to the sight of the gracefully laconic products of Japanese applied arts: wonderful lacquered objects, vases, various incrustations, bronze and ivory objects, fans, and so on. They were expensive, so for the most part we admired them at exhibits or through the windows of expensive jewelry stores. The subjects of these handmade wares, usually taken from nature, were frozen in sparsely elegant lines, and to this day remain one of the small bridges for understanding the culture of this country, so unusual and contradictory for a European.

By the middle of the 1930s, Japan had already established itself firmly on the Asian continent. Several years later it would begin a disastrous "Great Asian War," devastating in the numbers of victims and for the nation itself. However, life continued on this little island of spiritual life for old Russia, squeezed as it was by the hands of an alien power, although the subsequent pages of the history of Russian Harbin did not remain cloudless. And so Harbin, this island of Russian culture in China was, as they say, "on the seven winds." The East and West were strangely interwoven here without any assimilation of the Russian population. In the 1920s and 30s, the latter entered this area through guest artists from Europe and America—there were famous singers and musicians—but most of all, through movies and the press.

The movies were not only entertainment—for Harbin they were a window to the world.

While there were initially not many movie theaters in Harbin, later, when the silent movies began to speak, they began to spring up like mushrooms. The names were traditional: "Palace," Orient," "Star," "Giant" and others. In the 1920s and 30s, as in Europe and America, Ben-Hur (Ramon Navarro) was dying from thirst in the desert; Tarzan (Johnny Weissmuller) cavorted above the African jungles, hanging from the lianas; Fred Astaire and Ginger Rogers tap-danced on their glass stages; cowboys fired their shots without ever missing, and in that secret mountain country imagined by H. Rider Haggard, Ayesha ruled. The curly-haired Shirley Temple smiled both from the screen and from the many advertising photos and pins.

Western film stars (especially the Hollywood beauties) were greatly loved and read about in the American magazine *Photoplay*, which was always available for sale up until the beginning of World War Two. Fashionable tales about Hollywood were printed in the magazine *Borderland* and in other publications. We even wrote letters to our favorite performers and, amazingly, we received replies. During those years, Hollywood stars, as is well known, battled for popularity by corresponding with their male and female fans from around the world.

Pre-revolutionary Russian movies were represented by films with Vera Kholodnaia and Ivan Mozhukhin. Later on, Soviet films (from before 1935) also appeared though in small number. The only one I personally remember is *The Road to Life*. However, later, after the events of 1945, their pining countrymen were treated to such an emotional deluge of them that even now it is impossible to remember those impressions with equanimity. These were our encounters with our Motherland, and I think that only someone who had been separated from his native land can understand this burning feeling for one's country particularly if the separation from it was forced.

But let us return to Harbin in the 1930s and 40s. Before the war, American movies were shown very widely. One movie theater (the "Palace," I think, on the pier), specialized mostly in running cowboy movies. Later, the screens were monopolized by German reels, and Martha Eggert enchanted us, Zara Leander intrigued us with her unbelievable contralto, and Emil Jannings amazed us with his acting. Some movie theaters ran Japanese films, mostly about the samurai of years past.

With their pro forma happy endings, the hollow and banal—but beautifully produced—American and European movies of those years, inspired in us just the slightest hope that "all would end well" in life. The lovely, finely molded little faces, their elegant dress, extravagant villas and beautiful melodies created the illusion of possible happiness in the reader. From the viewpoint of today's "thinking" and its tendency towards harsh film critique, the movies of those years are, no doubt, naive as was much in the literature and art of that time. But in my view, the movies of the pre-war era had one indisputable quality: Good prevailed and preference was given to Beauty, which helped enormously in preserving our equipoise during those difficult years in that lonely sliver of Russia!

Translated by Natasha Kolchevska

China (1937)

Aleksandr Vertinskii

In her memoirs the writer Natal'ia Il'ina remembers being fourteen years old, sitting at home alone in her parents' dining room in Harbin. On the evenings when her parents were out, she would play recordings of Vertinskii on the gramophone and listen to him singing about places she would never see: San Francisco, the cafés and the elegant women of Paris. Unknown streets flew into her imagination. The places she dreamed of, the images in which she encased them came from the voice of Aleksandr Vertinskii, who traveled the world, touring Paris, Constantinople, Shanghai, and the United States, singing the songs of the homeland that tore at the hearts of the émigrés.

Vertinskii was born in 1889 in Ukraine. He dabbled in acting and had bit parts in silent movies before embarking on a singing career. He left Russia in 1920 and finally settled in Paris, where he performed for the émigré community for nine years. He went to the United States but left during the Great Depression to live among the émigré community in Shanghai. He was allowed to return to Russia in 1943 and died in 1957 in Leningrad.

A unique figure both on and off the stage, Vertinskii often performed as the Russian Pierrot, with powdered face and closed eyes. Elegant, refined, somewhat decadent, he was adored by prerevolutionary and émigré audiences alike. His lyrics are laced with the toska, *or anguish, that appealed to the émigré sense of anomie.*

Above the Yellow River—the blind white sky . . .
Sails twitter in the wind, like the wings of shot birds
And a black kite flies . . . probably thinking, "Where
Can I escape from this torrid heat, from this melancholy without
borders?"

Yes—from this melancholy . . . of dead, ancient China
From the melancholy of Emperors, Deceased Dynasties and powers
Of Sleeping Gods, of uninhabited expanses
Where centuries sleep by the feet of Great Tombs.

And in empty cities Jews, steadfast in their wise Talmud,
Patiently trade; Englishmen, Germans, and Italians
And various other white people bustle to and fro,
The Conquerors of the World, the merchants and seekers of profit.

But in China's slanted eyes, in its submissive smile
Silent serpents sleep and the lightning of distant thunderheads [broods].
The thunder will clap, and the shaking earth will begin to moan, breaking
The centuries-long silence of the great holy sepulchers.

Translated by Kenny Cargill

From Harbin, Home (1985)

Natal'ia Il'ina

Natal'ia Il'ina was a child of the Harbin emigration. Her father, an officer in the White Army, fled there with his family in 1920 after the Bolshevik Revolution. Il'ina was only seven at the time. She spent her growing-up years in Harbin and then moved to Shanghai in 1936, where opportunities were better. She began writing fillers and light satirical pieces for the local émigré newspapers but was also becoming increasingly disenchanted with émigré life. Longing for a homeland she couldn't remember, she joined an organization in 1941 called the Union for the Return to the Motherland and began working for a pro-Soviet newspaper in Shanghai. In 1946 she chose to repatriate, and in 1947, along with 2,500 other Russian families, she left Shanghai by steamer for Nakhodka and from there traveled by train deep into the country. Repatriation had been encouraged by Stalin himself, partly as a way of replenishing a population that had been decimated by the purges and the Second World War. Il'ina and several thousand others just like her were more swayed by the Stalinist propaganda machine luring them back to the Motherland than they were by news of the Gulag and the purges that had managed to find its way into the émigré press. Yet even as the returnees arrived in their own country, Stalinism sealed their fate. They were allowed to settle only in provincial cities, a measure put in place to protect the country from those who had seen a world outside the borders of Stalin's Russia.

Il'ina's physical journey back to the Soviet Union, recounted in the excerpt here, was the easy part. Much more difficult was the slow, often painful process of coming to understand the country and the system to which she had returned. The land she looks out onto from her train window is the one she initially mythologized and created in her mind's eye. Forty years later she would write memoirs that set forth a very different picture of the country, one that was no less home yet viewed with the experience of years through a sharper and starker lens.

My favorite photographs in mother's album: me all decked out in a white medical coat, smiling happily, leaning against the trunk of a birch tree. Summer. Everything's in full green. The garden at the Institute of Orthopedics and Reconstructive Surgery in Kazan'. Uncle Ivan Dmitrievich and I sit on the sofa side by side. In the background a carpet hanging on the wall. Moscow. My uncle's room on Gagarin Lane. Again, one of me full size taken from a distance, my face barely visible because the background is in focus—the fountains at Peterhof.

These photographs (there are lots of them!) and letters that I wrote to mother during our seven-year separation, allow me to remember with clarity times that have passed. Mother not only kept the photos and letters, but the postcards dropped into mailboxes during the long journey by freight train from Nakhodka to Kazan'.

The Soviet government assumed the expenses for transporting the former émigrés back to the motherland. The 2,500 families that were leaving were divided into five groups. The first left Shanghai in August of 1947; the last on the 30th of November that same year. I was with this last group. We went by steamship as far as Nakhodka, and from there by train into the heart of the country.

Letter #1 dated December 6, 1947. We arrived yesterday late at night and saw small fires burning. Now it's morning, and we are sitting in a small bay, still haven't moored. It's beautiful and stark here: the view right out of Jack London—a leaden green sea, rounded, snow covered hills. We had smooth sailing if you don't count the first two days when the seas were rough. Almost all the women and many of the men lay there, seasick. I have to give myself credit: I barely felt anything at all; that entire difficult Monday I was on my feet. I even worked at the typewriter in the ship's salon. The typewriter was moving around on the table, and I was trying not to look at the portholes where the sea would first appear and then the sky. I had promised myself to get the newspaper for the public bulletin board out towards five on Tuesday evening, and I made it! I wrote only a small feuilleton for it, since I was busy getting other people to contribute to it and trying to bring the artists together who had scattered hither and yon.

It's cold. Eleven degrees of frost [minus 11 c], but there is the open sea, and wind. But in general, Mama, everything is going well. I have bright hopes for the future. I am going to the country where everything depends on people's energy, activity, and work.

December 12. We are staying in Nakhodka. It's not particularly comfortable, but it's decent. But I'm glad you aren't here. Summer here is supposed to be spectacular, but winter not quite as upbeat. I've gotten used to the cold and am managing not to freeze. However, for the old men and children our life in the barracks is hard. What for me is an interesting adventure would be a hard trip for you. Morally I feel wonderful. I published my newspaper here. I believe in Socialism. I believe in myself.

In Nakhodka we were unexpectedly detained. We left here only on New Year's Eve, December 31, because a major snowfall had blocked any movement along the rail lines. We survived the monetary reform in Nakhodka. I traded in my card, and we all took part in the elections for the first time. Our heavy baggage, trunks, and large chests (several people brought furniture and even pianos with them!) stood on the pier in the open air. Our men took turns around the clock standing watch over our things. The barracks were all made of wood with two-tiered bunks. In the main room was a stove with burners. We stoked it with wood and made ourselves a home. We spread our blankets on the bunks and the place even started to look cozy. The only thing that was intolerable was the lavatory: two structures made out of frozen boards, each for ten people. The weather stayed clear and cold. In the morning the pipes emitted a rose-colored smoke. The local settlement with its market was far away. The barracks stood in the open field where the wind pushed its way in, unobstructed, from the sea. It was wonderful to open the padded door of one's own dwelling, to feel oneself surrounded in warmth and where someone's tea pot was boiling on the stove. We drank tea constantly.

In Nakhodka they gave us a list of cities where the local governments were supposed to look after those of us who were repatriating by providing us with work and, initially, with a place to live. All the cities with the exception of Kazan', were in the Urals or Siberia. We got to choose the city where we'd like to settle. Old men, women with small children and people in poor health were sent off from Nakhodka by normal rail transport. The rest of us left in freight cars.

14 of January 1948. I am writing on the train. I'll send a letter from Omsk, where we'll be, maybe, tomorrow morning. There are twenty of us plus our things in the freight cars. The heavy baggage is going in the other cars. We sleep side by side on the bunks. We're lucky with the weather! It's so warm that Yura, Roma and I went out twice between the cars. The names of the station do not bode well: "Winter," "Sheepskin Coat," and the temperature is minus 7 degrees! They say that it can reach minus 40 or 45! We drink fermented, boiled milk, and eat yogurt, and butter. We have enough money. I talk a lot with the local people here. They're all very happy with the monetary reform and with the repeal of the card system. The beauty around us is unbelievable. The woods, the fields, the countryside covered in snow. I feel as if I have already seen all this, that it is all

familiar to me, all part of my birthright. Don't worry about me. Every day I thank God that I came and that I'm in Russia.

We were young, healthy and weren't bothered by the hardships of the journey. Everything was interesting—for the first time we saw the country where we were born. We viewed it differently, however. The landscape reminded me of a picture painted by Russian artists; the log huts, the forest tinged blue in the distance, the snowy fields evoked literary associations. Overcome by it, I whispered lines of Blok: "How shall we live and cry without you!"

With Yura it was different. Raised in a Tientsin Catholic school, he knew English at that time better than he did Russian. In Shanghai where he worked for a foreign firm, someone gave him *The Communist Manifesto* to read. Everything stemmed from that moment. From there on in, Yura began to read only Marxist literature. It became his religion. He had the passion of a preacher and the impatience of a fanatic. I remember how struck I was hearing from him that Winston Churchill was an idiot. Yes. An idiot. His logic was that capitalism is doomed, the world is moving towards socialism, following the course of history; the idiots are those who don't see it. They didn't even offer Russian literature in the Catholic school, and so it completely passed Yura by. In general, art was foreign to his rational way of thinking. The woods, fields and huts that so stirred me didn't touch Yura. He wasn't returning to Russia but to a country that was the first in the world to decide to move from word to deed, to put into practice the great international system of socialism.

And Roma? Of the three of us, he was the more ironic and restrained. We couldn't remember his reactions and his impressions.

"I have a lot of conversations with the local people," I told my mother. It's interesting, what had I expected? Along the way the only people we were meeting were women wrapped in kerchiefs who came out onto the station platforms with pieces of frozen milk and pots of cooked potatoes. They looked at us in amazement. We were dressed oddly. In the summer of 1947 in Shanghai, American military uniforms were being sold cheaply—sheepskin coats, rough rust-colored boots, camouflage pants, and green army blankets and sheets. For many of us, these light, warm sheepskin coats with fur lining and a rough, tightly fitting material on top, and black, indelible letters on the back reading U.S.N. (United States Navy—USA) were comfortable clothes to travel in. Women in pants, in shoes that no one had ever seen before, with these letters on our backs were enough to astonish them. An old woman from whom I bought milk once (an amazing old woman, with wrinkles, and deep shining blue eyes, with a knotted shawl that was still white!) muttered "My dear ones! And who might you be? Not French?"

"What kind of French? We're Russian, grandma, Russian!" I told her firmly, repeating the word "Russian" with delight, barely restraining myself from embracing her.

"Where're you commin from?"

"From China!"

"Well, isn't that something. And is there white bread there?"

"There is, grandma."

"How come you left then?"

"But, but, we want to live in Russia!" My spirits flagged a little. The mercenary nature of the woman embarrassed me—do we really live by bread alone?

"Ah, so that's the way it is," the backward old woman muttered indistinctly.

In Sverdlovsk [Yekaterinburg] we stayed for five days. Most of the repatriates in our groups settled there. The two or three freight cars that were going to Kazan' were detached, reattached to another train and we were put onto another track. In the morning we jumped out onto the web of rails. It got light late in this Ural city. We glanced up at the sky and saw that it was finally getting light, and in the freight cars it was dark as night. We walked around somewhere in the merchant area in the darkness, holding each other by the hand. Unknown people were wandering in the dark forest thirsty for a profit off of these strange new arrivals. They called out to us "Citizens! Don't you want to sell something?" How we wanted to. Our echelon usually arrived in these big cities at night. We didn't see any cities in daylight until we got to Sverdlovsk. We saw only the countryside, the stations, the half-stations. After we walked around the streets on our first day, the three of us, Yura, Roma, and I, wanted something good to eat, some music, and a beautiful life. Once we sold our wristwatches to some passersby. Yura and Roma went right ahead, but I held back, thinking to myself how can I survive without my watch? The buyer cheered me with these words: "Don't worry over it, little citizen; there will be new ones. You won't fall into harm's way in your fatherland!" These words were balm for my soul, and I often cited them in my letters. I am in my homeland. Nothing bad will befall me.

Translated by Adele Barker

On the Banks of the Seine (1983)

Irina Odoevtseva

Paris in the 1920s was the center of Russian émigré life in Europe. Much of the émigré community there was made up of intellectuals—poets, writers, composers, philosophers, and artists who strove to preserve their cultural identity abroad while waiting for the opportunity to return home. They founded émigré newspapers, set up publishing houses, organized literary evenings, and waited. Among the literati who made Paris their home was Irina Vladimirovna Odoevtseva (1895–1990), who had become known for her poetry in Petersburg prior to emigrating. In 1921 she married the poet Georgii Ivanov and left with him for Berlin in 1923 and then moved to France. After Ivanov's death Odoevtseva began work on her memoirs while still in France. Ultimately in 1987, under Gorbachev, she accepted an invitation from the Soviet government to return to her homeland, where she died in 1990.

This excerpt is taken from her second volume of memoirs devoted to portraits of her literary contemporaries. For the most part Odoevtseva remains in the background of her writing, allowing the literary figures of her time to dominate her canvas. Here she describes her meeting with the poet Marina Tsvetaeva, one of the most remarkable literary figures of twentieth-century Russia. Tsvetaeva had emigrated with her husband and children first to Berlin, then to Prague, and finally in 1925 to Paris. Ill health, financial difficulties, and lack of reception for her poetry all weighed heavily on Tsvetaeva in Paris. Her daughter had already moved back to the Soviet Union in 1937, and her husband, Sergei Efron, who, it subsequently came to light, was working as an agent for the Soviet government, disappeared from Paris and turned up in Moscow that same year. In 1939 Tsvetaeva decided to follow them, and Odoevtseva's memoir catches her at this moment. Odoevtseva speaks movingly of her last meeting with the poet. Two years later Tsvetaeva's husband was executed, her daughter and sister imprisoned, and she herself evacuated to the town of Elabuga in Siberia, where in 1941 she hanged herself. One senses from this memoir that Tsvetaeva understood all too well her probable fate upon returning to the Soviet Union.

Paris. Summer 1938. In only two days Georgii Ivanov and I were heading to Biarritz for an entire three months. To the ocean. I was already filled with a light, joyful anticipation.

I spent the day running from store to store. I was quite tired. And yet, I didn't feel like staying home, spending the whole evening reading or listening to the radio.

"Georges, let's go out somewhere!"

Georgii Ivanov, as always, agreed. But where to go? All our friends and acquaintances had already parted for their own holidays. Even in Montparnasse you didn't see a single soul.

"How about the cinema?"

No. I had no interest in sitting motionless before the screen.

"What about the Gingers?" he suddenly recalled. "After all, they're still in Paris. Today is Thursday, on Thursdays they have their 'Gathering of Poets.' How about that, we'll go there. We've put off seeing them for ages, they'll be very pleased."

"More than pleased, they'll be delighted. Both Ginger and Prismanova love you. Let's go. But in a taxi, not the metro. A taxi there and back. I'm awfully tired."

And off we went.

Ginger himself answered the door. But to my surprise, he not only showed no pleasure in the unexpected appearance of Georgii Ivanov, he looked flustered, even upset, though he tried to hide it.

"Of all the people I was not expecting! Marvelous, wonderful, thank you," he said in a clipped voice, awkwardly lingering in the doorway, gathering our hats and placing them on the sideboard in the foyer as if to keep us from entering just a bit longer. Finally he announced, "We have Marina Ivanovna here. She has come to say goodbye before leaving for Moscow."

Ah, so that's it, Marina Tsvetaeva was there. She couldn't bear Georgii Ivanov or Adamovich or me, considering us all Petersburg snobs and aesthetes.

She especially disliked Georgii Ivanov since the time he mistakenly attributed Mandel'shtam's poem "How Quickly You Tanned" ["Kak skoro ty smugliankoi stala"], in reality dedicated to her, to a "little strumpet of a dentist" instead.

Few in Petersburg seemed to be aware that there was a romance between Tsvetaeva and Mandel'shtam. Mandel'shtam himself never brought up her name in conversation, whereas he often spoke with pleasure of the "nice little girl dentist" who once made him false teeth and let him pay her back later.

Marina Tsvetaeva considered herself slandered and decided to defend her rights in the press with an epistle that she wrote for *Poslednye novosti* [The Latest News]. But Miliukov didn't want to print it, which only upset her further and turned her all the more against Georgii Ivanov.

It was completely understandable that our inopportune arrival upset poor Ginger. No doubt this could have spoiled his "final evening with Tsvetaeva."

His worry was unfounded. In fact, we saw Marina Tsvetaeva rather regularly at literary evenings and at the salons of the wealthier "patrons of the arts." Occasionally we even exchanged a few innocent words, although she always made efforts to avoid us, and we her.

But now our retreat was cut off. Ginger led us into the room where Marina Tsvetaeva was seated at a table with a sheet of text set out before her. There was also Sofiev, Korvin-Piotrovskii, Zakovich, and a few more of the young poets' group.

Prismanova headed towards us. It would not enter her head that there could be some misunderstanding between us. She rarely had any idea of the personal relations among her friends and acquaintances. They simply didn't interest her. She was always whirling aloft in the ether worlds of poetry.

Georgii Ivanov greeted her earnestly.

Marina Tsvetaeva addressed us in with a squint. She was quite short-sighted, but with a coquettishness that was not characteristic of her, she refused to wear glasses.

Our arrival was clearly unpleasant to her. She proudly sat up straight and with hackles raised, turned into, as she herself sometimes put it, the "Kamchatkan bear off its ice floe," a pose I had seen her strike in the homes of the patrons, as if she was readying herself for attack. Here again she had assumed her battle stance.

But Georgii Ivanov quickly approached her and kissed her on the hand, a hand she extended with a certain hesitation.

"Marina Ivanovna! I'm so happy! I was afraid that we would not have the chance to see you before you left."

"Happy?" she repeated dryly. This she had not expected.

"Terribly happy!" he warmly insisted. "After all we may have little chance to visit again soon."

"We will never see each other again. Never," she coldly interrupted. She turned to me in a voice only slightly warmer.

"And you, tell me, are you happy too?"

"Awfully happy!" I said with complete sincerity.

She shrugged.

"Well miracles happen every day. I am almost ready to believe you. Most of my former acquaintances no longer greet me or even acknowledge me on the street, they turn away."

"Scoundrels!" Ginger said, projecting his voice. "Let them all hang, those bourgeois rich."

"While we," Zakovich interrupted, turning to Georgii Ivanov, "are preparing a collective request to one such bourgeois, at the initiative of Marina Ivanovna, in fact, to sponsor a holiday for N. N."

N. N. was a lovely young writer who had just gotten over a terrible illness. She really did deserve a rest somewhere in the mountains or by the sea. Georgii Ivanov and I readily joined in the "collective request." It was being overseen by Marina Tsvetaeva.

"Sofiev, do read what we have drafted so far."

Sofiev began aloud,

"Deeply respected, dear . . ."

"Not dear, but kind," she corrected him, "Kind and sensitive . . . after all the bourgeoisie are sentimental. Shall I continue?"

Sofiev continued,

"Knowing your golden heart and the generous help you always extend, we . . ."

"Golden heart, that's good," Marina Ivanovna interrupted. "You have to crawl! Crawl! Pour on the flattery, let him soak it up—he might fall for it."

"Don't worry, Marina Ivanovna, he'll fall for it. We'll catch him like a frog with this letter," said Georgii Ivanov pointing to the sheet of paper. "If any of us asked him in person, face to face, he would undoubtedly refuse, but here we have the spirit of revelation, the call to social conscience—he won't let us down."

We worked over the text by which, like a frog, we were to catch our wealthy miser, and rewrote it three times. Georgii Ivanov was as witty as ever and made everyone laugh. I never thought that Marina Tsvetaeva could laugh so heartily or so merrily. I had never seen her so animated or friendly. I was completely charmed by her.

At last the letter was ready, artfully and skillfully rewritten.

"Now for signatures. You are the first, Georgii Vladimirovich. Very nicely now, with a flourish. After all you are the darling of *Sovremennye zapiski* [Contemporary Notes], unlike me. They never gave me, nor my poems or prose the time of day. They always sent them back . . ."

We completed the signatures and even wrote out the address in calligraphy.

Marina Tsvetaeva looked up at the clock on the wall.

"Goodness! Half past eleven. Mur has not even dined yet and tomorrow I have to get up at five-thirty!"

"On the other hand," Piotrovskii announced importantly, "thanks to you, N. N. will now be able to have a rest at the seaside. You've done a good deed, Marina Ivanovna."

Everyone warmly and boisterously bid their goodbyes to Ginger and Prismanova. They were both radiant—there had never been such a successful "Gathering of Poets."

We stepped out *en masse* onto the quiet, sleeping street, filled with moonlight.

"Let's accompany Marina Ivanovna to the metro. We won't find a taxi here anyway," Georgii Ivanov proposed.

We headed to the metro in pairs. Marina Ivanovna and I walked in front, with the rest a short way behind us.

She hurried along with a quick and light step, frowning.

"How far they live from the metro."

Yes, it was far, but I wished it were even farther so that I could walk with her shoulder to shoulder just a little more.

"I like walking with you. You keep a good pace. I had thought that with those high heels you would be stumbling your way along with a lady-like hop. You can tell a person from their walk just as much as from their handshake," she said with conviction.

"Marina Ivanovna, are you happy to be returning to Russia?" I said, asking the question that had been with me all evening. "Very happy?"

She raised her head.

"Ah, no, of course not. It would be another thing if I could return to Germany, to the place of my childhood. I would like to go there—all those wide-open squares and gothic buildings. Russia is foreign to me now. And hostile to me. Even the people. I am a stranger there."

She breathed a sigh and slowed her pace.

"All the same I am satisfied to be leaving Paris. I have outlived it. Paris doesn't exist for me anymore. I knew so much grief and disappointment here. Nowhere have I been so unhappy. I remember once in Prague—I was quite at loose ends there—I dreamed of how good everything would be in Paris. Whereas in Paris, I began to think of Prague almost as a lost paradise. So, now I am going to Moscow. It is better for my son who is there. But for me? . . . My emigration has come to an end."

She sighed again.

The moon shone brightly. Too brightly. Under its light everything began to strike me as unreal. I was overcome by such a strange feeling, as if I were losing all sense of time and space. Was this really Paris in the summer of 1938?

Suddenly I remembered, as if through a dream, how on a similar warm, summer, moonlight night years ago, I had walked with Anna Akhmatova through the quiet, sleeping streets of Petersburg—for the first and last time in my life. Just as I was now walking with Marina Tsvetaeva. Yes, just as now, for the first and last time in my life.

Back then it was not Akhmatova who was leaving but I, full of joyful hopes. And this time it was not I who was leaving, but Marina Tsvetaeva, in deep anguish without hope.

I looked at her tired face, pale and sad.

My heart tightened. I felt so badly for her. And I feared for her. No, she can't go! Death would meet her there. She would die there like Mandel'shtam. And so many others.

I wanted to cry out, "Don't go! You can't go!" But I couldn't bring myself to say it. And she would not have listened to me anyway. Even if I got down on my knees and begged her.

I felt completely helpless. There was nothing I could do. But I could at least console.

"Marina Ivanovna, I want you to know that I have always adored your poems. Back in Petersburg Gumilev gave me a gift of your *Vechernii al'bom* [Evening Album], and I was simply delirious with it. He read me aloud your wonderful poems to Blok and Akhmatova. He greatly admired them."

"Really?" she asked, as if not sure to believe me. "Is that really true? For some reason I used to think that Gumilev was against me. And you too. The workshop apprentice. To be fair I thought the same of Adamovich. It's a good thing that you told me." She smiled slightly, and her face became younger. "I am glad that Gumilev liked my poems."

We reached the entrance to the metro, and it was time to part. I was so deeply sad that I barely held back my tears.

"You are quite different from how I thought you to be. What a shame. This means yet another chance to meet again that I will miss. How many of these have I had in my life, these moments that never repeat! And here is one more."

She extended her hand.

"Farewell. Farewell forever. Be happy. And wish me neither happiness nor a *bon voyage*. There is no point in it with me."

Georgii Ivanov and Piotrovskii caught up with us. She bid goodbye to Georgii Ivanov. Her silver rings shone dimly in the darkness as he kissed her hand again.

I looked at her, trying to commit her to memory as best and as carefully as I could—all of her, in full detail, to preserve her in my memory just as I saw her at that moment. For I would never see her again. Never.

Final handshakes.

"Don't forget about our missed dates," she said, smiling weakly. "And don't forget me either."

I wanted to reach out and make a sign of the cross to protect her, but I held back.

She had already set off down the stairs alongside Piotrovskii. My eyes followed her. But she did not look back.

And then she was gone.

Translated by Bruce Grant

108th Street (1986)

Sergei Dovlatov

"If you're interested in the latest news," wrote the Russian émigré writer Sergei Dovlatov in Forest Hills, New York, "stand in front of a Russian store." The world of the Russian émigrés in the borough of Queens was Dovlatov's home away from Russia, or better put, his Russia inside the United States. " 'Write about America,' " he recalls his American literary agent saying to him. " 'Take a story from American life. You've been living here a long time now.' He was mistaken. I didn't live in America. I lived in a Russian colony. There were no American stories here."

The experiences of third- and fourth-wave Russian émigrés living in the boroughs of New York are the subjects of Dovlatov's fiction and nonfiction. He brings to his descriptions of their new life in the States their memories of the complicated life they left behind in the Soviet Union. His portraits of family members in his book Nashi (Ours) are laced with frank, nonchalant humor that affords the reader a glimpse into everyday life in Stalinist and post-Stalinist Russia. A line such as "There's one thing I don't understand. How come my parents knew everything while Il'ia Ehrenburg (an influential Soviet writer) didn't?" opens the window just far enough to expose the lies of the Stalin era.

Dovlatov (1941–90) was born in Ufa in Bashkiria. He studied at Leningrad State University and was subsequently drafted into the Soviet Army, working as a prison guard in one of the high-security camps. After he was demobilized he returned to Leningrad and began writing stories. His affiliation with the samizdat group and his harassment by the KGB ultimately led to his decision to emigrate, first to Vienna and then to New York.

Among émigré writers in America, Dovlatov enjoyed rare success. Literary careers eluded many émigrés there who had been well known in the Soviet Union. Dovlatov's style, his sense of the comic and the absurd, won him an American audience. His books began to be translated into English, and his stories appeared in Harper's, The New Yorker, Partisan Review, and elsewhere. Though his works were read by both American and European audiences, it was not until glasnost that Soviet audiences, and later the newly reconstituted Russian reading public, were able to read him in their own country.

This is what happened in our neighborhood: Marusya Tatarovich couldn't help herself and fell in love with a Latin American named Rafael. She vacillated for two years and then finally made her decision. Although when you get down to it, Marusya basically had nothing to decide between.

Our whole street was worried—how would things turn out? After all, we're serious about things like that. We are six brick buildings clustered around a supermarket, inhabited primarily by Russians—that is, recent Soviet citizens. Or, as the newspapers put it, émigrés of the third wave. Our neighborhood stretches from the railroad tracks to the synagogue. A bit to the north is Meadow Lake; to the south is Queens Boulevard. And we're in the middle. One Hundred Eighth Street is our central highway.

We have Russian stores, day-care centers, photography studios, and barber shops. There is a Russian travel agency. There are Russian lawyers, writers, doctors, and real estate agents. There are Russian gangsters, madmen, and prostitutes. There's even a Russian blind musician.

For us, the native residents are like foreigners. If we hear English spoken, we grow wary. Sometimes we insist, "Speak Russian!" As a result, certain local individuals have started speaking our language. The Chinese counterman at the coffee shop greets me, "Good morning, Solzhenitsyn!" (It comes out "Solozenisa.")

We are ambivalent about Americans. I don't even know what we feel most—condescension or idolatry. We pity them for being irrational, feckless children. Yet our constant refrain is, "An American told me . . ." We use that phrase as the decisive, killer argument—as in, "An American told me that nicotine is harmful to your health."

The local Americans are mostly German Jews. The third-wave immigrants, with rare exceptions, are Jewish. So finding a common language is rather simple. The locals are constantly asking, "Are you Russian? Do you speak Yiddish?"

Besides Jews, we have Koreans, Hindus, and Arabs in our neighborhood. We have very few blacks. More Latinos. For us they are mysterious people with boom boxes. We do not know them. But just in case, we despise and fear them.

Squinty Frieda expresses her dissatisfaction. "Why don't they go back to their lousy Africa!" Frieda herself is from the city of Shklov. But she prefers to live in New York. . . .

If you want to get to know our neighborhood, you should stand outside the stationery store. It's on the corner of 108th and 64th Drive. Come as early as possible.

Our cabdrivers are setting off: Lyova Baranov, Pertsovich, Eselevsky. They are all stocky, grim, and determined.

Lyova Baranov is over sixty. He is a former artist, a follower of Molotov. In the beginning of his career, Lyova painted only Molotov. His works were displayed in innumerable housing offices, clinics, district party offices, and even on the walls of former churches. Baranov had thoroughly studied the minister's features, his qualified laborer's face. On a bet, he drew Molotov in ten seconds. Blindfolded.

Then Molotov was removed. Lyova tried to paint Khrushchev, but in vain. The features of a rich peasant were beyond his powers.

The same thing happened with Brezhnev. Baranov couldn't do the opera singer's face, either. And then Lyova bitterly turned to abstract art. He began painting colored blobs, lines, and curlicues. He also began drinking and debauching.

The neighbors complained to the local police. "He drinks, debauches, and is involved in some kind of abstract cynicism."

As a result, Lyova emigrated, got behind the wheel, and calmed down. In his spare time he paints Reagan on horseback.

Eselevsky was an instructor of Marxism-Leninism in Kiev. He defended his Ph.D. dissertation, was studying for further degrees. One day he met a Bulgarian scholar who invited him to a conference in Sofia. But they wouldn't give Eselevsky a visa. It seems they didn't want to send a Jew abroad. So for the first time in his life Eselevksy's mood was spoiled. "That does it!" he said. "I'm going to America!" And he did.

In the West, Eselevsky became completely disillusioned with Marxism. He began publishing incendiary articles in émigré newspapers. But then he became disillusioned with the émigré newspapers, too. The only thing left was to get behind the wheel.

As for Pertsovich, he had already been a driver in Moscow, so very little changed in his life. Of course, he was making a lot more money now. And he owned the taxi, too.

And here comes the owner of the photography studio, Yevsei Rubinchik. Nine years ago he bought his own business. Since then, he's been paying off his debts. The rest of the money goes toward buying modern equipment. This is the tenth year that Yevsei is living on spaghetti. The tenth year that he's wearing Armenian shoes with gum rubber soles. The tenth year that his wife is dreaming of going to the movies. The tenth year that Yevsei is consoling his wife with the thought that the business will go to their son. The debts will be paid by then. However—I sometimes remind him—there will always be ever more modern equipment. . . .

Here comes fledgling publisher Fima Druker, hurrying to get his newspaper. In Leningrad he was a famous bibliophile. He spent entire days at the book market. He had six thousand rare, even unique, books. In America, Fima decided to become a publisher. He couldn't wait to restore forgotten masterpieces to their place in Russian literature—the poems of Oleinikov and Kharms, the prose of Dobychin, Ageyev, and Komarovsky.

Druker got a job as a janitor at the trade center. His wife became a nurse. In a year they managed to save four thousand dollars. With that money Fima rented a cozy office. He ordered light blue office stationery, pens, and business cards. He hired a secretary, who incidentally happened to be Ilya Ehrenburg's granddaughter. He called his business Russian Book.

Druker met prominent American philologists, including Roman Jacobson, John Malmsted, and Edward Brown. If Jacobson happened to mention a little-known poem of Tsvetayeva's, Fima hurried to add, "The *Bridges* almanac, 1930, page 264." Philologists loved him for his erudition and lack of greed.

Fima attended symposia and conferences. Chatted in the hallways with Georges Nivat, Frederick Ottenberg, and Alexis Rannit. Corresponded with Vladimir Nabokov's widow. He treasured the telegrams she sent: "Definitely not," "Categorically against," "Unacceptable terms." And so on. He had a rubber stamp made that said, "Efim G. Druker, Publisher." There was also an emblem—a folio with a goose quill—and the address. Then the money ran out.

Druker appealed to Mikhail Baryshnikov. Baryshnikov gave him fifteen hundred dollars and some good advice—"learn to be a masseur." Druker ignored the advice and went off to a conference at Amherst. There he met Vladimir Weidle and Simon Karlinsky. He astonished them with his knowledge. He reminded the two elderly scholars of myriad publications they had forgotten.

On the way back, Druker visited Yuri Ivask. He spent a week at the old poet's house, chatting about Vaginov and Dobychin, debating which of them had been homosexual. (As it turned out, both were.) And the money ran out again.

Then Fima sold part of his unique library. With the proceeds, he reissued Feuchtwanger's *Jew Süss*. It was a strange selection for a publishing house called Russian Book. Fima assumed that the Jewish topic would interest our émigrés. The book came out with only one typo. In large letters on the cover it said: FEUCHT-WAGNER.

Sales were lukewarm. Back home there was no freedom, but there were readers. Here there was freedom enough, but readers were missing.

Druker's wife filed for divorce. Fima moved to the office. The place was filled with boxes of *Jew Süss*. Fima slept on the cartons. He gave copies to his many friends. He paid Ehrenburg's granddaughter with books. He tried to exchange them for sausage at the Russian store. The amazing thing was that everyone, except his wife, loved him.

Here's the owner of the Dnieper deli, Zyama Pivovarov, spreading out his wares. In the Soviet Union Zyama was a lawyer. In America he worked on a loading dock when he first arrived. Then he moved to a grocery store. In a year, he bought the store. After that it got its supplies from the well-known firm of Demsha and Razin. It offered butter from Vologda, sprats from Riga, tea from Georgia, and sausage from the Ukraine. You could buy an amber necklace, an electric samovar, a wooden *matryoshka* doll, or a Chaliapin record there.

Zyama labored almost round the clock. It was a rare unity of dream and reality, an astonishing equivalence between desire and ability, an unattainable identity of effort and result. . . .

I think Zyama is an absolutely happy man. Groceries are his element, his biological medium. He belongs in a delicatessen the way Napoleon did at Austerlitz, or Mozart did at the premiere of *The Magic Flute*.

Many people in our neighborhood owe him money. . . .

Zaretsky the columnist is walking his mutt near the fish store. He is wearing a running suit with a stripe and his bald spot is covered with a plastic bag. In the Soviet Union, Zaretsky was famous for his popular monographs on cultural figures. At the same time, his anonymous research was circulated in samizdat editions—particularly his voluminous work *Sex Under Totalitarianism,* which claimed that ninety percent of Soviet women were frigid.

The punitive organs quickly identified Zaretsky. He had to leave. At customs he made a historical statement: "I'm not the one abandoning Russia! Russia is abandoning me!" He asked everyone there if "Academician Sakharov" was present. A minute before boarding he rushed over to the grass. He wanted to bring a handful of Russian soil to the foreign land. The police chased him off the grass. Zaretsky exclaimed, "I'm carrying Russia away on the soles of my shoes!"

In America, Zaretsky became a teacher-without-portfolio. He lectured everyone: Jews about Russian Orthodoxy, Slavs about Judaism, American counterintelligence about vigilance. He fought for democracy with all his might. He said, "Democracy must be instilled by every available method. Including the atom bomb!"

Everyone knows that in order to be heard in America, you have to speak low. Zaretsky never figured that out. He shouted at everyone: at the social security people, at the editor of the daily emigrant paper, at the hospital nurses, even at cockroaches. As a result, no one listened. Still, he attended all the émigré meetings and continued shouting. He shouted that Western democracy was in danger, that Geraldine Ferraro was a Soviet spy, and that American literature did not exist. That they sold fake meat in supermarkets. That Harlem had to be bombed and welfare increased.

Zaretsky was a professional wrecker. The destructive instinct became almost a creative passion with him. In his hands, watches, tape recorders, and cameras immediately broke. Calculators, electric razors, and cigarette lighters malfunctioned. He broke the metal turnstile in the subway. His body blocked the revolving door at City Hall for an inordinate amount of time. On meeting an acquaintance, he'd say, "What's the matter, my friend? Your wife looks awful, and I hear your son is hanging out with a bunch of hoods. You look pretty pasty yourself—better go see a doctor, old chum!" Strangely enough, Zaretsky was respected and slightly feared.

Here comes retired dissident Karavayev, carrying a brown paper bag. You can see the shape of beer cans through it. His face shows a mixture of anxiety and enthusiasm.

In the Soviet Union he was a well-known human rights activist. He demonstrated exceptional courage in his struggle with the regime. He spent three terms in the camps, went on seven hunger strikes. Every time he was released, he started up again.

In his youth Karavayev wrote a fable. It takes place in a zoo. People crowd around the panther cage. There is a sign in Latin, plus information on habitat and feeding. The sign also says: "Does not breed well in captivity." The author pauses at this point and asks, "And what about us?"

After his third prison term, Karavayev was allowed to go to the West. At first he gave interviews, traveled the lecture circuit, and started up foundations. Then interest in him waned. He had to think about eating.

Karavayev spoke no English and had no degrees. His camp professions— loader, delouser, and bread cutter—didn't apply in America. So he worked for the Russian newspapers. He always wrote on the same theme—the future of Russia. And he saw the future much more clearly than the present. That happens with prophets.

America disappointed Karavayev. He missed the Soviet regime, Marxism, and the punitive organs. Karavayev had nothing to protest against. His camp illnesses allowed him to apply for disability. So Karavayev drank a lot and spent even more time having hair of the dog that bit him, since beer was sold round the clock in our neighborhood. The cabdrivers and businessmen looked down on Karavayev.

Now Lemkus, the mysterious social activist, gets behind the wheel of a Chevrolet. In the Soviet Union Lemkus had been a professional impresario.

He organized mass festivities, led triumphant cheers during May Day demonstrations, and wrote anniversary speeches, cantatas, and even instructions in verse for car aficionados. He moonlighted as master of ceremonies at young people's weddings. He wrote gags for circus acts:

"Vasya, what's the matter? Why do you look so sad?"

"I saw a guy fall into a puddle."

"And that upset you?"

"You bet it did! I was the guy."

Lemkus left because of political persecution. And the persecution was the result of nightmarishly ridiculous incompetence.

What happened was, Lemkus wrote a cantata dedicated to the sixtieth anniversary of the armed forces. It was performed at the Officers Club, with Lemkus himself reading the narration. A band was behind him. Over six hundred representatives of the army and navy were in the audience. The cantata was broadcast all over the city via loudspeakers.

Everything was going fine. As he recited the cantata, Lemkus put on a soldier's cap or a naval cap in turn.

At the end came these lines:

And protecting our peaceful sleep,
You are stronger than granite.
And our beloved party
Will reward you generously.

Just as Lemkus roared out the last line, a counterweight fell on his head—a canvas bag weighing fifty pounds. Lemkus was knocked out. The audience could see only the worn soles of his concert shoes.

Three seconds later the police ran down the aisles. In another three seconds the hall was surrounded. Lemkus was revived and arrested. A KGB major accused him of planning the diversion. The major was convinced that Lemkus had calculated it down to the last second, purposely had the sack fall on the narrator's head in order to discredit the Communist Party.

"But *I* was the narrator," Lemkus said in his defense.

"All the more so," the major replied.

In short, Lemkus was persecuted. He was not allowed to do ideological work. Lemkus couldn't even think of any other kind.

Finally, Lemkus had to emigrate. For about four months he worked at his old profession: He organized trips for émigrés to Niagara Falls; performed as master of ceremonies at bar mitzvahs; wrote poems, rhymed announcements, toasts, and cantatas. For instance, I well remember his:

Suffering from the KGB all our lives,
We remember the bitter hurt!
Let our dear America
Protect us from our enemies!

But the pay was low. And then he had a second child. And then he ran into the Baptists.

The Baptists were interested in the third-wave immigrants. They needed their own man in émigré circles. They wanted to get the attention of Russian refugees. The Baptists evaluated Lemkus. He was a good family man, didn't smoke, and drank moderately.

So Lemkus became a religious activist. He was put in charge of a mysterious radio station that broadcast worldwide. He had a regular show, "How Can You See God?" He became pious and sorrowful. Now he whispers, with eyes downcast, "If it pleases God, Fira will cook some veal for lunch."

In our neighborhood they're convinced he's a crook.

Around the corner comes real estate mogul Arkasha Lerner. Apparently he needs something for breakfast, some crazy condiment or other.

Lerner began his career as a director in Belorussian television. His wife worked there as an announcer. The Lerners lived happily. They had a good apartment, two salaries, a son named Misha, and a car.

Arkady Lerner was considered a solid professional. Even his penchant for slow motion could not spoil his TV documentaries. Kolkhoz horses galloped gracefully, flowers opened slowly, sea gulls soared. Lerner was enchanted by harmony per se. His short subjects were considered Impressionist.

But life bustled all around, imbued with socialist realism. In the next apartment the plumber Berendeyev beat his wife. Winos made rowdy noises under his windows. The television studio boss was a virulent anti-Semite. So the Lerners decided to emigrate, particularly since many people were leaving them behind, including their close friends.

In America, Lerner spent about a year lying on his couch. His wife worked as a saleswoman at Alexander's. Their son went to Hebrew school. Lerner dreamed of working in television. He was completely atypical as an émigré: He didn't pretend to have won State prizes, didn't invent a dissident past, or insist that Western art was in a state of crisis.

His friends set up a meeting with a producer who wanted to do screen versions of the Russian classics. He needed a director of Slavic extraction. The meeting took place on the terrace of the Blow Up restaurant.

"You're a director?" the American asked.

"I don't think so," Lerner replied.

"How do you mean?"

"I've gotten much worse this past year."

"But they say you used to be a director?"

"Used to be. Or rather, I was called one. I was upgraded in 1967. Before that I was an assistant."

"An assistant director?"

"Yes. The one who goes out for vodka."

"They say you were a talented director?"

"Talented? That's the first time *I've* heard it. I wasn't satisfied with what I did."

"Okay! I'm going to do screen versions of the classics."

"I think all screen versions are shit!"

"Is that a compliment?"

"What I mean is, I would prefer an original theme."

"Such as?"

"Something about nature . . ."

An abyss opened up between the two men, and widened with every passing minute.

The Yankee said, "Nature doesn't sell!"

Lerner replied, "Art doesn't sell out!"

With that they parted. Lerner lay around on his couch for another three months. But I must add that his financial status was not bad. Apparently, Lerner had a gift for material well-being. I'm convinced that poverty and wealth are innate qualities, just like hair color or perfect pitch. One is born either poor or rich. Money has almost nothing to do with it. You can be a pauper with money. And, conversely, a prince without a cent.

I've met rich men among the inmates of prison camps, and poor ones among the highest ranks of the camp administration. The paupers suffer losses in every possible circumstance. They are fined when their dogs relieve themselves in the wrong place. If they drop change, the coins inevitably roll through a grating. It's just the opposite with the rich ones. They find money in old jacket pockets. They win lotteries. They inherit country houses from distant relatives. Their dogs win dog shows. Apparently Lerner was born to be wealthy. So he soon had money.

First he was bitten by a Newfoundland dog that belonged to the local dentist, and was paid a significant compensation. Then Lerner was sought out by an old man who had borrowed thirty rubles from his grandfather before the imperialist war—that is, World War I; in the seventy years since, it had turned into several thousand dollars. After that an acquaintance said to Lerner, "I have some money. Keep it for me. And, if possible, don't ask any questions." Lerner took the money; he was too lazy to ask questions. A week later the acquaintance was shot and killed in Atlantic City. As a result Lerner bought an apartment. A year later it tripled in value. Lerner sold it and bought three others. And he became a landlord.

Now he gets up even less frequently from his couch. He has more and more money. Lerner spends it expansively, mostly on food.

In twelve years in America he has bought only one book. Its title is indicative: *How to Spend Three Hundred Dollars on Lunch*. After lunch Lerner naps, turning off the television set. He's too lazy to smoke.

But this prologue is running on too long. It's time to return to Marusya Tatarovich.

XIV

Life under Advanced Socialism

With Khrushchev's ouster in 1964, the Soviet Union entered an era commonly referred to as the period of stagnation, or *zastoi*. Leonid Brezhnev replaced Khrushchev as First Party Secretary and ushered in a period he termed "the stability of cadres." What he attempted to secure was a normal lifestyle for those who occupied the middle and upper rungs of both the Party and the state apparatus. Increasingly, the consumer sector and its inability to provide basic goods for Soviet citizens had become a source of concern. As a command economy with responsibility for the country's economic life emanating from the center, the Soviet Union had directed most of its resources toward the military and industry, often leaving the consumer without access to basic necessities. The question that leaders from Khrushchev through Gorbachev had to contend with was how to make the necessary reforms and adjustments in consumer life without sacrificing the basic principles of the socialist state.

Brezhnev had inherited an economy that was faltering badly. The annual rate of growth that had previously hovered between 5 and 6 percent in the late 1950s and 1960s fell to 3.7 percent and then even lower in the mid-1970s. The question was what to do about it. Under Khrushchev efforts had been made to decentralize the economy, thereby placing more responsibility on the factory managers themselves and allowing them greater freedom in production decisions. Prime Minister Aleksei Kosygin attempted to give local enterprises increased freedom in setting prices, in firing workers, and in absorbing new technology. To the Party heavyweights these reforms undermined the planned economy and the priority placed on military and industrial production.

Soviet citizens, both rural and urban, responded to the economic stalemate by engaging in an unofficial or second economy. To fully know Soviet society was to enter the world of *blat*, a world of reciprocal favors, networking, and informal exchange. So widespread became the phenomenon of *blat* that one could argue that it sustained a command economy otherwise unable to provide essential goods and services to Soviet citizens. It occupied the space between the legal and the illegal, between public and private. It was quietly condoned by the state because it provided commodities and solved everyday problems, from plumbing to the housing shortage, that the state failed to respond to. The pervasiveness of *blat* was reflected in the language itself. "How did you get that?" someone might ask of a friend with a new outfit, a bottle of Johnny Walker on the kitchen table, or a pair of tickets to the Bolshoi (whose tickets were for the most part held in reserve for top Party officials, foreigners, and delegations). *Po blatu* (through *blat*) or *Cherez zna-komykh* (through acquaintances) was the usual answer, pointing to the fact that these items had not been purchased (*kuplennye*) but "obtained" (*dostavlen-nye*). Unlike market economies in which almost anything was available to those with the money to buy it, the system of *blat* was based instead on a system of connections carefully nourished and developed by Soviet citizens in order to live decently.

People managed as well by cultivating their private plots on collective farms (see Lev Timofeev's "The Village of Posady" in part V). The kolkhoz market where the peasants sold their own produce was also a form of private enterprise, one, moreover, that was tolerated because it eased the conditions of the peasants as well as the plight of the Soviet consumer faced with constant deficits and empty shelves in state-run stores.

This second or shadow economy reached into virtually every area of Soviet life. The quota system in factories and enterprises created astonishing scenarios that fed the need for basic consumer goods. Workers at a factory outside Moscow that produced military hardware would rush to meet their production quotas well before the end of the month, saving as much raw material as possible so as to spend the last ten days of every month producing refrigerators which they then sold privately to Soviet citizens. People would take their cars in for a minor repair only to find when they went to pick them up that the seats, or in some cases even the engine, had been taken out and sold to the highest bidder, who, in return, could provide some essential service on the side. People moonlighted, hoarded, and resold. Black markets dealing in specialized goods sprang up. Even though this shadow economy was declared illegal, it permeated the highest rungs of government across the former Soviet bloc. Brezhnev's own family became implicated through his daughter's obsession with diamonds.

Soviet citizens came increasingly to depend on the second economy, and in the late 1970s and early 1980s they had every reason to believe that "the system," as such, was there to stay. The chaotic revolts of the 1920s and 1930s had given way to the forging of new solidarities through massive sacrifice in the Second World War and the celebrated victory that followed. The dark days of Stalinist violence brightened after Khrushchev's "Secret Speech" in

1956, and a solidly middle-class lifestyle began to take shape. Consumers might still wait in line for years for apartments, cars, clothing, and basic goods, but the horizon of expectation that every family, urban and rural, could hope for such a lifestyle rose considerably. A limited range of fruits and vegetables made often erratic appearances in state stores, but the legal recognition of rural private plots and urban farmers' markets eased food concerns for those with extra rubles. Most households, indeed, had more rubles than ways to spend them. The Soviet Union, by all official markers, was moving closer to fully housing, educating, caring for, and employing all of its citizens. In the absence of private motorcars, affordable mass transportation could be taken for granted by nearly all. The government proclaimed, with loose approximation, that the country's literacy rate was the highest in the world. For all of these and many other reasons, Leonid Brezhnev, the last real inheritor of this distinctly Soviet age, began declaring in the late 1960s that the USSR had reached the stage of "advanced socialism."

Brezhnev's tenure as First Party Secretary was characterized by backpedaling on many of the liberal reforms that impacted the intelligentsia under Khrushchev. In 1964 the young Leningrad poet Joseph Brodsky was put on trial and sentenced to hard labor for parasitism. Two years later the Sinyavskii-Daniel Trial forced writers who sought to write openly and honestly to henceforth publish their works underground through samizdat, or self-publishing. Eight years later Solzhenitsyn was deported.

The authorities were all too willing to rid themselves of these dissident writers even though many of them went on to publish material in the West critical of the Soviet Union. The intelligentsia and the dissident movement had become galvanizing points for Western journalists, and it was to the state's advantage to fragment these groups, leaving them without a centralized power base. This partly accounts for why the physicist Andrei Sakharov was sentenced to internal exile in the city of Gorky in 1980. Sakharov, the father of the Soviet hydrogen bomb, had become one of the leaders of the dissident movement, advocating democratization and warning of the peril of nuclear arms. By exiling him to Gorky, Soviet authorities succeeded in isolating him not only from the West but from the center of the dissident movement in the major cities of Moscow and Leningrad as well.

What then of the writers who did not leave and who did not become part of the dissident movement? For those whose writing was published through official channels, there remained the Soviet Writers' Union, a powerful agency providing its members with the longed-for perks and privileges. It would be a mistake, however, to assume that Soviet literary culture was made up of dissident writers on the one hand, who either fled the country or went underground, and official writers on the other, who produced production novels. There were writers in the 1970s such as Yury Trifonov and Natalia Baranskaia who functioned within the parameters of the official literary establishment yet still managed to take a hard look at areas of Soviet society that had come up short. In his novella *Obmen* (The Exchange, 1969), Trifonov looks at the morally corrosive effects brought about by the housing question, or *kvartirnyi vopros*, while Baranskaia in her work *Nedelia kak nedelia* (A Week Like Any Other Week, 1968) was the first to bring into the open the overburdened life of the average Soviet woman. What was possible on the literary front was an examination and critique of *byt*, or daily life. That much the official literary establishment and the Party could absorb. Any criticism of Soviet leadership or the Red Army was still outside the realm of what was permitted.

The late 1960s and early 1970s saw an increase in protests over the lack of human rights in the Soviet Union. In 1968 the samizdat journal *Chronicle of Current Events* published its first issue; it continued in operation through 1984. The journal published a list of human rights violations that occurred throughout the USSR, which made its way to the West through the diplomatic pouch and foreign correspondents stationed in the Soviet Union. As writers and members of the intelligentsia were put on trial, the *Chronicle* turned the tables on the Party by putting it and the state on trial on the pages of its publication.

Events both within and outside the Soviet Union fueled the protests and the dissident movement. The most spectacular of these was undoubtedly the invasion of Czechoslovakia by Soviet troops in August 1968. Gradually since the death of Stalin, Czechoslovakia had been moving toward more liberal reforms that culminated in its 1968 Action Program. The Czech Communist Party held that the goal of socialism could be reached differently by different nations. Moreover, it allowed for differing opinions among Party groups and warned against inordinate concentration of power in the hands of any one group. Alexander Dubček, who had become First Secretary of the Czech Communist Party that year, was overthrown when Soviet troops advanced into Prague. Later Dubček was allowed to return, but in April of the next year he was replaced once and for all by Gustav Husak, who was more than willing to do Moscow's bidding. But even with the invasion that smacked of the Hungarian Revolt of 1956, indisputably some things had changed. Sanctions and punishments were meted out differently now. No one was sent off to the Gulag. Instead Dubček was reassigned as a forestry inspector in Slovakia, not unlike the fate of Viacheslav Molotov, who, after Stalin's death, became ambassador to Mongolia.

As the invasion of Czechoslovakia suggests, Brezhnev's tenure was characterized by a precarious balance between domestic and international politics. At a time when the Soviet government was already dealing with unrest among the dissident community at home, it was less willing than ever to tolerate reformist movements such as those taking place in Czechoslovakia. The rationale that lay behind the invasion was that freedom to pursue one's own course toward socialism must not harm or hinder the advancement toward socialism in other countries. Out of the invasion came the onerous Brezhnev Doctrine, which essentially gave the Soviet Union the right to intervene in any of its satellite states where the road to socialism was viewed as imperiled.

There were, in addition, the intangibles that accounted for the loss of liberalizing momentum that had taken place during the Thaw. The age of upper-echelon Party cadres played a role in much of the decision making, as well as in much of the reluctance to reform and decentralize. In the late 1960s and the 1970s the Kremlin was looking increasingly like a gerontocracy. The average age of Politburo members rose to sixty-eight between the years 1966 and 1982. Perhaps learning lessons from Khrushchev's fate, his successors soon appeared to prefer to die in office. Brezhnev died in 1982 at the age of eighty, his last years spent in decidedly ill health, rendering him incapable of carrying out his functions in office. Surrounding him were the Party's leading cadres, many of whom had been educated and had risen through the ranks under Stalin and who still held the values and beliefs of that complex time in Soviet history.

Communal Living in Russia:

Stories and Thoughts (2000, 2003)

Ilya Utekhin, Alice Nakhimovsky,

Slava Paperno, and Nancy Ries

Shortly after the Revolution the famous, or infamous, communal apartment came into being and became the primary form of housing for millions throughout most of the Soviet era. The kommunalki, *as they were called, were part of the new collective vision of the future shorn of private property as well as the result of huge population shifts from the countryside into urban areas. Communal living consisted of an apartment space shared by anywhere from four to seven families. Each family had its own room, which functioned simultaneously as living room, study, bedroom, and dining room. Shared with other families were the corridor, the kitchen, the bathroom, and the telephone. Into these living spaces people were thrown together who otherwise had little or nothing in common, yet who shared their space and their lives until the end of Soviet power. For some who lived in these apartments, life approximated nightmare, with theft, denunciation, drinking, and lack of privacy the order of the day. Others, however, took solace in recognizing the footsteps of someone familiar coming home at night and the support of neighbors who became like family.*

The excerpts that appear here are taken from Communal Living in Russia: A Virtual Museum of Soviet Everyday Life, *on the website http://kommunalka .colgate.edu. The first is an interview with a resident of a communal apartment; the second, a denunciation of one communal apartment resident by another.*

"Stories and Thoughts: We're Like One Big Family"

SUMMARY

A woman who has spent her whole life in communal apartments explains why she likes it.

BASIC FACTS AND BACKGROUND

When: 2000

Where: A large communal apartment in a prestigious district of St. Petersburg. Fifty-five people once lived here; now there are 23.

Who: Ekaterina Sergeevna [E. S.], one of the apartment's oldest residents. Lena Utekhina does the interviewing.

What: E. S. ended up in this apartment with her two children as a result of an apartment exchange she undertook after her divorce. Apartment exchanges are discussed in the essay about ownership and the distribution of city housing in the Soviet Union.

Apartment meetings devoted to calculating the electric bill devolved into a ruckus because there was only one meter for the apartment. Until each family got an individual electric meter, it was hard for tenants to agree on how to divide the bill in accordance with their particular notions of justice.

The building's architect, Stepan Samoilovich Krichinsky (1874–1923), did indeed live in the apartment the last two years of his life.

Translation of the Russian Transcript

EKATERINA SERGEEVNA: So, when we moved to this apartment in 1971, there were 33 people here. There were people living in every room, it was very lively. Gradually it thinned out. Some people died, other people got new places to live, and now there are probably 23 of us. Yes.

What can I say, there were some very interesting people living in this apartment. Right across from me was an utterly unique woman, she was a librarian in a psychiatric hospital, but she was very erudite, educated, she had an enormous number of books in . . . in her little room, and was very eccentric. She never went into the kitchen, except to get water. She didn't use any gas and she didn't use the bathroom. Everything she had was electric. She had an electric teapot, and electric pots, in general everything she used was electric. She did use the toilet. But not the bathroom, ever. She was very old, 83, when she died.

Well, in the next room over there was Marya Ivanna with her son, but . . .

LENA: There was some horrible story connected with . . .

E. S.: Yes. This son turned out really badly, he was in prison a number of times, and in the end he fell asleep, drunk, on the couch and the couch went up in flames. They threw it out the window, because there was no way to put the fire out. After that he went to prison, and since his mother had died before, before this, the room didn't have anyone registered in it, and so he was left without a place to live. When he got out, he went to live with his ex-wife, and that's where he is now.

LENA: And when you moved in, what did they tell you about the history of the apartment?

E. S.: About the history . . . Well, that they wanted to give this apartment to the architect Krichinsky, who drew the plans for the building. I think that's the story. Here is where his study was supposed to go, and the room next to it should have been the library. Where Natasha is now was the large parlor and your room was the smaller one. Next to that was a room for serving coffee, and there was a room off the kitchen for the cook. Later they gave her a regular room and they took down the partition and the kitchen kind of expanded. Can you imagine, there were 55 people here, and the kitchen was only 15 square meters. There was an incredible ruckus, especially when the electric and gas bill came, and it had to be divided up—that was something to see. Well, eventually everybody got their own electric meters, and there were fewer and fewer people, so things quieted down.

LENA: How many generations of your family have lived in Petersburg?

E. S.: I've lived here all my life, all my life. I even was born . . .

LENA: And your mother also?

E. S.: And my mother . . . Actually, my mother was from Odessa, but she came here a long time ago, when she was around 25, and she lived in Petersburg for 60 years. My father was a real Leningrader, a Petersburger. We come from an old noble family, the Ryumins. My mother was a Polar Explorer, and my father also. I was born in the Far North House, 53 Vosstania Street. All the families there were like one big family. We were good friends, and children went to each other's birthday parties, because all the parents worked for the same organization, they all went on Far North expeditions, it was a very interesting life.

LENA: Why did you move here?

E. S.: We did a room exchange. I got divorced, I was left with two children, and my mother and I put our two rooms together and moved here.

LENA: How many years would you say you have spent in kommunalkas?

E. S.: All my life. All my life. I was born in a kommunalka. Of course there we had a three-family apartment, and then I lived on Petr Lavrov Street, there were nine tenants, and here there are 11. So, my whole life.

LENA: And every time a bigger one.

E. S.: Yes, yes, my whole life.

LENA: I see. And where is it better to live, in a new district in your own little apartment or despite everything . . .

E. S.: Yes, I like living here very much.

LENA: Since the film won't have my question, you should answer in a full sentence. Is it better to live in a kommunalka in the center of the city than in a private apartment in a new district?

E. S.: It's better to live in a communal apartment, a large one, in this kind of, in a historic district, a historic Petersburg district, than in a housing complex.

LENA: Why?

E. S.: There's some kind of disconnection, life is more boring. I don't know, it seems to me that people there are completely different. Everybody is on their own. And here we're like one big family. If someone is in trouble, it gets shared. Or a joy, you share that too. Today one person will be in a bad mood, and tomorrow it will be a different person. We somehow neutralize each other, and it works out very well.

LENA: I see.

E. S.: I like it. I love this apartment. I do. The bathroom has its problems, but we put up with everything. Of course, your own apartment is a good thing, but if I had to choose the lesser of two evils, then this is better.

"Letters from Soviet Citizens: A Denunciation Sent to a Foreign Consulate"

SUMMARY
One resident denounces a neighbor to foreign consulates in order to keep her from going abroad.

BASIC FACTS AND BACKGROUND
Denunciations of one resident by another, typical of Soviet times, can still occur. In this denunciation, which mimics an official letter, we see a Soviet-style enumeration of sins.

We cannot judge the extent to which the information provided in the denunciation is true. In principle, there is nothing unusual about a resident who steals, comes home intoxicated, or engages in prostitution. In a small apartment taking action against such a resident is difficult.

According to the Soviet view of things, the absence of a steady job is indication of a serious moral flaw: if you do not work, you are living at others' expense.

OHGK /St. Petersburg

3 0. Sep. 2003

Eingegangen

Генеральному консулу
Австрийской Республики

от С ------- Н -------
А ---------
проживающей по адресу:
1-----, г.Санкт-Петербург,
пр.Ч --------- д.1 --
кв.3 --
тел.: 3------- (раб.)
       2------- (дом.)

Уважаемый господин генеральный консул!

Обратиться к Вам меня заставляют следующие обстоятельства:

В коммунальной квартире по вышеуказанному адресу вместе со мной проживает гражданка М--------- С------- Н---------.

Гражданка М--------- С.Н. в течение длительного периода времени нигде не работает, имеет передо мной задолженность, постоянно мешает нормальному проживанию в коммунальной квартире, нарушая покой и тишину после 23.00., являясь домой в нетрезвом состоянии с посторонними гражданами, угрожает мне. Гр.М--------- С.Н. ведет беспорядочную половую жизнь с гражданами иностранных государств, используя их впоследствии в качестве финансовой поддержки.

18.09.03г. я обнаружила пропажу из мест общего пользования квартиры своих личных вещей. В их краже я подозреваю гражданку М--------- С.Н., так как следы несанкционированного проникновения в квартиру отсутствуют. По данному факту 19.09.03г. мной был вызван наряд милиции, который произвел задержание посторонних граждан, находившихся в нашей квартире, и в 7- отделение милиции Центрального района г.Санкт-Петербурга подано заявление с просьбой привлечь гр.М--------- С.Н. к ответственности, предусмотренной действующим законодательством.

Гр.М--------- С.Н. в настоящее время продает комнату в коммунальной квартире и пытается оформить выездную визу.

Убедительно прошу Вас в случае обращения г.М--------- С.Н. за оформлением выездной визы иметь в виду вышеперечисленные обстоятельства.

С уважением,

С   Н.А.

Letters from Soviet Citizens: A Denunciation Sent to a Foreign Consulate. Source: "Stories and Thoughts: We're Like One Big Family," from *Communal Living in Russia: A Virtual Museum of Soviet Everyday Life*, http://kommunalka.colgate.edu/. Copyright 2006–8 by Ilya Utekhin, Alice Stone Nakhimovsky, Slava Paperno, and Nancy Ries. Used with the kind permission of the copyright holders.

"Promiscuous sexual relations" is a Soviet formula. Soviet morality sharply condemned promiscuity, particularly among women, and considered transgressions of sexual moral norms to be a community matter. Thus, for example, issues of marital infidelity could be taken up by a Comrades' Court (courts run by non-professionals to adjudicate social disturbances in residences and workplaces, utilizing peer-pressure and social sanctions against offenders of public order and morality).

The lack of any specific reference to Austria suggests that similar letters may have been sent to other consulates in St. Petersburg.

TRANSLATION OF THE RUSSIAN TRANSCRIPT

To the Consul General of the Republic of Austria
From S. N. A., resident at the following address
(the address and work and home telephones are provided)

Honorable Consul General,

I am forced to contact you due to the following circumstances.

Ms. M. S. N. lives in my communal apartment (address given above).

For quite some time now, Ms. M. S. N. has not had regular employment, she has unfulfilled financial obligations toward me, continually interferes with normal life in the communal apartment, creating disturbances after 11 o'clock at night by returning home in a state of intoxication and accompanied by strangers, and she has made threats against me. Ms. M. S. N. engages in promiscuous sexual relations with foreign nationals whom she then uses as a source of financial support.

On September 18, 2003, I discovered that some items belonging to me were missing from common areas of the apartment. I suspect Ms. M. S. N. of stealing them, as there are no indications of unauthorized penetration of the apartment. In connection with this case, on September 19, 2003, a police squad was summoned by me. They took into custody some strangers who were present in our apartment, and a petition was filed at Police Station number 7 of the Central District of St. Petersburg to take action against Ms. M. S. N. pursuant to the law.

At the present time, Ms. M. S. N. is in the process of selling her room in the communal apartment and is attempting to file for an exit visa.

I urgently request that, should Ms. M. S. N. apply for an exit visa, the above mentioned circumstances be kept in mind.

Yours Truly,

S. N. A.

Trial of a Young Poet:
The Case of Joseph Brodsky (1964)

What follows is a partial transcript of the trial of the Leningrad poet Josef Brodsky (1940–96), which took place in 1964. Brodsky was twenty-four at the time. The case brought before the District Court of Leningrad rested on whether being a poet was "real work" as defined by Soviet law. The trial lasted two days. At the end Brodsky was found guilty of parasitism and sentenced to five years of forced labor on a state farm near the Arctic Circle. He was subsequently pardoned and released as a result of protests both from abroad and from within the Soviet Union, from no less than the poet Anna Akhmatova and the composer Dmitrii Shostakovich. Brodsky left the Soviet Union in 1972 and settled in the United States, where he taught at a number of New England colleges for years. In 1987 he won the Nobel Prize for Literature and was poet laureate of the United States in 1991–92. Like Vladimir Nabokov, Brodsky learned English well enough to advance his writing career in it. He said of his parents after they died (the Soviet government refused to grant either Brodsky or his parents visas to see each other), "I write this in English because I want to grant them a margin of freedom: the margin whose width depends on the number of those who may be willing to read this. . . . I want English verbs of motion to describe their movements. This won't resurrect them, but English grammar may at least prove to be a better escape route from the chimneys of the state crematorium than the Russian."

The transcript of the trial was made by the journalist Frida Vigdorova, who was present in the courtroom and managed to take down most of the proceedings, though forbidden to do so by the judge. The transcript was smuggled out of the Soviet Union soon thereafter and appeared in the West, in translation, in the summer of that same year.

Ukase

4 May, 1961

ON THE INTENSIFICATION OF THE STRUGGLE AGAINST
PERSONS AVOIDING WORK FOR THE COMMON GOOD
AND LEADING AN ANTI-SOCIAL PARASITIC LIFE.

It is ordered that adult citizens able to work who will not fulfill the most important duty laid down by the Constitution, namely to work honestly according to their abilities, who avoid work for the common good, who profit from gains not arising out of work, from the exploitation of land, automobile vehicles, living-accommodation, or who commit other anti-social acts that enable them to lead parasitic lives, in accordance with the decision of the People's Court of the City District are liable to deportation to places specially selected for the purpose for a period of two to five years and to forced labour in the place of their penal settlement, together with simultaneous seizure of their property not acquired by work.

> N. Organov, President of the Praesidium of the Supreme Soviet of the
> R.S.F.S.R.
>
> S. Orlov, Secretary of the Praesidium of the Supreme Soviet of the R.S.F.S.R.

SESSION OF THE COURT OF THE DZERZHINSKY
DISTRICT OF THE CITY OF LENINGRAD

FIRST HEARING OF THE CASE AGAINST JOSEF BRODSKY
ON FEBRUARY 18TH, 1964

PRESIDING JUDGE: MRS. SAVELYA.

JUDGE: What is your occupation?

BRODSKY: I write poems. I translate. I suppose. . . .

JUDGE: Never mind what you "suppose." Stand properly. Don't lean against the wall. Look at the Court. Answer the Court properly. Have you a regular job?

BRODSKY: I thought that was a regular job.

JUDGE: Give a clear answer.

BRODSKY: I wrote poems. I thought they would be printed. I suppose. . . .

JUDGE: We're not interested in what you "suppose." Answer why you didn't work.

BRODSKY: I did work. I wrote poems.

JUDGE: That doesn't interest us. We're interested in what institution you were in touch with.

BRODSKY: I had contracts with a publishing house.

JUDGE: Then answer. Did you have enough contracts to live on? Give us a list of them with the dates and the sums they were for.

BRODSKY: I can't remember exactly. All the contracts are with my lawyer.

JUDGE: I'm asking you.

BRODSKY: Two books containing my translations have been published in Moscow. (*Enumerates them.*)

JUDGE: How long have you been working?

BRODSKY: Roughly. . . . .

JUDGE: We're not interested in "roughly."

BRODSKY: Five years.

JUDGE: Where did you work?

BRODSKY: In a factory, on geological expeditions. . . .

JUDGE: How long did you work in the factory?

BRODSKY: One year.

JUDGE: What as?

BRODSKY: As a milling-machinist.

JUDGE: And what is your real trade?

BRODSKY: I'm a poet. And a translator of poetry.

JUDGE: Who has recognised you as a poet? Who has given you a place among the poets?

BRODSKY: No one. And who gave me a place among the human race?

JUDGE: Did you learn that?

BRODSKY: What?

JUDGE: To be a poet. You didn't attempt to go to a university, where people are trained . . . where they're taught? . . .

BRODSKY: I didn't think . . . I didn't think that could be done by training.

JUDGE: What by, then?

BRODSKY: I thought that . . . by God. . . .

JUDGE: Have you a request to make of the Court?

BRODSKY: I should like to know why I've been arrested.

JUDGE: That is a question, not a request.

BRODSKY: Then I have no request to make.

JUDGE: Has the defence any questions to ask?

DEFENCE COUNSEL: Yes. Citizen Brodsky, do you give what you earn to your family?

BRODSKY: Yes.

DEFENCE COUNSEL: Have you been under treatment in an institution?

BRODSKY: Yes. From the end of December 1963 to January 5th this year in the Kashchenko Hospital in Moscow.

DEFENCE COUNSEL: Don't you think that your illness prevented you from working for long in one place?

BRODSKY: Maybe. Probably. I don't really know.

DEFENCE COUNSEL: You have translated poems for an anthology of Cuban poets?

BRODSKY: Yes.

DEFENCE COUNSEL: I ask the Court to add to the papers of the case the expert opinion of the office of the Translators' Section. A list of the translated poems. Copies of the contracts. And I ask for Citizen Brodsky to be medically examined to ascertain whether his state of health has prevented him from doing regular work. Furthermore, I ask for Citizen Brodsky to be immediately released. I am of the opinion that he has committed no crime and that his arrest is illegal. He has a permanent place of residence and can appear before the Court at any time.

The Court retires for consultation and then reads out the following decision:

To be sent for a Court psychiatrist's report on the question: Is Brodsky suffering from some psychological illness and does this make it impossible to send Brodsky to forced labor in a remote area? To pass the papers of the case to the Militia to check Brodsky's employment contracts. . . .

JUDGE: Have you any questions?

BRODSKY: I have a request. To be given pen and paper in my cell.

JUDGE: This request must be addressed to the chief of the Militia.

BRODSKY: I asked him and he refused. I ask for pen and paper.

JUDGE: I shall pass your request on.

BRODSKY: Thank you.

(*A large crowd has gathered outside the Court, mostly young people*)

JUDGE: What a lot of people! I didn't think so many people would come.

VOICE: It isn't every day a poet comes before the Court.

SECOND HEARING OF THE CASE AGAINST JOSEF BRODSKY (FONTANKA 22, HALL OF THE BUILDING WORKERS' CLUB, ON MARCH 13TH, 1964). ANNOUNCEMENT:

"Legal Proceedings against the Work-shy Element Brodsky"

The psychiatric report reads: "Psychopathic character traits observable, but capable of working. Hence measures of an administrative character may be taken."

The Judge asks Brodsky what requests he has to make to the Court. It emerges that he has not yet seen a copy of the indictment. The hearing is adjourned, and he is taken out so that he can read the indictment. On being brought in again, he declares that several of the poems are not by him.

Furthermore, he requests that the journal which he wrote in 1956, when he was sixteen, should not be included among the documents of the case. The journal is not removed. The Judge asks him why he has changed his place of work thirteen times since 1956, and at intervals in between has not worked.

SOROKIN (*Public Prosecutor*): Is it possible to live on the money you earn?

BRODSKY: It is possible. Since I have been in prison I have signed a statement every day to say that 40 kopecks have been spent on me. And I have earned more than 40 kopecks a day.

SOROKIN: Don't you need shoes and suits?

BRODSKY: I have a suit, an old one, but a suit of sorts. I don't need a second.

DEFENCE COUNSEL: Have experts expressed approval of your poems?

BRODSKY: Yes, I've been printed in the almanac *For the First Time in the Russian Language* and have given readings of translations from the Polish.

JUDGE (*to the Defence Counsel*): You are supposed to be asking him what useful work he has done, and you ask him about his readings.

COUNSEL: His translations are useful work.

JUDGE: It would be better, Brodsky, if you would explain to the Court why you didn't work during the breaks between jobs.

BRODSKY: I wrote poems. I did work.

JUDGE: But you could have worked at the same time.

BRODSKY: I did work. I wrote poems.

JUDGE: But there are people who work in a factory and write poems. What prevented you from doing that?

BRODSKY: But people aren't all the same. Even the color of their hair, the expression of their faces. . . .

JUDGE: That's not your discovery. Everyone knows that. It would be better if you explained how you assess your share in our forward movement towards Communism.

BRODSKY: The building of Communism—that doesn't only mean standing at the work-bench or ploughing the soil. That also means intellectual work which. . . .

JUDGE: Never mind the high-sounding words. Tell us how you intend to arrange your working activity in future.

BRODSKY: I wanted to write and translate poems. But if that contradicts the general norm, I shall take a fixed job and write poems in spite of it.

JUDGE TYAGLY: In our country everyone works. How were you able to laze about for so long?

BRODSKY: You don't look upon my work as work. . . .

Josef Brodsky, the 24-year-old Russian poet and translator, who was condemned earlier this year [1964] in Leningrad to a five-year sentence of forced labor, has now been pardoned and released. We have this information from the Swiss playwright Friedrich Dürrenmatt who has just returned from Moscow (where he had been invited to attend two premières of his plays). According to Dürrenmatt, the mounting pressure—there were protests from leading Soviet writers and artists, including Anna Akhmatova, Dmitri Shostakovich, Samuel Marshak, Konstantin Paustovsky, among others (Victor Zorza reported this in *The Guardian* of May 13th)—has proved successful. Since his trial Brodsky had been working as a dung carrier on a State farm near Archangel. The text which we publish was brought out by a European journalist and is an almost complete "protocol" of the two-day legal proceedings in February and March of this year.

The Most Well-Read
Country in the World (1986)
Edited by S. S. Vishnevskii

From the postwar era on, in newspapers, on the radio, and at Party congresses, the Soviet Union touted itself as "the most well-read country in the world." The literacy statistics were indeed impressive. When Lenin took over in 1917, it was estimated that only one-fourth of the rural population was literate, compared to three-fourths of urban dwellers. With Lenin's commitment to universal literacy reading and writing clubs were set up in factories; there was an unprecedented push in education; newspapers were available for next to nothing; in fact one didn't even have to buy them: they were hung in the parks and along public thoroughfares for passersby to read. By 1927 70 percent of Soviet citizens were able to read and write. By 1939 the percentage rose to 94. As for books, they were cheap and easily available, often cheaper, it has been said, than bread and tobacco. But there was a catch: bookstores were piled high with books that no one wanted to read. If Soviet citizens had enough bread to eat, they were suffering from another kind of hunger, "book hunger." What then of the country that read more than any other country in the world?

Russia's book market during the Soviet era was nothing if not complex. Bookstores were owned by the state. What they stocked on their shelves was official literature that had undergone a great deal of ideological sifting. Certain authors who fell in and out of Party favor were available but in limited circulation. Complete collections of authors, however, including the nineteenth-century masters, were available through bookstores by special order. Anniversaries of the births and deaths of major Party figures produced new editions of their works, most of which sat on the shelves untouched or in storage rooms. Dissident and exiled writers were available only through samizdat or the black market, where the price of books was so high that groups of people would contribute money to buy one copy and then share it. There was also the phenomenon of the Berezka books, volumes published in the Soviet Union but for foreign purchase only, sold at special hard currency stores called Berezka (birch tree). Here one could find books that were not banned but were nevertheless deemed inappropriate for mass circulation and were hard to come by in state-owned stores. Thus a situation arose in which, alongside the impressive literacy statistics, there lurked the infinitely more confounding question of what it was that Soviets were encouraged to read, what was available to read, and what people really wanted to read. Often the answers to each question were different.

One of the characteristic features of spiritual life in an advanced socialist society and a way of life for millions of people is an attraction to reading. In the USSR, the press plays a huge role in the upbringing of the New Man. Its task is to instill a Marxist-Leninist worldview and communist morals in the Soviet people. The press strives to inspire them to fulfill the complex tasks of perfecting socialism, to facilitate the growth of culture and science, and to solve the nation's economic problems as well.

True to Vladimir Il'ich Lenin's teaching, the Communist Party of the Soviet Union (CPSU) and the Soviet government are doing everything possible to ensure that the intellectual values accumulated by mankind become accessible to every Soviet man and woman.

In the communist upbringing of the working people, the greatest significance is given to studying the legacy of the founders of scientific communism, Karl Marx, Friedrich Engels, and Vladimir Il'ich Lenin. Since the inception of Soviet power, the country has published more than 3,608 books and brochures of works by Marx and Engels, with a general circulation of 135.9 million copies, and 15,729 books and brochures of Lenin's works (whose general circulation number 604.5 million copies).

The current interest in political and socioeconomic literature is very high; its circulation figures continue to grow. For example, from 1940 through 1983 these figures rose from 127.3 to 218.1 million copies, and the number of books and brochures rose from 8,658 to 13,661.

The June 1983 Plenary Session of the Central Committee of the CPSU instructed the country's publishing houses to bring books out that promote a more active formation of scientific and Marxist-Leninist philosophy—the foundation of the Communist education of the Soviet people. A series of books such as *Plamennye revoliutsionery* (Fiery Revolutionaries); *Liudi, vremia, idei* (People, Time, Ideas); *Pamiatnye daty istorii* (Memorable Dates in History); *Lichnost', moral', vospitanie* (Personality, Morality, Education) and others are assigned an important role in this task. The creation of textbooks for the system of Party and economic education takes place at a high scientific level, as does the publication of literature about the Soviet way of life, the achievements and advantages of socialism, and the CPSU's peace-loving foreign policy.

Around 300 monographs and works of fiction for both adults and children were published for the 40-year anniversary of the Soviet people's victory over

 НЕГРАМОТНЫЙ тот-же СЛЕПОЙ
ВСЮДУ ЕГО ЖДУТ НЕУДАЧИ И НЕСЧАСТЬЯ ·

"He who is illiterate is like a blind man. Failure and misfortune lie in wait for him on all sides." From a 1920 poster.

Fascist Germany, dedicated to the heroic deeds of the Soviet people during the Great Patriotic War. These books reflect the organizational and mobilizing role of the CPSU in achieving that victory. A considerable part of these publications is devoted to the modern Soviet Army, vigilantly guarding the peaceful work of the Soviet people, and to the loyalty of young people to the military traditions of older generations.

The country publishes collections of classical Russian and Soviet literature, including those by Pushkin, Tolstoy, Dostoyevsky, Chekhov, Turgenev, Gorky, Sholokhov, Aleksei Tolstoy and others in large editions.

The world has never known, and still knows of no other literature whose highest accomplishments are the product of the talents of many different nationalities. One should remember that for many people in our country a writing system emerged only after the Great October Revolution.

Soviet writers are constantly sensitive to the concerns of the Party and the state. In their creative work, they are guided by the decisions of the Party Congresses and Plenary Sessions of the Central Committee of the CPSU, as well as Party documents. The Party and the government have adopted resolutions on the advancement and development of specific literary genres and other urgent problems of literature. Among these resolutions are "O literaturno-khudozhestvennoi kritike" ("On Literary Criticism" 1972), "O rabote s tvorcheskoi molodezh'iu" ("On Work with Creative Youth" 1976), and "O tvorcheskikh sviaziakh literaturno-khudozhestvennykh zhurnalov s praktikoi kommunisticheskogo stroitel'stva" ("On the Creative Ties of Literary Journals with the Practice of Communist Construction" 1982).

The Union of Soviet Writers has its own extensive list of periodicals. It publishes 86 journals, 16 newspapers, and tens of almanacs in various languages, with circulations of more than 10 million copies.

Translations of the best works of classical and contemporary foreign writers make up a large share of Soviet publications. According to current UNESCO data, the USSR is the largest publisher of translated literature. More than 2,000 titles by foreign authors from over 100 countries are published annually in the Soviet Union, with general circulations of more than 176 million copies. Over the course of the 10 years since the 1975 Helsinki Conference on Cooperation and Security in Europe, Soviet publishing houses have released more than 17,000 books, translated from foreign languages, with a circulation of more than 1 billion copies. Of that number, 242 million are works by French authors, 168 million are English, and 152 million are American. In the West today there is not one truly prominent writer whose name would not be well known in the USSR. The journal *Inostrannaia literatura* (Foreign Literature), with a circulation of more than 400,000 copies, familiarizes Soviet readers with new works of contemporary foreign literature. The 200-volume *Biblioteka vsemirnoi literatury* (Library of World Literature), which includes translations of the masterpieces by artists of the written word from all eras and nations, is published in the USSR with a circulation of 300,000 copies.

Newspapers and journals enjoy great popularity in the USSR. National newspapers such as *Pravda* (Truth), *Izvestiia* (News), and *Trud* (Labor) have a circulation of over 10 million copies; publications such as *Komsomol'skaia pravda* (Komsomol Truth) for youth, and *Pionerskaia pravda* (Pioneer Truth) for children enjoy large circulations.

The Soviet press, from the national to the regional, including those publications that circulate widely in factories and on construction sites, works toward the goals of building socialism and the Communist upbringing of the working people.

The network of libraries continues to spread throughout the country, and their book holdings continue to grow. In 1913 there were about 14,000 public libraries in Russia, with book and journal holdings of 9.4 million copies, or 6 books for every 100 people. In 1984 the number of public libraries was 133,700, with holdings of 2,050,400,000 books and journals, or 21 books and journals per person.

In 1974, the Central Committee of the CPSU adopted a special resolution "O povyshenii roli bibliotek v kommunisticheskom vospitanii trudiashchikhsia i nauchno-tekhnicheskom progresse" ("On Enhancing the Role of Libraries in the Communist Upbringing of the Workers and in Scientific and Technological Progress"). In accordance with this resolution, a great deal has been done to expand the work of scientific, technical, and public libraries, and to spread the achievements of science and technology. It has been equally important to provide economic specialists with scientific and technical information. In addition, readers receive individual help according to their age, educational level, and professional interests.

Public Libraries (End of year)

According to preliminary data, the total number of books in the country is now approaching 40 billion copies. Five billion of these are housed in state, trade union, and institutional libraries; the others are in private collections. At present practically every Soviet family has a personal library with more than half of family libraries averaging 100–200 books or more.

The public plays an important role in the promotion of books and the expansion of a reading audience. In 1974, the All-Union Society of Book Lovers was founded in the USSR. Today it is one of numerous public organizations, bringing 16 million people together in its ranks. In addition, 14,500 booklovers' clubs, 12,100 bookstores and newsstands nation-wide, and millions of volunteer booksellers are active in the All-Union system. Reader conferences and the promotion and dissemination of literature are only some of the interests of booklovers. The promotion of books in the countryside occupies a special place in their activities. Every member of the All-Union Society of Book Lovers has a task: to use books in every way possible to educate and mold the New Man.

1) *A Book is Great Power* (Lenin).
2) In 1983, the circulation of literary works in the USSR had increased more than twofold in comparison with 1965. In 1984, 935 million copies of adult fiction and children's books were published (30 percent more than in 1980). Today adult fiction and children's literature make up 51.4 percent of the country's book publishing. The publishing houses give special attention to bringing out children's literature. Since the inception of Soviet power, more than 110,000 different books and brochures have

	IN THE CITY		IN THE COUNTRYSIDE		TOTAL	
Year	Number of libraries (thousands)	Number of books and journals (millions of copies)	Number of libraries (thousands)	Number of books and journals (millions of copies)	Number of libraries (thousands)	Number of books and journals (millions of copies)
1940	18.5	135.5	76.9	64.2	95.4	199.7
1970	37.3	775.3	90.7	588.2	128.0	1363.5
1980	35.9	1079.8	96.1	744.0	132.0	1823.8
1984	36.5	1199.8	97.2	850.6	133.7	2050.4

been published for children, with general circulations of more than eight billion copies. Today the annual circulation of children's literature has exceeded half a billion.

3) Today, Soviet multinational literature is published in 89 national languages of the peoples of the USSR.

4) In 1984, 8,327 newspapers were printed in the USSR, with general circulations of more than 185 million copies. 5,231 journals and other periodicals are being published with a yearly circulation of 3,339 million copies.

5) Six periodicals are published on the average for every Soviet family.

6) The number of libraries of all types (public, scientific, educational, technical, and other specialties) numbered at 329,000 at the beginning of 1981, with total book holdings of 4.7 billion copies. The number of readers at public libraries in 1984 had reached 148 million. Every year 3.2 billion copies of books and journals are loaned out, which comes to 21 copies for every reader.

Translated by Larissa Rudova and Stephanie Wesley

International Relations at the

Lenin Library: From *My Life:*

The Diary of a Single Woman 1917–1997

Galina Koltypina

With the Thaw came the first chance for foreigners from capitalist countries to travel to the Soviet Union, if only in an official capacity. Even more slowly came the possibility for Soviets to begin contemplating trips beyond the traditional confines of the Communist bloc. Those who traveled initially were Party members who went abroad as part of scientific or cultural delegations. They moved in groups often accompanied by a rezident, *or member of the* KGB, *as part of the delegation. Their access to travel was predicated on leaving the rest of the family behind as an insurance policy against defection while abroad. Thus it was that the contact most Soviet citizens had with foreigners, if they had any at all, was limited to their homeland and usually confined to the major cities of Moscow, Leningrad, and Kyiv. Many cities were simply closed to foreigners both for security reasons and because officials were concerned that local conditions were not up to international standards.*

Galina Borisovna Koltypina was for many years the director of the Music Division of the Lenin Library in Moscow, one of the world's largest such institutions. This excerpt is taken from her unpublished manuscript, Moia zhizn': Dnevnik odinokoi zhenshchiny *(My Life: The Diary of a Single Woman), spanning the years 1917–97. Written with humor, it is an eye-opening account of her childhood, migration to Moscow from the Far East, her work at the Lenin Library, love and heartbreak, everyday life, housing, her first travel overseas, and her supervision of foreign delegations. She retired in 1997 and lives in Kaluga.*

We first heard about the possibility of associating with foreigners, and even traveling abroad as tourists, during the Khrushchev era, sometime in the 1950s. Up until then an impenetrable iron curtain had separated Soviet nations from that "other world." Moreover, during Stalin's rule any contact with foreigners was treated as espionage, with all the attendant consequences. In the first days after World War II, communication with our American and British allies was still possible. Sometimes the Americans—strong, noisy young men with an easy gait—dropped in on us at the Lenin Library and offered us candy and chewing gum. This, however, was quickly put to a stop. We bibliographers who served at the reference desk had to sign statements avowing that we were not to engage in conversations with foreigners, put foreign publications on display, or include information about them in bibliographic indices. There was a swell of exaggerated "patriotism," which under our conditions meant that no opportunity was lost to demonstrate the superiority of Russians on any given question. All of this taken together instilled an inordinate fear and caution in us and created an iconic "image of the enemy" of whom we needed to beware.

Khrushchev drew back the iron curtain somewhat. We started to display foreign publications, and significantly more foreign patrons began appearing at the Lenin Library. . . . My librarian's existence became a bit livelier through contact with foreign guests, mostly librarians who were visiting our country. At that time contact with foreigners, formerly forbidden (under Stalin we had to sign a statement that under no circumstances would we engage in conversation with foreigners), was increased significantly and was legalized. Unbelievable rumors circulated that it would even become permissible to travel to other countries. Foreign guests were usually received at the Office of the Library Directorate and then guided around the library and shown the packed reading halls, which invariably caught foreigners by surprise, as did the official slogan: "The Soviet People Are the Most Well-Read People in the World."

In September 1956 a delegation of Swedish library workers headed by Uno Willers, the National Librarian of Sweden, arrived to visit our library. In addition to touring libraries in Moscow and Kiev, the Swedes wished to visit the Black Sea. The Directorate thought it over and proposed that they visit the city of Krasnodar, where a new library had recently opened, and then travel from there to the sea coast. My boss, Abrikosova, decided to dispatch me to Krasnodar so that I could oversee the necessary preparations. The following is an excerpt from a detailed account of this episode in my diary.

I went to Krasnodar on business with two main goals, chief among which was to prepare the local library for the visit by the Swedes, who would arrive in five days, on the 12th of September, and to organize their trip to the Black Sea. A secondary goal was to familiarize myself with the library's bibliographic work. I had little experience with business trips, and therefore I worried about whether I would be able to secure a place to stay in a hotel. But my anxiety turned out to be unfounded, as Moscow had clearly notified the local authorities about my arrival. As soon as I disembarked from the train, a voice over the radio invited "Comrade Koltypina" to come to the information desk. I was met by the Deputy Director of the Regional Bureau of Culture and the Deputy Director of the Regional Library. They quickly collected me, put me in an automobile, and took me to a hotel, where a room had been reserved. It was—to my delight—a single. I wasn't given the chance to change clothes or even grab a bite before they collected the director of the hotel, and we set off to see the head of the Regional Committee of the Communist Party. All of this commotion ensued because the Regional Committee had received a telegram from the Ministry of Culture of the USSR informing them that Swedes were coming to their city. In those days we were still not accustomed to the arrival of guests from capitalist countries, and Krasnodar had never before hosted such visitors. Therefore the matter was sent up to the appropriate heights. I laid out our requirements: first of all, the hotel had to be clean, especially the toilet (this made the party chief look menacingly at the hotel manager). Secondly, Moscow had allotted a maximum of eighty rubles to take care of the Swedes, per day, per person (at this the chief snorted disdainfully, saying that Moscow had given no orders to them about this matter, and that Krasnodar would host the guests as is customary). I remarked that it was not necessary to go overboard, since Swedes eat very little in the morning, only coffee and fruit, but they did not listen to me. I added that in addition to visiting the library, whose preparation was my task, they might also wish to visit the local museum.

What could be done about the queues outside the shops? People would start sitting on the sidewalk in front of them early in the morning, as the food supply in the city was very bad. One couldn't allow the Swedes to see this, let alone to enter a shop. Besides, Moscow had given orders that they were allowed to take photographs of anything they wanted. The head remained anxiously silent on this point, saying simply: "We'll think of something."

And what about the fact that the Swedes had expressed a desire to swim in the Black Sea? Well, that was easy enough to arrange. We would take them to Gelendzhik by car to a regional resort where they would take care of everything. On that note we all went our separate ways.

I returned to the Hotel Krasnodar (the best in the city) and, along with the terrified hotel manager, started to look over the "deluxe" rooms on the second floor. Businessmen were sitting around in these deluxe rooms drinking vodka. The walls were quite filthy, spattered with champagne. The only luxury in the rooms consisted of a sink. The most frightful thing of all was the "toilet": a wooden seat laid directly on a filthy floor. I was horrified. The manager broke out in a sweat and sprung into action. First of all, he threw out all of the business travelers (where he sent them I do not know) and prohibited entry onto the second floor. All staff on hand started washing, scrubbing, and painting. They were especially zealous about the toilet. In the evening the exhausted director, drenched in sweat, invited me in for an inspection. The rooms were clean, extra beds had been removed, carpets had been laid, clean curtains had been hung, the sinks had been washed, and pictures had been hung over the champagne stains. I approved and said that vases filled with flowers and fruit should be placed in each room on the day of the Swedes' arrival. Then we went to look at the toilet. The floor had been scrubbed and the walls had been painted. A lock (which they gave to me) had been hung on the bathroom door. In so far as this was the only toilet, I asked where the other business travelers would go, to which the hotel manager answered: "They can go in the courtyard." The manager then ordered the entrance to the second floor to be locked up and installed a guard, who was to open the door only for me.

While the hotel was being cleaned and tidied, I went to the library to establish a plan for meeting the Swedes. I looked over the catalog and the international holdings and offered a range of advice. On the way back I stopped at the museum to verify that there was something worth seeing, and then returned to the hotel for lunch.

It turned out that the Swedes' plane was delayed and that they wouldn't arrive until the following day. Finally, I was at the library when someone ran up to me with the news that the Swedes were expected any minute. I ran back to the hotel. The first thing I saw was a line of staff that stretched along the entire staircase. Some nicely groomed, well scrubbed women were standing there: one of them held flowers, another towels, and a third one, an iron (!). They were clearly all terrified, and the hotel manager rushed around giving them orders. Managing to contain my laughter, I went to my room feeling highly amused. The poor woman holding the iron, extended straight ahead, was particularly funny.

At last they arrived. There were four men, plus two Russian escorts: Mr. Mirnyi, the translator (he worked for our Collections Division) and Ms. T. L. Postremova (Vainer), the Scientific Director. I went back to my room and continued laughing, especially when Mr. Willers poked his head in and said perplexedly that they did not need an iron, since their shirts were made out of wrinkle-free material. They removed the lock from the toilet, but the hotel manager left a guard at the entrance to the second floor, with strict instructions to stop anyone who might try to gain access.

After the Swedes had freshened up, we set off for breakfast in the restaurant. It was completely empty, since the manager had given orders to throw everyone out. The table was overflowing with a great variety of delicacies. Behind each chair stood a waiter who incessantly changed the plates. I sat down next to the representative from the local government, Mr. Kachalovyi, a very cultured and kind person. Among the Swedes was again Mr. Willers, the National Librarian, who had auburn hair and blue eyes and was a man of high culture and great intellect. He gave a short speech with generalities about international friendship and about how books unite people. The others included a Mr. Von Feilitsen, whose aristocratic background was quite clear from his manner and appearance; and Mr. Kharnesk, the portly Director of the Uppsala University Library, who was polite but a bit reserved. Of course, such an abundance of food at breakfast surprised them. They ate very little.

After breakfast we proceeded to drive to the library. Although it would have been possible to go on foot, instructions had clearly been given to go by car. It was sprinkling lightly, and I was glad that the Swedes would stay inside the car, for I was very afraid that they would poke their noses into the shops. To my great surprise there were no queues outdoors. It seems that the wise men from the regional party committee had solved the problem quite simply: they closed all the shops for a "cleaning day."

I won't begin to enumerate all the other visits by foreigners, as they are recorded in our department's records in the library. I only want to emphasize that the policy of openness was carried out quite cautiously. Guests of our department (the Music Division) were often accompanied by a representative from the Department for International Relations (along with a translator). If there was no escort, then I myself reported on the interaction. To characterize the politics of the time, I can offer the following record of a memo we received on how to behave during the 1980 Olympic Games. This briefing was issued by Mr. Riazhskikh, the Deputy Director for Cadres and Protocols (my comments are in italics).

IN THE EVENT THAT FOREIGN PARTICIPANTS IN THE
OLYMPICS ARRIVE AT THE LIBRARY:
- Do not permit guests to enter on their own. Suggest that they should join a group. The Library's tour guides lead groups of up to fifty people.
- It is permitted to photograph everything except for literature.
- Do not allow foreigners into the cafeteria; only Russians may enter. (*This was due to the abominable quality of the food and service.*)
- Take any gifts offered by our guests, but deposit them at the Information Desk with a written receipt (even fountain pens can contain explosive devices).

- Get rid of any notices, leaflets, or proclamations immediately, if any should appear.
- All manner of parcels for staff should be handed over to the Information Desk. Open the contents very carefully; letters may also contain explosive powder.
- It is permitted to write notes in guests' comment books if they are patriotic.
- In difficult situations refer to the special official posted at the Information Desk. In extreme situations call the Regional Committee of the Communist Party or the KGB (telephones are located at the Directorate's reception desk). On May 1st there was an incident in which a mentally ill man from the city of Dnepropetrovsk threw a bottle with red paint at a passing car with members of the Central Committee inside.
- If anyone asks whether the library has the works of Solzhenitsyn, answer that it does. They are used by specialists. (*This was a form of progress. Before we had to respond, "The works of enemies and renegades are not kept here."*)
- Exercise caution with forgotten items; immediately call the police. (*Here I will recount one instance that happened to me while I was on duty at the Directorate. A worker in the cloakroom reported that a reader had forgotten his briefcase. The police were called in. A police officer carefully approached it and put his ear up against it: "It's ticking!! That means there is a time bomb in the briefcase!" After a while I was informed that, thank god, it was much ado about nothing—it turned out that the briefcase merely contained an alarm clock. But why it was in the briefcase, and why a reader left it in the cloakroom, remained a mystery. And so, we remain vigilant.*)
- Don't gawk at foreigners. (*This was an actual order.*)
- Don't ask foreigners for anything. This especially applies to youth, who are wont to beg for various items.

These instructions were issued on July 8, 1980, the year in which the International Olympic Games were held in Moscow. By the way, the athletes did not come to the library, and they did the right thing.

Translated by Jane Zavisca

Moscow Circles (1969)

Benedict Erofeev

Vodka has been an all too consuming facet of Russian life since early chroniclers first noted the proclivity of the Russians for imbibing. Indeed, over the centuries the Russian government developed what might be called a schizophrenic attitude toward vodka by lobbying against its corrosive moral and social effects while using vodka sales as one of the chief sources of state revenue. Originally vodka consumption was largely confined to Russia's rural regions and was a feature of peasant life associated with holidays and celebrations. It was during these times that Russian villages engaged in protracted vodka drinking (zapoi), often lasting for days. As taverns became a regular feature of rural life in the nineteenth century, vodka consumption and public drunkenness became a growing problem as Russia's peasants no longer needed a holiday in order to engage in a protracted zapoi.

Benedict Erofeev's novel, Moskva-Petushki (Moscow Circles), written in 1970, is one of the best-known paeans to the art and virtues of Russian drink. The work chronicles the completely inebriated train journey of Erofeev's thinly disguised fictional counterpart from Moscow to a place called Petushki, where his lover and child are presumably awaiting him. As the train moves closer to its final destination, Erofeev's Venichka falls into ever deeper drunken ruminations and hallucinations. Through it all, however, emerges the portrait of a man steeped in religion, literature, and history, a man who drinks with decisive pleasure to thumb his nose at a society that rewards only conformance and adherence to the Party line. Venichka's recipes for "killer" cocktails are a drunken and humorous comment on the products, both cosmetic and ideological, that were being dished out for the Soviet consumer.

Initially the novel circulated in the underground and was published in Paris in 1977 in Russian. It was not until Gorbachev came to power that the work appeared, though in a greatly abridged form, in a short-lived Soviet government journal called Sobriety and Culture, *circulating as part of Gorbachev's anti-alcoholism campaign. In 1995 the novel finally was published in full in Russia.*

Moscow to Kursk Station

Everyone talks about the Kremlin. I have heard about it from many people, but I have never seen it myself. How many times when drunk, or even crapulous, have I crossed Moscow, north to south, east to west, from one end to the other, through the centre, or any old way—but I have never seen the Kremlin.

It wasn't there again yesterday, and yet I spent the whole evening staggering about somewhere in the vicinity, and I wasn't even all that drunk. When I got out at Savelovsk Station I had a glass of Bison Grass vodka, because long experience has taught me that this is the best available cure for a heavy head in the morning.

Yes. Bison Grass it was. And then, at Kalyaev Station, I had another glass, only this time it was coriander vodka. A man I knew used to say that coriander vodka does not have a humanizing effect for, while it refreshes all bodily parts, it weakens the soul. For some strange reason the opposite happened to me, that is, my soul was wonderfully refreshed, but my limbs weakened. I agree, its effect was not humanizing. That is why I added two pints of beer and some egg liqueur straight from the bottle.

What next, Benny, what did you drink then? I hear you ask. A most natural question, but I cannot answer it properly. I remember quite clearly that on Chekhov Street I had two glasses of Hunter's vodka. But could I have got across the Sadovaya Ring Road without a drink? The answer is no. So I must have had something else.

And then I went to the centre of town, because that's what always happens: whenever I go looking for the Kremlin I end up at Kursk Station. Actually, I was supposed to go to Kursk Station, and not to the town centre, but that is where I went, so as to see the Kremlin, just this once. I knew anyway, that I wouldn't see the Kremlin and that this way I'd end up at Kursk Station.

It's enough to make one weep. Not because I never made it to Kursk Station (so what: if I didn't get there yesterday, I'll get there today). Not because I woke up this morning in the hallway of some blocks of flats (it seems that yesterday I sat down on the fortieth stair from the bottom, and, hugging my little suitcase, fell asleep). All that is unimportant. What matters is the fact that I have just discovered that between Chekhov Street and that hallway I managed to drink another six roubles' worth—what was it, and where? And in what order? And did it make me feel better or worse? No one knows, and now no one will ever find out. Just as no one knows to this day whether Prince Dimitry was killed by Boris Godunov. Or was it the other way round?

Where was this hallway? I still haven't the faintest idea, but that's as it should be. All is well. Everything in this world must be slow and wrong. That way man avoids hubris and remains unhappy and confused.

It was light by the time I went out into the street. Everyone will know—everyone, that is, who has spent a paralytic night in a strange hallway and has left it at dawn—that my heart was heavy as I descended those forty steps and that it was very heavy as I came out into the light.

Never mind, said I to myself, never mind. Over there is a chemist's—see? And over here a silly bugger in a brown jacket is sweeping the pavement. You can see that too. So keep calm. Everything's as it should be. If you want to go left, Benny, then go left. I'm not forcing you to do anything. If you want to go right—go right.

I went right, swaying slightly from cold and misery, that's what did it, the cold and the misery. How heavy lies the early morning burden on the heart! How illusory yet inevitable the distress! What does it consist of, that burden which dare not give its name? Two parts paralysis to one part nausea? Is it more an exhaustion of the nerves or a mortal anguish somewhere near the heart? And if it consists of all these in equal parts, then what does it add up to: stupor or fever?

Never mind, said I to myself, put your collar up against the wind, and keep going, slowly. And take very, very shallow breaths. That way your feet won't keep catching on your knees. And go somewhere. Never mind where. If you turn left, you'll end up at Kursk Station. If you turn right, you'll still end up at Kursk Station. So turn right, just to make sure. Oh, vanity of vanities.

How insubstantial life is during that most impotent and shameful interlude in the life of our people—the hours which stretch from dawn to opening time. How many are the needless silver threads on heads without a home! Keep going, Benny, keep going.

. . . .

Orekhovo-Zuevo–Krutoe

and out came Tikhonov, looking very sleepy and shading his eyes because of me and the sun.

—What are you doing here, Tikhonov?

—I'm working on my theses. We've been ready for action a long time now, but we didn't have the theses. But now they're ready too.

—So you think the situation is ripe?

—God knows! When I've had a drink I think it is, but as soon as my head clears a little, I think, no, it's not ripe yet, it's too early to take up the gun . . .

—Drink some Juniper vodka, Vadim, that'll help.

Tikhonov drank some Juniper vodka, burped and became depressed.

—Well, is the situation ripe enough now?

—Very nearly. Give it a moment or two and it will be.

—So when do we advance? Tomorrow?

—Oh, God knows. When I've had a drink I think it is best to advance straight away, but really we should have advanced yesterday. But as soon as the drink begins to wear off, I think no, yesterday would have been too soon and the day after tomorrow won't be too late.

—Go on, Vadim, have another Juniper vodka.

He did and got depressed again.

—Well then, is it time to advance?

—It is time!

—Don't forget the password. And remind everybody—rendezvous is at 0900 hours Greenwich Mean Time tomorrow morning, between the villages of Gartino and Eliseykovo, near the cattle yard.

—Goodbye, comrade. Try to get some sleep tonight.

—I will. Goodbye comrade.

I must say straight away, since the entire human race is now standing in judgement, that I was opposed to this escapade from the start, knowing it would be as barren as a fig tree (a good expression, that, barren as a fig tree). I said from the beginning that a revolution achieves something only if it takes place in the hearts of men and not in the hay. But once they'd started the revolution without me, I couldn't stand aside from my comrades. I hoped at least to prevent their hearts from getting too hard and their hands from spilling unnecessary blood.

Just before 0900 hours Greenwich Mean Time we were sitting by the cattle yard in the hay, waiting. To each man who came up to us we said: "Sit down and join us, comrade—you won't find the truth by looking at your feet." But everyone remained standing and, gun at the ready, responded with an agreed quotation from Antonio Salieri: "Nor is there truth up above." The password was a joke and had a double meaning, but we were thinking of something else. 0900 hours Greenwich Mean Time was approaching.

Where had it all started? It all started with Tikhonov nailing his Fourteen Theses to the gate of the Eliseykovo village council. Or rather he didn't nail them to the gate, he wrote them in chalk on the fence, and they weren't so much theses as words, clear and terse words, and there weren't fourteen of them, just two. Anyway, that's where it all started.

We marched out in two columns, carrying banners.

One column advanced on Eliseykovo and the other on Gartino. We marched unopposed until sunset. There were no dead or wounded on either side, and there was only one prisoner: the former chairman of the Larionov village committee, thrown out of work in his declining years for drunkenness and congenital idiocy. Eliseykovo fell. Cherkassovo was at our feet, Neugodovo and Peksha begged for mercy. All the key centres of the Petushki region, from the shop at Polomy to the Andreyevskoe warehouse, fell into the hands of the insurgents.

After sunset the village of Cherkassovo was proclaimed the capital. Our prisoner was transported there, and that is where we held our victory congress. All the speakers were smashed, and all were mumbling one and the same thing: Maximillian Robespierre, Oliver Cromwell, Sophia Perovskaya, Vera Zasulich, punitive expeditions from Petushki, war with Norway . . . and then it was back to Sophia Perovskaya and Vera Zasulich.

People in the audience were shouting: "Where's Norway?" "Oh, God knows where!" others answered. "Somewhere in the middle of nowhere, at the back of beyond."

—Wherever it is, I tried to silence the noise,—we can't manage without an invasion. To rebuild an economy destroyed by war you've got to destroy it first, and to do this you need at least one war, civil or otherwise, and you need a minimum of twelve fronts.

—We need White Poles! shouted Tikhonov, wild-eyed.

—You idiot! I shouted at him,—why can't you keep your trap shut! Vadim, you are a brilliant theoretician and we all carry your theses in our hearts, but when it comes to practical matters you're a shit! Tell me, what do you want White Poles for?

—All right, who's arguing? said Tikhonov, capitulating.—As if I needed them any more than you! Let it be Norway then!

In our excitement and elation we somehow forgot that Norway had been a member of NATO for the last twenty years, and so Vladimir T. rushed to Larionov post office with a bundle of postcards and letters. One letter, posted "Recorded Delivery," was addressed to King Olaf of Norway and carried a declaration of war. Another letter, or rather a blank sheet of paper in a sealed envelope, was sent to General Franco. Let it serve as a warning to the old sod, the effing old Caudillo will get shit-scared!

The demands we sent to Prime Minister Harold Wilson were very moderate: "Withdraw your gunboats from the Gulf of Akaba, and then you can do just as you like." Our fourth and last letter was addressed to Wladislaw Gomulka, to whom we wrote: "You, Wladislaw Gomulka, have full and inalienable rights to the Polish Corridor but Josef Cyrankiewicz has no rights to that Corridor at all."

And we sent off our postcards: to Abba Eban, Moshe Dayan, General Suharto and Alexander Dubček. All four postcards were very pretty, with flowers and acorns. Let them get a little pleasure, we thought, and then they might realise that we too are subject to international law.

No one slept that night. We were all gripped by enthusiasm, we all gazed into the sky and imagined how pleased Wladislaw Gomulka would be and how Josef Cyrankiewicz would tear his hair in despair.

Our prisoner, Anatoly Ivanovich, former chairman of the village council, did not sleep either. He howled from his barn like a banshee:

—Boys! Does this mean that I won't get a drink tomorrow morning?

—Listen to him! Be glad that you'll be fed in accordance with the Geneva Convention!

—What does that mean?

—You'll soon know! It means that you'll be able to walk, but you won't feel like whoring!

Krutoe–Voinovo

Early next morning, even before the shops opened, we held a Plenary Meeting. It was an Extended October Plenary Meeting. Since all four of our Plenary Meetings were October Extended ones, we decided to number them: first Plenary, second Plenary, third Plenary and fourth Plenary.

The main item on the agenda was the election of a chairman, that is, the election of me as chairman. That took no more than two or three minutes. The rest of the meeting was spent in pure speculation on the theme: whose shop will open first—Auntie Masha's in Andreyevskoe or Auntie Shura's in Polomy?

I sat in my chair listening to the discussion and thinking that a discussion may be a necessary thing, but decrees are an absolutely necessary thing. Why had we forgotten the crowning achievement of every revolution? How about this for a decree?: "Auntie Shura will open her shop at six a.m." What could be simpler? Now that we were vested with power by the people we could easily make Auntie Shura open her shop at six a.m. instead of 9.30! Why hadn't I thought of it before?

And how about a decree on land: "All the land of the region, with all the produce and property thereon, with all its alcoholic drinks, shall be the property of the people outright, with no reparation." Or how about this: "The hands on the clocks will be moved two hours forward." Or two hours back. Never mind where to, so long as they're moved. And: "The word 'devil' will henceforth be spelt 'divel.' " Oh, yes, and we must think of a letter of the alphabet to abolish. And finally Aunty Masha in Andreyevskoe must be made to open at 5.30 instead of 9.30.

Thoughts were crowding in my head, so much so, that I got depressed, called Tikhonov out into the corridor, where we drank a little Coriander vodka and I said:

—Listen, chancellor!

—What?

—Nothing really. It's just that you're a shitty chancellor, that's what.

—Find yourself another, then, said Tikhonov, offended.

—That's not the point, Vadim. The point is this. If you want to be a good chancellor, sit down and write decrees. Have another drink and then sit down and write. I've heard that you lost control over yourself and pinched our prisoner. Why? Do you want to open the floodgates of terror?

—Well, just a little . . .

—What terror do you want? White?

—Yes.

—A pity, Vadim. But never mind, there are more important things to deal with first. First you must write a decree, any decree, however bad . . . Have you got a pen and paper? Right then, sit down and write and then it'll be time for another drink and for the declaration of human rights. And then we can have a look at the Terror question. Time enough. And then we'll have another drink and study, study and study.

Tikhonov wrote down two words, had a drink and sighed:

—Yes. I shouldn't have started the terror. But mistakes are inevitable when you are embarking on such a new undertaking as ours, and there are no precedents to guide you. Well, there were some precedents, but . . .

—What precedents! That was nothing! Just a flight of the bumble bee, a children's game played by grown-ups, not a precedent! Do you think, we should introduce a new calendar?

—No, let's leave it as it is. You know what they say: leave the shit alone and it won't stink.

—You're absolutely right, let's leave it. You are a brilliant theoretician, Vadim, and that's good. Do you think it's time to close the Plenary Meeting? Auntie Shura in Polomy must have opened by now. They say she's got Rossiyskaya in stock.

—Yes, we'll close the Plenary Meeting. There'll be another one tomorrow anyway. Let's go to Polomy.

It turned out that Auntie Shura didn't have any Rossiyskaya. As a result of this—and of our expectation of punitive raids from the centre of the region—

it was decided that our capital should be temporarily transferred from Cher-kassov to Polomy, twelve versts from the borders of the Republic.

And that is where we held our second Plenary Meeting next day. The main item on the agenda was the resignation of me as chairman.

—I rise from my chair, I said in my speech,—in order to spit on it. I consider that the post of chairman should be held only by a man who is capable of staying blind drunk for three days. Are there such men among us?

—There aren't, the delegates answered with one voice.

—I mean, don't you think that I could stay blind drunk for three days?

For a moment or two they all stared thoughtfully at me and then they chorused:

—It's possible.

—Well, then, I continued—We'll manage without a chairman. Let's go out into the fields instead and prepare the punch. Boris here is a man of sterling moral qualities, so let's lock him up and leave him to reshuffle the cabinet.

My speech was interrupted by an ovation and the Plenary Meeting was over. The fields were illuminated by a blue glow. I alone did not share the universal excitement and faith in the success of our enterprise and I wandered among the fires troubled by one thought: Why is the world silent? Why doesn't anyone in the world seem to care about us? The whole district is aflame and while the world might be silent because it is holding its breath, why doesn't anyone, from east or west, extend a helping hand? What is King Olaf up to? Why aren't the regular troops attacking from the south?

I took my chancellor quietly aside. He was reeking of punch.

—Vadim, do you like our revolution?

—Oh, yes, he replied,—it may be feverish but it is beautiful.

—I see. And how about Norway, Vadim, have you heard anything from Norway?

—Nothing so far. Why do you want to know about Norway?

—How can you ask? Are we or aren't we at war with Norway? It's all rather stupid. We have declared war, but Norway doesn't want to take part . . . Listen, if we don't get bombed by tomorrow, I'll get back in that chair and then you'll see!

—Do, said Vadim,—who's stopping you, friend? Get back in your chair, if you like.

Voinovo–Usad

There was not a single bomb the next day. So, opening the third Plenary Meeting, I said:

—Senators! I see that no one in the world wants friendship with us or war with us. Everyone has turned away from us with bated breath. Since the Petushki punitive squad will arrive by tomorrow evening and Auntie Shura's shop will be out of Rossiyskaya by tomorrow morning, I take all power into my own hands. Let me explain to any fool who does not understand that I am introducing a curfew. Moreover, I hereby declare that the powers of the President are extraordinary and plenipotentiary, and I hereby declare myself President. That is, I declare myself to be "a man above the law and the prophets."

No one made any objections. Only the Prime Minister, Boris S., shuddered at the word "prophets," and the upper part of his body shook with vengeance.

Two days later he died of anguish and an excessive tendency towards generalization. There didn't seem to be any other cause of death and we didn't hold a post-mortem because those are unpleasant. And the same evening the telex machines of the world received the following statement: "Death from natural causes." There was no mention whose death, but the world guessed. The fourth Plenary Meeting was sad. I rose to make my speech and I said:

—Delegates! If I should ever have any children I will hang a portrait of the Governor of Judea, Pontius Pilate, on their wall, as an example of cleanliness. The portrait will show Pontius Pilate washing his hands. I too am washing my hands. I joined you in a moment of drunkenness and against the advice of my reason. I told you that our hearts must be revolutionized, that our souls must strive towards the assimilation of eternal moral values—and everything else is in vain, useless. It is just spiritual torment and bugger-all else. What now? We won't be allowed to join the Common Market. The ships of the U.S. Seventh Fleet can't get to us, even if they wanted to.

Here the audience objected:—Don't despair, Benny! They'll send us some B52s!

—What? B52s! You must be joking!

—And Phantom jets!

—Ha-ha! Phantom jets did I hear you say? You just mention "Phantoms" again and I'll die laughing.

That was when Tikhonov rose and said:—All right, they might not give us Phantoms. But at least we can be sure of the devaluation of the franc.

—Tikhonov, you're an idiot, and that's all there is to it. You may be a valuable theoretician, but the things you say . . . But that's not the point. Why is the whole of Petushki region aflame, but no one notices it, even in the Petushki region? In short, I hereby shrug my shoulders and resign my chairmanship. Like Pontius Pilate, I will wash my hands before you and finish what's left of the Rossiyskaya. To hell with all my plenipotentiary powers. I'm off to Petushki.

You can imagine the storm of protest among the delegates, especially when I began to polish off the Rossiyskaya.

You can also imagine the sort of words they addressed to me when I made to leave, and when I left. I won't bother to quote them.

There was no repentance in my heart. I walked through pasture and meadowland, through rose-hip thickets and herds of cattle. The wheat bowed down to me and the cornflowers smiled up at me. And I repeat, there was no repentance in my heart.

At sunset I was still walking. Queen of Heaven, I thought, where is Petushki? I keep walking and still there is no Petushki in sight. It is getting dark . . . where is Petushki?

Where is Petushki?, I thought as I came up to someone's lighted veranda, which appeared out of nowhere. Then again maybe it wasn't a veranda at all, perhaps it was a terrace, a mezzanine or a wing, I can't tell them apart and I always get them mixed up. I knocked on the door and asked:—Where is Petushki? Are we a long way from Petushki?

Instead of an answer, all those on the veranda roared with laughter. I knocked again, feeling insulted, the laughter on the veranda burst out again. How very strange! What was even stranger was that someone was roaring behind me.

I looked back—and I saw the passengers on the Moscow–Petushki train, all with revolting grins on their faces. So that was it! I was still in the train!

Never mind, Erofeev, I thought, never mind. Let them laugh. Take no notice. Follow the precepts of Saadi, be straight and simple as a cypress and as generous as a palm. I don't know what palms have got to do with it, but never mind, be like a palm anyway. Have you any Kuban vodka in your bottle? You have. Right then, go to the end of the carriage and drink it. Drink it, and then you won't feel so sick.

I went to the end of the carriage, accompanied on all sides by stupid smirks. I felt a vague unease rising from the very bottom of my soul and I couldn't understand what it was and why it was so vague.

"We are coming to Usad, aren't we?" I addressed those who were waiting to get off. "This is Usad, is it not?"

"You should be at home, not asking people stupid, drunken questions," answered a little old man. "You should be at home, doing your homework. I bet you haven't done your homework for tomorrow. Your mother will be very angry." And then he added: "You're only knee-high to a grasshopper, yet you think you have got a right to argue."

Was he crazy? What mother was he talking about? What homework? What grasshopper? And then I realized it was me, and not the old man, who was crazy, because I saw another little old man, with a very white face, who stood near me, looked into my eyes from way down below and said:

"Why do you want to travel anywhere, anyway? It is too late for you to go courting and too early to lie in your grave. Why do you want to travel anywhere, dear lady?"

"Dear lady!!?"

I shuddered and went to the opposite corner of the corridor. There's something funny going on. The whole place seems to be rotting and everyone is nutty. I had a feel all over just in case, but there was no doubt—I was no dear lady. So what made him say that, and why? It might have been a joke, of course. But what a stupid joke!

I am sane and they are all crazy. But maybe it is the other way round? Maybe they are all sane and I am the only nut. The unease kept rising higher from the bottom of my soul. And when the train stopped and the door opened I couldn't restrain myself from asking one of the men getting out:

"This is Usad, isn't it?"

To my enormous surprise the man stood sharply to attention and bellowed:

"No, sir!"

And then he shook me warmly by the hand and, bending down towards me whispered in my ear:

"I will never forget your kindness, comrade Lieutenant Colonel!"

And he left the train, wiping away a tear.

The Soviet Middle Class (2002)

Maya Turovskaya

The middle class has always been a problematic concept in Russia and the Soviet Union. Russia never had a middle class in the conventional sense. To remain faithful to Marx, who saw socialism as the next evolutionary stage after capitalism, the early Bolshevik ideologues found themselves inventing a capitalist system and, by extension, a middle class for prerevolutionary Russia. For whatever its tenuous roots, this was a class that, in theory at least, was to have no place in Soviet society. Yet something approximating it came into being under Stalin as the technical intelligentsia was recruited into the building of a new society. One of the features of this group was its access to perks and privileges such as travel (within Soviet borders), dachas, and special goods.

In her essay, the film and theater critic Maya Turovskaya discusses what it meant to be a member of the Soviet middle class in the post-Stalin era and how differently that class functioned in the Soviet Union than in the West. Money played its own pivotal and peculiar role in the way this class navigated the Soviet system. While the members of this class had money to spend, there was either nothing to buy in the stores (all were owned by the state) or nothing that one wanted to buy. Imported items were sold only in special stores to which only high-ranking Party members had access. Private enterprise was prohibited. Deficits were common, resulting from a command economy that determined supply not by local demand, but by decisions made at the center. Basically the amount of money one had was of less consequence than one's cultural capital. If a Soviet citizen was highly educated or in the medical field or, in the case of Turovskaya, in the arts and theater, he or she could barter and trade access to tickets or medical treatment in order to get everything from a hair cut to car repair. What Turovskaya had to peddle was her access to culture: tickets to a performance could put meat on the table. People's professions became convertible, and thus in a very real sense culture played a defining role in driving the economy during the later days of socialism.

A conjecture about the existence of a Soviet "middle class" first came to me precisely 35 years ago, one fickle February, in that selfsame Munich where I am now.

Instead of racking my brains for a definition of the middle class, I will quote the Oxford English Dictionary: "Middle class—social class between the upper and the lower, including professional and business workers." There is nothing to add or to delete here, except perhaps that in the post-Stalin USSR, the *nomenklatura* may be likened to an "upper class," while the "lower class" was made up of the so-called "people." Business was illegal; more often than not, it was not so much a noun as an adjective, one more attribute of that same *nomenklatura's* privileges.

In that memorable year of 1967, Mark Donskoy and myself were sent to the "far abroad" to show the film "Ordinary fascism." The Central Committee sternly warned us about Nazi and Banderist plots in the Bavarian capital, but already at the airport we were greeted by multiple black-and-white reproductions of a portrait of Che Guevara. We had arrived at the height of the (as yet undeclared) "youth revolution." In the club that had invited us, portraits of Stalin, Trotsky and Mao hung next to each other with a post-modern ease above an enormous samovar. The language of conversation was that of Marxism-Leninism—but one that had little to do with what was tested in the lifelong Soviet exam. The club's director (I don't know what line of work he was in when free from "voluntary work") had a wife who worked at TV, which had not yet become the powerful medium that it is now. As much as we could, the two of us indulged in satisfying our mutual feminine curiosity about each other's everyday life: "we" were just as exotic to them as "they" were to us.

Strange as it may seem, our "starting conditions" appeared almost symmetrical. Our German host treated us to a "reception" in a three-and-a-half room flat just like mine, in a similar *art nouveau* style house. However, she had to heat an extra room for this: in winter, they huddled in just one room, since heating their stoves took time and effort. But their nicely located flat was spacious and inexpensive. She was impressed when I mentioned central heating, while we had not yet been sufficiently upset by dug-up sidewalks to question its profitability and see the advantages of autonomous boilers. (Now these Munich houses have been renovated and become expensive, though one still has to climb the beautiful wooden stairs on foot.) Their son was with us at table: it turned out that our children were both of the same nursery school age. She complained that the kindergartens were only from 8 to 12, after which you had to tug your child around with you. My own nursery school—run by the municipal district, not the Writers' Foundation—not only ran from 9 to 6; it even took the children to the Black Sea in the summer.

But then she had a marvellous, albeit second-hand Mercedes (cars were cheap in Germany then by today's standards) the back seat of which was cluttered with enviable toys—it was used as a children's room. As for me, I had been waiting for a Moskvich for years (and didn't even have a Zhiguli).

"Where did you buy this elegant dress?" she asked me once. I hadn't bought it, I'd had it made by my tailor at the Writers' Foundation. Blinded by the abundance of "Ladies' Paradise" shop windows, I confessed this not without shame. "Are you saying you have a tailor of your own, and that this dress was made especially for you?" "Well, she doesn't even cut out the clothes, she just pricks them." "I know a tailor too, but who can afford this?" It wasn't easy to explain to her that tailors and "commercial shops" were all we had (what modest socialist block lines of ready-made clothes there were to be, were only just starting to appear). But what she found even stranger was my request to be taken to "her" hairdresser's to have my hair done (I was preparing for an important lecture on Russian drama at the university). "There's no point in wasting your money," she said sternly, "I will give you a hairdryer, and we will buy curlers" (another novelty to us). Again: how to explain to her that "one's own" hairdresser means much more than just getting one's hair done? Explaining our cumbersome "socialist" everyday life was almost as difficult as translating Stanislavsky's terminology into the Brechtian conceptual framework then dominant in Germany.

But our definitive divergences cropped up when we discussed . . . tidying up. She was lucky: she had managed to agree on a good price with her *Putzfrau* for two hours twice a week. Now I understand her very well indeed, but then . . . Then I had a nanny, a "domestic worker" in Soviet jargon; she came at 9 am and left when she wanted, i.e. not before 10 pm: she was my socialist butler, my socialist servant, my good wizard (when my mother-in-law turned 90, then 100), my burden. Nanny would continue to live with me for a long time, almost up to her death, and in the end it wasn't clear who was looking after whom. But that was later; then I mentioned the mornings but didn't mention the evenings: my German friend wouldn't have believed me anyway. "Well, you know," she said, "only millionaires live like that." I have never felt so much like a millionaire since.

In our "Munich Marxist debates," as they would have been called then, I tried in vain to argue that the advantages of socialism (cheap labour) were a result of patriarchal backwardness. The word *sputnik* had just entered all languages, and Yury Gagarin's trademark smile doomed all talk about under-development in advance (by the way, the former homeland of the elephants honours him much less than the Americans celebrate their astronauts). Moreover, we were in turbulent 1968. But it was our mutual "Lancaster instruction" that—then and there, in a very practical way rather than by hearsay—first made me realise the existence of a Soviet "middle class." Or at least, its pseudomorphosis.

Middle Middle

The Soviet middle class's survival kit (which didn't always have to be complete) of "apartment, dacha and car" roughly corresponded to the European one's (leaving out electronic and other innards). *Dacha* is a Russian word, but it does stand for the concept of leisure that is so important in the everyday life of the middle class. The USSR had its own leisure stereotype: the one-month holiday (sometimes with one's children and other family members) "in the South" or in the Baltics, but always within the Soviet Union. Isn't this why former Soviet people, at home and in emigration, rushed to foreign beaches [after the end of the Soviet Union] and now travel no less than the Germans? Foreign travel existed, too, but only in groups, instructed to "look left, look right." Elderly Americans and young Japanese, not to mention others, also board buses and look left and right, but in our times one had to have the (sometimes insufficient) guarantee of official references and a family back home.

Culture, however, meant more than just leisure in Soviet practice, more even than culture itself ("In Russia, a poet is more than just a poet . . ." etc.). It was both affordable and scarce. It was at the core of the middle class's identity and, at the same time, of the way it distinguished itself from others. (This is why Russian emigrants feel a cultural hunger wherever on the planet they may be.)

Of course, rumours about empty museums in the West (a mainstay of Soviet propaganda) turned out to be exaggerated: I have never seen Washington's National Gallery or Munich's *Pinakothek* empty. In Germany, any "events," even exotic ones such as Russian authors reading from their works, always attract a grateful audience: the Western middle class is curious and active. But this is not to be compared with the symbolic status that culture had in the USSR.

Sports as part of leisure, even expensive ones such as alpine skiing and tennis, also branded the "middle" as a class. Not to speak of active tourism, which the USSR catered for with unlimited resources of wilderness. "Fitness," however, that emblem of the Western middle class, was something that the latter's poor relation had only a vague idea of, including those who frequented the *banya*.

Education (which turned out to be largely convertible) and medicine were a matter of course.

"The Whole Family
on Vacation." Poster,
1957. Courtesy of
www.plakat.ru.

The medical system was different, too; it had its good and bad sides (until
it imploded). Maybe the polyclinics (including the "departmental" ones) were
as cumbersome and unprofitable as central heating, but for the patient they
had advantages compared to the system of autonomous specialist doctors. I
confess that I miss the once-hated preventive check-ups with their tiresome
blood and urine analyses and summons to the gynaecologist's. But most of all
I miss "our" doctors, who knew us in and out, who didn't need to be instructed *ab ovo* and who, most importantly, followed the old Russian tradition
of healing the sick, not the sickness. My respects to them. Sometimes backwardness has advantages, too. Though Western medicine is much better
equipped, and, if one is insured, much more comfortable.

There was one all-embracing concept, however, which cannot be translated into the Western way of life, but which defined the everyday life of the
Soviet middle class in all its grotesqueness. That concept was *shortage*.

Neighbourly Book-keeping

Once, when I was working at the Institute of the World Economy and International Relations, a colleague from a kindred research institute gave a lecture there on the work of an international commission on comparing life standards in different regions and countries. The USSR turned out to be a difficult case: all attempts by our "junior" and "senior" researchers and the foreign experts to find a clear measure for these standards failed. Using Marx's universal equivalent—money—didn't work out. Salaries, taxes—none of these statistics contained any information. In the end the international commission concluded that the only scientifically reliable source was . . . neighbours' opinion. The point was not that salaries were low, but that one couldn't "buy" anything with them; everything had to be "got hold of." The shortages made life basically non-monetary. Everyday life consisted of permanent "extra-vocational" efforts. The life structure of the Soviet middle class reminds one of the elevator in Vassa Zheleznova's *art nouveau* house in Panfilov's film: on the outside, everything is normal; the cabin moves as expected; but in fact, instead of a mechanism, there is a guy who pulls it up and down. The elevator was driven by "pure manpower." How else could a "junior researcher" have survived on his 120 rouble salary invisible to the world?

My above-mentioned apartment in a house built in 1912, with its stucco mouldings, parquet, old redwood elevator and all the rest constantly prompted my foreign friends to ask misconceived questions about rent. The amount of the latter just as constantly shocked them. Even compared to our scanty salaries, the figure was negligible. Only now do I realise the weighty share of a "normal" middle class person's budget that is made up of lodging expenses. In Munich, rent has reached astronomical levels, and bankrupt Berlin refuses to follow Munich's example of total privatisation, since a lack of subsidised housing means that there are no more levers to influence prices.

But could my friends, even Slavic studies experts, have understood Voland's judgment on Soviet people: "they're normal people, but they've been corrupted by the housing issue"? Or the sacramental meaning of the title of one of Trifonov's novellas, *Exchange*? Even the most innocent "amelioration of dwelling conditions" meant melodrama, comedy, and farce, and at times even something epic in the Brechtian sense. When, after my husband's death, I moved from my *art nouveau* house to the co-operative ghetto of Moscow's *Aeroport* district, I had to use "pure manpower" to organise a cyclopean exchange involving 11 flats, pull it through the Scylla and Charybdis of bureaucracy (real estate agents didn't exist)—and, when this effort, so alien to my impractical and un-heroic character, was over, the last bureaucrat suddenly refused to sign. I had to run to see Misha Ulyanov, a "people's artist" in the true sense of the word. He put on all his regalia and off we went; *en route* he told me about the "three peg rule." Whenever he called a big boss about someone's request (which is what he, his partner Yuliya Borisova and a host of other bearers of famous names did all the time, unselfishly, for friends, acquaintances and strangers), a subordinate would note the call and peg the note somewhere, hoping his boss would forget about it. The game continued up to three calls, after which the subordinate would willy-nilly take down the request. "So you'll see, we will get off lightly."

I remember how Raya Orlova, when she was an unofficial consultant, vainly proposed Voinovich's *Ivankiad* to American publishers. They had trouble understanding not just the humour of the situation, but the situation itself. "A high-ranking bureaucrat wants to buy a room from an intellectual—so where's the problem?" This is where the watershed difference lay between their fairly hierarchical, but monetarised way of life and our pseudomorphosis.

The legendary standardisation of life in the USSR concerned ideology and, probably, lists of staff members. In the sphere of everyday life, every administration, every institution, every local party committee excelled in overcoming the shortages autonomously, wringing out privileges large and microscopic.

In my sister's hush-hush aviation institute, "orders were taken." In Mosfilm's cafeteria, one could get meat on Thursdays (or Fridays). A friend of mine got a "voucher" for a carpet in the hospital where she was working. My brother-in-law was "attached" to a polyclinic belonging to the Academy of Sciences, while I was "attached" to that of the Writers' Foundation. Their institution had rest homes in the Crimea, ours had "creative resorts." My local nursery school was administered by a secret military factory. The network of tricks was infinitely diverse. One would get a plot of garden land, another would obtain tours abroad (the prices were laughable, one could have travelled around the world, but there were the officially imposed "years without travel," the issue of registration etc.). One would get manufactured goods at his workplace, another would get a subscription to whole series of collected works etc. etc. But personal effort was much more important. Everyone was a trapper hunting for his prey under conditions of total scarcity. One would have "their own dealer," another would have access to a *Berezka*, still another would get one of the rare commissions to countries of the "socialist camp"—it's impossible to remember everything. The well-known paradox whereby the fridges were full while the stores were empty, was rooted in private initiative. One of my friends "shopped" at the Central House of Writers, another had "her own" butcher, where she entered through the back door. As for myself, whenever I had lots of visitors or was in need of boots, I would ask "my" hairdresser. She did the hair of all the ladies in the area, so she had *blat*, connections—the decisive word in a Soviet middle class man's thesaurus. One could survive without money, but not without *blat*.

Looking back, I keep marvelling at the high status of culture. Of course, I topped up Lyusya's fee to get my hair cut without having to queue; but in all other instances, she wanted nothing from me except news about theatre and cinema (Lyusya was a theatre lover). The young urologist from the Botkin whom I consulted at the polyclinic, was a film freak. I had to give him detailed surveys, recommendations and reviews of the latest films. Once I found him cheerful and suntanned after a holiday—he had been to the United States at his cousin's invitation (such visits had only just been allowed). His cousin was a director and wanted to know whether his new movie could have any success in Russia. The movie was called *Jaws*. I nearly fell off my chair: the cousin was Spielberg (indeed, Russia is the home of the elephants—but elephants need the right conditions to prosper). Maybe my doctor is now living in California (he mended my kidneys, and they haven't caused me any trouble since). By the way, throughout my long life no medic, from nurses to famous professors, ever accepted money from me—they were all among the foremost con-sumers of culture. But part of the print run of each of my books went into a "medical fund."

Well, of course, apart from one's personal "database," there was the "com-munal network," which my friend dubbed the "Do-you-happen-to-know-where-to-have-a-fan-mended." True enough, we couldn't have survived with-out the famous "Let's take each other by the hands . . ." But I'm not talking about favours and services. The trademark Soviet friendship was a political, moral and personal refuge, yet another element of identity; it was what our fellow middle class men from abroad fell for in bureaucratically unfriendly, uncomfortable Moscow. Even now neither distance nor changes of place can alter it; though perhaps age can. However big the income differences were (some were better off, others were substantially poorer), they didn't play a significant role.

Anecdotes of the Times

The anecdote was a staple of Soviet life. Whatever the topic—communal living, lines, shortages, alcoholism, climbing divorce rates, declining political leadership—nothing but nothing was beyond the reach of the Soviet anecdote. There were, of course, the more official venues where one might encounter anecdotes, such as the magazine Krokodil' (Crocodile). But Krokodil', like every other official publication in the Soviet Union, was subject to the censor's pen, and thus the anecdotes found between its covers lacked the bite of those that circulated by word of mouth at home, at the office, at the institute and the factory. They couldn't solve the problems, but they helped to blow off steam!

Many Soviet anecdotes took the ethnic minorities as their subjects. Jokes about Ukrainians, Jews, Georgians, and the Chukchi were particular favorites. Some were built around traditionally perceived stereotypes. Georgians, for example, were seen as people who managed to thumb their noses at Soviet power, amass enormous wealth, often through unsavory dealings, and live well while the rest of the Soviet Union was standing in line and coping with deficits. Anecdotes about the Chukchi, one of Russia's indigenous people who live in the far northeast on the Chukotka Peninsula, reflected the changing political climate. Certain anecdotes about them point to the Party's failure to fulfill its promises to improve the lives of the indigenous peoples through culture, education, and material well-being. Other anecdotes contained biting critiques of the Chukchi themselves as ignorant simpletons who lived far away from the major centers of Russian life in so-called backward conditions. Jewish anecdotes too proliferated and changed with the times. From the 1970s on, many addressed the theme of Jewish emigration and discrimination at home, despite the fact that Jewish candidates for jobs were often the best qualified by virtue of their education.

Two alcoholics are tying one on and [had] run out of vodka.

"Petya," one of them says, "go into my bedroom. Behind the curtain there's a half bottle of vodka."

Petya comes back.

"Vasya, I'm not one to gossip, but back there in the bedroom some guy is sleeping with your wife."

"Quiet!" says Vasya. "This is his vodka."

QUESTION TO RADIO ARMENIA: "What is the definition of the Supreme Soviet of the USSR?"

ANSWER: "The Supreme Soviet is a collective organ of Soviet power, consisting of two sorts of people: those who are absolutely incapable of anything and those capable of doing absolutely anything."

A woman asks a man she has just met: "What is your alcohol consumption like?"

"Only on holidays and when I go to the bath," he answers.

The woman thinks it over and says to him, "I think you meet my standards."

Two hours pass, and the prospective husband says to her, "What holiday is it today?"

"There's no holiday today," she answers.

"Then I'll go to the bath."

A teacher asks her class, "Class, do you know what is tragedy?"

The class sits silently for a while. Finally a hand goes up.

"Yes, Boris, can you tell me what is tragedy?"

"Yes, I can" says Boris. "It is when there is a terrible airplane crash and everybody is killed."

The teacher responds, "No, it is a terrible accident but it is not tragedy. Can anyone tell me what is tragedy?"

Everyone thinks for awhile. Finally another hand goes up.

"Yes, Tanya, do you know?"

"Yes, it is when they plant a lot of grain in Ukraine. There is no rain so no harvest."

"Ah, Tanya, that is a terrible misfortune, but it is not tragedy."

Finally, after a prolonged silence another hand goes up.

"I know what is tragedy, teacher. It is when Brezhnev and Kosygin stand in the middle of Red Square. Terrible bomb goes off. Both are killed."

"Yes, that is tragedy," says the teacher. "Now do you know why?"

"Yes, because it is not a terrible accident and it is not a terrible misfortune."

During the NEP period [in the 1920s] a class was in session at school.

"Children," said the teacher." Here is an icon. But we all know that there is no God. So I want each one of you to come up and spit on the icon."

All the children except for Moishe did as they were told.

"Moishe, why didn't you spit? You know that there's no God."

"If there's no God," says Moishe, "then why spit on him? And if there is, it won't do me any good arguing with him anyway."

After listening to the news about Gagarin's space flight, Rabinovich shrugs his shoulders: "To leave the Soviet Union, to fly around the world—and all this only in order to come back? One has to be crazy."

At the time when Israel attacked the Arabs, a certain citizen in Moscow beat up two Jews. They took him off to the police station and questioned him:

"What did you beat them up for?"

"In the morning I hear on the radio that Israel had attacked the Arabs. Then in the afternoon I find out that the Jews have gotten as far as the Suez Canal. In the evening I go down to the metro, and they're already here!"

A Chukchi became a member of the prestigious Writers' Union.

He was interviewed by a score of journalists.

"Tell us please," asked one of them. "What books that you've read have made a strong impression on you?"

The Chukchi smiled. "You are mistaken. A Chukchi's not a reader. A Chukchi's a writer."

Ivan used to come to a Chukchi's tent and get him accustomed to vodka. The Chukchi decides not to drink any more and warns his wife:

"As soon as Ivan comes, tell him I'm not at home. And I'll hide meanwhile."

Ivan comes with a bottle of vodka, and the Chukchi's wife tells him that her husband isn't home. Ivan makes her drink vodka and seduces her. The Chukchi lies behind the bed-curtain and thinks: "What a predicament! I should be beating Ivan up—and I'm not home."

Partisans of the Full Moon (1970s)

Akvarium

When Paul McCartney performed in Red Square in 2003, Russian Defense Minister Sergei Ivanov told him that he had learned English by listening to the Beatles.

Rock arrived in the Soviet Union in the late 1950s and early 1960s, at approximately the same time it took off in the West, with the one difference that it was immediately forced into the underground as ideologically suspect. Although Western rock was banned from the Soviet Union, Soviet citizens throughout the decades found ways to listen to it. Those who lived close enough to the western borders could sometimes pick it up on the VOA (Voice of America) or the BBC. Tapes were smuggled in by tourists, by sailors, and sometimes by Russians themselves returning from conferences abroad. The prevailing Party line was that rock-and-roll was a short-term phenomenon that would soon play itself out. What happened instead is that Russian rock began to take off, developing its own style, though it was initially heavily influenced by singers from Chuck Berry to Bob Dylan. Leningrad became the center of the music renaissance, with bands such as Argonavty (the Argonauts), Mify (Myths), and Mashina vremeni (Time Machine) expressing through their songs the inner world of Soviet youth who stood on the cusp of adulthood. Over time Soviet rock groups became increasingly defined by the quality of their lyrics, their poetic style, and their overtly political texts. In the 1970s the songs found their way out to the provinces and the other republics on tape, bypassing official channels.

"Partisans of the Full Moon" is a song by the St. Petersburg group Akvarium, founded in 1972. The group attributes the idea for the song to Bob Dylan's "Father of Night." The title alludes to the fact that many of these groups recorded their songs at night since recording outside official venues was illegal.

To those who hold stones[1] for the long day,
To the brothers of the grapes and the sisters of fire
[A song] about what exists inside me,
Though joyfully it is not only for me.

I see the signs of a great spring,[2]
A silver flame in the night sky.
We have everything that exists.
The time has come—will we open the doors?

Here come the partisans of the full moon . . .
My place is here.
Here come the partisans of the full moon . . .
Let them come . . .

They have knowledge on the other shore.[3]
White reindeer on black snow.
I know everything that exists.
My love . . . but can I really?

Then who can tell us what to do and where is his lash?
Fear is his holiday and guilt is his net . . .
We shall only sing,
My love, but we will open the door.

Here come the partisans of the full moon.
My place is here. My place.
Here come the underground partisans of the moon.
Let them come.

Translated by Kenny Cargill

Notes

1. An idiomatic expression: "to hold a stone" (*derzhat' kamen' [za pazukhoi]*) means "to be ready to take revenge."
2. This may refer to the Russian sociocultural concept of the Thaw. In other words, spring is the coming of liberalization and democratization.
3. A metaphor for the West made famous by the title of Alexander Herzen's *From the Other Shore* (*S togo berega*).

XV

Things Fall Apart

Brezhnev's death in 1982 led the USSR into a period of significant uncertainties. His successor, Yuri Andropov, the savvy former-KGB chief, died in office after only fifteen months, and Andropov's successor, the decidedly less charismatic Konstantin Chernenko, died after only thirteen months in the same post. Mikhail Gorbachev, an ambitious former law student and agronomist from the Russian South, would serve as the Soviet Communist Party's last General Secretary and, perforce, as the Soviet government's last leader, from 1985 to 1991.

More was afoot than just a change of scenery at the top. The collapse of global oil markets that sent so many Western countries into recession in the early 1970s also deeply affected the USSR's ability to provide basic goods for its people, as well as to finance its extensive military goals, foreign aid to socialist bloc countries, and its extensive domestic social programs. The Polish cardinal Karol Wojtyla, crowned Pope John Paul II in 1978, set the stage for a public debate over Communism in the Eastern bloc that would soon have far-reaching effects. In such an economic and political climate the ill-fated Soviet invasion of Afghanistan in 1979 drew wide international opprobrium. Perhaps the single most telling event, however, was the Chernobyl nuclear disaster in Ukraine in April 1986, coming only one year into Gorbachev's leadership. In a terrifying flash Chernobyl came to symbolize what was, at times, the perilously ambitious reach of Soviet modernization given the uneven, often crumbling infrastructure straining to support it. Like imperial Russia's defeat in the Russo-Japanese War eighty years earlier, the disaster evoked public humiliation for the government and widespread calls for reform.

Gorbachev was careful to repeat, and repeat often, that *perestroika*, or restructuring, was intended to improve and upgrade an existing system, not overthrow it. Alongside perestroika came *uskorenie*, an "acceleration" of reform efforts, and the very platform for these efforts, *glasnost'*. Often translated simply as "openness," glasnost in fact means revealing (and, more so, publicly discussing) that which had previously been kept under wraps.

As happens so often in politics, cultural issues played out first. Less than two months after taking office Gorbachev urged the Soviets to confront the country's high rate of alcoholism and the attendant problems created for the health sector in crime, suicide rates, and life expectancy. Despite the high-profile destruction of some of the finest vineyards across the country, moonshine consumption and alcohol poisoning only rose in response. On intercultural fronts, reformers from non-Russian regions took to challenging the deeply layered Soviet state that had long prided itself on international solidarities. One of the first and best-known events came in December 1986, when the Kazakh capital of Almaty saw three days of rioting and protest after Gorbachev dismissed an ethnic Kazakh as General Secretary of that republic and replaced him with a Russian. Not long afterward an acrimonious, decades-long struggle between Armenia and Azerbaijan over the mountainous southern Caucasus region of Karabakh reopened in 1988. From then on, there was little turning back in public understanding of what could be challenged. Daily life became harder as the pace of change sped up. Gorbachev's ambitious economic reforms, angling for the very first time in Soviet history for state enterprises to be entirely responsible for their own budgets, led to dramatic and unpredictable lurches in both industrial and consumer supply. By the end of the 1980s stores filled one week could be empty the next.

In terms of media, citizens accustomed to a steady diet of state-controlled information soon had a veritable smorgasbord of new information to consume. Around the country, people became glued to frequently startling television documentaries and news programs. Readers lined up at news kiosks in the early hours of the morning to be the first in line to buy the coveted issues of the "thick journals," the most prestigious publications of the country's sophisticated literary circles, to read the complete works of long-repressed novelists and poets. For many the deluge of historical revelation meant a loss of the sacred; for more still, it meant simply an absence of traditional constraint.

Some were less happy than others with this new policy of openness. Perestroika is considered to have formally ended when an eight-member team calling themselves the State Committee on Emergency Measures launched a bungled coup to unseat Gorbachev in August 1991, just days before he and regional leaders were set to sign a new union treaty expanding the rights and privileges of all fifteen of the Soviet republics. The coup failed, but Gorbachev conceded defeat when it became clear that it was a politically more limber Boris Yeltsin whom the country rallied behind. On the eve of its very reinvention, the Soviet Union dissolved entirely.

Between 1985 and 1991 some lost the only world they had ever known, while others jettisoned it with abandon. What all citizens of the Soviet Union were actualizing, perhaps for the first time since Marx and Engels had long ago called for the masses to recognize their true circumstances—and what continues to make modern Russia so distinctive—was an intensely reflexive public scrutiny of the world around them. It was a time like no other for millions of highly educated citizens, urban and rural, down to the person. After seventy-four years the world's first Communist state came to an end.

The Most Responsible
Phase of Perestroika (1990)

Mikhail Gorbachev

*The French writer Roland Barthes once wrote that mythic narratives—those funda-
mental underpinnings that uphold the integrity of persons and entire states—are
harder to sustain when radical change is under way. "Myths of the right," he wrote,
are conservative by nature, regardless of political stripe. They succeed not necessarily
by the content of their messages, but by their links to a stable past and an equally
stable present. They are timeless and enduring. "Myths of the left" are a much trickier
affair: they want to overthrow old orders, but they walk a fine line. Too much change
can raise too many questions, so many, in fact, that it makes it difficult to restore
order once reform is set in motion.*

*Barthes's words tell us about the difficult line walked by Soviet leaders in the
1980s, calling upon what by then was an established socialist public, with its own
understandings of history, and seeking, however tentatively, to reorganize the very
same world—to upgrade socialism—and to rewrite history yet one more time.*

*In his speech to the Twenty-eighth (and last) Communist Party Congress of the
USSR, Mikhail Gorbachev makes a telling observation that "real Soviet power is
being restored," reminding listeners that grassroots-level soviets, or "councils," are
what the Soviet Union was originally meant to be based on. Such grassroots organizations, according to Lenin's plan, however, were also supposed to be scenes of active
experiment, the refusal of fixed, authoritarian structures. Gorbachev's ability to
reinvent Soviet power, in this respect, may have gone a long way to undoing it.*

The principal positive result is that society won freedom, which unfettered
popular energies, offered scope for ideas previously gripped in the vice of
dogmas and old formulas, gave vent to concern about the future of the nation
and the future of socialism, and made it possible to involve millions of people
in politics and launch vital change.

Without freedom, this Congress would not have been held, or it would not
have been held in the atmosphere we have here now.

Mikhail Gorbachev, General Secretary of the Soviet Communist Party, at the Congress of Peoples' Deputies of the USSR, 1990. Courtesy of ITAR-TASS.

Much of what accumulated in the stifling and repressive atmosphere of Stalinism and stagnation, and is now surfacing, is far from pleasant and constructive. But this has to be tolerated. This is what a revolution is all about. Its primary function is always to give people freedom. And perestroika with its democratization and glasnost has already fulfilled its primary task.

Society needs spiritual revival as much as air. It takes place right before our eyes. With all the twists to this process, it has already exerted a huge impact. Society has changed. All of us have changed.

It is entirely another matter that neither the party nor the country as a whole, neither the old nor the newly formed organizations and movements, neither of us, comrades, have yet learned how to use the freedom that we attained. Therefore the priority task is to learn how to do this sooner and better.

We have made considerable progress in the political reform. We have created new structures of power from the top to the bottom on the basis of the democratic expression of the people's will.

They continue to be perfected, but we have already started to act, giving real substance to our democracy and the notion of a law-governed state.

It has been said more than once that there are many shortcomings in the work of these new structures, that experience is lacking, that procedures and mechanisms are not yet operating smoothly and that political culture, competence and specific knowledge are lacking at times.

The shaping of the personnel of elected councils has not yet been completed. Nevertheless, the new councils got down to business: people's deputies assumed a more responsible attitude and are striving to tackle specific problems and meet the needs of the people as soon as possible.

Real Soviet power is being restored, and this is a gratifying factor, one of the most important achievements of perestroika, in which Communists and party organizations have been and are participating.

Still there is a certain distance, I would say, coolness between elected councils and the party. And here Communists should be more attentive. They should first of all consider how they should act. They should consider if this alienation is not linked with the fact that we still cannot abandon the former methods of dealing with local councils, methods inherited from the command-administrative system. New government bodies, in turn, react painfully to such methods.

. . . .

The party will be the vanguard of society and will be able to act successfully only if it wholly realizes its new role and completes within a brief period of time its reforms on the roads of democracy, and more promptly learns to work with the masses in a new way.

It is necessary to overcome the alienation from the people inherited from the previous times. This is to be achieved first of all by renewal of the activity of primary party organizations, renewal of cadres and enhancing their prestige.

I am deeply upset by the misunderstanding that emerged here. We shall fail to advance unless we are able to consolidate the party's positions, to offer an effective policy to society and thus impart fresh dynamism to perestroika, unless we realize that everything that took place in the past is now dated and unacceptable.

From the atmosphere of the Congress, from many speeches and the manner of debating employed by some delegates, I sensed that far from everyone has understood that the party is living and working in a different society, that a renewed party with a different style of activity is needed.

We are not changing our line or our choice and are committed to socialist values. But, believe me, the party's success depends on whether it realizes that this is already a different society. Otherwise it will be marginalized by other forces and we shall lose ground.

We now have immense possibilities, and the main thing is to realize that we shall not achieve much without renewal, democratization, without strengthening the living bond with the people or without active work among the masses.

I had a lot of personal conversations with comrades during the Congress, and I must say that I came to feel more understanding of the unconventionality and novelty of the situation in which the party has found itself, from, so to speak, rank-and-file comrades—workers, farmers, intellectuals and secretaries of primary party organizations. Generally speaking, though, this is an expression from the lexicon of the past, and maybe I should not have used it.

Comrade Gaivoronsky from Donetsk spoke here. He correctly recalled that the most important thing is for the party to increase broad and deep contacts with the working class. This was also illustrated by a meeting with worker delegates and with those invited to the Congress.

Party committees, including the Central Committee, are to blame for the fact that during major political campaigns they were unable to uphold the interests of the working class. They pondered for too long over their attitude toward emerging new forms in the working class movement. We have lost a good deal because of that. The working class puts this question squarely before us.

Another lesson from the discussion is that we must continue to act in the main directions of perestroika. The party and state leadership were scathingly criticized for the economic situation, the state of affairs on the market and the provision of goods.

To solve the food problem is the key task in this respect, and I put it to the fore. Once we remove its acuteness, 70–80 percent of the acuteness of the situation in the social sphere—the transition to a regulated market and the housing shortage—will be eased as well.

In this connection, and I will not conceal it, I was worried when three-quarters of the Congress decided to change the name of the Commission for Economic Reform, excluding the word "market." This means that there is a persisting lack of understanding of the need for an abrupt turn in order to radically change the economic situation.

Has our entire history not shown, comrades, the futility of attempts to get out of the plight in which both the state and the people have found themselves, by patching up the command-and-administrative system?

We have already incurred tremendous losses by stubbornly clinging to it for decades and continuing to cling even now, thereby putting the brakes on renewal and the transition to new forms of economic life in the country.

If we continue to act in this way, then, I shall be frank, we will bankrupt the country. I am expressing my viewpoint explicitly.

The advantages of the market economy have been proven on a world scale and the question now is only whether the high level of social protection—

which is characteristic of our socialist system, the system for the working people—can be ensured under market conditions.

. . . .

I repeat from this rostrum for the Congress, the party and the entire country to hear: Our position is, first, that it is essential to give full freedom to all types of economic management in the countryside on the basis of a completely free choice.

Second, it is necessary to establish reasonable exchanges between town and countryside, industry and agriculture, exchanges which would promote the advance of the countryside within the shortest period of time.

Third, the state should promote as fully as it can a solution of the urgent problems of the countryside, primarily the creation of worthy living conditions for our farmers. These are the three major strategies, on the strength of which it is possible to revive the countryside and provide the country with food. None of these principles can be removed from this triad, for the entire system would collapse.

We should make major decisions on matters concerning the agrarian sector, the countryside as a whole, and the position of farmers. This is, so to speak, my summary of the discussion which has been held here.

Yet another two subjects were raised here sharply and it was not easy to listen to all this because they concerned people's lives and have already had damaging consequences. There are, to begin with, the ecological problems, one of the acutest issues. We should not put its solution off. We came to realize the acuteness of the problem too late. But much, comrades, can still be rectified. This is illustrated by foreign experience.

Approximately three decades ago, dozens of towns in the United States were within an ecological disaster zone. Rivers were literally dead and the Great Lakes were on the verge of ruin. But large inputs and the implementation of special programs made it possible to drastically improve the situation. The same is being done in Europe, which is saturated with industry and chemical businesses.

Therefore, however hard the situation we now find ourselves in, it is necessary to make large inputs of funds in the nature conservation sphere, regarding it absolutely on a par with such vital tasks as the provision of people with food and housing.

Clean air and water are essential for people in a no lesser degree than bread, comrades. I think state programs will be needed, of course, to tackle the sphere of ecology as a whole and major ecological problems.

The aftermath of the Chernobyl accident causes anguish in all of us. Comrades from Byelorussia, the Ukraine and the Bryansk region must come to realize that we partake of their misfortune.

We face a situation that confronts us with more and more problems, and this is a cause for deep reflection. Just one reactor, and what consequences! Imagine what would happen if a nuclear war breaks out. Nuclear reactors will be destroyed even in a conventional war, and the consequences will be similar to those at Chernobyl. Our country is unable to cope with these consequences. Billions of rubles have been spent and will be spent, while new needs are emerging.

I want people in Byelorussia, the Ukraine and the Bryansk region to hear my words; I want them to know that the entire country is at their side, is aware of their tragedy and will continue to help. Similarly, we have mentioned the Aral problem here and the people there should feel that we will come to their aid as well.

. . . .

I do not doubt the gravity of the situation in some spheres of intellectual development. And I share the alarm over morals which have become widespread and which are incompatible with the ideals of humane socialism. This is not only a legacy of the past but also the result, I repeat, of the explosion of freedom, which society experienced all of a sudden, after being confined for a long time in a room with stale air. We were simply unaware of many things. All this demands great attention by the party, intellectuals, the schools, the entire system of our cultural and educational establishments. This is so.

But I also felt in the criticism of the ideological situation the strong breath of old attitudes. In the report I tried to approach the problem of ideology in its new form. The problem is what we understand by socialism. Some comrades believe that if we write down now in the policy statement and other documents that we remain loyal to old attitudes, everything will click into place. What place? Won't we find ourselves where we have been for more than 60 years, with the known consequences?

The ideology of socialism is not a textbook where everything is compartmentalized by chapters, paragraphs, rules and principles. It will shape up together with socialism itself, as we will facilitate the development of a well-fed, civilized, spiritually rich, free and happy country, as we come to embrace universal human values again not as something alien from the class point of view, but as normal for man. These values have been worked out throughout centuries and millennia. What their neglect has brought us is well known.

Causes of the Collapse

of the USSR (1992)

Alexander Dallin

*The years leading up to perestroika and the naming of Mikhail Gorbachev as General
Secretary of the Communist Party set the stage for rapid change in key ways. While
the years of Leonid Brezhnev, the most significant period of advanced socialism and
perhaps the first and last era of relative stability in the USSR, are often known as a
time of stagnation (zastoi), the previous section of this volume hoped to show that it
was anything but. Prosperity greater than any the country had known began to be felt
across city and countryside. The effect—barring the fact that food shortages continued to interrupt daily life and hundreds of thousands of educated urban residents
could still be found in cramped communal apartments decades after the promise of
dignity for all—was to create a rising tide of expectation. The country was extraordinarily literate by any standards. Intelligentsia and workers alike (still known as
"intellectual laborers" and "manual laborers," respectively) could find reprieve from
the frustrations of limited or cramped housing by taking annual trips for rest and
relaxation in the Baltics, on the shores of the Black Sea, or in Eastern Europe.
Through travel many became aware of the significant alternatives that existed across
the considerable diversity of the socialist bloc.*

*While it is most common to suggest that ethnic conflicts sundered Soviet stability
and brought down the state—among the highest profile events that undoubtedly sped
the collapse—Alexander Dallin here reminds us of the wide range of circumstances in
play. Not least was the USSR's dwindling ability to maintain its hard-won standard
of living. In spring of 1986 crude oil revenues, on which the USSR was heavily
dependent (unsteadily so, after the upheavals governing OPEC in the 1970s and the
Iran-Iraq War that closed out that decade), plummeted from just over thirty U.S.
dollars a barrel to under ten, devastating the Communist country's limited foreign
currency reserves. Thus Gorbachev's ability to patch budget shortfalls and appease
alienated sectors of the population when necessary, as his predecessors had done, was
considerably constrained. To this one can raise questions of the enduring legitimacy of
a state that bravely opened up its founding decades to widespread criticism, alongside*

contemporary revelations of enduring corruption and a rapid pace of change few modern governments have willingly embraced.

Against Predetermination

Identifying the sources of historical events is a notoriously chancy and disputed business. We have no experimental method, nor proof that would stand up in a scientific court of law. Etiology—the search for causes—is not a science, nor is there any reliable technique for weighing the relative importance of different inputs. The archives will reveal no documents that will conveniently spell out the causes of the Soviet collapse. Moreover, the assessment of causes may well change with the distance in time from the events. Finally, as with an earthquake, at times subterranean processes are at work without our being able to track them in advance of their eruption.

Research will help, as will a commitment to making assumptions explicit. At the very least, it is often possible to tell who has gotten it wrong, without being sure who has gotten it right. But, ultimately, we have to rely on an individual analyst's scholarly intuition and empathy, and on his or her implicit philosophy of history. It is only fair to indicate that my own inclination is to distrust both conspiracy theories and flukes, and to be suspicious of all manner of determinism and inevitability, mysterious "essences" and broad *a priori* philosophical schemes. It is far better, I would maintain, to examine the empirical evidence without prejudging the case.

I find no grounds for arguing that the outcome—the disintegration of the Soviet system—was predetermined, let alone inscribed in the "genetic code" that went back to October 1917 and the origins of that system. How do we know what, if anything, was preordained? More concretely, the system withstood many tests far more severe than what it experienced in the 1980s (for example, in the first Five-Year Plan and in World War II) and survived: its institutions and controls were scarcely brittle then, and popular attitudes— admittedly, difficult to probe in retrospect—scarcely bore out the neo-totalitarian argument that the regime never had any legitimacy in the eyes of the population.

Of course the seizure of power in 1917 was illegitimate. But it is impossible seriously to derive the events of 1991 from that fact. It is far more sensible and far more persuasive to argue that what we see in the Soviet collapse is the product of unintended results, both of socioeconomic development and of earlier policy choices. According to the neo-totalitarian argument, the Soviet Union remained totalitarian after Stalin—not because the reality of Soviet life was so, but because of a continued commitment of the decision-makers to a

Rallying at the statue of
Dzerzhinskii in Moscow's
central Lubianka Square, 1991.
Courtesy of the Hoover
Institution, Russian Pictorial
Collection, Envelope CT, Item 1,
Hoover Institution Archives.

totalitarian vision. By the same token, it is precisely the extent to which Soviet
reality diverged from that vision that provides evidence of social autonomy—
of what is properly referred to as unintended consequences.

What we are really puzzling over is how as thoroughly controlled, as
tightly disciplined, as rigidly programmed, and as heavily indoctrinated a
system as the Soviet managed to fall apart, unravel so easily and so completely, and in the process prompt in its citizenry an utter scorn for authority,
and a disregard for laws and regulations.

The answers, I believe, have to go beyond social psychology, for they
centrally involve political institutions and behavior. They involve both broad
secular changes and particular individual choices. There is, I suggest, a cluster
of interrelated developments that together, and in their interaction, formed
the essential preconditions—necessary but not sufficient—for what occurred
in the 1990s. In brief, they are: (1) the loosening of controls; (2) the spread of
corruption; (3) the erosion of ideology; (4) the impact of social change on
values and social pathologies; (5) the growing impact of the external environment on Soviet society and politics; and (6) the consequences of economic

constraints. Against these background conditions, certain decisions of the Gorbachev regime, in turn, appear decisive as catalysts for collapse.

The Loosening of Controls

One thing that held the Soviet Union together, exacted obedience and compliance, and provided the framework for its *sui generis* development, was the sweeping Stalinist system of controls. Stalin died in 1953. In retrospect, what we see during the following 30 years is a gradual, unheralded loosening and then breakdown of these controls.

An essential part of the control structure and process was the terror that had reached unbelievable proportions and exacted such an incredible cost in the Stalin years. In the Khrushchev years it was the abandonment of mass political terror that provided the conditions for reducing the scope of controls. It ended the atomization, the silencing of that society—with an impact that did not become fully apparent until a generation later.

. . . .

At the same time, the post-Stalin years unintentionally conveyed to the Soviet citizen a sense of fallibility and uncertainty in the country's leadership. This was suggested both by the tinkering with institutions . . . and the "bifurcation" of the party, for instance, and by the continuous struggle over power and policy within the elite, which found policy expression in, among other things, the anti-Stalin campaign, and which culminated in the ouster of Khrushchev.

In the Brezhnev years a remarkable change in mood became apparent. Whether or not it accurately reflected reality, Soviet observers began to speak —rather more candidly than before—of stagnation and the leadership's failure to come to grips with urgent problems, and foreigners noted the change.

. . . .

[John] Bushnell detected "mounting skepticism and cynicism about the values and performance of the regime in other areas as well."

And Dusko Doder recalled:

When I arrived in Moscow on temporary duty in the summer of 1978, it was apparent that incremental changes had taken place over the past decade. . . . In the narrow circle of my friends I found something that was new, or at least more pronounced than before—the quest for the comforts of middle-class life: a car, a place in the country, a tiled bathroom, a Japanese stereo, a chance to travel abroad—at least to Bulgaria.

By the early 1980s it was apparent to him that

> Brezhnev's stable regime had produced an amazing proliferation of cor-
> ruption, a cynicism that undermined all enterprise. An air of stagnation,
> the timeless inertia of the bureaucracy, a crisis of spirit—all characterized a
> system that seemed to have accompanied the aging leaders into exhaus-
> tion and debility.

. . . .

The Spread of Corruption

Far more serious is the massive spread of corruption, in all its many aspects, as
a way of life. In a powerful account based on personal experience and replete
with well-documented anecdotes, Konstantin Simis, in his *USSR: The Corrupt
Society*, is compelled to conclude:

> The Soviet Union is infected from top to bottom with corruption—from
> the worker who gives the foreman a bottle of vodka to get the best job, to
> Politburo candidate Mzhavanadze who takes hundreds of thousands of
> rubles for protecting underground millionaires; from the street prostitute,
> who pays the policeman ten rubles so that he won't prevent her from
> soliciting clients, to the former member of the Politburo Ekaterina Fur-
> tseva, who built a luxurious suburban villa at the government's expense—
> each and everyone is afflicted with corruption.
>
> I was born in that country and lived there for almost sixty years. Year
> after year since childhood and throughout my whole conscious life I
> watched as corruption ate more deeply into society until it turned the
> Soviet regime in the sixties and seventies into a land of corrupt rulers, ruling
> over a corrupted people.

. . . .

No doubt, many instances of corruption remained unexposed. But what is
known argues strongly that the corruption presupposed a loosening of controls, permitting a wanton violation of law to take place in the interstices. It
also implied and fostered a new measure of cynicism about the "radiant
heights" of communist morality.

Much of this "quiet revolution" became possible because the end of mass
terror also meant an end to the individual's paralyzing fear, and because
bureaucratic actors saw opportunities for self-aggrandizement with minimal
risk or cost. But in Stalin's time, in addition to both outer constraints and

often simply the lack of opportunity for autonomous corruption, there had been psychological inhibitions on many well-placed individuals, rooted in their belief in the system and in the cause in the name of which it was all being done. Later, with a change of generations and apparently a change of values, one began to observe an erosion of ideological commitments and a more single-minded pursuit, and at times also a more explicit articulation, of personal priorities.

. . . .

The Erosion of Ideology

Beginning at an earlier point but most explicit and tangible in the post-Stalin years, some of the millions of communists who made up the Soviet elite, and who were slated to become the regime's next generation of leaders, experienced an unadvertised but far-reaching crisis of identity and self-doubt.

One facet of this crisis was in the subtle erosion of faith in the future and of the belief that the Bolsheviks alone had all the answers. This disillusionment, greatly intensified by Khrushchev's anti-Stalin campaign, was accompanied by an unheralded transformation in the dominant orientation: a shift from the pursuit of the millennium to compromising with reality.

. . . .

Strikingly, a similar decline may be noted in the rulers' self-confidence concerning their right to rule. Unwittingly, memoirs such as those of Khrushchev's son Sergei and of others close to the leadership testify to this point. A number of former Soviet academics have privately related their difficulties in coming to terms with the Stalin phenomenon. How had it been possible in the first place, and how could Stalinism now be explained to the next generation? What were the implications for the Soviet experiment? Within the limits of the permissible, serious questions were raised from within the Marxist-Leninist tradition: for instance, on the nature of "contradictions" under socialism, and the phenomenon of bureaucracy.

. . . .

Indeed, it was during the Brezhnev years that we witnessed an unprecedented surge of dissident literature—not from people who had never shared the regime's values or goals but from prominent individuals well within the system's elite. In retrospect, the number of dissidents appears to have been greater than was commonly assumed at the time. In 1970, Andrey Sakharov, Roy Medvedev, and Valeriy Turchin addressed a letter to the Soviet leadership, arguing in favor of far-reaching democratization.

> Over the past decade menacing signs of disorder and stagnation have begun to show themselves in the economy of our country. . . . The population's real income in recent years has hardly grown at all; food supply and medical and consumer services are improving very slowly, and with un-evenness between regions. The number of goods in short supply continues to grow. . . . What is the source of all this trouble? The source lies in the antidemocratic traditions and norms of public life established in the Stalin era, which have not been decisively eliminated to this day. Noneconomic coercion, limitations on the exchange of information, restrictions on intel-lectual freedom, and other examples of the antidemocratic distortion of socialism which took place under Stalin were accepted in our country as an overhead expense in the industrialization process.

. . . .

Social Change

The Soviet era witnessed a remarkable process of social change. In some measure it had begun even before the 1917 revolutions: urbanization and higher educational attainments are the universal by-product of economic development. To a significant degree, this was ideologically welcome to the Leninists as it promoted "proletarianization" at the expense of the peasantry. Later, the "liquidation of the kulaks as a class" was a conscious policy decision buttressed by ideological, economic, and security considerations (whether spurious or not). Similarly, the massive employment of female labor, the wholesale resettlement and migration, as well as the expansion of labor camps and forced settlements, were willed by the regime. And to some extent, the new social stratification was the inevitable by-product of choices made on behalf of rapid industrialization, bureaucratization, and centralization. But, whether willed or not, these developments had unforeseen, unintended, and (from the regime's point of view) often undesirable consequences.

The magnitude of the transformations is suggested by Soviet census fig-ures: the urban share of the population rose from some 18 percent in 1926 to about 65 percent in 1985. The number of "specialists"—the so-called intelli-gentsia—grew from some 2 million before World War II to over 30 million in the 1980s, of whom more than half had specialized training or higher education. The government, party, police, and military bureaucracies grew at a comparable pace.

. . . .

An additional factor in the 1970s and early 1980s was the (accurate) perception, spreading in urban society, that the previously axiomatic opportunities for upward social mobility were no longer there. With the slowdown of economic growth, the more or less stable size of administrative and military cadres, the end of massive purges (and the widespread retention of older officials in office), it was plausible that there should be fewer vacancies to be filled. The resulting effect on morale, especially among ambitious younger people, was obvious.

We find then an unmistakable spread of skepticism and widespread cynicism, particularly in the 1970s. Along with the "weakening belief in ideals," cited above, observers pointed to a career-mindedness and materialism, and a combination of consumerism and consumer pessimism. Moreover, it was pointed out, "because economic performance has been so central to socio-political stability, the consequences of this stagnation are potentially serious." There was also a lack of fit between educational opportunities and career needs; and high aspirations combined with a disdain for manual labor to create further tensions. High rates of labor turnover, low productivity, and low worker morale were additional indicators of growing problems.

The loss of optimism and the loss of purpose readily led to a change of attitude. This was reflected, for instance, in the jocular remark, "We pretend to be working, and they pretend to be paying us," as well as in the middle-class view of corruption reported by Bushnell: "It's a crime *not* to steal from them," which is revealing also for the use of "them" for the authorities. It easily spilled over into antisocial behavior. Alcoholism, in particular, became even more of a severe problem than before, with manifest consequences from industrial accidents to family life. Lying and cheating seemed to become pandemic in Soviet society.

One conclusion of particular interest, prompted by studies of Soviet refugees, émigrés, and "displaced persons," concerns variation of grievances by age groups. The so-called Harvard study of Soviet refugees in the 1950s had concluded that young people were more thoroughly indoctrinated and less critical of the Soviet system than their elders. But in the early 1980s a corresponding study of Brezhnev-era émigrés found evidence that, on the contrary, young people (as well as those with more education) now tended to be more negative and more disenchanted with the performance of the system than their elders.

. . ∴ .

Economic Decline

Specialists told us that the Soviet economy needed structural reform long before 1985. Above all, the central command economy had failed to keep up its previously impressive growth rate, the GNP plummeting (by Western estimates) from some 6 percent growth rates in the 1960s to perhaps 2 percent or less in the early 1980s. Per capita real income declined as well. One reason was that earlier on, inputs—capital, labor, energy—had been ample and cheap. By the 1970s this was no longer so, and it was necessary to switch from a strategy of extensive development to an intensive one. Moreover, productivity was low, and the system failed to provide adequate incentives for harder work or for technological innovation. If anything, the technological gap and lag behind the West were increasing. Typically, the quality of production and services was substantially below world standards. This reduced Soviet ability to export goods and also added to consumer dissatisfaction, given the rising expectations of the new elite.

. . . .

Interaction among the Variables

All this adds up to a subtle change in the relationship of state and society on the eve of the Gorbachev years. Society gains greater autonomy, grievances and expectations become more critical and more overt, and there occurs an implicit shift to some expectation of accountability. If there is an increasing inclination to judge the regime by its performance, in the 1980s the regime falls short. And, more immediately important in 1985, it is essentially this perception of the same trends that shaped the conviction of Mikhail Gorbachev and his friends that "things cannot go on like this."

I have argued that none of the trends we have examined was the prime motor in this process of change. It is precisely the interaction among these variables that was critical. While we cannot "replay" the events with one variable left out, some inferences as to relative weights are plausibly strong. Thus, had the whole control structure not loosened up, much of the articulation of grievances could not have occurred, acquaintance with the outside world would have been far more modest, and the assertion of autonomy in various venues could neither have been undertaken nor succeeded to the degree that it did. Similarly, the effect of the loosening up on the spread of corruption, the perception of stagnation, and contact with the West all facilitated the erosion of ideological commitments. So manifestly did the social pathologies, the value shift and the rising expectations among the new urban middle class erode the faith among officials and non-officials alike.

True, the economic constraints alone should have been enough to engender doubts, comparisons, and grievances. However, the true economic facts were not widely known; indeed, some "derogatory" facts were scarcely known even in the highest leadership circles. Furthermore, at earlier times of economic difficulty—be it 1930 or 1946—there had been no such articulation, essentially because both the actors and the political environment had been so different. We must then conclude that the cluster of trends we have focused on provided a set of necessary conditions for the changes that ensued.

The Gorbachev Factor

Taken together, the trends and developments discussed above suggest a number of serious flaws and fragilities in the Soviet system. But there are no grounds for arguing that they doomed it. If we had seen them as clearly as we do now in, say, 1984, would we have been led to conclude that a collapse of the Soviet Union was inevitable in the foreseeable future? I think the answer has to be "no."

In that case, do we mean to say that, had Gorbachev and his associates *not* come to power, the Soviet Union would have hobbled along, and might have continued to muddle through without overt instability? That is the only possible conclusion. If we reach that conclusion, based on those premises, then we must give serious weight to the proposition that the much-touted "collapse of communism" was perhaps not nearly so inevitable and surely not necessarily so imminent as it has been made out to be.

. . . .

If my argument has merit, the implication is that the Gorbachev years, and what is now called *katastroyka* [a word formed from the Russian words for "catastrophe" and "building"], are an essential part of the explanation of the collapse. They are not sufficient by themselves to explain it, but they are, ironically or tragically, a vital link in the chain of destabilization, delegitimation, and disintegration that led from the superpower status of the 1970s to the new, shrunken, confused, and impoverished Russian Federation of the 1990s.

Unlike some of the earlier trends that we can label impersonal or secular, in the Gorbachev period we are dealing with very distinct acts of will, acts that in retrospect should deaden any temptation to agree with those who seek to transform history and politics into mathematical formulae of rational choice. It did make a lot of difference that these particular individuals, beginning with Gorbachev and soon Yakovlev and Shevardnadze, were the ones taking charge in Moscow. Suffice it to contemplate counterfactual scenarios in which, say, Chernenko remained in office for another five years, or was succeeded by Grishin or Romanov: how different would the country have looked?

Those who see the Soviet period and the dominant Leninist ideology as a seamless web have difficulty explaining how a Gorbachev and his cohort could have emerged in charge of such a system in the first place. Whatever happens elsewhere, here personalities have certainly played a significant part. The fact that they, and not any others, came to power in 1985 also serves to torpedo the "inevitable collapse" argument. To claim that the Soviet system was bound to crash amounts to committing what Reinhard Bendix called "the fallacy of retrospective determinism"—denying the choices (however constrained) that the actors had available before acting.

But what was it about the Gorbachev policies—so many of which were brilliant—that contributed to the system's collapse? First and foremost, Gorbachev put an end to the claim that there was one single truth and therefore one single party that was its carrier. In association with this argument, he fostered *glasnost'*, an end to censorship, an end to widespread political repression, and an end to the official monopoly on rewriting the past. In terms of sociopolitical impact, all this brought about a remarkable sense of having been lied to, of having been deprived of what the rest of the world had had access to, a "desacralization" of the system and delegitimation of the authorities, a transformation of the Communist Party from the unchallenged clan of privilege to a hollow institution without a rational task other than self-preservation. This in turn opened the floodgates to massive and varied grassroots organization and articulation outside the party.

Our Fairy-Tale Life (1997)

Nancy Ries

For all the rapid unfolding of events throughout perestroika, few observers took the time to pause and consider specifically Russian cultural interpretations and under-standings of those events. Many scholars indeed did seek to illuminate the stresses of such transformation: basic foodstuffs were disappearing from shelves, public services were in gradual decline, and new means of bureaucratic obstruction appeared every day. In this context, the anthropologist Nancy Ries questioned the role of "the Russia tale" she was constantly hearing, an epic genre coupling heroism and absurdity and echoing so much of Russian literature, from Gogol to Bulgakov. She also wondered how these epic and absurd tales were cross-cut with elaborate talk about suffering and misfortune.

In this lively take on Russia's famously "mysterious Russian soul," Ries focuses on the ways Russian culture is continually constituted and reconstituted through dis-course. Uzhas ("How awful") and Koshmar ("What a nightmare," in a Russian borrowing of the French cauchemar) are two terms that, on the surface, are perfectly sensible responses to tales of life collapsing all around. Yet in what she called "litanies and laments," Ries found remarkably patterned responses that echoed familiar folk-tales, songs, and sayings. Shoppers who stood in lines for hours were not merely heroic; when people told about their shopping torments, they evoked bogatyri, epic figures of Russian myth and history. In such a context, perestroika replayed earlier revolutionary transformations in Russian society, pulling at long-standing tensions—between the haves and the have-nots, mischievous men and steadfast women—in a world where suffering and misfortune render new worlds from old.

At a small gathering over tea one afternoon in 1990, conversation turned to "the complete disintegration" (*polnaia razrukha*) of Soviet society. As people traded examples of social chaos and absurdity back and forth, and the conver-sation reached its climactic pitch, Volodia, a writer, turned to me and deliv-ered a punch-line, with a sardonic glee typical of certain kinds of Russian pronouncements: "You know what this country is, Nancy? This country is *Anti-Disneyland*." He was justifiably proud of his precise symbol for Russia, one that described quite well the sense of inhabiting a mythical land where everything was geared toward going wrong: a gargantuan theme park of inconvenience, disintegration, and chaos. Indeed, the most popular thrill of the day seemed to be wondering, aloud, "How bad can it get?" and spinning wickedly frightening but fascinating scenarios about the dissolution of order. This was precisely what we around the table had been doing when Volodia tossed in his metaphor.

His idea of Russia as Anti-Disneyland also conveyed Volodia's impression that Russia and America are inherently opposite kinds of realms, based around opposite cultural fictions. If Disneyland celebrates a mythic American prosperity, if it is conceived around the ideology that life can be a boundless magical realm of cheerfulness and fun, then Anti-Disneyland is fashioned around a spectacular commitment to poverty, humorlessness, and travail. The one is captured in the image of a high-turreted fairy castle; the other is represented by the image of a grungy, overcrowded communal apartment where everyone fights for access to the bathroom.

His image also aptly hinted at the inventedness of the Russian world, which often seems like a fairy-tale land to insider and outsider alike, a product of mythic imagination. Zara Abdullaeva recently declared: "The fabled realm inhabited by this nation is indeed enchanted: the most common things go astray here, while extraordinary ones come to pass. Cause-effect connections have been severed for good, common sense casually defied, and some impenetrable magic rules that fools smart people and gives fools a break."

Russians regularly use the phrase "our fairy-tale life" (*nasha skazochnaia zhizn'*); referring to the October revolution, one journalist lamented: "This fairy tale was popular for so long." Satirical writers from Saltykov-Shchedrin to Sinyavsky have expanded this type of conceit into whole sagas of the fantastic and absurd. Many of these literary sagas take advantage of the fantastic, mythic, always huge and often monstrous productions of the state. There has long been much to parody in these utopian attempts to invent and secure a fantasy reality (attempts that occurred regularly well before 1917).

But there is a distinctly fairy-tale quality to the reality conveyed through average, day-to-day conversation as well. A conventional inventory of generic forms, images, themes, and figurative devices supplies the collective imagination with the materials to create magically charged narratives within daily talk and gossip. These narratives, in turn, help to fashion the cultural realm which is Russian "fairy-tale life." Certain meaningful symbolic keys serve as a discursive frame for the constant recreation of the Russian life-world. In his essay "Blurred Genres" Clifford Geertz refers to these structures when he writes of "the repetitive performance dimensions of social action—the reenactment and reexperiencing of known forms" and to "reiterated form, staged and acted by its own audience."

All this pivots around the creation of self or selves. The structures that mold a social world inhere first in the person; local worlds are, as it were, by-products of people's productions of themselves. As Barbara Myerhoff writes, "One of the most persistent but elusive ways that people make sense of themselves is to show themselves to themselves, through multiple forms: by telling themselves stories; by dramatizing claims in rituals and other collective enactments; by rendering visible actual and desired truths about themselves and the significance of their existence in imaginative and performative productions."

Much of the examination of Russian talk that follows focuses on the modes of production and representation of the Russian "characters" who inhabit, as subject and object, the Russian "Anti-Disneyland," and who often seem to have stepped out of the rich fairy-tale land of Russian epics and tales.

The Perestroika Epic: "Complete Disintegration"

One evening in March 1990, at a festive dinner with some friends, tales of "complete disintegration" circled the table almost to the exclusion of other topics. "Did you know that by now everything in Kaluga Province is under rationing?" "My parents in Kiev have planted their own potatoes." "I heard they are now selling sausage so contaminated with pesticides, hormones, and radiation from Chernobyl that you should not feed it to children—but still people are buying it, so starved are they for meat." "What we are seeing is complete ruin." "Yes," said one young man who works for the transport system. "At work we heard, some Japanese came, inspected our rails—and said that they had never seen such a nightmare, the rail beds are crumbling and the rails are in terrible condition—they said we will have terrible crashes, especially on the busy Moscow–Leningrad line." "Yes," said another man, "complete disintegration." At one point in this litany of ruin, I naively tried to interject the question: "Well, what can be done to remedy these problems?" My question was met with silence; I had failed to understand the ritual nature of this kind of repartee.

The phrase "complete disintegration" and similar phrases such as "complete breakdown" or "collapse" (*polnyi razval, raspad*) resounded through many of the Moscow conversations in which I participated. *Polnaia razrukha* was an abbreviated reference to everything that was supposedly disintegrating in Russian society at the time: it was a discursive signpost which embraced the escalation of crime, the disappearance of goods from the stores, the ecological catastrophes, the fall of production, the ethnic violence in the Caucasus, the "degradation" of the arts, the flood of pornography, and other signs of immorality which some people saw everywhere. Though these tales had their basis in the social concerns and changes of the time, the animated performances whereby people circulated them—vividly embroidering them with personal details, experiences, and emotions—functioned to create a very specific, local sense of that reality. *Polnaia razrukha* became a folkloric genre: it manifested a particular structure (litany), took a particular approach to the subject (portentous), focused on certain subjects (the gorier and more horrible, the better), and it maneuvered its audiences to a desired response (alarmed astonishment). More than this, however, these stories helped to fabricate a sense of shared experience and destiny.

In the late 1980s, a frenzy developed in the mass media to portray the kinds of horrors that were the main and driving ingredients of the *polnaia razrukha* genre. The tabloid news broadcasts that became a regular feature on Soviet television in these years were almost ritualistic inversions of the utopian portrayals of Soviet life that had been a staple of the pre-perestroika media. The December 17, 1990, broadcast of the popular TV show *Completely Secret* (*Sovershenno Sekretno*) featured a segment on the awful conditions in the morgue of a hospital; interspersed with interviews with doctors and workers were shots of a room full of human corpses—several rows of decaying bodies sprawled on tables. The workers reported that the temperature and sanitary controls were very bad, and that rats regularly nibbled the corpses, a comment that was followed by a shot of rats scurrying along the decaying floor of a corridor.

In March 1990, the popular television show *Vzgliad* did a piece on the Moscow zoo. The punchline was a comment by a zoo worker who reported that he overheard parents saying to their kids: "Look what nice meat there is on that animal." This was followed by a story about a home for the aged where some criminals were sent to live and subsequently spent their time beating and robbing the elderly. There was a panoramic montage of scenes of old people lying in bed, and a mood of intense pathos was established by the music used and the images chosen. Nobody said the words "total disintegration" but the implication was clear. At the end, one announcer intoned: "This is where we are going, friends."

One *polnaia razrukha* tale combined the typical litany of horrors with a tone of moralistic cant: a TV news piece (December 11, 1989) about frostbitten alcoholics displayed the scarred, bleeding, and skinless hands, noses, and lips of drunks who had passed out on the street during bitter cold days. The interviewer asked, "How did this happen to you?" in order to deliver a message about the immorality and pathos of alcoholism, then added, porten-tously, "This is what we have come to" (implying, rather disingenuously, that such problems had never occurred before perestroika).

The social horror stories fetishized in the media helped greatly to fuel the growth of a sense of cataclysm in day-to-day narratives. Topics featured in broadcasts were quickly drawn into private conversations where they could be related to actual personal experiences, and one effect of this dialectic was that national problems came to seem very immediate, while personal or familial woes were made epic, invested with historical resonance.

In one conversation I had with a friend while waiting for a bus, the *polnaia razrukha* tale began with empty shelves and circled round and round the various crises of the day all the way to an envisaging of the future destruction of the world at the hands of terrorists with access to the USSR's nuclear weapons, ending with a chorus of "How awful," "What a nightmare," and "What are we going to do?"

Typical incidents of urban disorder—fist-fights, drunks careening along the street, people butting in line or using obscene language openly in public—could stimulate exclamations of "complete ruin." So too could the private vending activity on busy streets or outside metro stations, which during perestroika began to evolve into a huge cultural and economic phenomenon, with dozens of older women standing side by side holding up their wares—a pack of cigarettes, a dried fish, a bottle of vodka—commodities that they had stood in line to purchase from state stores and sell for higher prices to pas-sersby; this kind of activity was snarlingly referred to as "speculation," but the epithet *"polnaia razrukha"* drew it into the broader picture of social disintegra-tion. All these phenomena were construed as proof that the Soviet Union was collapsing into chaos and anarchy (both favorite words of the perestroika period).

One irony here is that many of the people with whom I spoke did not express concrete anxiety about the possibility of personal suffering; there seemed to be more exhilaration stimulated through the sharing of these stories than there was anxiety. It was primarily older people who expressed great alarm at these developments, in part because they recognized the vulnerability of their social position, and in part because the events of the perestroika years completely contradicted all their expectations; for them, perestroika brought a collapse of their whole cultural world. Younger, less immediately vulnerable people, raised on the ubiquitous and only somewhat underground spirit of irony of the 1970s and 1980s (and inexperienced in war or famine), were much more likely to speak in an idiom that expressed their fascination with possible danger. As if from morbid curiosity, such people often said, "How far do you

"I need a guy to split the cost
of a bottle." From *The
Dictionary of Russian Gesture*.
Courtesy of Hermitage Press.

think we will go?" and then went on to try to imagine how far, competing with
one another through their various fantasies of ruin.

The situation in stores, however, was the favorite topic of *polnaia razrukha*
tales, as it had the most immediacy in people's lives. During the long Brezhnev period known as the era of stagnation (it is enough to say that one word
in Russian to invoke the entire period, which only ended with the coming of
Gorbachev), economic growth was low, but the Moscow stores were usually
stocked with the supplies routinely called for in daily existence, though lines
to purchase them could be long. During "stagnation" there were sometimes
shortages of particular items, and most people tried to keep an extra supply of
certain things on hand. Matches, lightbulbs, soap, toothpaste, toilet paper,
salt, and sugar were commonly hoarded. During perestroika, the economic
system heaved a great nationwide sigh—and instead of stagnation there were
suddenly odd and unnerving patterns of shortages of every kind. This was
basically the result of the combination of wage inflation, on the one hand, and
declining production, on the other: people had more money to purchase
fewer goods. This led to cycles of panic buying and hoarding (on both individ-

ual and regional levels), further depleting the availability of goods in the stores. As part of the policy of economic "shock therapy," designed to increase production, the government announced that the prices of basic foodstuffs—including bread—would be raised in the late spring of 1990; this increased hoarding, and, worsening matters still further, caused enterprises to hold back shipments in anticipation of receiving higher prices for their goods after price freezes were lifted.

As Moscow stores became emptier than they had been, and as crucial commodities (sugar, dairy products, meats) vanished from state stores one after another, people began to speak with real agitation. When, in the spring of 1990, internal passports proving Moscow residency were required to make certain food purchases, the *polnaia razruhka* tales became quite intense. It seemed to me, then, that at the same time that these developments made them quite anxious, my interlocutors were electrified by this intrusion of economic calamity into their personal lives; having to show their passports (and then being able to tell about it) gave them a sense of connection to the more abstract turmoil of larger social levels. And this, I daresay, made them feel personally part of the intense Russian drama widely described as being an interminable cycle of chaos, calamity, and ruin.

One afternoon in April 1990, I passed an acquaintance in the corridor of an office and asked how she was doing. "Everything is alright," she reassured me, "but what a time we are living through!" She went on to tell me the following tale, whispering the whole time as if letting me in on a mystery. "Everything is alright, but it is becoming such a nightmare trying to buy anything!" she said.

> Every store you enter is empty. This is the end, I do not know, maybe we have come to the point of complete ruin. A friend of mine told me about a store he went to, a supermarket, where they were selling nothing but one kind of canned fish, and not just canned fish, but fish of such an awful quality that even drunks would not buy it to go with their vodka. But some enterprising managers, and clerks, having nothing else to do, of course, had carefully arranged all of these thousands of tins—and so there were Eiffel towers of canned fish, and pyramids, and Great Walls—a whole world, the seven wonders of the world, constructed from—sardines.

She finished her depiction of this fairy-tale place by adding the following fairy-tale phrase: "Such a thing is only possible in one country—here, in Russia."

The story itself was quite probably true—the Moscow supermarkets, never super to begin with, in 1989 and 1990 did become like fairy-tale places. One

Car in a forest. Courtesy of Donald Weber, www.donaldweber.com.

spacious store that I wandered into was selling nothing but half-kilo boxes of salt, and although their display had fewer architectural pretensions, the store clerks had made some effort to display the cardboard boxes attractively throughout the place. If there were nothing else to do, if there were nothing to sell and nothing to buy, shop clerks and shoppers alike could use the materials at hand (or the material lack at hand) to build—from whispered words or from boxes of salt or from tins of fish—"tales" that drolly and adroitly commented on the very lack of consumable substances.

But such tales, whether communicated by means of visual or verbal media, were more than simply commentaries on the situation in the stores. They all served, more generally and more durably, as chronicles of the fabulous-terrible conditions of mythical Russia, Volodia's "Anti-Disneyland."

Getting By (1995)

Valerii Pisigin

In the early 1990s Russians in the new federation were reeling from the "shock therapies" let loose upon the land by predominantly Western economists hired by the Yeltsin administration. Their goal was to try to right the dramatic imbalances between newer market-driven and older Soviet, command-style economies of scale. World agencies such as the International Monetary Fund were pleased, but few others rejoiced. Stores newly filled with consumer goods long sought after were often the subject of trauma rather than delight for the millions of citizens who could only look through the windows. In this essay from 1995, the Russian writer Valerii Pisigin mordantly captures some of the humanity in the struggles to stay afloat.

It's common knowledge that millions of Russians today are engaged in trade. In many instances, this is their only source of income. They exert every effort to move goods from one end of the country to the other, and from other countries as well. They move everything they possibly can.

Perhaps this kind of trade isn't all they once dreamed of. But, all the same, it's more honorable than stealing, and, of course, better than begging.

But, there are those who can neither steal nor transport the simplest little things. A certain elderly resident of Donetsk sells live gray mice at the city market. He's not selling them for breeding, but as cat food. The product is nutritious, ecologically pure, and offers the thrill of the hunt to the predator. What wealthy owner wouldn't buy it for his pussycat?

While in Donetsk they sell live mice, in Cheliabinsk they sell dead ones.

Locals recalled an elderly woman standing in the center of town, delicately holding a dead mouse by its tail, and in all seriousness asking 300 rubles for it [about six cents at the average 1995 exchange rate of 5,000 rubles to a U.S. dollar].

The commentary of the passersby was unanimous: "Well, if they're going to sell tree branches for people to beat themselves with in the bania . . ." (!) Readers might react similarly, but don't rush to judgment. As the saying goes, "Everything has its time and place," and so the dead mouse had a buyer. (There's also a law of economics that says, if you can sell it, they'll buy it.)

Counting change.
Courtesy of Rick Hibberd.

The eighteen-year-old buyer didn't regret the 300 rubles he had spent on the mouse, explaining that he was on his way to a date where his purchase "would get a squeal!"

In order to survive, people engage in fraud and all kinds of cunning little devices, illustrating that "necessity is the mother of invention."

But what sort of "necessity," and what kind of "invention"?

At the central Perm market a Chinese citizen was taken into custody, not for not carrying her required documents (the usual problem), but for being in possession of three Russian passports registered in Perm and Nizhnevartovsk. According to the detained trader, "People pass by, try on leather coats, and say that they don't have enough money. So they take the coats and leave their passports as a deposit, promising to exchange them later for money, and then never return." Such a tale is perfectly plausible: the buyers report their lost passport and receive a new one, paying a fine on the order of 2,050 rubles. Since a coat is considerably more expensive, the advantage is obvious.

In Moscow, at the exit to the Skhodnenskaia metro station, forty-nine-year-old Nikolai Kimovich V. bought a couple of bottles of alcohol from a little granny. "I'd returned from Karelia," he says, "and wanted to make home-made fruit liqueur from the wild whortleberries and bilberries I'd gathered. I open a bottle and it's water!" He ran back to the metro. The granny was still selling her wares. Without complaint she took back the opened bottles, returned his money, and told him about the scoundrel of a wholesaler who had sold her the entire phony case. She also shared the fact that Nikolai Kimovich was only the third out of dozens of buyers whose money she'd returned and she therefore was intending to stay there until midnight to get rid of the whole case.

Nikolai Kimovich shouldn't get mad or cuss the old woman. On the contrary he should be eternally grateful. Water is life. He's well aware that pure poison can come in bottles with pretty labels. Health officials constantly advise against buying alcohol in commercial kiosks. There are tons of victims of counterfeit alcohol.

Here's just one typical scenario:

In the village of Tarasovo in the Pavlovo-Posad district of the Moscow region, eleven people died in one night. One of the residents brought back to the village a half-filled, eight-liter bottle purchased somewhere in the Nogin-skii district. From a report on the tragedy:

A seventeen-year-old neighbor invited a group over for snacks and drinks. They returned the favor with the aforementioned bottle of spirits; after partaking, she later died at a hospital. During their drinking bout, one of the drinking buddies poured himself a half-liter and organized an alterna-tive party at the other end of the village. Literally within the hour the local rescue squad was putting the pedal to the floor to transport the dying from the village to the central hospital of Pavlovo-Posad. The first five to arrive were admitted to intensive care in a comatose condition. Two of them died within forty minutes; the others a short time later. In the course of the next few hours, another four were admitted; they couldn't be saved either. Besides those who died at the hospital, two died at home.

Let us repeat that there are countless examples of similar poisonings. People pay with their lives not only because of their belief in and love for strong drink but because of their resourcefulness and inventiveness with whatever is at hand. No one set out to kill those villagers; it's just that someone needed to make a little on the side.

Business isn't founded just on natural cunning, but on exceptional courage as well.

Kazan' resident N., a man without occupation, adores winter storms, snowfall, and black ice. On bad weather days, on a narrow little street, where there aren't any traffic cops, he suddenly jumps into the road directly under the bumper of a Zhiguli and lands in a snowdrift. The terrified driver leaps out of the car, trying to come to his aid. Groaning and moaning, he gets up and, limping, takes a few steps. Then in a weak voice he says that he won't press charges, but it wouldn't hurt to relieve his stress a little. The relieved driver shoves some cash in his hand and leaves, and the "stunt man" stays there waiting for his next victim. Usually he gets off easy, but sometimes he sustains bodily injury when he runs up against tough guys.

How expensive bread is when you have no money!

Not always, however, is business so manifestly dangerous. There are also smart, inoffensive ways of getting things done.

From St. Petersburg it's reported that only 15 percent of the "Whiskas" cat food available in the city is bought up by pet stores. The remaining 85 percent, according to informed sources, is acquired by representatives of Petersburg pizzerias. The subsequent fate of this "feline joy" is not hard to surmise.

In the once brotherly republic of Turkmenistan, the health department staff in the town of Nebit-Dag made the residents happy with an interesting discovery: a popular chewing gum made in Iran, delivered by local merchants familiar with the product who sold it in all the kiosks, turned out in reality to be a birth control preparation and, furthermore, to be hazardous to the health of adolescents. Someone turned up who translated the unintelligible writing on the colorful package.

Swindlers exist alongside the serious and enterprising. Such is the law of primitive accumulation. At the end of October cockroach races took place in Kostroma.

Insects seven centimeters in length arrived from Madagascar and stayed at the Volga Hotel during the competition.

It's not known whether the distinguished "athletes" fraternized with the unofficial residents of the hotel's cracked walls and floors, or haughtily brushed them aside.

Similar contests took place in Rostov-on-Don. At the *Las Vegas* casino, "sportsmen" from Argentina joined the starting line, with an average of seventy bets placed on six races. The roaches ran along electrical rigging while guests in evening attire observed the racetrack on two monitors. As the local newspaper *Our Times* reported on it, the winner of one of the heats was a female roach, who passed her more prominent rivals to "bring" 300,000 rubles in winnings to a young lady who had placed a 50,000 ruble bet on her.

Cockroaches are cockroaches, but note this: Where Rostov, Las Vegas, and Argentina meet, now that's "convergence"!

Enterprise and native wit are beginning to prevail everywhere.

Workers at the Green Grove resort in Sochi have turned Stalin's dacha into a business. They put together looted furniture and recreated the interior according to recollections of eye-witnesses, and for seven million rubles even seated the supreme genius of mankind in the living room.

"They brought a dissembled wax figure and proceeded to assemble it," said Comrade Shishkin, the assistant director of the resort. "Now guests take pictures of themselves near the figure. Joseph Vissarionovich promises to repay the costs in the near future."

Important people stay in these apartments—businessmen, government figures, other well-to-do clients. The prices are reasonable. For example, a night in Stalin's daughter Svetlana's bedroom costs a mere 360,000 rubles, according to February 1995 prices. But then how many memories!

The most expensive apartments at the dacha cost half a million rubles a night; that's without food. With food, spa treatment, and so on, it could be just under a million. Clients are steady and families come for vacation. An article titled "A Night Alone with Stalin" reports that even important government functions are held at the dacha. They say that it's easy to think in Stalin's chamber, but more significantly—important problems are quickly resolved with no bureaucratic tangles. Maybe that's why the all-Russian meeting of the president's regional representatives was held there.

Translated by Sara Lomasz-Flesch

XVI

Building a New World, Again

Much political history in the Soviet period, as in tsarist Russia before it, hinged on the repression of the powers that had been: Lenin lamented the capitalist degradation into which Russia had fallen and exploited the exploiters, Khrushchev denounced Stalinism's excesses in his famous "Secret Speech," Brezhnev sent Khrushchev into early retirement, Gorbachev set out to revive Communism, and Yeltsin shed his own Communist past in order to renounce it. With the fall of the USSR came mourning, a time to bury the bones of the past (literally, in dealing with the remains of Russia's royal family and the victims of years of repression), together with a fantastic social energy for discovery and rediscovery. The much-heralded "New Russians" of nouveaux riches status took center stage alongside monarchists, new religionists, and nationalists of all possible stripes. Cities such as Moscow and St. Petersburg transformed with astonishing rapidity while the countryside struggled to cope with the heavier payloads of unemployment from the collapse of a command economy that had been elaborately designed to suture supply and demand across a complex array of geographical spaces and politically driven personal networks.

Yet as all the new forms of consumerism and information flow reorganized life across the vast country, it was also a time to wistfully, sometimes bitterly appraise all that had been left behind: the solidity of near-full employment, mobility across a vast portion of the socialist bloc, higher education, accessible health care, housing to which one could at least aspire, and so forth. Many certainly have seen poetic justice in the return of capitalist entrepreneurs after seventy-four years of socialist rule. Yet limited private enterprise never entirely disappeared during the Soviet period. Lenin's New Economic Policy (1922–28) temporarily loosened the initial claims of the state over the means of production, and Stalin soon after denounced the "leftist" practice of wage equalization that had been favored early on. In the agricultural sector small private plots of land became one of the few ways for collective farmers to sustain their household during the economy's dimmest years. The system of perks and privileges that emerged under the Soviet socialist banner became legendary, as did the trading strategies of Soviet factory managers who routinely ordered too many supply goods in order to participate in expansive circles of barter and influence. Nonetheless a generalized ambiguity about the culture of material gain, long prominent in Russian society, endured. As the historian Jeffrey Brooks wrote of the Russian middle classes of the late nineteenth century, "Money [gained from business or commerce], although clearly sought after . . . was regarded with ambivalence and hostility by much of Russian society, both because it was not old . . . and because commerce and industry were associated with the exploitation of others." The same sentiment, nurtured under Soviet tutelage for decades, is witnessed still in the marked distaste so many Russians have for open discussions of money and property.

In December 1993, when the new constitution of the Russian Federation asserted that "every person has the right to freely use his abilities and property to engage in entrepreneurial and other economic activities unrestricted by law," few might have gauged the extent or irony of the "unrestrictions." By 1996 the federal government had transferred over 100,000 commercial entities, large and small, to private ownership. The ultimate privatization of over 15,000 factories affected more than 60 percent of the industrial workforce. But the move toward privatization, or *privatizatsiia*, was quickly likened to "grabi-fication," *prikhvatizatsiia*. The most common scenario was for managers of state firms to install themselves as de facto owners, using their influence to run their new companies as small satrapies which often buckled from the weight of their inherited debt loads. At one stage the more spectacular robber baron successes led men like the now exiled former auto dealer Boris Bere-zovskii to insist that he and six other men controlled over 50 percent of the Russian economy. The loosening of state controls all around has also height-ened rates of violence, with almost anyone doing business in a major city the potential target of extortion.

At the forefront of Russia's postsocialist merchant classes are a group known, appropriately, as *Novye Russkie*, or "New Russians." In Moscow per-haps more than any other city they have come to personify the nouveaux riches lifestyle that has transformed the gray capital into a sea of fur coats, Mercedes, Rolexes, protection services, nightclubs, and casinos. Such sudden rises in fortune illustrate how high the stakes can be. In 1996 one British investment prospectus for a Russian satellite telephone company opened with an array of caveats so dizzying it is difficult to imagine how investors could have proceeded. The promise of investment was evident: only a few years before, the company had been a wing of Soviet satellite military surveillance, and it was able to enter the market with considerable inside influence over radio frequency regulators. But among the risks potential foreign partners faced were nationalization and expropriation of property, the instability of market legislation, the falling value of the ruble, limited repatriation of profits, the inexperience of the Russian courts in commercial and corporate law, the frequent legislative contradictions between different levels of government, the near impossibility of honoring erratic tax regulations, the absence of insurance on bank deposits, and, finally, the high cost of bodyguards. Yet upon their opening on the foreign stock exchange, the company's stock tripled almost overnight.

"Russian mafia" in the 1990s soon became a metaphor for all things unseen and not fully known to the public. In the world of the 1990s old chestnuts of Soviet social wisdom were revealed as canards and nothing was quite what it seemed; it was a world oscillating between socialism and the social honor it was meant to uphold, between market relations and the rapacious path of the government, between new world orders and organized crime.

Awakening from a deep slumber, rebuilding civil society, and making a transition ever in progress from communism to capitalism, closure to openness, and Orient to Occident—these are the new stereotypes of Russia's latest revolutionary rite of passage. They are also stereotypes worth moving beyond. In the emphasis on awakening, rebirth, and reconstruction, the tendency has been to presume dramatic departures for a country that never physically went anywhere. Thousands of political leaders, for example, did little more than change their office letterhead, while citizens continue to negotiate a concept of "transition" that is far from self-evident and by no means always benevolent.

With the passing of the first presidents of the Russian Federation into the political twilight and an oil boom that has sustained a significant economic recovery for a country that went through more forms of "shock therapy" over the twentieth century than most historians can keep up with, Russian life is moving slowly to stability again. Yet the country remains an extraordinary site of reflection on the kinds of political, social, and economic commonplaces that most citizens of longer-standing market-run societies long since conceded as part of the natural landscape. What, after all, does the development of "civil society" mean for a post-Soviet age when, at least by dictionary definition, the Communist Party was a putatively voluntary, nongovernmental organization? Was not the USSR the greatest example of civil society's reach? What does democracy mean when a society moves from full employment and the furnishing of extensive social supports to deep class stratification and the routinization of a level of poverty unseen for decades?

Burying the Bones (1998)

Orlando Figes

In July 1998 the bodies of Nicholas II, tsar of Russia, king of Poland, and grand duke of Finland, his wife, Aleksandra, and three of his daughters were laid to rest in a funeral at the St. Peter and Paul Cathedral in St. Petersburg. It was exactly eighty years to the day after their collective executions. Overwhelmed by the First World War and massive unrest at home, the tsar abdicated in March 1917 at the behest of the newly formed provisional government. Over the next sixteen months his family was shuttled from one temporary location to another, each less luxurious than the last. In the early morning of 17 July they were awakened and led to their deaths in the basement of Ipat'ev House in the city of Yekaterinburg.

The elaborate funeral brought what Orlando Figes calls "unfinished business" to a partial conclusion. Some figures in the Russian Orthodox Church continue to dispute the provenance of the remains, identified by international forensic testing. Formal recognition of all the royal remains would leave only one last piece of business at hand: the corpse of a very unroyal but even better known Russian leader, Vladimir Lenin, who lies under a plexiglass shield, steeped in chemicals, in the center of Moscow's Red Square.

"How long did he rule for anyway?" The question from a man in a Yankees baseball cap was met by silence from his fellow Russians. Did anybody know? We were a small crowd waiting in the late afternoon sun for the cortège of black cars carrying the bones of the last Tsar and his descendants to arrive at the Troitsky Gates of the Peter and Paul Fortress. The Romanovs were late and most of the people around me were coming home from work when they came across the police barriers on Troitsky Square which should have cleared by three. There was a long silence. None of these commuters, it seemed, knew their history. Then an old man (who looked like a professor) spoke out in a voice of authority: "Nicholas ruled for thirty-five years." Someone immediately disagreed: "It was less than that." But nobody was sure.

The people of St Petersburg were not much disturbed by the burial of the bones of Nicholas II—who ruled Russia from 1894 to 1917—aside from the traffic jams it caused. The next day, 17 July, the day of the funeral itself, the Nevsky Prospekt was gridlocked when I set off for the ceremony. I had come to the city for a week to report on the funeral for a German newspaper, and to finish a book I had been writing with a Russian friend on the political culture of 1917. I stepped out into the middle of the traffic, opened the door of the nearest car, and took the driver's nod towards the empty seat as an invitation to get in. Every car in Russia is a part-time taxi. I've had rides in lorries and snow-clearers, the ZIL limousines of the old Party chiefs, and ambulances—although not (as yet) one with patients inside.

My driver—a suntanned watermelon trader in shorts and a string vest—was not in a good mood. He was cursing Boris Yeltsin, whose motorcade was at this moment speeding through the police-cordoned streets, as his own clapped-out Lada repeatedly stalled. "Get a move on," he shouted through the window to the bus in front of us. "These can't wait all day." He was referring to the melons piled up on the back seat. I asked him what he thought of the funeral. "What am I to think? I don't have time to think. The Tsar will be able to go to heaven. I am glad for him. Life up there is better than down here."

In 1998, most Russians had too many contemporary problems to be bothered by the events of eighty years before. Political turbulence, poverty, crime, unpaid wages—who, in these circumstances, would worry about the fate of the Romanovs? Yet the funeral held a kind of passive interest for the people of St Petersburg (one poll suggested that nearly half the city's residents intended to watch it on television) and there was a general sense that the burial was right.

But would I make it to the ceremony? It seemed not; the traffic was still not moving and my driver still cursing. I paid him off and settled in a bar on the Nevsky Prospekt where a small group were watching the live broadcast on a portable television. "I think it's right that they should have a Christian burial," said the peroxide blonde behind the bar as she poured me out a beer. "It is a matter of human decency." She was wearing a necklace with a cross together with a silver chain made up of the letters G-U-C-C-I. "It's the children I feel sorry for," said a businessman as we watched another sequence of sepia photographs of the Tsar and his daughters playing tennis and rowing in a boat. "The Communists were savages to murder them."

Then we heard the Russian President give his funeral oration. This was Yeltsin at his most solemn and articulate. The murder of the Tsar was "a shameful act which the Communists concealed." His family were "innocent victims of repression" which should have no more place in Russian history. Their burial was a "symbolic moment of national repentance and unity." It was "time to tell the truth . . . we are all guilty." We watched as Yeltsin slowly bowed down before the congregation of Romanovs and only then did it become clear that those words, for him, were more than a cliché. In his old life, as the Party boss of Sverdlovsk (Yekaterinburg), Yeltsin himself had ordered the destruction of the Ipatiev House, where Nicholas and his family were murdered by the Bolsheviks in the small hours of the morning of 17 July 1918. This was a personal repentance. I looked across at the blonde behind the bar and her eyes were full of tears.

The Tsar and his family were the first victims of the Terror which their deaths announced. The slaughter of the children, in particular, has become a symbol of the moral degradation of a regime which went on to kill millions of other innocent people who do not have a grave that anybody knows. This is a nation, like the Jews, where nearly every family has part of itself missing— grandparents who died "in the camps" or disappeared in the war—and no place to mourn and commemorate that loss. I bought a cognac for Nastya, the tearful barmaid, and she began to tell me about her grandfather. He was arrested in 1938.

Unfinished business—that is what the bones are all about. For seventy years the nine skeletons (of the Tsar, his wife, and three of his daughters, along with a cook, a maid, a valet and the family physician) had rotted underground in a wooded spot twelve miles north-west of Yekaterinburg. The records suggest that the corpses of Alexis, the Tsar's only son, and a fourth daughter, Maria, were burned to ashes by their executioners, but that in the rush to dispose of all the bodies before the White forces arrived in the city they had simply buried the other skeletons. The Bolsheviks said nothing about the murder—other than a mendacious official announcement that the former Tsar had been executed and his wife and son removed to a "safe place." This, after all, had long been planned as a secret execution. Lenin, who it seems had ordered it, rejected the idea of a trial or public execution—such as the Jacobins had given Louis XVI in 1793 or the English revolutionaries Charles I in 1649—on the grounds that a trial would presuppose the possibility of his innocence (and that in effect would put the Bolsheviks on trial). For seven decades his successors hid the truth—until the bones were finally exhumed in 1991 (twelve years after their discovery by a geologist named Alexander Avdonin) and subjected for the next six years to forensic tests around the world. By comparing their DNA to that of the Tsar and Tsarina's relatives, including the Duke of Edinburgh (Empress Alexandra's great-nephew), scientists are as sure as scientists can be that these are the bones of the Romanovs.

. . . .

The White myth dominated the media's coverage of the funeral. Anything approaching an objective view of the historical role of Nicholas was not to be seen on the television. He was presented, together with his lovely daughters, as the innocent victim of a barbaric revolution—as if his own policies and attitudes had nothing to do with its cause. What might have been a day of national mourning for *all* the victims of the Terror had been hijacked by television as a purely monarchist event, with all the nation's grief focused on the royal coffins, Diana-style. Television pictures from the ceremony were intercut with photographs of the Tsar and his family on happy picnics and boating trips in some summer before the First World War. A Chopin prelude played in the background, and the commentator told us (as if he knew): "What a wonderful family it was! How beautiful and graceful were the Grand Duchesses! All so soon to be senselessly destroyed!"

Legends, nostalgia: and at the heart of them a yearning for the bourgeois family ideal, for the genteel and decent life the Romanovs enjoyed but the common Russian people never had. As my old acquaintance, Vitaly Startsev, sometime Professor of History at the Herzen Institute, explained over coffee when I visited him at his apartment the following morning: "People do not know their history. They look at Nicholas and see a charming man who loved his family and was kind to everyone. These are qualities which they never saw in their Soviet leaders—and so they conclude that the Tsarist government was, or must have been, more humane as well."

And so the media peddled the idea of Tsarist Russia as a lost idyll. "Russia was embarking on a period of greatness and well being in 1913," Valery Ostrovsky told his viewers, as they watched (again) those lovely scenes of the Tsar and his daughters dancing on the deck of the imperial yacht. "The rouble, which today is the weakest in the world, was then one of the strongest currencies." Ostrovsky is a well-known television don, a historian young and bright enough not to have been corrupted by the old Soviet system. Under Gorbachev he used to preach the liberal virtues of democracy. But throughout this coverage he spoke the language of a monarchist. "Nicholas was one of the world's most important statesmen. He was a great patriot and thought only of Russia and the people. He gave them freedom and the people enjoyed freedom and loved their Tsar."

Even Dmitry Likhachev, who is perhaps the most respected voice of the nation's liberal consciousness, was not immune. Likhachev, at ninety-two, has lived through Russia's century of terror and upheaval. He has always been a figure above politics, a spokesman for the humanist ideals towards which the Westernist intelligentsia in Russia has always aspired. His books on Russia's cultural history have been read by millions; he has been enormously influential. Yet in those days of the funeral he too showed his political colours. "The Revolution," he said on television, "was simply a nightmare. When the Tsar was murdered it felt as if the sun had left the world. This was the end of a relatively humanitarian period in Russian history and the start of a new barbarian epoch."

No serious effort, then, to explain the Revolution and Nicholas's role in bringing it about. Almost nothing about his lack of talent as a politician—of his rigid adherence to the archaic vision of autocracy which he inherited from his father; nothing of his refusal to face up to the new social forces of capitalist and industrial Russia; nothing of his contempt for liberalism and the rule of law; or of his obstinate unwillingness to delegate his powers to able ministers, such as Witte or Stolypin, who alone had projects of reform that might, just might, have saved his dynasty. And nothing, or nothing much, about his adamant refusal (once the danger of the 1905 revolution had been dealt with) to grant more freedoms to the new parliamentary parties, or to local government and trade unions, the effect of which was to force these potentially loyal elements into the revolutionary underground and to direct it towards violent extremes. This was a man who did not have the wits to understand the challenge of his reign, a man who devoted all his energies to the minutiae of his autocratic office (even sealing envelopes with his own gentle hand) as a catastrophe gathered outside his door. Indeed, he barely seemed aware of it as he retreated more and more from public life and took refuge in the private and equally damaged realm of his family. While Petrograd sank into chaos, he wrote in his diary on 26 February 1917: "At ten o'clock I went to mass. The reports were on time. There were many people at breakfast. Wrote to Alix and went for a walk near the chapel by the Bobrinsky road. The weather was fine and frosty. After tea I read and talked with Senator Tregubov until dinner. Played dominoes in the evening." The next morning he lost his throne.

Pyramids and Prophets (1999)

Eliot Borenstein

Despite the earnest rise of new financial institutions in the building of the Russian Federation, few had forgotten that Soviet-era banks were long run by the government and for the government. In the most comfortable days of the 1970s and early 1980s, most citizens still held whatever cash they had at home, and almost no one had pension savings, as they could expect a complete range of government services upon retirement.

With the Wild West atmosphere of the early 1990s, distrust of institutions carried over into financial markets, and trade of all kinds—an advanced art form in the Soviet period—thrived foremost among friends, friends of friends, and friends of acquaintances. Thus was the stage set for the events of 1988 to 1994, narrated here by Eliot Borenstein, when the Moscow entrepreneur Sergei Mavrodi operated MMM, a financial services agency that fed pipe dreams (and remarkably few payouts) to tens of thousands of Russian investors. At its height the pyramid scheme's fictitious everyman, "Lenia Golubkov" (portrayed in a series of popular television commercials by the actor Vladimir Permiakov), ranked higher than President Yeltsin in public opinion polls.

In the more than a decade of legal wrangling that followed the pyramid's collapse, government officials estimated total losses of one hundred million dollars, coming largely from the pockets of average Russians. Despite the collapse, Mavrodi continued to enjoy support. He was elected to the country's governing Duma the year of the scheme's collapse, claimed parliamentary immunity from prosecution until ejected by the government, and then disappeared from Russia entirely. Returning years later, he served four and a half years in prison for his crimes. Pensioners welcomed him on his release from prison, insisting to reporters that they believed Mavrodi would have honored the company's payout obligations had the government not intervened to stop him.

Initial Mystery

To understand the MMM phenomenon, a few words about the nature and history of the company are in order. MMM was founded by Sergei Mavrodi as a cooperative in 1988. A 1979 graduate of the Moscow Institute of Electronic Machine Building, Mavrodi's involvement in "business" dates back to 1981, years before Gorbachev's reforms would render such activity legal. Over the years, Mavrodi slowly climbed the black-market ladder, selling first jeans and records, then eventually computers and other expensive consumer goods. According to the newspaper *Moskovskie novosti,* Mavrodi spent most of the 1980s registered as an elevator attendant, janitor, and night watchman in order to avoid prosecution for "parasitism" (lack of an official job) while developing his black-market career. For the first few years of its existence, MMM kept a low profile in both the markets and the media; in the late 1980s it was the Alisa company, with its ubiquitous barking dog, that dominated the airwaves. As MMM expanded, its troubles with the law also grew, most notably over the question of taxes. In January 1992, MMM's accountants were arrested for nonpayment of taxes and for presenting false balance sheets. In April of the following year, Makhaon, an MMM subsidiary, was prosecuted for hiding one billion rubles. MMM Bank, another affiliate, was closed in the fall of 1993, but its money disappeared before unpaid taxes could be collected. Soon MMM's run-ins with the law took a burlesque turn that strained credibility even more than its ad campaign: in May 1944, a Toyota carrying important documents relating to eighteen divisions of MMM was mysteriously hijacked on its way to the offices of the tax police: the car was later found, but the documents had vanished for good.

Perhaps not surprisingly, the beginning of MMM's troubled relationship with the authorities roughly coincided with the company's rise to prominence in the public consciousness (1992–94). If the government was intrigued by MMM's activity, ordinary Russians were no less so. From the very beginning, MMM was a creature of Moscow's equivalent of Madison Avenue, a set of mysterious initials and enigmatic advertisements that seemed designed to arouse the public's curiosity. In the early 1990s, MMM lavished money on exquisitely produced billboards displayed in metro stations throughout the country's major cities: one would have had to be blind not to recognize MMM's ever-present butterfly symbol, often accompanied by the enigmatic slogan "из тени в свет перелетая" (Flying out of the dark into the light). Perhaps these words were an announcement that MMM would indeed finally "come to light" and reveal its true nature, but its early television advertisements only increased the mystery, even as they emphasized the company's widespread name recognition. One ad in particular comes to mind, the commercial that might best be called "The Annunciation of MMM." This TV spot immediately stood out for its high production values (still a rarity in 1992) and excellent direction; it was a combination of Western quality with Russian faces. In it, the camera shows us people from a wide variety of backgrounds, at work, at play, engaging in casual conversation. One after another, each one sees a light emanating from the heavens and looks up. Finally, we see what they see: the huge letters "ммм," accompanied by a God-like baritone proclaiming: "нас знают все" ("Everyone knows us," or, more literally, "We are known by all"). In effect, the ad worked like an incantation: endless repetitions of the words "everybody knows us" ultimately rendered them true: who didn't recognize ммм? At the same time, the ad played on a variety of mass traditions: the ever-present Soviet мы (we) that was the subject of so many political slogans had now become an object, нас (us), while the masses became the subject, все (everyone). Although both Soviet propaganda and post-Soviet advertising target the "masses," their different approaches to the populace reflect contradictory metaphors of the body politic: for Soviet propaganda, with its roots in the collectivist romanticism of the proletarian culture movement, the masses moved as one body.

When the masses become consumers, however, the once-nationalist public body becomes fragmented, privatized. Although the advertiser operates on a large scale, he must nevertheless develop the illusion of a personal relationship between the product and the consumer. The ммм ad treated consumers as anything but undifferentiated masses or class types: the revelation of ммм was, like the revelation at Sinai, a collective event experienced by each person individually. Moreover, the Sinai comparison leads to an important point: the advertisement is suffused with a distinctly nonsecular glow. In the United States, such an approach fairly reeks of Protestantism: the skeptical housewife comes to accept Clorox bleach as her personal saviour. Appropriately, this ммм ad appeals to a closer, Russian Orthodox context: as the individuals who make up the Russian все each, in turn, look up and display their profiles to the camera, their poses effortlessly switch from the casual to the iconic, and each one basks in the reflected halo of corporate transfiguration.

Eventually, the advertisers lifted the veil of mystery from their product, and ммм was revealed to be an investment group. This, however, was no ordinary fund: first of all, it did not involve the direct purchase of stocks. Instead, ммм's "partners" bought pieces of paper that gave them redemption rights to stocks, which in turn might someday earn dividends. Most investors never redeemed their paper for actual stock; instead, the paper itself was the source of unheard-of profits. ммм newspaper ads repeatedly crowed that "our shares are guaranteed to be liquid"—they could be bought and sold at any time. Moreover, whereas the new capitalist stock market was a source of potential anxiety for consumers who were only just being weaned from a planned economy, ммм's shares came with a guarantee: not only would they always go up in price faster than the rate of inflation, but, in the best traditions of Gosplan (the Soviet governmental entity in charge of central economic planning), their future value was announced several days in advance. There was, however, no rational explanation for such profits; certainly, no investments in Russia at the time could yield such returns, nor could the currency markets (despite the inexorable decline of the ruble); even drug trafficking was less lucrative than the 3.000% annual dividends promised by MMM.

Although a number of hypotheses have been proposed to explain MMM, the prevailing mode is quite simple: it was a pyramid scheme that operated on an elegant and simple premise: if enough people were convinced to buy the shares at 1,000 rubles (the original price), even more investors could be persuaded to buy them at 1,200. Some of those who bought in at 1,000 took their money and ran, but others kept it in because the price went up as promised, suggesting further profits. When the company increased the price again, its proven track record of profitability lured new buyers, whose higher investment paid off the old buyers. In a pyramid, old investors are paid off thanks to new investments, but pyramids usually collapse when the price for new stocks gets too high to be affordable, driving down the number of buyers and, eventually, the value of the shares. Shareholders panic and ask for their money back, but the company cannot oblige: the stock undergoes a kind of physical sublimation, and "guaranteed liquidity" gives way to hot air. Investors can certainly make money on pyramids, but only if they get in early enough, since the scheme is based on an inflationary spiral. To put it bluntly, pyramid schemes function very much like a notoriously unreliable method of contraception, in which a calamitous outcome can be avoided only given a timely withdrawal.

Playing the Market

. . . .

Since MMM was trying to soak up the paltry savings of engineers and pensioners, the heroes and heroines of the company's mini-melodramas were carefully designed to be ordinary: "New Russians" need not apply. Thus Russia was introduced to its new national hero, a man who would displace the butterfly as MMM's primary symbol: Lenia Golubkov, construction worker. Lenia Golubkov was a cross between a Horatio Alger success story, a Russian fairy tale, and a socialist realist nightmare. If the much-maligned protagonist of the socialist realist novel developed an unhealthy attachment to his tractor, machine operator Lenia Golubkov, the Soviet hero's capitalist grandson, was only too happy to strike it rich and give his unlamented excavator a divorce. When first we meet Lenia, he is a typical working stiff who jumps at the chance to buy ммм shares and make money from thin air. Initially, his goals are small, hence the oft-quoted refrain from Lenia's first commercial: "Куплю жене сапоги" (I'll buy my wife some boots . . .). The boots are followed by a fur coat, a dacha, and even, eventually, a trip to California to attend the World Cup soccer championship: indeed, Lenia needed a "family growth chart" to keep track of his burgeoning wealth through 1993, all thanks to ммм. As numerous commentators pointed out at the time, Lenia is a postmodern Ivanushkadurachok (Ivan the Fool), a fairy-tale hero who found the secret to success that involved no effort on his part.

Lenia was quickly joined by an equally colorful supporting cast: his plump, fur-clad wife and his tattooed brother Ivan often shared the camera with him. But there were also other heroes, each designed to appeal to different segments of the audience: Nikolai Fomich and his wife, Elizaveta Andreevna, pensioners who can barely make ends meet. What can possibly save them, other than ммм? Igor and Iuliia, the young, party-loving would-be entrepreneurs of the ммм-тv generation, advise their friends to invest in ммм in order to make money to pay off a business debt. And, of course, there was Marina Sergeevna, a lonely, single woman of a certain age. As we see her leaving her apartment, the announcer tells us that "Марина Сергеевна никому не верит" (Marina Sergeevna trusts no one). Even though she has seen ммм's commercials, she is on her way to the Sberbank to give her hard-earned rubles to the state-owned entity that has defrauded its customers so many times. One of her neighbors tells her about her own success with ммм, and finally she is convinced to put part of her money in the bank and invest part in ммм. A nervous week goes by, and Marina Sergeevna cashes in her shares at an ммм trading point in order to receive the promised profit. Her reaction: "Надо же, не обманули!" (How about that! They were telling the truth!) To which the announcer responds, "Правильно, Марина Сергеевна!" (That's right, Marina Sergeevna!) Like the Wizard of Oz, ммм provides something for everyone: a dog for Nikolai Fomich, a pair of boots for Lenia's wife, and even new love for Marina Sergeevna. Just as Vladimir Zhirinovsky would promise to personally console all of Russia's lonely women with his sexual favors, Marina Sergeevna not only gains much-needed cash, she also meets a man, Volodia.

> ANNOUNCER: Marina Sergeevna arrived at her friend's birthday party. But she didn't come alone. There were congratulations. And, as is the custom, they drank and had snacks. Then they danced. And then they talked. The men had their own conversations, and so did the women.

WOMAN: You're so lucky, Marinka! How I envy you! How I envy you, how I envy you!

ANNOUNCER: Marina! You do have something worth envying. А / О ммм.

Ведущий: Марина Сергеевна пришла на день рождения к своей подруге. Но не одна. Звучали поздравления. И, как водится. выпивали и закусывали. Потом были танцы. Ну, а потом разговоры. У мужчин—свои. А у женщин—свои. Женщина: Счастливая ты, Маринка. Я так тебе завидую! Так завидую, так завидую!

Ведущий: Марина! И есть чему позавидовать А/О "ммм."

Marina Sergeevna's friend feels compelled to express her envy three times in a row. While one might be tempted to ascribe this repetition to the laziness of the script writer, this folkloric triple invocation of envy is actually the key to the commercial. One of the appeals to socialist ideology (if not Soviet reality) is that it promises to eliminate envy by eliminating discrepancies in wealth: while the Soviet Union was hardly egalitarian, the conspicuous consumption of the post-Soviet New Russians has provoked the scorn (and envy) of the majority of citizens still hovering around the poverty level. Marina Sergeevna's economic success is portrayed almost exclusively in terms of her personal happiness, which may be "worth envying" but could hardly invite the hostility so often provoked by wealth. Moreover, even as the woman "envies" Marina Sergeevna, she is also able to celebrate with her, to share in her happiness. To some extent, this is an oblique expansion on Mavrodi's euphemism for his investors: "partners." ммм struck a devious compromise between the values of state socialism and "wild" capitalism: the success of individuals spreads happiness to everyone around them.

. . . .

MMM *as Shadow Cabinet*

Of course, the greatest challenge to Golubkov's creators was the pyramid's collapse in the summer of 1994. As the value of ммм's shares continued to rise, the government intensified its scrutiny of the company's operations. On July 18, the State Anti-Monopoly Commission urged television stations to stop broadcasting ммм's commercials, but the plea fell on deaf ears; 2,666 ммм ads had aired on Russian television in March, April, and May 1994, bringing financially strapped stations much-needed cash. Of far greater consequence was an announcement made by the Tax Inspectorate three days later: ммм's subsidiary Invest-Consulting owed 49.9 billion rubles in taxes, payable immediately. Mavrodi responded the next day (July 22) by upping the ante: if forced to pay, he would shut down MMM and let the government deal with his outraged shareholders. By the time MMM shut down all its trading offices on July 26, panic had already erupted. Huge crowds gathered outside the company's main office on Varshavka—from two to three thousand people on July 26 to an estimated thirteen thousand the following day. Independent dealers were already buying up MMM shares at 65,000–75,000 rubles on the twenty-sixth, down from 115,000–125,000 before the crisis began. Typically, the government and MMM moved to calm down the unruly crowd in their own fashions: Mavrodi recorded a soothing message, while the authorities sent in OMON, the "special forces" that are as inevitable in any post-Soviet mass crisis as a chorus is in a Greek tragedy. On July 29, MMM, laying the responsibility for the panic entirely at the feet of the government, announced that circumstances had forced it to drop the official price of MMM's shares from 115,000 rubles to 950. By evening, the crowd had stopped traffic on Varshavka, and only OMON could restore order. The next day, Mavrodi issued new MMM "tickets," which the Ministry of Finance announced it would not recognize; for its part, MMM designated these tickets "promotional material"—truth in advertising at last, even if only in the fine print. The new tickets also differed from their predecessors in bearing the likeness of Sergei Mavrodi himself, a wise move from the standpoint of publicity, if not aesthetics, for it suggested that MMM's founder had no plans to try to slip out of the country unnoticed. The tickets' official rate was 1,065 rubles, and despite the assault on MMM's reputation, brisk trading began.

One would think that the results of a battle between the central government and one private company would be a foregone conclusion, and yet the government's campaign against MMM was foundering, at least in part because it did not know how to fight an enemy based entirely on image rather than substance. The government's lack of comprehension of the rules of the narrative game was a definite obstacle to its belated attempt to clamp down on MMM's operations, and it allowed Mavrodi to outmaneuver his enemies every step of the way. As a result, officials made themselves look foolish when they engaged in a war not just with the company, but with its fictional creations as well. One of the more memorable moments came when Prime Minister Viktor Chernomyrdin addressed Marina Sergeevna and Lenia Golubkov on national television, warning them that they should be more careful with their money. Mavrodi then turned the tables on Chernomyrdin: "So, the authorities do not like Lenia Golubkov and Marina Sergeevna," he responded in the nation's newspapers. "But do Lenia Golubkov and Marina Sergeevna like the authorities? No one's asked about that. Yet." If the prime minister and Mavrodi were engaged in a war of words, then Chernomyrdin was well on his way to defeat. He had already ceded important rhetorical ground by invoking MMM's characters as if they were real: in his response, Mavrodi also referred to Lenia and Marina Sergeevna by name, but their enemies, "the authorities," remained abstract. As a result, MMM's heroes not only appeared to be classic "little men" victimized by inhuman bureaucratic forces, they also seemed more "real" than the nameless governmental authorities who opposed them. Moreover, Mavrodi's words contained a thinly veiled threat: if the government closed down MMM, then Mavrodi's "partners" would get their revenge at the ballot box.

Indeed, as events unfolded over the next two years, it became more and more clear that MMM and its "partners" were styling themselves as an alternative not only to the current "party of power," but to the Russian state itself. Mavrodi claimed that MMM was the most powerful political force in the entire Russian Federation, large enough to gather the one million signatures needed to call a referendum on the current government and the constitution. Yeltsin's government was particularly vulnerable at that point, having just put the country through an almost interminable four-question referendum process in a failed attempt to resolve the country's constitutional crisis. By August 8, Mavrodi's "partners" were openly talking of nominating him for president. If only a few years ago the greatest threat to Yeltsin's government seemed to be from the Communists, now MMM appeared to be on its way to taking over the mantle of the opposition: when diehard Communists organized a demonstration commemorating the failed coup attempt against Mikhail Gorbachev on August 19, an MMM rally held on the same day had a far greater turnout.

My Precious Capital (2002)

Mikhail Ryklin

"Art belongs to the people," Lenin once famously pronounced, and from the country's inception Soviet leaders encouraged public participation in all manner of public art. As the new government labored within the walls of the medieval Kremlin, Lenin urged that Moscow's surrounding "grey squares" be turned into "living museums" through spontaneous, temporary art installations that would change with each passing season. Stalin, by contrast, appreciated the gravitas of a capital city laid in granite and built to impress. In the Soviet Union and its successor states, art and politics have gone hand in hand much more closely than in most older market economies.

In 1999 the Russian critic Mikhail Ryklin paused to survey the transformations under way in the new Russian capital after eight years of capitalist entrepreneurship. He found much to remind him of sovereign rules of old. Reeling from the financial crash of 1998—when the Russian government defaulted on external debt payments as well as internal salary transfers, the stock market lost 90 percent of its value, and the ruble's value plummeted—the city's breathless pace of construction briefly halted. Moscow's recovery from the crash was swift. Rising world oil prices sent profits surging into the capital again, elevating the city's status to that of staggering global metropolis. By 2006 Moscow had unseated Tokyo as the world's most expensive city.

To many observers, especially foreigners, the changes that have taken place in Moscow's appearance over the last ten years seem unprecedented. "In the West this would have taken much more time," they insist. They overlook the fact that sixty years ago their grandfathers considered the "General Plan for the Reconstruction of Moscow" (1935) unprecedented, followed by yet further mass constructions thirty years later. Here we must remember: In Russia, for power to exist, it constantly requires the presence of something unprecedented. This is a kind of alibi for the inhuman treatment of its own citizens. What is happening out on the street, we are told, is so grandiose that our own "petty" troubles may entirely fade against the background. Contemporary Russia inherited (in somewhat altered form) this particular vision of the future from the USSR. It's just that now the future appears in the form of an idealized prerevolutionary past.

For many years the attitude of foreign travelers to Muscovite architecture was distinguished by extreme ambivalence. The famous Marquis de Custine saw two Moscows instead of one: one Moscow seen from a distance, a phantom city consisting of hundreds of gold cupolas, "a poetic city, which resembles no other city in the world, a city whose architecture has neither a name nor anything similar to it"; and another Moscow which (if you are inside this city and look at it from within) is "a big city without monuments, that is, without a single work of art that might be seriously worthy of admiration. Glancing at this clumsy, unwieldy copy of Europe, you ask yourself: Where has Asia disappeared to, after appearing before your eyes for just a moment?" The center of poetic Moscow was the Kremlin, especially in the moonlight. Any attempts to draw a new building into the historical ensemble of the Kremlin was taken as a personal insult. Custine was mortally offended at Nicholas I because, having begun construction of the Great Palace in the Kremlin, he ruined this unique work of "tsarist architecture," this original work of national genius, built, true enough, by Italians. Dumas was also irritated by everything in Moscow that reminded him of Paris, depriving this Asiatic capital of its exotic aura.

For others Moscow has always been a village city, a city with an urban façade that conceals something else, something non-urban, non-European, also unprecedented. Walter Benjamin wrote about this with particular beauty in his book, *Moscow Diary*. The waves of modernization squeezed but did not destroy these strange spaces behind the façades, where a city of many millions comes into contact with its village essence. The first powerful wave of "Haus-mannization" (named for the baron who reconstructed Paris under Napoleon III) rolled through Moscow in the Stalin era, when the central streets were widened, the basic means of transportation (first and foremost, the metro), the sky-scrapers, and the All-Union Agricultural Exhibition were built. The 1960s are dominated by the romance of mass construction: millions of people who lived in communal apartments had the first chance to get their own apartments. The state makes haste to declare an unprecedentedly high rate of housing construction. The idea of "a model communist city" concealed the attempt to create a privileged class of capital residents by exploiting the resources of an enormous empire. This attempt was successful thanks to the system of registration, which still exists today in an altered form, and which turned Moscow into a half-closed city.

However, the main building of the Soviet period, the famous Palace of

Soviets, for whose sake the Cathedral of Christ the Savior was destroyed, was never built. The project was delegated to Stalin's "court architect," Boris Iofan, but, perhaps symbolically, was never realized. This utopian building was conceived as a synthesis of all cultures of the world: "The whole millennial culture of human art will enter the walls of the people's building. From the golden faïence tiles of Mauritanian Spain to the architecture of American glass. From the majolica decorations of Florence to metal alloy. From the carved mosaic of Byzantium to contemporary industrial plastic. The old-fashioned art of Gobelin lace, ebony carving, the reborn fresco, the technical achievements of photoluminescence, the folk art of Palekh lacquer—it is impossible to enumerate the riches of the artistic decorations. The technical comforts of the twentieth century—amid porphyry and marble, crystal and jasper—will have an invisible effect." It is not surprising that such a building could not be constructed. However, as a linguistic ideological construct it exerted tremendous influence on the whole Soviet period. Moscow was built full of imperfect likenesses of this symbolic structure, which in its eclecticism comes closest of all to the post-war metro station (especially those on the Ring line). It is precisely in these (imperfect constructions) that the authors of the time saw "manifestations of Stalin's concern for the simple Soviet man."

It is natural to evaluate post-Soviet architecture vis-à-vis Soviet predecessors. First of all people notice the coexistence of various styles: from glass and concrete "corporate architecture" to buildings in the "Muscovite style" ("a good imitation of bad nineteenth-century eclecticism," in the words of one foreign architect) and the numerous restorations of monuments destroyed during the Soviet period. After the Soviet period's dreary monotony (especially the 1960s–1980s), Russian specialists take a positive view of the mixture in a single urban milieu of late modernism, postmodernism, vernacular architecture, the numerous "new buildings" and vacation spots of the "New Russians," which take the form of small-scale fortified edifices with towers and battlements that have no analogue in twentieth-century work. Judging by these structures, Russian capitalism is strikingly dissimilar to its western prototype, as is especially evident in the case of overt imitations. What might be considered unambiguous kitsch in another city is welcomed in Moscow, in its contrast to the semi-official style of the preceding seventy years, as a step forward, "a breath of fresh air."

This concerns among other things the "New Russian" architecture (which professionals, as a rule, will not condescend to discuss), Tsereteli's "monumental propaganda," and the *grands travaux* of Moscow mayor Yuri Luzhkov. If we equate anarchy with freedom, then we are indeed faced with an unheard-of freedom, connected with post-Soviet society's lack of any kind of consensus, even of a simple common denominator. For the overwhelming majority of Russian citizens, the Soviet period has not yet ended (materially they are still living in the USSR, which has entered a phase of disintegration); a small layer, called for some reason the "middle class," strives to attain comfort on the western model (hence such linguistic neologisms as *evroremont* [Euro-renovation], and *inomarka* [foreign brand]). A quantitatively insignificant percentage of the rich aims at something unprecedented as they satisfy their often extravagant caprices, falling into mild aesthetic chaos. Under such conditions it is impossible to realize the Grand Style that professionals still dream of.

The financial crash of August of 1998 brought an end to the era of excessive expectations, when the city that was heretofore "capital of the world proletariat" hoped to become one of the world's largest capitalist metropoles in a single bound. I am inclined to see a Stalinist moment of declared de-Stalinization in this megalomania. The needs of the private person are sacrificed for the *Nth* time to a splendid future, which never actually materializes. Instead of consulting firms, which draw up plans at least a few years in advance, in Russia numerous officials and businessmen are overcome by an enthusiasm for change. These people's peculiar recklessness takes the form of striving for total planning, unmediated foresight which will not stoop to calculation. The reverse side of this "dreaminess" are shopping centers, unrented business spaces in half-occupied buildings, built in expectation of an enormous income which the vast majority of Muscovites were supposedly going to have, but in reality do not. But where a businessman loses his own money, the official wastes the budget. Capitalism is being constructed in Moscow by more or less Soviet methods. The state remains personified to the highest degree: it is no accident that the city's mayor Luzhkov, a compact, short man, is one of the key personages of the last ten years, first strolling in a cap, then chasing a soccer ball, then going down through an ice hole. Just as it is no accident that Yeltsin's presidential career began as first secretary of the Moscow Committee of the Communist Party of the Soviet Union—that is, the head of the city of Moscow.

While the state remains deeply unpredictable and so oddly personified, it is only reasonable to want to insure oneself against its vagaries. Had there been no such mechanisms of resistance, the crisis in 1998 could easily have resulted in total financial collapse. Fortunately, there are people in Russia today who have learned how to put the brakes on fairly effectively, thereby softening the results of the policy of good intentions carried out by the state. These are the first manifestations of a genuine private interest: if officials in other countries insure society against the unpredictable actions of private persons, then in Russia, on the contrary, individuals insure themselves against the dangerous

improvisations of the state. But for now their possibilities are limited. Therefore the new spiral of reconstruction in Moscow is turning out to cause
tremendous damage to the surrounding environment: striving to minimize
financial outlays, they are maximizing ecological outlays. As in many other
countries with relatively impoverished populations, Russia still has few people
who dare to question the price of progress. Development as such continues to
be fetishized, and is considered a good in itself. As a result, enormous sacrifices are made for insignificant goals.

In Brezhnev's time architects considered themselves victims of the regime,
forced to grind out standardized buildings, "stepping on the throat of their
own song." Now, it would seem, the hour has come for genuine architecture.
There are clients with money, a developed market for construction materials,
and a qualified work force. In the early 1990s offices in Moscow were paid for
100 percent in advance—a situation unlike any other construction practice in
the world in recent decades. Even after that, conditions were auspicious until
August of 1998.

But here too the architects met with disappointment: "We were fobbed off
with some kind of counterfeit dream." Once again they did not succeed in
carrying out their social-critical function, in deconstructing the figures of
power. "What was imagined as a deconstruction of power became its expression," writes critic Grigorii Revzin. Dissolution into the surroundings is transformed into the concept of the "unnoticeable" underground Manège, and
postmodern irony into buildings of corporate architecture (mostly banks,
which aimed to uphold their international image). The client is interested not
in the quality of the architecture but in the most rapid return on the money
invested; the builder wants to make the project as cheaply as possible, the
government of Moscow creates commissions, councils, administrations,
which "approve" the project. Here is the opinion of the editor-in-chief of the
journal *Proekt Rossiia* [Project Russia], Dutch architect Bart Goldhoorn: "It is
naïve to presume that architecture flourishes when everyone wants it to. In
fact the opposite is true. The more money and politics that participate in it,
the worse the result." He also draws attention to "the overwhelming resemblance [of buildings erected by the municipal government] to the architecture
of Disneyland, where architecture is dictated by the laws of public success. . . .
Moscow is the only place in the world where popular Low Culture has been
upgraded as the official State Culture." If Stalinist Moscow aspired to become
a model for the rest of the world, contemporary architecture is dominated by
a reproductive tendency. From an inimitable model, Moscow is becoming an
exceptional copy that pretends to originality.

It would seem that the worst of the old travelers' prophecies is being realized: Moscow, losing the exoticism they so loved, is becoming a world city. However, a new exotic quality is arising to take its place: the exotic quality of original copying. Transplanted to new soil, the copy masters the features of the original. It is surprising to find the copy in such an unusual place, and the act of copying itself is presented as something arbitrary. In some sense, from the 1930s to the present, Moscow has been living through changes like the ones St. Petersburg underwent in the eighteenth century. The exception is that, if St. Petersburg was a fresco realized by Peter I on the damp ground of the Finnish swamps, in Moscow's case we have a palimpsest, where new writing is laid over multiple old layers. Besides that, the variety of contemporary architectural styles is significantly greater than what existed three centuries ago. Muscovite style is significantly broader than the eclecticism of the pseudo-Slavic style; it absorbs everything up to postmodernism (for example, the Atrium restaurant by "paper architects" Brodskii and Utkin). These productions become Muscovite circumstantially, in that they function in a certain context, created under a charismatic personality's direction. How could it happen, well-known art historian Oleg Grabar wondered, that the participation of Italian, German, Dutch, French and Russian master-craftsmen in the construction of St. Petersburg did not lead to stylistic anarchy? Why has this city preserved its national physiognomy? The answer is simple: "the enormous, decisive role of the personality of Peter in creating the appearance of Petersburg." The author of the Petrine Baroque style was Peter himself. Moscow was also reconstructed, thanks to "Stalin's concern for the human being," whose executor in the 1930s was Lazar Kaganovich. In both cases external imitation of Europe only distances the copy from the original, giving it a particular originality.

Yuri Luzhkov plays a similar role in the current spiral of modernization in Moscow. The *grands travaux* that the Mayor has tied to his name, as well as all new commercial structures are expected to adhere to the "Muscovite style." Almost all these buildings are built by anonymous architectural studios, often with serious departures from the blueprints. I cite Bart Goldhoorn again: "Although the current Mayor's office has less real ability to influence the process of construction it had than in Soviet times (when financing was a government monopoly), the desire to oversee everything is still present just as before. Having received support from citizens in elections, the city powers along while the residents enjoy keeping themselves busy with the renaissance of the Soviet metaphor of 'leader-builder,' personified by the mayor himself." In other words, real authorship is alienated yet again to the benefit of symbolic authorship. A question arises à propos of this: should we adopt an attitude of pathos towards architecture and sculpture? Do we have the right to condemn new monuments because they disfigure the appearance of the city? (This has been written about all of Tsereteli's works and the grand projects of the Moscow government.) At one time the Eiffel Tower and the Cathedral of Christ the Savior were also considered models of bad architecture, and people felt that tearing them down would restore the historical appearance of Paris and Moscow. Architecture and art cannot be better than their times. I think that the new urban milieu of Moscow reflects the spirit of our dynamic and unprincipled time no better and no worse than the other spheres of life in Russia. Authoritarian (not to be confused with totalitarian) tendencies are present in Tsereteli's works, and are present in the absence of real competition among monumental sculptors. But does such competition really take place in the sphere of banking, say, or in the academic sphere? It is hard to understand why we decry things in one area while tacitly accepting them in others.

Today's Moscow is a city that, in fact, has no demand for works of contemporary art, where the market in photography is in an embryonic stage. Therefore contemporary architecture is also possible, for now, only as an initiative from above or as a whim of the sudden *nouveaux riches*. Many people evaluate its coexistence in this context with obvious kitsch positively because they are comparing this milieu not with Europe or America, but with the Soviet one that preceded it.

If this is a continuation of the Soviet period, it is one that lacks the previous totalitarian gleam. If it is capitalism, then in the best case it is a passé version of the period of primitive accumulation. This is one reason why contemporary Russian art is so hard to write into the world context. What worked in the first Russian avant-garde has turned against the people who are making art in Russia today. Politics may be art's great competitor, but it also strives for artistic status.

Translated by Sibelan Forrester

Fade to Red? (1996)

Masha Lipman

The oppositional logics of cold war life, solidly in place from the 1950s onward, dictated that the USSR had to be everything that the West was not. If daily life under perestroika made all of Russia into an "anti-Disneyland," as Muscovites insisted to Nancy Ries (part XV), the USSR, we learn from Masha Lipman, was also the inheritor of an "anti-style." Lipman, a political analyst at the Carnegie Moscow Center, wrote this essay just after the financial crash in 1996. By conventional wisdom, drab gray urban boulevards were the showcases for thousands of identically drab apartments with their identically drab inhabitants. Zapretnyi plod sladok, goes the Russian saying: "The forbidden fruit is sweet." Throughout the Soviet period, despite extensive media restraints, all urbanites knew what was available to them and what was not, relative to the West. The long forbidden status of luxuries, however, also led to an extraordinary ingenuity for their local conjurings. One Moscow cultural historian found that, to bring the Soviet period alive for women with whom she was working, all she had to do was ask them about the outfits they took the most pride in. Assembling a really good outfit proved a full-time job unto itself.

Kuznetsky Most is a short, narrow shopping street not far from the Kremlin. In the nineteenth century, it was famous for its fashion boutiques; in the late twentieth century, there are boutiques and an art gallery and several Soviet-style stores. Names like Christian Lacroix and Versace, CK Calvin Klein and Donna Karan, Trussardi and Kenzo, Gianfranco Ferre and Gucci, Armani and Yves Saint Laurent are familiar in Moscow, and those who can't afford their products—which is just about everybody—see the advertisements or hear Russian celebrities talking on television about their favorite designers.

At the Christian Lacroix boutique, two armed guards stood at the door, but inside I was greeted by three young saleswomen. We got to talking, and at first they sounded confident. They had been in business since December, and they had special clients whom they rang up whenever there was something new and chic on sale. Right now, they were running low on merchandise, but they really did expect the fall collection to arrive any day. Furthermore, they assured me, Christian Lacroix was coming in person to introduce it. Maybe, I thought, Donna Karan was right—Moscow *is* the place to be—and yet I couldn't help asking, "Don't you expect this crisis to affect your business?"

"Not unless there's revolution and people begin to kill each other," one of them said.

The conversation continued in a casual, friendly fashion, but the mood abruptly changed when I asked, "Do you think a revolution is likely?"

"Of course it is," another said. "I'm talking not as a boutique representative but as a woman and as a mother. Anything can be expected in this country. And nobody trusts this country. Over the past year and a half or two years, nobody has trusted Russia." Apparently, Christian Lacroix's faith in Russia is fading, too. After my visit to his boutique, the designer's Paris headquarters said that his trip to Moscow had been postponed.

Not far away is the Gianfranco Ferre Studio boutique, which opened in June. It is in a large, gleaming mall called Petrovsky Passage, near the Bolshoi Theatre. The mall features all manner of international boutiques: Kenzo, Givenchy, Lancôme. But the foot traffic here, once brisk, is somewhat hushed. At Gianfranco Ferre, the last remnants of the summer collection are on sale at forty to fifty percent off. (A suit that was once five thousand three hundred rubles, or eight hundred and fifty dollars, is now three thousand rubles.) Despite the bargains, there are few takers.

"All through the summer, we might sell as many as twenty articles a day," one saleswoman told me, smiling with pride. "Even though we've been in business only since June, we have already begun to form a permanent clientele. They call us asking when the new collection is arriving. They even called after the crisis began. Unfortunately, we can't tell them anything about prices."

"There's always a crisis in this country," another salesgirl said. "It will calm down." Then a little chill of anxiety seemed to hit her and she added, "Do you think it's worse this time?"

Around the corner from Christian Lacroix there's a jeans store called Big Star. An English-language notice on the door reads "Closed." There's also a Russian sign saying "Closed for technical reasons," a newly coined euphemism meaning "We haven't figured out any new prices yet."

I can't say that all of this is not strange sometimes, even for those of us who have spent half our lives yearning for a radical change. After decades of solemn reports on the wheat harvest, our journalism now occasionally uses the hermetic style of the fashion press, which we parse at our peril. Even seven years into "post-Communism," the Russian ear (or mine, at least) has a hard time adjusting. Not long ago, a miniskirt was described as "reminiscent of patchwork"; it took me a minute to figure out that the barbarous-sounding Russian word *pechvork*, which I came across in the August issue of *Woman*, was, in fact, "patchwork." I suppose most fashion readers know the word, because it was not included in the accompanying glossary, which did include the words "teddy," "bodysuit," and "French knickers."

Over the years, foreign friends—mostly Americans—were always shocked by the idea that Russians might take any interest in fashion. To them, the Soviet Union was the incarnation of anti-style, so much so that the Wendy's hamburger chain used to run commercials featuring a Soviet "fashion show," which featured a very fat woman wearing burlap. Well, no one would deny that we are still a poor country, and poverty does not allow for much crêpe de chine, but for decades our realities and private aspirations—even our rebellions—have been reflected in what we've chosen to design and wear. A riddle wrapped in an enigma wrapped in a cocoon of flair, you might say.

Fashion has almost always come to Russia from the West. In the nineteenth century, Russian noblemen emulated their European counterparts in attitudes, literary taste, life style, even language. And, of course, clothes. Here is Pushkin (in Babette Deutsch's translation) on Eugene Onegin, a Russian aristocrat:

> What London haberdashers hallow
> We buy with timber and with tallow:
> 'Tis here, to please a lavish whim,
> With all a dandy's mind can limn,
> And all that Paris in her passion
> For the most costly merchandise
> So elegantly can devise
> To tempt the sporting man of fashion
> Observe his closet well, and gage
> Thereby our eighteen-year-old sage.

In the early twentieth century, however, Europe was overrun by a wave of Russian refinement, particularly Serge Diaghilev's extravagant Ballets Russes, which came to Paris in 1909. Audiences were taken as such by the innovative sets and elegant costumes by León Bakst, Alexandre Benois, and Nikolay Roerich as by the dancing of Nijinsky, Fokine, and Karsavina. Suddenly, the stereotypical Russia of Tolstoy and Dostoyevsky—the literary Russia, eternally in search of truth, the obsessive country that rejects the banality of surfaces—displayed a grace and a subtlety unfamiliar to European audiences. Yet all the stylish promise of the Ballets Russes never spawned a lasting Russian fashion designer, to say nothing of a Russian fashion industry. If there was a fledgling elegance in the country, it disappeared shortly after Lenin arrived at the Finland Station. And, at the same time, all our would-be fashion titans (many of them White Russians) left for Paris and elsewhere. Little did we know that the son of one of Lenin's confidants, the young Alexander Liberman, would emigrate and go on to shape the American tastemaker Condé Nast.

The October Revolution tried to cast aside the old world: anything deemed bourgeois was condemned, and dressing nicely was distinctly—fatally—bourgeois. Out went anything remotely feminine for women and formal suits for men. In came the leather jacket of the commissar (with Mauser revolvers as accessories). My grandparents, who saw the Revolution as the coming of a new world, adopted the ascetic style of the Bolsheviks. Not only did they reject fashion; they stopped celebrating birthdays and anniversaries, threw out all their furniture, and ate their meals off butcher paper.

Lenin himself, after spending so many of his pre-Revolutionary years as a political exile in Europe, continued to wear a three-piece suit and a tie. But, unlike his ideas, Lenin's fashion statement never became the rage. The generation of the twenties combined *narodny,* or folk, style with the severe utility of military dress. "A service jacket cut from a gray blanket together with a *malorossijsky"*—Ukrainian—"embroidered shirt showing from underneath": such is the outfit of a Soviet bureaucrat disguised as the devil in Mikhail Bulgakov's novella "Diaboliad." Most of Bulgakov's works were inspired by his hatred of the Revolution and of the Bolsheviks' elimination of individual style. In photographs, Bulgakov invariably appears in a conservative suit and hat, an outfit that underscored his alienation and made him a suspicious figure in a world in which a fellow-playwright, such as Vsevolod Vishnevsky, appeared at rehearsals wearing a politically correct leather jacket and, to be sure, a Mauser.

In the early twenties, the New Economic Policy brought back some elements of capitalism—the taste for the good life, good clothes and food, music and entertainment—and genuine revolutionary spirits were disgusted. Nevertheless, the Russian avant-garde took a keen interest in fashion—although, to be sure, revolutionary fashion. Alexander Rodchenko designed his own overalls. Kazimir Malevich's paintings suggested a kind of Suprematist color scheme— all bold, stark shades. Lyubov Popova brought a Cubist edge to her costume designs for the theatre, and she designed coats and dresses as distinctive as any abroad.

Even beyond the artistic world, the yearning for style blossomed under the New Economic Policy. In Ilf and Petrov's novel "The Twelve Chairs," a Soviet engineer's wife is obsessed with emulating a rich American woman she reads about in a French fashion magazine. The scene is Moscow, 1927: "The glossy photograph showed the daughter of the American billionaire Vanderbilt wearing an evening dress. There was fur and feathers, silk and pearls, extraordinary lightness of design and a mind-boggling haircut." The engineer's wife buys "a dog skin which was meant to look like a muskrat. This was used for the adornment of the evening outfit."

Yet even in the most terrible days of the Stalin era, after the New Economic Policy was crushed, citizens remained aware of style. Movies from the West were occasionally shown, and one could try to copy the clothing worn by such movie stars as Mary Pickford. Meanwhile, Communist Party officials and secret-police bosses, diplomats and bureaucrats enjoyed the privilege of foreign trips on business or for medical treatment; they brought back from Paris and London crates of dresses, bottles of perfume, and, generally, a sense of style, however rudimentary. Years later, high Party officials would establish top-secret tailor shops; in the most élite of those shops, tailors with security clearances made mannequin replicas of Politburo members so that the men of the Party leadership could order their new gray suits on the telephone without wasting precious time.

In the late fifties and sixties, as the Iron Curtain pulled back slightly, we began to see Soviet versions of Western hipness. The *stilyagi* (our Beats) adored Dizzy Gillespie and Charlie Parker and craved outfits consisting of skintight pants, a big-shouldered jacket, and thick-soled shoes. The lucky *stilyagi* bought their clothes from the rare foreign visitor; others had to make do by taking in their Soviet-made trousers. They would strut along the streets of Moscow and Leningrad in their stylish stuff, defying the police, who would sometimes chase them down and "slash open their seditious narrow pants," as Vassily Aksyonov recalls in his autobiographical novel "The Burn."

Young people in big cities tried to keep up with their Western counterparts, but Soviet industry kept grinding out the same drab, gray stuff. Legend has it that, sometime in the sixties, the French actor and singer Yves Montand was titillated by a kind of Soviet women's underwear called a *shtany*—a longish, baggy, thick, ugly thing. The writer Tatyana Tolstaya recalls, in an article in Russian *Vogue,* that there was nothing more shameful for a girl than for somebody to see her *shtany*: "Maletskaya fell down and her *shtany* could be seen—warm, flannelette, lilac. How horrible!" As for Montand, the story is that he bought a collection of Soviet undergarments to take back home to Paris, where he planned to organize a private exhibition.

Under Brezhnev, the U.S.S.R. became a consumer society without consumer goods; in the face of shortages, the Soviet people developed clothes obsessions. The tiniest detail—a collar line, the shape of buttons or pockets— would be reproduced at home by self-taught tailors. To create the flared trousers you saw in foreign films, you sewed in a wedge running from the knee to the rim of your old trousers. You'd spend an entire day waiting in line for a rare imported article; you'd think nothing of spending a month's wages on a pair of tight knee-high boots; you dreamed of a suède jacket. And if you had the privilege of foreign trips, you could take everyone's breath away. The symbol of all we did not possess was a pair of bluejeans. "A boy from a rich jeans family," a girlfriend of mine would say dreamily as she described somebody whose *nomenklatura* parents worked abroad and spoiled their pampered son with denim. To have both jeans and a jeans jacket—this was the fulfillment of an impossible Soviet dream. In Aksyonov's "The Burn," a foreign wife of a Russian playboy longing to outdo and outdress all the local women adorns herself in a "long suède skirt with a front cut running up to her pelvis, suède underwear, high suède boots, suède jacket, suède . . . pelerine, suède umbrella and a suède bag for vegetables."

More recently, in the post-Gorbachev, post-perestroika years, clothes have returned to the Russian market. This has produced some distinctly un-Soviet situation comedy. Russian *Vogue*'s editor-in-chief, Aliona Doletskaya, described her delight in finding a terrific Issey Miyake outfit in London and then her disappointment to discover, at a Moscow soirée, that someone else was wearing the same garment.

For others, fashion developed as a semiotic system indicating degrees of economic position and even of physical threat. The leather jacket, once the symbol of selfless struggle against capitalism, became in the early nineties the preferred garment of the post-Soviet hustler. The new gangster capitalists, much like their revolutionary forebears, wore their leather jackets with firearms as accessories and were no less ready to use them. Unlike their predecessors, however, they wore heavy gold chains and were often accompanied by underdressed women.

In a recent interview in *Kommersant*, an Italian tailor tells the story of his first Russian client: "It was like in a bad thriller. Two minutes before lunch break a handsome guy entered my shop. After he made sure that I was the man he was looking for, he announced, 'I wear two pistols on me. Make me a suit that would hide them even with the coat buttoned.' "

But in the age of reform, as business life became respectable and a middle class began to emerge, people became more sophisticated about clothing. Now this tailor has permanent clients in Moscow. Some of them are members of the Duma.

Probably the person hurt most by the invasion of foreign fashion designers to the Russian market was Slava Zaitsev, who was for years the only clothing designer of note in the Soviet Union—in fact, the only designer authorized to introduce Soviet haute couture to the world. Zaitsev's House of Fashion, on Prospekt Mira, is a multistory building in the bland Soviet style. His look—close-cropped hair, black suit, tuxedo shirt, and bow tie—is familiar to all.

The other day, I stopped by to see Zaitsev, who is a youthful sixty. His office is decorated in fashionable black wood and features elegant lamps and a framed picture of the designer with Boris Yeltsin. When the economic reforms began, Zaitsev told me, he lost many customers to his Western competitors. "Now is the first year when I've begun to win back clients," he said. "I think the Russians have had enough of mass-produced imports. And all these clothes in the boutiques lack soul, they lack my energy. I charge every piece. My clothes are alive."

Perhaps. What is true is that, in an empire of uniformity, of burly outerwear and industrial undergarments, he was the exception. (Like the poets Yevtushenko and Voznesensky, he was given official license to be rebellious, not least because Soviet officialdom could trust him not to take his rebellions very far.) Even in the gray days of late Communism, Party officials put up with Zaitsev's orange pants and tomato-red shirt, his canary-yellow maxicoat and white fur hat. He was the token designer, and he played the role with panache.

In 1988, in the full flower of perestroika, Zaitsev became his own boss at the House of Fashion and a true celebrity. People waited in line to buy Slava Zaitsev clothes. (Even Raisa Gorbachev, the first Kremlin clotheshorse, took an interest. According to Zaitsev, Mrs. Gorbachev used to insist that her clothes had been designed by him—which he says wasn't the case.) After the collapse of Communism, he endured, and prevailed: he was entrusted to design robes for the justices of the Constitutional Court, the first such court in the history of Russia.

These days, Zaitsev tries to show a certain magnanimity toward his Western competitors: "In principle, I salute the appearance of their boutiques," he said. "They exist all over the world, so why should we be different? It's especially good for our young designers and for the older ones who cannot afford to travel abroad." Zaitsev conceded that if Western boutiques have to leave Russia as a result of economic collapse and political backlash, it will be good for his business. "But, as a person, I highly respect my colleagues," he said. "My ambitions yield to my benevolence." His alarm about the current crisis is tied, above all, to his fears about the look of Russia, and Russians: "If, God forbid, something happens, and an embargo is imposéd upon us and borders are closed, what will people wear?"

What *will* people wear if the Communists succeed in turning back history? Zaitsev recalled the early days of his career, when he designed his first collection for peasants and workers—padded jackets, skirts, and *valenki* (felt boots). But these days even Gennady Zyuganov, the Communist Party leader, is looking rather natty as he seeks to defeat his capitalist enemies. Indeed, when I see him wearing elegant suits I find myself wondering where in the world he bought them.

Casual (2005)

Oksana Robski

"The East aestheticizes its monstrosity to the West—its ruins, its fake, its own end,"
the Bulgarian writer Vladislav Todorov wrote of post-Soviet culture, cited at the
outset of this volume. "The West pays for the danger because the West has been
investing in the thrills of the ruins from the very beginning. Danger impregnated with
money becomes a thriller." Todorov was writing on the legacies of cold war life, years
that all on both sides of the Atlantic were supposed to be glad to see end, but that
nonetheless were hard to shake after so many years of watching each other's lives from
afar. The mafia, for example, became the natural successors to Communist rule in
Western media eyes. A real Russian mafia did exist and was ready for prime-time
viewing, to be sure. But had it not existed, it surely would need to have been invented.

In her blockbuster novel, Casual, *published in 2005, the Russian writer Oksana*
Robski takes a world that the country's storied "New Russians" and Jackie Collins
fans alike would find at the ready: a life of bodyguards, errant spouses, errant lovers,
thieving housekeepers, and the high costs of self-fashioning. For the very narrow
stratum of robber-baron society, a world that Russians copied from the European
experience in capital accumulation, the Russian femme fatale found her new narra-
tor. She is the example par excellence of the world of glamur *(glamour), a word*
currently in vogue in Russia. Consumption, luxury, and fashion are all used to
highlight the economic and social stability that the Putin era has brought many
Russians.

It was bath day. Wednesday. The best time for it.

At the beginning of the week you have to catch up on everything that
accumulated over the weekend. At the end of the week you want to hang out
in restaurants and go to clubs.

But on Wednesday you can get together with the girls and heat up the
sauna. I have a Turkish steam bath at my house.

Veronika came. Her husband, Igor, had a cold and was home being watched
by the bodyguards and the housekeeper. Veronika could relax without wondering where he was—or with whom.

Lena came. Her husband left her for his secretary two years ago. She was wearing fake diamond earrings, but in our little village, it would never occur to anyone that fake diamonds existed. Just as, for instance, in the housewares store in Mnevniki, nobody would have thought that the round piece of glass on my finger cost more money than the whole store.

Katya came. Her friend Musya, a famous party animal and homosexual, was waiting patiently for Katya to give up on finding a husband and agree to have his baby before her biological clock stopped ticking. None of his pretty, muscular lovers could give birth.

We lit candles, wrapped ourselves in bath sheets, and Galya served the tea that was reserved for Wednesdays, a special herbal mix.

No one mentioned Serge.

Katya told us about a unique old woman who could tell your fortune with her dreams. She would pray all day and get the answer to her question that night. The questions were almost always the same.

After Katya's visit, the old woman dreamed that Katya was at a beach at the ocean, feeding bread crumbs to small ocean fish. That meant pregnancy.

Katya was pleased with the old woman.

The only inconvenience was that you might run into someone you knew when you went to see the old woman. Everyone in Moscow was going to her.

I wondered what she would dream about me?

Long ago someone told me that you shouldn't go to fortunetellers unless you had nothing to lose. So I never went.

Veronika came out of the steam room and, squealing, jumped into the cold plunge pool. Galya greeted her with a big bath sheet. All wrapped up, Veronika lay down on a soft chaise. Galya put a bright-blue cleansing mask on her face.

Some women look glamorous even in a facial mask.

Lena, who had recently started dating an attractive man from BMW, was worried about his financial status.

"What would the old woman dream if you asked her how much money he had?"

"If he had ten million, she'd see two sharks." Katya lay down for a massage. "Fifty million would be three sharks."

"And five hundred million would be a jackpot," chuckled Veronika, even though you're not supposed to talk during the facial. "Imagine the old woman dreaming about a jackpot and not knowing what it is, because she's never been in a casino!"

Galya took no part in our conversation. I had strictly forbidden her to talk.

After a second session in the steam, it was my turn for a massage.

Veronika had a cup of tea while Lena and Katya splashed around in the cold water.

We've known one another for a long time, around fifteen years. We've had fights and broken up several times. For a while I was friends with Lena against Katya, and Veronika wouldn't be friends with any of us. Or did we lock her out? Once Katya broke up my friendship with Lena and Veronika, and then betrayed me herself. But she was going through a difficult period, and a year later I forgave her. Now we were all friends and cherished the time, suspecting that it would not last. I wouldn't say that we loved one another very much. But we knew more about one another than our parents and husbands put together. We knew what we could expect. We had long accepted our faults and foibles. We could be ourselves without worrying about making an impression. We were cozy with one another, the way you can be cozy in a child's playroom.

Lena was talking about a miserable date with some new admirer. She had brought Katya with her. "I told Katya, 'If I like him, I'll say: I have gum. And if I don't, I'll say: I don't have any gum.'"

They came to the café near Red Square and sat down on the plastic chairs. It was 2 PM, and her date was drunk. He ordered cognac for all of them.

"Do you have any gum?" Lena asked Katya.

"I don't know. Maybe yes, maybe no."

They drank the cognac. Then they started talking about gum again.

"I must have some in the car," Katya said. "How about you?"

"I don't have any."

"Neither do I, come to think of it."

"Would you like me to ask the waiter for some?" asked the date.

"No. No!" They shook their heads like crazy.

They started up again a few minutes later.

"Well?"

"I don't have any."

The young man asked the waiter to bring gum and ordered more cognac. He was surprised that they weren't drinking and suggested getting something to eat. He chugged down the cognac. A girl in fashionable jeans from Lagerfeld's latest collection came down the street. She came over to kiss him. They were friends.

"Maybe there is some gum," Katya said, "but it's sugar-free."

"You mean it's in tablets rather than sticks?" Lena asked.

Katya nodded without the slightest idea of what Lena meant.

The young man said good-bye to the girl and ordered more cognac. He asked where they wanted to go next. He suggested his place.

"One hundred percent sugar," Lena concluded, while their date looked at them in suspicion. "You know, I've decided we're not going to have any gum today. Let's go!"

We all laughed and Veronika asked them to bring her on the next date.

Then Katya told us about photo-rejuvenation. It's expensive, but it doesn't work. She had four sessions for $730 and then stopped.

I told them about pregnant Svetlana.

Veronika was a mother of two children and she knew Svetlana.

"Maybe we should chip in to help her?" she exclaimed enthusiastically.

I knew what that meant. First Veronika would give some money. Buy presents when the baby arrived. She would spend a lot of time thinking about what to get for his first birthday. But she wouldn't even bother to call. By the time he was two, she would sit in a bar with the girlfriends and bitterly denounce herself for being such a bad person, having completely abandoned Svetlana and the child. She would dream about buying a carload of furniture, clothes, and toys any day now and showing up on Svetlana's doorstep, her modest smile stopping the flow of gratitude. More than likely that would never happen.

"That bitch wanted to steal your husband! And now she has the nerve to look you in the eyes!" Lena was talking about Svetlana, but she meant the woman who stole her husband. "Let her starve to death, we're not going to help her!"

"Give her money for an abortion," Katya said and gave me a look.

I was the only one who knew her secret. Seven years ago, her fiancé, one of the richest men in Russia, fell in love with another. Practical Katya wept over her lover's treachery and then began thinking about how to guarantee her lifestyle. Until he announced they were separating, she had time to think of something. And we did. Katya announced she was pregnant—she even quit smoking. A few months later she began complaining of morning sickness. Even to me. By that time her tycoon's affair with another became well known. She demanded an explanation. He left slamming the door. The next day she told people she had lost the baby. And as a result, she was sterile. The tycoon broke up with the new girl very quickly. He treated Katya warmly to this day, never forgetting to transfer ten thousand dollars to her account every month.

Katya had no children. Or any long-term relationships. It's not easy finding a fiancé when you're well off.

"What do you think?" asked Veronika.

I thought that she probably had Svetlana's phone number.

"Scratch her eyes out," I replied.

"What about the baby?"

Lena beat me to an answer. "She has to prove that it's Serge's first!"

"Now, that's right," agreed Katya.

"Impossible. There's nothing for DNA analysis."

If only . . . I don't know . . . I do know. If only we could exhume him and take a lock of his hair. I thought how much I wanted to see Serge again. I missed him terribly, as if he were a living person. Sometimes I thought that he was just away on a trip and all I had to do was call to bring him home. I was so ready to call!

But I wasn't ready to see him under those circumstances.

"Girls, let's talk about something else," I asked.

And we started on thieving housekeepers. Veronika has an extra refrigerator-freezer in the basement. She bought a rabbit and put it in the downstairs freezer, having no plans for rabbit in the near future. But three days later she wanted rabbit and asked the housekeeper to make some. She and Igor got home at the same time, the table was set, and dinner was prepared: veal roasted in the oven with cheese and mayonnaise. "There is no rabbit," the housekeeper explained. Veronika, furious, went down to the cellar and saw that the housekeeper was right. About the rabbit.

"But I'm not an idiot." Veronika made it almost a question. "I put it in there myself!"

Katya said that it's too bad about the rabbit, but she was much sorrier to lose her silk scarves. She kept them neatly folded in her wardrobe, and the housekeeper was stealing them one at a time, figuring that Katya couldn't remember all of them. Katya suspected after the second one vanished and caught her red-handed with the third. She pulled her scarf out of the housekeeper's bag and demanded the others.

"I won't give them back," said the housekeeper. "You have plenty as it is." She slammed the door so hard that Katya sat for a long time, afraid that she might come back for something else.

"Do you know her address?" Lena asked. "That has to be punished. She'll go work for someone else."

"I know it."

Veronika took the initiative. "Give it to me. I'll ask Igor to send our Borisych to see her. She'll stop stealing forever."

Borisych was a former major in the Fraud Squad. Igor kept him on the payroll for when anyone had to be given a scare. For instance, if a travel agency takes your money and then doesn't do your visas, or if you buy something that is a lemon but the store won't take it back. Borisych would surround the store or travel agency with a squad of sturdy men in black masks, go inside, make all the staff lie on the floor, and instantly solve all the issues.

We talked more about all kinds of things and Veronika started heading for home. Katya and Lena were in no hurry. We went upstairs to the living room, opened a bottle of Beaujolais and chatted lazily, lying on the couches.

They went home around midnight.

Anecdotes about New Russians

With the collapse of the Soviet Union, the new class of people who had emerged, the New Russians, or Novye Russkie, *quickly became the butt of much Russian humor. Many of the New Russians with little education had acquired fabulous wealth in a relatively short time and became known for their freewheeling lifestyle, corrupt business practices, and coarse behavior.*

In a restaurant the maître d' points at a drunk New Russian in a stained, ruby-colored jacket lying comatose with his face in the salad and his hands splayed out on the table. He says to the waiter: "Why don't you kick this jerk out onto the street?"

The waiter replies: "What for? Every time I wake him up, he thinks I brought him something to eat and he pays the bill."

Two classmates meet up, one a new Russian, the other a university graduate. While they're talking about this and that, the university graduate says: "Hey Petya, you were nothing but a complete dunce in school—you couldn't even memorize your multiplication tables, and now look at how nicely you're dressed; you've got money, a car. How is it possible? My whole life I've worked, I finished school with a gold medal and I'm barely making ends meet. What are you living on?"

"I'm living on three percent."

"What do you mean?"

"Well, it's like this. I go one time abroad. I look around me. There's a can of something there. Let's say it costs a dollar. So I buy it, I bring it back and say I sell it for four dollars. There's the three percent that I'm living on."

Translated by Adele Barker

Return to the Motherland (2001)

Irina Sandomirskaia

What does it mean to belong to a country? In her reflections on one of the greatest Russian symbolic powerhouses of all, "the Motherland," Irina Sandomirskaia reminds us that, though all Russians are by no means the same, virtually everyone raised in the former Soviet Union stands an excellent chance of recognizing the very same fragments and images that once constituted the government's official vocabulary of patriotism. Following the October Revolution, generations of émigrés had to ask themselves whether one could still belong to a place that one had physically left. (The answer was, most often, and painfully, yes.) Following the collapse of the USSR, Russians and many others have had to ask a different question: Can you still belong to a country if you have not physically gone anywhere, but the country itself has departed? Today of course the Russian government is not the only powerful body in the business of articulating what counts as patriotic. Between children's books written afresh, renovated public spaces, and savvy media efforts to power an ever expanding market, "the Motherland" is at the center of public life, as always. Mother Russia calls, read the posters of wartime, and it calls still, in times of upheaval, and restoration.

What does the Motherland begin with?
A picture in your ABC-book.

According to a popular Soviet song, the story of *Rodina*, or Motherland, begins with a "picture." For Soviet schoolchildren and the parents who were reading along with them, Motherland arrived as something ready-made, created without personal participation. It was an unquestionable given. Together with the "picture," the Motherland, thus, "begins" not in personal experience, nor in any immediate emotional kinship with what is a collective self, but with an ideology that supports the picture and grants it the status of authoritative prototype.

I remember the picture from my own ABC-book forty years ago, as well as from the primers that belonged to my children: a blue sky, a green hill, a

Alpinists renovate the "Motherland Calls You!" monument, a 52-meter-high
sculptured female incarnation of the Russian Motherland with a sword in her
hand, the central figure of the memorial complex in honor of the Battle of
Stalingrad. Photograph by E. Kotliakov. Courtesy of ITAR-TASS.

couple of birches, a river in the background, and a caption saying: "Our
Motherland." I remember other pictures representing the Motherland: the
war-time propaganda poster "Motherland Calling," the Stalingrad war memorial with its monumental sculpture of Glory in the city of Volgograd, the
countless allegories of the Motherland in mosaics, frescoes, and sculptures
that adorn the Moscow subway system, patriotic songs on TV and radio,
poems about the Motherland from school readers, the text of the Oath of the
Young Pioneer of the Soviet Union that was printed on the back covers of
school notebooks (together with multiplication tables), fragments of military
texts, patriotic events in which one had to participate on the order of the
school principal, red banners and slogans in the streets by way of festive
decoration on days marking official celebrations, and many, many other
things. These images of patriotic life that the Soviet regime was directing at us

all have by now already blended with the landscape of personal memory. The language of doctrine has mixed with individual recollection and caked into an indivisible, inalienable whole: the symbolic landscape of my country.

My generation knows many contexts from which we memorized the obligatory reading lists for school courses on Russian literature. These quotations may be cliché, seem even trite or worn-out, but they are by no means dead, these commonplaces found in millions of classroom essays. They are produced by *grazhdanskaia lirika*, Russian socially conscious poetry. These are almost anonymous quotations, semi-proverbs, hackneyed phrases that our instructors sentimentally called *krylatye slova* or "winged words," the standard lexicon of more or less every educated Soviet individual.

These fragmented, almost forgotten quotations have almost come to be detached from their original authors, those anonymous images, time-worn memories, the eternal anxiety of our youth with its tedious Pioneer pageants and endless Komsomol meetings, scraps of song lyrics and public appeals, official slogans and private jokes, the recollections of childhood and the nostalgias of older age. Such is the material that my Motherland uses to build its reality. It is an assortment of isolated, barely coherent verbal, visual, and gestural fragments. Yet, incoherent as they may be, all such fragments are included in the basic alphabet, the lexicon of culture that unites us, the speakers of contemporary Russian language, into a collective body. All of us, the daughters and sons of the Motherland, are members in Motherland's community, subscribers to its language, and agents of its practices.

The Soviet Motherland demanded sacrifices but promised us a radiant future of Communism. Lately, in communication with us, our luminous future has chosen a new rhetoric. In the 1990s, the streets of Moscow were adorned with a billboard featuring the face of an anonymous woman smiling down upon the traffic jams below. The inscription on the billboard was "I Love You." In the Soviet period, the most popular visual representation of a female figure in public places would have been one or another image of the Motherland—the goddess of victory in wartime, as in Volgograd, or the sturdy Komsomolka—but this was different. This new messenger of love took over the Motherland's place in the language of the street, suggesting that, even if she might appear different, our blue-eyed nymph angled for the same attention. The effects of this facelift were amazing. Formerly, the Motherland would address her children with an appeal, her mouth open in a war-cry, one arm hoisted in an emphatic gesture of appeal, and the other pointing at the text of the Military Oath. Now, what I assumed to be the Motherland was mysteriously silent; she was young and attractive, and she was looking at me with a tender understanding smile. The Motherland used to send her sons to gun-ports with their chests bared. Her substitute seemed to be spreading invisible wings over the insane traffic of the new Moscow, showering citizens of the market economy with the simple human gifts of love and peace. In contrast to the Victorian morals of the Soviet Motherland, these were more ambiguous: as rumour had it, the unknown woman in the picture was actually a *hetaira*, an expensive fashion model kept by some new Russian millionaire who wanted to share her love with everyone. The Motherland was acting liberally, in all senses.

The stress of transition to a market economy, however, creates a demand that seeks its own therapeutic responses. Messages of the "I love you" sort offered a strong anaesthetic effect. It is not so much the content but the tone, one of loving interest and support. This therapeutic effect savvily reached out to an electorate that is nostalgic about the Soviet past, signaling a new public discourse driven by strategies of seduction rather than coercion. As in the 1920s, when Lenin cast aside ponderous monuments to usher in a new era of mobility and flexible citizens, the staggering solidity of Stalinist architecture rarely finds a place anymore. Durable materials are good for the embodiment of eternal values. But it is precisely eternity and immortality that find less home in a society moving as fast as Moscow's in recent years, one shifting from the mode of coercion into one of seduction. The main thing is mobility. Formerly a "civic temple," with its icons, anthems, altars, and sacrifices, today the language of the Motherland works more like a flying circus: it sets up its brightly coloured tents for the attraction of the public. That is where it finds its market. And just as quickly, it disassembles those attractions and relocates them when consumer interest fades. This is what Marx told us years ago in *The Communist Manifesto*—that love of country is easily manipulated by business elites. Post-Soviet elites have done a rather good job of reminding us of this, mobilizing Stalinist sentiment anew for love of country. Who knew that the fall of the Marxist state would make us think of Marx again?

Consider the construction boom that swept up all the capital since 1992, and the principles by which buildings have been razed or risen anew, clad in new facades, or shorn of old ones. No single word better captures this fevered movement than *evroremont*, short for "European," or "Western-style renovation." Here, home repair seeks to express belonging to a global establishment, and its technologies are designed to superimpose a "global" high-tech look over the sometimes bizarre exteriors and rough textures of works designed by Stalinist architects and executed by the low cost labor of Soviet workers and engineers, sometimes prisoners of war, or simply prisoners. Thus, the global finds itself determined by the local, while the local finds itself determined by the Soviet, both amounting to a longing for "our own" space:

a space that will give peace and comfort for the former Soviet body with its new experiences and privations, as well as a look that will please the nostalgic patriotic gaze, without, at the same time, abusing capitalist taste by the memory of repression that Stalinist architecture carries in its every element.

Under socialism, for example, the borderline between private and public was marked by the railing of the balcony in a private apartment. Divided from the outer world by long plastic strips woven into iron fencing, or by a home-made set of additional glass frames (*osteklenie balkonov*—the enclosure of balconies with a glass wall, the only initiative that was allowed to the Soviet tenant in his attempts to win a few more cubic meters of privacy), the individual home thus expropriated a little bit of the outer world. This was a gesture of expropriation of the outer, but also an exposition of the inner, and the sight of ragtag belongings that were traditionally stored on such balconies, sometimes even the sounds of chickens that people started raising there during the worst of Gorbachev's *uskorenie*, or "accelerated reform," became an unavoidable compromise in the balcony's ambivalence as a private space wholly exposed to the public. How does the post-Soviet *evroremont* deal with such compromises?

One day, passing through a Moscow square, I came across two Stalin-era apartment buildings that sit like candlesticks on either side of a broad public space. They were two housing blocks that had been constructed, in their time, to form an architectural ensemble. The ensemble never worked out, as it happened, and the square still stretched in an impossible gape, as it always had, since Soviet city planning too rarely knew how to deal with the width and breadth of its own urban landscapes. One of the houses had by that time just undergone a "Western-style renovation," *evroremont*, while the other still stood untouched. The ensemble thus represented a perfect case for "before" and "after."

What one noticed in the renovated building was the "global design" of the new facade, reminiscent of the original, and at the same time very different. This signifier of Stalinist culture now had all its crenellated, turreted surfaces smoothed out—not in any metaphoric sense, but literally. The original facade bore the characteristic exuberance of its time, ringed with small sculptural ornaments once called "architectural excesses" (*arkhitekturnye izlishestva*) and later purged from architectural practice during the Khrushchev era. This unevenness of the surface of the wall, with its chaotic shadows, sometimes deep and sometimes shallow, produced a rich and varied texture. During regular upkeep over succeeding years, repairmen never strained to match the original plaster, so the effect often made for extremely impressionistic, even picturesque exteriors. By contrast, these "excesses" are resolutely eliminated by the technologies of *evroremont*. In the building before me, surfaces had been smoothed over with stucco, the walls of the ground floor were reclad with expensive looking polished granite, and sagging window frames were replaced with darkly tinted, one-piece sashes to create the effect of having no windows at all, just black rectangular gaps along the smooth surface of the walls.

By minimizing the ornamentation of the renovated facade, the building signalled the arrival of a new political economy in the distribution of beauty and comfort to the private citizen. The idea conveyed by Stalinist design is that of affluence and abundance on a strictly collective, shared basis. This was the goal of the Communist Party as declared in each of its documents and represented as already achieved in the Stalinist visual canon of the post-war period—a time when the country was, in fact, destroyed, famished, and anything but affluent. It is this ideological abundance that represents itself, among other ways, in the notorious over-ornamentation peculiar to the Stalinist grand style. The new Euro-renovated facade carries, instead, a message of solid moderation. Minimalism renders the idea of affluence: expensive affluence, far from the cheap abundance of the Stalinist age. Naturally, these new public scenes no longer welcome the rank-and-file Soviet citizen to partake of the pleasures of the feast of postsocialist well-being.

The economic motives that dictate such minimization are quite understandable, if not paradoxically so. Eager as they are to make their real estate look affluent, developers act out the theatre of solid austerity to reduce costs. By contrast, generations back, in the designing of their bizarre facades, Stalin's architects could afford as many "excesses" as they liked because their budgets were as unlimited as the labour available for building. Yet likewise today, *evroremont* is often performed by inexpensive, illegal guest workers, hired through bribes and by dint of the hurried constraints on the country's most profitable growth sector. And, it must be sadly noted: by eliminating ornamental excesses, the new builder pursues this dream at minimal cost. Hence, bad maintenance and cheap materials—long the curse of a Soviet construction industry that has yet to be lifted—remain the benchmarks of an urban transformation that relies heavily on re-cladding rather than rebuilding. Walls of dark glass descend over good old post offices and savings banks (the once omnipresent *sberkassa*) across the former Soviet Union. Local imitations of an imagined Wall Street, they pledge a life of new smoothness by way of hiding, rather than recognizing, the old.

In the meantime, a smooth facade is an ideal surface for forgetfulness. Future history can stream down its vertical heights without leaving a trace. New facades provide no cavities for sedimentation, no reliefs to hang on, no frictions to arrest a fall. Similarly, smoked glass offers the ideal surface, gesturing to the transparency of a democratic institution without actually disclosing its operations inside. The viewer encounters a mirror and thus, only herself.

As Susan Buck-Morss points out, in the drive to renovate lives and country, there has been much concern in the West over the development of "civil society" in Russia, somehow forgetting that the former Soviet Union was a country once run by one of the world's largest, allegedly voluntary, non-governmental organizations ever, the Communist Party. The Soviet version of transparency was formulated by Lenin and developed by Stalin in the quite Machiavellian terms of "democratic centralism" as the organizing principle of the Party, the Komsomol, and other allegedly non-governmental bodies. Following the demise of "democratic centralism," the Kremlin has taken to representing civil society and today's rival NGOs as a lost cause, wrought by Western provocation to imbue the Russian soul with something dangerously inorganic, unnatural to the Russian tradition. In the Kremlin as elsewhere, Motherland regenerates itself instead through a language of smoothness and seduction. These new rhetorics, found in fragments of beloved texts, in new children's primers, and in the buildings that surround us, are joined by a microsurgery of meaning in an attempt to restore blood circulation in the collective symbolic body of all Russians known as "We." One can therefore fast recognize the Motherland in the smiling face of the kept woman on an "I Love You" billboard, or across evroremonts whose impenetrable dark glass suggests a powerful economy that no longer invites or even requires the participation of average citizens. We recognize the Motherland because her very nature is that of a vague recognizability, a kind of hyper-quotation, a powerful reality cloaked in metaphor. The once violent Motherland is believed to have retreated into history, yet she is still everywhere around us.

In recent years, on the road heading from Moscow's Sheremet'evo International Airport into the city, weary passengers were greeted by another towering billboard, featuring an enormous bottle of Coca-Cola. Importantly, it faced the arriving traveller, not the departing one. As if a fountain, the globally preferred beverage burst out in foam and promised to quench the traveler's thirst on days warm or cold. This encounter always made me think of Rabelais' Temple of the Holy Bottle, with Pantagruel's long pilgrimage in search of a revelation from the Oracle within. Shuttling from one country to another, I imagined my own pilgrimages as those of Pantagruel, waiting for revelation of greater things to come—apparently to be expected from a bottle of soda. Below the bottle read the caption: "Welcome Back!" (*S vozvrashche-niem!*). Not simply "welcome," but "welcome back." This bottle does not speak to just anyone. It speaks, most tellingly, to the Russian and the Russian alone. It calls to me, the prodigal daughter of the Motherland who has fled its

Picture of Donskoi Monastery, 1933. Courtesy of the American Geographical Library at University of Wisconsin–Milwaukee libraries. Photographer William O. Field.

borders, and it welcomes my return as the end of my prodigality, it meets me on my way *here*, not *there*. To welcome me back, the Motherland performs one of her many tricks: here, she dons the uniform (a red one, by the way) of one of the world's largest global corporations. And, of course, I do return. Because apart from the Motherland, I have no other place to come back to.

Translated by Bruce Grant

Suggestions for Further Reading

Histories of Russia and the Soviet Union

Brumfield, William. *A History of Russian Architecture*. Seattle: University of Washington Press, 2004.

Figes, Orlando. *Natasha's Dance: A Cultural History of Russia*. New York: Henry Holt, 2002.

Hosking, Geoffrey. *The First Socialist Society: A History of the Soviet Union from Within*. 2nd ed. Cambridge, Mass.: Harvard University Press, 1992.

——. *Russia and the Russians: A History from Rus to the Russian Federation*. Cambridge, Mass.: Belknap Press, 2001.

Lincoln, W. Bruce. *Between Heaven and Hell: The Story of a Thousand Years of Artistic Life in Russia*. New York: Viking, 1998.

Malia, Martin E. *The Soviet Tragedy: A History of Socialism in Russia, 1917–1991*. New York: Free Press, 1991.

Raeff, Marc, ed. *Russian Intellectual History: An Anthology*. New York: Harcourt, Brace and World, 1966.

Riasanovsky, Nicholas. *A History of Russia*. New York: Oxford University Press, 2000.

Rzhevsky, Nicholas, ed. *The Cambridge Companion to Modern Russian Culture*. New York: Cambridge University Press, 1998.

Service, Robert. *A History of Modern Russia from Nicholas to Putin*. London: Penguin, 2003.

Stephan, John. *The Russian Far East: A History*. Stanford, Calif.: Stanford University Press, 1994.

Vernadsky, George. *Kievan Russia*. New Haven, Conn.: Yale University Press, 1973.

I. Icons and Archetypes

Bailey, James, and Tatyana Ivanova, editors. and translators. *An Anthology of Russian Folk Epics*. Armonk, N.Y.: M. E. Sharpe, 1998.

Berdyaev, Nikolai. *The Russian Idea*. Translated by R. M. French. Hudson, N.Y.: Lindisfarne, 1992.

Billington, James. *The Icon and the Axe: An Interpretive History of Russian Culture*. New York: Vintage, 1970.

Cherniavsky, Michael. *Tsar and People: Studies in Russian Myths*. New York: Random House, 1969.

Hubbs, Joanna. *Mother Russia: The Feminine Myth in Russian Culture*. Bloomington: Indiana University Press, 1988.

Monahan, Barbara. *A Dictionary of Russian Gesture*. Ann Arbor, Mich.: Hermitage, 1983.

Nakhimovsky, Alexander D., and Alice Stone Nakhimovsky, eds. *The Semiotics of Russian Cultural History*. Ithaca, N.Y.: Cornell University Press, 1985.

Pesmen, Dale. *Russia and Soul: An Exploration*. Ithaca, N.Y.: Cornell University Press, 2000.

Sinyavsky, Andrei. *Soviet Civilization: A Cultural History*. Translated by Joanne Turnbull. New York: Arcade, 1990.

II. From Kyiv through Muscovy

Baron, Samuel H., editor and translator. *The Travels of Olearius in Seventeenth-Century Russia*. Stanford, Calif.: Stanford University Press, 1967.

Birnbaum, Henryk. *Novgorod in Focus*. Columbus, Ohio: Slavica, 1996.

Custine, Marquis de. *Letters from Russia*. Translated and edited by Robin Buss. London: Penguin, 1991.

Fennell, John. *The Crisis of Medieval Russia, 1200–1304*. New York: Longman, 1983.

Kivelson, Valerie. *Cartographies of Empire: The Land and Its Meanings in Seventeenth-Century Russia*. Ithaca, N.Y.: Cornell University Press, 2006.

Pelenski, Jaroslaw. *The Contest for the Legacy of Kievan Rus'*. New York: Columbia University Press, 1998.

Platonov, Sergei Fedorovich. *The Time of Troubles: A Historical Study of the Internal Crises and Social Struggle in Sixteenth- and Seventeenth-Century Muscovy*. Translated by John T. Alexander. Lawrence: University Press of Kansas, 1970.

Poe, Marshall. *A People Born to Slavery: Russia in Early Modern European Ethnography, 1476–1748*. Ithaca, N.Y.: Cornell University Press, 2000.

Zenkovsky, Serge, editor and translator. *Medieval Russia's Epics, Chronicles and Tales*. New York: Dutton, 1974.

III. Reform to Revolution

Bassin, Mark. *Imperial Visions: Nationalist Imagination and Geographical Expansion in the Russian Far East, 1840–1865*. New York: Cambridge University Press, 2006.

Berlin, Isaiah. *Russian Thinkers*. Edited by Henry Hardy and Aileen Kelly. New York: Viking, 1978.

Catherine the Great. *Memoirs*. Translated by Mark Cruse and Hilde Hoogenboom. New York: Modern Library, 2005.

Chernyshevsky, Nikolai Gavrilovich. *What Is to Be Done?* Translated by Michael R. Katz. Ithaca, N.Y.: Cornell University Press, 1989.

Dostoyevsky, Fyodor. *Notes from Underground*. Translated and annotated by Richard Pevear and Larissa Volokhonsky. New York: Knopf, 1993.

Emerson, Caryl. *The Life of Musorgsky*. Cambridge: Cambridge University Press, 1999.

Engel, Barbara Alpern. *Mothers and Daughters: Women of the Intelligentsia in Nineteenth Century Russia*. Evanston, Ill.: Northwestern University Press, 2000.

Engelstein, Laura. *The Keys to Happiness: Sex and the Search for Modernity in Fin-de-siècle Russia*. Ithaca, N.Y.: Cornell University Press, 1992.

Herzen, Alexander. *My Past and Thoughts*. Translated by Constance Garnett. Revised by Humphrey Higgens. New York: Knopf, 1968.

Hingley, Ronald. *Russian Writers and Society, 1825–1904*. New York: McGraw Hill, 1967.

Hughes, Lindsey. *Peter the Great: A Biography*. New Haven, Conn.: Yale University Press, 2002.

Jackson, David. *The Wanderers and Critical Realism in Nineteenth-Century Russian Painting*. Manchester, England: Manchester University Press, 2006.

Madariaga, Isabel de. *Russia in the Age of Catherine the Great*. New Haven, Conn.: Yale University Press, 1981.

Pushkin, Alexander Sergeevich. *Eugene Onegin: A Novel in Verse*. Translated by James E. Falen. Oxford: Oxford University Press, 1995.

Tolstoy, Lev Nikolaevich. *Childhood, Boyhood, Youth*. Translated by Rosemary Edmonds. Harmondsworth, England: Penguin, 1964.

Turgenev, Ivan. *Fathers and Sons*. Translated by Michael R. Katz. New York: Norton, 1994.

Valkenier, Elizabeth. *Ilya Repin and the World of Russian Art*. New York: Columbia University Press, 1990.

——. *Russian Realist Art, the State and Society: The Peredvizhiniki and Their Tradition*. New York: Columbia University Press, 1989.

Wortman, Richard. *Scenarios of Power: Myth and Ceremony in Russian Monarchy*. Two vols. Princeton, N.J.: Princeton University Press, 1995–2000.

IV. Far Pavilions: Siberia

Balzer, Marjorie Mandelstam. *The Tenacity of Ethnicity: A Siberian Saga in Global Perspective*. Princeton, N.J.: Princeton University Press, 1999.

Bassin, Mark. *Imperial Visions: Nationalist Imagination and Geographical Expansion in the Russian Far East, 1840–1865*. New York: Cambridge University Press, 1999.

Bloch, Alexia, and Laurel Kendall. *The Museum at the End of the World: Encounters in the Russian Far East*. Philadelphia: University of Pennsylvania Press, 2004.

Diment, Galya, and Yuri Slezkine, eds. *Between Heaven and Hell: The Myth of Siberia in Russian Culture*. New York: St. Martin's Press, 1993.

Grant, Bruce. *In the Soviet House of Culture: A Century of Perestroikas*. Princeton, N.J.: Princeton University Press, 1995.

Hawes, Charles Henry. *In the Uttermost East*. Reprint, 1904; New York: Arno Press, 1970.

Humphrey, Caroline. *Karl Marx Collective: Economy, Religion, and Society on a Siberian Collective Farm*. Cambridge: Cambridge University Press, 1983.

Rasputin, Valentin. *Siberia on Fire*. Translated by Gerald Mikkelson and Margaret Winchell. DeKalb: Northern Illinois University Press, 1989.

Slezkine, Yuri. *Arctic Mirrors: Russia and the Small Peoples of the North*. Ithaca, N.Y.: Cornell University Press, 1994.

V. A Changing Countryside

Aksakov, S. T. *A Family Chronicle*. Translated by Olga Shartse. Moscow: Raduga, 1984.

Blum, Jerome. *Lord and Peasant in Russia from the Ninth to the Nineteenth Century*. New York: Atheneum, 1966.

Buckley, Mary. *Mobilizing Soviet Peasants: Heroines and Heroes of Stalin's Fields*. Lanham, Md.: Rowman and Littlefield, 2006.

Frierson, Cathy. *Peasant Icons: Representations of Rural People in Late Nineteenth Century Russia*. New York: Oxford University Press, 1993.

Hindus, Maurice. *Red Bread*. New York: Jonathan Cape, 1931.

Hoch, Steven L. *Serfdom and Social Control in Russia: Petrovskoe, a Village in Tambov*. Chicago: University of Chicago Press, 1986.

Ioffe, Grigory, Tatyana Nefedova, and Ilya Zaslavsky. *The End of Peasantry? The Disintegration of Rural Russia*. Pittsburgh: University of Pittsburgh Press, 2006.

Paxson, Margaret. *Solovyovo: The Story of Memory in a Russian Village*. Bloomington: Indiana University Press, 2005.

Robinson, Geroid T. *Rural Russia under the Old Regime*. New York: Macmillan, 1949.

Roosevelt, Priscilla. *Life on the Russian Country Estate: A Social and Cultural History*. New Haven, Conn.: Yale University Press, 1995.

Semyonova Tian-Shanskaia, Olga. *Village Life in Late Tsarist Russia*. Edited by David L. Ransel. Translated by David L. Ransel with Michael Levine. Bloomington: Indiana University Press, 1993.

Venturi, Franco. *Roots of Revolution: A History of the Populist and Socialist Movements in Nineteenth Century Russia*. Translated by Francis Haskell. New York: Knopf, 1960.

Vucinich, Wayne, ed. *The Peasant in Nineteenth Century Russia*. Stanford, Calif.: Stanford University Press, 1968.

Worobec, Christine D. *Peasant Russia: Family and Community in the Post-Emancipation Period*. Princeton, N.J.: Princeton University Press, 1991.

VI. Near Pavilions: The Caucasus

Babchenko, Arkady. *A Soldier's War in Chechnya*. Translated by Nick Allen. London: Portobello Books, 2007.

Breyfogle, Nicholas B. *Heretics and Colonizers: Forging Russia's Empire in the South Caucasus*. Ithaca, N.Y.: Cornell University Press, 2005.

Chenciner, Robert. *Daghestan: Tradition and Survival*. New York: St. Martin's Press, 1997.

Colarusso, John. *Nart Sagas from the Caucasus: Myths and Legends from the Circassians, Abazas, Abkhaz, and Ubykh*. Translated and annotated by John Colarusso. Princeton, N.J.: Princeton University Press, 2002.

Derluguian, Georgi M. *Pierre Bourdieu's Secret Admirer in the Caucasus: A World-System Biography*. Chicago: University of Chicago Press, 2005.

Gammer, Moshe. *The Lone Wolf and the Bear: Three Centuries of Chechen Defiance of Russian Rule*. Pittsburgh: University of Pittsburgh Press, 2006.

Gamzatov, Rasul. *My Daghestan*. Translated by Julius Katzer and Dorian Rottenberg. Moscow: Progress, 1970.

Grant, Bruce. *The Captive and the Gift: Cultural Histories of Sovereignty in Russia and the Caucasus*. Ithaca, N.Y.: Cornell University Press, 2009.

Grant, Bruce, and Lale Yalcin-Heckmann, eds. *Caucasus Paradigms: Anthropologies, Histories, and the Making of a World Area*. Berlin: LIT, 2007.

Haxthausen, August Freiherr von. *Transcaucasia: Sketches of the Nations and Races between the Black Sea and the Caspian*. London: Chapman and Hall, 1854.

Iskander, Fazil. *The Gospel According to Chegem: Being the Further Adventures of Sandro of Chegem*. Translated by Susan Brownsberger. New York: Vintage, 1984.

Jersild, Austin. *Orientalism and Empire: North Caucasus Mountain Peoples and the Georgian Frontier 1845–1917*. Montreal: McGill-Queen's University Press, 2002.

Khodarkovsky, Michael. *Russia's Steppe Frontier: The Making of a Colonial Empire, 1500–1800*. Bloomington: Indiana University Press, 2002.

Layton, Susan. *Russian Literature and Empire: Conquest of the Caucasus from Pushkin to Tolstoy*. Cambridge: Cambridge University Press, 1994.

Politkovskaya, Anna. *A Small Corner of Hell: Dispatches from Chechnya*. Translated by Alexander Burry and Tatiana Tulchinsky. Chicago: University of Chicago Press, 2003.

Saroyan, Mark. *Minorities, Mullahs and Modernity: Reshaping Community in the Former Soviet Union*. Edited by Edward W. Walker. Berkeley: International and Area Studies, 1997.

Suny, Ronald Grigor, ed. *Transcaucasia, Nationalism, and Social Change*. Ann Arbor: University of Michigan Press, 1996.

Tolstoy, Lev. *Hadji Murad*. Translation, preface, and notes by Aylmer Maude. Introduction by Azar Nafisi. New York: Modern Library, 2003.

VII. Revolution

Farnsworth, Beatrice. *Aleksandra Kollontai: Socialism, Feminism, and the Bolshevik Revolution*. Stanford, Calif.: Stanford University Press, 1980.

Fitzpatrick, Sheila. *The Russian Revolution*. New York: Oxford University Press, 2001.

Fitzpatrick, Sheila, and Yuri Slezkine, eds. *In the Shadow of Revolution: Life Stories of Russian Women from 1917 to the Second World War*. Translated by Yuri Slezkine. Princeton, N.J.: Princeton University Press, 2000.

Miliukov, Pavel Nikolaevich. *Political Memoirs, 1905–1917*. Translated by Carl Goldberg. Ann Arbor: University of Michigan Press, 1967.

Pasternak, Boris. *Doctor Zhivago*. Translated by Max Hayward and Manya Harari. New York: Pantheon, 1991.

Reed, John. *Ten Days That Shook the World*. New York: Vintage, 1960.

Serge, Victor. *Memoirs of a Revolutionary, 1901–1941*. Translated by Peter Sedgwick. Oxford: Oxford University Press, 1963.

Shapiro, Leonard. *1917: The Russian Revolutions and the Origins of Present-Day Communism*. London: Temple Smith, 1984.

Sukhanov, N. N. *The Russian Revolution: A Personal Record*. Translated and edited by Joel Carmichael. Oxford: Oxford University Press, 1955.

VIII. Building a New World from Old

Bergan, Ronald. *Sergei Eisenstein: A Life in Conflict*. Woodstock, N.Y.: Overlook Press, 1999.

Clark, Katerina. *Petersburg: Crucible of Cultural Revolution*. Cambridge, Mass.: Harvard University Press, 1995.

Ellis, Jane. *The Russian Orthodox Church: A Contemporary History*. Bloomington: Indiana University Press, 1986.

Fainsod, Merle. *How Russia Is Ruled*. Cambridge, Mass.: Harvard University Press, 1963.

Hirsch, Francine. *Empire of Nations: Ethnographic Knowledge and the Making of the Soviet Union*. Ithaca, N.Y.: Cornell University Press, 2005.

Kataev, Valentin. *Time, Forward!* Translated by Charles Malamuth. Evanston, Ill.: Northwestern University Press, 1995.

Kenez, Peter. *The Birth of the Propaganda State.* Cambridge: Cambridge University Press, 1985.

——. *Cinema and Soviet Society from the Revolution to the Death of Stalin.* London: I. B. Tauris, 2001.

Martin, Terry. *The Affirmative Action Empire: Nations and Nationalism in the Soviet Union, 1923–1939.* Ithaca, N.Y.: Cornell University Press, 2001.

Starr, S. Frederick. *Melnikov, Solo Architect in a Mass Society.* Princeton, N.J.: Princeton University Press, 1978.

Stites, Richard. *Revolutionary Dreams: Utopian Vision and Experimental Life in the Russian Revolution.* New York: Oxford University Press, 1989.

Taylor, Richard, *The Eisenstein Reader.* Translated by Richard Taylor and William Powell. London: British Film Institute, 1998.

Trotsky, Leon. *Problems of Everyday Life: Creating the Foundations for a New Society in Revolutionary Russia.* New York: Monad Press, 1973.

IX. Rising Stalinism

Clark, Katerina. *The Soviet Novel: History as Ritual.* Chicago: University of Chicago Press, 1985.

Djilas, Milovan. *Conversations with Stalin.* Translated by Michael Petrovich. New York: Harcourt, Brace, and World, 1962.

Dobrenko, Evgeny, and Eric Naiman, eds. *The Landscape of Stalinism: The Art and Ideology of Soviet Space.* Seattle: University of Washington Press, 1993.

Dunham, Vera. *In Stalin's Time: Middleclass Values in Soviet Fiction.* Durham, N.C.: Duke University Press, 1990.

Figes, Orlando. *The Whisperers: Private Life in Stalin's Russia.* New York: Henry Holt, 2007.

Fitzpatrick, Sheila, ed. *Cultural Revolution in Russia, 1928–1931.* Bloomington: Indiana University Press, 1978.

——. *Everyday Stalinism: Ordinary Life in Extraordinary Times: Soviet Russia in the 1930s.* New York: Oxford University Press, 1999.

Getty, J. Arch, and Oleg V. Naumov. *The Road to Terror: Stalin and the Self-Destruction of the Bolsheviks, 1932–1939.* Translations by Benjamin Sher. New Haven, Conn.: Yale University Press, 1999.

Graham, Loren. *The Soviet Academy of Sciences and the Communist Party 1927–1932.* Princeton, N.J.: Princeton University Press, 1967.

Gronow, Jukka. *Caviar with Champagne: Common Luxury and the Ideals of the Good Life in Stalin's Russia.* Oxford: Berg, 2003.

Hellbeck, Jochen. *Revolution on My Mind: Writing a Diary under Stalin.* Cambridge, Mass.: Harvard University Press, 2006.

Kelly, Catriona. *Comrade Pavlik: The Rise and Fall of a Soviet Boy Hero.* London: Granta, 2005.

Kotkin, Stephen. *Magnetic Mountain: Stalinism as a Civilization.* Berkeley: University of California Press, 1995.

Lewin, Moshe. *Russian Peasants and Soviet Power: A Study of Collectivization*. New York: Norton, 1975.

Medvedev, Roy. *Let History Judge: The Origins and Consequences of Stalinism*. Edited and translated by George Shriver. New York: Columbia University Press, 1989.

Radzinskii, Edvard. *Stalin*. Translated by H. T. Willetts. New York: Doubleday, 1996.

X. The Great Terror

Adler, Nanci. *The Gulag Survivor: Beyond the Soviet System*. New Brunswick, N.J.: Transaction, 2002.

Applebaum, Anne. *Gulag: A History*. New York: Doubleday, 2003.

Barnes, Steven A. *Death and Redemption: The Gulag and the Shaping of Soviet Society*. Princeton, N.J.: Princeton University Press, 2010.

Conquest, Robert. *The Great Terror: A Reassessment*. New York: Oxford University Press, 1990.

Getty, J. Arch, Gabor T. Rittersporn, and Viktor N. Zemskov. "Victims of the Soviet Penal System in the Pre-War Years: A First Approach on the Basis of Archival Evidence." *American Historical Review* 98, no. 4 (1993), 1017–49.

Gheith, Jehanne, and Katherine Jolluck, eds. *Stories from the Gulag*. New York: Palgrave Macmillan, 2010.

Ginzburg, Eugenia. *Journey into the Whirlwind*. Translated by Paul Stevenson and Max Hayward. New York: Harcourt Brace, 1967.

Larina, Anna. *I Cannot Forget: The Memoirs of Nikolai Bukharin's Widow*. Translated by Gary Kern. New York: Norton, 1993.

Mandel'shtam, Nadezhda. *Hope Abandoned*. Translated by Max Hayward. New York: Atheneum, 1974.

——. *Hope against Hope: A Memoir*. Translated by Max Hayward. New York: Atheneum, 1970.

Merridale, Catherine. *Night of Stone: Death and Memory in Twentieth-Century Russia*. New York: Penguin, 2000.

Shalamov, Varlam. *Kolyma Tales*. Translated by John Glad. New York: Norton, 1980.

Solzhenitsyn, Aleksandr. *The Gulag Archipelago, 1918–1956: An Experiment in Literary Investigation*. Translated by Thomas P. Whitney and Harry Willetts. New York: Harper and Row, 1985.

Vilensky, Simeon, ed. *Till My Tale Is Told: Women's Memoirs of the Gulag*. Translated by John Crowfoot. Bloomington: Indiana University Press, 1999.

XI. The War Years

Adamovich, Ales', and Daniil Granin. *A Book of the Blockade*. Translated by Hilda Perham. Moscow: Raduga, 1983.

Beevor, Antony. *Stalingrad*. London: Viking, 1998.

Garrard, John, and Carol Garrard, eds. *World War 2 and the Soviet People*. New York: St. Martin's Press, 1993.

Ginzburg, Lidiya. *Blockade Diary*. Translated by Alan Myers. London: Harvill Press, 1995.

Grossman, Vasilii. *Life and Fate: A Novel.* Translated by Robert Chandler. New York: Harper and Row, 1985.

Kirschenbaum, Lisa A. *The Legacy of the Siege of Leningrad 1941–1995.* Cambridge: Cambridge University Press, 2006.

Norman, Geraldine. *The Hermitage: Biography of a Great Museum.* London: J. Cape, 1997.

Salisbury, Harrison. *The 900 Days: The Siege of Leningrad.* New York: Harper and Row, 1969.

Stites, Richard, ed. *Culture and Entertainment in Wartime Russia.* Bloomington: Indiana University Press, 1995.

Tumarkin, Nina. *The Living and the Dead: The Rise and Fall of the Cult of World War II in Russia.* New York: Basic Books, 1994.

Werth, Alexander. *Russia at War 1941–1945.* New York: E. P. Dutton, 1964.

Zhukov, Georgii Konstantinovich. *The Memoirs of Marshal Zhukov.* New York: Delacorte Press, 1971.

XII. The Thaw

Davies, Robert W. *Soviet Economic Development from Lenin to Khrushchev.* Cambridge: Cambridge University Press, 1965.

Khrushchev, Nikita Sergeevich. *Khrushchev Remembers.* Translated by Strobe Talbott. Boston: Little, Brown, 1970.

Lakshin, Vladimir. *Solzhenitsyn, Tvardovsky and Novyi Mir.* Translated by Michael Glenny. Cambridge, Mass.: MIT Press, 1980.

Siniavskii, Andrei. *The Trial Begins.* Translated by Max Hayward. London: Collins and Harvill, 1960.

Smith, Gerald Stanton. *Songs to Seven Strings: Russian Guitar Poetry and Soviet Mass Song.* Bloomington: Indiana University Press, 1984.

Taubman, William. *Khrushchev: The Man and His Era.* New York: Norton, 2003.

XIII. Russians Abroad, Near and Far

Baschmakoff, Natalia, and Marja Leinonen. *Russian Life in Finland 1917–1939: A Local and Oral History.* Helsinki: Studia Slavica Finlandensia, 2001.

Berberova, Nina. *The Italics Are Mine.* Translated by Philippe Radley. New York: Harcourt, Brace and World, 1969.

Boyd, Brian. *Nabokov: The American Years.* Princeton, N.J.: Princeton University Press, 1991.

Brodsky, Joseph. *Less Than One: Selected Essays.* New York: Farrar, Straus and Giroux, 1986.

Glad, John. *Russia Abroad: Writers, History, Politics.* Tenafly, N.J.: Hermitage and Birchbark Press, 1999.

Harbin and Manchuria: Place, Space and Identity. Edited by Thomas Lahusen. Special issue of *South Atlantic Quarterly* 99, no. 1 (2000).

Ilf, Ilia, and Evgenii Petrov. *Little Golden America.* Translated by Anne O. Fisher. New York: Princeton Architectural Press, 2007.

Johnston, Robert. *New Mecca, New Babylon: Paris and the Russian Exiles, 1920–1945.* Montreal: McGill-Queen's University Press, 1988.

Karlinsky, Simon, ed. *The Bitter Air of Exile*. Berkeley: University of California Press, 1977.

Nabokov, Vladimir. *Speak Memory: An Autobiography Revisited*. New York: Putnam, 1966.

Pereleshin, Valerii. *Russian Poetry and Literary Life in Harbin and Shanghai, 1930–1950: The Memoirs of Valerii Pereleshin*. Amsterdam: Rodopi, 1987.

Raeff, Marc. *Russia Abroad: A Cultural History of the Russian Emigration, 1919–1939*. New York: Oxford University Press, 1990.

Stone, Norman, and Michael Glenny, eds. *The Other Russia: The Experience of Exile*. London: Faber and Faber, 1990.

Williams, Robert. *Culture in Exile: Russian Émigrés in Germany, 1881–1941*. Ithaca, N.Y.: Cornell University Press, 1972.

Wolff, David. *To the Harbin Station: The Liberal Alternative in Russian Manchuria, 1898–1914*. Stanford, Calif.: Stanford University Press, 1999.

Yakobson, Helen. *Crossing Borders: From Revolutionary Russia to China to America*. Tenafly, N.J.: Hermitage, 1994.

XIV. Life under Advanced Socialism

Bonavia, David. *Fat Sasha and the Urban Guerilla: Protest and Conformism in the Soviet Union*. New York: Atheneum, 1973.

Boym, Svetlana. *Common Places: Mythologies of Everyday Life in Russia*. Cambridge, Mass.: Harvard University Press, 1994.

Buchli, Viktor. *An Archaeology of Socialism*. Oxford: Oxford University Press, 1999.

Condee, Nancy, ed. *Soviet Hieroglyphics: Visual Culture in Late-Twentieth-Century Russia*. Bloomington: Indiana University Press, 1995.

Cracraft, James, ed. *The Soviet Union: An Interpretive Guide*. 2nd ed. Chicago: University of Chicago Press, 1988.

Cushman, Thomas. *Notes from Underground: Rock Music Counterculture in Russia*. Albany: State University of New York Press, 1995.

Gellner, Ernest. *State and Society in Soviet Thought*. New York: Blackwell, 1988.

Goscilo, Helena, and Beth Holmgren, eds. *Russia—Women—Culture*. Bloomington: Indiana University Press, 1996.

Lapidus, Gail, ed. *Women in Russia*. Brighton, England: Harvester Press, 1978.

Millar, James R. *The ABCs of Soviet Socialism*. Urbana: University of Illinois Press, 1981.

Sakharov, Andrei. *My Country and the World*. Translated by Guy V. Daniels. New York: Knopf, 1975.

Tillett, Lowell. *The Great Friendship: Soviet Historians on the Non-Russian Nationalities*. Chapel Hill: University of North Carolina Press, 1969.

Yurchak, Aleksei. *Everything Was Forever, Until It Was No More: The Last Soviet Generation*. Princeton, N.J.: Princeton University Press, 2006.

XV. Things Fall Apart

Brown, Archie. *The Gorbachev Factor*. Oxford: Oxford University Press, 1996.

Feshbach, Murray, and Alfred Friendly Jr. *Ecocide in the USSR: Health and Nature under Siege*. New York: Basic Books, 1992.

Gorbachev, Mikhail. *Perestroika: New Thinking for Our Country and the World.* New York: Harper and Row, 1987.

Hosking, Geoffrey. *The Awakening of the Soviet Union.* 2nd ed. London: Mandarin, 1991.

Humphrey, Caroline. *The Unmaking of Soviet Life: Everyday Economies after Socialism.* Ithaca, N.Y.: Cornell University Press, 2002.

Remnick, David. *Lenin's Tomb: The Last Days of the Soviet Empire.* New York: Random House, 1993.

Ries, Nancy. *Russian Talk: Culture and Conversation during Perestroika.* Ithaca, N.Y.: Cornell University Press, 1997.

Smith, Kathleen. *Remembering Stalin's Victims: Popular Memory and the End of the USSR.* Ithaca, N.Y.: Cornell University Press, 1996.

Suny, Ronald Grigor. *The Revenge of the Past: Nationalism, Revolution, and the Collapse of the Soviet Union.* Stanford, Calif.: Stanford University Press, 1993.

Walker, Martin. *The Waking Giant: The Soviet Union under Gorbachev.* London: Michael Joseph, 1986.

XVI. Building a New World, Again

Aslund, Anders. *How Russia Became a Market Economy.* Washington, D.C.: Brookings Institution, 1995.

Barker, Adele Marie, ed. *Consuming Russia: Popular Culture, Sex, and Society since Gorbachev.* Durham, N.C.: Duke University Press, 1999.

Borenstein, Eliot. *Overkill: Sex and Violence in Contemporary Russian Culture.* Ithaca, N.Y.: Cornell University Press, 2008.

Boym, Svetlana. *The Future of Nostalgia.* New York: Basic Books, 2001.

Buyske, Gail. *Banking on Small Business: Microfinance in Contemporary Russia.* Ithaca, N.Y.: Cornell University Press, 2007.

El'tsin, Boris. *The View from the Kremlin.* Translated by Catherine A. Fitzpatrick. London: HarperCollins, 1994.

Erofeyev, Victor, ed. *The Penguin Book of New Russian Writing.* London: Penguin, 1995.

Garrard, John, and Carol Garrard. *Russian Orthodoxy Resurgent: Faith and Power in the New Russia.* Princeton, N.J.: Princeton University Press, 2008.

Gessen, Masha. *Dead Again: The Russian Intelligentsia after Communism.* London: Verso, 1997.

Klebnikov, Paul. *Godfather of the Kremlin: Boris Berezovsky and the Looting of Russia.* New York: Harcourt Brace, 2000.

Ledeneva, Alena. *How Russia Really Works: The Informal Practices That Shaped Post-Soviet Politics and Business.* Ithaca, N.Y.: Cornell University Press, 2006.

Mickiewicz, Ellen. *Changing Channels and the Struggle for Power in Russia.* Oxford: Oxford University Press, 1997.

——. *Television, Power, and the Public in Russia.* Cambridge: Cambridge University Press, 2008.

Sakwa, Richard. *Putin, Russia's Choice.* New York: Routledge, 2004.

Acknowledgment of Copyrights and Sources

Index

ADELE BARKER is a professor of Russian and
Slavic studies at the University of Arizona.
BRUCE GRANT is an associate professor of
anthropology at New York University.

Library of Congress Cataloging-in-Publication Data
The Russia reader : history, culture, politics /
edited by Adele Barker and Bruce Grant.
p. cm. — (The world readers)
Includes bibliographical references and index.
ISBN 978-0-8223-4656-2 (cloth : alk. paper)
ISBN 978-0-8223-4648-7 (pbk. : alk. paper)
1. Russia—History. 2. Soviet Union—History.
3. Russia—Civilization. 4. Soviet Union—
Civilization. 5. Russia—Social conditions. 6. Soviet
Union—Social conditions. 7. Russia—Politics
and government. 8. Soviet Union—Politics and
government. I. Barker, Adele Marie, 1946– II. Grant,
Bruce, 1964– III. Series: World readers.
DK18.R874 2010
947—dc22   2009050791